Anger

With blessings offered to the
Roseville Public Library.

Lawrence Holiday Harris

The Origins and Growth
of
BAPTIST FAITH

Twenty Baptist Trailblazers in
World History

The Origins and Growth
of
BAPTIST FAITH

Twenty Baptist Trailblazers in
World History

Lawrence Holiday Harris

THE REPRINT COMPANY, PUBLISHERS
SPARTANBURG, SOUTH CAROLINA
2001

An original publication, 2001
The Reprint Company, Publishers
Spartanburg, South Carolina 29304

ISBN 0-87152-534-8
Library of Congress Control Number 2001048216
Manufactured in the United States of America

The paper used in this publication meets the requirements of American National Standard for Information Science—Permanence of Paper for Printed Library Materials, ANSI Z-39.48-1984.

Portraits of Trailblazers by Richard "Rick" C. Lico

Library of Congress Cataloging-in-Publication Data

Harris, Lawrence Holiday
  The origins and growth of Baptist faith : twenty Baptist trailblazers in world history / Lawrence Holiday Harris
    p. cm.
  Includes bibliographical references and index.
  ISBN 0-87152-534-8 (alk. paper)
    1. Baptists—Biography. 2. Baptists—History. I. Title.

BX6493 .H335 2001
286'.092'2—dc21
[B]   2001048216

The Light of the World Is Jesus

The whole world was lost in the darkness of sin,
The Light of the world is Jesus;
Like sunshine at noonday His glory shone in,
The Light of the world is Jesus.
Come to the Light, 'tis shining for thee;
Sweetly the Light has dawned upon me,
Once I was blind, but now I can see:
The Light of the World is Jesus.

— Philip P. Bliss (1838-1876)

Contents

Preface

It has given me immense pleasure all my life to be a member and admirer of the Baptist Faith. Baptists are an awe-inspiring Christian family, because of their love of God and His son Jesus, who as individuals sense the leading of the Holy Spirit, and who nourish their tenacious belief in the Bible as the Word of God, their governance through grassroots democracy, and their evangelical zeal. The greatest gift conferred on the world by Baptists, in my opinion, is the doctrine of the Separation of Church and State, sometimes mistakenly attributed to Thomas Jefferson. In fact, that magnificent doctrine is the bequest of Baptist Trailblazers Thomas Helwys in England, Roger Williams in Rhode Island, and legally in republican America, the hand-work of John Leland of Virginia and Isaac Backus of Massachusetts. Almost like a twin to the Separation doctrine, Baptists, from their founder John Smyth in the seventeenth century, proclaimed tolerance and freedom of worship, not only for Baptists but also for Catholics, Quakers, Unitarians, and Muslims. Roger Williams gave life to those visions by sheltering Sephardic Jews and Free Thinkers in Rhode Island, where he built the first Baptist Church in the New World.

Baptists are a robust presence throughout the world, numbering in 2000 A.D. over forty-three million baptized believers. In the United States and Canada alone, there are thirty-three million Baptists, divided into thirty denominations; some of these functional groups are huge, like the Southern Baptist Convention (nearly sixteen million) or almost invisible, like the Two-Seed-in-the-Spirit Predestinarian (201 members, 16 churches). Two of the most prominent Baptist bodies in North America are composed almost entirely of African-Americans: National Baptist Convention of America (over three million) and National Baptist Convention, USA, Inc. (over eight million). It would be unthinkable to study Baptist progression in philosophy, leadership, missions, and theological training without frequent reference to the Northern Baptist Convention, now called the American Baptist Churches in the USA. Then, there are numerous thriving ethnic Baptist groups, such as the Vietnamese, Koreans, Chinese, and the Hispanic branches.

An evangelical zeal to expand Home and Foreign Missions is a characteristic of many, perhaps most Baptists. This predisposition to conquer the world for Christ had much to do with planting missions overseas and nurturing large clusters of Baptists in Brazil, the Caribbean area, China, Germany, India, Korea, Nigeria, Philippines, Romania, and Russia. The United Kingdom, home to the earliest Baptists, and mother-soil of the Faith, has a quarter of a million believers, with influence far exceeding those numbers. On the other hand, there are Baptist branches in the United States, such as the Primitive Baptists (Hard-Shell) and similar churches with a strong Calvinistic orientation, that are not evangelistic and oppose missionary activities, because of their doctrines regarding the Elect. While it is evident that Baptists are a tough, and without dispute, a contentious people, their survival skills have been sharpened in centuries-old Scriptural debates over the means God has chosen to convert the unsaved, as well as His leading on church policy and growth. But the Missions Question was resolved for many generations, by a largely nineteenth-century Gospel Revolution, when the Good News was spread in India by the gifted linguist William Carey; in Germany and most of Continental Europe by Johann Gerhard Oncken; and in Russia and its bordering states by Vasili G. Pavlov, and by a host of others.

My impulse in writing *The Origins and Growth of Baptist Faith* was to spread the knowledge about our theological roots and Baptist heroes, both men and women, and with little regard for color, sex, and nationality. Some of these Trailblazers (not all of them elaborately described) were brilliant like Harry Emerson Fosdick, others were rock-bound independents like John Bunyan, some were humble and gifted like Luther Rice, and some were as eloquent as Martha Marshall. Many of them overcame enormous odds to follow their Calling, such as the freed slave George Leile (Lisle) and the Russian Vasili G. Pavlov. Numbers of them were imprisoned, isolated, or killed—as Thomas Helwys, Lottie Moon, and Martin Luther King. For every stripe and deprivation they suffered, their Baptist grit was a manifestation of obedience and faithfulness to their Lord. From their simplest beginnings, stemming from Independent and Anabaptist forebears, they would not tolerate the interference of monarchs, magistrates, and governors in their sacrosanct privilege of direct worship. Often they chose the prison cell, rather than sign a document of forced compliance. Having been tortured and abused for their faith, these great Christians demanded religious freedom, not only for themselves, but for all people.

While undertaking the detailed research and writing of this book, in a period lasting five years, I have not disregarded the imperfections of those Baptist saints, but I have had to observe reasonable restraints required by charity and common sense. I have portrayed the Trailblazers largely as they lived. As the German-Baptist reformer Walter Rauschenbush stated it, "we [Baptists] are not a perfect denomination," and many of the best people we know follow other lights. As an interesting case, in assessing the roles of America's presidents of Baptist persuasion, Jimmy Carter has been adjudged by many as a vacillating and only moderately effective chief executive. However, when he assumed a private life and the role of ex-president, public opinion turned in his favor because of his social and peace-making activities, to rank him in nobility, wisdom, and Christian charity with such a revered notable as George Washington.

The denominational partisan struggle among Southern Baptists, particularly between moderate conservatives and their more loyalist Convention-oriented brothers and sisters, sometimes defined superficially as an ideological contest between moderates and Fundamentalists, has played no part in the selection of Trailblazers. To the contrary, most of the selected heroes were conservative Baptists. Some like merchant-preacher William Kiffin and Texan B. H. Carroll were ultra-conservative while only one, Walter Rauschenbusch, could be regarded for a time as a radical. Two major figures, Roger Williams and John Smyth, would leave the Baptist Faith but sustain many of its basic tenets, and one of the greatest, John Bunyan, while conservative in his theology, simply cannot be defined. Instead of being discomfited by the diversity of these wonderful Trailblazers, I am encouraged and my admiration whetted that the Baptist Faith can sustain such a multi-hued leadership.

In my search for the truth, I rediscovered a major clue as to why Baptists are so constantly at war with each other: There has been a dualism in the Baptist Faith from its inception in England, marked by its double origin from the General Baptists and the Regular Baptists. The General Baptists assumed as a primary doctrine the theology of Jacobus Arminius, that emphasizes that Christ died for all men ("whosoever believeth in Him should not perish"). The Regular Baptists, on the other hand, cited the doctrine of the French-Swiss theologian Jean (John) Calvin (Calvinism) that mankind was predestined and salvation was limited to the Elect (the few). The doctrine of the Elect is most clearly upheld by the Primitive Baptists, and Calvinism has surged back into the Baptist mainstream through the teachings of some Baptist seminaries. Despite many struggles and compromises over the centuries, this dualism still persists, although modified, and Baptists continue to differ on missions, theology, national and congregational leadership, and other lingering questions concerning the roles of societal structure (weak centralism) or convention structure (strong centralism). Meanwhile, the dual roots of the Baptists both bless us and distress us.

The Baptists in the twenty-first century continue to evolve in complex ways. And their microdebates and differences frequently have proven to be blessings in disguise; often the church insurgents, feeling passionately about their newly-surfaced beliefs, simply move to a new locale and constitute there a new church. However, any assessment of that phenomenon, the Southern Baptist rift, beginning around 1979, must reflect a significant and complicated development, touching all fifty states in subtle ways and affecting the world through missions, foreign relief, theological training, and financial and scientific initiatives. Those other Baptists in the United States alarmed by the Southern Baptist "new direction" have built or have assisted in creating eleven new schools of theology, which in turn, have further diversified religious education in the United States. So, continuing in a high-tech cosmos, the hardy Baptists—nearly two hundred world varieties—will optimistically survive, adapt, and thrive—while carrying out their paramount mission, conveying the Good News of Jesus Christ.

LAWRENCE HOLIDAY HARRIS

Acknowledgments

My wife Thelma L. Harris, jewel and inspiration, who was my companion during this five-year project.

Mrs. Marilyn Howard, to whom I owe a world of gratitude, who typed the entire manuscript many times and stuck loyally with me to the end.

Mrs. Nan Bell, who began the work with me and typed the first eight chapters.

The Rev. Frank Johnson, my pastor, who "knew" I could complete such a difficult undertaking.

The Rev. Jake Holland, who assisted me in selecting the Baptist Trailblazers, heroes of this book.

Dr. Waldo P. Harris, a source of kindly support and reviewer of the chapter on Martha Marshall.

Mrs. Ray Kitchens, former church historian, Isle of Hope Baptist Church, whose keen literary skills and friendly advice greatly assisted me.

Mr. Charles W. Howle, my friend, who abbreviated the chapter on Luther Rice.

Mr. James Richardson, Professor Paul A. Richardson, and the Rev. Bill Gardner for supplying materials and tendering advice on the chapter on hymn composer Philip P. Bliss.

Dr. Robert G. Gardner for his suggestions and critical analysis of the chapter on Martha Marshall.

Mrs. Igor (Yelena) Kulikov for expertly reviewing the chapter on Vasili G. Pavlov.

The Rev. James A. (Jimmy) Long, II, for his review and suggestions on the Preface.

The Rev. Matthew Southall Brown for his review and suggestions regarding the chapter on Martin Luther King, Jr.

Mrs. Suzanne Woodrum for supplying materials and patiently reviewing the chapter on Philip Bliss.

Dr. John Finley for his kindness and scholarship in reviewing the entire manuscript.

The Rev. Earnest T. Pirkle for his kindness and scholarship in reviewing the entire manuscript.

The Rev. William Neal, editor, *Baptist Index*, for his kindness and scholarship in reviewing the entire manuscript.

Taken in May 1995, by the tomb of John Bunyan outside London Wall.

LAWRENCE HOLIDAY HARRIS

Lawrence Holiday Harris was born in China, the son of Southern Baptist missionary to China Dr. Hendon Mason Harris, and grandson of missionary to Mexico William David Powell. He served in the Battle of the Bulge in World War II and rose to become an Army Lieutenant Colonel.

In the State Department, he served as Education Officer (Refugee Relief Program), Intelligence Research Officer (Europe/China), and American Consul to Hong Kong and Manila. His writings include: *American Business Opinion and the Ruhr Occupation*, 1923 (Berkeley, Cal.); *India: A Study of National Integration* (University of Santo Tomas, Manila); *Spanish Internal and External Policies* (NIS/State Department); *Italian Political Dynamics* (NIS/State Department); and *History of Refugee Relief Program* (State Department).

His education was acquired at Baylor University (B.A.), University of California (M.A., History), and the University of Santo Tomas (Ph.D., Political Science). He has taught at the University of Santo Tomas (Graduate School), Chapman College, Orange, Cal. (World Campus Afloat), and Savannah State University, where he was for years Director of International Studies. His name is included in *Personalities of the South* and *Dictionary of International Biography*.

Chapter 1

John Smyth
(c.1570-1612)

Progenitor of Baptist Doctrine

In the inchoate and turbulent process of the Protestant Reformation, begun by Martin Luther in 1517, there emerged in Europe other dynamic religious innovators, such as John Calvin in Geneva and Ulrich Zwingli in Zurich. Zwingli's break with the Roman Catholic Church and his profession of the Bible as the supreme doctrinal authority inspired some of his students to die for their beliefs, as the earliest Anabaptist martyrs. As the most radical elements of the Reformation, the Anabaptists suffered hideously from Catholics and Protestants, alike, because of the Anabaptists' inspired zeal, their refusal to allow princes or councils to dictate their beliefs, and a complete reliance on the Scriptures for spiritual guidance. For this, they were burned alive or drowned in Switzerland, Bohemia, Germany, and England. Although the Anabaptists evolved into the current Amish and Mennonite churches, at this earliest time they had a profound influence on John Smyth and the unique character of the Baptist Faith.

John Smyth (c.1570-1612), an English theologian and writer, was the progenitor of the General Baptists of England, and, thus, guardedly, is the father of the Baptist movement. Between 1609 and 1611, Smyth founded a church in Amsterdam, Holland, of English

Anabaptists, whose tenets of faith and practices were remarkably similar to those of modern Baptists. However, that church was not called a Baptist church, for even the word "Baptist," a pejorative term, was not accepted until about 1654.[1] Despite the probable greater influence in history of the Particular Baptists (Calvinistic), John Smyth as the motivator of the earlier General Baptists was the first great leader to emerge from the founding Baptists.

This remarkable man was molded by a discordant England, torn between Anglicans, Calvinists, and Separatists. He migrated through religious communities as varied as Anglicans, Puritans, Separatists, and Baptists. Even though with poetic license he may be called the "Founder of the Baptist Faith," his link with Baptists (as that of Roger Williams in Colonial America), lasted only a few short months. He attempted without success to become a Mennonite, and most of his followers became Mennonites after his death. The remnant of his followers became the first Baptists known to history.

Smyth apparently entered Christ's College, Cambridge University in 1586 in order to prepare for the Anglican ministry. He graduated with a B.A. degree in 1590, earned an M.A. from the college in 1593, then remained as a teaching fellow from 1594 until 1598. In 1594 he was ordained an Anglican priest by Bishop Wickham of London. Smyth has been described as learned, able, forceful, and engaging but also possessed of "an unsettled head"; this forces the conclusion that he was a person whose philosophic parameters cannot be defined. In his break from the Anglican Church, he was audacious, for clearly he was molded in the rugged image of John the Baptist.

This was a chaotic period, and Puritans were tireless in attempting to simplify the established Anglican Church. At Cambridge, Smyth in temperament and religious practice became a moderate Puritan, identifying with the majority of the faculty of that university. Smyth is believed to have been greatly influenced by the Cambridge teacher Francis Johnson, who was to become prominent as a

Separatist leader. In the town of Campen, Holland, Johnson organized the first congregation of English Anabaptists of whom there is certain knowledge. At this stage, Smyth accepted vocal and instrumental music in church, a degree of government regulation of religion, and established prayers. However, he became sharply critical of the Anglican state church, and soon he found himself in the Clink, an English prison, for not adhering to the teachings and rituals of the State Church.[2]

His career advanced through a series of pastorates and appointments. On September 27, 1600, by a vote by the authorities of eight to seven,[3] he became the city preacher at Lincoln. His effective ministry and the approval of the municipal "Fathers" were manifest when, on August 1, 1602, he became "city lecturer" for life, a prestigious post that paid forty pounds a year, plus house rent. This was an ironical appointment, because he was forced to relinquish this last office in five weeks.[4]

The reason for Smyth's dismissal was that he was venturing toward Separatism, a step to the left of the Puritans. In his sermons from the pulpit he strongly criticized the sins of prominent leaders, including many Anglican priests that he designated as "Papists," and the rite of infant baptism that they were practicing. After a few weeks of study, he became a practicing physician. He also produced at this time two major writings: "The Bright Morning Starre" (1603) and "A Paterne of True Prayer" (1605).[5]

By 1605 Smyth lived in the Midlands, at Gainsborough on the Trent. During the frequent absence of the parish priest, Smyth would serve unofficially as the preacher. The Anglican hierarchy disapproved his preaching and ordered him to cease. The breach widened until Smyth broke completely with the Church of England and began to associate exclusively with a Separatist congregation that organized in 1602 and met in Gainsborough. He thus became a pastor within this Pilgrim congregation, some of whom later escaped persecution by sailing to America on the *Mayflower*.

Separatist Church Evolves

Part of the small Separatist congregation worshipped under the leadership of Richard Clyfton at Scrooby Manor House and included the prominent lay leaders John Robinson, William Brewster, and William Bradford. Many of these Separatists were natives of Norfolk, Suffolk, Essex, Kent, and London.[6] In order to escape persecution from King James I, who threatened to "harrie them out of the land" for their refusal to adhere to the English state church, they divided in 1606 into two groups. The Robinson-Brewster-Bradford group, forerunners of the Congregational Church, separated from the Smyth-Thomas Helwys group, some of whom became the progenitors of the English Baptists.[7] This separation of a congregation of about eighty persons was for practical reasons and safety from the English authorities and the persecution of Anglican Bishop Bancroft, and not because of doctrinal differences.

Some of these Separatists were frightened by the memory of the Dissenters Barrowe, Greenwood, and Penry, who were executed in England in 1593. Led by the Gainsborough congregation in 1607, both groups migrated to Protestant Holland, a tolerant state that welcomed Separatists from about 1595. However, once overseas the English Separatists began to diverge. The Smyth-Helwys group adopted "believer's baptism," that is baptism after confession of faith in Christ, as responsible believers, and became Baptists or Proto-Baptists.[8]

The other group, from Scrooby Manor Church, led by John Robinson and layman Richard Clyfton, moved to Leyden and then sailed to America and eventually became the Congregational Church in New England.[9]

As the Smyth-Helwys group from Gainsborough departed for Amsterdam in 1607, they were not yet Baptists. In their shared leadership, Helwys, from a landed family, brought stability, while Smyth was more creative and dynamic. The group was only another refugee English church in Amsterdam. This company of believers was largely from Yorkshire, Lincolnshire, and Nottingham, England. The members of the congregation took lodging and employment at the old East India Bakehouse, owned by the Mennonite merchant Jan Munter, located near Amstel, in the current Rembrandtsplein sector of the city. While Smyth was busy as a medical doctor, the congregation made a living by baking hardtack biscuits for the many ships in the harbor.

Shortly after his arrival in Holland, Smyth accepted the theology of Jacobus Arminius. Arminianism subsequently became a critical doctrine for many Baptists through the ages, since it proclaimed that atonement was available to all mankind through the sacrifice of Jesus. This doctrine became a principal tenet of those who were to call themselves General Baptists and for others, including the Free-will Baptists. In contrast, in generations to follow, other Baptists advocated a "particular" atonement, of a limited number of persons to be saved, a belief sustained by orthodox Calvinists.

At first the Smyth group had fellowship with the Anabaptist Ancient Church, led by English expatriate Francis Johnson, but Smyth soon found himself at odds with his old mentor from Cambridge. Smyth ascribed the disagreements with Johnson to procedures of worship, means of financial support of churches, and the role and duties of ministers. These differences were explained in Smyth's book, *The Differences of the Churches of the Separation* (1608).[10]

Smyth insisted that worship be spontaneous and inspired by the heart, and not written or mandated. He was against reading even from the Bible during the worship service, so as not to hinder the Holy Spirit.[11] Smyth's model for not reading Scriptures in the service was the example of Jesus, who closed the scroll before he began to preach (Luke 4:20). In his opinion, the English translations of the Scriptures reflected inadequately the direct word of God. Prayer, preaching, and the singing of Psalms were to be undertaken without written help, such as some Separatists sought from the Prayer Book of the Church of England. In his literalism and individualism, Smyth went far beyond the views of most Separatist leaders.

Even before moving to Holland, Smyth's beliefs were changing as reflected in his book, entitled *Principles and Inferences concerning The visible Church*. In this work, he defined the church as: "A visible Communion of Saincts is of two, three, or moe Saincts joyned together by covenant with God and themselves, freely to vse al the holy things of God, according to the word, for their mutual edification, and God's glory."[12] This concept of the church would change drastically, as Smyth interacted with his congregation and the Anabaptists, both from England and the Continent.

In 1608, while in Holland, he offered his views on church government and the ministry, that touched on his greatest disagreement with the Ancient Church of Francis Johnson. "We hould that the Presbytery of the church is Vniforme: and that the triformed Presbytetie [Presbytery] consisting of three kinds of Elders viz. Pastors, Teachers, Rulers is none of God's Ordinance but mans devise."[13] Thus, Smyth in the beginning spoke against a three-tiered church government influenced by the thoughts of the Geneva reformer John Calvin, and advocated a two-layered leadership of the Church through pastors and deacons.[14]

In a unique challenge to the Christian world—and establishing a distinctive Baptist concept—Pastor Smyth asserted that infant baptism as practiced by many churches, including the Roman Catholic and Anglican, was not warranted by the Scriptures. The scriptural church, he held, should consist of the regenerate only, of those who had been baptized after a personal confession of faith. These views were contained in a tract called "The Character of the Beast" (1609). Even earlier, Smyth wrote to Richard Clyfton that infants were not to be baptized, because "there is neither precept nor example in the New Testament that they were baptized by John or Christ's disciples."[15]

He repeated these arguments to the Ancient Church of Francis Johnson, that did not require persons leaving the Anglican Church to be re-baptized. If persons defecting to the Ancient Church were not baptized again as believers, they should return to the Anglican Church, he asserted.

Taking Refuge in Holland

Through a series of theological discoveries, John Smyth's religious positions evolved until they assumed the basics of the Baptist faith. In 1607, when Smyth and Helwys left England for Holland, they led a congregation based on an Old Testament covenant, accepted some government control of religion, but gave no attention to believer's baptism. After two years, all of these positions had been discarded, and by 1609 Smyth had established a church, essentially Baptist, based on the baptism of mature believers.[16]

In a radical move—amazing to both his friends and enemies—Smyth in 1609 decided to establish a new, pure church, based on the baptism of professed believers. Smyth persuaded his followers to disband, and convinced the deacons to surrender, along with himself as pastor, their offices in the church; with Smyth they were again baptized in order to create a new church. Thus, Smyth, Helwys, and thirty-six other English citizens formed on foreign soil the first Proto-Baptist church. Properly speaking, it was not until a remnant of this group regrouped in England under Helwys that the organized denominational history of the General Baptists begins. However, its spiritual and belief structure was established principally by John Smyth at Amsterdam.

Smyth solved the problem of baptism by baptizing himself first, through affusion, that is by pouring. Immersion was rare even among the Anabaptists and not practiced by General Baptists for another generation. For this act of self-baptism Smyth is sometimes called a Se-Baptist, along with the early "Colonial Father," Roger Williams. He then baptized Helwys and the others in the congregation, as related in Smyth's work *The Last Book of John Smyth*. Smyth wrote: "Seeing ther was no church to whome wee could Joyne with a Good conscience to haue baptism from them, therfor we might baptize ourselves."

The unusual baptism was generated by Smyth's belief that the practices of true apostolic succession were sustainable only if they were based on true belief and practice. The basis of the reconstituting of the church was to acquire a new baptism, since the former baptism through a corrupted church, namely the Church of England, was not believed to be sanctified.[17] The succession of pastors, as practiced by the Waterlanders, would become the model for Smyth, but be rejected by Helwys.[18] In the written words of John Robinson, pastor of the Pilgrim Church, who was present:

> Mr. Smith [Smyth], Mr. Helw: & the rest haveing vtterly dissolved, and disclaymed their former Ch[Church]: state, & ministery, came together to erect a new Ch: by baptism: vnto which they also ascribed so great virtue, as that they would not so much as pray together, before they had it. And after some streyning of courtesy, who should begin, . . . Mr. Smith baptized first himself, & next Mr. Helwis, & so the rest, making their particular confessions.[19]

After their leader's self-baptism, Smyth's congregation issued the "Confession of Faith of John Smyth and His People in 102 Articles," which was published about 1612. That statement of beliefs asserted that a church should be composed of baptized believers only and that only such believers should partake of the Lord's Supper. In the same manuscript, John Smyth set forth in Article LXXXVI his sturdy views on magistrates and interference with religious beliefs by public officials:

> That the magistrate is not by virtue of his office to meddle with religion, or matters of conscience, to force and compel men to this or that form of religion or doctrine, but to leave Christian religion free to every man's conscience, and to handle only civil transgessions [*sic*] (Roman. XIII. 3.4), injuries and wrongs of man against man, in murder, adultery, theft, etc. for

Christ only is the King and Lawgiver of the church and conscience (James IV. 12)[20]

This, for its day, may be the most emphatic expression of religious freedom written in English. It is notable that Smyth and a small assembly of Baptists should proclaim it and make it a precursor of tolerance in England and America. However, this doctrine was denounced by John Robinson, one of the Pilgrim fathers of New Plymouth.

John Smyth, as the earliest great Baptist, if we exclude Helwys, quickly regretted his se-baptism, probably within months, as hasty and disorderly. He had come to believe that the Waterlander Mennonites in Amsterdam, who baptized by affusion, that is pouring, comprised a true church, from which could be derived a holy succession. Once again he abruptly changed his course and repudiated his se-baptism and church membership. He became convinced that true baptism could only be obtained from someone who scripturally possessed the right to baptize. Most of his followers then repented of their error, unchurched themselves, and adopted the belief that baptism must be by succession, that is administered by someone who had been properly baptized.

The great Baptist movement that was to largely implant the doctrine of separation of church and state in America, and to encircle the world with its vitality, nearly died in its cradle with the defection of John Smyth. Even the rise in England of the Particular Baptists (Calvinistic) may not have balanced this loss of doctrine. However, Thomas Helwys and a small band of about ten were satisfied with their baptism and found fundamental differences between their practices and the Mennonites, and, in England in 1611-1612, founded the General Baptists. Although Baptists have regarded Mennonites as a kindred faith, Baptists generally have not adopted the Mennonite positions on pacifism, unwillingness to serve in the government, and refusal to pledge oaths.

Although the parting of the Smyth and Helwys groups was in an

atmosphere of love and respect, Helwys advised the Dutch Mennonites to be cautious about Smyth's application for membership. Smyth
was never received by the Mennonites, although most of his followers were absorbed into the Waterlander church. Smyth died from
consumption on August 20, 1612, without membership in any church.
In a strange evolution of religious history, this rugged seeker, neither
a Baptist in the beginning nor a Baptist in the end, would formulate
the outlines of Baptist faith and serve as its Trailblazer.

Chapter 2

Thomas Helwys
(c.1570-c.1616)

Planter of the Baptist Church

Thomas Helwys is the founder of the first Baptist church on English soil, at Spitalfield, outside the London walls. His motive in leading a courageous flock of ten from Amsterdam to England in 1611 or early 1612 was in part to strengthen the witness of those being persecuted and martyred in England by the Anglican Church and government authorities. Thus Helwys, in his homeland, established the first permanent English congregation of the General Baptists, who espoused the Arminian doctrine of unlimited atonement and were baptized at first by affusion or pouring. Like the catacomb churches of early Christianity, Helwys's congregation met secretly, and he would die in prison for his beliefs.

Helwys, like a number of early Baptist leaders, rose from the educated classes of England, some of them former Anglican priests, not a few who had attended Oxford and Cambridge. Other Baptist leaders had little formal education.[1] In just a few years, colleges and universities would be closed to these Dissenters and the Baptist clergy. Helwys, from Broxtowe Hall, England, was a country squire, of "good background," and educated in law at London. He was a fearless preacher and co-leader in the Separatist church at Gainsborough, and while living at Amsterdam was offered the honor—but refused it—of baptizing John Smyth and the entire company of Baptists. His wife Joan and their children remained in England when the Smyth flock, including Helwys, fled to Holland.

In an oppressive Stuart age, when even upright Separatists, such as General Thomas Harrison (d. 1660), a prominent military officer under Oliver Cromwell, were drawn and quartered, Thomas Helwys wrote an appeal for tolerance for all believers in God, whether Muslims, Jews, Roman Catholics, Anglicans, or Dissenters. He was perhaps the greatest spokesman for religious liberty to that time, and the scope of this Baptist statesman exceeded that of John Smyth. Smyth had largely appealed against interference by magistrates in the Christian religion, but Helwys asked for religious freedom for all people. The tradition of Baptists, both in England and the United States, of demanding freedom of conscience and religious practice for themselves but equally for others, was enlarged by Smyth, Helwys, and, later, by another early Baptist, Leonard Busher. The struggles that then led to the Act of Toleration (1689) in England and the doctrine of the "Separation of Church and State" in the United States were inspired by Baptists and English Congregationalists, but not exclusively so. Partially, these efforts stemmed from the bedrock of Anabaptist tolerance and practice.

The Baptists, from the period of Helwys, became the foremost champions of religious liberty and conscience in England and the New World. In his writing, *A Short Declaration of the Mistery of Iniquity*, published in England, Helwys became a major spokesman for religious liberty. He demanded for Baptists and all other Christians "blessed liberty to understand the Scriptures with their own spirits." In the tolerant views of Helwys, as well as his theology, can be seen the extending of the concepts of John Smyth and the reinforcement of concepts on separation of church and state held by the Anabaptists. While, in the historic Baptist view, kings, Parliament, lords, and magistrates would be given utmost honor and respect in temporal matters, no supremacy would be given to them in religious matters. Thus, Baptists as a whole accepted service in the government, including the military, but rejected completely any effort by the government to regulate their relationship to God. The creative mind of Helwys developed a dynamic that protected religious freedom but allowed participation in government.

Helwys had been the staunch colleague of Smyth from the period of Separatist meetings at Gainsborough, from about 1602 to the group's exile in Amsterdam in 1607. Separatists did not like the terms priest or even preacher, which were to them pretentious. So "teacher" Helwys developed theologically with his colleague, "teacher" Smyth, until 1610, when the small Baptist remnant under Helwys separated from the Smyth congregation. Throughout their relationship, Smyth as the primary leader was the explorer of primal church doctrine, providing direction and restless inquiry for the congregation and himself, while Helwys gave constancy to the church and maturity to the evolving doctrines.

Smyth's Proto-Baptist church had been established in Amsterdam, Holland, from about 1609, but increasingly it found doctrinal similarities with the Waterlander Mennonite (Anabaptist) church. These early Baptists preferred fellowship with the mild Waterlanders rather than the more rigid Flemish church or the Frisons element of the United High German Anabaptists. Following a controversy with Richard Clyfton,[2] Smyth told his congregation that he repented of his self-baptism.[3] Smyth, in progressive steps, had migrated from the Anglican Church to the Baptist faith. Now he convinced the majority of those who were Baptists to seek membership with the moderate Waterlanders of Amsterdam and embrace their Hofmannite Christology,[4] which virtually denied the humanity of Christ. In February 1610 Smyth's group wrote a petition in Latin, since Dutch was a new language to them, confessing error for baptizing themselves, and requesting admission to the Mennonite Church.[5]

The Mennonites were cautious in receiving the Smyth congregation and required first an examination of their doctrine. Before the inquiry was completed, and admission authorized, the Smyth group would submit to or prepare four sets of documents: (1) twenty articles written by Smyth; (2) a Dutch confession of beliefs prepared by Mennonite elders and signed by Smyth and forty-three members of his Congregation; (3) nineteen articles written by Helwys and his Baptist associates, and; (4) a confession of one hundred propositions as part of *The Last book of John Smyth*, called "The Retraction of His Errors." There was no mention of immersion in these early documents, since both the Smyth group and the Mennonites used affusion. The twenty Latin articles by Smyth and the nineteen articles by Helwys are the earliest English Baptist confessions.[6]

The Believers Divide

In reaction to Smyth's chameleon-like change of direction, at least among a small sector of his church, there was consternation, perhaps fury. Helwys accused Smyth of sinning against the Holy Spirit, in doubting the correctness of his own baptism, since Smyth recognized ordination when privately given.[7] Ten members, led by Thomas Helwys and John Murton and including William Piggott and Thomas Seamer, refused to admit that their baptism was not sanctified. In 1610 Helwys and John Murton led the small Baptist remnant in excommunicating John Smyth and the majority with whom they recently were in close communion.[8]

Despite their discouragement because of the break, the Baptists remained in Holland, at least until July 8, 1611. Helwys utilized this troubling period to examine the differences among the various kindred groups, including his own, those led by Smyth, and the other English Separatists. The chronicler Christopher Lawne reported that there were three English groups in Amsterdam at this time: one of them led by Leonard Busher, who probably had been with Helwys at one time; the Helwys congregation; and the Smyth group.[9]

The Baptists presented to the Mennonites a "Confession of Faith," so that the Mennonites might discern the differences between them and the diminished Smyth group. Along with the "Confession," Helwys and John Murton sent to the Mennonites a letter written in

English urging them not to receive John Smyth.[10] Smyth, although anxious to join the Mennonites, did not press matters. He died in August 1612 without membership in any regular church and was buried in the Nieuwekerke at Amsterdam.[11]

The doctrinal differences between John Smyth and Thomas Helwys were not significant, except in regard to the legitimacy of Smyth's self-baptism. However, Baptist history, and Baptist characteristics of vitality, tolerance, missionary zeal, and evangelism, could have been altered critically with the absorption of the major part of Smyth's group into the Mennonite congregation. That Baptists did not evolve quite differently may be due to the heritage left by the ten survivors that included Helwys.

Before their break, the two groups, led separately by Smyth and Helwys, had agreed on basic beliefs: the authority of the New Testament; believer's baptism; falling from Grace; loyalty to the State; sovereignty of the conscience; and strict Christian morality. Helwys's theology permitted taking an oath and would have allowed members to serve as magistrates. Helwys and Smyth agreed, even while separating, in denying original sin. However, Helwys would later change his position and proclaim: "men are by nature the children of Wrath, born in iniquitie and in sin conceived, wise to all evil but to good they have no knowledge."[12]

The practices of these earliest Baptists are clarified in the "Declaration of Faith of English People Remaining at Amsterdam," drawn up in 1611. Baptism by pouring was applied to believers only and never to infants. Freedom of conscience required the consent and knowledge by candidates of their baptism, but it also allowed falling from Grace. The Calvinism that was embraced in the beginning was now abandoned. The church authorized the election of officers, including men and women deacons and preaching elders.[13] And while the differences between Smyth and Helwys were small, the Smyth group would be absorbed as a single wave into the sea, whereas the Baptists under Helwys, on the other hand, would become a leaven that would expand and greatly affect the religious world.

Return to England

Before John Smyth died in Holland in 1612, Helwys and John Murton led the little flock of refugee Baptists back to London, to join the other besieged Dissenters. There, in 1611 or 1612,[14] at the Spitalfield suburb of London, they founded the first Baptist church on English soil. The persecution of non-Anglicans was being pursued relentlessly, and church services were carried out in secret. The Baptists were aware that, in 1612, two Dissenters, Bartholomew Legate and Edward Wightman, were burned to death in England for their Non-Conformist religious views.[15] Among the persecuted Dissenters was Helwys's wife Joan, who had been imprisoned for joining the Separatists. Despite the stern persecution that assailed Baptists, Quakers, Congregationalists, and others, the General Baptists founded by Helwys grew slowly, and in 1626 could claim five churches. By 1644, while still persecuted, and with Helwys long deceased, the association numbered at least forty-seven churches.[16]

Helwys was an active scholar, who between 1611 and 1612 wrote four books, three of them in Holland and a fourth in England.[17] Before returning to England, driven as he was to suffer with the other English Dissenters, he prepared a list of beliefs to which he subscribed and which separated him from Smyth. These differences were:

  I. that Christ took his flesh of Marie [Mary], having a true earthlie, naturall bodie.
 II. that a Sabbath or day of rest is to be kept holy everie first day of the weeke.
III. that ther is no succession or privilege to persons in the holie things.
 IV. that magistracie, being an holy ordinance of God debarreth not any from being of the Church of Christ.[18]

The articles of Helwys asserted doctrines easily recognizable by later Baptists: the humanity, as well as the divinity of Christ; the strict observance of Sunday, similar in respects to the Puritan prac-

tice; the priesthood of the believer, distinctive in its doctrinal difference with the Roman Catholic position on its priests; and acceptance of magistrates as members in the Baptist Church.

In England, shortly after arriving from Holland, Helwys published his great defense of religious liberty in the writing, *A Short
Declaration of the Mistery of Iniquity* (1612). Helwys sought with
boldness extraordinary to present a copy of his work to King James.
Not successful in this, he then sent the book to the king, with a
personal note on the flyleaf. The proud monarch, advocate of the
"Divine Right of Kings," must have been astounded when he read
the following words:

> Heare, O king, and dispise not ye counsell of ye poore, and let
> their complaints come before thee. The king is a mortall man,
> and not God therefore hath no power over ye immortall soules
> of his subiects, to make lawes and ordinances for them, and to
> set spirituall Lords over them.
>
> If the king have authority to make spirituall Lords and lawes,
> then he is an immortall God, and not a mortall man.
>
> O king, be not seduced by deceivers to sin so against God
> whome thou oughtest to obey, nor against thy poore subiects
> who ought and will obey thee in all things with body life and
> goods, or els let their lives be taken from ye earth.
>
> God save ye king.
>
> Spittlefield neare London
>
> Tho. Helwys[19]

This letter and the book, *The Mistery of Iniquity*, was to cost Thomas
Helwys his liberty and ultimately his life.

In *The Mistery of Iniquity*, Helwys acknowledged that in the Old
Testament period, kings had supremacy in directing religion. For the
New Testament phase, he did not concede similar authority to the
rulers. Helwys alluded to Jesus, who would not call down fire on
those who differed with Him on religious interpretation. The king
was to be in charge of laws, despite the English struggle between
Parliament and the haughty Stuarts: "Let the king command what

ordinances of man he will, and wee are to obey it." However, the king could not exercise similar power over the Church, for "with this Kingdom, our lord the King hath nothinge to do."[20]

In this final book, *The Mistery of Iniquity*, Helwys wrote one of the greatest petitions for freedom of worship ever published:[21]

> Let the King judge, is it not most equal that men should choose their religion themselves, seeing they only must stand themselves before the judgment seat of God to answer for themselves. . . . [We] profess and teach that in all earthly things the king's power is to be submitted unto; and in heavenly or spiritual things, if the king or any in authority under him shall exercise their power against any they are not to resist by any way or means, although it were in their power, but rather to submit their lives as Christ and his disciples did, and yet keep their consciences to God.[22]

Freedom of expression was extended by Helwys, as pastor of the London Spitalfield Baptist Church, to his close associates. Leonard Busher, reportedly a member of the same congregation, and possessed of some learning, championed adult baptism through immersion thirty years before the Particular Baptists (Calvinistic) adopted it. In 1614 Busher was not barred from issuing a tract that offered the argument that Jews and even "Papists" (Catholics) should have the right of law to write, dispute, or print any matter relating to religion.[23]

Helwys distanced himself from the doctrine of the Anabaptists, who did not allow magistrates or judges to be church members. Ultimately, Baptists found government service compatible with faith and took their lead from Helwys's words contained in "A Declaration of Faith of English People Remaining at Amsterdam in Holland" (1611).[24] Helwys declared: "And therefore they [magistrates] maybee members off the Church off CHRIST reteining their Magistracie, for no Hoile Ordinance off GOD debarreth anie from being a member off CHRISTS church."[23] In the same writing, Helwys affirmed the authority of magistrates, who "beare the sword off God—

which sword in all Lawful administracions is to bee defended and supported by the servants off God that are vnder their Govrnment."[26]

This valiant Baptist Trailblazer showed Christian audacity not only in returning to England in the teeth of persecution, but also in asserting his religious views. He did not hesitate to attack the chief religious groups of his day, the Roman Catholic and Anglican hierarchies, for robbing mankind of their freedom in Christ. He assailed Puritan preachers, who in order to avoid controversy with the Anglicans over rites that the Puritans abhorred, sought appointments as private chaplains or city preachers. Helwys criticized the Mennonites for refusing government service, their emphasis upon apostolic succession, and on their adherence to the doctrine of free will. Helwys replied that only Adam before his fall enjoyed true freedom of choice. Finally, he criticized the Calvinists for their predestination doctrine, giving man no free choice in accepting God's grace.[27] Attacking on all sides, it is remarkable that Helwys found believers who would sacrifice their security and positions for an austere, persecuted faith that relied for salvation on Jesus' sacrifice and doctrines defined by the New Testament, instead of rituals, councils, priests, and ancient documents.

Step by step, we can trace the evolution of Baptist theology through the earnest searching of the Scriptures, first by John Smyth and then by Thomas Helwys. Mistakes were made, for despite their submissions, first to God and then to the demands of their faith, these Trailblazers were human and fallible. As an example, of his first statements on dogma, Helwys aligned himself with Smyth in rejecting the doctrine that from Adam man was tainted with original sin. In a later version of his confession, Helwys changed his theology to embrace the Biblical position that men and women are "children of wrath" and conceived in sin.[28] This took the Baptists in a different direction from some Anabaptists, who held that man was essentially good.

Distinctive to Helwys was the idea of the Puritan Sabbath, to be observed on the first day of the week. He also advocated the weekly observance of the Lord's Supper, which differed from the Anabaptist practice. Helwys also authorized oath-taking as an acceptable practice.[29]

The intensity of the opening struggle in England for religious freedom is illustrated by Helwys's depictions of the Church of Rome as the first beast of the Revelation, while the second beast is identified as the Church of England (Anglican Church). In the table of contents for *A Short Declaration of the Mistery of Iniquity*, Helwys limited the powers that the king had the right to employ. However, men provoked the great Stuart kings at the peril of their bodies, and by writing his book, Helwys in an act of supreme courage advocated full religious freedom. The title of his book shows the apocalyptic influence and fervor of the period, but Helwys's call for tolerance is revolutionary.

Helwys's admonitions to the monarch on religious freedom included the following eloquent appeal:

> What Great Power and authority: what honor, names and titles God hath given to the King.
>
> That God hath given to the K. [king] an earthly kingdome with all earthly power against the which, none may resist but must in all thinges obey, willingly, either to do, or suffer.
>
> That Christ alone is K. of Israell, & sitts vpon Davids Throne, & that the K. ought to be a subject of his Kingdome.
>
> That none ought to be punished either with death or bonds for transgressing against the spirituall ordinaces (sic) of the new Testament, and that such Offenses ought to be punished onely with spiritual sword and censures.[30]

The doctrine of succession, through which the Roman Catholic Church could establish validity as the true church, stemming from Peter, has held an esteemed place in its dogmas. For the Church of England, the historical succession of churches and bishops also is revered. But for a new, radically different church, such as the Baptists represented, succession had little merit, logic, or spiritual basis. The Baptists, instead, preferred to look to the Scriptures for examples, or else to the history of early Christian churches of the first centuries. As Helwys declared: "There is no succession in the outward church, but that all succession is from heaven." Later he was to state: "I deny all succession except in the truth."

Even in the earliest formative period of the Baptists in Amsterdam, Helwys, in warning the Mennonites about receiving the restless John Smyth into their community, aimed an arrow at successionist beliefs. [Shall you ever] "prove, that he or they from whome you have your beginning were the first? No man can ever prove it . . . Cast it away, seeing there is not warrant in God's word to warrant it unto you, that he or they were the first." Thus Helwys rejected succession as historically unprovable and spiritually not necessary.[31]

In asserting their distinctiveness, Baptists through the ages have affirmed that the Bible with its sixty-six books—omitting the Apocrypha—is the unique doctrinal source. No other documents, church councils, or creeds share or even approach the same elevation of reverence that the Scriptures, in particular the New Testament, hold for Baptists. The General Baptists that appeared in England with Helwys regarded the Scriptures as the Word of God and the source of doctrinal truth. Baptists of this period insisted that every believer, not only the elders, had the right to read and interpret the Bible, thus indirectly giving an impetus to literacy.[32]

The Helwys confession of 1611 confirms the centrality of the Bible to Baptist belief:

> That the scriptures off the Old and New Testament are written for our instruction; 2 Tim. 3.16 & that wee ought to search them for they testifie off Christ IO. 5.39. And therefore to be vsed with all reverence, as conteying the Holie Word off God, which onelie is our direction in al things whatsoever.[33]

The importance of baptism was emphasized by Helwys but not as a necessity for salvation, since baptism from the beginning was symbolic of cleansing from sin. The Helwys confession of 1611 affirmed: "That Baptisme or washing with Water, is the outward manifestacion off dieing vnto sinn, and walkeing in newness off life. Roman. 6.2,3,4. And therefore in no wise apperteyneth to infants."[34]

The doctrine of believers baptism was asserted again in Helwys's Propositions and Conclusions (1612): "outward baptism of water, is to be administered only upon such penitent and faithful persons as are (aforesaid), and not upon innocent infants."[35] Thus, from the seventeenth century, Baptists enjoined against baptism of infants, since infants could not be saved by actions of an adult and were not held to be responsible for their own actions, due to their immaturity.

The struggle between Arminianism and Calvinism would be an important issue to John Smyth, Thomas Helwys, and their contemporaries. Later in history, this doctrinal struggle would contribute to the beheading of Charles I of England, who offended Parliament and the Puritans by confirming Arminian bishops, who then aligned themselves with the king. The Arminian positions, which Puritans found so offensive, rejected the Calvinist interpretation of total predestination, asserted that Christ had died for all persons rather than only the elect, and affirmed that all sinners had the freedom to accept or reject divine grace.[36]

John Smyth opposed the Calvinist concept of original sin and held that, instead, God deals with each person and his personal sins. Smyth rejected the notion that God predestines some for salvation and others for damnation. Smyth stated that "as no man begetteth his child to the gallows, nor no potter maketh a pot to break it; so God doth not create or predestinate any man to destruction."[37]

Thomas Helwys built on these premises and employed predestination as a positive doctrine. He wrote:

> That God before the Foundation off the World hath Predestinated that all that beleeve in him, shall-be saved, Ephes 1.4, 12; Mark 16.16 and al that beleeve not shalbee damned. Mark 16.6 . . . and not that GOD hath Predestinated men to bee wicked, and so to bee damned, but that men being wicked shallbee damned, for GOD would have all men saved, and come to the knowledg off the truth.[38]

Still, the General Baptists, of which Helwys was prominent, held that men could fall away from the grace of God, and lose their salvation.[39]

Considerable attention has been given by William R. Estep and other historians to the influence of the Anabaptists in the lives and beliefs of Smyth and Helwys. But truth is truth. Despite the picture of two strong, creative Christian pioneers carving a unique road for Baptists, there appears to be ample evidence that much in their doctrine and practice originated with the Anabaptists. The Anabaptists refused to take oaths, and probably influenced some General Baptists to refuse to take on oath of loyalty to the state, and such Baptists suffered severely for it.

Historically, General Baptists repeatedly affirmed their loyalty to the crown and native land, but not all. The Helwys congregation in 1611 declared:

"That it is Lawful in a just cause for deciding of strife to take an oath by the Name off the Lord."

This position was re-affirmed by 1678, when the General Baptists formally encouraged oaths under proper circumstances.[40]

Other than the assertion of the priesthood of the believer, the greatest unique Baptist doctrine may be the sanctity given to the individual conscience and the obligation by Baptists to protect the religious freedom of all people. Baptists in the seventeenth century scandalized some English citizens and frightened others with their claims for freedom of conscience, even for Jews, Muslims, Catholics, and atheists. Helwys denied that religious uniformity was a necessary ingredient for tranquillity. In one of the most generous statements of the age, Helwys wrote:

"Let them be heretickes, Turkes, Jewes, or whatsoever it apperteynes not the earthly power to punish them in the least measure" in spiritual matters.[41]

Thomas Helwys, the Baptist pioneer, is one of the most illustrious universal exponents of religious freedom. He actively sought protection for the stern faith of Baptists, but also for Muslims and atheists, who were burned in Spain and hounded out of Puritan New England. He advocated religious protection even for the persecutors of Dissenters, Baptists, and Quakers, namely, the Church of England and the Roman Catholic Church, that dominated much of the Christian West. Thus, in a true sense, he was possessed of a great soul.

While not consciously self-destructive, Helwys willingly faced torture and death by returning in 1611-12 to England from Amsterdam to present James I with a plea for religious toleration. He freely sought to join the imprisoned and persecuted Dissenters of England, and was, in a sense, a spiritual precursor of the Lutheran pastor, Dietrich Bonhoeffer, who centuries later returned from America to Nazi Germany and death. Helwys would publish in England his masterpiece, *A Short Declaration of the Mistery of Iniquity*, and would then be confined to Newgate Prison by James I until his death in 1616.

He was a careful theologian and convincing advocate. But his greatest act, from the Baptist perspective, was to salvage in Amsterdam the Baptist remnant of ten persons, and give them the firm backbone and doctrine to refuse John Smyth's enticements to join the Dutch Mennonites. Thus, he saved the Baptist cause, at least those who called themselves General Baptists. At London in 1611 or 1612, Helwys would establish the first Baptist Church on English soil, but the word "Baptist" would not appear in its name.

Thomas Helwys, the Baptist Trailblazer, is unforgettable for the supreme courage shown when he confronted King James I on matters of religious freedom, and, because his fate was determined by Christian free will, he died in prison the freest man in England.

Chapter 3

John Bunyan
(1628-1688)

The Gifted Tinker

John Bunyan was a Baptist Trailblazer, who rose through his conversion experience from village prankster to one of Christendom's illustrious preachers and perhaps its most renowned and effective author. For the strict conformist, he is a disturbing saint. For others, inspired by his Christian compassion, audacity, and individualism, Bunyan is a singular flame. In his labors and imprisonment, he sought to reflect the concern of Jesus Christ for his people's salvation and welfare, in preference to a concern for the restrictive laws of the Church. This is a plain accolade for the writer of sixty works, including the classic *The Pilgrim's Progress*. He is memorable, for the mold that shaped Bunyan shaped no other human, so unique was his witness and person.

Bunyan was born in the significant year of 1628, a year in which Charles I was compelled by the House of Commons to sign the Petition of Right, a landmark in the struggle for civil rights in England. He lived through the period of the English Civil Wars and the establishment of the Commonwealth by Oliver Cromwell, and died just before the Glorious Revolution of 1688, which became a centerpiece of constitutional liberties.

*John Bunyan (1667) Blesses his Blind Daughter
from Bedford Jail*

John Bunyan began his life in the village of Elstow, near Bedford, England, the son of Thomas Bunyan, the latter a tinker or brazier who mended and sold pots, lanterns, and kettles. The Bunyan family filled a respectable niche in the village and had even owned land in Bedfordshire as early as 1199. Margaret, John Bunyan's mother, was Thomas's second wife, and she bore two other children, Margaret, young John's constant companion, and William. As a youth, John sometimes worked at the forge by the family cottage or stirred up business by traveling from door to door as a tinker.[1]

He was a reckless young man, high spirited and imaginative. More fortunate than some of his economic class because of his parents' ambitions, he was able for a short time to attend grammar school, possibly at nearby Houghton Conquest, where he learned the rudiments of reading and writing. Discipline in village schools was severe and education was minimal, and at Elstow a teacher was removed for cruelty and drinking, not uncommon vices.[2] John's chief diversions, however, were engaging in mischief, playing bowls and tipcat (a game similar to cricket), and dancing on the village green. In an age of Puritan ascendancy, he enjoyed those outlets, regarded by some pious neighbors as sinful but tolerated by others.

Later, Bunyan would say about his childhood: "Even as a child, I had few equals in cursing, swearing, lying, and blaspheming the holy name of God." More than once he had given himself up as lost eternally. While Bunyan later called himself the vilest of sinners, he was clearly exaggerating the depth of his depravity, and in time hotly denied that he was unchaste.[3] As he was growing up, however, Bunyan was disturbed by intrusions of religious feelings, while at other times he experienced terrifying visions and remorse about his aimless life. In 1644, at age fifteen, his boyhood would end with the death of his mother Margaret and his sister.

In this stormy period, Bunyan, age about seventeen, was enrolled in Lieutenant Colonel Richard Cockayne's regiment in the Parliamentary Army and served from 1644 until 1647, or two and a half years. In order to create a professional army in place of the depleted levies of generals Manchester, Essex, and Waller, Parliament began impressment and promised regular salaries to the men. As part of Cromwell's New Model Army, Bunyan spent most of his military career at the fortress of Newport Pagnell, twelve miles from Elstow, in company with Presbyterians, Congregationalists, and, on the left, Baptists and Levellers. Under Cromwell, every combatant knew that he was engaged in a righteous war and carried *The Soldier's Pocket Bible* on his person.[4] Cromwell's army was a praying, singing battle force, and although lay preaching was forbidden, soldiers often exhorted their comrades as lay preachers and suffered arrest. The soldiers of Lord Essex kept fasts, listened to sermons, advanced to battle singing hymns, and when victorious sang in the field among their dead.[5]

Baptist fervor was shown by two officers, Lieutenant Paul Hobson and Captain Beaumont, who were arrested and imprisoned by Sir Samuel Luke, governor of the fortress, for holding an unauthorized preaching service on Sunday, June 15, 1645, at the village of Lathbury, near Bunyan's garrison at Newport Pagnell. The uproar from the arrest was to resound to the farthest nooks of England. The Baptist officers were on travel orders to London, and not under local command. Their galling offense to Sir Samuel was that they ignored the Presbyterian-style celebration for the parliamentary victory at Naseby, which he had ordered in the form of a thanksgiving service. Hobson and Beaumont absented themselves from the official service and drew a larger group to Lathbury, where Hobson, a Baptist, preached the sermon. Sir Samuel Luke was disliked both by soldiers and townsmen, and the incident near Newport Pagnell probably hastened Sir Samuel's resignation. The embroglio involving the preaching officers was settled at a higher level by General Fairfax, who asked for apologies from both sides.[6] But Non-Conformists, including the Baptists, attracted new converts because of the preaching.

However, Bunyan, at this stage a rustic soldier, gave no evidence of having any exact knowledge of the great civil and religious issues at stake in the Civil Wars. It is only a speculation that in his soldier years he met the literary characters that enlivened his books, including Mr. Greatheart, Captain Boanerges, Talkative, Mr. Live-Loose, Ignorance, and Pickthank. He volunteered for the Irish campaign in his last days in the army, to serve under Captain O'Hara, as one of seventy-nine privates. However, the unit was abruptly disbanded at Newport Pagnell on July 21, 1647, and Bunyan's war was over.[7]

After his return from war, at the probable age of twenty, he resumed his trade and married a religious orphan girl, whose name is not known.[8] This future great Baptist pastor and author commented briefly about his extreme poverty: "This woman and I came together as poor as poor might be, not having so much household stuff as a dish or spoon betwixt us both." It is significant that he selected a pious wife, who brought as her sole possessions two books that awakened in Bunyan an interest in religion: *The Plaine Man's Pathway to Heaven* and *The Practice of Piety*.

Bunyan endured a long period of spiritual conflict, including horrific childhood dreams of hell, devils, and monsters. The standard Calvinist practice was to count sins done during the day and to beg God's forgiveness before sleeping at night. As reflected in his book, *Grace Abounding to the Chief of Sinners*, Bunyan's conscience was quickened by Pastor Christopher Hall of the Elstow church through a sermon on keeping the Sabbath. The freedom of Sunday afternoon for music, dancing, and games allowed by the *Book of Sports* (1617) was deplored by strict preachers.[9] Yet soon Bunyan was engaged in the game of tipcat. As he was about to strike the six-inch "cat" or shuttle with his bludgeon or "catstaff," a voice seemed to say: "Wilt thou leave thy sins and go to Heaven, or have thy sins and go to Hell?" He imagined that he saw Jesus looking sternly from Heaven. But fearing that he had sinned beyond all hope, he returned to his game. After a long struggle, Bunyan repented and felt free of his sin and guilt. He was confident of God's grace, began to study the Bible earnestly, and became a man of exemplary behavior. He was baptized, probably in the dead of night in the Baptist way (as testified by an unnamed friend in *Grace Abounding*, seventh edition[10]), at Bedford, where he later served as pastor for his entire life.[11]

The influence on Bunyan's conversion by ordinary Christians, unremarkable books, and common events is striking. His first wife's books were read and made a mark on him. A poor man "spoke pleasantly of the Bible," and kindled his interest. Four village women of Reverend John Gifford's congregation at Bedford discounted their own righteousness, and over the course of several meetings, spoke joyfully of a "new birth."

John Gifford, formerly a major in the Royalist Army, had been taken prisoner at Maidstone in 1648, and after escaping, practiced medicine briefly. Around 1650, Gifford was converted, organized a small Independent church (later to become a Particular Baptist church), of twelve Bedford citizens, and served as Bunyan's spiritual guide and mentor. Kindly and tender, Gifford became the prototype for Evangelist in *Pilgrim's Progress*.[12] In that same church at Bedford that Bunyan later served as pastor, he followed the lead of Gifford in accepting into the communion of saints some persons that were not immersed but had been christened as infants. Bunyan pursued during his lifetime the principle that the inner experience was more important than the outward form.[13]

The five years following Bunyan's departure from the army were to be the defining years of his life. At its climax, and near his twenty-fifth birthday, he was set on a godly course. Although lacking in formal training, Bunyan began preaching in familiar villages with such effectiveness and eloquence that people flocked to hear him. He sometimes alluded to the divine protection that God had given him in his youth, in an encounter with a poisonous adder, whose fangs he had extracted with his fingers, and, again, in falling from a boat on the Bedford River.[14] He gradually became less dependent on his tinker's trade, although among early Baptists it was considered honorable and even desirable for a preacher to have a trade.

When Charles II was recalled to the throne in 1660, the Anglican Church also returned to power, and Bunyan was arrested for disobeying the laws prohibiting services by Non-Conformists. His only crime was preaching the Gospel. For this, he was thrown into prison at Bedford in 1660, and, except for brief intervals, would remain incarcerated for more than twelve years, until 1672. He could have obtained his freedom at any time by promising not to preach. But as he said, "If you let me out today, I will preach again tomorrow."

Bunyan's first wife had died, and shortly before his arrest he married Elizabeth, a "noble-hearted woman," who nurtured his four children, one of them blind Mary, particularly loved by Bunyan. Eventually Bunyan and Elizabeth would have two children of their own.[15] In prison, he preached to prisoners, read the Bible and John Foxe's book about martyrs, and wrote religious books and papers.[16]

Bunyan was imprisoned at age thirty-two, because his unauthorized preaching was considered a threat to religious conformity. But also, the authorities regarded his religious activities as evidence of sedition. In the official mind, Baptists and Anabaptists were mistakenly identified as the same religious group and were viewed as equally reprehensible as Quakers and Levellers. Anabaptists were associated with the anarchy and excesses in the sixteenth century that convulsed the German city of Muenster, in an episode of murder, immorality, and destruction. The Fifth Monarchists, that now prophesied the imminent return of King Jesus, and the Thomas Venner "insurrection" in London (during which fifty men sought to overthrow the government and their leader was hanged) accentuated the sense of danger. The constables with warrants in their hands did not stop to listen to the Dissenter field preachers, whose simple message was for listeners to repent and be saved, but who did not challenge the authority of the king or Parliament. Both Baptists and Quakers were to suffer unjustly for the Venner affair.

Bunyan's congregations customarily met with the Bible in their hands and listened, while pastor and people examined the Scriptures. Bunyan's preaching in 1660 had no prophetic quality. He was a man with a single purpose, preaching the Gospel and seeking souls for the Kingdom Eternal. "Discretion was not in his books." Oth-

erwise, the world would never have heard of him. King Charles II
had just returned in 1660 to Dover from abroad, and partially because of fear of the Fifth Monarchists, the Declaration of Breda,
which had protected citizens from arrest because of religious differences, was withdrawn.

Thus, when the congregation began assembling at the Lower
Samsell farmhouse near the great elms, Bunyan's name was almost
certainly on the list of those to be arrested by newly-appointed Justice Francis Wingate. Bunyan's supporters warned him that an armed
force had gathered nearby to arrest him if the meeting proceeded.
After walking alone among the trees for an hour of meditation and
prayer, Bunyan began the worship service and resolved to face imprisonment, rather than turn his back on his beliefs and fellow
Christians. Sustained by the Scriptures and John Foxe's *Actes and
Monuments*, Bunyan welcomed the opportunity to suffer for Christ.
His answer to the fears of his fellow worshippers was: "Come, be of
good cheer; let us not be daunted; our cause is good. We need not
be ashamed of it."

Rather than be a traitor to his faith, he resolved to face the test:

> If I should now run and make an escape, it will be of a very
> ill savour in the country. For what will my weak and newly-
> converted brethren think of it, but that I was not so strong in
> deed as I was in word."[17] In Justice Wingate's first case, having
> assumed a new office, Bunyan was remanded to the Bedford
> County jail, where he would spend twelve years. Against a pro-
> posal for release, if he promised not to gather his fellow-Chris-
> tians again, he answered calmly: "I durst not make any further
> promise, for my conscience would not suffer me to do it."[18]

In prison from 1660 to 1672, Bunyan earned an income for his
poor family and paid his prison fees by making thousands of tagged
shoelaces. His prison, like others in England, was a stinking over-
crowded enclosure, with men and women pushed together, sleeping
on straw, with no water closer than the courtyard. A quarter of a loaf

England and Scotland and Their Major Cities

of bread daily was the allowance for food, if paid for by the prisoner. Families could bring additional food. Bunyan, never forgetting he was a preacher, proclaimed the gospel through the bars to crowds on Sunday morning. A kindly jailer allowed him once to preach in London, possibly during the period of the Great Plague, but such liberties were unusual, and the jailer was threatened with the loss of his position.[19]

For social exchange, Bunyan preached to his fellow inmates or counseled his parishioners from Bedfordshire, who visited him from time to time. He derived comfort from his knowledge that the greatest number of prisoners around him were not felons, but Non-Conformists like himself. Therefore, there were daily gatherings for prayer, singing, and Bible reading. Bunyan's book *The Holy City* was conceived as the consequence of a sermon given in prison. Also in prison, he wrote his classic, *Grace Abounding to the Chief of Sinners.*[20]

In 1672, in a ploy to gain support among the Non-Conformists, Charles II suspended the laws against religious Dissenters, an act which allowed Bunyan to be released from prison. In 1676-77, just three and a half years later, he would be incarcerated a second time, for six months. It is believed likely that in this second imprisonment he wrote the first part of *The Pilgrim's Progress*, published in 1678 as one of the greatest works of literature and forerunner of the modern novel. In 1684, possibly after a third brief imprisonment, he would complete this major work.[21]

In writing *Pilgrim's Progress*, Bunyan did not know that he was creating an epic work of literature, "for of literature he knew almost nothing except the Bible." He merely wanted to tell in simple English the story of Christian the hero, who flees from the City of Destruction on a pilgrimage that takes him from the Slough of Despond to the River of Death and, finally, to the Celestial City. His book is an allegory of the human soul, of suffering, temptation, trials, and, ultimately, salvation through Jesus Christ. It, in essence, is Bunyan's quest for God's favor, that embraces his entire life. His characters are real people of England, speaking the lively and humorous language of shopkeepers and peasants: Mr. Worldly Wiseman, Mr. Talkative, Hopeful, and Faithful.

It was a "happy accident" for the world that Bunyan had little education and knew thoroughly only one book, the King James Version of the Bible, the work of fifty-five men and published only seventeen years before he was born. Bunyan "lived in the Bible until its words became his own." Bunyan had experienced spiritual struggles and seen visions, and thus he created reality for the readers of his book through the credible characters of his story. Paradoxical as it may be, Bunyan's legend of Christian became the most popular English-language book, next to the Bible, for three hundred years.[22] *Pilgrim's Progress* has been translated into more languages than any other book except the Bible. Thus, it may have been, next to the Scriptures, the most effective moral teacher in the Western World, serving as a prime source of enlightenment for children and a character guide for adults.[23]

This "ignorant" tinker's son—and renowned Baptist—would eventually write sixty published works, including: *Grace Abounding to the Chief of Sinners* (1666); *The Life and Death of Mr. Badman* (1680); and *The Holy War* (1682).[24] In English literature, Bunyan shares a secure place with the great Puritan writer John Milton.

Until the last years of his life, Bunyan in the public mind was the man of the pulpit, rather than master of the pen. Tradition holds that his out-of-town congregations would arrive at dawn to hear him at noon. Men of letters, as well as tailors, farmers, and smiths, were awed by his words of eloquence and spirit. "I bowed myself with all my might," Bunyan wrote, "to condemn sin and transgression wherever I found it." None of his sermons survive intact, but from his sermons expanded into treatises it is possible to capture the mood that prevailed when men and women met in forest glades at midnight, packed into barns, convened behind locked doors, or listened in hushed silence after walking miles following a day engaged in plowing. His power lay not in forensic tricks or emotional outbursts but in his complete reliance on the Word of God. As the Earl of

Clarendon, Edward Hyde, is reported to have said: "The Bible in English under every weaver's and chambermaid's arms hath done us much harm."

To the loyalists of the formal churches, Bunyan represented only one more bumpkin, who felt empowered through preaching. As the "Water Poet" John Taylor expressed it in 1641:

> Extemp'ry without any meditation,
> But only by the Spirit's revelation.
> Tis madnesse, that a crew of brainless blocks,
> Dares teach the learned what is Orthodoxe.
> These kind of Vermin swarm like Caterpillars.
> And hold Conventicles in Barnes and Sellars.
> Some preach (or prate) in woods, in fields, in stables,
> In hollow trees, in tubs, on tops of tables,
> To the expence of many a Tallow Tapor,
> They tosse the holy Scripture into Vapor.[25]

Yet for all his singularity and uniqueness, John Bunyan as the Baptist preacher did not depart from the Bible or generally from orthodox doctrine, nor engage in unbiblical speculations or "Chaotic nonsense."[26]

The preaching career of Bunyan probably began with the statement of his conversion delivered to the Bedford church and likely assumed direction with the encouragement of that church's pastor, John Gifford. When Bunyan was arrested and tried in 1660, he gave testimony to preaching for five years, but it is reasonable to believe that Gifford and the Bedford church had encouraged his first efforts from about 1657.

In 1671, while Bunyan was still in prison, the Bedford church weighed the calling of Bunyan as its pastor, after the death of John Gifford. After much deliberation and prayer, the church proceeded to "seeke God about the choice of Brother Bunyan to the office of an Elder that their way in that respect may be cleared up to them." Then, on January 21, 1672, at a full assembly of the Bedford church, "After much seeking God by prayer, and sober conference formerly had, the Congregation did at this meeting with joynt consent (signifyed by solemne lifting up of their hands) call forth and appoint our brother John Bunyan to the pastorall office or eldership."[27]

With the relaxing of the Act of Uniformity by the king, Bunyan occasionally was allowed to leave prison, and he was present at a church meeting to give himself to "serve Christ and his church" as pastor of the Bedford congregation. Bunyan was released from prison after the king's pardon of May 17, 1672, because magnanimous Quakers petitioning for the release of their own believers included the names of Bunyan and other Dissenters. Bunyan received a license to preach, along with twenty-five other preachers, on May 9, 1672. So, armed with his freedom, an appointment as pastor at Bedford, and a license to preach, he departed the Bedfordshire jail. He would be returned to prison after three and a half years had passed.[28]

As an itinerant preacher, with his base at Bedford and a widening span of believers, he would ultimately preach near London and receive the un-Baptist honorary title of "Bishop" Bunyan. Until his final acclaim, he would largely preach in secret places, removed from the notice of the king's officers, such as a shed with an escape door at Bendish, a tree at Tinker's Hill, or, more openly, with the congregation of John Gibbs at Newport Pagnell. He preached about men's sins, about their separation from God, and of the punishment with Hell-fire if salvation was not obtained. He was a compassionate man, but the Puritan tenor of the age affected his message. By foot or horseback, he pursued his tinker's trade and delivered week by week the Gospel message to a multitude of distant villages.[29]

In the years between his first and second imprisonment, Bunyan was able to preach in a real "church," a barn and orchard for the congregation of Baptists purchased by Josias Ruffhead for fifty pounds. The church members would worship in this setting, "the Meeting Barn," for the next thirty-five years, until a new sanctuary, the Old Meeting House, was erected on the same site. Sixteen years of Bunyan's devoted ministry began with the "Barn," in which clustered his scattered flock that had previously met discreetly or not at all.

The original twelve members of John Gifford's church were joined by others. Prominent members now included two haberdashers, two linen drapers, a shoemaker, a lastmaker, and a tinker (Bunyan). This church, in seventeenth-century terminology, belonged to the Open Communion branch of the Particular Baptists. The church government was in true Baptist expression individualistic, with all lay members free to express their opinions in a congregational setting. However, members would have been quick to remind each other of Scriptural restraints. In Bunyan's beliefs, the inner Christian experience took precedence over outward church form. In permitting membership in the church to persons that were not immersed, he was severely criticized by other Baptists and not welcomed to the pulpits of churches that followed the "strict communion."[30]

Bunyan was tolerant and fiercely loyal to his Non-Conformist Christian principles. While his basic beliefs were Baptist, and he was pastor of a Particular Baptist church at Bedford, he preferred to be called a "Christian" rather than a Baptist. This was so because he felt that all sects and denominations were destructive of the harmony of God's family. In two publications, *Heavenly Footman* and *Peaceable Principles*, Bunyan warned his readers about Quakers, Ranters, Freewillers, Anabaptists, Independents, and Presbyterians.[31] His unorthodox style greatly disturbed strict Particular Baptists such as William Kiffin. With his unique faith, Bunyan vigorously defended the practice of serving the Lord's Supper to persons who were not immersed. By exalting Christ as the Messiah, by giving testimony that the Bible is the fundamental document, and through suffering for long years in prison for his faith, he followed in the main the Baptist way.[32]

Bunyan was the leading elder or pastor at the Bedford church, but the dynamics compelling religious change induced him to become active as a public debater. Public disputations, where often prominent priests and pastors argued theological points on opposite sides, became a principal means by which Baptists made converts. Between 1641 and 1700 at least 109 public debates were held in England involving Baptist champions. Some of the leading Baptists who were involved in the public debates included Christopher Blackwood, Henry Jessey, and articulate, university-educated John Tombes. Tombes became a specialist in arguing against infant baptism, while Bunyan involved himself in six debates refuting Quaker doctrines.[33]

In his attitudes and beliefs, Bunyan could be almost as surprising and shocking as the great Master he followed.[34] He and his fellow-Baptist, John Dell, disapproved of the baptism of infants, yet they tolerated the sprinkling of infants for the sake of "pious and grieving wives" who had left the Anglican Church.[35] While Bunyan was baptized by immersion and advocated that practice for all who would accept it, he did not require immersion for membership in the Bedford church.

His church had a "mixed" congregation, meaning that some were not Baptists. Although personally "orthodox," as that term had meaning to seventeenth-century Baptists, he apparently was sympathetic to those who experienced the stress and trauma induced by religious societies that were breaking down and re-forming. Bunyan, who in his church allowed "open" membership and "open" communion—that is, not limited to Baptists or immersed Christians—stands in stark contrast to the merchant-pastor William Kiffin. The most steadfast of Particular Baptists, Kiffin stood firmly for "closed" communion, celebrated only by immersed Baptists and "closed" membership, by mature believers, who were saved by Christ and baptized in the Baptist way.[36] The Bedford Church, actually a Meeting Barn, under the leadership of Ebenezer Chandler, Bunyan's successor, would become as strict as most Regular Baptist congregations.[37]

Defining Baptist Practice

Bunyan and Kiffin had serious differences, which both clarified in their writings. These differences were most notably over who should be baptized and what persons could be admitted to take the Lord's

Supper. Before his release from prison in 1672, Bunyan published "A Confession of Faith," which contained viewpoints that alarmed Kiffin. Kiffin responded in 1673 with a work entitled "Serious Reflections." Bunyan answered this treatise with "Differences in Judgment Concerning Water Baptism No Bar to Communion" (1673). Bunyan complained that he had been "assaulted" for sixteen years by other Baptists, who "have sought to break us in pieces" over the issues of baptism and communion.[38]

In reply to criticism of his publication, "A Confession of Faith," Bunyan answered:

> I own Water-Baptism to be God's Ordinance, but I make no Idol of it.
>
> I will not let Water-Baptism be the rule, the door, the bolt, the bar, the wall of division between the righteous and the unrighteous.
>
> I am for communion of saints with saints, because they are saints; I shut none of the brethren out of the churches, nor forbid them that would receive them.
>
> I am not against every man though by your abusive language you would set everyone against me; but I am for union, concord and communion with saints as saints, and for that cause I wrote my book.[39]

Again Bunyan agreed to the validity of water baptism [immersion] but did not set it up as a bar or "Idol." In spirit, virtually all Baptists would agree that baptism in any form is not essential to salvation, but the practice follows the example of Jesus Christ and the intent of the Holy Spirit.

From the beginning, there was a difference among Baptists as to who should be accepted into the membership of a congregation and who should be welcome to take the Lord's Supper. Baptists like William Kiffin, John Spilsbury, and Hanserd Knollys stood firm that the church should be composed of baptized believers only, and only those were acceptable in the New Testament to receive the Lord's Supper. On the other hand, Baptists like Henry Jessey, John

Tombes, and John Bunyan favored accepting all Christians to communion. Beyond this, Jessey and Bunyan preached in churches whose members were not all Baptists. Such "mixed churches" and "open communion" were the practice of a large number of English Baptists and were advocated by some of its greatest preachers.[40]

The main ideas of Bunyan on ordinances are found in his words:

> Touching shadowish, or figurative ordinances; I believe that Christ hath ordained but two in his church, viz., Water baptism and the supper of the Lord: both of which are of excellent use to the church in this world; they being to us representations of the death and resurrection of Christ; and are as God shall make them, helps to our faith therein. But I count them not the fundamentals of our Christianity, nor the grounds or rule to communion with saints: servants they are, and our mystical ministers,—I therefore here declare my reverent esteem of them; yet dare not remove them as some do from the place and end, where by God they are set and appointed; nor ascribe unto them more than they were ordered to have in their first and primitive institution. It is possible to commit idolatry, even with God's own appointments.[41]

Bunyan taught that since God could save a person without immersion or any kind of baptism, as Jesus did to the malefactor beside him on the cross, then any Christian must be welcome at the Lord's Table. Otherwise, said Bunyan, the Church would be in the position of rejecting those whom the Lord accepted. He concluded his argument with: "All I say is, That the Church of Christ hath not warrant to keep out of their communion the Christian that is discovered to be a visible saint by the word, the Christian that walketh according to his light with God."

Kiffin, in great disagreement, answered that the New Testament communion comes only after baptism, and not before. The acceptance of Bunyan's beliefs on this matter would ultimately, according to Kiffin, lessen an esteem for Christ, disregard the Bible that prescribed it, and finally eliminate baptism, an ordinance given by God.

This tough theological struggle, comparable in a lesser way to the debate over sacramental cleanliness between apostles Peter and Paul, was won in the short-term among Particular Baptists by Kiffin. In the long-term, Baptist churches in England and America generally would adopt open communion, and leave to individual conscience, rather than church discipline, the determination as to who should take the Lord's Supper.[42]

Despite the popularity of singing with modern Baptists and its prominent part today in worship services, singing was not readily accepted in the early church. Benjamin Keach is given credit for introducing hymn singing to Baptists, at first to men only. But several Baptist women, Anna Trapnell and Katherine Sutton, reinforced the adoption of singing by introducing their separate books of hymns. John Bunyan also wrote songs for children, but he was unable to induce his adult congregation to sing, so novel was the practice. Even for the persistent Keach, congregational singing involved a "grueling controversy" over the practice.[43]

Two years before his death, Bunyan wrote a book of seventy-four poems for children, reflecting his love of music and verse. Seventeenth-century English children who were trained to think that life's main purpose was to prepare to die must have squealed with pleasure over Bunyan's Country Rhimes for Children. Snails, spiders, moles, and frogs acted as moral instructors of children, because of a lively creator with a droll insight. In such animals, bugs, and birds, there was one part reality and another part allegory, as any Midland child knew well. The Frog could be a large-mouthed Hypocrite, that mounts his Head, as if above the World and seeks in Churches to hoarsely croak, for "He neither loveth Jesus, nor his Yoak." As Bunyan wrote it:

> The Frog by Nature is both damp and cold,
> Her mouth is large, her Belly much will hold.
> She sits somewhat ascending, loves to be
> Croaking in Gardens, tho unpleasantly.

The sting of the bee was the similitude for sin, and the black wise spider taught mankind the way to Heaven. So, in his doggerel, and all else, Bunyan directed the focus onto God and salvation.

The last great phase of Bunyan's life was to begin with his return to prison. The king's Proclamation of February 3, 1675, suppressed Non-Conformist assemblies and ordered the listing of all persons who did not take communion at Church of England parish churches. Accordingly, on March 4, a month after the Proclamation, a warrant contained the charge that Bunyan "preached or taught at a conventicle meeting or assembly under colour or pretence of exercise of Religion in other manner than according to the Liturgie or Practice of the Church of England."

The king had issued The Act of Indulgence, and now three years later, the king would reverse himself. Charles II, the "Merry Monarch" and ally of Louis XIV, bribed his enemies and cooperated with Parliament in order to retain his power, but adhered to firm personal policies of raising a standing army, seeking an absolute monarchy, and restoring Catholicism. He would not succeed in his major aspirations, but he would be the instrument to place Bunyan again in confinement, where he would begin *The Pilgrim's Progress*. Also, the few years of freedom had blown the seeds of Non-Conformism too far, and that which once was regarded as radicalism would now be perceived by many in England, Ireland, and Scotland as correct, honorable, and even holy.

As established by a bond dated June 1677, Bunyan was sentenced to prison "for continued absence from communion at St. Cuthbert's Church." Since there was no ecclesiastical prison at Bedford, he would have served his time at the county jail, and not, as tradition would have it, the jail under the bridge. It is not likely that Bunyan sought vigorously to avoid prison, for his parishoners could not easily have paid the fines of twenty pounds for a first offense or forty pounds for the second offense. Further, he had too much integrity to make promises not to preach the Word of God. Therefore, he was incarcerated again in the Bedford County Gaol, where recently he had endured twelve years of confinement.[44]

Bunyan was released from prison, after serving six months of imprisonment, about July 1677. However, his imprisonment afforded him the opportunity to write in prison the first part of *The Pilgrim's Progress*, that was entered in the Stationer's Register on December 22, 1677, and published shortly thereafter by Nathaniel Ponder.[45] The power of this book is that in its simplicity it transcends Puritanism, Calvinism, sectarianism, and embraces the Christianity of Antioch, as well as that of the Christ-follower in the twentieth and twenty-first centuries.

At the time of his second release from prison in 1677, Bunyan had eleven more years to live. These were the most productive years of his life. He preached Sundays at his Bedford church, but taking to the saddle, he preached weekdays on invitation in many other churches. Now as "Bishop" Bunyan, a title conferred at first in derision, but later accepted as an honor, he took the risks of being an open Dissenter, and followed the invitations bravely. Twelve hundred faithful heard his seven o'clock morning sermon, while nearly three thousand worshipped with him at London, at a Towne-end Meeting House, or again at London's Pinner's Hall, a favorite meeting place for Non-Conformists. He frequently reminded his listeners that every act on earth has eternal consequences. His congregation knew the Bible thoroughly, but he reminded them of Heaven, Hell, a means of salvation, and the grace of God. His sermons gave no partiality to novelty but dwelled on accepted doctrine.[46] It was apparent to his flock that the power and authority of God were revealed in his words.

The dangers of dissent were still present. Reverend Francis Bampfield was dragged from his pulpit by soldiers armed with halberds, while Reverend Thomas Jolly ingeniously protected himself with a guard in front of the chapel and a pulpit that disappeared through a stairway. When James II offered Bunyan an official position in the Bedford Corporation to express the Monarch's tolerance, Bunyan ignored the request.[47]

Last Decade

In his last decade, 1678 to 1688, Bunyan was at his most productive as a writer. He expended two years in writing *The Holy War*. In it, he told the story of his religious conversion under the cover of military maneuvers, sieges, skirmishes, and retreats.

Bunyan's end came suddenly. He had traveled by horseback to Reading to reconcile a young man and his father. Then he rode forty miles from Reading to London in a driving chilly rain. His mission was to preach as the guest of the "Anabaptist" Lord Mayor of London, Sir William Shorter. Although sick, Bunyan preached on August 19 in the Boar's Head Yard in Whitechapel on the text from John 1:13: "Which were born, not of blood, nor of the will of flesh, nor of the will of man, but of God."[48] Two days later, Bunyan became very ill, and twelve days later, on August 31, 1688, he died, three months short of his sixtieth birthday, at the home of his host, John Strudwick. According to tradition, he was buried in the Baptist Corner of the Non-Conformist cemetery at Bunhill Fields, near other notable dead, including Vavasor Powell, Samuel Wesley, and Daniel Defoe. In 1695 Bunyan's bones were placed in a vault, upon which his effigy rests. Bunyan left his entire estate of a cottage and forty-two pounds and nineteen shillings to his wife Elizabeth.[49]

In an age of radical reformers and preachers, Bunyan was a Baptist Trailblazer. That Bunyan was individual and personal in his devotion to God is Baptist to the core. All clues and reports from friends and foe alike support the premise that he was converted and immersed as a Baptist. His pastorate radiated from a Regular Baptist church at Bedford. Even his place of burial was attributed to the Baptist section of Bunhill Fields. That he was attacked so doggedly by some Regular Baptist pastors, infuriated by his individualism, may well reinforce, not diminish, his witness as a unique Baptist preacher, in some ways far in advance of others in kindliness, tolerance, and humility. He loved God more than conformity and formal organizations. He was more attuned to the Christians of Jerusalem and Antioch than to new church affiliations. His first loyalty was to the Bible, not to his great work, *Pilgrim's Progress*.

This was an original man, preacher and writer, inheritor of Baptist and Puritan traditions, touched by a fire that came from the Holy Spirit. He felt no call to reform, like Oliver Cromwell, and received no summons to public service, like John Milton. While his culture was narrow, he was neither ignorant nor uncultivated. His genius was to use the simple to glorify God with all that he possessed.

Chapter 4

William Kiffin
(1616-1701)

Baptist Merchant-Minister

The rise to prominence of William Kiffin, wealthy London merchant and Baptist minister, coincides with the emergence of the Calvinistic Particular Baptists as the future dominant element of the Baptist movement. This Calvinist dominance, both in England and America, would last until the nineteenth century. The Calvinists, whether French Huguenots, Scots Presbyterians, or Particular Baptists, were heirs of the great Reformation leader, John Calvin. Calvin established a stern theocracy after 1536 in Geneva, Switzerland, spread his Protestant concepts through his book *The Institutes of the Christian Religion*, and proclaimed a strict morality and the doctrine of predestination. It would be predestination—the doctrine that God would save only a few—the Elect—that would define the critical difference between William Kiffin's Particular Baptists and Thomas Helwys' General Baptists, the latter advocates of the Arminian doctrine that through Christ all mankind could be saved.

Kiffin, having risen from poverty to vast wealth through his woolen trade, was the friend and financial resource of the Stuart King Charles II, and thus was able to protect and nurture the Particular Baptists. Although he had no great education, he helped formulate and sign every major Baptist confession of his time. He stood for closed

William Kiffin (1656)—Portrait Study

communion and closed membership. Kiffin was the contemporary and associate of other eminent Particular Baptists of the period, including Richard Blunt, Praise God Barebone, and Hanserd Knollys. It was during the life of William Kiffin that the Particular Baptists, around 1640-41, probably were the first Baptists of any kind to adopt immersion as the standard practice for baptism, although Leonard Busher, a General Baptist leader, had advocated in 1614 baptism by immersion in his treatise "Religion's Peace."[1]

Kiffin, of Welsh extraction, was born in London in 1616. He became an orphan when both parents died in the London plague of 1625. He charged the relatives who assumed his care with misappropriation of his estate. He was apprenticed to a brewer, and from that "mean calling" he ran away in his fifteenth year.

While a vagrant, he wandered into a Puritan church. The minister preached so effectively on the Fifth Commandment, "Honor thy Father and Mother," and of the obligations of servants to masters, that young Kiffin returned to his master. Inspired by the minister, Kiffin embraced the Puritans, was convicted of his sins, and found peace in salvation. He then joined a Separatist church, probably the JLJ Church, whose Pastor was Henry Jacob,[2] and moved after some time to a Baptist congregation in London, of which John Spilsbury was the pastor. It is variously argued that the first Particular Baptist church was organized in 1638, but other historians maintain 1633 as the proper date.[3] At any rate, the Baptists and Kiffin had found each other, and Kiffin prior to 1644 became the pastor of a newly constituted Baptist church. Kiffin was to devote almost his entire adult life as elder (pastor) of the Devonshire Square Church in London.[4]

Approximately at the same time that he assumed his calling as minister, Kiffin became a merchant in a profession that would make him affluent. He first began in 1643 a trading voyage to the Netherlands, and then undertook a joint venture in the Netherlands with a Christian man of his congregation. As Kiffin stated: "It pleased God so to bless our endeavors, as from scores of pounds to bring it to many hundreds and thousands of pounds." Through his wealth, he became one of the most influential merchants in England, and he shrewdly used his wealth to protect and advance the Baptists and preach the Gospel without hindrance.[5] He valued success as a means to reach men for God.

Kiffin's wealth made him the object of envy but also obtained for him prestige and influence with the Stuarts and high government officials. In one instance, Charles II requested from Kiffin a substantial loan of forty thousand pounds. With his ready wit, Kiffin replied with all respect to the king that he could not lend so large a sum, but he would be honored to make a gift to the king of ten thousand pounds. The king was delighted to so "honor" his subject. Kiffin, in the privacy of his home, laughed merrily about how his gift had saved him thirty thousand pounds, since a loan to the King was uncollectable.[6]

Some idea of the diversity of the English Baptists that were already in existence in the 1730s, including the Calvinists in their strongholds of London and Bristol, may be derived from the works of William T. Whitley. The twenty-five Baptist ministers in London in 1731 included: seven Calvinists; seven hyper-Calvinists (Antinomians, who believed predestination guided their daily actions and felt that sin was not a menace to their salvation, because of God's bestowed grace); six Arminians (General Baptists); two Seventh-Day Baptists; and even three Unitarians.[7] In the long stretch of history, the weakness of the General Baptists would be a drift by some churches to liberalism, and even Unitarianism, while the defect of the Particular Baptists (Calvinistic) would be an evolvement by some churches into stifling ultra-conservatism.

The Particular Baptists (Calvinistic) flourished in England in the period 1638-41, led by Henry Jessey, John Spilsbury, and William Kiffin. While emerging a generation after the General Baptists, the Particular Baptists ultimately became more numerous, developed strong attachments and controls in each church, and gave to church associations little power and only advisory functions. The Particular

Baptists had seven churches in 1644, and together those churches in that year issued a testimony of their beliefs in the First London Confession.[8] These Calvinistic Baptists laid great stress on loyalty to the state and participation in civic affairs. This was in contrast to the General Baptists of Smyth and Helwys, who in the seventeenth century often were hostile to a government that persecuted them. Some General Baptists, but not all, refused to bear arms or take oaths, although Helwys had approved taking oaths in a just cause. Perhaps reflecting the Anabaptist influence on their origins, some General Baptist churches refused church membership to government officials. On the other hand, despite their philosophic roots in John Calvin, the early Particular Baptists were less rigid in practice than their brethren in the General Baptist congregations. This moderate trait was shaped in part by the Separatist groups, from which the Particular Baptists sprang. Unlike the General Baptists, the Particular Baptists were more tolerant of the Church of England, despite its imperfections, and regarded that body in some ways as a true church.[9]

The JLJ Mother Church

The Calvinistic or Particular Baptists of Kiffin, according to Thomas Crosby, the earliest historian of the Baptists, originated from Separatists or Dissenters from the Anglican Church. Some of these Separatists assembled together in the Southwark section of London in 1616, as a church organized by a non-Baptist minister, Reverend Henry Jacob. This was the famous JLJ Church, so named for the initials of its first three pastors, Henry Jacob, John Lathrop, and Henry Jessey. The Separatists, unlike the Puritans, completely left the Church of England because it was structured like the Catholic Church and the services were too liturgical and ceremonial. The Separatists, in contrast, centered their beliefs on the Bible, favored simplicity in style, and adopted participatory church government. The Baptists, influenced by such beliefs, later faulted the Separatists for not accepting believer's baptism and religious liberty.[10]

The JLJ "mother church" was an independent church but not in a hostile relationship with the Church of England. However, it was comprised of strong-minded, variously-oriented Non-Conformists, and this church was troubled frequently by dissension. Shaken by the discord, Jacob left England for Virginia about 1622. During the tenure of Pastor John Lathrop, "of tender heart and humble spirit," a dispute arose when church members sometimes attended the Anglican church. Also there was continuing unrest about acknowledging the Church of England as a valid church. Debates also ensued about the purpose of baptism. Because of its vitality, the JLJ Church attracted members, and thus its size increased the danger of notice by the city authorities, since such Independent churches were illegal. In 1633 seventeen persons led by Samuel Eaton, some of them with Anabaptist views, were granted dismission and received a "further Baptism."[11] Were these now Baptists? Tolerant Henry Jessey was called as pastor of the JLJ Church in 1637, but defections occurred again in 1638, this time by six members who had religious views like Eaton, and joined the Baptist church of John Spilsbury.[12] The Spilsbury Church, thus, is guardedly called the first Particular Baptist church in England.

Although baptism by immersion was advocated first in 1614 by Leonard Busher, probably a member of Helwys' General Baptist church, it was the Particular Baptists who practiced it first in the congregations of Praise God Barebone and Henry Jessey. The records of the JLJ "mother church" make this clear, after the departure for New England of its pastor, John Lathrop:

> 1640. 3rd Mo: The Church became two by mutuall consent just half being with Mr. P. Barebone, and ye other halfe with Mr. H. Jessey. Mr. Richd Blunt with him being convinced of Baptism yt also it ought to be by dipping in ye Body into ye Water, resembling Burial and riseing again Col.2.12, Rom.6,4 had sober Conferance about in ye Church, & then wth some of the forenamed who also were so convinced; and after Prayer & Conferance about their so enjoying it, none having then so practiced it in England to professed Believers, & hearing that

some in and ye Nether Lands [Holland] had so practiced, they agreed and sent over Mr. Rich'd Blunt (who understood Dutch) with Letters of Commendation, and who was kindly accepted there, and Returned with Letters from them Jo:Batten a teacher there, and from that Church to such as sent him.

1641. They proceed on therin, viz Those Persons yt were perswaded Baptism should be by dipping ye Body had mett in two Companies, and did intend so to meet after this, all those Agreed to proceed alike togeather: and then manifesting (not by any formal Words) a Covenant (wch Word was Scrupled by some of them) but by mutuall desires and agreement each Testified: Those two Companyes did set apart one to Baptize the rest: so it was Solemnly performed by them.

Mr. Blunt baptized Mr. Blacklock yt was a Teacher amongst them, and Mr. Blunt being baptized, he and Mr. Blacklock Baptized ye rest of their friends yt ware so minded, and many being added to them they increased much.[13]

In this manner began the Baptist ordinance of baptism through immersion, not as necessary for salvation, but essential to following in correctness the will of the Father, as expressed in the New Testament. Initially, immersion was not accepted by all Particular Baptists, but eventually it became the standard practice.[14]

In the 1640s the Particular Baptists experienced rapid growth, partially because of Baptist books, tracts, and public debates between Baptists and their Anglican, Quaker, and Independent opponents. While many Baptist debaters were university graduates, such as John Tombes, Henry Jessey, and Christopher Blackwood, other Baptist speakers had risen from common stock and used "plain talk" arguments, emphasizing the Scriptures and logic on such topics as immersion, the nature of Christ, and the meaning of ordinances. Perhaps the most publicized Baptist debate was held on October 17, 1642, between four Baptist speakers, including William Kiffin, and the distinguished and arrogant Anglican churchman Daniel Featley. Featley gave his side of the disputation in a tract entitled: "The

Dippers Dipt, or the Anabaptists Duck'd and Plung'd over Head and Eares."[15]

Featley attacked his Baptist opponents as illiterates, who worked at secular occupations, were members of a "sottish sect," that did not know the original languages of the Scriptures. Despite being erroneously called Anabaptists and other epithets, Baptists often fared well in such debates, and their congregations grew as a result.[16]

During Kiffin's lifetime, he participated and signed nearly every important Baptist document issued by his own Particular Baptist church or jointly crafted by the General Baptists and Particular Baptists. By 1650 the General Baptists numbered at least forty-seven churches, while the Particular Baptists had at least seven churches by 1644. The Particular Baptist churches acted together in 1644 to issue a confession of faith of great importance, the First London Confession, composed of fifty articles.[17] This important document, that expressed Calvinistic theology, limited baptism to immersion, and advocated religious liberty, was signed by William Kiffin, Hanserd Knollys, and others.[18]

The first London Confession pronounced baptism "as an ordinance of the New Testament given by Christ." Baptism was required before the believer could take the Lord's Supper. The Confession then proceeded to specify the details of the baptismal ceremony:

> "That the way and manner of the dispensing this ordinance is dipping or plunging the body under water; it being a sign, must answer the thing signified, which is, that interest the saints have in the death, burial, and resurrection of Christ: and that as certainly as the body is buried under water and risen again, so certainly shall the bodies of the saints be raised by the power of Christ in the day of the resurrection, to reign with Christ."[19]

The baptizing official and the new convert were enjoined to conduct the service "with all modesty," since Baptists had been falsely accused of exposing bodies and other scandalous behavior during such ceremonies.

Procedures for the Lord's Supper

The First London Confession seems to have required "closed communion," while the Second London Confession makes no mention of the subject, suggesting a drift to "open communion." Individual churches, both of the Particular and General Baptists, divided over the point of whether the Lord's Supper should be limited to those Christians who were immersed ("closed communion"), as against allowing professed Christians to partake of the Lord's Supper regardless of the manner of baptism ("open communion"). This question would divide church from church into the twenty-first century.[20] Perhaps the major debate on this issue occurred between Kiffin and John Bunyan, the celebrated author of *The Pilgrim's Progress*. Bunyan, an interesting and unusual Baptist preacher, alarmed Kiffin, inasmuch as Bunyan, while recommending immersion at his Bedford church, did not require it for church membership.

After Bunyan published his confession of faith (1672) and another work on the significance of baptism, Kiffin responded with his publication "Serious Reflections" (1673), and his final arguments in "A Sober Discourse of Right to Church Communion" (1681). Apparently Kiffin's alarm was generated in part by Bunyan's contention that it was possible to commit idolatry even with baptism and the Lord's Supper. Bunyan taught that since sinners could be accepted by God without immersion or other forms of baptism, then any Christian must be made welcome at the Lord's Table. Kiffin feared that the doctrine of Bunyan would weaken both communion and the strict requirements of church membership.

Kiffin proclaimed that in the New Testament communion comes after baptism; and that to change the order, both would be weakened. He warned: "Nor may the Lawes, Orders, and Prescriptions of Christ be altered, or varyed, in any tittle. . . ." Kiffin feared that communion served to the unbaptized would open the door to "Popish Purgatory, and Monkery and ten thousand other things." The short-term victory went to Kiffin, not Bunyan, since most Particular churches in Kiffin's lifetime adhered to "closed communion." However, Bunyan could have claimed the long-term victory, since "open communion" would ultimately triumph in Baptist churches.[21] In Kiffin's church, however, no one would receive communion or church membership that had not been baptized by water.

From the first, Baptists were divided over the question of whether to admit to membership only those converts who were baptized as responsible persons, also known as believer's baptism. Churches differed as to who would be served the Lord's Supper. Particular Baptists, like William Kiffin, John Spilsbury, and Hanserd Knollys, asserted that the church should consist of baptized believers, and that only they should come to the Lord's Table. Others like Henry Jessey (a Particular Baptist), John Tombes, and John Bunyan favored the laxer practice of partaking of the Lord's Supper with all Christians. Some churches were mixed, containing a number of Congregationalists and Independents who did not immerse, and this shaped the less rigid requirements of other Baptist churches.[22]

In 1642 and again in 1648, the English Civil Wars broke out between King Charles I and Parliament, the latter supported by Puritans, Baptists, and the English industrial South and East. The struggle had ensued, with the calling of the Long Parliament in 1640: (1) to fight off the Scots (who later joined the king) that initially rebelled because of the Anglican liturgy and Book of Prayer forced on fellow Presbyterians; (2) to obtain funds for a struggle for constitutional reforms; and (3) to gain control by Parliament of the militia loyal to the king. Charles I was an absolutist, who was married to a French Catholic, Henrietta Maria, and who sought to impose religious uniformity on his subjects through the Archbishop of Canterbury, William Laud. He would pay dearly for his autocratic rule, first by the Civil Wars and then finally by his beheading. The heroic figure, who would emerge dominant with the victorious Parliamentary New Model Army, was the audacious Puritan Oliver Cromwell, friend and supporter of the Baptists, who in gratitude flocked to his army.[23]

As his price for gaining the support of the Scots, Charles I tolerated a Church of England dominated by Scots Presbyterians and a Long Parliament led by Presbyterians. This situation was unpleasant for Baptists and other Independents, but it did not last long. One of the last acts of the Presbyterians in 1648 was to pass a law assigning death for eight errors of doctrine, including denial of the Trinity. Sixteen other "errors," including the denial of infant baptism, were punishable with imprisonment.[24]

Under laws promulgated by the Presbyterians, William Kiffin, on July 12, 1655, was charged before the lord mayor of London with heresies and blasphemies, including the specific charge that he preached "that the baptism of infants was unlawful." The influential and affluent Kiffin was treated with great respect by the mayor, who on the plea of being very busy, deferred the case to another day. The records do not indicate that the accusation was ever afforded a hearing. Other Non-Conformists, with less influence, were not so fortunate. But the excesses of the Presbyterians eventually would cause their expulsion from Parliament. The real power in the state was the army, which was composed mainly of Independents, including many Baptists. These strong Dissenters would squelch the power of the Presbyterians, who threatened to tyrannize them.[25] In fact, the Baptists in Cromwell's army have been given the credit for preventing the Presbyterians from establishing their own state church. This the army did in 1648, by purging Parliament of members who did not favor a free church as well as a free state,[26] resulting in the formation of a "Rump" Parliament.

The Fifth Monarchy Movement created problems for some Baptists and Separatists during the period of Oliver Cromwell, who from 1653 to 1658 served as protector of the Commonwealth of England, Scotland, and Ireland. The Fifth Monarchists, excited by the millennialist hopes raised in the seventeenth century, were agitated by unsound interpretations of the seventh chapter of the Book of Daniel. According to some accounts, four major kingdoms (represented by four beasts that symbolized Assyria, Persia, Greece, and

Rome) would pass away, to be followed by an eternal kingdom—the millennial rule of Christ. Some Biblical authorities agreed that at this period Christ would turn the government over to His "Saints," who would then eradicate the depraved conditions by effecting economic and religious reforms. The greatest benefactors would be the humble and poor, whereas the oppressors would be subdued. It would be an epoch of contentment, good health, and plenteous food. The stern Puritanical period of Cromwell seemed for some oppressed people to presage the beginning of such a Kingdom of Heaven.

Most Fifth Monarchists were willing to await peacefully the unrolling of God's designs. Elements of these were trained soldiers, prepared to fight in battle for the Fifth Monarchy, but only on signal from Christ himself. A small but radical group were willing to accelerate the advent of Christ by resorting to military force, but few Baptists joined these fanatics.[27]

The regicide of Charles I by Cromwell—a terrible deed to most of Europe—built up a backlash, through the offended English, Scots, and Irish high churchmen, monarchists, and Stuart supporters. Still, Cromwell had promulgated a fair amount of religious liberty and came close to adopting the Baptist concept of equal religious tolerance for all men.[28] Many Baptists joined Cromwell's army, with some of them writing infantry and cavalry drill books and creating new churches near Irish military campgrounds. After the death of Cromwell in 1658, and the rise to power of Charles II, the protective coat for Independents was gradually removed and persecution began once more.

Pastor-Evangelist Thomas Collier, "Apostle to the West," neither an adherent of General or Particular Baptists, but a type of Baptist theological bridge,[29] and William Kiffin, of the Particular Baptists, sought to reduce the involvement of Baptists in the Fifth Monarchy Movement. A letter to the Baptists in Ireland expresses the views of Kiffin and others opposed to protesting publicly against Cromwell:

> And this we are clearly satisfied, in that principles held forth
> by those meeting in Blackfriars, under pretense of the Fifth

Monarchy, or setting up the kingdom of Christ, to which many of those lately in power adhered, had it been prosecuted, would have brought as great dishonor to the name of GOD, and shame and contempt to the whole nation, as we think could have been imagined.[30]

The letter of Kiffin on the Fifth Monarchy, expressing loyalty to the state, continues. He states: "—That our [Baptist] principles are not such as they have been generally judged by most men to be; which is, that we deny authority and would pull down all magistracy. And if any trouble should arise, either with you or us, in the nation, which might proceed to the shedding of blood, would not it all be imputed and charged upon the baptized [Baptist] churches?"—-[31]

Baptists as a body were loyal to the Commonwealth. And Cromwell was always reluctant to move against them, in particular since Baptists were among the most loyal of his men in the military ranks, whether private or general. Included among his leading officers, Major General Thomas Harrison became a Baptist in 1657,[32] adhered to Fifth Monarchist beliefs, suspected correctly that Cromwell aspired to be king, and in his vulnerability as a rebel was tried and executed. The story of Harrison is exceptional, as he sought to block the ambitions of Cromwell. Many Baptists and Separatists were also involved in the disbanding of an entire regiment under the command of Cromwell and his lieutenant, the Earl of Essex,[33] the latter suspected of being too sympathetic to his Non-Conformist soldiers.

The Fifth Monarchists, whose main activities were verbal outbreaks, consisted of Congregationalists and some well-known Baptists, the latter including Hanserd Knollys, Henry Jessey, and Vavasor Powell. But the principal leaders of the movement were non-Baptists, General Thomas Harrison (not yet a Baptist) and Thomas Venner. In the public mind, a false relation was contrived between the Fifth Monarchists and extremists, some of them Anabaptists who seized in the 1530s the German city of Muenster. Vavasor Powell added to these negative impressions, when he asked crudely: "Lord, wilt Thou have Oliver Cromwell or Jesus Christ to reign over us?"[34] In 1656 the funeral of a Baptist pastor became the rallying occasion of Fifth Monarchists and some Baptists, who reportedly declared: "God's people must be a bloody people."[35] Is there any wonder that a fraction of English people were edgy about Baptist political motives?

In the first known document in which General and Particular Baptists cooperated, Kiffin, John Spilsbury, and other Baptist leaders signed a document to disassociate themselves from the Fifth Monarchists and the abortive Venner insurrection of 1661 to overthrow Charles II. The document was entitled, "The Humble Apology of Some Commonly Called Anabaptists." And, as late as 1678, Baptist leaders were still trying to distance themselves from Muenster and the Fifth Monarchy Movement.[36] Most Baptists of this period were not obsessed with apocalyptic speculations. Their views and sermons were balanced, but expressed the certainty that Christ would ultimately return in triumph and judgment.

Kiffin also was embarrassed by an episode during the reign of James II. James reigned from 1685 to 1688, until his Protestant daughter Mary and her Protestant husband William of Orange arrived in England from Holland with a huge army. The so-called "Glorious Revolution" solidified Protestant dominance in England and resulted in the flight of James II to France, where he was protected by Louis XIV until his death.

Prior to the enthronement of William of Orange and despite the death of his father, Charles I, James II had learned little from the English religious revolution. James angered his people by setting aside the laws against Roman Catholics and Dissenters and attempted to restore Catholicism as the religion of England. He appointed many Catholics to office and even named some Catholics as bishops in the Church of England. In trampling on his pledge to maintain the Anglican Church "as by law established," James infuriated many Protestants, not only the supporters of the Church of England.

However, the king required allies, and thus he curried the favor of the Independents, including Baptists. In some cases, the king exercised his powers to protect Baptists from intolerant laws. Baptists, while accepting this protection, gave no approval to an autocratic king and his religious policies. However, the fear of Roman Catholic supremacy drove Protestants to establish closer political and religious cooperation with James II. In pursuance of his policy of seeking Independent support, the king appointed Kiffin alderman of the Ward of Cheap. Kiffin was aware of the trap the king had set, and was genuinely unhappy, but he was forced to take the office rather than pay thirty thousand pounds in penalty if he refused. After serving as alderman for nine months, he was able to be discharged. "Neither Baptists nor any other Non-Conformists were to be hoodwinked, nor could they be flattered or bribed into approval of the overriding of the laws of England."[37]

The Confession of 1644, signed by Kiffin, Hanserd Knollys, and others, is a towering monument to religious liberty and good citizenship. As a great landmark for Baptists and all enlightened Christians, the Confession encapsulates Baptist beliefs on religious freedom, that all men should be allowed to worship God according to the dictates of personal conscience. As the historian Henry C. Vedder states: "On the strength of this one fact, Baptists might fairly claim— they were the pioneer body among modern Christian denominations to advocate the right of all men to worship God, each according to the dictates of his own conscience, without let or hindrance from any earthly power."[38]

The following article from the Confession reflects the strength of the advocacy for tolerance in religious matters:

> XLVIII. A civil magistracy is an ordinance of God, set up by him for the punishment of evil doers, and for the praise of them that do well; and that in all lawful things, commanded by them, subjection ought to be given by us in the Lord, not only for the wrath, but for conscience sake; and that we are to make supplications and prayers for kings, and all that are in authority, that under them we may live a quiet and peaceable life in all godliness and honesty.

The supreme magistracy of this kingdom we acknowledge to be King and Parliament—And concerning the worship of God, there is but one lawgiver—which is Jesus Christ—So it is the magistrate's duty to tender the liberty of men's consciences (Eccl.8:8), (which is the tenderest thing unto all conscientious men, and most dear unto them, and without which all other liberties will not be worth the naming, much less the enjoying), and to protect all under them from all wrong, injury, oppression, and molestation—And as we cannot do anything contrary to our understandings and consciences, so neither can we forbear the doing of that which our understandings and consciences bind us to do. And if the magistrates should require us to do otherwise, we are to yield our persons in a passive way to their power, as the saints of old have done (James 5:4).[39]

Thus, this great document established, as in a contract, the link between Baptists and religious freedom. Those two, through history, have remained inseparable. The endorsement by Kiffin gives profound proof of the endearment that Baptists placed on religious liberty, especially at this early time. Also the First London Confession of 1644 had its effect, both in England and Colonial America, because its moderate and rational tone disassociated Baptists everywhere from the extravagant fanaticism of a few Anabaptists at Muenster during the sixteenth century.[40]

William Kiffin was the great merchant-preacher of the Particular Baptists, whose long life was adorned with steadiness and profound faith in God. Not equipped with a formal education, he was remarkably intelligent and sagacious, and preached from the Bible on the level of university-educated pastors, such as Hanserd Knollys and John Spilsbury. His prestige and wealth gave him ready access to judges, princes, and the Stuart kings. Thus, in an age of persecution of Dissenters, he could and did protect the Baptist faith. He was attentive to the primal conferences and documents of the Baptists, notably the First London Confession of 1644, and manuscripts rejecting the Fifth Monarchy Movement. He signed numerous accords and confessions, including some with the General Baptists.

While his firm stance on closed communion and mandatory baptism by immersion for church members may appear to some non-Baptists as rigid and intolerant, his pronouncements gave clear definition to Baptist beliefs. In the chaotic religious and political world of the seventeenth century, Kiffin is distinct, determined, and dependable. He stands singular as a great Baptist Trailblazer, and one of the most notable Christians of the ages. He was signer and co-author of a magnificent statement in the London Confession of 1644 that all men were entitled to worship God in freedom under their lawgiver Jesus Christ. In his unique life, Kiffin served England and its rulers, his Christian flock, and, above all, his God. Although no burial stone remains, he was buried in 1701 in Bunhill Fields, London, along with two eminent Baptist pastors, Hanserd Knollys and John Bunyan.

Roger Williams (1639) Fur Trading with the Indians

Chapter 5

Roger Williams
(c1603-1683)

Standard Bearer of Religious Freedom

Roger Williams (c.1603-1683) was a Separatist preacher and Seeker for most of his eighty years. He adopted the Baptist faith in the period 1636-39, while in exile from Massachusetts, and served as a Baptist pastor for a short time, inspiring him in 1639 to establish the first Baptist church on North American soil at Providence, Rhode Island. He was almost certainly the first great evangelical preacher in the New World to proclaim collectively the doctrines of: soul competence, religious freedom, and separation of church and state, among the most precious tenets of the Baptist faith. The city he founded, Providence, and the state of Rhode Island that he co-founded with Baptist physician-minister John Clarke were the first governments in the world to authorize by law complete religious freedom. His missionary zeal extended to the Wampanoags in Plymouth and the Narragansett Indians in Rhode Island, whose languages he mastered, and, who, in return, trusted his friendship and protection.

Roger Williams was one of the world's greatest advocates of human freedom, and, deservedly is proclaimed as one of the fathers of American democracy. No civilization has yet attained the political and religious freedom envisaged by this complex, tolerant, but controversial Trailblazer, who throughout his entire life was both a Christian activist and political visionary.

Williams was born in 1603 in London, the son of merchant tailor James Williams and his wife, the former Alice Pemberton, faithful members of St. Sepulchre's Anglican Church. Roger's father was a moderately affluent middle-class manufacturer of ceremonial robes, canopies, and pavilions. The family had several properties, including a new house on Cow Lane in the West Smithfield neighborhood of London. However, we know little of Williams's heritage, because the records of St. Sepulchre's Parish and the family entries were destroyed by the great London fire of 1666.[1]

At an early age, Williams was markedly studious, religious, and sensitive to the plight of religious Dissenters. He read the Bible earnestly and with conviction. Several Dissenters that repudiated the Church of England, including Bartholomew Legate, were burned to death close to the Williams's home in 1611-12. Among Legate's alleged crimes were the heresies that as a lay preacher he had stated that Christ was "begotten and made" and that Jesus had not "existed from everlasting," and that Christ had not made the world. Other martyrs had died in the past in the same London suburb, including in 1555, John Rogers, Vicar of St. Sepulchre's, who had gone to his burning "as though he had been led to a wedding." West Smithfield had many Dissenters, and numbers of Anabaptists and Baptists. As a mature man, Roger Williams became a facile speaker of French and Dutch, the latter probably learned at an early age through the presence in London of Dutch children, who attended the Dutch Reformed Church that met in Austin Friars, the worship place of 450 Dutch families.[2]

Three men were to exert a profound effect on Williams' life, two as his earliest friends, namely Sir Edward Coke and Sir Harry Vane the Younger; the third figure, John Winthrop, as governor, was to banish him from Massachusetts and remain his political opponent, but in a paradoxical sense was his true friend. Sir Harry Vane, from a distinguished Anglican family, became a Separatist, to his father's disappointment, and was in time appointed governor of Massachusetts Bay Colony, with Winthrop as vice governor. After serving as a high official in England under Oliver Cromwell, Vane in his later career was to die on the scaffold because of his involvement in the death of Charles I. However, he was on many occasions able to facilitate Roger Williams's requests. But it was Sir Edward Coke, whose friendship and actions were to change forever the life of young Roger Williams.

While taking shorthand notes of a sermon at St. Sepulchre's Anglican church as a young lad, Williams attracted the attention of Coke, renowned as one of the greatest lawyers in England. Sir Edward, then in his sixties, employed the young man as a court recorder. Then Coke obtained for him in 1621 a scholarship at Sutton's Hospital, later named the Charter House School, where Williams studied Latin, Greek, and Christianity. His excellent grades enabled him to earn a further scholarship in 1625 to attend Pembroke College of Cambridge University, where students were trained for the Anglican ministry. Sir Edward, Chief Justice of the King's Bench, and prominent in Star Chamber proceedings, served as a character model for Williams, by standing up to King James I, and, after election to Parliament, asserting the right of the freedom of speech. Coke paid the price for this pluck, by spending nine months in prison. But it is reasonable to believe that Williams was permanently influenced by his eminent friend in his own determination and life goals. Ultimately the brave Coke, as a prominent Puritan involved in the death of Charles I, would be drawn and quartered; the severed head of Major General Thomas Harrison, a Baptist, would face him, as he rode on a sled to meet the executioner.[3]

The influences that led Roger Williams from the Church of England to Puritanism and then to the Baptist faith are not clear. He might logically have had contacts with the JLJ Independent Church or the Baptist church of John Spilsbury, for he certainly knew of their half-secret existence. He also owned a Dutch Bible and knew enough Dutch to establish a close contact with Dutch Anabaptists.

In his mature years, Williams would write of his "being persecuted in and out of my father's house."[4] The records show that for some unknown reason, possibly discontent over religious matters, Williams, the bright scholar, who graduated with a Bachelor of Arts at Cambridge in 1627, discontinued his work for a Master's degree, after eighteen months of study. Cambridge at that time was a hotbed of Puritan philosophy and agitation. Upon graduation from Cambridge, he signed the obligatory oath that affirmed the Book of Common Prayer and the Thirty-Nine Articles, marker stones of faith of the Anglican Church. When his graduation was completed, he was ordained as a priest in the church.

Like many young prelates, Williams became a private chaplain at Otes, the estate in Essex County of Puritan leader Sir William Masham, in a stronghold of Puritan opposition to the King.[5] But the true leader of that manor and Hatfield Broad Oak, as well, was the widow of Sir Francis Barrington, Lady Joan Barrington, high principled and tenacious, against whose will and authority no one dared to cross. Lady Barrington and her daughter Elizabeth Masham were brought up in the womanly ideals of the time: to fear God, love the Gospel, and hate Popery. This also was a critical period in English history, with King Charles conceding to the Petition of Right in June 1628, that ended imprisonment without stated cause, billeting of soldiers without Parliamentary approval, and forced loans. Otes was an important stopping place for Puritan political leaders, and from their spirited conversations at dinner or during their leisure, Williams was able to absorb considerable political philosophy and method.

In his first efforts in romance Roger Williams was soundly defeated, not by the object of his love, but by the redoubtable Lady Joan Barrington. His fault was that he had aimed too high. Williams's choice was Jane Whalley, niece of Lady Barrington, who quickly returned his love, but would never get the approval of the grand lady of the estate. He then turned his attention to Mary Barnard, the lady-in-waiting or companion to Jug (Johanna) Altham, Lady Masham's daughter by a former marriage. Mary Barnard is believed to be the only daughter of Richard Bernard (Barnard), respected minister of Worksop in Nottinghamshire. Then, Williams the poor preacher, with only "seven score pieces & a little (yet costlie) studie of books," married the minister's daughter on December 15, 1629, at the parish church of High Laver, Essex.[6] She would endure with him to the end, in the distant frontier state of Rhode Island.

Aside from his decision to accept the call as minister, his most fateful choice was to seek a mission field in the New World. The intervention of Lady Barrington to terminate his first romance with Jane Whalley must have been one factor in determining that he must move on. Another cause was a meeting in 1629 of Dissenting clergy attending the Lincolnshire session of the Massachusetts Bay Company at Sempringham, county seat of the Earl of Lincoln. That meeting was attended by John Cotton, Thomas Hooker, John Winthrop, and probably Roger Williams, all of them to meet again in the New World, but with Williams in religious contention with the majority Puritans of New England.

However, for the moment, the preachers among these potential emigrants expressed sorrow and contempt for many practices in the Anglican Church; the offenses included giving a ring in the marriage ceremony, kneeling at the Lord's Supper, wearing priestly vestments, and signing the cross at baptisms. Williams' discontent, however, lay not so much in details of ritual as they related to his desire for a full divorce of the congregations from the Church of England and the complete separation of church and state in England. Apparently, Williams had not openly discussed his unhappiness with the Anglican Church to John Winthrop, who would be shocked in Colonial America by the Separatist direction of Williams.[7]

The leaders made a decision to transfer the headquarters of the Massachusetts Bay Company to America, and some of them chose to settle near Salem, founded by Puritan gentry in 1628. Among the new planters would be the Earl of Lincoln's sister and his steward, Thomas Dudley, and the most distinguished of all, John Winthrop, intelligent, genial, and well-dressed. Williams also was influenced by this company and their deliberations, particularly in the light of an offer from abroad to become the pastor of a church in Massachusetts.[8]

All of this discussion, dissension, and talk of emigration stemmed from the tidal wave precipitated by Martin Luther at Wittenberg, Germany, in the sixteenth century. But the cataclysm gained strength, animated in unique ways by John Calvin and Ulrich Zwingli. In England, Henry VIII had displaced the pope by the Act of Supremacy (1534) and assumed the role of "Supreme Head of the Church of England" (formerly the Catholic Church in England), but the monarch left many of the Catholic forms, powers, and rituals intact. Great reforms were undertaken: the Bible was translated into English, monasteries were dissolved, and church properties were seized. In Roger Williams's day, the religious storm that now created Baptists, Quakers, Presbyterians, and Antinomians (ultra Calvinists) also had created a modified doctrine in the Anglican Church. "High Churchmen" in the Anglican Church, under William Laud, archbishop of Canterbury, as the enforcer of uniformity, sought to retain in the English Church much of the symbolism and ritual of the Catholic Church, except that the Church would be disciplined and directed by the king and his servant Archbishop Laud. "Low Churchmen" wanted a reformed Church, Puritan in character, with a simple service and a godly group of bishops and leaders, who would be spiritual shepherds only. Distinct from these were the more radical Separatist reformers represented by Williams, that had left or were leaving the Anglican Church and now sought to create new Separatist churches, free of bishops, Prayer Book, and rituals. Already in Roger Williams's mind, the Anglican Church was corrupt and cruel and had lost the spirit of Christ.[9]

The most impelling reason for immediate flight to New England was a note signed by "A Friend," warning that Williams had been identified by Archbishop Laud as an enemy of the king and the Church of England and that steps were being taken to bring him to trial before the King's Council.[10] In a later stage of his life, Williams would write that "Bishop Laud pursued me out of the land."[11] Already Williams had found himself sharply changing from the views of John Cotton and others who wished to remain in the Church of England, but as reformist Puritans. Then, after he secured an Independent parish in Essex, his advocacy of a church free from the authority of king or bishop were views far too radical for Sir William Masham and his old mentor Sir Edward Coke. Even in the circle of his distinguished admirers, Williams was sometimes referred to as "divinely mad." In time, the New World would adopt his perceived extremism as its highest principles. But in view of the danger, he quickly resolved with Mary to take voyage on December 1, 1630, for the New World, aboard the ship *Lyon*, loading at Bristol and bound for Boston; there he would begin a new life in a lush and rugged wilderness.

After landing at the crude new town of Boston, in February 5, 1631, and finding dissatisfaction in a government under John Winthrop, Sr. (that imprisoned lax citizens who did not attend church services), he made his first theological stand. He was offered membership in the Boston church, then meeting in an unfinished hut, but, even more, unexpectedly, was asked to serve as the church's leading teacher or minister. Facing the principal officers and elders of the community, Williams refused the pastoral office, principally because the church was still a corporal part of the Church of England, and, in the words of the young minister an "unseparated people." It was a disturbing meeting that continued for hours, until early dusk. Williams, also, was perturbed by the entanglement of government and religion, from which he sought relief with some new form of government. Afterwards, Williams was grateful for a kind message and a packet of books as a gift from Winthrop, for despite their heated political differences, he would always regard Governor Winthrop as his true friend. The confrontational meeting was the talk of Plymouth, as well as Massachusetts, with some regarding him as a brazen upstart, but many poor folks, mavericks, rebels, and liberals hailing him as a kind of prophet. The controversial nature of the man, his arguments, and his name, would be widely discussed throughout New England.[12]

Here was Roger Williams at his boldest—living in a savage land, with a young wife, dependent upon the assistance of the Puritan community, and being offered one of its greatest honors as pastor-replacement for the departing Reverend John Wilson. But he had refused the post on a principle not understood by the most brilliant community leaders. He had no trained skills, except as minister. The corn harvest was still many weeks away, and the settlement had barely escaped starvation. Despite all this, he refused to join in communion with the Boston church and spoke against the magistrates, who, he asserted, had no right as lay officials to punish religious offenses such as swearing and Sabbath-breaking.[13]

After his stand in Boston, Williams was again offered the post of minister at Salem, then under the jurisdiction of the Massachusetts Bay Company. Since he did not believe in "hireling ministers," he would take no pay. He was installed as minister at Salem on April 12, 1631, but stayed only a few months because of the displeasure of Governor Winthrop and the General Court. Williams, with justification, became upset with a new Massachusetts regulation that no one should have a vote in the colony that was not a member of an accepted church. As only one-fourth of the settlers were church members, Williams responded that this law was tantamount to establishing a theocracy.[14] In view of his "dangerous opinions" he was forced to leave, seeking refuge in Plymouth, about thirty-eight miles from Boston, under Governor Bradford, and not subject to the regulations of Massachusetts.

The Plymouth Colony, of three hundred inhabitants, was Separatist, and Williams became in 1631 the assistant minister under the Reverend Ralph Smith. However, his livelihood was achieved by learning the realities of frontier life, including much "hard digging" in his plot of land.[15] He subsisted in a small house, and working hard with a hoe, planted, tended, and reaped. Williams served two years at Plymouth, 1631-33, during which time he preached, farmed, and developed his most permanent lay profession, trading with Indians for their furs and wampum.

Beginning in this period, Roger Williams commenced something that few Anglo-Saxons had ventured, namely a serious study of Indian culture and languages. Williams developed first a friendship with the nearby Wampanoag Indians and their Sachem Massasoit, and then learned their language. The Indians took Williams to sea in their canoes, and complained about the English that had pushed them away from the best lobster beds in the bay and allowed their pigs to root up the clams on the beaches. Within a year, Williams the fur trader and preacher would be visiting the Narragansett Indians on the western side of Narragansett Bay. Williams was realistic about Indians, never attributing to the Native American such naive idealistic titles as "the noble savage," derived in a later time from the French-Swiss philosopher Rousseau. He made lifelong friends of the great Narragansett paramount chief Canonicus and his nephew and co-chief Miantunomi.[16] He knew that Indians could be charitable and kind, as the Wampanoags were, but that acting in other circumstances, and responding to pressures from land-hungry Englishmen, Indians could be treacherous and murderous, and capable of destroying every settler in reach.

These years were a vital period for Plymouth. Faced by an economic crisis, the colony radically changed its economic basics. Originally, the colony had sought to be a communal government embodying principles that imitated the earliest Christians. Land was held in common and produce was sent to England for sale, and the profits were to prosper the whole colony. The result had been hardship and sometimes near-starvation. It was manifest that the system must be changed, so that private investment and effort would be rewarded, and the colony could benefit from the prosperity of its private citizens. Williams rejoiced that through the changes each person now could improve his economic condition through his own efforts.[17]

In 1634, upon the death of its pastor, Roger Williams was offered and accepted the spiritual leadership of the Salem church. It was well that he accepted, for he was in deep trouble in Plymouth. Although Plymouth was Separatist and not under the authority of the Bay Colony, its affairs were closely observed by Governor Winthrop, who reported to London and the other governors from neighboring colonies. Plymouth Governor William Bradford believed that Williams was "a man godly & zealous, having many precious parts, but very unsettled in judgmente." Roger Williams's fault was that he undiplomatically contested the validity of the "King's Patent." In his written *Treatise* (1633), which alarmed both Plymouth and the Massachusetts Bay Company, Williams held with the Indians that despite the exploration by John Cabot and other English mariners, the land belonged to the Indians and should be paid for.[18] This was a critical moment for Massachusetts, since the royal land grant or patent was guarded zealously, and even then pressures were being exerted by the Crown and Archbishop Laud to rescind it and place the colony under a royal governor. Even more, in his arguments, Williams faulted King James I for granting lands to Massachusetts and wrote that James lied when he claimed to be "the first Christian prince" to discover those lands, and assaulted Charles I for being on the side of the anti-Christ.[19] The assumptions from other New England pulpits was that God had given the English the land. Williams was calling this taking of land a great "sinne." Those amazing positions by the isolated and Separatist pastor alienated him from Massachusetts, and made him, because of his criticism of that colony, a figure of controversy. Then the Plymouth church, acting on the advice of Elder Brewster the peacemaker, agreed to Williams's "dismission" from the Salem church, since the controversies imperiled church unity.

Williams was a marked man in Salem, even at the church where he nurtured a few Separatists and inspired others who would follow him to Rhode Island. After writing his *Treatise*, the shadow of exile was on him. Lesser men in England, for such an offense as writing the *Treatise*, would have been branded, whipped, or had their ears sheared off. Salem was already in trouble, because some of its men sought a piece of land for pasturing cattle on Marblehead Neck. Then Governor John Endecott of Salem, hot-tempered and bold, was stripped of his office for one year for disfiguring the royal ensign, by using his sword to cut out the red cross of St. George. Endicott's motive was to remove one more sign of idolatry. Williams spoke again against the new Residents Oath that concerned all males over sixteen, as an attempt by the authorities to gain peace, since new immigrants were passing through the colony.

Then he showed again his stubborn and fearless but exasperating character by raising anew his demand that magistrates, as lay officials, should not punish religious offenses. Thus he challenged one of the very basics of New England society, that magistrates, as God's deputies, had the right to punish infringements of the "First Table," embodying the first four Commandments, concerned with man's relations with God. If Roger Williams had been successful in his efforts, the punishing stocks and cages of New England would have been nearly empty.[20]

The man had clearly gone too far, and the Boston authorities were obliged to act. At the General Court session of July 5, 1635, he was charged with four "dangerous opinions:" (1) rejecting the magistrates' right to punish religious offenses of the First Table; (2) rejecting the right of government to administer a sacred oath to an unregenerate man; (3) rejecting a prohibition against a man's praying with an unregenerate person; and (4) rejecting a prohibition for giving thanks after a meal.[21] As the pressures from Massachusetts mounted, John Cotton wrote Williams about his "errors," and his close friend Thomas Hooker was sent to debate him. The Salem church began to relinquish its support of Pastor Williams, as the price for opposing the magistrates was now too high. Williams remained unchanged and wrote the Salem church that he would not have communion with its members unless they refused communion with the "unseparated" churches of the Bay. He then abandoned the church, and never, as far as is known, returned to the Salem pulpit.

On October 9 he stood before the Massachusetts Court to hear his sentence:

> Whereas Mr. Roger Williams, one of the elders of the church of Salem, hath broached & dyvulged dyvers newe & dangerous opinions, against the aucthoritie of magistrates, as also writt l[ett]res of defamacon, both of the magistrates & churches here, & that before any conviccon, & yet mainetaineth the same without retraccon, it is therefore ordered, that the said Mr. Williams shall dep[ar]te out of this jurisdiccon within sixe weekes nowe nexte ensueing, wch if he neglect to p[er]forme, it shalbe lawfull for the Govnr & two of the magistrates to send him to someplace out of this jurisdiction, not to returne any more without licence from the Court.[22]

Escape to the Wilderness

He was placed under an order of silence, but did not obey it. The magistrates convened again and agreed to return him to England by ship, but since he pled that he was grievously sick at Salem, Captain Underhill and fourteen armed men were sent to his home by pinnace to return him to Boston. Three days before the arrival of Captain Underhill, Williams, in the terrible winter of 1635-36, was headed for safety over a snow-covered wilderness, toward the land of Massasoit, called Sowams. His only companion was his servant, young Thomas Angell. Williams already knew how he would support himself, for he had discussed with John Winthrop the possibilities of establishing a trading post in the Narragansett Country.[23] Although he was aware of the tough barriers of language and culture, he also would go as a Christian missionary to the Indians.

The first efforts by Williams to carve a new settlement ended in failure. He procured land on the Seekonk River from the Sachem Massasoit, built a house, and was soon joined by miller John Smith, Richard Watermans, Thomas Angell, Francis Wicks, and a penniless attorney's clerk William Harris, who in the end would be a thorn in his flesh.[24] Others in the Salem church expressed interest in joining him for the cause of religious freedom. However, after the first crops were sown, an Indian runner brought word from the governor of Plymouth, Edward Winslow, that the grant received from Massasoit was in Plymouth territory; therefore, the exiles would have to move farther west. In any case, the notion of an independent colony for religious dissenters had been awakened.

Since a free religious community must be in safe territory, the party, at first alarmed, quickly reconsidered and by the next morning were headed for the land of the Narragansetts. In a session that lasted nearly three days between Williams and Canonicus, the great Indian made a grant to Williams, with no payment beyond the services Williams had rendered to the Indians; his gift was a rich peninsula between the Moshassuck and Woonsquatucket rivers, abounding with game, clams, and strawberries. The settlers were fortunate, for they had also been given a tract on the western shore of the Bay, that included islands covered with grass, which could provide fodder for cattle.[25]

The new settlement, on Williams suggestion, was called New Providence. The main town would be laid out on the east bank of the Moshassuck River, with ten-acre lots, each resident also to have six acres of woodland, and all to share a common pasturage. Williams asked only that in time he should be paid thirty pounds from a common fund for his expenses and that all settlers should pay thirty shillings into the central fund.[26] Williams's medieval idea of holding title to all lands in New Providence would eventually conflict with William Harris's view that all settlers were entitled to their own free title.

Soon Williams was thrust into a role that he would take on many times over the years—as intervener and peacemaker between the Indians and the English in New England. The Pequots of Connecticut, once conquered by the powerful Narragansetts, had murdered in 1636 a trader on Block Island, and his goods and two sons were carried away. This was another incident in an on-and-off four-year war between the Pequots and Narragansetts. Despite Williams's plea for peace, two hundred painted Narragansett warriors under Miantunomi set off in long canoes to restore Narragansett dominance. The issue had to do with the concern that the misdeeds of the Pequots might bring retribution by the English on all Indians.[27] In New England, there were only a few thousand Indians, but these were formidable warriors. There were five major tribes: Pawtuckets, near Salem, Massachusetts, dwelling near Boston Bay; Pequots in Connecticut; Pokanokets, near Plymouth; and the most powerful, the Narragansetts, located west of Narragansett Bay.[28] The first English Pilgrims at Plymouth had been succored through a famine by Massasoit, sachem of a small tribe subordinate to the Pawtuckets.

Roger Williams was burdened to bring Christ to the Indians, but because of his knowledge of the barriers of tradition and language, he knew the task was imposing. Williams's style was to ask the Native Americans about their religion and then to tell them about Jesus, bringer of love and light. He did not try to discredit their religion, but rather led them to a knowledge of God through the Son. As Winslow said, "Roger Williams was farmer and trader by necessity but he was still preacher by choice." The Reverend John Eliot disparaged Williams for "trucking with the Indians." This was only true in part, for from his trading post he preached to the Native Americans simply and with some regularity, reaching out for "the natives soules." Because of the Indian sense of awe and reverence, the Bible had an impact on them as God's Word, and as Roger Williams stated it, "for by Nature they are much affected with a kind of Deity to be in Writing."[29]

In one of the first serious books on Indian culture and language—as contained in Roger Williams's *A Key into the Language of America*—he wrote the creation story for Indians:

> Friend, I will aske you a Question.
> Speake on.
> Who made the Heavens?
> The Earth, the Sea?
> The World.

Some will answer Tatta' I cannot tell,
some will answer Manittowock the Gods.

How many gods bee there?
Many, great many.
Friend, not so.
There is onely one God.
You are mistaken.
You are out of the way.
A phrase which much pleaseth them,
being proper for their wandring in the
woods, and similitudes greatly please them.

Friend, I will tell you newes.
One onely God made the Heavens, &c.
Five thousand yeers agoe.
And upwards.
He alone made all things.
Out of nothing.

In six dayes he made all things.
The first day Hee made the Light.
The second day Hee made the Firmament.
The third day hee made the Earth and Sea.

The fourth day he made the Sun and the Moon.
Two great Lights.
And all the Starres.
The fifth day hee made all the Fowle.
In the Ayre, or Heavens.
And all the Fish in the Sea.
The sixth day hee made all the Beasts of the Field.

Last of all he made one
Man
Of red Earth,
And call'd him Adam,
or red Earth.

Then afterward, while Adam,
or red Earth slept,
God tooke a rib from Adam,
or red Earth,
And of that rib he made One
Woman,

And brought her to Adam.
When Adam saw her, he said,
This is my bone.
The seventh day hee rested,
And therefore Englishmen
Worke six dayes.
On the seventh day they
praise God.[30]

Although he spent many hours and dozens of days in stinking, smoky lodges mollifying the Indians and preventing wars, and in so doing endangering his own life, he was not able finally to end the Pequot War nor prevent the eventual destruction of the Narragansett nation; he could not even save his own house in Providence, which was burned to the ground in the last wars. Perhaps no combination of well-meaning people could have avoided the disasters. But the trust that Indians expressed by designating him as their official peace-maker and by Canonicus, who referred to him as "my son," may have few, if any, counterparts in the relationships of Europeans and Native Americans.

In the end, New England, not just Plymouth or Rhode Island, would become fearful and aroused and send an army to destroy the Narragansetts. The desultory raids for English horses and cattle, and the attacks on women and men by the Pequots in 1636-37, involved a long-range plan to totally eradicate the English. But because of the intricacies of war and alliances, the conflict also involved the Mohegans, whose territory extended to the Connecticut River, the Mohawks of New York, and the Pequots, who were most inclined to hostility to other Indians but unsuccessfully sought an alliance with the formidable Narragansetts. At one stage, Narragansett chief Miantunomi sent a severed Pequot hand to Massachusetts Governor Winthrop to prove his loyalty to the English.[31]

On May 1, 1637, the Hartford Court declared war on the Pequots and prepared to send ninety men under Captain John Mason, along with one hundred Mohegan Indian allies under Uncas their sachem, to destroy the Pequot fort on the Mystic River. In order to calm Canonicus and the Narragansetts, who feared the English schemes, Williams wrote letters to his old friends Harry Vane and John Winthrop, governor and deputy governor of Massachusetts; he asked them to placate the Narragansett chief by sending him a ten-pound box of sugar and a gift of powder. Later in the month, Miantunomi, with his warriors and nobility, came to New Providence for an extended conference and camped closely around Roger Williams's small two-story house. This encampment would be repeated many times during the life of this Trailblazer. Roger Williams and Miantunomi, aided by a drawn diagram of the Pequot defensive positions, worked out an attack plan. In the two battles to follow, Miantunomi carried out a successful attack on Block Island and then assisted in the surprise attack on the Pequot fort on the Mystic. In that last ghastly battle on May 25, the fort and nearby wigwams were set on fire, and seven hundred Pequots were hacked or burned to death by the combined forces of Captain Mason, Captain Underhill of Massachusetts, and the Indian chieftains Uncas and Miantunomi.[32]

The quiet aftermath of the victory could have been modified, if not nullified, by the absence of a treaty defining the terms of peace. In the negotiations that followed the battle, Miantunomi was pacified, and a treaty was achieved by the chief meeting in Boston with Governor Winthrop. The Pequot War was over, but no young colonial soldier would ever forget the blood-letting at the fort on the Mystic. Peace would largely reign until King Philips War in 1675, nearly forty years later, ignited by the son of the friendly sachem Massasoit.[33]

Roger Williams may not have been the first Baptist pastor in the

New World, but that matter is conjectural. The honor arguably could be given to physician-pastor Dr. John Clarke (c.1609-76), who may have encountered Baptist concepts in England or Holland, and in 1638 was the minister of a church in Newport, Rhode Island (now known as The United Baptist Church, John Clarke Memorial). The United Baptist Church, renowned over the years for its organization, evangelism, and loyalty to Baptist principles, may be second in longevity to the church pastored by Roger Williams in Providence.[34] Dr. Clarke was a remarkable man, who mortgaged his property and exiled himself in England for twelve years, 1652-64, in order to write the charter enjoining religious freedom for the Colony of Rhode Island and Providence Plantations; this document was signed by King Charles II on July 8, 1663.[35] Clarke was a Particular Baptist, inspired by John Calvin, as were the majority in his church; but some of his flock were General Baptists, often called "Six-Principle Baptists" for the practice of laying hands on new converts. In 1671 Stephen Mumford led a schism of minority Seventh-Day Baptists, who left the Clarke church in order to worship on Saturday instead of Sunday.[36]

Roger Williams, the Baptist

Roger Williams, whose life was recklessly bold, took another audacious step, this time in the progression of his religious life. He became a Baptist in the period 1636-39, and soon would be a Baptist elder or minister. In order to adopt the Baptist way, Williams had evolved through churches that were Anglican, Puritan, and Separatist. In his own town of Providence, and perhaps previously influenced by Dr. John Clarke and Mrs. Richard (Catherine) Scott, a believer from England,[37] he was baptized by Ezekiel Holliman, who had been a member of Williams's Separatist church at Salem. Williams then baptized Holliman and ten others, probably by immersion,[38] but the form of baptism is not verifiable. In March 1639, in the crispness of early spring, water was disturbed in a creek or river, to immerse the "Saints" who had renounced liturgy and form for the simple Christian life. Thus was established, in 1639, with twelve believers and no church sanctuary, the first Baptist church in the New World, with Williams assuming the role of its pastor.[39] History was repeating itself, for Thomas Helwys in 1611-12 had led ten members from Holland to become the first Baptist church in England.

There is little information to confirm how Williams preached and advised his little Baptist frontier flock. He believed in baptism as a symbol of new life and rejected the practice of sprinkling infants.[40] Perhaps the best lessons of his sermons and life are from his dealings with Native Americans. He had not encouraged Miantunomi to declare that Sunday would be observed as a day of worship, for God's way was not to force anyone to worship against his will. He would have followed this rule with the Baptist church at Providence.[41] He did not try to make converts by frightening his listeners with illustrations of Hell-fire and eternal damnation.[42] Unlike the Reverend John Eliot, who disparaged Williams for not keeping records, he did not generalize about numbers of persons who were saved through his ministry. In this there would have been no problem, for in that remote area there were few persons except Indians. Of a certainty, he would have spoken of a risen Savior, who had died for the sins of mankind, and he would have directed all to read the Bible, God's Holy Word, and to follow the precepts of Christ in daily living. Although a moderate Calvinist, Williams insisted on the General Baptist position, of laying on of hands after Baptism and before the Lord's Supper. In 1652 this practice would split the Providence church.[43]

In just four months, in 1639, after organizing the Baptist church, Williams, like John Smyth in Amsterdam, would have serious doubts, not about the form of his baptism, but about its validity, and whether it should be administered by a person without a proper succession. Baptists were scattered and few in number in this earliest America, and innovation was a necessity for converts who had never seen a

Baptist church or encountered many persons of their new faith. Thus, the scarcity of resources influenced the terms by which the Holy Spirit was to be followed. Having served as a Baptist pastor, Roger Williams would withdraw from the church he founded and for his remaining life would refer to himself as a "Seeker." Thomas Olney succeeded him as pastor.[44] Tradition, but not documentary evidence, asserts that the present First Baptist Church of Providence is the lineal successor of the church organized by Williams. Williams as a Seeker would retain many Baptist concepts in his core beliefs, including the one he asserted boldly—the separation of church and state.[45]

The greatest public service given by Williams was as the fearless advocate of religious freedom. He had refused to be minister at the Boston church, because it had not severed ties with the Church of England. He was driven from the Salem Separatist Church for challenging the King's Patent that granted land to Massachusetts but archly ignored any consideration of payment for lands owned by the Indians. He rejected the right of magistrates as lay officials to punish religious offenders. He had also demanded that the Salem church clearly separate from the Church of England, which prescribed the terms of prayer, worship, and even religious thought. Most of those that agreed with him in Salem would eventually join him in Providence.

Williams advocated religious liberty for all, not only the persecuted Baptists. Despite his running battle with George Fox, leader of the Quakers, Williams, as president of Rhode Island, 1654 to 1657, invited the troublesome Quakers to make a home in the colony, despite their exclusion from Massachusetts and New Amsterdam.[46] Even more, in 1658 Massachusetts passed a death penalty for all Quakers found in its territory.[47] As a ship bearing Quakers left anchorage at New Amsterdam (later New York City), the records read: "We suppose they went to Rhode Island, for that is the receptacle of all sorts of riff-raff people, and is nothing else than the sewer (latrina) of New England. All the cranks of New England retire thither. We

*First Baptist Church, Providence, Rhode Island
(building erected in 1775).*

suppose they will settle there, as they are not tolerated by the Independents in any other place."[48,]

As early as 1652, Williams endorsed the idea of having Jews "whose conversion we look for" to settle in Rhode Island.[49] A ship landed fifteen Jewish families of Sephardic stock at Newport in 1658. Williams sailed to Newport, spoke to them in Dutch, and welcomed them to the Colony, and predicted that other Jews would come to Portsmouth and Providence. Williams's open acceptance set a pattern of hospitality, whereas some of his compatriots were hesitant.[50]

The two most important publications of this epoch on religious liberty, aside from John Clarke's "Ill Newes from New-England," were Roger Williams's "The Bloudy Tenent of Persecution" (1644) and "The Bloudy Tenent Yet More Bloudy" (1652). In "The Bloudy Tenent" he argued for complete religious freedom for all people, including atheists, Papists (Catholics), Turks, and Jews. Parliament ordered that the book be burned, but a new unlicensed edition appeared quickly in England and then in America. John Cotton, the leading Puritan minister in New England, answered with his own publication, "The Bloudy Tenent Washed and Made White in the Bloud of the Lamb" (1647), which asserted that minor deviations could be allowed on less important doctrine but that the church and the magistrates were empowered to use even force to uphold the basic doctrines of Christianity.[51]

The vision of Rhode Island and Providence Plantations as a single colony was not a concept born in a flash. It had evolved with Williams's New Providence and Clarke's Newport, but also with the development of the towns of Warwick and Portsmouth. The ambitions of Massachusetts, and even Plymouth, to acquire land played a part; but also their designs to restrain unredeemable Dissidents, such as John Clarke and Roger Williams, entered into the picture. The Separatists of Rhode Island acted in self-defense to preserve their freedom, but in so doing they created a tolerant society. The idea of a separate colony of Providence Plantations was formulated by practical Separatists led by Roger Williams. The immediate chief catalyst was the coalescing of a Federation of New England out of the four colonies of Massachusetts, Plymouth, New Haven, and Connecticut. In 1643, in response to supplications from disturbed Rhode Islanders, Williams bade a hasty farewell to Mary and five children and set sail for Dutch-ruled Manhattoes (Manhattan) and on to England to seek a patent for a new colony.[52] Aboard a Dutch ship bound for New Amsterdam, Williams worked on his book, *A Key into the Language of America*, which became popular in England for its depiction of Indian customs and culture.

He arrived in 1643 in England in the middle of an English Civil War, with Parliament and its Roundhead Army facing King Charles I and the Cavaliers. Williams, through the support of such new friends as John Milton and Oliver Cromwell, and old ones like Sir Harry Vane, was able to forestall an effort by Hugh Peters and his allies. Peters sought expansion of the grant to Massachusetts to cover the entire Narragansett Bay area, including Rhode Island. In a rebuff to Massachusetts, the English authorities granted in 1644 "a free Charter of civil incorporation and government to the Providence Plantations on Narragansett Bay."[53]

The key to success was Williams and his infinite patience for about ten months, during a Civil War not yet won. He cultivated friendly relations with important members of the eighteen-member Board of Commissioners, headed by Sir Robert, second Earl of Warwick, that had taken from King Charles his control of all English colonial affairs. The opposition was formidable, counseled by Massachusetts agents Thomas Welde and Hugh Peters, who sought a patent over Rhode Island not only for its land but also to suppress Rhode Island as a sanctuary for heretics. No speech was as useful to Williams as his book *A Key into the Language of America*. This publication was read by literate and common citizens alike, because of its appeal to Christianization of the Indians. No friend was more helpful than Sir Harry Vane, soon to be second in line to the protector, Oliver Cromwell. Vane's prominence occurred in part because Vane negotiated a Covenant with the Scots, that freed twenty thousand Scotch soldiers to join the forces of Parliament against the King. This new coalition broke the military stalemate.[54]

The success achieved by Williams was narrow, and by only two votes when ten votes was required, but the victory was momentous. A charter was granted on March 14, 1644, that permitted total religious freedom, not only for the Rhode Island mainland or the Island of Aquidneck, but for both. The commissioners had given full authority and power to Providence Plantations to rule themselves, provided only that the government should be "Comformable to the laws of England." When Williams returned from England he would learn that at Newport, John Clarke's home, the island colony had officially changed its name to Rhode Island.[55]

Another event, years later, would hasten the consolidation of Providence Plantations and Rhode Island. On July 16, 1651, the Baptist pastor John Clarke, his assistant pastor Obadiah Holmes, and layman John Randall (or Crandall) held a worship service at the home of Witte (or Wittes), an elderly, almost-blind man, in Lynn, Massachusetts. This unlawful service, during which Clarke denounced infant baptism, was reported to the Boston Court. As a result, Clarke was fined twenty pounds and Randall fined five pounds. Obadiah Holmes was assessed thirty pounds, far more than he was capable of paying. He refused any effort to pay and stated bravely: "I bless God I am counted worthy to suffer for the name of Jesus." At this point, the Reverend John Wilson, "long accounted one of the holiest among the Boston orthodox," slapped Holmes in the face.[56]

Holmes preached to the onlookers, as the official whipper cut his back to ribbons with thirty strokes of a three-corded whip. At the thirtieth stroke of the whip, the sympathetic crowd surged forward, praising God. Holmes was forced to recuperate for several weeks in Boston, crouched on elbows and knees.[57] After his ordeal, Holmes told the magistrates, "You have struck me as with roses." His wounds would scar him for life. This story of Christian heroism was related by John Clarke in his "Ill Newes from New England." It was read over the whole realm of England and contributed greatly to the success of the supreme diplomatic mission of Clarke and Williams in England, in November 1651.[58]

In November 1651, Williams had sailed to England, with John Clarke and secretary William Dyer to forestall another dangerous situation for Rhode Island. William Coddington, an Antinomian (hyper Calvinist) and later a Quaker, but foremost an ambitious troublemaker, announced plans to set up a separate colony on Aquidneck Island, with himself as the autocratic head. When Coddington suddenly departed for England, responsible persons in Rhode Island feared he would work there to destroy their charter. Those fears were well founded, for in 1651 he returned with a full grant of power from the Council of State and also a life governorship over the entire territory of Rhode Island. The jurisdiction of the 1644 Charter was cut almost in half and deep resentment stirred the majority of Rhode Island citizens, who now would be forced to endure an autocracy.[59]

After endorsement of their commission by the disturbed citizens, Williams and Dr. John Clarke were authorized to represent Rhode Island and Providence Plantations in England. Williams was paid one hundred pounds for the expenses of his last voyage to England, seven years after his services were rendered. Now he was obliged to sell his fur-trading station to provide for himself and his family. The party of three, which included a secretary, sailed in November 1651 from Massachusetts with the permission of Governor Endecott but not his blessing. England was in a state of high excitement, for King Charles II was a refugee in France, and a tug of war for power lasting a year was being pursued between the Rump Parliament, headed by Sir Harry Vane, and the army led by Oliver Cromwell. Tired of the impasse, Cromwell invaded Parliament in April 1653, with soldiers led by Major General Thomas Harrison (later a Baptist). Cromwell reportedly shouted to the Parliament that was forced to end its deliberations: "Your hour has come—The Lord is done with you."[60]

Williams had been in England without his family for two and one-half years, before he decided he must depart. Before the ending of the Rump Parliament, Cromwell served as chairman of the Council of State. Petitions were submitted from Clarke and Williams asking that Coddington's life commission as governor be revoked and that the former Royal Charter of 1644 be confirmed. Despite the hectic pace of events, at long last, in a new hearing, the fraudulent grant was revoked, and the 1644 Charter of Providence Plantations was confirmed.[61] During the waiting period, Williams had frequent contacts with the printers and received completed from the firm "The Bloudy Tenent Yet More Bloudy."[62] The diplomatic work was half completed, and Clarke, in residence with his wife, was left behind to negotiate a new charter for Rhode Island and Providence Plantations.

John Clarke succeeded in writing and obtaining approval of the Charter of 1663. It was an achievement almost without parallel. Here was a remarkable Baptist pastor, who was to serve his church for forty years and to endure exile in England for twelve years, and with Roger Williams was to be the founder of the state of Rhode Island.[63] Under the influence of Williams and Clarke, these words at last were sealed in the 1663 Royal Charter given by Charles II:

> Our royal will and pleasure is, that no person within the said colony, at any time hereafter, shall be in any wise molested, punished, disquieted, or called in question, for any differences of opinion in matters of religion, and do not actually disturb the civil peace of the said colony.[64]

This legal exclusion of religion from persecution did not arrive too soon, for in 1654 the Baptist president of Harvard College, Henry Dunster, was removed from his office, and in the dead of winter refused the right of remaining for six months in the house he had built, because of Dunster's newly acquired Baptist faith and his preaching against infant baptism. He died five years later.[65]

The genius of Williams is that he strengthened principles that prevented the United States from accepting a national church. He worked in his colony for a government of the people, organized a system of courts, and wrote a just penal code.[66]

Williams lived a long life, and although always a turbulent and controversial Trailblazer, he was honored in the end as one of the greatest men of America. His fellow Rhode Islanders admired him for his brilliance, tenacity, and character, and through their respect, he was elected president of the colony. His personal tolerance established a new standard for the colony and then the nation, in the protection of Quakers, Jews, Catholics, and Dissenters, as well as Baptists. Although the certain friend of the Indians, and loved in return, he was unable to shield the Narragansett nation from extermination, but he tried tirelessly.

He is the father of the largely-Baptist basic doctrine of separation of church and state. Baptist as he was in his fundamental doctrines, even as an old man, he was convinced that converting men to Christianity, particularly Native Americans, was not a matter of baptism, ritual, or prayers, but rather achieved through practicing Christian beliefs with passionate conviction. During the last forty years of his life he was the strong friend of the Baptists and wrote in defense of Baptist principles as late as 1676.[67] His book, *The Bloudy Tenent of Persecution*, the Charter of 1644, and the First Baptist Church in America at Providence are his monuments. At Geneva, Switzerland, at the International Monument of the Reformation, his statue depicts the only North American among the founding great Protestants.

Roger Williams died in 1683, busy to the end. As Winslow says, "there was nothing of other worldliness about him—, nothing of Puritan austerity. . . . He was impulsive, lovable, warmhearted, and magnetic." A great contemporary said that he was "a man lovely in his carriage—the sweetest soul I ever knew."[68]

Isaac Backus (1744) at Philadelphia Presenting Religious Freedom Cause before Congressional Committee

Chapter 6

Isaac Backus
(1724-1806)

Historian and Freedom Advocate

Isaac Backus, Baptist historian and preacher, had an important impact on a creative and expansive period in American religious history. This was the epoch marked by the Great Awakening (beginning about 1726), the American Revolution (1775 to 1781), the second Great Awakening (1798 to 1820), and the rapid growth of the frontier-nurtured Separate Baptists, forerunners of the Southern Baptists. Backus exerted his most powerful influence as the chairman of the Baptist Committee on Grievances for the Warren Association, Rhode Island, and as the meticulous and reliable historian of the Baptist faith, who penned *A History of New England, with Particular Reference To The Denomination of Christians Called Baptists*. He signed or had a part in composing almost all of the major Baptist declarations written in New England during his lifetime. However, his greatest role—shared with Baptist minister John Leland of Culpeper County, Virginia—was as a great advocate of religious freedom in early America.

Backus was born in 1724 in Norwich, Connecticut, of wealthy parents, who also were independent adherents in religious thought of the "pure" Congregational faith, that opposed the Saybrook Platform and the Established Church. The "Platform" in Connecticut restricted the authority of the local Congregational church and tended to protect orthodoxy[1] during the period of New Light ascendancy. Backus was converted at age seventeen, in 1741, and joined a New Light church, organized in response to the influence of the great Methodist evangelist George Whitefield, Oxford colleague of John Wesley. Though by nature shy and introverted,[2] Backus began preaching without church approval, and in 1746 was exercising the functions of a minister. Troubles arose in his first church, and he left the congregation to begin work that led to establishing the Congregational Titicut Church of New Lights, near Plymouth, Massachusetts, situated between Bridgeport and Middleborough.[3]

The principal influences in his life, especially the revivalist style of preaching and Calvinistic theology, had begun with the preaching of Jonathan Edwards in 1734 at Northampton, Massachusetts. The intensity and style of Edwards affected many churches, both in Massachusetts and Connecticut. Regular Baptist churches of this time largely were uninspired and spiritually dormant, and as Whitefield's dynamic preaching, similar to that of Edwards, swayed hosts of people, the Regular Baptists became adamantly anti-revivalist. Regular Baptists tended to dwell in the more developed tidewater and urban areas and continued to favor a restrained and orderly style of worship. Besides the Regulars, there were a variety of other Baptists scattered thinly throughout Colonial America: Six-Principle, General, Seventh-Day, Dunkards, and Freewill, who were influenced in varying degrees by the evangelical fervor of the "New Lights."

The Edwards-Whitefield preaching and doctrine spawned a new variety of Baptists, the "New Light" Baptists, also known as Separate Baptists, the spiritual forebears of the Southern Baptists. Separate Baptists tended to penetrate into the frontier lands, were resourceful but poorer than the settled Regular Baptists, and worshipped in a style that frequently was emotional and sometimes noisy. At first, the New Lights were Arminian in adherence to a doctrine that proclaimed God's willingness to save all repentant sinners, but later they became assertive Calvinists,[4] narrowing the field to the "Elect." In the South, both Regulars and Separates became distinct disciplines, although in New England they never divided.[5] This era also produced a host of energetic Separate Baptist preachers, male and female, ordained and unordained, including Backus, Daniel and Martha Marshall, her brother Shubal Stearns, and in Virginia, Colonel Samuel Harris and Hannah Lee Hall. Over one hundred Congregational churches were overwhelmed by the revival spirit and joined the Baptists in a new faith.[6]

Separates, in particular, were persecuted cruelly by the Established churches—the Anglican/Episcopal and Congregational churches, and the civil authorities supporting them. The rationale for mistreatment was that Baptists were violating the restrictive laws of the colonies. But those laws also prevented or obstructed Baptists from obtaining legal marriages, closed their churches, and barred "unauthorized" ministers from preaching. The net result of the persecution was demonstrably futile, since Baptist churches and believers multiplied dramatically. Another effect of persecution was to induce Separates to move into the Middle and Southern colonies, where they sought better treatment or hoped that sheer distance would make persecution more difficult.

In 1751 Backus, the Congregationalist minister, departed from his tradition to submit to believer's baptism by immersion. This occurred when the Titicut Congregational Church (New Light) organized in 1748, with Backus as pastor. This church began in 1749 a prolonged and tortuous discussion of the meaning and form of baptism. Backus accepted and then backed away from believer's baptism. The struggle became increasingly uncomfortable and embarrassing as the congregation divided into factions of immersionist Baptists and christening Congregationalists.[7] After a "long and bitter struggle with himself," Backus was convinced by his reading of the Scriptures that believer's baptism was the correct biblical position, and he submitted himself for immersion to elder (preacher) Benjamin Pierce of Warwick, Rhode Island. This action left Backus for a time excluded from the Congregational church but not attached to the Baptists, as he was initially opposed to joining that faith.[8] However, Backus had voluntarily burned his bridges, and, much more, he was a new creature in a Baptist embrace, although he did not yet comprehend it.

He pursued his labors as a convinced Calvinist, in the style of Jonathan Edwards, and as an enthusiastic evangelist. In 1756, with six baptized believers, he constituted a Baptist church in Middleborough, Massachusetts. Backus was ordained as its pastor. In 1754, at Stonington, Connecticut, a ministerial conference of Separate Baptists and Congregational Separates decided that sprinkling and immersion were incompatible. Presumably, the directive stemming from this conference had an influence on Backus, who in 1756 decided he could not pastor under one roof Baptists and Congregationalists. After this conference, Separate Baptists became simply Baptists.[9] Like "beloved" Bunyan in England; he would accept members into the church that had been christened as infants, in the mode of the Pedobaptist (Congregational) churches. He also ordained Minister Ebenezer Stearns of Easton, Massachusetts, in a church that did not require immersion.[10] But unlike Bunyan, Backus was soon convinced that believer's baptism must precede the taking of the Lord's Supper.

While the Congregationalists and Baptists, both children of the Great Awakening, often shared the same church in New England and the same minister, in the end they would diverge. This was because of conflicting theology, that from one perception encouraged acceptance of infant baptism by Congregationalists. This contrasted with the insistence by Baptists on a conversion experience, followed by believer's baptism through immersion, as a demonstration of faith. Neither faith held that salvation was obtained by baptism. But the Baptists would not compromise their belief in soul competency. Baptism, Baptists assert, involves a personal commitment to Christ, and therefore infant baptism is meaningless for infant salvation, since babies have no free will or faith to accept God's grace. In Baptist theology, personal faith in Christ always precedes baptism. Nothing accentuated the differences between the two denominations more than the Congregational Half-Way Covenant of 1662. The Congregationalists and Baptists could not overcome the incompatibles, which included the different styles of worship. Thus, they parted, or else as happened, many New Light Congregationalists became Baptists.[11]

Backus's life, while not untroubled, was set on a noble course. Near the time of the baptism controversy, in 1748 or 1749, he married Susanna Mason of Rehoboth, who would prove to be his greatest earthly blessing in a companionship that would endure for about fifty-one years.[12]

In his personal appearance, Backus was about six feet tall, and on the corpulent side. His mien was grave and venerable, and often when conversing or preaching, he would shut his eyes, the effect, some said, of his modesty. His voice was clear, sharp, and distinct. In the words of his intimate friend, Dr. Thomas Baldwin of Boston: "In both praying and preaching, he often appeared to be favoured with such a degree of divine unction, as to render it manifest to all that God was with him."[13] As a preacher, he was completely evangelical, and despite the power of his discourse, his sermons were not embellished with rhetorical language but rich in scriptural truth.[14] His burning desire was for the sinner to make a personal decision to accept Christ.

While serving as a New Light Baptist preacher, Backus was a convinced Calvinist, but not extreme in style or personality. Through his influence and patience, he helped keep the Regular Baptists and Separate Baptists in New England from forming distinct denominations and influenced many Regular churches to adopt a moderate form of revivalism. In theology and church polity, during his lifetime, he was probably the leading religious influence in the Baptist faith in New England.[15]

At Middleborough, Backus remained the faithful pastor for sixty years until his death. Although poorly paid, he was able with patience and frugality to accumulate "an estate of considerable value."

However, the church he nurtured at Middleborough was small for many years. Because of the revival of 1779, the church flock grew from 59 members to 138. This church produced several distinguished ministers of the Gospel and was the mother-church of several other Baptist churches.[16] The devotion of its servant-leader is testified amply by his activities between 1756 and 1767, beyond the perimeter of his church, when he traveled 15,000 miles and preached 2,412 sermons.[17]

Pre-Revolutionary New England was intolerant of Baptists, particularly the New Lights or Separate Baptists, whose ministers often would not register for preaching licenses, refused to submit to infant baptism, and would not attend the state churches as required by colonial laws in Massachusetts, Connecticut, and Virginia. Among the most grievous laws were those requiring Baptists, Presbyterians, and other dissenters through taxes to support the Established churches.[18] The penalties for violating the religious laws included imprisonment, beatings proscribed even for women (including Margaret Meuse Clay of Virginia), confinement with shackles, and the selling of personal property, land, and homes through public auctions. In 1774 Backus was chosen agent of the Baptist churches of Massachusetts, and for ten years he labored to exempt Baptists from their unfair burdens. These burdens would not be lifted until 1833, when church and state were finally separated in Massachusetts.[19]

Baptists Drift Toward Organization

America was in flux, and the political and religious changes influenced the life of Backus at a time when individualist Baptists began groping toward cooperative efforts and even forming associations of like-minded churches. Baptists, reflecting attitudes derived from the Particular Baptists in England, were reluctant to join inter-church bodies that might then direct and control them. Therefore, when they formed Baptist associations, individual churches gave them only limited power. Associations in this early time were largely religious and fellowship bodies, to exchange information, reinforce resolve against external oppressors, and define and support doctrines. Discipline was the responsibility of each church—a distinctive Baptist notion—although associations assisted, when requested, in the recommendation for pastors or in their dismissal. Although associations were not usually coercive bodies, they gave fraternal support when asked to calm church disputes.

The Philadelphia (Baptist) Association, the first such body, was formed in 1707, in a major area of Baptist concentration. In 1742 the Philadelphia Association adopted a modified version of the Westminster Confession,[20] a confession that had a profound effect on Baptist theology for several centuries. During its development, the Philadelphia Association debated the concept of a Baptist organization that would embrace the entire country, sent missionaries abroad, and founded the Baptist College of Rhode Island (later called Brown University), with Princeton graduate James Manning serving as its first president. For many years the college was the seminary and chief training ground for Baptist ministers.

The second Baptist Association (and the first in the South) was the Charleston Association, organized by Oliver Hart in 1751 in South Carolina. The Philadelphia Association became the model for the new body. Only four churches were affiliates of the Charleston Association in 1751, but there were twenty-six churches as members in 1796. In 1790 the Association managed a fund to assist young ministers. And throughout its existence, it sent preachers to the frontiers, helped establish new churches, and did yeoman service in filling pulpits and advising churches seeking pastors.

The Warren Association of Rhode Island, closely intertwined with the life of Backus, was the first Regular Baptist association in New England. It represented ten churches, only four agreeing to affiliate at its inception. There was apprehension that the new association might encroach on church prerogatives. And even Backus, although agreeing to serve as its clerk, refused for a while to join it. The Warren Association sponsored the new College of Rhode Island in a colony that Baptists viewed optimistically because of its tolerance and sound government. Most importantly, the Association correlated the Baptist resolve and research in the struggle for religious liberty. In 1769 the Warren Association created an eight-member "Grievance Committee," headed by Backus in 1772 (after its former head, John Davis, became ill),[21] to seek redress for persecuted Baptists. Careful research was made in each legal case to accumulate evidence and present witnesses before the courts and legislatures.[22] His efforts while serving as defender of Baptist rights led him to collect the largest number of Baptist-related documents in any colony.[23]

In his writings Backus recounted the intolerance of the state authorities and the seizure of property belonging to Baptists: houses, oxen, land, and orchards, all to be sold for a small fraction of their true value to pay taxes for the support of the Congregational Church. The Exemption Laws passed by several states, beginning in 1727, allowed dissenters to be refunded state taxes under certain circumstances, but the laws were temporary and were modified frequently. The obtaining of "certificates of exemption" from church taxes for Baptists required regular church attendance by each applicant, the verification by three Baptist churches in close proximity (often not possible, since the population was thin), residence within five miles of the church, and often a substantial fee for the license.[24] Baptists were distressed, moreover, because more often than not officials addressed them as "Anabaptists," which to Baptists was a term of reproach. Also grievous to Baptists was the implied concession to the authorities that government officials had a right to control conditions of worship and even to determine the sincerity of one's personal faith. Backus feared that the temptation to obtain "certificates of exemption" might encourage some Baptists to be baptized carelessly, without true conviction, that is "to come under the water when they have not been under the blood."[25]

Backus rejected the church tax from the beginning, and on February 6, 1749, he was imprisoned. However, he was released shortly through the intervention of persons in his congregation. He would not pay the tax but was sternly warned that he faced a long-term imprisonment. Undaunted, he assumed leadership of a group of "saints," who assembled on May 24, 1749, at Attelborough "to seek the Lord's direction" on the matter of "support of a worship that we can't in conscience join with. . . ." Backus carried to the Cape a copy of the group's petition addressed to the authorities, which was read and warmly seconded by the New Light supporters there. After the laws of Massachusetts and Connecticut were modified to exempt faithful Baptists from the church tax, Backus denounced the change and its civil authorities for still exercising the power of God and favoring one religion over another.[26] As Backus stated it: "In all civil governments some are appointed for others, and have power to compel others to submit to their judgment; but our Lord has most plainly forbidden us, either to assume or submit to any such thing in religion."[27] The "certificates of exemption," to allow exceptions, were regarded as tolerant expressions by Massachusetts and Connecticut authorities, and most Baptist congregations signed them to avoid inconvenience. But to Backus, who would not bend, the measures were odious, ungodly, and unjust in principle.[28]

Injustice Against Baptists

The Massachusetts and Connecticut authorities had not expected the Separate Baptists to expand so quickly, nor anticipated the concurrent loss of revenue because of the applications for certificates. In government action around 1750, against the congregation of Elder John Blunt and his new Baptist church at Sturbridge of mixed believers, the tax collectors took the following measures:

> stripped the shelves of pewter, of such as had it; and of others that had not they took away skillets, kettles, pots, and warming pans. Others they deprived of the means they got their bread with, viz., workmen's tools, and spinning wheels. They drove away geese and swine from the doors of some others; from some that had cows; from some that had but one they took that away. They took a yoke of oxen from one. Some they thrust into

prison, where they had a long and tedious imprisonment. One brother [Abraham Bloss or Bloice] was called from us and ordained a pastor of a Baptist church [in Upton] and came [back to Sturbridge] for his family; at which time they seized him and drew him away, and thrust him into prison, where he was kept in the cold winter till somebody paid the money and let him out [after 43 days].[29]

Symptomatic of religious oppression but probably the greatest mistake ever made by the oppressors was the imprisonment of widow Elizabeth Backus, the mother of Isaac Backus. For failing to pay her church taxes on time, and while sick and reading her Bible before a fire, she was seized at night and dragged away to jail. The highly respected lady recounted this misfortune to her son in the following letter:

Norwich, November 4, 1752

DEAR SON: I have heard something of the trials among you of late, and I was grieved till I had strength to give up the case to God, and leave my burden there. And now I would tell you something of our trials. Your brother Samuel lay in prison twenty days. October 15, the collector came to our house, and took me away to prison about nine o'clock, in a dark rainy night. Brothers Hill and Sabin were brought there next night. We lay in prison thirteen days, and then were set at liberty, by what means I know not. Whilst I was there, a great many people came to see me—Though I was bound when I was cast into this furnace, yet was I loosed, and found Jesus in the midst of the furnace with me. O, then I could give up my name, estate, family, life, and breath, freely to God. Now the prison looked like a palace to me. I could bless God for all the laughs and scoffs made at me——We are all in tolerable health, expecting to see you. These from your loving mother.

Elizabeth Backus[30]

Elizabeth Backus was released from jail because a friend paid the tax for her.[31]

Another respected Christian leader suffered persecution in 1752 for a similar "offense." Elisha Paine, ordained Baptist pastor of Long Island, "was seized and imprisoned at Windham for a tax to [support] the minister [Rev. Cogswell, Congregational clergyman] whom the church rejected." Paine the Baptist retorted: "I believe the same people who put this authority into the hands of Mr. Cogswell, their minister, to put me into prison for not paying him for preaching. . . ." Paine accused the rejected Congregationalist preacher of acting against justice, "yet he hath taken from me by force two cows and one steer, and now my body held in prison, only because the power is in his hands."[32]

Backus showed ingenuity and grit in facing the Establishment in 1770 with a threat to carry the battle for religious liberty to London. Such a confrontation in the epicenter of Imperial and Parliamentary power was to be avoided at all costs by the New England dignitaries. On August 20, 1770, the Colonial authorities, whose provincial charters were always vulnerable and subject to forfeiture to the Crown for good reason, were startled to read the following item by Backus in the *Boston Evening Post*:

> To the Baptists of the Province of Massachusetts Bay, who are, or have been oppressed in any way on a religious account. It would be needless to tell you that you have long felt the effects of the issue by laws by which the religious of the government in which you live is established. Your purses have felt the burden of ministerial rates; and when those would not satisfy your enemies, your property has been taken from you and sold for less than half its value. These things you cannot forget. You will therefore readily hear and attend, and when you are desired . . . and bring or send such cases to the Baptist Association to be held at Bellingham; when measures will be resolutely adopted for obtaining redress from another quarter than that to which repeated application hath been made unsuccessfully.[33]

The Baptists never carried out the threat to direct their appeals to "another quarter" (London), but they did raise funds in case they needed to dispatch an agent overseas.[34] This undoubtedly infuriated some of the leading citizens of Boston.

The ultimate test of Baptist courage was in 1773, when the Baptists chose to stop paying church taxes or even applying for exemption certificates. According to historian Leon McBeth, through civil disobedience the Baptists in 1773 made more progress toward religious liberty than had been made in the preceding decade. This new strategy developed from the frustrations of the Grievance Committee in Boston, which in its meeting of May 5, 1773, determined that several members could not recover their taxes, even though they had submitted exemption certificates.

Increasingly after 1770, Separate Baptists adopted civil disobedience as their weapon against mistreatment by either government or persons. This was in emulation of tactics used by the Sons of Liberty but also in response to violence and mob intimidation used on the frontier. Separate Baptists became less willing to endure force with meekness and humility. On May 5, 1773, Backus persuaded the Grievance Committee to consider jamming the Massachusetts and Connecticut judicial systems and presenting the authorities with the dilemma of jailing hundreds of protesting Baptists at the same time. The plan envisaged sending a letter endorsed by the Warren Association to the twenty-one Baptist churches, with congregations of 1,161, asking the Baptists to withhold tax certificates. The tactic did not succeed. For, although in the September meeting of the Association, when thirty-four votes were cast in favor of the plan, six opposed, and six were undecided—the vote was non-binding on the churches. Backus, on his part, refused to issue any certificates, but other churches issued them if requested. Also, some towns and parishes allowed tax exemption without certificates, as the approach of the American Revolution generated a need for cooperation and goodwill.[35] However, all was not well, for in Warwick, as late as February 7, 1774, eighteen Baptists were taken to jail for refusing to pay taxes in support of the Church Establishment. They remained in prison for eighteen days and were exposed to derision as tax dodgers.[36]

Presenting the Baptist Case

Backus and his Baptist colleagues were well aware that unless the American colonies placed in their laws provisions ensuring religious freedom, the old tyrannies would be extended. It was no easy task to advance the Baptist case in a favorable light, since intolerance in religious matters was written into the law in most colonies. However, the prelude to the American Revolution was another phase of history. The struggle over tax issues between the colonists, on the one hand, and England and its king, on the other, presented a rare opportunity for the Baptists to seek legal redress and a new direction for the wrongs done them in the name of religious conformity. However, in Philadelphia in 1774, after waiting to appear before members of Congress, Backus was vilified by newspapers, as he had been by members of the Established churches. He responded to some criticisms in writing, but ignored other insults. In one news article, Backus was threatened with a halter and the gallows.[37]

The First Continental Congress, attended by delegates of twelve colonies (not including Georgia), met in Philadelphia on September 5, 1774. The delegates had come to address the Five Intolerable Acts that closed the port of Boston and established the southern border of Quebec at the Ohio River. After its deliberations, the Congress sent a petition to King George III, asking that the Intolerable Acts be rescinded. If this was not done, the colonies threatened to impose an embargo on all commerce to and from England and the British West Indies.[38] When this petition, framed like an ultimatum, was treated with contempt in London, the colonies increased their acquisition of arms and intensified the training of militia. On April 19, 1775, the Revolutionary War, lasting five and one-half years, began at Lexington and Concord, with armed farmers and townsmen engaging His Majesty's regular forces in battle.[39]

During the 1774 Philadelphia session of the Continental Congress, joint measures were taken on September 13 to raise the Baptist issues before Congress by the Philadelphia Baptist Association, in collaboration with the Warren Association of Rhode Island. Despite this action, many Baptists had a genuine wariness of Baptist associations, because of their potential to control churches. Not surprisingly, Backus, clerk of the Warren Association, did not join it until 1770. Meanwhile, the Warren Association grew from four churches in 1767 to twenty-one by 1772, most of those churches situated in Massachusetts.[40] In part, the confrontation in Philadelphia was to declare the necessity of inserting clauses on religious freedom into the laws of the land.

While Baptists were rallying to the Colonial cause against Great Britain, a large committee of Baptists met four Congressional delegates from Massachusetts, and several members of Congress from other states, on the evening of October 14, 1774, at Carpenter's Hall. James Manning, president of Baptist Rhode Island College, read to them a memorial of grievances, while Backus rose to explain it. Two of the Congressional delegates, John and Samuel Adams, were irritated and declared that the Baptists had no reason to complain, since, in their opinion, Massachusetts had religious freedom and the fault, if any, lay with local officials.[41] Also there was much impatience with the Baptist position, until one Baptist messenger stated: "Only allow us the liberty in the country that they have long enjoyed in Boston, and we ask no more.[42]

Determined to stop the sun in its course, if necessary, Backus and his committee presented a direct plea to John Hancock, presiding over the Continental Congress. As a result, the members of Congress passed this resolution:

> In Provincial Congress, Cambridge, December 9, 1774: On reading the Memorial of the Reverend Isaac Backus, agent to the Baptist churches in this government: Resolved, that the establishment of civil and religious liberty, to each denomination in the province, is the sincere wish of this Congress; but being by no means vested with powers of civil government, whereby they can redress the grievances of any person whatever, they therefore recommend to the Baptist churches, that when

a general assembly shall be convened in this colony, they lay the real grievances of said churches before the same, when and where their petition will most certainly meet with all that attention due to the memorial of a denomination of Christians, so well disposed to the public weal of their country. By order of the Congress, John Hancock, President.[43]

These were fine words, but nothing would be done, that is until after the Revolutionary War. Backus and the Baptists presented the matter of the "injustice of being taxed where we are not represented" before the General Court meeting at Watertown in July 1775. A bill was drafted but tabled, according to Backus, because John Adams did not favor it.[44]

Effects from the War

Several years after the American victory at Saratoga, New York (1777), with the American Revolution neither won nor lost, a Congress convened in Boston on September 1, 1779. The purpose of this colonial assembly was to write a constitution, the final result to be the Articles of Confederation. The war had been fought by thirteen separate colonies, that raised troops and provisioned an army led by George Washington as commander, but no written constitution or even a permanent government was in place. During the war, very few Baptists were pacifists, except Dunkards (Tunkers) and Pietist Baptists that had originated in Germany, and many Baptists fought bravely for freedom in colonies that had badly oppressed them. Baptists were so generally supportive of the Revolutionary War that, when a list of enemies was posted by the general court of Boston in October 1778, Backus reported that there was not one Baptist among the 311 men named.[45]

The September 1779 meeting of Congress was significant and a crossroads for the Baptists. An article was presented by non-Baptists to further the support of ministers of the Episcopal and Congregational established churches through legal measures. Baptists, during the same war, often could not get sanctions to marry or hold services, but when Baptist chaplains served with largely-Baptist military companies, no authority was brave enough to remove these "illegal" military ministers. In order to obtain a favorable vote for the force measure, John Adams (later president) accused the Baptists of sending an agent, namely Isaac Backus, to Philadelphia during the session of the first Congress in order to break the union of colonies and obtain an advantage for the Baptist petitioners. The attack on the Baptists was joined by Robert Treat Paine. Paine accused the Baptists of reading a long memorial at Philadelphia in October 1774 that contained falsehoods against the Patriot Union. Because of these misrepresentations, delegates to the Congress were inflamed, producing the right atmosphere to pass the force provision for the Established ministers. Backus was informed of the fallacious accusations; he wrote a summary of the events as published by the *Chronicle* in Boston, challenging his accusers to a hearing before judges. Backus never heard from his accusers.[46]

After the war, George Washington wrote a letter to the Baptist churches of Virginia, commending the Baptists for their loyalty and dedication to the Patriot cause. "I recollect," he wrote, "with satisfaction that the religious society of which you are members have been throughout America uniformly and almost unanimously, the firm friends to civil liberty and the persevering promoters of our glorious Revolution."[47]

Disestablishment was demanded *in toto* by the Baptists, whereas the Presbyterians and Methodists asked only for the safeguarding of their rights. Before the Revolutionary War, the Congregational Church was the state religion of Connecticut, Massachusetts, and New Hampshire. The Anglican/Episcopal Church was favored by law in New York, Virginia, Maryland, North Carolina, South Carolina, and Georgia. Rhode Island, with twenty to thirty thousand Baptists after the war, had complete freedom of worship. New Jersey, Delaware, and Pennsylvania had no established religion. However, the elimination of religious intolerance was pursued during the war, first in New York and then in the southern states.[48]

The Man of Letters

Although known best to many as a formidable advocate of religious freedom, Backus also was a prolific writer of books and tracts, who in his nearly eighty-three years of life produced forty publications. Though he had only seven years of formal education, mainly obtained in winter studies, he modestly asserted: "Let none think me to be an enemy of learning." Indeed not, for Backus had digested and could freely quote from the philosophies of the Enlightenment, as espoused by John Locke and Thomas Jefferson, as well as the doctrines of religious liberty formulated by Roger Williams and John Clarke. He used the arguments of the Enlightenment to buttress his Bible-centered faith, as expressed in Calvinistic language. But Calvinism was on the wane, and Thomas Jefferson would proclaim Enlightenment's highest moral plane in a century dominated by the American and French revolutions. Backus was particularly fond of Locke's expression found in his treatise "On Toleration": "Civil laws are not to provide for the truth of opinion but for the safety and security of the commonwealth, and of every particular man's goods and person. And so it ought to be, for truth certainly will do well enough if she were once left to shift for herself."[49] Backus read much and widely, from the Bible daily, from writers in England and Colonial America on politics and government, and on religious history.

In 1769 Backus was asked by the Warren Association through "two gentlemen of note," to write a history of Baptists in America. His response was to complete in about twenty-seven years the monumental *A History of New England with Particular Reference to the Denomination of Christians called Baptists.* This difficult task enabled him to locate and conserve a variety of authentic materials concerning Baptists and others that would have been lost forever.[50] The finished work finally appeared in three parts: Volume I (1777), Volume

II (1784), and Volume III (1796).[51] The first volume, dealing with the history of the colonies and church affairs, was produced in 1777, during the confusion of the American Revolution.[52] He completed the last volume in 1796, near the end of the eighteenth century, when he was about age seventy-two, shortly before the Louisiana Purchase of 1803, with the American Republic striding forward briskly. His Baptist history is the earliest publication of the Baptist story in America, best known in a two-volume format.

In Backus's Baptist history, his insight is formidable and far-ranging. His remarks contain speculations on how Roger Williams became a Baptist, including the almost certain influence of Mrs. Catherine Scott, the sister of Anne Hutchinson.[53] He concludes that the second Baptist church had been established in America at Newport, Rhode Island, and that Dr. John Clarke, its pastor, had become Baptist around 1644, but conceivably before or after that date.[54] He noted that preacher John Gano, riding from his base at New York City, had established churches in several states, and was as much admired as George Whitefield.[55] Also he reflects on the hesitancy of Baptist churches in joining church associations, that hindered until 1767 the beginning of the Warren Association of Rhode Island.[56]

Other literary works written by Backus include "An Appeal to the Public in Defense of Religious Liberty" (1773); and "An Answer to Wesley on Election and Perseverance" (1789).[57] Scholars consider two of his most effective treatises (both of them to repel efforts by Massachusetts to control religion after the Revolutionary War) to be: "Government and Liberty Described; and Ecclesiastical Tyranny Exposed" (1778), and a companion piece, "An Appeal to the People of Massachusetts, State against Arbitrary Power" (1780). Both appeals were written to induce Massachusetts to alter its new constitution, so as to allow full religious freedom. Under the Massachusetts government, Backus asserted, Baptists were forced to support a religion (Congregational) with which they did not agree and to pay church taxes without any voice; this constituted taxation without representation. Backus requested that the government simply leave religion alone, since in the logic of Roger Williams, true religion was unfettered obedience to God.

The proposed Massachusetts Constitution of 1778 was defeated, an outcome attributed by many to Backus. In 1779 Massachusetts wrote a new constitution, but with contradictory language in Article III that could allow taxing of all persons in the support of state-supported ministers. Against this Constitution Backus wrote his treatise "An Appeal to the People." While his treatise failed to overcome the state constitution and its disturbing article, the public was alerted to a religious problem. In October 1780 Backus and his associates protested the provision in the Massachusetts constitution that placed public education under the control of Congregational Church leaders. The Baptists attacked the provisions for allowing a majority in each town and parish of "covenanting" for religious teachers, an obsessive concern for money and not the church of Christ, and for failing to afford equal protection to all sects.[58] Massachusetts did not adopt separation of church and state until about fifty years after the Revolutionary War, when constitutional remedies were made.[59]

Elder Backus was an elected delegate to the Massachusetts convention called to ratify the Federal Constitution of 1787. He was gratified to verify that the Constitution contained the words: "No religious test shall ever be required as a qualification to any office or public trust under the United States." Still, Baptists felt that a positive assertion in the Federal Constitution should be made for religious rights. Baptists applauded the contributions of James Madison in writing much of the Bill of Rights, especially the First Amendment that (in the words of Thomas Jefferson) erected a "wall of separation between church and state." Baptists, who had fought for religious freedom since the days of Governor Winthrop of Massachusetts, saw nothing remarkable about the provision that "Congress shall make no law respecting an establishment of religion, or prohibiting the free exercise thereof."[60] They also recognized as their sentiment, long expressed, contained in the Fourteenth Amendment of the Constitution:

> No state shall make or enforce any law which shall abridge the privileges and immunities of citizens of the United States, nor shall any state deprive any person of life, liberty, or property without due process of law, nor deny to any person within its jurisdiction the equal protection of the laws.[61]

In his beliefs and in his life, Backus remained a tenacious and conservative Baptist. He was a steadfast admirer of the preaching style and eloquence of Jonathan Edwards and read his sermons assiduously. Although Calvinism and closed communion, both dear to him, were espoused with vigor, Calvinism was declining at Backus's death in the early nineteenth century, and "closed communion" was hard pressed. "Closed communion," as practiced by Baptists, was the custom adopted by some Baptist churches, but rejected by other churches, from the seventeenth century; the practice restricted the serving of the Lord's Supper to the "saved" (immersed Baptists with a redemptive experience) and no others. But the practice was rejected by some churches from the beginning, and ministers including Bunyan refused to adopt it. At different stages of history, the practice was not wholly accepted by Backus's own Separate Baptists or fully approved in all periods by the Regular Baptists, the General Baptists, or the Six-Principle Baptists. Backus failed in his attempts to persuade the Groton (Baptist) Association to abandon "open communion," that permitted Pedobaptists (Congregationalists) and others to take communion with born-again Baptists.[62] But infant baptism was rejected by Backus, and virtually all Baptists, as unscriptual and misleading, as the child growing up might believe that he had been brought into God's kingdom by another person's act of faith.

Backus's life is a chronicle of constant activity to stimulate church growth, including far-ranging travel in New England and the South. His trips took him to virtually every cranny of Massachusetts, Connecticut, and New Hampshire but also to Virginia and Rhode Island. For thirty years he served as trustee of Rhode Island (Baptist)

College (later Brown University), doing much to increase the prestige of the institution.[63] In his lifetime, he would play a prominent part in converting the Baptist New Lights or Separates from a pesky and obscure element of Dissenters into a resolute and cohesive minority. They, with the help of Presbyterians and Methodists, withstood and defeated the "Standing Order." He arduously wrote, organized, and presided, as the second head of the Warren Association "Grievance Committee." Much of his world was affected by the New Lights, and the inspiration of Jonathan Edwards and George Whitefield. He was aware that in 1743 Whitefield's preaching induced seven church members to leave the "cold, cadaverous formalism" of the First Baptist Church of Boston to form the Second Baptist Church (Separate), with Ephraim Bound as pastor. This new church had 120 members within five years,[64] and its beginning was a dynamic early element in the surge of the Separates.

In the mid-stream of Backus's life, between 1740 and 1770, Baptist leaders had developed coherence and toughness, and churches had grown from three to twenty-three churches in Connecticut and from eight to thirty-two churches in Massachusetts. These had lit the bonfire that spread the illumination of the New Light Gospel to Virginia and North Carolina.[65] In 1789 he made a tour of Virginia[66] and was present at the conference of the Kehukee Association of Regular Baptists (Calvinist) that met on the Isle of Wight, Virginia.[67] This association of churches, represented in Virginia and North Carolina, would nurture a new variety of Baptists, the antimissions "Hardshell" or Primitive Baptists, that sometimes bore the term "Kehukeeism."[68] However, in 1755 Baptist life would change throughout the South, with the arrival at Sandy Creek, North Carolina, of the evangelizing Separate Baptists of New England. These Separates were led by Shubal Stearns, Daniel Marshall, and his wife Martha, and formation of the Sandy Creek Association would follow quickly.

In personal ways, Backus was adaptable and considerate. Against the injunctions of another preacher who believed inoculations were sinful, Backus in 1778 had his family immunized against smallpox. This did not inhibit his feeling that the smallpox plagues that struck Boston and other cities were the expressions of God's vengeance against their wickedness.[69] Backus was disturbed by an assistant pastor who reflected a modified Calvinist view, but Backus was generous in crediting this minister for winning many converts.[70] Thus, the Trailblazer Backus displayed a Christian kindness that generated effectiveness in his work. Even in his advocacy of government toleration of Dissenters, there was a link that he called "sweet harmony."

Backus had grown old, but the urge to preach the message of Christ and to struggle against injustice had not grown cold. When the General Assembly of Connecticut began its sessions in the fall of 1791, tension was in the air, for the Assembly was to debate a new "certificate law." The Baptists held a large mass meeting in the courthouse, with Backus, now sixty-seven years old, as a speaker. Backus recorded in his diary that he said, it is "heresy for any men to make any laws to bind others in religious matters or to loose any from the laws of Christ in the government of his church."[71] This time things would be different, for the Baptists and their Methodist allies won the day against Governor Huntington. Isaac Backus railed against the law in meetings of the Warren Association and wrote letters to leaders of the Baptists throughout the state. Backus thundered from his pulpit: "This is not right!" Influenced by the Baptists' determination, a new law was written that authorized each dissenter to write his own certificate, and, thus, to worship without a tax. According to historian William G. McLoughlin, "It was the highlight of Revolutionary liberalism in Connecticut."[72]

Meanwhile, as Backus approached his final days, John Leland, a younger and more radical Baptist champion of religious rights in Virginia, was attacking certificate laws in New England and advocating the disestablishment of religion.[73] Disestablishment did not occur painlessly, or as part of a natural order, for the contest for religious equality lasted until the presidency of James Madison in

New Hampshire, of James Monroe in Connecticut, and Andrew Jackson in Massachusetts.

Epilogue

Backus, the great Baptist Pathfinder of religious freedom, died in 1806. He is regarded by some scholars as the leading Baptist minister of the second Great Awakening, but not its most eloquent orator, for John Gano of New York or President James Manning of Rhode Island College may have been that. But Backus was the strongest voice of the religious dissenters against religious oppression. His treatise on "Defense of Religious History" (1773), absorbing arguments from Roger Williams, was written before the publication of the "Virginia Statute for Religious Freedom" stemming from the pen of Thomas Jefferson.

He was not all things to all men, for he represented the Baptist Warren Association's "Committee on Grievances," when the Baptists were a rugged but despised and abused minority in New England, Virginia, and elsewhere. Traveling thousands of miles to preach in New England and the South, he spoke for disestablishment of the Congregational and Episcopalian churches and against taxes to support another's religion. Government, he boldly asserted, had no moral or Scriptural right to control or limit a person's relationship to God.

Through his writings, Backus changed Colonial history. He could be daring, and sought on one occasion, by his letters, to influence dissenters to clog the judicial system in Massachusetts and fill the jails rather than submit to a religious tax. He also appealed to the inheritors of the Enlightenment on the basis of reason and simple justice. "Taxation without representation" was applicable to oppressed religious minorities as well as to colonies appealing to Great Britain for relief. Presbyterians and Methodists sought to protect their own parishioners from harm. Backus, in contrast, led the Baptists to advocate the exclusion of government from control of all religion, whether Quaker, Catholic, or Jewish, echoing the noblest sentiments of other Baptist writers.

Backus was a notable scholar and the most eminent Baptist historian in Colonial America. As the careful conservator of precious documents and books, he authenticated the unique Baptist positions and activities with regard to church and state. In his writing, and echoing a general Baptist conviction, religious liberty was presented as a fundamental issue of the American Revolution. He was the author of forty publications on freedom, state, and Baptist history. His most notable work is *A History of New England with Particular Reference to the Denomination of Christians called Baptists.* His scholarship added stature to the College of Rhode Island (later known as Brown University), of which he was a co-founder and trustee.

The Anabaptists and Thomas Helwys taught Baptists how to suffer. Roger Williams taught Baptists how to achieve statecraft and an all-embracing tolerant government. But Isaac Backus taught Baptists how to protect themselves and all persecuted faiths through the careful collection of evidence and the making of a proper presentation to courts and assemblies. These presentations invoked legal principles, noted the Scriptural basis, and appealed for religious freedom on the platform of reason and justice. Because of his selfless efforts, Backus has been acclaimed one of the greatest if not the ultimate Baptist architect of religious freedom. But as a faithful preacher of the Gospel, he would have consigned that title to the humble Nazarene.

Chapter 7

Martha Stearns Marshall
(1722-1793)

Frontier Woman Preacher

A tidal wave of Separate Baptists, the so-called New Light Baptists, swept from New England into the southern states around 1755, twenty years before the American Revolution. These aggressive evangelizers brought with them a new element for most Baptists—unordained women preachers or "Exhorters." The most successful of these female soul-seekers may have been New England-bred Martha Marshall, second wife of Daniel Marshall. She did not dominate the New Lights, forerunners of the Southern Baptists, nor did she eclipse Shubal Stearns, Daniel Marshall, or Colonel Samuel Harris, among the primary evangelists and church planters of the Baptist New Lights. But, winsome and feminine as she was, yet not restrained by her co-leaders or the new customs of the Separates, she was an extraordinary female preacher. Her courage, Christian conviction, and determination define her as one of the greatest Baptist Trailblazers.

Between 1740 and 1770, the Baptists of New England emerged from being an obscure and so-called "ignoble" small sect into a serious threat to the existing church order. One of the early builders was William Screven, who in 1696 was driven from Kittery, Maine, to Charleston, South Carolina, where he founded the first church of

**Martha Marshall Studying the Bible
at Abbots Creek, North Carolina (1761)**
Artist's concept not based on physical description.

the future Southern Baptist Convention.[1] The revival spirit developed other innovative leaders, including scholarly Hezekiah Smith. Some of these pioneers stemmed from respectable well-to-do Congregational families, as Isaac Backus, and others were honed as a new breed of Separate Baptists with natural talents—such as John Leland, Shubal Stearns, Daniel Marshall, and an array of unordained women preachers including Martha Marshall, wife of Daniel. This new type of Baptist was energetic and sometimes even truculent in facing the "Standing Order." They were not willing to accept denials or delay in redressing their mistreatment, and in attitude were quite unlike the General and Regular Baptists, who were polite supplicants on the occasion of misdeeds.

The New Light Baptists boldly asserted baptism by immersion and set in motion a lively evangelical thrust that won over many of their Congregational neighbors. This was at a time when the "Standing Churches" (Congregational and Episcopal) were gradually retreating from religious taxation and the Half-Way Covenant (where children became Congregational church members without a religious experience). Thirty-two new Baptist churches were formed in Massachusetts in the period 1740-1770, of which twelve were created from new converts. In Connecticut, fourteen Separate churches became Baptist, while nine other Baptist churches were established by former Congregationalists or Baptists leaving their old churches. In this exchange, the new churches often adopted "closed communion," accepting to the Lord's Supper only these who had been immersed.[2]

Before the emergence of the Separate Baptists, the role of women among the Baptists was limited except among Freewill Baptists, who had women preachers. Social progress has led modern women into a new examination of the priesthood and ministerial ordination, based on the capabilities of women and the attitude of Jesus toward women.[3] There was a limited but visible role for church women even from the ancient days. Some of the foremost women were: the prophetess Miriam, sister of Moses; Jael, who slew with a tent peg the sleeping General Sisera; and Judge Deborah, who around 1220 B.C. left her palm tree and went into battle with Barak at her side.[4] In the early Christian Church, there clearly were positions filled by women, notably deaconess Phoebe (Romans 16:1-2), about 300 A.D., whose duties included preparing women for baptism, going into the water with them, and anointing them.[5] Also, Pliny the Younger writes that there were deaconesses in the second century church at Bithynia.

In the seventeenth century English Baptist congregations, a few Baptist women preached and others served as deacons. But most early Baptist confessions limited preaching duties to men. Many churches had one man deacon and one woman deacon, the latter generally women over sixty years of age, financially supported in some cases by the church. Women deacons were expected to speak in support of their faith, assist other women at baptism, visit the needy, and enforce discipline. However, in the ordination of four women deacons at the Bristol, England, church in 1679, the church affirmed: "It is theire duty alsoe to speake a word to their soules by (persons under their care) as occasion requires, for support or consolation, to build them up in a spirituall lively faith in Jesus Christ; for, as some observe, there is not an office of Christ in his Church, but it is dipt in ye blood of our Lord Jesus."[6] Still, the role of women preachers and deacons was more common among the General Baptists than the Regular Baptists.

The Separate Baptists that between 1740 and 1770 penetrated the pioneer lands of North and South Carolina, Virginia, and Georgia were venturesome, evangelistic, and aggressive. Their women leaders also were fearless in proclaiming the Word before their small congregations and with the strangers they encountered. Thus, without the approval of parish, diocese, church council, or overseer, under the freedom of the Holy Spirit and in the openness of the frontier, where men and women bore hardships equally, numbers of Baptist women proclaimed the Gospel as New Light unordained exhorters, most notably Martha Marshall.

There were other outstanding Baptist women church-builders of the period, never encountered by Martha Marshall. One of these was Margaret Meuse Clay (1735-1832), wife of James Clay of Chester-field County, Virginia. Receiving her Christ-given salvation at a Baptist "unauthorized" church, she was baptized secretly in the moonlight on the James River by the Reverend Jeremiah Walker. Her piety, intelligence, and charm were widely recognized, with ministers frequently asking her to lead in public prayers. Her home appears to have been a guest stop for itenerant Baptist preachers before a church was organized in 1773.

She was rounded up with other Baptist teachers in the Chester-field area by the arch persecutor of Baptists, Colonel Archibald Cary. Margaret Clay and eleven Baptist men were tried in a crowded courthouse and convicted of unlicensed preaching. She went alone for the trial, with her husband unable or unwilling to attend. Unsubstantiated tradition supports the view that the defense plea was given by Patrick Henry, but if so his arguments were unsuccessful. The Baptists were the losers, and the eleven men bared their backs and were soundly lashed. Margaret Clay prepared to take her blows, when an unknown man pushed through the crowd and paid the fine to the authorities, sparing her the whipping. As Margaret Clay returned to her husband, she was singing: "Children of the heavenly king, as ye journey sweetly sing." As the result of her testimony, men stood in awe of her spiritual gifts, and her witness was fruitful in the conversion of sinners. After the death of James Clay in 1790, Margaret Clay and her family moved to Mississippi, where her story is still venerated.[7]

Another Baptist exhorter was Hannah Lee [Corbin, Hall], third child of Thomas Lee of Stratford Hall, Westmoreland County, Virginia. Five of her brothers were illustrious in the American Revolution and the founding of the Republic: Richard Henry, Francis Lightfoot, William, Arthur, and Thomas. Her avocation as a growing woman was reading, inasmuch as her father had one of the finest private libraries in the region. She married, at Stratford, Gawen Corbin, member of the House of Burgesses, and the couple moved to his residence, Peckatone Plantation on the Potomac River. However, he died in 1759, with a will that deprived his widow of thirty-two years from inheriting most of the estate if she should remarry or leave the county.

Hannah Lee Corbin openly left the Church of England (Episcopal), the affiliation of her parental family, and became a Baptist. This conversion resulted from the preaching in Northern Neck by David Thomas, a Baptist Calvinist evangelist of Fauquier County, Virginia, who visited the Westmoreland area between 1760 and 1762. The young widow "straightway" was converted to the Baptist faith, and in 1764 was called to appear before the grand jury of Westmoreland County for absenting herself for six months from worship at the State (Anglican) Church.[8]

Around 1762 Hannah Corbin married Dr. Richard Lingan Hall, an educated man of social standing. She was probably "illegally" married by a Baptist preacher, since dissenting marriages were not legally recognized in Virginia until 1780. In 1769 Hannah's eldest daughter married and inherited Peckatone Plantation. Then Hannah and her family moved to Richmond County, where the Hall home became a refuge for itenerant Baptist preachers. As the consequence of preaching performed by Baptist Separate preachers James Greenwood and William Mullen, the Morattico Church was organized in 1778 in Richmond County. Dr. Hall and his wife Hannah appear to have been charter members. She was forthright in all that she did, as a Baptist of convictions, both fervent for the American Revolution and an advocate of the rights of women. To her Anglican sister she wrote: "I am not surprised that you seem to have a mean opinion of the Baptist religion. I believe that most people that are not of that profession [Baptist] are persuaded we are either Enthusiasts or Hypocrites. But, my dear sister, the followers of the Lamb have been ever esteemed so; that is our Comfort. And we know in Whom we have believed." Hannah Hall died in 1783, leaving part of her estate to her "Baptist daughter."[9]

Neither Margaret Meuse Clay nor Hannah Lee Hall overshadow

that inspired missionary tornado, Martha Marshall. Martha is believed to have been a major factor in moving her distinguished brother, the Reverend Shubal Stearns, from the Presbyterian Church to the New Light Baptists (Separates). In all probability, she influenced her husband Daniel Marshall to become a Baptist frontier evangelist. At other times, she asserted herself boldly as a Spirit-filled unordained preacher and rose as the fearless court defender of her husband at his trial in Georgia for his unlicensed preaching. Under the spell of her biblical and righteous oratory, judges recanted, men wept, and women and children succumbed to the Holy Spirit. She was not the commander of the New Light army that swept from New England into the South, but among that Baptist host there were only a few that might have been her equal.

Martha was the second wife of Daniel Marshall (1706-1784), the Baptist Separate pioneer in the South. She was also the sister of Shubal Stearns (1706-1771), paramount leader of the New Light Baptists that gathered at the Baptist hub of Sandy Creek, North Carolina. The Stearns family roots were planted in Connecticut and in the Presbyterian faith, and Martha's earliest religious encounters would have been as a non-immersionist (Pedobaptist) Presbyterian.[10] In 1751, under the influence of the New Lights, Shubal Stearns was baptized by Baptist preacher Wait Palmer at Tolland, Connecticut, and soon afterwards ordained by Palmer and Joshua Morse.[11] The baptism of Shubal, approximately forty-five years old, and his impulses to become a missionary were conceivably influenced by his strong-willed younger sister Martha. There is a mystery as to why the winsome Martha married the middle-age, widowed Daniel Marshall, for historian David Benedict describes Daniel Marshall as "not possessed of great talents."[12]

However, Daniel Marshall had some extraordinary hidden gifts that unfolded in time. Marshall presumably was taller than his diminutive Martha, since her brother Shubal was short in stature. Daniel spoke and preached with a convincing and "fervent" voice, and, although his style later in life was imitated by young preachers, he never became a great orator. In the beginning, however, he "was neither profoundly learned nor very eloquent,"[13] but he did have a driving vision and knowledge acquired through experience. His character, like that of Shubal Stearns, was indisputably good, as a Christian man and a preacher. History would prove him to be wiry, tenacious, and staunchly courageous. Martha was probably a few or many years younger than the widower, whose potential she correctly assessed. Later, he, through his pastoral experience and support by her Christian prayers and fortitude, would make his mark as Shubal's chief lieutenant and as a remarkable, "indefatigable" church planter and winner of souls.[14]

Martha Stearns and Daniel Marshall, the latter about forty-one years old, were married on June 23, 1747, almost certainly in Connecticut. Martha would assume the care and instruction of her husband's son Daniel. In addition, she would bear ten other children: Abraham, John, Zaccheus, Levi, Moses, Solomon, Joseph, Eunice, Mary, and Benjamin (who died in his youth).[15] Although raised as a Presbyterian, Daniel around 1745 became a proselyte of "Methodist" George Whitefield and felt led of the Spirit to seek the conversion of the Mohawk Indians. He, Martha, and three small children left a comfortable home and in 1753-54 existed with few comforts in New York, as New Light missionaries to the Mohawks. War among the tribes and terrible danger during the French and Indian War (1754-1763) compelled them to move on to Pennsylvania and then to Virginia.[16]

Throughout these first missionary trials, Martha was far more than a pioneer woman boiling and beating clothes, rocking cradles, mending sweaters, and exchanging small talk with Indian women. She was a stalwart New Light missionary-partner of her stout-hearted husband. Neither of them was a Baptist at this time. All writers familiar with the saga of the Marshalls agree that Daniel's success then and later was "ascribable, in no small degree, to Mrs. Marshall's unwearied and zealous cooperation."[17]

It was near Winchester, Virginia, that the Marshalls became con-

verts to the Baptist faith. There, at Mill Creek in 1754, Daniel and
Martha Marshall and their associates Joseph Breed and his wife were
immersed by Baptist preacher Samuel Heaton.[18] Daniel was licensed
by the Mill Creek Baptist Church. Although Martha later served as
a Baptist lay preacher or exhorter, she was never ordained. Mill
Creek became virtually a clan gathering ground, for in August 1754
Shubal Stearns, brother of Martha, left his pastorate at Tolland,
Connecticut, and led a large party to join the Marshalls. Stearns,
before his Christian conversion, reportedly "was once wicked to a
proverb" but now he was set on a straight course.[19] His purpose was
to serve as leader-evangelist in an unsettled frontier, for Stearns was
"filled with missionary zeal to carry light into dark places."[20]

Three years before their arrival at Mill Creek, the Stearns party in
1751 was baptized in the Baptist way at Tolland. This was a climactic
moment for the Baptist preacher Wait Palmer, for among the new
converts was not only Shubal Stearns, but Shubal Stearns, Jr., Peter
Stearns, Ebenezer Stearns, Enos Stinson, Jonathan Polk, and their
wives.[21] The Stearns party that had combined with the Marshall
party in Virginia, now settled for a while at Cacapon in Hampshire
County, about thirty miles from Winchester. However, Shubal Stearns
was disappointed in the results of his missionary endeavors in Virginia, and a decision was made by the band of Christians to cross
into North Carolina, the new "Promised Land."[22]

Pioneer Work in North Carolina

In 1755 Shubal Stearns, Martha, and Daniel Marshall began their
work in the Granville District of North Carolina, close to Virginia.
They preached and gathered a Baptist following until 1758, sometimes in the vicinity of the extensive "parish" of the Reverend John
Gano of New York. Martha's Christian exuberance led her in time
to become an exhorter or unordained lay preacher; that position was
a unique feature of the Separate Baptists.

Neither Shubal Stearns nor Daniel Marshall had a certificate from

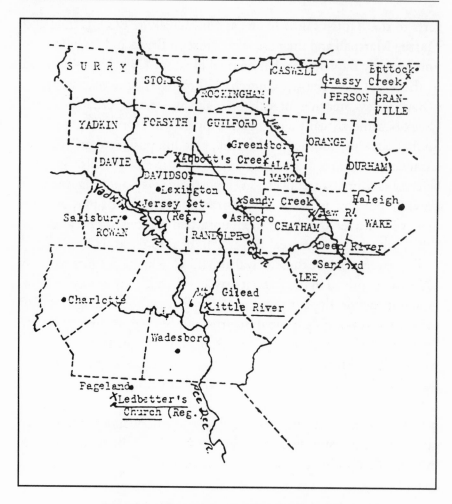

Separate Baptists in North Carolina
in the Eighteenth Century

the bishop of London or was supported by the Vestry Tax, since only Anglican ministers could be supported by that levy. By the Act of 1751 Baptist clergy could not unite couples in marriage nor collect a sizable marriage fee, available only to the Established Church. None of the Baptist preachers would have accepted the state-paid wages at any rate, or the tax proceeds, for Baptists disdained a "hireling ministry." All Baptist preachers in North Carolina were supported only through their useful labor and infrequently small freewill offerings. Thus, the support often was in kind: chickens, a pig, venison, corn, animal skins, rarely a frock coat, and perhaps "mountain dew" (or corn liquor) from members of their churches. This was a rough frontier, and drinking liquor was permissible, but not drunkenness, even at this early period. There was no record of Anglican ministers visiting, so they preached without hindrance for three years to the religiously-famished frontier families. There were few amenities of the type later available at Buffalo Settlement, now near Greensboro. George Soelle, Moravian missionary, reported in 1772 that "All the residents here [Buffalo Settlement] were Presbyterians, rich and well satisfied with themselves."[23]

Immediately after the small party of Separates arrived at Sandy Creek, Orange County, North Carolina, Stearns began his preaching and baptizing on the Yadkin River in Rowan County. Tidence Lane saw him under a peach tree, gathering his thoughts to preach. Marshall preached in the same year on the Uwharrie River and at Abbott's Creek, after which both men joined in organizing the Abbott's Creek Church. They traveled long distances, including a return to the Granville district to preach and baptize.[24]

On June 2, 1758, Stearns organized the Sandy Creek Association. By 1761 the Association consisted of three churches, namely Sandy Creek, Abbott's Creek, and Deep River, with an aggregate of 900 members. The Sandy Creek Church had 606 believers, and Baptists became the majority of the population in Rowan County. In 1758 there were probably no more than twenty Anglicans in the area, most of these county officers appointed by the Governor. The only other English-speaking Christians of any number were Quakers at Cane Creek, New Garden, and western Orange County; these became allies of the Baptists on the Regulator question.[25]

The Sandy Creek Association became a kind of Baptist Zion. The area that today is between Alamance County and the Yadkin River country in North Carolina contained the largest concentration of Baptists in the world, with Baptist meeting houses and preaching places rising like spring flowers, some of the more notable being Sandy Creek, the Jersey Settlement, and Bethabara near Shallow Fords. Of Sandy Creek churches, the Baptist nucleus, Morgan Edwards wrote in 1772:

> Very remarkable things may be said of this church, worthy of a place in Gillis's book, and inferior to no instance he gives of the modern success of the gospel in different parts of the world. It began with sixteen souls, and in a short time increased to six hundred and six——Sandy Creek is the mother of all the Separate Baptists. From this Zion went forth the word, and great was the company of them that published it. The church in seventeen years [1755-1772] has spread her branches westward as far as the great river Mississippi, southward as far as Georgia, eastward as far as the Potomac; it, in seventeen years, is become mother, grandmother and greatgrandmother to forty-two churches, from which sprang 125 ministers, many of which are ordained, and support the sacred character as well as any set of clergy in America.[26]

Paschal indicates that the people of Rowan County, west of Orange County (where the Battle of Alamance was fought) was inhabited by some of the "best type" of settlers that populated North Carolina, including the parents of Daniel Boone and relatives of General Nathanael Greene. Some of them from Delaware, New Jersey, Pennsylvania, and Rhode Island clustered in Jersey Settlement in the Granville District and were organized into the Jersey Baptist Church by the distinguished Particular Baptist pastor, John Gano of New York. Paschal states that in all North Carolina, the

Church of England had no vicar equal in religious capacities or ability to Particular Baptist Gano, or Separates Shubal Stearns[27] and Daniel Marshall. With the exception of Quakers and a few Presbyterians and Moravians, the people were Baptist and sympathized with the Regulators (or the "mob," as derisively they were called by the supporters of Governor Tryon). In the Upper Yadkin Valley (Rowan County) and all around Salem the people were Baptists. These Baptists detested the Vestry Act that gave legal authority to impose taxes on settlers, that would be used to pay the salaries of clergymen of the Church of England.[28]

If Sandy Creek under Shubal Stearns's ministry was the New Jerusalem, in the language of the Apostle Paul, then Abbott's Creek, North Carolina, for Martha and Daniel Marshal was its Damascus or Corinth. The Marshalls established a vigorous church there, from which, in radiating impulses, Daniel established meeting places and extended his labors as far as Virginia. However, Daniel's finest "catch" was the future leading Baptist Separate preacher, Colonel Samuel Harris, a respected landholder and militia officer, who did astounding things as a preacher and was widely-called the "Apostle to Virginia." This conversion occurred in the vicinity of the Dan River church—the first New Light church in Virginia—established in 1760 by Daniel Marshall and Philip Mulkey, with a mixed congregation of white and black members.[29] Colonel Harris, as a preacher, was accused of subverting "true religion" (Anglican variety) in Halifax, Virginia, was pulled from the pulpit and dragged about by his hair in Orange,[30] and attacked by a mob in Culpeper. Because Harris possessed a noble character and humility (and friends who would use fists in his defense), he suffered less than some other Baptist preachers in Virginia.

Both Sandy Creek and Abbott's Creek, and member churches of the Sandy Creek Association, had ruling elders, eldresses, and deaconesses. There were two exhorters at the Sandy Creek Church. Therefore, there would have been no aberration in Martha Marshall's serving as an exhorter at Abbott's Creek. These forerunners of the

Southern Baptist Convention followed the nine Christian rites: baptism, Lord's Supper, love-feast, laying-on-of-hands, washing feet, anointing sick, right-hand of fellowship, kiss of charity, and devoting children. Wine, not grape juice, was used with the Lord's Supper and administered every Sunday.[31] There was no bishop, following general Baptist tradition, but Shubal Stearns exercised the authority of a founder. However, for allowing women preachers, the New Lights were called "disorderly" by supporters of the Church of England.[32]

This is an appropriate opportunity to examine Martha Marshall in more detail. It is obvious that she was a bold and gifted exhorter, but not in a manner to upset men of the eighteenth-century American frontier. This was because she had genuine character, a profound love and knowledge of the Bible, and the ability to sway crowds with her eloquence. She performed the varied menial duties of cutting firewood, nursing ten children, washing clothes in streams, spinning and sewing, visiting the sick, praying for sinners, picking blackberries, roasting acorns and corn on an open fire, boiling mush, baking hoe cakes, and comforting her husband. Food certainly must have been sparse at times, when the corn was blighted and deer were scarce. She undoubtedly had miserable moments, giving birth to a huge family, one child followed rapidly by another. She restrained her fear of Indians in warfare and rough men who had primitive standards of justice. The travails of winter, with dwindling supplies and too few blankets, must have wracked her soul. But note the lack of condescension when the knowledgeable historian Robert B. Semple describes her religious role: "Without the shadow of an usurped authority over the other sex, Mrs. Marshall, being a lady of good sense, singular piety, and surprising elocution, has, in countless instances melted a whole concourse into tears by her prayers and exhortations."[33] There can be no doubt that Daniel Marshall's success was "ascribable, in no small degree to Mrs. Marshall's unwearied and zealous cooperation."[34]

Among the three dedicated male leaders the work of the New Light Baptists was divided. Shubal Stearns made his operational center Sandy Creek; Daniel Marshall developed the Abbott's Creek area; Colonel Samuel Harris planted and preached mainly in Virginia. After years of Christian ministry, Marshall was ordained by his brothers-in-law Stearns and Henry Leadbetter, in response to a letter to Stearns as senior pastor from the Abbott's Creek Baptist Church. This particular ordination was a difficult matter, since a plurality of ordained elders was required to constitute a presbytery. A Regular Baptist preacher on South Carolina's Peedee River was requested to assist, but he refused, sending word that Stearns's religious congregation was a "disorderly set," allowing women to pray in public and "ignorant men" to preach.[35] The part about women and unlettered preachers was true, for in this great geographical area, including the Carolinas and Virginia, there were only five college graduates among the Baptist preachers, including John Gano and Hezekiah Smith. This Separate group was a great contrast to the first English Baptists, some of whose leaders stemmed from Oxford and Cambridge.

Shubal Stearns in this milieu was the towering noble Christian spirit and catalyst. It was Stearns, the little man, with "good, natural parts," as Edwards put it, who principally determined that the Separates would establish themselves at Sandy Creek. It was Stearns who persuaded his young co-believers, with their cold attitudes, to accept the sermons of John Gano, the educated New York Regular. It was Stearns again who would persuade the majority of the New Light Baptists to avoid a bloody war against the tyranny of North Carolina's Governor Tryon. It would be Stearns who would die at his post at Sandy Creek, the Baptist Zion. In the Episcopal Church, he would have been an archbishop, in Jewish ancient history, a patriarch or prophet. And Martha would have been following in the footsteps of Miriam the prophetess, the sister of Moses.

Daniel Marshall, the "indefatigable" missionary, ventured into Virginia. As described by historian Robert Baylor Semple:

> The gospel was carried by Mr. Marshall into the parts of Virginia adjacent to the residence of this religious colony

(Abbott's Creek) soon after their first settlement. He baptized several persons in some of his first visits. Among them was Dutton Lane, who shortly after his baptism began to preach. A revival succeeded, and Mr. Marshall at one time baptized forty-two persons. In August, 1760, a church was constituted, and Mr. (Dutton) Lane became their pastor. This was the first Baptist Separate Church in Virginia. The church prospered very much under the ministry of Mr. Lane, aided by the occasional visits of Mr. Marshall and Mr. Stearns.[36]

When a branch church of Separate Baptists, ministered to by the mother-church, had seven to thirteen members and was able to provide for its own ordained minister, it could form an independent church. Its members petitioned the parent church, asking for letters of dismission for the new charter members. The appointed day normally was a day of fasting, with two or more presiding ministers present. This is the further procedure:

> The ministers inquire whether it is their desire to become a church, whether their habitations are near enough to each other, conveniently to attend church conferences? Whether they are so well acquainted with each other's life and conversation to coalesce into one body, and walk together in love and fellowship. Whether it is their intention to *keep* up *a regular discipline* agreeably to the Scriptures, to make *God's word* the rule of their conduct in church government, obeying his ordinances, and in matters of faith, and all other things relative thereto in a church relation, and by these things distinguish themselves as a true church of Christ? These things being answered in the affirmative, then a covenant is produced,—and being read, consented to and subscribed, the ministers pronounce them a church in some such words as these: "In the name of our Lord Jesus Christ, and by the authority of our office, we pronounce you, (mentioning their names) a true *Gospel church*; endowed with all necessary power towards becoming a complete organized body, and the due government of yourselves; and therefore stand bound

to make proper use of that power, as ye shall answer it to the
Head of the church, on whose name let us further call.

Then they pray to God for a blessing on them, and conclude by
singing His praise, and giving each other the right hand of fellowship. The church thus constituted have full power to choose their
officers, receive members, and deal with offenders."[37]

Baptist Separate churches had a pastor, often unordained, and
usually two deacons who served until resignation or death. If there
was no pastor, then the church had a ruling elder, but he could not
ordain or officiate at marriages. In many churches also there were
one or two men, known as "gifts," with a talent for prophesy. Pious
and devout, and with little education, they could talk or lead in
prayer.[38]

The people who gathered for preaching were motley. They were
an amalgam of white men and women, only some of whom could
read the Bible, some blacks, many zealous persons, and all participants in a lively faith. Typical of the houses of worship was the
shelter thirty feet by twenty-six feet built for 32 members by the
Reverend Joseph Murphy and his congregation, about 1769, at
Shallow Fords. In three years, this church had two branches, serving
about 350 families and gathering a total church membership of 185.[39]
Scattered flocks were served by "packhorse" preachers, living on the
edge of survival through prayers and wit, and little else. The families
they rallied were dirt-poor.[40]

The preachers on the frontier had no pay and in most cases no
promise of support. They traveled long distances between settlements on Indian trails or overland, wearing deerskins or homespun
clothes, often wringing wet and cold from fording streams. Their
parishioners were poor frontier people, always living on the margin
of death from starvation, Indians, or murderous neighbors. The
preachers often were greeted with tears of joy, and little else, except
parched corn and a roof for the night. And at a cluster of cabins,
although weary from travel, the preacher unloosed his Bible and
hymnbook from the saddlebag and under the prairie sky delivered a

message of God's grace. The backwoodsmen had no respect "for a preacher who couldn't shoot without a rest."[41]

On the frontier, there was passed around a proverb that the "preacher seldom rode a fat horse." And, generally, New Light preachers were not well supported. The Reverend George Soelle, the Moravian minister, respected by Baptists and a speaker at Baptist assemblies, wrote of the wretched livelihood of some preachers. Soelle visited Rocky River near Jersey Settlement, frequented by John Gano, and encountered the Baptist preacher Sims. "He is a very poor man, for it is the method and plan of the Baptists to give their preachers nothing; and they must support themselves by the work of their hands although they are expected to care for and visit those entrusted to their care, which does not meet with the approval of some of their members. . . ."[42] The Reverend Samuel Harris, seeing a Baptist minister suffer from lack of support, changed his first opinions and urged that preachers should be supplied with money and food.

Soelle in 1772 witnessed at Caraway Creek, branch church of the Haw River Baptist Church, the baptism of four adults, who joined six others in taking the Lord's Supper. These services were held at the Uwharrie River by Baptist minister Elnathan Davis, who invited Soelle, a Moravian, to preach but did not ask him to partake of Communion.[43]

Frontier life, around the Revolutionary War period was hard and cruel, and drinking liquor to excess was common among male and even female church members on the Forks of the Yadkin and elsewhere. Sometimes the men shamed their churches with heavy drinking at public gatherings and during elections. Two churches, around 1782, accused Reverend William Cook of excessive drinking. Cook, although a successful church planter, was dismissed as pastor. The Moravian Church at Wachovia, on the other hand, fostered the construction of a brewery and tavern, where beer was sold. At this time, there were one hundred Baptist ministers in the Yadkin Association of North Carolina, and their "use of strong drink was temperate," at least in most cases. Drinking by church members was common, but heavy drinking and drunkenness was not tolerated, as the church records fully testify. At monthly church meetings, the disorderly drinkers were admonished, and, if not repentant, were discharged.[44] Even stronger Baptist attitudes on drinking liquor were to come much later.

Even humor intruded into the serious business of saving souls. The Reverend Elnathan Davis, born in 1735, was baptized by Shubal Stearns and ordained by Samuel Harris. Davis, about twenty-two years of age, a pagan youth reared by a Seventh-Day Baptist family, attended the New Light baptism on the Haw River in order to obtain diversion, or possibly view a drowning. He had heard that John Steward, a huge man, would be baptized in the river by the spunky but small Shubal Stearns. So Davis, with eight to ten mischievous friends, "companions in wickedness," went to the site.

Davis listened as Stearns began to preach. Some of the people began to tremble, while another man leaned on his shoulder, weeping bitterly, and wetting with tears his new white coat. Davis shoved the man away and joined his friends sitting on a log. One of them said, "Well, Elnathan, what do you think now of these damned people?" He replied, "There is a trembling and crying spirit among them: but whether it be the spirit of God or the devil I don't know; if it be the devil, the devil go with them; for I will never more venture my self among them." He stood in the distance, but Stearns's voice drew him again to the crowd, where he was seized with trembling. He attempted to withdraw, but he became confused, and he sank to the ground devoid of strength, along with others. After he began to get control of himself he was overcome with a sense of "dread and anxiety, bordering on horror." This dreadful pall shadowed him for days, until he found relief by faith in Christ. Unlearned in the Scriptures and raw in technique, he began preaching immediately to the unconverted,[45] and, later on the Uwharrie River, where he met Soelle.

Contributing greatly to the phenomenal growth of the Separate Baptists was the Sandy Creek Association, organized in 1758, that met for three or four days in each year at the mother-church. Great crowds assembled, sometimes from forty or more miles away, to attend the preaching and experience the "great power of God." Through fascination with these extraordinary people, hosts of un-churched strangers attended and were converted. Some visitors pe-titioned the Association to send preachers into their neighborhoods. The modern misconception is that North Carolina and the South were always open to the preaching of the Gospel, but that view is not based on historical soundness. However, the meetings resounding with exhortations, preaching, and singing redoubled the enthusiasm of the preacher-missionaries.

Until its division, because of the great size of the Association and a desire for independence by its affiliates, the Sandy Creek Associa-tion maintained relations for twelve years with churches in North Carolina, South Carolina, and Virginia.[46] In 1771, in part because of its excessive powers, the Association divided into (1) the General Association of Virginia; (2) the Congaree Association (South Caro-lina); and (3) the Sandy Creek Association (North Carolina).[47]

The Baptist New Lights that met in the Sandy Creek Association were both evangelical and emotional. By today's standards they seemed to worship more like Holiness and Pentecostal churches than all but a minority of the most informal Baptist churches of today. If the crowds were large, the small meeting houses were left behind, and the meetings were held in fields or shaded groves, sometimes in unison with Methodists and Presbyterians. Under the increasing voice crescendo of the evangelist and responding to his pleas to allow the Holy Spirit to do a work for repentance, the crowds became moved, responding with tears, cries, fainting, falling down, praying, singing, and dancing.[48]

The revivals in the Sandy Creek Association, close to 1800, that followed the death of Stearns, duplicate in some manner the exhor-tative meetings of the early Separates. The revivals brought tears, trembling, screams, and exclamations. In such demonstrations there were some hypocrites who pretended. Some others, the non-believers, watched the emotional expressions from the fringe, with curled lips and loud scoffing laughter. But many sinners that were shaken and pierced by the Holy Spirit left the carnal world forever and became pillars of the Church.[49] In some meetings, remarkably, the Methodists and Presbyterians were more vociferous than their Baptist brethren, and became involved in so-called "religious epilepsies."[50] It is precisely in the fervent atmosphere of religion-hungry frontier people that an exhorter like Martha Marshall could stand and affirm the wonder of her salvation. "Great numbers turned to the Lord" through Daniel Marshall and "the assistance of his saintly and gifted wife" Martha.[51]

What religious principles were taught by these pioneer forerunners of the Southern Baptists? George Soelle, the Moravian missionary, reflecting in his *Diary* about the Baptists, after the departure of the Marshalls for South Carolina, about 1760, wrote that Reverend Stotzmann (Stotsmann), a Baptist, laid great stress on self-denial, abstinence from fleshly lusts, and a "change of life" that signified that the sinner had become a child of God. Although preachers went through a period of informal examination lasting several years before being ordained, according to Soelle,

> there was no necessity that he [the repentant sinner] should undergo a long period of probation and instruction before he was admitted to the fellowship of the saints. Only let him deny himself and take up his Cross and follow Jesus; this was the one thing needful. From the moment of his rebirth, the child of God was a Christian, should and could live as a Christian and be accepted as a Christian. It was this Gospel that Stearns and Marshall had preached in North Carolina, and Dutton Lane, Samuel Harris, and James Read had preached in Virginia. In their enthusiasm, men of little training in the schools were able to give a reason for their faith, as Soelle (the Moravian preacher) found on this occasion.[52]

Marshall's Separate Baptist Church at Abbott's Creek was organized in 1756-57 but re-organized after the departure of Daniel and

Martha for South Carolina in 1760. During his ministry at Abbott's Creek, Daniel preached far and wide and was more enterprising even than the aging Shubal Stearns. There are no records of the active and vigorous ministry that radiated from Abbott's Creek. The first recorded historical note is after the departure of the Marshalls: "North Carolina, Roan County, Janevary ye 4 day 1783. For the Baptis Church in Abets Crick." Obviously, the church clerk was no schoolmaster or attorney.[53]

The 1783 Confession of Faith of the re-organized Abbott's Creek Church (after the departure of the Marshalls) probably reflects a freedom from strict Calvinism (or else indifference to it) by Martha and Daniel Marshall and Shubal Stearns. It also mirrors their view of the church as a body of Christians, living "in sweet charity," who have surrendered themselves unreservedly to the service of God.

The Confession, probably written by Martha's brother Shubal Stearns, reads:

> Believing the Old and New Testament to be the perfect rule for life and practice and 2ly [secondly] Repentance from dead works and 3ly [thirdly] Faith towards God and 4ly [fourthly] The doctrine of Baptism and 5ly [fifthly] laying on of hands and 6ly [sixthly] the perseverance of the saints and 7ly [seventhly] The resurrection of the dead and 8ly [eighthly] Eternal judgment.[54]

Against such Baptist solidity and incessant ant-like activity, George Soelle, the old Moravian missionary, grumbled (literally, writing it) three months before his death on February 6,1773: "I cannot deny that there is some good in the Baptists, but there are too many who run about in their own spirit and do themselves and others harm. They are numerous in this neighborhood [Hunting Creek, North Carolina?] and preach industriously."[55] Baptists continue in the twenty-first century to "run about in their own spirit," doing some good.

The gulf between the Calvinistic Regular Baptists (who believed that God had given salvation to a limited number, the Elect) and the

Separate Baptists, who believed that salvation was available to "whosoever believeth in Him" (the many) was narrow or wide, depending on the narrowness or breadth of the preachers or the associations that supported them. In the northern states, despite their differences, the Regulars and Separates did not evolve into distinct denominations, as they did in the South. As examples, the eloquent John Gano, a Regular Baptist minister, worked in harmony with Separates Daniel and Martha Marshall, while the case of the Reverend John Newton is a picture of denominational doctrine narrowly applied.

John Newton, a Separate Baptist preacher affiliated with the Sandy Creek Association, preached for many years as a layman in North Carolina. He was born in 1732 in Pennsylvania and was baptized about 1752. He offended the Sandy Creek Association by the manner of his ordination in 1768, at Congaree, South Carolina, because the ordination service was administered by two Regular Baptist Ministers, the Reverends Oliver Hart and Evan Pugh. Another Separate Baptist preacher, the Reverend Mr. Reese, also was ordained on the same occasion.

Responding to the displeasure of the Sandy Creek Association in regard to the ordination by Regular Baptists, Mr. Reese humbled himself, acknowledged his error, and was restored to his ministerial work. It was a different story for Separate Baptist Newton, the successful preacher, who felt he had acted correctly, but made no acknowledgement of error, and was silenced in his own church by instructions sent from the Sandy Creek Association. Rejected by his own church, Newton never fully returned to ministerial work. Afterwards, the restored Reese and his church were convinced that in error they had complied with the mandate of the Association.[56] However, on an individual basis, there were many examples of cooperation between Baptist ministers of different strains.

Finally, the Regulars and Separates of Virginia united in 1787 at the Dover Meeting House on the James River. This was followed by a merger of the two Baptist branches uniting in North Carolina

(1788), South Carolina (around 1789),[57] and Kentucky (1801).[58] The Baptists united in these southern states began more strongly to accept Calvinist beliefs, through adoption of the Regular Baptist Confession, derived from the Philadelphia Confession. The Philadelphia Confession, in its turn, was simplified into "an abstract of Baptist principles," most of it stemming from the Westminster Confession,[59] first issued in 1647 by English Presbyterians. The Second London Confession (1677,1689) of the Particular Baptists was based substantially on the Westminster Confession; it was the first Baptist Confession to refer to the Bible as "infallible."[60] One of the practical aspects of the merger was the abandonment of the preaching and exhorting by women, typical and accepted by Separate Baptists. The practice was deplored by the more formal Regular Baptists, who believed women should be silent in church. Separates were opposed in principle to confessions, and asserted that the Philadelphia Confession was of lesser significance than the Scriptures; therefore, they would not require strict observance of it.[61]

Regardless of mergers and later denominational practices, the contributions of Martha Marshall at Abbott's Creek, and later in South Carolina and Georgia, are matters of significance. Paschal stated that at Abbott's Creek "great numbers turned to the Lord" because of Daniel Marshall, in whose work "he doubtless had the assistance of his saintly and gifted wife Mrs. Martha Stearns Marshall."[62] It would be apparent, from this statement, that Martha was a front-line warrior for Christ and not in any sense only an incidental bench warmer.

God's "mysterious ways" had led Martha and Daniel Marshall first to the Mohawk Indians, then to Sandy Creek in 1755, and the founding of a ministry at Abbott's Creek in 1756-57. Now those "ways" would lead into South Carolina and Georgia, where Martha would not be so much a sewing Dorcas—although she had eleven children—but, far more, "a flaming evangelist, stirring the convictions and consciences of strong men."[63]

Powerful forces of Christian reform, the European "Enlightenment," and available land produced a *zeitgeist* in the New World that would not tolerate permanent repression. Thus there were unleashed the great land migrations, fierce Native American resistance, and then a revolution that would tear Colonial America away from Mother England. In the critical years that followed the establishment of Sandy Creek, there were three major events that would explode the Baptists into all sectors of the South: (1) the Cherokee and Creek Wars against the settlers (1757-61 and 1774-76); (2) the Regulator Uprising and the "Battle of Alamance" (1771); and (3) The American Revolution (1775-81).

Indian Warfare

In North Carolina, the Cherokee Indians became restive during the French and Indian War (1754-63), when the English and French fought for mastery of North America. Indian tribes raided each other and the settlers, as they variously aligned themselves with the great European powers. The Creeks, who occupied rich lands in Georgia and Alabama, allied themselves with the Cherokees in 1759-60. Some white settlements were poorly defended since some of the militia had departed to fight on the side of the British Regulars.

The Cherokees, numbering about 2,390 warriors in 1755, inhabited a stretch of land from Savannah to Kentucky. They had no villages east of the Catawba River in North Carolina nor the Blue Ridge Mountains in Virginia. These Indians were friendly to English agents, but resentful of settler incursions into their hunting areas, and presented a danger on the Virginia frontier and western North Carolina during the French and Indian War. Marauding bands of ten to twelve braves would prey on unprotected families, until they were defeated in the Cherokee War of 1757-61. Forts were built by the colonists at Fort Dobbs on Third Creek (1755) and at Fort Defiance in Wilkes County. In 1759 the Cherokees and Creeks joined forces against the whites in western North Carolina.[64] In 1760, Elder John Thomas (preacher) of Toisnot Baptist Church was killed by Cherokee Indians while traveling with two others from Bethabara to Abbott's Creek.[65]

Much Baptist work ceased when the Indians became more aggressive. John Gano, Regular Baptist missionary for the Charleston Church, who labored in an area east of the Yadkin River, and from 1756 to 1759 at Jersey Settlement, had to abandon his pastorate because of marauding Cherokees.[66] The tempo of the Cherokee attacks increased in 1760-61, affecting churches on the Yadkin River and at Wachovia. The work of Daniel and Martha Marshall at Abbott's Creek stopped because of the danger. Paschal writes that the Indian menace did not cause the Marshalls to leave North Carolina for South Carolina, but certainly it must have been a factor, if only considered as a temporary measure of safety.[67]

Responding to immediate needs to shelter a large family, Daniel and Martha departed in 1760 for Beavers Creek, and by stages to Stevens Creek, South Carolina. But probably in their long-nurtured plans, conceived through prayer, they had planned to find a mission field of "widest expansion." This new field would not be as closely hedged as in North Carolina, where Colonel Sam Harris, John Gano, and Shubal Stearns had their extensive "parishes."[68] In North Carolina, Daniel Marshall had performed heroically, preaching as far east as New Bern and as far north as Virginia, where in Semple's words, he "planted the Redeemer's standard in many of the strongholds of Satan."[69]

In 1760, after much deliberation and prayer, affected by a vision for a wider ministry but also feeling a sense of urgency because of Indian incursions, Daniel and Martha Marshall crossed into South Carolina. They were not alone, for they took with them a portion of the Abbott's Creek Church. Including Daniel and Martha, the party embraced nine of the sixteen constituent members of the Sandy Creek Baptist Church, namely Joseph Breed and wife, Peter Stearns, Ebenezer Stearns and wife, and Enos Stinson and wife.[70]

These were not the initial Separate Baptists to penetrate the forest vastness of South Carolina. The Deep River Baptist Church held that honor as the audacious first body of Separates to leave North Carolina for South Carolina, going in 1759 to Broad River, with a fragment going farther South to Fair Forest. The pastor-leader of that caravan was Philip Mulky, with a "sweet voice" and "smiling aspect," who was baptized in 1756 at Sandy Creek.[71]

At Beaver Creek, South Carolina, on the Broad River, the Marshalls organized a large church. There had been some religious developments before the Abbott's Creek contingent arrived. The scattered Christian community expanded greatly through the solicitous ministry of the Marshalls, and the inspired preaching of Daniel. Seeking the direction of Divine Providence with prayers, the Marshalls in 1766 moved on with a few of the faithful to the Stephen's Creek area, where the Horse Creek meeting house was erected. Stephen's Creek was about fifteen miles north of Augusta, Georgia. This church was augmented with some members from Beaver Creek and became strong and influential. The Marshalls also preached in the Bush River area and at Congaree, there baptizing Timothy Dargan and Thomas Norris, both of whom became Baptist ministers. This produced a Christian ripple-effect, for Dargan preached in North Carolina's Bertie County, among people "wild and barbarous."[72] Dargan's pioneer efforts, in turn, may have prepared the way for the conversion of another great Baptist leader in 1770 or 1772, the celebrated Dr. Richard Furman. Dr. Furman, a slave-holder but moderate Separate preacher from Charleston, was prominent in bridging the differences between the Separates and the Regular Baptists. Furman served as the first president of the missionary Triennial Convention (1814) and assisted Luther Rice in establishing Columbian College, later George Washington University.[73] Despite the powerful counter-current of Calvinistic theology, Furman was a dominant figure in establishing the special blend of conservative theology and missionary zeal that characterizes most Southern Baptists.

The Regulator Movement

The Regulator movement shortly before the American Revolution would have a lasting effect on Martha Marshall and Baptist
expansion in the South. Between 1765 and 1771 Baptists and Presbyterians were mistreated because of enforcement measures imposed
by Governor William L. Tryon of North Carolina. Legal restrictions
prevented valid marriages between Non-Conformists. In the back
country, corrupt judges, sheriffs, clerks, and officials, loyal to Governor Tryon, over-taxed and abused Baptists. Tryon's troops raided
farms for food and targeted Baptist communities. This resulted in an
uprising that culminated in the 1771 almost-bloodless "Battle" of
Alamance in Orange County,[74] a confrontation between four thousand Regulators and two thousand of Tryon's supporters.[75]

Baptists were numerous in Orange County, and when Governor
Tryon called on troops to suppress the unrest and violence, the Orange
County militia refused to serve. In 1769 the Sandy Creek Baptist
Association in Orange County[76] forbade its members from taking up
arms against the state government, in violation of which church
members would be disbarred. Shubal Stearns was undoubtedly the
primary factor in this prohibition. Only seven Baptists were on the
armed Regulator side at Alamance, and these were expelled from
their churches and executed by the North Carolina officials. Captain
Benjamin Merril, a Baptist deacon and one of these seven, who was
condemned to be drawn and quartered by the authorities, spoke
bitterly of two men who seduced him into joining the Regulators.
Merril, who had a plantation near Jersey Settlement, had been told
that Governor Tryon intended to lay waste the country and destroy
its inhabitants. After his death, Merrill would leave a blind, deeply-
religious widow and ten children. Merrill said: "I received by the
grace of God, a change fifteen years ago—yet providence, in which
is my chief security, has been pleased to give me comfort under these
evils in my last hour."[77]

When Tryon's "gentlemen" army in 1771 invaded and engaged in a virtual anti-Baptist sacking of a peaceful area, it received assistance in intelligence, food, and supplies from the pacifist Moravians (United Brethren) and their leader, Frederic William Marshall. This created a rift lasting several years between the Baptists and the Moravians.[78] It should be noted that the Moravians had all the rights and immunities of the Church of England.[79]

However, with a few exceptions, Baptists were not forbidden by their churches to join the Regulator movement and prevent injustice. It is a certainty that many Baptists did join the Regulators, or by conviction were wholly on their side, in the efforts to redress the wrongs done to them and their neighbors. For example, nearly all the Baptist families of North Carolina's Chatham County signed the Regulator petitions. Moreover, these were Separate Baptists with strong impulses to confront political abuse as well as religious intolerance.

After the defeat of the Regulators at the Battle of Alamance, with twelve Regulators and three of Tryon's supporters killed, there was a general exodus of Baptists from the North Carolina countryside to Tennessee, South Carolina, and Georgia. In one surge, fifteen hundred families left their homes, with many more selling their estates in preparation to leave.[80] This flight was precipitated in large part by the excesses of Governor Tryon's army, which encamped near Jersey Church, burned homes and farm buildings, destroyed grain in the fields, and sacked the Baptist neighborhoods. In all likelihood, Tryon's men, without any justification, destroyed the old Jersey Settlement Church. More than forty men were made prisoners by Governor Tryon, who hurried them to Hillsboro, where they would be tried for treason.[81]

The North Carolina migration to get away from oppression had occurred even earlier. In 1768, three years before the Battle of Alamance, Baptists that "despaired of seeing better times" began to drift away from Orange County to the Holston River country in Tennessee. Alamance and the Regulator strife turned the trickle into one of the greatest religious migrations in history—the movement of the Separate Baptists to other southern states.[82]

The Southern Baptist Convention was in the process of being formed from the New Lights, although no one had the prophetic vision to call it that. The dissemination of John Locke's concepts of democracy by an unbending, stubborn people, and the spread of Baptist Separate doctrine and fervor, would proceed together, as if borne by a storm. The great liberation of Baptists and other Non-Conformists from churches they did not believe in, and taxes they would not bear, would climax after the Revolutionary War, but the changes—religious, intellectual, and economic—were already in progress.

The ravages by Tryon's "gentlemen" on both sides of the Yadkin River created for a time a "Baptist desert." However, most transparent was the campaign's effect on the Sandy Creek Church. Morgan Edwards says:

> It (the Sandy Creek Church) is reduced from six hundred and six to fourteen souls. The cause of this dispersion is the abuse of power which too much prevailed in the Province, and caused the inhabitants at last to rise up in arms, and fight for their privileges. But being routed, May 16, 1771, they despaired of seeing better times, and therefore quitted the Province. It is said that 1,500 families departed since the Battle of Alamance, and to my knowledge a great many more are only waiting to dispose of their plantation in order to follow them. This is to me an argument that their grievances were real, and their oppressions great, notwithstanding all that has been said to the contrary.[83]

Another historian described the depredations as follows:

> The Governor (of North Carolina) now had the opportunity to smite the Baptists. It was skillfully and cruelly done. Marching his army to Sandy Creek he encamped for a week,—levying contributions and terrorizing the neighborhood. Ruin fell on the church, from which it has not recovered to this day (1898).

Heavy requisitions for beeves and flour were made on Haw River, Deep River, Rocky River, Grassy Creek, Abbott's Creek and the Forks of the Yadkin.[84]

Baptist development in a wide area was truncated for one hundred years, but the Baptist faith, confined for years, would now surge into far greater frontiers of the South and West.

The frightening development of a North Carolina fratricidal war, in the midst of the geographical area ministered to by the Sandy Creek Association, was a consideration that influenced many Baptists to scatter to several other states. Whole Baptist communities to the north of Sandy Creek fled to Tennessee over several years, while those from Little River and the southeastern parts of the province went to South Carolina. Pastors and church members often moved as a single group, becoming in effect a traveling church. Some of these migrating parties maintained connections with the Sandy Creek Association. However, in 1786, because of the great distance from Sandy Creek, the Tennessee churches organized the Holston Association.[85]

The last great act of Shubal Stearns was to prevent a great loss of life among Baptists by intervening to prevent all except a handful from fighting at Alamance. What might have happened, if tough Baptist settlers numbering in the thousands had been freed to fight there, is conjectural. And it was at this climactic time that the great Shubal Stearns left the earth to appear before his Heavenly Father. Stearns, sixty-five years old, died at Sandy Creek on November 20, 1771. He had married Sarah Johnstone but left no children.[86] He was undoubtedly the most dynamic leader of the early Separate Baptists and had the supreme grace to maintain friendships with the Regular Baptists of John Gano and the Moravians of George Soelle. His manner of preaching, which served "to shake the very nerves" and "fetch tears from the eyes," was the model for a generation of young preachers.[87] His death also removed the final barrier that might have deterred Martha and Daniel Marshall from traveling on to their final destination in Georgia.

The Marshalls arrived in Georgia in 1771 and settled in the Kiokee Creek area, about eighteen miles north of Augusta in present-day Columbia County. Their permanent home became Horse Creek, where a church was organized in 1772. The first preaching created an incident that illuminated the character of Martha Marshall.[88]

On Daniel Marshall's second or third visit to Georgia in St. Paul's Parish, Augusta area, he was arrested by Constable Cartledge. It was Marshall's custom to preach in private homes, or under the open sky, and kneeling with a congregation in a grove of trees. "On the second or third of these, while in prayer, he was seized, in the presence of his audience, for preaching in the Parish of St. Paul, and made to give security for his appearance in Augusta, on the following Monday, to answer this charge. Accordingly, he stood a trial and, after his meekness and patience were sufficiently exercised, was ordered to come, as a preacher, no more into Georgia."[89]

The original charter of Georgia guaranteed religious liberty except to papists (Catholics), but Georgia had become a royal province in 1754. In 1758 the Second General Assembly meeting in Savannah enacted a law that imposed religious assessments, created parishes, and decreed that the Church of England stood as the Established Church. No other church was permitted to hold meetings, without a special license, that was rarely granted.

This early Baptist seed in Georgia could have died immediately because of the legal restrictions, if not for the intervention of Martha Marshall. She appeared, along with Daniel, for the hearing in the court at Augusta on the following Monday. When ordered not to preach any more in Georgia, Marshall meekly replied, "whether it be right to obey God (rather than men), judge ye."[90]

Then Martha Marshall rose to speak ardently. "With the solemnity of the prophets of old, she denounced such proceedings and such law, and to sustain her point quoted many passages from the Holy Scriptures, with a force and pertinency that carried conviction to the hearts of many. The very constable himself, Mr. Samuel Cartledge, was so deeply convicted by the words of inspiration that fell from her lips that his conversion was the result." Also the magistrate, Colonel Barnard, was converted and became a zealous Christian.[91] As the result of Martha's stirring defense, all charges were dropped, and the Marshall party sowed the Gospel message in the Kiokee Creek field and preached the Gospel in every direction. Two preaching stations in Georgia, Quaker Settlement and Kiokee, became branches of Stephen's Creek Church in South Carolina. Kiokee Creek would be the Marshalls' home and anchor for the rest of their lives.

The American Revolution

Even the approach of British troops in the Revolutionary War did not daunt Daniel Marshall, as it did the majority of Protestant ministers, who fled from Georgia. The Marshalls remained as the intrepid buttresses of Baptist faith, in the character of the Separates of Sandy Creek.[92] They continued their Christian work "with unabated missionary zeal."

The American Revolution was a long war, and meted out important consequences for the history of the world. Out of the war's ashes, in 1781, there arose a government of the people, unlike any the world had ever seen, and a principle of religious freedom never before endorsed by any government except that of Rhode Island, which had been founded by a philosophical Baptist, Roger Williams, and a Baptist physician John Clarke. Except idealists in Europe, few thinkers and philosophers gave the American republic any chance of succeeding. Even the fight for the Revolution's success was borne arduously only by one-third of the people of the Colonies, while one-third retained loyalty to the Crown and another third was largely indifferent. The Baptists, on the other hand, were almost completely on the side of independence, for to them this was a religious war. Baptist companies and battalions formed up under their elected officers and fought for Christ the King, as well as the republic, and brought along their musket-slinging Baptist chaplains, whether the Establishment would allow them or not.

Almost all the Baptists of North Carolina and Virginia were on the side of liberty and the Continental Congress. But in 1774, before the issues were clearly defined, Reverend William Cook and five members of Dutchman's Creek Baptist Church in Rowan County, North Carolina, signed a paper, "The Protest," circulated by Tory sympathizers. Twenty others from the church were outright Patriots. Reverend Cook repented his early action, and, as a result of his humility and statements of loyalty to Congress and the emerging nation, was restored to the esteem of his church and community. Cook's recanting occurred at a meeting of the Patriot Committee on July 18, 1775, and again on September 30, 1775, before his church, which chose not to censure him.[93] The five Tory members of the church were not "speedily excommunicated," as reported, for this was the prerogative of God alone, but they were disbarred from membership.[94] Dutchman's Creek had a large population of derivative Germans and Tories, and, to avoid conflict, meetings of pro-Congress Baptists were moved ten or fifteen miles away to the Baptist Deep Creek meeting House.[95]

The Revolutionary War (1775-1781) divided fathers, loyal to King George, and sons, loyal to the Patriots, and terribly split whole kinship groups. In several states, notably New York, North Carolina, and Georgia, the war became a civil war and was bitterly fought, as neighbor engaged neighbor with curses and terrible revenge. In North Carolina, the Timber Ridge Church, located west of the Yadkin River, was in the middle of a zone of bitter hostility between Tories and Patriots. The Moravian records reflect that the "King's Men" and "Liberty Men" were "very hot against each other," even after Gideon Wright's Tories lost the battle of Shallow Fords in October 1780. Both armies and their stalwarts crossed the Yadkin at Shallow Fords, ravaging their enemies, robbing homes, and seizing farm animals and grain.[96]

Two of the Baptist churches broken up during the Revolutionary War contributed a "large contingent" of men who fought the Loyalists at King's Mountain, North Carolina (1780) and assisted in the capture or death of a thousand Tories. They also contributed to the force of George Rogers Clark that in 1778 captured the Illinois outpost settlements of Kaskaskia, Cahohokia, and Vincinnes.[97] During the Revolution, when the Cherokee Indians rose against the settlers in May 1776, forty-five hundred militiamen from the Carolinas and Georgia combined to defeat the Indians decisively.[98] Thus, those people that Governor Tryon sought to make submissive would be a sturdy military resource against tyranny in any form.

The Timber Ridge Church, caught in a raging war, began as a Separate Baptist church, and its first pastor was Joseph Murphy, a Separate Baptist, who preached the same Gospel of love voiced by Martha Marshall and her fellow evangelists Shubal Stearns and Daniel Marshall. In its reorganization in 1787 or 1788, the Timber Ridge Church was declared to be a Regular Baptist Church ("Hard Shell"), that proclaimed the "Higher Calvinism" of the Philadelphia Confession. Thus, it embraced an anti-missions doctrine that accepted the salvation of the few, the Elect, while Pastor Murphy, who guided the church in its infancy, would have preached as a Separate Baptist that the love of Jesus was available to the many, the doctrine of Arminius.[99] Later, periodic general revivals led to cooperation between Baptists of various leanings. The Regular and Separate Baptists declared a union in eastern North Carolina in 1777, and unified in the western part after the Revolutionary War.[100]

The Buffalo Church, in York County, South Carolina, was organized about 1775 by the Sandy Creek Association, and the community was thought until 1774 to be in North Carolina. This church was in a perilous position because of the Revolutionary War, and after 1777 all religious activity was suspended. In the North and South Carolina border area occurred some of the bitterest struggles between Whigs and Tories. Neighbor fought neighbor at Ramsour's Mills (June 1780) and King's Mountain (October 1780). Also some Carolinians joined the American general Daniel Morgan in his startling classic victory over Tarleton at the Battle of Cowpens in January 1781. However, even in this hazardous period, Baptist pastor Joseph Camp of the Buffalo Church remained at his post.[101]

John Gano served as a chaplain in the Colonial Army during most of the war. He encouraged the Patriot troops through his prayers and counsel to resist the oppressive rule of the British. He commanded the respect of officers and men, while exposing himself to their privations and dangers. After the war, he returned to his flock at Jersey Settlement, North Carolina, that had dwindled to thirty-seven communicants. However, his church, which once had two hundred members, would become large again.[102] Gano had the supreme privilege of baptizing General George Washington in the Hudson River near Newburgh in 1783, with forty-two witnesses present. Washington made his decision after searching the Scriptures, as contained in Matthew 3:16.[103]

The American Fabius, Rhode Islander Nathanael Greene, nipped at the heels of General Charles Cornwallis as he pursued his Southern Campaign in 1780-81 into the Carolinas. Although the British Regulars were better trained, they would be defeated in 1781 at Cowpens, and mauled and barely victorious in the battles of Guilford Courthouse and Eutaw Springs, near Charleston.[104]

Baptist preachers joined the Episcopal, Methodist, and Presbyterian clergymen in serving as military chaplains. They set up altars on Sunday and spoke warmly to grimy and wounded men returned from battle. In Georgia, Daniel Marshall joined the forces of General Nathanael Greene as a spiritual comforter. Tory sympathizers captured him, but he "preached" them into releasing him. Once free, he quickly joined General Greene's army, which was harassing the troops of Cornwallis as the latter sought shelter in Virginia. Elder Oliver Hart, pastor of Charleston's First Baptist Church, visited the troops of "Swamp Fox" Francis Marion and Nathanael Greene, bringing with him boxes of food, clothing, and equipment for the relief of the fighting men. While the war was being fought, Isaac Backus and other Baptists protected the Quakers, Moravians, and Mennonites, who would not fight because of religious convictions. The Warren Association passed a resolution asking that such pacifists be permitted "to pay such equivalent" in lieu of military service.[105]

The Journey Ends

Daniel Marshall, age seventy-eight, died at Kiokee Creek on November 2, 1784, approximately one year after the Treaty of Paris (September 3, 1783) that formally ended the Revolutionary War. He had been both a soldier of Christ and a chaplain to the Patriot army. Before expiring, the old minister had preached, with these words: "I am resolved to finish my course in the cause of Christ."[106] There have been few church planters in history that have exceeded his noble work. During the Revolutionary War, until he assumed the role of chaplain, other ministers had fled from the scene, but he remained. As David Benedict recounts it:

> But the intrepid Marshall stood his ground and never deserted his post; like an Apostle, having his dear people in his heart, to live and die with them. Though the din of war was heard, and rapine, violence, and bloodshed, filled the land with consternation, the zeal and perseverance of this brave soldier of the Cross were not in the slightest degree abated. Assisted by a few licentiates, who remained on the field with him, the good work went on; the spirit of pure religion was progressive, and even in those times that tried men's souls, very many were converted to God.[107]

On the day of his death, Marshall turned his burdens over to Martha and not to his son, the Reverend Abraham Marshall, who would serve as moderator of the Kiokee Association for twenty years.[108] Abraham wrote these words: "To the venerable partner, who was sitting by his side bedewed with tears, he said, 'Go on, my dear wife, to serve the Lord. Hold on to the end. Eternal glory is before us.'"[109] And Martha Marshall continued praying, singing, and exhorting until the end.

Martha Stearns Marshall, as a frontier exhorter (c.1722-1793),[110] was empowered by the Holy Spirit. Without the title, she had the character of a prophetess among the Separate Baptists, forerunners of the Southern Baptists in the Carolinas and Georgia. She embodied a unique feature of the New Light tidal wave, an unfettered woman preacher. She loved the Lord with all her heart. Thus she had no fear of releasing emotions and eloquently quoting the Gospel to large crowds of stunned men and women.

Her husband Daniel was an average man, except in his faith and tenacity in spreading the Word, in which he was extraordinary. He was above all a brave and committed missionary. But it was undoubtedly the winsome and modest Martha, with the bloodline, polish, and leadership of her brother Shubal Stearns, that helped mold Daniel Marshall into one of the most successful church planters in eighteenth-century America.

This intrepid woman willingly shared with her husband the wilderness of New York as missionary to the Mohawk Indians. She then enthusiastically took her faith to the raw frontiers of North Carolina, South Carolina, and Georgia. If the half-savage Scotch-Irish and Germans that tamed the frontiers could be touched by Christ, the soul of the emerging nation could be critically shaped. Thus Sandy Creek, perhaps more than Charleston, became the Zion of the Southern Baptists and others. There and at Abbott's Creek, this great woman, mother of ten children, rose above her homefire commitments to become the Deborah of the New Lights. Her supreme moment was near Augusta, Georgia, when with fiery Scripture-filled eloquence she electrified the Court, the constable, and the magistrate, and reversed the decision that prohibited Baptist teachings from entering Georgia. Martha Marshall, the flaming evangelist and Gospel-warrior, was one of the greatest Baptist Trailblazers. She died with her boots on, faithful in her love of Jesus, the Scriptures, and the Church.

Chapter 8

John Leland
(1754-1841)

Fighter for Disestablishment and the First Amendment

John Leland, as a Baptist preacher from New England, was shunned for a time in the South and regarded with suspicion by ministers in the North. But during his lifetime, he probably became the Baptists' foremost advocate of the doctrine of the separation of church and state. He was popular with the people, but remained eccentric, and his religious views shifted from mild Calvinism to the modified Arminianism of the Separate Baptists. However, his place in Baptist history is firmly established as the major spokesman for religious liberty in the South, although he lived only fifteen years in Virginia (1776-91). As an advocate for religious freedom in early America, he shares the national honors with his predecessor and friend, historian Isaac Backus.

Leland spent his entire life in New England, with the exception of the critical Revolutionary War period. He was shrewd, witty, and pious, but often at odds with other Baptist ministers. His status was marred for nine years among Baptist congregations because of his ordination by lay members of his congregation at Mount Poney, Virginia in 1776[1] and with the laying on of hands as required by the (Virginia) Ketockton Association[2] and against the practice of the

John Leland, about 1814, Baptizes a Convert in Virginia.

Charleston and (New England) Warren associations. He also embraced the Messianic views of the growing Baptist Separates. Through his skills as a traveling evangelist and orator, he was able to organize Baptists, both Regular and New Light, on questions of religious freedom during the crucial war years of the struggle against Great Britain. Although he lacked a formal education, his keen intelligence and research enabled him to become a mentor to Baptist leaders and their congregations. Incessant in his endeavors, he preached 3,009 sermons and baptized 1,278 converts.[3]

As a prolific writer, Leland combined the best of the First Awakening and the Enlightenment. He also composed hymns and wrote on devotional and theological topics. Leland, independent in his theology, and attracted to the views of Separates like John Waller and Colonel Samuel Harris, spread a moderate evangelical message in the South. Still, his diluted Calvinism disturbed the Regular Baptists, who exerted increasing influence as the Revolutionary War terminated. He planted the concepts of the Enlightment and diffused Thomas Jefferson's philosophy among the common people. As a goal, he sought to improve the life of slaves and work for their final liberation. After his return to New England in 1791, Leland as a self-proclaimed "old grey-headed sinner" indulged even further his gift for writing,[4] as well as venturing to eliminate the Congregational Establishment in Massachusetts and Connecticut.

Leland was born in May 1754 at Grafton, Massachusetts, where his father was a Presbyterian farmer and his mother "a high-flying Separate" Congregationalist. As a youth, young John was apprenticed to a shoemaker in Hopkinton, and he became an expert cobbler.[5] Among his customers was Sallie Devine, who fell in love with Leland. Sallie's parents were devout Baptists, members of the Hopkinton Baptist meeting house. Sallie persuaded John to hear Preacher Everett Jones, who had experienced a brutal whipping as punishment for preaching without the authorization of the Massachusetts authorities.[6] In 1772 Leland, in the manner of Roger Williams, was converted and immersed by Elder Noah Allen of

Bellingham. Then he received a divine call in 1775 to become a Baptist minister.[7] Six months later he was licensed by the Billingham Church. After he and the gifted Sallie Devine married in 1776, they walked to Virginia, where they shared their lives until 1791. As a brave woman, Sallie mothered eight children in Virginia and would save her husband's life by grabbing the arm of a ruffian who attacked Leland with a sword while he was preaching.[8]

Leland established churches in Virginia and finally settled in Orange County. He became known as the outstanding Baptist preacher in Virginia[9] and his sermons sometimes were attended by Thomas Jefferson. He was a "born preacher," leading seven hundred persons in Virginia to confess Christ. Cathcart stated: "We doubt if his equal will ever be seen again."[10]

Because of the influence of the Baptist Separates on his theology, Leland viewed from the twenty-first century appears to have been a moderate Baptist. Leland said that the best theology provided enough Calvinism to believe that a man was lost and enough Arminianism to believe that he could be saved. The aberration of the "irregular" ordination at Mount Poney was corrected in 1787, when a presbytery of Baptist ministers "properly" confirmed his calling to the clergy.[11] He was an evangelical minister who centered his faith on Jesus Christ and regarded the Holy Scriptures as the Word of God. An intelligent observer stated that he was not a "sensational preacher" nor a "bundle of eccentricities."[12] He was politically a liberal but theologically a New Light Baptist.

Leland's core religious beliefs are contained in his letter of February 1788 to Robert Carter: "The Creed, that I could die for, may be registered on a small Piece of Paper; which is as follows:

> I believe there is a God, possessed with all glorious Perfections. 2. That the Book called the Bible, is of divine Authenticity. 3. That Jesus Christ is the Messiah, properly God and Man. 4. That Men are all fallen from God. 5. That absolute Necessity of a Death unto Sin and a new Birth unto Righteousness to be either safe or happy. 6. That what System or Spirit soever a Man

have that does not leave him to love God, hate Sin, deny himself and follow after Holiness, is certainly wrong."[13]

Notably, there is no mention of baptism, the Lord's Supper, grace, or, from the Calvinist viewpoint, predestination; however, this omission does not infer that these elements did not constitute matters of importance to him. Nevertheless, it became known that he cared little for predestination.

Intolerance in Early America

The period of John Leland in Colonial America was a religious crossroads and an epoch of trials for Baptists. The "Pilgrim Fathers," recently persecuted in England, established the Congregational Church by law as the official church in New England and began persecuting dissenters who did not agree with them. The Congregational theocracy was defined by the Cambridge Platform (1648) and bolstered by legislation that allowed taxing and enforcement measures that would support only the Congregational faith. John Cotton, religious spokesman for the Established Church (Congregational), allowed religious differences only on peripheral matters. However, he advocated severe punishment if these differences constituted blaspheming "the true" God and his true [Congregational] religion. Roger Williams objected strenuously to such a confining and narrow "freedom."[14]

Similarly, in Virginia, North Carolina, South Carolina, and Georgia the Anglican Church (later Episcopal) asserted its exclusive validity as "the Church." This translated into harsh persecution of Baptists in Virginia, especially the New Lights or Baptist Separates formed in the mold of John Waller or Colonel Samuel Harris. In Virginia, the Anglican authorities did not recognize the legality of Baptist marriages and were reluctant to register Baptist meeting houses. In addition, the authorities imposed tithes, through enforced contributions of cotton and other farm products, on the entire population, whether Anglican or not, in support of Anglican clergymen.[15]

In Virginia, as early as 1611, Governor Thomas Dale required all citizens to strictly conform to the practices of the Anglican Church. He enforced the laws with whippings, fines, and mutilations. These laws were reinforced with the Tobacco Laws, in support of the Anglican clergy, and, after 1660, the expulsion of the Non-Conformists. Despite the severe measures, a few Baptists apparently had penetrated the Virginia Commonweatlh, because some persons "refuse to have their children baptized—[and in punishment] shall be amerced two thousand pounds of tobacco; halfe to the informer and halfe to the publique."[16] Still, Baptists arrived with other colonists; in 1714 two Baptist preachers ordained in London, Robert Nordin and Thomas White, sailed for Virginia. Also, Reverend Robert Jones preached in 1727 in Prince George County.[17]

Severe religious persecution prevailed in the South from the 1750s to 1783. There had been only limited religious turmoil in the South before this time, except during the Regulator "uprising" around 1771, in North Carolina. So what caused the new repressions? There were two principal reasons for the new religious afflictions: (1) the lashing out of the Anglican Church, stung by its declining congregations and the indifference and worldliness of its clergy, and the rising anti-Colonial and pro-Congress feelings of the population. All of these developments isolated the pro-Tory Anglican Church, as it desperately sought through intimidation to assert its old authority; (2) the swarming into Virginia in 1750-70 of the Baptist Separates or "New Lights," who, filled with missionary zeal, would not cower before the intolerant authorities and refused to obey the state religious laws or the restrictions imposed by the Anglican Church. In case after case, Baptist preachers submitted to beatings, jails, and deprivations for proclaiming the Gospel, while winning the masses over to their side.[18] Thomas Jefferson wrote in 1781 that "Two-thirds of the people had become Dissenters [mainly Baptist] at the commencement of the present revolution."[19]

The religious struggle in Virginia produced a maelstrom involving religious persecutors and Christian heroes. Baptists, the chief cause of the turmoil, bore the brunt of its fury. Some of the protagonists of this period were Colonel Samuel Harris, converted by Daniel Marshall and later attacked while preaching and dragged by his hair; Lewis Craig, one of the thirty Baptist preachers who in the period 1768-77 were stoned, whipped or jailed; and "Swearing Jack" (John) Waller, who was deeply touched as he sat in the jury box to hear Craig declare: "I thank you, gentlemen of the grandjury, for the honour you have done me. While I was wicked and injurious, you took no notice of me; but since I have altered my course of life, and endeavored to reform my neighbors, you concern yourselves much about me."[20]

Fiercely independent, each following of Baptists, from its founding, differed from other Baptists on such matters as: Saturday worship (Seventh-Day Baptists), the elements of good and evil (Old Two-Seed-in the-Spirit Predestinarian Baptists), emphasis on Calvinism and a tranquil and orderly worship style (Regular Baptists), a heightened emphasis on the work of the Holy Spirit (Separate Baptists), adherence to private interpretation of the Scriptures and aversion to slavery (North American Baptists), and a concentration on evangelism and Sunday School (Southern Baptists). Leland, verging toward the doctrines of the Virginia Baptist Separates, did not embrace Calvinism nor pretend any understanding of it.[21] He deplored the chasm that developed in the South between the two largest groups of Baptists, the Regular Baptists and the prolific evangelizing Baptist Separates. Leland's comments were that the worship of the Regulars was "solemn and rational," whereas the Separates' style of worship was "very noisy," although they were "most zealous."[22]

The Regulars and Separates voted to merge in Virginia in 1787 and in North Carolina in 1788. In the northern states, the two bodies never sought complete separation, despite the emotional style of the Whitefield-inspired Separates. In the South, encouraging the unification, was the eminent Richard Furman of New York, who was converted as a Separate Baptist in 1770 and became a prominent minister in Charleston, South Carolina in 1814; he was installed as the first president of the Triennial Convention,[23] predecessor of the Southern Baptist Convention. Initially the Separates resisted union, in part because they feared the dilution of their beliefs as the result of a common confession of faith. Leland added that, "Confessions of faith often check any further pursuit after truth." He persisted: "Why this Virgin Mary [a confession] between the souls of men and the scriptures," alluding to one of the theological mountains blocking the unification of Catholics and Protestants. Both Baptist groups finally united on the basis of the Philadelphia Confession. But in formalizing the union, the Regulars assured the Separates that they were free to retain "liberty" in the interpretation of certain contested articles in the Confession.[24]

The Approaching Revolutionary War

In the ten-year period before the military skirmishes in 1775 (Lexington and Concord), an array of economic and political measures—the Sugar Act, the Townshend Duties, the Tea Act, and the closing of Boston harbor—signaled the approach of a defining war between the colonists and Great Britain. The critical matters producing the war were restrictions on commerce and the denial of political rights to the colonists. Ecclesiastical matters, particularly the protection of religious minorities such as the Baptists, were of lesser or no concern to the political authorities on both sides. The British, in their defense, had passed an Act of Toleration in 1689 that gave relief in the United Kingdom to the persecuted dissenters and ended the licensing of preachers but still required tithes in support of the authorized Church of England.[25] However, in the colonies, Roger Williams's concepts of the unfettered conscience and the existence of local governments without an official religion (as in Rhode Island), and Leland's concept of the separation of church and state, were ideas barely heard and rarely heeded. However, the Revolutionary War, with its pressures for the enlistment of thousands of

Baptist yeomen in the war, would serve Leland and the Baptists well; Baptist military assistance to the cause was urgent. The Revolutionary War would ultimately provide a tool to the Baptists, Quakers, Mennonites, and Presbyterians to pry away the mantle of oppressive privilege long afforded the Anglican and Congregational state churches.

Reform Moves in the South

The leading Baptist spokesman for disestablishment in the South was John Leland, friend of Thomas Jefferson, and, later, as a Jeffersonian Republican, the supporter of Andrew Jackson. He had much to do, for the colonial government of Virginia placed the narrowest interpretation on the Act of Toleration, unwilling to grant licenses to Baptist preachers or grant authorization to open religious meeting houses. Local sheriffs were often loathe to enforce licenses, even when they were legally issued to Baptists. The situation was exacerbated because Baptist Separate ministers frequently refused to seek licenses to preach, believing the practice to be against their moral and civil rights.[26]

Leland's views often seem to reflect the general premises of the great English political philosopher John Locke, in maintaining that republican government is the best form of government since its power is derived from the people. He also embraced the Lockian concept that between the government and the people there is an unwritten but sacred compact impelling the government to act on the highest moral principles for the people. If the government failed to discharge its obligations, according to Locke, the people had the right to overthrow that corrupt government. Leland held similarly that new laws were not binding if inconsistent with the nation's Constitution.

Influenced by new political currents, the Baptists and Presbyterians joined forces in 1758 to send petitions to the Virginia General Assembly. The two religious groups requested that the Anglican Establishment in Virginia be disestablished and that the clergy of

Non-Conformist religious groups be authorized to perform the marriage ceremony. Long afterwards, in 1779, in their support, Thomas Jefferson introduced the Bill for Religious Freedom, that did not pass.[27]

In 1770 the Baptists of Virginia began to petition the Virginia House of Burgesses for relief from various religious encumbrances. At first the complaints were about Baptist ministers not being permitted to preach in meeting houses, other than those previously registered, and obligations from the provinces that required licensed preachers to bear arms and attend muster.[28] James Madison, hearing of the injustices done to "persecuted Baptists" and harassed Presbyterians, was not optimistic about remedies, in view of the report of "monstrous effects of the enthusiasm [unrest] prevalent among the sectaries" (Non-Conformists). Madison showed skepticism about immediate solutions. He wrote a friend: "That liberal, catholic, and equitable way of thinking, as to the rights of conscience, which is one of the characteristics of a free people, and so strongly marks the people of your province [Pennsylvania] is but little known among the zealous adherents to our hierarchy" [in Virginia].[29] In 1773 the Ketocton Baptist Association in Virginia petitioned for the liberty to preach in all proper places. In 1775 Baptists and other Protestants petitioned against the prohibition of worship services at night. In August 1775 occurred the first thoroughly organized Baptist action for religious freedom and the separation of church and state, stemming from a joint meeting of northern and southern district associations.[30] In 1784 the Virginia Baptists went further and organized a general committee to act as the guardian of Baptist rights against future religious discrimination.[31]

When war first loomed between Congress and the British Crown, Baptists with few exceptions were loyal to the ideal of freedom. In August 1775 the Virginia Baptist Association addressed the following petition to the Virginia Convention (state legislature) meeting at Richmond:

> Alarmed at the shocking oppression which in a British Cloud hangs over our American Continent, we, as a society and part

of the distressed State, have in our Association considered what part might be most prudent for the Baptists to act in the present unhappy Contest. After we had determined "that in some Cases it was lawful to go to War, and also for us to make a Military resistance against Great Britain, in regard of their unjust Invasion and tyrannical Oppression of, and repeated Hostilities against America," our people were all left to act at Discretion with respect to inlisting without falling under the Censure of our Community.[32]

The Continental Congress needed every man it could muster to fight the British. Fully mindful that Baptists could press an advantage, in what to them was a religious war for freedom, the Baptist petition continued:

And as some [Baptists] have inlisted, and many more likely to do so, who will have earnest Desires for their Ministers to preach to them during the Campaign, we therefore delegate and appoint our well-beloved Brethren in the Ministry Elijah Craig, Lewis Craig, Jeremiah Walker and John Williams to present this address and to petition you that they may have free Liberty to preach to the Troops at convenient times without molestation or abuse.[33]

Under the practical needs of the hour for more loyal troops and against the fulminations of the Established Church, the Virginia legislators gave way to Baptist pressure. As Baptist historian McBeth states, Baptists more often than not achieved victories not through skillful articulation of principles, but because of the necessities for a united front against the Crown.[34]

A single Baptist church in Prince William County made this petition to the Virginia Convention in order to bolster "unanimity":

". . . that they be allowed to worship God in their own way, without interruption; that they be permitted to maintain their own ministers, and none others; that they may be married, buried and the like without paying the clergy of other denominations;

that, these things granted, they will gladly unite with their brethren to the utmost of their ability to promote the common cause."

Another petition in October 1780 from the Baptist Association
meeting at Sandy Creek, Charlotte County, before the battle of
Yorktown (October 19, 1781) expressed appreciation for "heaven-
born Freedom" and pain over continuing religious bias. The petition
spoke of "religious oppression" as "the most inhuman and insupport-
able." The petitioners were in "Grief," inasmuch as "Religious Liberty has not made a single Advance in this Commonwealth without
some Opposition." The petition called for the fulfillment of religious
liberty and the eradication of all relics of religious oppression.[35]

These and other petitions had a significant impact on the Virginia
legislature. First, the Baptist arguments were similar to those framed
by the colonial governments against British imperial oppression.
Second, the loyalty of the Baptists would have to be nurtured to
secure the manpower necessary to defeat the British armies.

Leland Involved in Religious Controversy

Into this military-taut milieu, in 1776, ventured John Leland,
disciple of Isaac Backus of Massachusetts. Leland's early ambitions
were to help free from prison all the Baptist pastors incarcerated
under the rules of the Anglican Establishment, and to assist in this,
"to get himself elected to the Assembly."

As a boy, Leland had read and reread *Pilgrims Progress*, written by
Baptist martyr John Bunyan, who endured twelve years in Bedford
Jail for the grave offense of preaching the Gospel. At the age of
eighteen, young Leland heard a warning from Heaven: "You are not
about the work which you have got to do."[36] He spent the winter and
spring of 1775 exploring his future home in Virginia. After his final
move with Sallie in 1776, he accepted the call to preach at Mount
Poney, Virginia. The suspicion that his conversion was influenced by
a Universalist, his submission to an "improper" ordination, and his
Arminian views clouded his relations with Regular Baptists, even as

far as Massachusetts, where his old colleagues were members of the Warren Association. Leland gained some acceptance by a new "proper" ordination in 1786.[37] Although soon the most popular preacher in Virginia, he was a disturbing factor to many Regular and General Baptist preachers for his unorthodox views. He strongly supported adult baptism and excommunicated some church members for keeping loose company and engaging in excessive drinking, but he opposed theological seminaries, mission activities, and the Sunday School movement.[38]

Leland maintained a friendship with Thomas Jefferson and became a strong advocate of Jeffersonian democratic concepts as embodied in Jeffersonian republican philosophy. He also developed a cordial relationship with James Madison, author of the Bill of Rights. Jefferson, an indifferent Presbyterian-turned-deist, disliked the Presbyterian clergy and attended on occasions Leland's preaching in Orange County,[39] where Leland by 1779 was pastor of a half-dozen country churches. Jefferson was attracted to the message preached by Baptists and found kinship with Baptist preachers. During his presidency, Jefferson frequently attended the sermons of the Reverend William Parkinson, Baptist chaplain to the Congress.[40] Jefferson undoubtedly was influenced by Leland in his tolerant religious concepts. Madison, Leland's neighbor and a friend of the Baptists, would be pushed by the Baptists and pulled by Leland to promulgate the First Amendment to the Constitution. Another powerful figure in the political fight for Disestablishment was Patrick Henry, who on occasions rode his horse thirty to forty miles to assist Baptist preachers threatened by zealous sheriffs or magistrates. Sorely abused by the Anglican Church and its state supporters, Leland and the Baptists won these effective parliamentarians to their side in the fight for religious freedom.

Leland, in addressing the questions of religious freedom and soul competency, spoke in words similar to those of Roger Williams: "every man must give an account of himself to God, and therefore every man ought to be at liberty to serve God in a way that he can best reconcile to his conscience." For these reasons, one must not surrender his conscience to other men, for man's faith is sacred and the future faith of the unborn should not be restrained or inhibited. Thus, Leland asserted that religion is not a public concern but a private matter between the soul and God. Because of this, the religious opinions of men should not be subject to the control of civil government.[41]

Leland asserted that the establishment of religion, as in Massachusetts and Virginia, corrupts both the state that enforces it and the state church that receives the benefits.[42] The "uninspired, fallible" system of man then becomes the yardstick of religious goals and attainments. Established religion, he argued, alienates man from man, and man from God. These strictures then "metamorphose the church into a creature, and religion into a principle of state,—while preaching is made a trade of emolument [monetary gain]."[43]

Referring to Martin Luther's combative injunctions to "cut, stab, and strangle" peasant insurgents in order to end the attacks on lordly manors and castles in the German Peasant Revolt of 1524-25,[44] Leland justified force to restore law and order, even against the church. He affirmed that the government could punish those who harmed others during a "religious phrenzy," but only against their actions, not their beliefs. Truth, he asserted, needed no civil ruler to steady the Ark of God. Leland concluded:

> Government has no more to do with the religious opinions of men, than it has with the principles of mathematics. Let every man speak freely without fear, maintain the principles that he believes, worship according to his own faith, either one God, three Gods, no God, or twenty Gods; and let government protect him in so doing.[45]

In order to counter those who argued that Christianity would perish without state support, Leland maintained, "It is error and error alone, that needs human support."[46] Religious establishments, on the other hand, operated from a desire "to dictate to others—to have a halter around the necks of others." In order to cinch the point,

Leland concluded that the Roman emperor Constantine, who protected the Christian faith by law, did more harm than all the persecuting Roman emperors.[47]

The Virginia legislature and its leaders were hammered to end support for the Established Church. The issue was confronted by means of the General Assessment Bill; this proposal was written to end Anglican Church (Episcopal) privilege in Virginia and was at first supported by George Washington (Anglican), Patrick Henry (Presbyterian), and other leaders of the Anglican and Presbyterian churches.[48] Under this compromise measure, which emerged after 1770 in the tense confrontational national period, all citizens would be taxed for religious support; under its terms the taxes would go to the denomination selected by the taxpayer. This concept was seriously considered in 1784 in connection with a bill for the support of teachers of religion. The bill was supported in a lukewarm way by the Anglicans and strongly so by Presbyterian pastoral and lay members. However, the Baptists led by Leland firmly dissented and pressed against enactment. Some historians give the Baptists the primary credit for derailment of a bill that would give them funds collected by the state.

The Virginia Baptists responded with their own resolution:

> Resolved, That it be recommended to those counties which have not yet prepared petitions to be presented to the General Assembly against the engrossed bill for a general assessment for the support of the teachers of the Christian religion; to proceed thereon as soon as possible; that it is believed to be repugnant to the spirit of the Gospel for the Legislature thus to proceed in matters of religion; that no human laws ought to be established for this purpose; but that every person ought to be left entirely free in respect to matters of religion; that the holy Author of our religion needs no such compulsive measures for the promotion of His cause; that the Gospel wants not the feeble arm of man for its support; that it has made, and will again through divine power, make its way against all opposition; and that should

the Legislature assume the right of taxing people for the support of the Gospel, it will be destructive to religious liberty.

Therefore, This committee agrees unanimously that it will be
expedient to appoint a delegate to wait on the General Assembly with a remonstrance and petition against such assessment.[49]

James Madison threw his considerable weight on the side of the
Baptists and won the battle against general assessment for religion
in Virginia. In 1784 Madison gathered the opinions of American
thinkers in regard to the relationship of state and church. These
reflections were contained in his "A Memorial and Remonstrance on
the Religious Rights of Man," which condemned general assessment
in Virginia and other states. Madison summarized his views with
words reflecting that religion should be "wholly exempt" from government."[50]

In 1785, with the support of Madison and the Baptists, Thomas
Jefferson introduced his "Bill for Establishing Religious Freedom" in
Virginia. The bill contained these words:

> Be it enacted by the General Assembly, That no man shall be
> compelled to frequent or support any religious worship, place or
> ministry whatsoever, nor shall be enforced, restrained, molested,
> or burthened in his body of goods, nor shall otherwise suffer on
> account of his religious opinions or beliefs; but that all men
> shall be free to profess, and by argument maintain, their opin-
> ions in matters of religion, and that the same shall in no wise
> diminish, enlarge, or affect their civil capacities.[51]

The acceptance of this bill effectively ended the dominating role
of the Anglican Church in Virginia, as well as terminating the persecution of the Baptist and Presbyterian churches. Disestablishment,
including the loss of glebe lands, was to emerge, and other states
would follow the example of Virginia. Virginia and the nation now
turned their attention to the new Federal Constitution.

During the war years, Leland had traveled often on foot and
horseback between Orange and Yorktown, some 120 miles. He was

in constant demand as a revival preacher, sometimes preaching a dozen sermons in a week. In one instance in 1779, when his horse was ailing, he walked twenty miles to Culpeper to preach a funeral service, and then returned on foot. In the Baptist style, he expounded on the concept that every person is "precious in the sight of the Lord." When challenged by an Anglican minister as to whether he could preach on Numbers 22: 21, "And Balaam . . . saddled his ass," Leland explained that Balaam represented the state-hired clergy, the saddle represented the tax burden of their salaries, and the dumb ass represented the people who bore the burden.[52]

Ratifying The Constitution of 1787

Under the old Articles of Confederation of 1781 the American government could neither regulate commerce nor collect taxes from its four million citizens. Therefore, fifty-five statesmen met at Independence Hall in Philadelphia from May 25, 1787, to September 1787 to write a remarkable document, the new United States Constitution.[53] Unfortunately, the new Constitution could not adequately protect the religious rights of the nation's citizens as perceived by John Leland and the Virginia Baptists, who were unwilling to ratify the document unless amendments were added. In the process of ratification, the favorable vote of populous New York and Virginia was crucial if the new nation was to hold together.

The United States Constitution of 1787 contained nothing about religious liberty and little about religion, except several references to the "Deity." The exception was Article VI: "no religious Test shall ever be required as a Qualification to any office or public Trust under the United States." This satisfied George Washington and the intellectuals who wrote the Constitution. However, it was disquieting to the Baptists, who had suffered whippings and the stocks for merely worshipping in a grove or a neighbor's house.

Baptist opposition to the Constitution quickly gathered. As the Philadelphia convention ended, a letter arrived from James Gordon of Orange, Virginia informing Madison that several men, some of them Baptists, including Colonel Charles Barbour, planned to oppose his election to the Convention on Ratification. The majority of Madison's constituents were Baptists, who were also the vast majority in the counties of Orange, Goochland, and Culpeper.[54] Vigorous discussion of the issue occurred among members of the Virginia Baptist General Committee, in which Leland was prominent.

Leland and Madison had been good friends, and Baptists had admired Madison's strong positions in support of religious liberty. Madison, in 1772, as an Episcopal student, writing from the College of New Jersey (Princeton), attacked intolerance in New Jersey as a "hell-conceived principle of persecution."[55] Later, he was won over to the Baptist position that government should have no control over religion. As the youngest delegate to the 1776 Virginia Constitutional Convention, Madison made the motion, with the amendment accepted, that in the "Declaration of Rights," the words "religious liberty" should be substituted for the word "tolerance." "Toleration," he stated, presumed a favored church. In the House of Burgesses, Madison won the plaudits of the Baptists by his insertion in the Declaration of Rights for Virginia the amendment that "all Citizens of the Commonwealth shall be free from coercion by the State in matters of religion."[56] Thus Madison and Leland were fighting on the same side, but Madison for a time ignored Leland's pleas for specific language protecting religious practitioners under the new United States Constitution of 1787. Apparently Madison, and Washington as well, could see no possible danger.

The proceedings involving the writing of the Constitution in 1787 were supposedly discreet, but fairly accurate accounts of the proceedings filtered throughout the new nation in the form of letters, newspaper items, and rumors. But John Leland questioned:

> Where are the guarantees of complete religious liberty? . . .
> Where is the protection for the individual to believe or not to
> believe, to worship or not to worship, to be free to support his
> church or any religious cause, and free also from all compulsion

of the government to support some church? Remember we stand for religious liberty![57]

The urgency for protection from religious tyranny would lead eventually to the Bill of Rights as an integral part of the Constitution. Meanwhile the questions raised by Leland were debated by religious and civil leaders of every following from the Tidewater to the Blue Ridge Mountains.

The Baptist General Committee of Virginia in 1789, alarmed by the lack of specific articles protecting religious liberty in the Constitution, authorized John Leland to convey its fears to President George Washington. Leland wrote:

> When the Constitution made its first appearance in Virginia, we, as a society, had unusual strugglings of mind, fearing that the liberty of conscience, dearer to us than property or life, was not sufficiently secured. Perhaps our jealousies were heightened by the usage [treatment] we received in Virginia under regal government, when mobs, fines, bonds and prisons were our frequent repast.[58]

Washington replied: "If I could have entertained the slightest apprehension that the Constitution framed in the convention, where I had the honor to preside, might possibly endanger the religious rights of any ecclesiastical society, certainly I would never have placed my signature to it."[59] But Baptists, realists in a frontier setting, knew that Washington the man of honor would not always be there as protector, even when he added: "I beg you will be persuaded that no one would be more zealous than myself to establish effectual barriers against the horrors of spiritual tyranny, and every species of religious persecution."[60]

At first, Madison and Jefferson had differing views of the protective cover that the Constitution afforded or failed to supply for religion. Madison, in January 1789, wrote that he did not see in the defects of the Constitution any of the "serious dangers" that had alarmed some citizens. But Thomas Jefferson, writing from Paris, felt some concern and stated that he would assist in writing a bill of rights that would include planks for freedom of religion and freedom of the press.

The Revolutionary War, from the Baptist standpoint, had been a war of religious liberation. The Baptists, along with Episcopalians, Congregationalists, Quakers, Methodists, Presbyterians, and Catholics, had favored the proposed constitution and the vision of the federal government. However, the Virginia Baptists, almost alone, rallied to fight against ratification, since the Constitution did not specify clearly the national law regarding religious freedom. Leland, as a young preacher of twenty-two or twenty-three years, had had ambitions to run for the House of Burgesses, but now he found himself propelled along as a candidate against his friend James Madison. Since Madison initially would not heed the urgent Baptist call for religious protection, the Baptists would select their own delegate to face Madison, and, in Virginia, defeat the new Constitution. Madison disappointed the Baptists by agreeing with James Wilson that no bill of rights was needed. Then Madison aligned himself with John Adams, champion of the Massachusetts Establishment, who gave oral assurances that "Congress would never meddle with religion."[61] John Adams had been less than cordial to Baptist protests, and Baptist agent Isaac Backus in New England and the Virginia Baptists did not trust Adams.

Historian Joseph Dawson states that there is less than full knowledge of the circumstances of Leland's candidacy for delegate to the Ratification Convention in Virginia.[62] However, if Leland chose to run against Madison, as the Baptists desired him to do, it was evident that Madison would lose the election and Virginia would have been lost to the Union. On January 30, 1788, James Madison, Sr., had written his son: "The Baptists are now generally opposed to it [the Constitution], as it is said; Col. Barbour has been down on the Pamunkey amongst them, and on his return, I heard, publicly declared himself a candidate" [for the Ratification Convention]. James Gordon, also running as delegate, informed Madison that Leland was opposed and added this compelling message, "Upon the whole I think it is incumbent on you without delay to repair to this state, as the loss of the Constitution in this state [Virginia] may involve consequences the most alarming to every citizen of America."[63]

In March 1788 the General Committee met in Goochland County and under Leland's guidance passed a resolution that caused ripples throughout the nation and later the world. That statement was:

> We the Virginia Baptist General Committee, unanimously hold that the new federal constitution, proposed to the States for their ratification, does not make sufficient provision for the secure enjoyment of religious liberty; and therefore it should be amended to make such provision.

Among those present at the General Committee meeting was a veteran of the Revolutionary War, Colonel Charles Barbour, who offered to withdraw as delegate to the Virginia Ratification Convention if Leland would represent the largely-Baptist county of Orange and block the ratification of the Constitution.[64] There was no illusion on the part of the politicians about Baptist political power, if mobilized. Thomas Jefferson in his autobiography (1821) wrote: "By the time of the Revolution, a majority of the inhabitants [of Virginia] had become dissenters from the established church."[65] Leland was deeply troubled by the consideration that he might be forced to run against his good friend James Madison, "father of the Constitution." Leland promised only to consider the matter of running in the election, and after reflection, to be a candidate only for a short time.

Leland's objections to the Constitution were written and circulated. His primary concerns were that "There is no Bill of Rights" and "Religious Liberty, is not sufficiently secured." He continued:

> No religious test is required as a qualification to fill any office under the United States, but if a majority of Congress with the President favour one system more than another, they may oblige all others to pay to the support of their system as much as they please, and if oppression does not ensue, it will be owing to the mildness of Administration, and not to any Constitutional de-

fence, and if the manners of people are so far corrupted, that they cannot live by Republican principles, it is very dangerous leaving Religious Liberty at their mercy.[66]

Madison, returning from Philadelphia, passed through Fredericksburg, where supporters warned him that he should immediately confer with Leland if he wished to survive politically. Madison, half-sick and traveling in a gig made of a jerry-built seat and carriage wheels, stopped at the spacious Leland home. The two men talked earnestly for several hours under the great oaks of the estate. Various biographers attribute to strong-willed Sallie Leland or Colonel Barbour a logical proposal to end the crisis, namely that Madison accept the amendments proposed by Leland and that Leland then throw his support to Madison.

Madison had to be persuaded, as a man of principle, that additional guarantees of religious liberty and other rights must be erected. The outcome was that Leland gave his public support to Madison shortly afterwards at a picnic at Gum Spring, about six miles from Orange.[67] Madison stood on a hogshead of tobacco and confirmed that he would run for the First Congress, and, if elected, would introduce the amendments proposed by John Leland. As a consequence, Virginia supported the Constitution but only by a narrow margin.

In June 1789 Madison introduced his amendments to the Constitution. The first of them reads: "Congress shall make no law respecting an establishment of religion, or prohibiting the free exercise thereof."[68] The Baptist tenet embracing the separate responsibilities of God and Caesar, so long upheld by Baptist Trailblazers Roger Williams, John Clarke, Isaac Backus, and John Leland, was now destined to become a core belief of the American people, as well as an integral part of the Constitution.

Despite his deep involvement in the philosophical battles that made the American Constitution unique, Leland was always the Baptist pastor. In 1787, at a time of general spiritual revival and with Leland's enthusiastic support, the Regular Baptists and Baptist Separates united, although each group retained some cultural distinctives. Then Leland made a startling proposal in harmony with Thomas Jefferson's personal desires, that slaves should be gradually freed.[69] The Great Awakening had aroused humanitarian concerns among Presbyterians, Methodists, and Baptists. The Baptist Ketockton Association in 1787 declared "that hereditary slavery was a breach of the divine law." However, other Baptists became so disturbed and divided over efforts to achieve "gradual emancipation" that the matter was dropped.[70]

In 1788 President James Manning of Baptist Brown University urged Leland and the Virginia Baptists to establish "a seminary of learning." As a consequence, Leland and nine other men were empowered to devise seminary plans.[71]

Leland then returned to the issue of slavery, which would force his departure from Virginia. At the General Committee meeting on August 8, 1789, at Richmond, he voiced a ringing resolution against slavery, which was adopted and would shake every slave-holder:

> Resolved, That slavery is a violent deprivation of the rights of nature, and inconsistent with a republican government, and therefore recommend it to our brethren, to make use of every legal measure to extirpate this horrid evil from the land; and pray Almighty God that our honorable legislature may have it in their power to proclaim the great Jubilee, consistent with the principles of good policy.[72]

Because of a lack of substantial support, this measure was not sustained. Leland was confronting the same stone wall that blocked Thomas Jefferson's lofty attempts to eradicate slavery and its justification in the legal code of Virginia, the Declaration of Independence, and the Ordinance of 1787; the latter limited slavery north of the Ohio River.[73] Until the Civil War, most Americans, including the Baptists, would sidestep responsibility on the slavery issue, and alleging that it was a secular matter, not an issue for the church. Leland and Jefferson in their idealism were like two lonely figures obscured in a vast forest or a marginless sea.

Again in 1791, preparatory to his leaving Virginia for New England, Leland brought up again the question of "the Negro Question." As a New Englander with no slaves, he did not wish to meddle in southern customs. He was unwilling to inflame the passions of slave-holders, who might resort to abusing slaves. He admonished slaves to "obey them who have the rule over you in the fear of God." Still, while giving political speeches in support of Andrew Jackson (who equally hated abolitionists and secessionists), he expressed strong faith in the ability of the "Negro" to be a good citizen who could take care of his own needs. Leland had never designed a practical way to pay for the manumission of slaves. However, he urged that slaves who had lived worthily for many years in America should be liberated and that compensation should be paid to their owners.[74]

Catholics, Quakers, and Jews had been received with Christian charity into the Baptist enclave of Rhode Island, in the era in which Quakers could be sentenced to death in New Amsterdam. Leland displayed the same generosity toward Catholics that characterized Roger Williams. This attitude was derived not from expediency but from high principle. Leland lived in advance of his time in asking equal rights for Catholics. With nobility of purpose and mindful of the needs of the Irish immigrants to New England, Leland spoke for the Roman Catholic's right to absolute religious freedom in America. In 1836, having returned to the East, he summarized his feelings: "No man who has the soul of an American, and the heart of affection for our democratic institutions will either fear or wish to injure the papists" (Catholics). He could be certain that only a minority of the religious believers in America in that generation would agree with him.[75]

Return to New England

While the slavery question compelled Leland to confront his future, it is unlikely that it was his only consideration in returning to his nurturing ground in New England. In 1791 Leland, the doughty

Sallie, and their eight children sailed from Fredericksburg, Virginia, to New London, Connecticut. They stayed in New London only two months before moving on to Cheshire, Massachusetts, where Leland spent his remaining life as a gallant Trailblazer, fighting for disestablishment in Massachusetts and Connecticut.[76] Here was Daniel leaping back into the lion's den, after having been spared once before. The Congregational Church was the established institution. Exemptions from the religious tax by non-Congregationalists required the issuance of certificates. Real power in Connecticut lay with a half-dozen families and the Governors Council (Upper House), to which only Congregationalists could belong. At the apex of power was the Reverend Timothy Dwight, popularly called "the Pope," who as president of Yale could and did crack the whip on religious and civil matters. Resolutely, Leland set out to attack the system, but this time with a subtle twist. Leland launched his literary offensive under the title of "Yankee Spy," by fictional Jack Nips.[77]

Leland was never given a warm-hearted embrace by the Baptist clergy of New England. He was an evangelical Separate Baptist pastor and regarded by the Shaftesbury Association as "this eccentric but useful minister."[78] He preached fervently, favored revival meetings, and felt himself to have no power without the support of the Holy Spirit. On the other hand, he visited Philadelphia in 1784 with Elhanan Winchester, who defected from the Baptist faith to Universalism, and the Philadelphia Baptists feared incorrectly that Leland was leaning toward Universalism. Another peculiarity occurred in the ministry of Leland, mostly at the Cheshire Church, after 1798, when for twenty or more years he refused to allow the administration of the Lord's Supper.[79] His reason for this strange deviation may have reflected somewhat the opinion of John Bunyan, who rejected no Christian from the Lord's Supper, whether immersed or not. Bunyan had declared: "It is possible to commit idiolatry even with God's own appointments."[80]

Leland was a prolific and effective writer, not infrequently resorting to sarcasm or wit. His major treatise was notably on religious

liberty, *The Rights of Conscience Inalienable*. He argued that the rights
of conscience are not subject to government permission and that the
establishment of a state religion always damages true religion. The
evil enticement is that the practice bolsters the state church superficially, while enriching its clergy at the expense of Non-Conformists.[81] This outstanding literary work, published in 1791 at New
London, was employed to fight the church establishment in New
England. The tract's impossibly-long title is: *The Rights of Conscience
Inalienable, and Therefore Religious Opinions Not Cognizable by Law
or, The High-Flying Churchman Stripped of His Legal Robes Appears a
Yaho[o].*[82]

Leland drafted many "Memorials" addressed by the Baptists in
Virginia to its governor and the General Assembly and one to President George Washington. Also, he is believed to be the author of the
Baptist Memorial of 1777, which influenced Jefferson to formulate
his bill on religious liberty that was enacted into law years later. This
literary gift and his personal support made Leland the "foremost"
supporter of Jefferson in effecting the disestablishment of the Anglican (Episcopal) Church and the obtaining of relief for dissenting
churches.[83]

Attributed to John Leland, under the pseudonym John Enon, is
an attack on the christening of infants, entitled "Watery War Continued." A portion of this long poem will clarify the message:

> Sometimes you hear the learned assertion,
> There were no places for immersion;
> Your friends have taken it for granted,
> Your geographic skill was wanted;
> And kindly, for your information,
> Have told to stop your innovation,
> That Jordan was a little stream,
> To talk of dippings all a whim.
> At Aenon, too, and all around,
> No dipping-places could be found.
> What though there was much water there?

> T'was in small brooks! You often hear.
> Ye baptists dare not controvert
> What learned men so oft assert.
> This country, though exceeding dry,
> Yet brooks and fountains could supply;
> Full large enough, 'tis thought, for John
> To sprenkle people one by one.
> And had he used them sparing, too,
> As moderns are inclined to do,
> These many brooks, we make no doubt,
> For sprenkling might have long held out."[84]

Leland wrote more than twenty hymns and encouraged congregational singing, a practice that carried back to the Anabaptists. On a cold, icy winter day in 1779, while preparing to baptize five converts, he composed the following verse:

> Christians, if your hearts are warm;
> Ice and snow can do no harm;
> If by Jesus you are prized
> Rise, believe, and be baptized.[85]

The episode of a sixteen-hundred-pound cheese presented by Leland to newly-elected President Thomas Jefferson on January 1, 1802, in behalf of the Baptist Church and the community at Cheshire, Massachusetts, attracted wide attention. After the townspeople gathered and the gargantuan cheese was presented, Leland led in prayer, and the people sang a hymn. Leland and his friends delivered the cheese in Washington, after a five-hundred-mile trip by sled, boat, and horsecart. Later, Leland addressed both houses of Congress, after an introduction by Thomas Jefferson.[86]

Although Leland gave most of his time to preaching and itinerant evangelism, he served two terms in the Massachusetts legislature. In that state he was a leading Jeffersonian Republican and, later, an ardent political supporter of Andrew Jackson. But after preaching, his principal ardor was thrown into the fight for the disestablishment of the Congregational State Church, both in Massachusetts and

Connecticut.[87] This would be a tough, extenuated battle, lasting far beyond 1785, and would culminate in the liberation of Virginia from its religious intolerance and exclusivity. Not until 1817 would the Congregational Establishment be overthrown in New Hampshire, followed in 1818 by Connecticut[88] and 1833 by Massachusetts. Meanwhile, Baptists in Massachusetts had grown from 530 baptized members and eleven churches in 1770 to 8,463 members and 136 churches, after a twenty-five year period, as recorded by the Warren Association. A realistic projection for the Baptist believers in Massachusetts in 1795 would be 42,000 or twelve percent of the population.[89]

There was plenty of scorn and bitterness between Baptists and the "Standing Order." Baptists were discriminated against by judges and juries and subjected to mob violence as late as 1782. Baptist preacher Hezekiah Smith, a Princeton graduate called "the Baptist Whitefield," was lampooned on his death as "a man of little learning, small pulpit talents, and no dawn of genuis."[90] Isaac Backus, Leland's old friend and mentor, was singled out as one of the Baptist fanatics and ignoramuses. An anonymous writer to the *Boston Gazette* in 1779 stated that "I love the Baptists, but I hate Backus," whose books were not worth reading, but since paper was scarce it could "be of use in a certain servile office." Further, "Backus and his informers deserve to have their noses wrung and their arses kicked."[91]

Baptists Gain Respect

After the Revolutionary War ended in 1781, the Baptists, now more numerous and accepted, had not given up on reform. But Baptists were now members of a denomination or religious family, rather than a sect, and the new inertia of respectability exerted its toll. Instead of concentrating mainly on disestablishment, they now diverted much of their energy to home and foreign missions, Sabbath schools, temperance, and social programs.[92] As McLoughlin states it, a new generation of Baptists came of age, unaware of the

First Great Awakening or the full difficulties experienced by their fathers, and these young Baptists sought to bring change in part through the strength, and respectability of the Baptist movement.

Part of the change of attitude was due to the heavy contribution Baptists had made in the War for Independence. During that war the Reverend Oliver Hart was compelled to leave Charleston, South Carolina, when the British besieged the city in 1780, and he was forced to retire to New Jersey. Hart, at the request of the Council of Safety, had been sent to persuade some "dissaffected" Royalists to join the Revolution. The Reverend Edmund Botsford fled from Georgia in 1779, losing his library and home. On the invitation of General Andrew Williamson, Botsford served as chaplain for several months. The Reverend Richard Furman was so successful in rallying the people of the High Hills of Santee to the Continental Congress that he attracted the adverse attention of British General Cornwallis, who put a price on his head. John Hart of Charleston, another Baptist minister, served as an officer of the Continental line.[93] Of the estimated fifteen hundred Baptists of military age in South Carolina during the war, six hundred actually served.[94]

Never adequately recorded has been the vicious civil war during the Revolutionary War waged between Tories and the Sons of Liberty in the South, which subsided only when both sides joined forces to fight the Indians, who undertook dangerous raids into the Carolinas and Georgia. The Baptists, along with others, made substantial contributions to freedom and earned the plaudits of George Washington and James Madison. In fact, Madison often declared "that the Baptists had been in all his time the fast and firm friends of liberty."[95] The post-war period also would test the mettle of the Baptist veterans and their children. After 1811 the Baptist fight for disestablishmentarian principles was joined by Methodists and Universalists.

Leland settled in western Massachusetts among Baptist partisans, and from there he mixed his religious duties with a heavy dose of support for Jefferson's Democratic-Republican Party. Most Baptists, both in Massachusetts and Connecticut, joined the Republican Party, opposed the Federalists, and sought to bring down the religious Establishment, in a loose alliance with moderate Congregationalists and Unitarians.[96] However, those "allies" did not share a common vision of separation of church and state, as held by the Baptist leaders Backus and Leland. Nor did the moderate Congregationalists and Unitarians share Jefferson's and Leland's antipathy to the concept of a "legal" Christian nation or religious taxes to support any religion. What the "allies" wanted foremost was that the old-line Congregational ministers stop using their pulpits for attacks on the Jeffersonian movement; they were not interested in radical goals or in sharing their substantial power with less wealthy Baptists.[97]

In Connecticut, Leland had defended Jefferson against charges by the Congregational clergy that Jeffersonian democracy was dangerously anti-clerical, atheistic, and could destroy religion and society. In his book *A Storke [Stroke] at the Branch* (1801), he reminded citizens to support John Locke's and Jefferson's concepts of life, liberty, and property. He then prepared arguments for promoting the separation of church and state, as advanced in *The Dissenter's Strong Box.* Contained in the *Strong Box* is this advice borrowed from Jefferson:

> It is error, and error alone, that needs human support; and whenever men fly to the law or sword to protect their system of religion, and force it upon others, it is evident that they have something in their system that will not bear light, and stand upon the basis of truth.[98]

The long campaign by John Leland, the Baptists, and others led to: the disestablishment of Connecticut in 1818; the Federal Judiciary Act of 1789, creating U.S. courts; and the case of *Marbury vs. Madison* (1803), which established the supremacy of the national government. In the final victory, a Baptist-Episcopalian-Methodist coalition would be reinforced by Universalists, Unitarians, Quakers, and disaffected Congregationalists. The chief opponent had been the brilliant Lyman Beecher, who after several years, acknowledged: "That which I thought was the worst thing . . . turned out to be the best thing that ever happened in the state of Connecticut."⁹⁹

The Massachusetts Constitution of 1780 compromised its promises of allowing the worship of God "agreeable to the dictates of his conscience" by requiring in Article III taxes to support religion.

> Taxes paid by any dissenter may be applied to the support of teachers of his own religious sect or denomination, provided there be any on whose instructions he attends; otherwise it may be paid towards the support of the teacher or teachers of the parish or precinct in which said moneys are raise[d]."¹⁰⁰

The message was clear, that non-church persons and small churches with no minister would be obliged to support the Congregational Church.¹⁰¹

In 1801 at Cheshire, Leland, bristling with sarcasm, pulverized the logic supporting an exceptional tax for religion, his sermon circulated from Maine to Georgia. The sermon, "A Blow at the Root," contained these words:

> My dear hearers, I come to address you in the name of the authority of Massachusetts: the presbytery has approbated me, and the laws of the state have declared me learned and orthodox: I am not one of them who vainly imagine they are moved by the Holy Ghost to preach, but I have entered in at the door of lineal ordination, succeeded from the apostles, through all the whoredom and murders of Rome: I am not of that class who harangue the people extempore without sense of grammar; but I have my sermon all written down, and shall read it distinctly: And now, my hearers, as the law obliges you to have a teacher, I exhort you to be subject to every ordinance of man, for the Lord's sake.¹⁰²

In 1810 John Leland was elected to the General Court, and this afforded him an opportunity in 1811 to attack the employment of religious teachers supported by public funds. By 1820 even Daniel Webster conceded that the days of Article III, as a barrier to disestablishment, were coming to an end. The sheer variety of churches not sympathetic to the old arrangement foretold its demise. In 1820 the Congregationalists in Massachusetts numbered 373 churches, the Baptists 153, the Methodists 67, the Quakers (Friends) 39, the Episcopalians 22, the Universalists 21; and the remainder 23.[103] The famous Dedham case gave the Unitarian faction within the Congregational Church the right to hold church property when it was a majority. The Congregationalists began to understand the logic of Baptist complaints against providing money for another religious group. Now taxes were levied against Trinitarian Congregationalists to support the hated Unitarians when the latter were in the majority.[104]

In 1833 the "Standing Order" fell, when the people of Massachusetts in a public referendum voted ten to one against Article III and voted all faiths equal under the law. Massachusetts belatedly surrendered religious privilege with reluctance, and only because the change was profitable. If the greatest contribution of America is religious liberty, as expressed by Troeltsch, then the squalling and laborious surrender by Massachusetts was almost ignominious. The Congregationalists, with a common origin in England, and, except for their practice of christening infants, the twin-brother of the Baptists, had proven to be intractable and exclusionary in their policies.[105]

Leland would not surrender his public voice with the long-delayed victory at Boston.

> I have publicly pledged that as long as I can speak with my tongue—wield a pen—or heave a cry to heaven, whenever the rights of men, liberty of conscience, or the good of my country were involved by fraud or force, my feeble efforts would not be dormant.[106]

Facing the Sunset

Leland, after the Massachusetts victory, was past eighty years of age, but he had visited Virginia again and returned to Middleborough to exchange views with the venerable Isaac Backus.

The end was coming to old Leland. By foot or horse, he had traveled the equivalent of three times around the world, most of them to serve fervently as a Separate Baptist evangelist. He had preached eight thousand sermons and written eighty-six books and pamphlets, and an additional assortment of short speeches that absorbed a total of about 744 pages. Even as he headed for the distant harbor, he spoke of himself as "an old weather-worn sailor, yet on the deck, in a boisterous sea, not at the helm . . . but sounding the deep . . . watching the winds and pirates." He was alert, a tenacious adversary, an indefatigable Christian advocate. He kept on, almost to the hour of his death at eighty-seven, in the year 1841.[107]

John Leland's life had the Non-Conformist, even eccentric qualities observed in the lives of other great Baptists, notably John Bunyan and Roger Williams. Like them in his gifts, Leland helped alter the religious-political world of Virginia and Massachusetts. In Virginia, he was the close ally and advisor of Thomas Jefferson and James Madison. Leland and the Baptists (not Madison, according to Dawson) were the true fathers of the First Amendment to the Constitution. In Massachusetts, Leland may have played a lesser role than the admirable Isaac Backus, but both Baptist preachers and their Baptist colleagues exerted a critical role in the long tortuous process of disestablishing the Congregational Church in Massachusetts. Backus was more conservative, Calvinistic, and acceptable to the Regular Baptists of New England, and Leland was more amenable to the Baptist New Lights of Virginia. Both Trailblazers were essentially New England-bred and preachers steeped in Congregational traditions, and both were to become fierce Baptist warriors against the Congregational Establishment in New England and the Anglican (Episcopal) Establishment in Virginia.

There is much to suggest that Thomas Jefferson enjoyed the preaching and doctrine of the Baptists, possibly because of John Leland, whose church Jefferson attended. Likewise, Universalists, Catholics, and Quakers should share warm feelings for Leland. Dawson suggests that Leland may have been "saved" through the influence of a

Baptist holding the Universalist belief,[108] and Leland traveled in 1784 to Philadelphia with Universalist Elhanan Winchester.[109] In 1836 in New England, Leland loudly proclaimed the right to complete religious freedom for the Irish Roman Catholics. He also found allies, that included Quakers, to finally destroy the chokehold of the Congregational Church in Connecticut. He railed against slavery and prayed for it to end, while supporting the potential of liberated blacks.

But despite his great curiosity, his friendship with deists like Thomas Jefferson, and travels with Universalists, Leland knew himself to be a Baptist preacher of the Gospel. His love was enwrapped in Jesus, and he felt powerless without the aid of the Holy Spirit. This was a man of brain and discernment, but that great insight was in submission to Christ. Therefore, no person he knew could be outside the embrace of God's love. His greatest civic contribution was to advance the separation of church and state, but all along the way he was primarily an evangelist of Christ, not a statesman.

Chapter 9

George Leile
(c1750-1815)
and the Negro Pioneers

Founding Fathers of the Black Baptists

During the Revolutionary War, as British armies captured Savannah, Georgia, in 1778 and Charleston, South Carolina, in 1780, British arms provided shelter for Tory native sons, Indian allies, and escaped slaves, who had been promised their freedom. Among the many blacks that joined the British was George Leile [Lisle] (c.1750-1815), earlier freed by his white master to serve as a Baptist minister and one of the first clergymen of his race in North America, but in imminent danger of being returned to slavery after his master's death.

Leile (sometimes called Lisle, or Sharpe after his master, but more often Brother George) was born in Virginia and converted and baptized about 1773-74 near Kiokee, Burke County, Georgia, by Baptist minister Matthew Moore.[1] Leile was told by both fellow slaves and whites that his father was the first Christian convert of African lineage they had known. In recognition of Leile's faith and gifts, he was "approbated" to preach by a white church near Kiokee.[2] The future black preacher had been sold by speculators as a slave to Baptist deacon Henry Sharpe, either in Virginia or Georgia. Sharpe, after recognizing Leile's talents and Christian fidelity, gave him his freedom on August 17, 1777,[3] along with the documents of manu-

George Leile (Lisle), 1780, Preaching in Savannah

mission. This liberation enabled Leile to preach at Silver Bluff in Jasper County, South Carolina (a black church founded about 1773), at Brampton and Yamacraw in Georgia, both close to Savannah, and at other plantations.[4]

George Leile, as an eminent Baptist Trailblazer, was not only the founding father of the black Baptist churches of Savannah but also the first black Baptist "missionary" to Jamaica, and in missions the forerunner of the great William Carey and Adoniram Judson. If his attainments had been limited to establishing and pastoring the flock that became the First African Baptist Church in Savannah and gaining the conversion of Andrew Bryan, its second pastor, that in itself would be sufficient to merit scholarly research. Even if the Savannah church under Leile had been amorphous, out of fear of white patrols, and was not formally organized as early as sometimes portrayed, the Savannah church has been identified as among the first black Baptist congregations in America. The First African Baptist Church of Savannah is almost certainly the longest continuing black Baptist church in North America.[5]

The research performed by the First African Baptist Church in Savannah (sometimes at variance with the rival claims of First Bryan Baptist Church, Savannah) indicates that George Leile was ordained on May 20, 1775. In 1796 Leile, about age forty-five, sent a parcel from Jamaica, where he was living, to Mr. W. H. Leichestershire in England. Leile's parcel contained a copy of a church covenant, confirming that December 1777, during the American Revolution, was the constituting date for the Savannah church.

Leile was converted by the Holy Spirit through the ministry of a Tory (pro-British) preacher, Matthew Moore, whose sister Mildred was the wife of Henry Sharpe. Henry Sharpe, Leile's master, had three children and nine slaves, and farmed 1570 acres on the Savannah and Ogeechee rivers. Although magnanimous in his treatment of George Leile, he had much trouble with the authorities, perhaps because of his Non-Conformism. He was charged in 1773 with stripping boards from a public bridge, and before that was publicly whipped for trading with the Indians without a permit. Also, Sharpe was a deacon in the Big Buckhead Church started by the Reverend Matthew Moore, and thus was sometimes in trouble with the Established Church over matters of religion.[6]

George Leile was convicted of his sins while attending Moore's preaching. Leile wrote: "This state I laboured under for the space of five or six months." As he realized that he was saved, he said: "I felt such love and joy as my tongue was not able to express. After this I declared before the congregation of believers the work which God had done for my soul, and the same minister, the Rev. Matthew Moore, baptized me, and I continued in this church about four years, till the [e]vacuation [of Savannah, by the British army]."[7]

Fired by his faith and encouraged by a tolerant Christian mentor, formerly his master, Leile preached over a wide area, often traveling a twelve-mile stretch on the Savannah River by bateau. But the institution of slavery also produced patrols watching over roads and waterways and inhibited the meeting of sizable groups of black slaves for any purpose. Those slaves without passes suspected of overstepping the bounds of propriety or indulging in conspiracy would be seized, manacled, and savagely beaten.

Georgia was officially Anglican Church "territory" and repressively so for Non-Conformists immediately before the American Revolution. Then an avalanche of irrepressible Separate or New Light Baptists swept into the state from North and South Carolina, led by Daniel and Martha Marshall and, later, by Daniel's son Abraham Marshall. The New Light Baptists had stemmed from New England Congregational and Presbyterian revivalism that produced in its Baptist adherents, including the founding leader Shubal Stearns, a fearless opposition to persecution, a literal and absolute belief in the Bible, attuned to the anticipated and imminent return of Christ, and accompanied by high emotion. The Separate Baptists in Virginia, the Carolinas, and Georgia, like swarms of army ants, captured almost the entire country they invaded, convicting and baptizing, but producing a sense of desperation and a harsh backlash from the Anglican magistrates, sheriffs, and bureaucrats.

Kiokee, near Augusta, was the first white Separate Baptist church in Georgia, founded in 1772, with Daniel Marshall as pastor. Even earlier, in 1771, a branch of Stephens Creek Church, South Carolina, had a meeting house at Heggie Rock, near Kiokee, on the Little Kiokee Creek. Daniel Marshall, a Baptist convert from Congregational doctrine, became a prodigious church organizer in South Carolina and Georgia, although a stammerer and weak in build.[8] His wife Martha, who interceded at the trial of her husband after he was charged with unauthorized preaching near Augusta, Georgia, was one of the most valiant Baptist exhorters (unordained lay preachers) in history.

The Separate Baptists by 1801 had fourteen churches in Georgia, ten of which became members of the Georgia or Hephzibah associations. George Leile had attended a Separate church with many Tories among its members, namely Big Buckhead Baptist Church in Burke County, which disbanded about 1776. Gradually, most of the Separate Baptist churches by the early nineteenth century merged with the Regular (Particular) Baptists, absorbed their Calvinist doctrine, and adopted their more orderly church service and often their interest in education. This amicable transition in style and organization is attributed to the early friendship and cooperation of Separate Baptist patriarch Daniel Marshall and Regular Baptist preacher Edmund Botsford, leaders of the two groups.[9]

Blacks had become Baptists in small numbers from the seventeenth century. The first black Baptist in America may have been "Jack, a colored man," who as a slave was baptized in 1652 into the Newport, Rhode Island, Particular (Regular) Baptist Church. In or after 1773 there were seven organized or unorganized black churches in America. By 1790 there were 7,707 black members in white-controlled churches.[10] These numbers scarcely hint at the multitude of blacks that ultimately would flow into the Baptist churches. Reverend Botsford in 1790 reported that sometimes he preached in South Carolina to groups of three hundred slaves, who "sing delightfully; and those who are truly religious, in general far exceed the *whites* in love to each other, and in most other duties. Many of them can read, and are remarkably fond of hymns."[11] However, numbers of these early black converts, until their profession of Christian faith, firmly attached to Africa's animism and ignorant of Christian doctrine and theology, were on occasions rejected for church membership. However, others mastered their theology and became mature believers, such as the deacons of the Third Baptist Church in 1832 in Savannah. One of the most distinguished and insightful black preachers was John Jasper, born about 1812 and a slave for fifty years near Richmond, Virginia, who became famous for his extraordinary sermons, "The Sun Do Move" and "Whar Sin Kum Frum," heard by thousands of people.[12]

The slow emergence of the black preacher proceeded both in the North and South during the Revolution. In Salem, Massachusetts, around 1791, a black minister, Thomas Paul, preached in the white Baptist church pastored by Elder Lucius Bolles. Apparently only one white family was disturbed by this innovation.[13] In the South during the war years, a few white Baptist churches selected outstanding black preachers, former slaves, rather than less compelling white preachers. In one instance, the Roanoke Association of Virginia purchased a slave to serve as minister.[14] In the South and North, the churches imposed a strict discipline on members, primarily for drunkenness on the part of whites. On occasions, church bodies called for repentance and reform, and often resorted to exclusion of white or black members from the congregation.

The moral code was imposed on slave-masters as well as common members. The Turkey Creek, South Carolina, church in 1797 had seven black members. In 1799 a white woman was excluded from the church for abusing a black servant.[15] The Buffalo Church inquired of the Bethel Association, South Carolina, first, whether a Christian master could beat a black church member, and, secondly, if a black slave could remarry, if forced by the system to leave his wife in a distant area. The Association answered both questions in the affirmative, but with many qualifications to the second answer.[16]

In the first stages of the Christianization of slaves, and long thereafter, blacks usually sat in a raised gallery or a special section of the church. Black Christians generally were called Brother George and Sister Mary, and, on occasions, by their master's name, as Thompson's Harry or Blackstone's Harriet. In writing about black Baptists, reference was sometimes made to Black Sampson or the "Ethiopian Paula." In Baptist churches, the distinctions between races were often narrowed, such as in the Charleston and Beaufort area, where Baptist ministers baptized whites and blacks together.

Some of the hidden thoughts about white reactions to their black brethren in the church were revealed by Thomas Fuller of Beaufort in this vignette:

> Sunday, Nov. 6, 1803. I was baptized in the river with several Negroes who had been received the afternoon before. This act has caused some estrangement between my friends and myself. Nevertheless, I shall ever have cause to rejoice that the blessed Lord my God led me in the way and plucked me as a brand from the burning. Let every one act as he has light. We would do well to attend to what our Lord on his baptism said to John: "Suffer it to be so now; for thus it becometh us to fulfill all righteousness."[17]

The conversion of large numbers of blacks became a pattern in the last quarter of the eighteenth century. The Welch Neck Church in South Carolina received 87 blacks for baptism in 1779. In 1800 the Charleston, South Carolina, Baptist Church had about 63 black members.[18] George Leile preached in South Carolina at the Silver Bluff Church, an all-Negro church, with about 60 members. Silver Bluff, twelve miles below Augusta on the Savannah River, under its black pastor Jesse Galphin (or Jesse Peter) possibly began in 1773,[19] dissolved in 1778 with the capture of Savannah by the British, and reconstituted in 1791. The church grew to have 210 members, before its disappearance about the time Galphin began his work in Georgia.[20]

Baptists Move into Georgia

Most black churches, or those churches predominantly black, were composed of Particular (Regular) Baptists. This persuasion of Baptists was the largest of five groups that, at different periods, migrated to Georgia. The first contingents of white Baptists to arrive in Georgia, but limited to about ten families, were the Seventh-Day Baptists, who followed either Calvinistic or Arminian theology, but always worshiped on Saturday as the Lord's Sabbath. The first congregation of these from England settled about 1661 in Newport, Rhode Island. Their greatest strength was in Rhode Island, New Jersey, and Pennsylvania, where they formed associations. The pioneer band in Georgia, at Tuckasee King, Effingham County, were persecuted by their neighbors, so the Sabbatarians, after a four-year stay, left that province for South Carolina.[21]

The second Baptist group to infiltrate Georgia were the Particular (Regular) Baptists, who originated among the Independents in seventeenth-century England. The Particular Baptists favored an educated clergy, orderly services, and limited atonement (only the Elect to be saved) as derived from the teachings of Augustine of Hippo and John Calvin of Geneva. They also taught unconditional election (man's choice of no avail), irresistible grace, and the perseverance of the saints (once saved, always saved). The first Regular (Particular) church in America was organized by Roger Williams in 1639 at Providence, Rhode Island, but some of its members represented other Baptist strains. The Regular (Particular) Baptists in Georgia began at Bethesda Orphanage near Savannah (founded by Congregationalist George Whitefield) when the manager, Nicholas Bedgegood (1751-59), became a Baptist and in 1763 returned from South Carolina to immerse five persons and administer the Lord's Supper at Bethesda. The Bethesda group became a branch of the Charleston,

South Carolina, (Regular) Baptist Church.[22] In 1773 Baptist Edmund Botsford, "the flying preacher," established a church near New Savannah, now known as the Lower Brier Creek or the Botsford Church. [23] The Botsford Church joined the Georgia Baptist Association in 1788.

By 1790 the largest group of Baptists in the former British colonies were the Particulars (Regulars) who nationwide had 809 churches and congregations and 57,327 members. By 1801 the Particulars, black and white, with 105 churches (some of them absorbed from the Separates) and 5,272 members, comprised ninety-nine percent of all Georgia Baptists.[24]

The growth of the third group, the New Light Baptists or Separate Baptists that invaded Georgia near Augusta at Kiokee, was phenomenal. Also the quick absorption of this dynamic group by the Particular Baptists in Georgia in three decades was mystifying. The Separate Baptists, inspired by the preachings of George Whitefield and Jonathan Edwards, Congregational firebrands, found fertile ground, first in New England and then in the frontier South. Many of the great Separate proclaimers left the Congregational Church and became New Light (Separate) Baptists, such as Daniel Marshall, Martha Marshall, and Shubal Stearns. They brought the Great Awakening revival fire, preached the Gospel with intense emotion, and transfixed the sinner with the Word of God. They were emotional and noisy, whereas the Particulars were solemn and dignified. Although a number of the foremost New Light Preachers were intelligent, well-read men, such as Hezekiah Smith and John Leland in Virginia, many others were inspired ordinary men, and often illiterate. They expected the Lord Jesus to come at any moment.

The Separates nationwide reached their apex in 1780 with 221 churches and branches and 9,842 members. Ten years later they had declined to 69 churches and branches, with 3,572 members.[25] Their Bible-based faith, open democracy, including acceptance of women preachers, honesty, burning evangelism, and courage have left permanent traces on the Baptist psyche and message. During the Revolutionary War, some Separates that preached non-resistance were buffeted both by the Tories and the Whigs.[26]

The fourth Baptist group to develop in Georgia represented the black churches, which at first aligned with the Georgia Baptist Association and adopted Particular (Regular) doctrine. After the black Silver Bluff, South Carolina, church and its black pastors, David George and Jesse "Peter" Galphin, dispersed in 1779 for protection to Savannah and Charleston, apparently the Springfield Baptist Church of Augusta, Georgia, with 210 members, became its successor and joined the largely-white Georgia Baptist Association.[27] The black slaves remained with their pious white pro-Congress Baptist master, George Galphin, despite the British Emancipation of 1775, until the church broke up in 1778 with the fall of Savannah, when their master fled for his own protection.[28]

The second Baptist black church in Georgia was established at Savannah in December 1777, "without white notice or approval," with George Leile as pastor. The proof of this is the belated revelation of Leile's confirmation of the existence of *The Covenant of the Anabaptist Church begun in America, Dec. 1777, and in Jamaica Dec. 1783*.[29] With the augmentation of members from the disbanded Silver Bluff Church, including Leile, Jesse "Peter" Galphin, and David George, the Savannah church had about 38 members in 1780. A third Georgia black Baptist congregation, Beaverdams, organized by 1796 in Burke County with 228 members, had disbanded early in the nineteenth century. Also, there is every reason to believe that, with the residence in Georgia prior to 1772 of ten affluent white Baptists, each the owner of one hundred or more slaves, some of their servants became baptized Christians.[30]

The black church members, whenever feasible, moved into their own organizations. Thus forty-eight percent of black Georgia Baptists were in two black churches in 1790. Eleven years later, more than sixty-two percent were in three black congregations. In 1801, the 1,705 black Georgia Baptists were thirty-two percent of the total Baptist population. But a massive influx of blacks into Baptist churches did not occur until after 1800.[31]

There was a fifth group of Baptists in Georgia, namely the General Baptists. The General Baptists, the original group in England bearing the name of Baptists, blossomed in 1609 from Anabaptist roots in England and the Netherlands. The General Baptists were founded by John Smyth and Thomas Helwys, and immigrated in small numbers to Colonial America. In the 1720s, one of their churches emerged in Newport, Rhode Island, and from there spread to Massachusetts, New Hampshire, and Maine. Their theology embraced general atonement (all that believed in Christ could be saved), conditional election (repentant believers welcomed to God's throne), human choice manifested in receiving salvation as God's gift, and the possibility of falling from grace. General Baptists usually, but not always, practiced the laying-on of hands for the ordaining of preachers, deacons, and all new baptized believers.[32] One element of those who rigorously practiced the laying-on of hands were called General Six-Principle Baptists.

The General Baptists or Freewill Baptists (as one group was called after 1780) practiced open communion and sometimes foot washing, after the example of Jesus. In 1790, nationwide, there were three broad groups, comprising 4,453 members and 76 churches. In Georgia, by 1791, the General Baptists consisted of only three ministers and a few members organized into several small congregations and one association.[33]

Emergence of George Leile

In this potpourri of Baptists, the ex-slave pastor George Leile was a phenomenon both to whites and blacks, most remarkably as a gifted, inspired preacher. He was neat in dress and humble in his manner. Even while preaching from a hollow or tree stump, he was a powerful and persuasive man of God. We have insight into a clergyman of stubborn resolve, reflecting perseverance in preaching the Gospel in the face of threats near Savannah. There is evidence of a leader with unusual vision, who could organize a black-led Savannah church and later construct a church edifice in Jamaica.

The black missionaries sent to Africa by Leile's congregation in Jamaica give evidence of the preacher's world vision and pure Christian commitment. He willingly ventured to minister among the humble people in the back-country.

He was not a great scholar, for slavery taught no person to think or study, but he accumulated, after years, "a few books, some good old authors and sermons, and one large Bible that was given me by a gentleman."[34] He had only a self-taught education, but somehow he learned to read and write; he corresponded overseas through many letters to Christian brothers in England and Georgia. In the end, he won the highest respect of blacks and whites. "The slaves loved him and their owners honored him."[35]

His beliefs were orthodox Baptist doctrines, expressed with clarity. He later wrote, "I agree to election, redemption, the fall of Adam, regeneration and perseverance, knowing the promise is to all who endure, in grace, faith and good works to the end, shall be saved."[36]

There were only a few pro-British Baptist churches in the South during the Revolutionary War. The Patriots' cause was supported by almost all white Baptists in the southern provinces, not only for separation from the Crown but for religious freedom from the British-born institution, the Anglican (later Episcopal) Church. Conversely, it is logical to believe that many if not most blacks, whether Baptists or not, prayed for a British victory that would rescue them from slavery. An interesting exception to the general white pro-Congress sentiment was the Big Buckhead Baptist Church of Burke County, Georgia, the church of Deacon Sharpe, and in existence only from 1774 to 1776. Leile was a member of this congregation that manifested strong Tory loyalties,[37] but possibly it had a few Whig members, including John, the brother of Henry Sharpe. Influenced by that church, pro-British black preacher Jesse Galphin (Jesse Peter), the fortunes of war, and his own desire to remain free, George Leile was caught in an increasingly dangerous situation.[38]

Favored by eloquence and spiritual fervor, Leile preached in the evenings to mixed congregations, sometimes at the Reverend Matthew Moore's church near Kiokee.[39] He expounded the Gospel along the Savannah River, among both blacks and whites. Leile was regarded as a wonder, possibly a prophet; nothing like him had ever been seen.

Then, inexplicably, as the war enveloped the area, Leile ceased his preaching for the duration of the war. This gifted free man may have been cautioned by his friends, white and black, to stick to reading the Bible and to limit himself to private meditations, but not to indulge in political fantasies. The pro-Congress militia won their first battle in Georgia, at Burke County Jail. This victory established the reputation of Baptist chaplain Silas Mercer, who told his troops to stand their ground, because the Lord would deliver a victory to the Colonials, because of the "justice of their cause." Then, Leile's chief bulwark was killed in a minor fight that followed: Deacon Henry Sharpe of Big Buckhead Baptist Church (now Major Sharpe of the Loyalist Militia) died in 1779 after a skirmish at Spirit Creek, Burke County.[40]

Tradition, but no written records, suggest that Leile relinquished his pastoral duties during the war to fight on the British side. But, if this is true, no solid proof has been uncovered until this time.[41] On the other hand, he encouraged black people to assist the British during Savannah's occupation; he spent much time at Tybee Island, the British base, and worked ceaselessly for the king's soldiers. He continued to minister to his Christian flock by commuting to Savannah in his boat.[42]

One or more heirs to the Sharpe estate, not having the same esteem for ex-slave Leile as did Henry Sharpe, undoubtedly resenting his Tory activities, and probably short of money and other resources because of the British occupation of Charleston and Savannah, reportedly sought to return Leile to servitude. As a consequence, Leile was placed in jail until his official papers confirming his free status could be procured and his release obtained. It is not known what role was played in this situation by his new protector, British Colonel Kirkland.[43]

British military policy during the Revolution included efforts to encourage slaves to desert their pro-Congress masters for freedom; possibly four thousand slaves left Savannah for the Caribbean islands and conceivably six thousand fled from Charleston. Other slaves, under Leile's associate David George, escaped to Nova Scotia in the far North, but because of the hard life there, they settled in 1792 in Sierra Leone on Africa's west coast. Blacks remaining behind in Savannah, who had collaborated with the British military, were enslaved onced more. But the prodigious efforts of Leile resulted in black churches evolving in Savannah, near Augusta, Georgia, and in Nova Scotia and Jamaica.[44]

Colonel Kirkland, as chief British occupation officer,[45] advised Leile to leave when the British forces left the Low Country. Leile then became an indentured servant to Kirkland, a common expedient to pay sea passage. The British had lost the war, with the capitulation of General Cornwallis at Yorktown, Virginia, on October 19, 1781. Then, Leile, the ex-slave, and Kirkland, the British officer, with no future in the new republic, sailed for Kingston, Jamaica, on July 11, 1782.[46]

However, the ship's schedule was altered by a change in the sea weather, which caused an interruption in the voyage, which in turn changed the destiny of George Leile and the future of the First African Baptist Church. Before arriving in Jamaica, Leile's ship was held at anchor for several weeks by adverse weather at Tybee Island, ten miles from Savannah. Leile returned to Savannah by land and there baptized Andrew Bryan (Leile's successor as pastor), Bryan's wife Hannah, Kate Hogg, and Hagar Simpson, all of them slaves. After this momentous rite, Leile's ship departed with the great Trailblazer on board.[47] George Leile's life in Jamaica will be discussed in the last portion of this chapter.

Andrew Bryan Carries On

The black congregation that had been assembled by George Leile at Brampton Plantation might have floundered and died had it not been for that last-minute convert, Andrew Bryan. They were a little core of slave believers, recorded in 1777 as "the Anabaptist Church," meeting in a plantation barn, that became in time the First African

Baptist Church of Savannah, Georgia. That church at Brampton's Barn, through many struggles, would have a phenomenal growth, expanding from six church members during the Revolutionary War to thirty,[48] and then to forty-five new members in 1788. The Reverend Abraham Marshall, the white moderator of the Association, assisted by young black minister Jesse Galphin, ordained Andrew Bryan in 1788, and in 1790 organized the church and its 381 members.[49] In 1832 Andrew Marshall, Bryan's successor, would lead his 2,795 members to purchase a fifteen-hundred-dollar sanctuary, financed by the church and its white trustees.[50] Leile and Bryan's work for the Lord would produce the intertwined relationship of First African Baptist Church and its daughter churches, the Second Baptist Church and the First Bryan Baptist Church.

Andrew Bryan, Baptist preacher and convert of George Leile, purchased his freedom in 1790 for a nominal sum.[51] Formerly he was a slave owned by kindly Jonathan Bryan, owner of Brampton Plantation, three miles from Savannah, now located on the site of the National Gypsum Company, at the Georgia Ports Authority. Bryan's master had prestige as a member of the British Crown Council. However, as the Revolutionary War drew near, Jonathan Bryan resigned from the Council to become one of the Sons of Liberty that met at Tondee's Tavern and conspired to produce a rebellion against the Crown in Georgia.[52] The landholder Jonathan Bryan was a respectable master and advised his heirs not to break up slave families.

Andrew Bryan, the future church leader and successor to George Leile, was a slave born near Goose Creek, sixteen miles from Charleston, South Carolina. At the early stages of his life, he would become a Regular Baptist preacher in Georgia, and at midstream he would purchase freedom for himself and his small family. Remarkably for a black person of that time, at his death he would have an estate valued at about three thousand dollars. More than that, he would be regarded by some as the "Founding Father" of the Black Church in Savannah.

As a Baptist preacher and leader of his people, Bryan was grave and always polite. He was deferential to whites, and to have been otherwise in a slave-holding society would have been foolish. He didn't have to prove his staunch character or his bravery and piety, for the incidents in his life would bring these to the surface. His civility caused him to develop powerful white friends that aided his efforts to strengthen his church. In public he always appeared "decently clothed."[53] Bryan would be tested severely, and a true Christian character would be refined in the crucible.

Other blacks were emerging as preachers, visibly so in Baptist churches, since neither a long novitiate nor formal education was required. Dozier described "Negro Jacob, a slave," who preached in 1789 in Virginia as "a most wonderful preacher." He also told of a black named Lewis in Essex, Virginia, "with the greatest sensibility I ever expected to hear from an Ethiopian. . . . His gift exceeded many white preachers." In 1795 a black preacher, Jacob Bishop, was so much admired in Northhampton County, Virginia, that county friends purchased freedom for him and his wife.[54] In 1791 a church numbering five hundred, composed mainly of "people of colour" had as its first pastor, Moses, a black man, "often taken up and whipped for holding meetings." William Lemon, black, was sent several times as a "messenger" (delegate) to the (Baptist) Dover Association. Also, Davenport Church in Prince George County, Virginia, a mixed church, was regularly ministered to by black preachers.[55]

About nine months after his baptism in 1783, Andrew Bryan began preaching at Brampton Plantation and then on the rice and indigo plantations along the Savannah River. He had been encouraged by Leile to take the mantle of leadership over the little flock, and once he assumed the pastoral role for about three years,[56] even in an unordained capacity, nothing would deter him. His own freedom would be obtained in 1790, for he was blessed, despite the cruel system of slavery, to have an enlightened master and patron of integrity, Jonathan Bryan, who gave him great freedom and protected him from hostile whites.

He was an eloquent preacher, relying on the Bible for his inspiration, expounding an orthodox Regular Baptist message: Christ had died on the cross to save sinners, even black slaves, whose sins could be washed away by His blood. By faith, all sinners could be redeemed, and through baptism they could manifest to mankind that they were born again. Around this faith and a flock first gathered by George Leile and regenerated by Andrew Bryan, there was created, first at Brampton Plantation and later at Yamacraw (the old Indian village site) and Savannah, the longest continuously-existing black Baptist church in America. Initially it was called "the First Colored Baptist Church," and later it would be known as the First African Baptist Church. In its dissent, the First Bryan Baptist Church maintains that First Bryan is the "true" church, for, in the church battle over the Campbellite heresy, it was uncontaminated and never left the original Bryan Street site.[57]

This church of slaves indulged in foot-washing and laying-on of hands, the latter practice adopted from the General Baptists or the Separate Baptists. In addition, all Baptist churches followed two ordinances: Baptism through immersion (usually in a spring, creek, or river) and the Lord's Supper, the latter in remembrance of Christ's sacrifice. These two rites were simple, never referred to as sacraments, and had no saving or miraculous features in their observance. Then to this ceremony was added the special spiritual uniqueness of the swaying Negro saint, praising his Lord with his melodious or plaintive high-arching notes. Bryan, as evidence of his orthodoxy, required all candidates for baptism to show proof of marriage. However, the state of Georgia recognized no marriage between slaves. Therefore, if single because of the institution of slavery, the candidate for baptism was required to have a proper period of separation before engaging in a new marriage.[58]

At baptism, great dignity and reverence were observed. The men would dress in their best attire. The senior women would be clad in snow-white aprons and head handkerchiefs. Then they would march in procession to the river by Fahm Street for the immersion, presided over by Andrew Bryan. On the river bank, they sang melodiously the old hymns of redemption:

> I am bound for the promised land,
> Oh, who will come and go with me?
> I am bound for the promised land.

Some sentences of the Bible would be chanted in paraphrase form by gifted local folk-poets, and the improvised verses would be sung by the entire group as a chorus.[59]

The area of Bryan's preaching was constantly being enlarged. Since Andrew Bryan preached to whites as well as blacks, his greatest "catch" in terms of worldly influence may have been in Effingham County, where he converted Major Thomas Polhill and his wife. Polhill was the son of an Episcopal minister, stemming from a church that severely persecuted the Separate Baptists, who carried the gospel to Virginia, the Carolinas, and Georgia. Thomas Polhill energetically assisted Bryan in his land purchases for the church. Also, Polhill attempted to build a Baptist church for blacks on Franklin Square, but the venture failed.[60] In church-building, with God's help, the black ministers and flocks would prove to be the instruments of their own destiny. As newly-imported African slaves were brought into Georgia, Bryan found new work in converting them. Some of these "Africans" became outstanding Christians, and not infrequently held the position of deacons or "householders," the last a term applied to Christians who were requested to serve as the church leaders at various plantations.[61]

Not every white was a generous Henry Sharpe nor a compassionate Jonathan Bryan, although a cruel master was despised by the other squires and gentlemen. However, there were sharp-eyed, even vicious militia and patrol guards, who feared the possibility of an uprising such as that led by Nat Turner in 1831 in Virginia, where fifty-five white residents were murdered. More likely, the patrols were alerted to prevent the kind of slave revolt generated by Gabriel Prosser in 1800, near Richmond, Virginia, and Denmark Vesey in

1822, near Charleston, South Carolina. Both of these slave revolts resulted in mass executions of the leaders of the uprisings.

The patrol system was elaborate, with drums signaling when all blacks had to be behind their own doors, normally 8:00 P.M. in winter and 9:00 P.M. in summer. Any slave even fifteen minutes late in meeting a curfew at night was confined at the guardpost, and if his master did not pay his one-dollar fine in the morning, he would be whipped.[62] Church services were generally limited to the time between sunrise and sunset, and were seldom held at night unless there was a white minister present. For good behavior or meritorious services, masters issued "tickets" or passes for slaves to attend services or to visit another plantation. No slave could be baptized in Georgia without the written permission of his master.[63] Servants attending worship without passes were sometimes seized and sharply beaten by the patrols.

Like the underground church of ancient Rome, the black Christians on various plantations under Bryan, Galphin, and others, cunningly developed a system called the "Society." On each plantation, a black convert was appointed as the "watchman" or "householder" to take charge of the little flock and open and lead the prayer meetings. These sometimes apprehensive believers met at the watchman's small house, or, if the owner or overseer prohibited worship, in the woods or swamps. When a prayer meeting could be gathered during the day or evening, against the wishes of a harsh master, the work gangs would sing the message: "steal away, steal away to Jesus." If the master was not tolerant nor a genuine Christian, the risk was considerable. As the nebulous and growing church met more frequently, at first at Brampton Plantation and later at Savannah, usually every three months for baptism and celebration of the Lord's Supper, those servants with the passes and cypress canoes could paddle to the meeting place to hear Bryan's sermons.[64] In such a manner and place, about 1785, Bryan converted and baptized his brother Sampson Bryan (later to become a deacon) and seventeen others. Many other blacks were saved at this time, but they could not obtain their masters' authorization to be baptized.[65]

Large numbers of Bryan's flock were whipped by the guard patrols, some even while the baptismal services were in progress at the Savannah River, the victims in most cases having failed to obtain tickets or passes from their masters. Then came the day, about 1789-90, when Bryan, his brother deacon Sampson Bryan, and about fifty believers became the targets, and with whips were "inhumanly cut." Local whites feared a plot and, incited by their own clergy, became incensed that Bryan had refused to dissolve his church as ordered. Bryan, with blood dripping to the earth from his deep cuts, lifted both hands to the sky and cried to the Lord. He would not terminate his sacred work nor close the church. Then, turning to his persecutors, he proclaimed: "If you would stop me from preaching, cut off my head! for I am willing not only to be whipped, but would freely suffer death for the cause of the Lord Jesus."[66] Then the meeting house was ordered closed, and fifty persons of the congregation, including Bryan, were locked up in prison.

This outrageous action against a peaceful church congregation astounded and infuriated one sector of the white community. Jonathan Bryan, their white protector, and his influential friends, intervened with the authorities, pleading that the black Baptists were martyrs to evil and prejudice.[67] In the court proceedings that followed, Chief Justice Henry Osbourne, and Justices James Habersham and David Montague in the Inferior Court of Chatham County, ruled in favor of the prison inmates and released them.[68]

Despite his freedom from jail, Bryan was barred by the mayor and council from Savannah and had to petition the city fathers to preach at Yamacraw.[69] Jonathan Bryan, the concerned master, then allowed worship in a barn on his Brampton Plantation, given to the congregation as its church. The church, nevertheless, was watched and spied on by distrustful patrol guards, both at the believers' barn and at their nightly prayer meetings. At the Reverend Andrew Bryan's private house an intruder overheard Bryan praying earnestly for the men who mercilessly whipped him. Shocked by the Holy Spirit with fear and remorse, this white witness reported to his friends on what became the talk of the community, eliciting general sympathy for the black congregation. Permission was then granted by Chief Justice Osbourne for the black church to worship in his jurisdiction any time between sunrise and sunset.[70]

The church had met for two or three years at the Brampton Plantation barn. Some of the flock congregated periodically in the woods at Yamacraw near the Savannah black hamlet of St. Gall and baptized the new converts in the Savannah River. In the period 1788-89 a rough wooden meeting house was built on the property of Edward David at this Yamacraw location. Then, with titles dated 1790 and 1791, notice was made that "Free Andrew" was involved in a land acquisition by gift from Thomas Gibbons, Esquire; this location became the temporary meeting place of the church, Lot 12, bounded by Savannah's Mill and Indian streets.[71] At the Mill Street site a crude shelter for worship was constructed.

This beginning of a black church in Savannah was to be turbulent, for the congregation now numbered in the hundreds and posed a special hazard to some whites, who had observed only recently the departure of a multitude of slaves who had sided and fraternized with the British during the American Revolution. Whites also were not unmindful that in the Low Country at the end of that war, slaves outnumbered white citizens.[72]

Organizing the Colored Church

Notwithstanding the dark clouds, the year 1790 was a high watermark for the Colored Church of Savannah, with its 381 members,[73] for despite the harassment of the church and the oppression of its members by suspicious whites, it would be formally organized, join an association of white Baptist churches, and be granted added protection by the militia commander. Through the intervention of several white friends sympathetic with the goals of Reverend Bryan, the commander of the county militia, Major D. B. Mitchell, on March 19, 1790, issued the following permit to preach on Sundays:

> I do hereby give unto the Said Andrew as Pastor, and to his Elders and Society, my full approbation to meet and perform Divine Worship, in the Meeting-house at Yamacraw, on the Sabbath day, between Sun Rise and Sun Set, so long as they conduct themselves with due decency and order; and that the persons attending thereon have a pass from their masters or Mistresses for that purpose. . . .[74]

The dignity of the Reverend Andrew Bryan and the discipline of his church was demonstrated by their letter in May 1790 to the white Georgia Baptist Association. At that time the Association was meeting ninety miles away at Brier Creek in Burke County. The black church asked for a review of its church's constitution and a confirmation of the ordination of Andrew Bryan, initially performed alone and in disregard of Baptist precedent by Separate Baptist pastor Abraham Marshall of Kiokee.[75] Fortunately, Abraham Marshall in 1790 was the white moderator of the Association, and he dealt with the matter forthrightly.

> There I was alone," he said, "and no other minister within call. I felt it might appear an assumption of episcopal power; yet all things were ripe, and the interesting body of converts was suffering for want of organization and an administrator. The thing wanted doing, and I did it.[76]

Afterwards, from 1790 until 1795, the black Baptist church joined and participated as an active member of the Georgia Association. It also became in 1802 a founding member of the Savannah River Association, an association predominantly white. When the Savannah River Association divided a few years later, the Sunbury Association was formed with a majority of the people from black churches, including Bryan's church.[77] The "Colored Church" of Savannah never joined the largely white Hephzibah (Baptist) Association.[78]

The freeing of a slave involved some strict legal procedures. So, in 1790, legal notice was given that Pastor Bryan had purchased his freedom from William Bryan, son of the benevolent plantation owner Jonathan Bryan. Later, Andrew Bryan would buy the freedom of his wife Hannah and his only daughter.[79] Andrew had passed through the various stages of slave development, probably first as a field worker, then house servant, waiter, coachman, and trusted body servant, and finally a free man.[80] This was exceptional, and not the lot of thousands of slaves.

In 1794 there began the construction of a permanent church structure. Services were continued on Mill Street in Savannah until a small temporary church building, 42 feet by 49 feet, was completed and rolled to the new property on Bryan Street in Oglethorpe Ward. The newest property, Lot 7, was 95 feet by 132 feet, and on it Andrew Bryan built his own small house. The price of the Bryan Street property was thirty pounds sterling, with the deed dated 1793, paid by Andrew Bryan, and then sold as required by law to white trustees.[81]

But nothing could have obscured the joy of the congregation after the completion in 1795 of the "big meeting house." The finished church was a boxy two-story wooden building, adorned only by a few plain windows and surrounded by a wooden fence for privacy. Nothing about it spoke of grandeur, but the exultation that rose from the hearts of its members must have reached to Heaven. It had been built from hand-hewn timbers, hacked from the woods by the believers themselves and then constructed mainly by the men, but on many occasions assisted by women, who held the beams straight or hoisted equipment and tools. This probably was the first black church built in North America solely for Baptist worship.

The problems of obtaining approval for worship and gathering the church together were still to be solved. This church had a far-flung congregation, at least three-fifths of its members meeting mainly at Brampton's barn. Their suffering was reported and received with

The first black Baptist church in North America was erected in Savannah in 1794.

sympathy by sensitive whites.[82] An influential attorney, Lachland McIntosh, then intervened to ask the Savannah authorities in 1795 to grant the church permission to worship in its own church. McIntosh's petition was presented by the Reverend Andrew Bryan to leading citizens in the Savannah community, including its mayor and aldermen. It reads in part:

> . . . The influence of vital religion on the human Heart . . . is to subdue the turbulent passions—promote a spirit of meekness & moderation . . . a resignation to the will of Providence. . . .
>
> . . . as individuals and a Society, they [church members] have been eminent for thier (sic) meek and inoffensive carriage towards the Citizens . . . & obedient behaviour to thier (sic) Masters and Mistresses . . . there are many instances . . . [in Savannah] . . . of bad and evil disposed Negroes & Slaves . . . but since thier (sic) becoming members of Andrew's Society [they have become] the most valuable & trusty slaves thier (sic) Masters have in thier (sic) possession. . . . The desire they have to assemble is to get good, to become better slaves & better Christians—Your petitioners therefore humbly pray that a society of Christians . . . may no longer be deprived of the privilege of worshiping the God of thier (sic) existance, according to the dictates of their consciences and in thier (sic) own way. . . .

The Campbellite Controversy

The approval to worship was received with rejoicing in 1796 from the pulpit. The church would remain unified until 1832, long after the death of Leile and Andrew Bryan, until white evangelist Alexander Campbell arrived in Savannah to disturb the black and white Baptist believers with his doctrines. Campbell stemmed from Presbyterian stock and was only a transient Baptist, and his movement would do the Baptists much harm and evolve into the formation of the denomination of the Disciples of Christ. He was anti-missionary, anti-Sunday School, anti-institutional, and believed that salvation was completed only with baptism, the so-called heresy of baptismal regeneration.[83] The Campbellite "heresy" would split the historic black church in Savannah in 1833, resulting in the majority of the church being "dissolved" by the Sunbury Association, along with their pastor Andrew Marshall. Those blacks not joining the so-called heresy numbered 132 and were largely the males led by Deacon Adam Arguile Johnson; they remained on the property at Bryan Street and then were given the original building purchased in 1790 by the Reverend Andrew Bryan.[84] This body was organized as the Third Baptist Church, an affiliate of the white church. Later this congregation became the First Bryan Baptist Church. The Reverend Andrew Marshall was partially "silenced" by the Sunbury Association. He and his followers withdrew from Bryan Street eventually and moved to Franklin Square, where the present First African Baptist Church began its separate existence. However, the First African was far-sighted enough to purchase the large wooden church vacated by the white Baptist church. A reconciliation was effected in 1837 between Deacon Johnson and Andrew Marshall,[85] which resulted in Marshall and the First African Baptist Church receiving authorization by the Sunbury Baptist Association to resume normal church activities, although Marshall throughout the alienation quietly kept most of his flock together through prayer circles and informal meetings.

The influence of Andrew Bryan on his communicants and even on white Savannah was substantial. He was a strict disciplinarian, visiting those members who were absent from church services as well as the sick. The owners of unruly slaves often called on him to correct a dangerous or unbending servant. This was far better than a lashing that cut to the muscle, or a public sale that split a wife and children from the husband and father. Bryan's fatherly admonitions, along with a certain severity meted out to the unwise, often restored a bad servant to a course of civility and restraint.[86]

There was evoked genuine respect, and even fear, when he warned a church member of the possibility of removal of Christian privileges and even excommunication: The "colored church" had captured the hearts of the blacks and to be excluded from the service was a disaster, bringing the miscreants to the gateway of hell itself. Bryan was dominant in his community and exercised a commanding presence in the slave world into which he was born.

During baptisms old Bryan would sit in a horse-pulled two-wheeled gig, while younger preachers did the more arduous work. In his advanced years, he relied more and more on ministers Evans Grate and his nephew Andrew Cox Marshall, both of them members of the Second Colored Church.[87] At the baptism, he would give the charge to the candidates, extend the right hand of fellowship, and welcome the newly-baptized to the Lord's Table.[88]

It is fortunate that there is a vivid description of Bryan by his friend Dr. Henry Holcombe, depicting his sunset years, but striking in its detail:

> His fleecy and well-set locks have been bleached by eighty winters; and dressed like a bishop of London, he rides, moderately corpulent in his chair, and, with manly features of jetty hue, fills any person to whom he gracefully bows with pleasure and veneration, by displaying in smiles even rows of natural teeth white as ivory, and a pair of fine black eyes sparkling with intelligence, benevolence and joy.[89]

Andrew Bryan died on October 6, 1812, believed to be ninety-six years old. His funeral became almost a state affair, with five thousand people mourning his death, and the ceremonies were attended by white Baptist, Presbyterian, and Episcopalian ministers and dignitaries. He was interred at the black cemetery in Troup Ward, Habersham Street, but his remains were removed later to Laurel Grove Cemetery.[90] Historian Benedict reflecting on his death stated:

> This son of Africa, after suffering inexpressible persecutions in the cause of his divine Master, was at length permitted to discharge the duties of the ministry among his colored friends in peace and quiet; hundreds of whom through his instrumentality were brought to the knowledge of the truth, as it is in Jesus.[91]

Simms saw a parallel between Bryan and "the history of Moses and the Israelites," because it was "perhaps the first time in the history of the State that one of this despised race commanded the respect of a community and an acknowledgment that in the negro character, even under the conditions of slavery there is true manhood and virtue developed by Christianity."[92]

The final benediction, years later, was inscribed in marble and placed beside the grave, as probably influenced by his nephew Andrew Cox Marshall:

> Sacred to the memory of Andrew Bryan, pastor of the First Colored Baptist Church in Savannah. God was pleased to lay his honor near his heart, and so impressed the worth and weight of souls upon his mind, that he was constrained to preach the gospel to a dying world, particularly to the sable sons of Africa. Though he labored under many disadvantages, yet taught in the school of Christ, he was able to bring new and old out of the treasury, and he has done more good among the poor slaves than all the learned doctors in America.
>
> He was imprisoned for the gospel and without ceremony was severely whipped, but while under the lash he told his persecutors, he rejoiced not only to be whipped, but he was willing to suffer death for the cause of Christ. He continued to preach the gospel until Oct. 6th, 1812. He was supposed to be ninety-six years of age. His remains were interred with peculiar respect. An address was delivered by Revs. Mr. Johnson, Dr. Kollock, Thomas Williams, and Henry Cunningham. He was an honor to human nature, an ornament to religion and a friend to mankind. His memory is still precious in the mind of the living.[93]

Andrew Marshall Leads the Church

After the death of Andrew Bryan, his nephew, Pastor Andrew C. Marshall, would endure travails but lead the First African Church to an astonishing growth. Marshall (1755-1856) was a former slave (one of 530 free blacks in Savannah in 1810), and although he could not write, he learned to read, acquired a slave and other substantial assets, and lived in a brick house. He worked tirelessly to convert his people to Christ, baptizing about thirty-eight hundred persons, and, in return, was greatly loved. During his career as a drayman and preacher, he narrowly escaped a brutal whipping, when he was accused of purchasing stolen bricks to build his house. However, he was fortunate in having an influential white friend, Mr. Richard Richardson, who had purchased Marshall's freedom for two hundred dollars[94] so that he could preach. In order to satisfy the letter of the law, Marshall got a few restrained strokes during the ritual flogging. However, Richardson and his white friends stood by to see that the constable, as ordered, should not draw blood or scratch Marshall's skin.[95]

The real crisis for Andrew Marshall would originate, as referenced, in 1832, with his dabbling in the doctrines of Alexander Campbell[96] that resulted in the split in the Savannah church. The chief alarm was manifested in the white churches that guided the black believers, for every black church had white ministers present during the services.[97] Campbell was teaching doctrines that would cause the loss of many Baptist churches in Kentucky and Indiana. The turmoil regarding the doctrinal issues produced in the short run an excommunicated scattered church in Savannah under Marshall, and an orthodox remnant under Deacon Adam Johnson that continued to worship at Bryan Street with the blessings of the white Baptists and the Sunbury Association.[98] Marshall, at last, would disavow the Campbellite "heresy," and a public reconciliation would occur between Marshall and Johnson

Before his church was admitted again to the Sunbury Association in 1837, Marshall was described as a mistaken old man, "struggling to extricate himself from the dilemma in which he had placed himself and people, panting to use that great power he felt moving within his heart, and like a caged eagle, beating itself against the bars of the cage."[99] However, the restored 1,810-member First African Baptist Church (now at Franklin Square and in the old white Baptist Church, which had been purchased for fifteen hundred dollars)[100] and the First Bryan Baptist Church would follow their separate destinies, each claiming to be the original church.

Leile in Jamaica

In order to describe the development of the black church established by Leile in Savannah, and to tell the story of its dedicated long-lived second pastor, Andrew Bryan, we have only hinted at the success in Jamaica of the Trailblazer, that first black missionary George Leile.

Leile landed at Kingston, Jamaica, owing seven hundred dollars to Colonel Kirkland for the passage of himself and his family. His occupation was that of farmer and produce hauler in support of a wife and eventually four children.[101] He was fortunate once more in the patronage of a fine master, this time the British officer Kirkland, who obtained work for him as a drayman for the governor of Jamaica, General Campbell. His duties were performed so efficiently, that surprisingly, after about two years, in 1783-84, he was granted papers that made him a free man once more.[102]

Leile did not describe his family, or much about himself in his correspondence from Jamaica. Hardly anything is known about his family, except their ages and sex.[103] However, in a letter from Jamaica in 1791 to the Baptist preacher and editor, Dr. John Rippon, in London, he wrote: "I cannot tell what is my age, as I have no account of the time of my birth [in Virginia]; but I suppose I am about 40 years old. I have a wife and four children," their ages: 19 (son), 17 (son), 14 (son), and 11 (daughter). He remained a faithful Particular Baptist and preached its doctrines of election (Calvinistic), redemption through Christ, and the promise of salvation to all who would endure.[104] He was diplomatic in handling men and enjoyed reading good literature. And as he aged, he was given the love of the slaves and the profound respect and admiration of their masters.

The departure of many blacks from Georgia after the Revolution spread the Baptist message to several islands in the Caribbean. Mr.

Amos, a black preacher, left Savannah during the exodus for New Providence, Bahama Islands, and the British West Indies, where he established a vigorous Baptist church. Leile, with four men from the American colonies, founded in 1784 the first black Baptist church in Jamaica. But the difficulties that assailed the Separate Baptists in America oppressed him on the island. His powerful effective preaching that was winning the hearts of black slaves aroused the stiff opposition of the Anglican Church.[105] His meetings were frequently interrupted and he was cruelly persecuted. Then Pastor Leile stood in grave peril. He was imprisoned with others and charged with preaching sedition, an offense that bore the death penalty. Leile, standing before the court, barely escaped the death penalty, but another preacher-companion was hanged.[106]

This spiritual Trailblazer, with the aid of people of great influence, was able to build a permanent edifice for the First Baptist Church of Jamaica. The chief supporter of the church was Steven A. Cook, a member of the Jamaican Assembly who solicited funds in England.[107] As Leile reflected on his church work, through correspondence to Dr. Rippon in London:

> There is no Baptist Church in this country [Jamaica] but ours. We have purchased a piece of land at the east end of Kingston containing three acres for the sum of Pounds 155, currency, and on it have begun a meeting house [1791], 57 feet in length by 37 in breadth — Several gentlemen, members of the House of Assembly, and other gentlemen, have subscribed towards the building about Pounds 40.—And Rev. Sir, we think the Lord has put it in the power of the Baptist Societies in England to help and assist us in completing this building—the greatest undertaking—in this country for the bringing of souls from darkness into the light of the gospel. . . ."[108]

Thus, Leile led a flourishing church, baptized some converts that migrated from Georgia, and guided its expansion until it became a congregation that numbered in the hundreds.[109] With the assistance of deacons and elders, the church work was extended far into the rural districts. In 1791 Leile wrote that he had baptized in his ministry about five hundred persons. In all of his activities, he was industrious and practical.[110]

Summary

Leile in 1777 organized on Brampton Plantation, Georgia, the first permanent black Baptist church in America and, indirectly, became the founding father of three churches in Savannah. He converted Andrew Bryan, who led the church through its turbulent early stages from Brampton Plantation to Yamacraw Village, Savannah. Bryan then strengthened the church by preaching along the Savannah River. However, the supreme achievements of Bryan may have been the acquiring of legitimacy for the slave society to operate as an all-black church within the (Baptist) Sunbury Association and in the confines of Savannah. Then the congregation to its glory built with its own hands a plain two-story Baptist edifice, the first black church structure in America.

The gifted Andrew Marshall, the congregation's third pastor, another heir of George Leile, despite the schism Marshall created, gathered some 2,795 members by 1831 to the fellowship from Savannah and the nearby plantations.[111] After nearly four years of isolation and humiliation, about 1857, the majority of the congregation under Marshall would occupy a fine wooden church on Franklin Square that had been vacated by the Savannah white Baptists. The congregation would be restored to the Association, and take the proud name of the First African Baptist Church. The First Bryan Baptist Church, stemming from a minority that remained steadfast to Baptist doctrine and practice, believes that it is the "true" church and was dealt an unfair blow on the matter of heritage when the state Missionary Baptist Convention of Georgia ruled in 1888 that First African was the mother church and First Bryan its daughter church.[112] However, the First Bryan Church acknowledges also that its existence stems from that original, spirit-filled and amazing pioneer, George Leile, the black Tory Baptist preacher.

There are many firsts that accrue to George Leile. He was the first ordained black Baptist preacher in America. He or his converts began Baptist work near Augusta, Georgia, in Savannah, in Nova Scotia, and Sierra Leone. He was the first black missionary and the first Baptist preacher of African descent to do mission work abroad. His activities in the mission field in Jamaica precede by fifteen or more years the foreign mission work of Presbyterian David Livingstone and Baptists Robert Morrison, and Robert Moffatt, and all their illustrious contemporaries. He was the first black clergyman to send missionaries back to Africa, the land of his ancestors, and in 1842 more than fifty missionaries were sent from Jamaica to Africa, largely the result of his work.[113] This great black saint and Trailblazer is scarcely known, but his place in history is among the greatest religious figures of Christendom.

William Carey Translating the Scriptures into Sanskrit
at Serampore, India

Chapter 10

William Carey
(1761-1834)

Father of Modern Missions

The English Baptist cobbler and preacher William Carey is the "Founding Father" of modern Christian missions. It is a present-day myth, sometimes promulgated even at prestigious universities, that Christian missionaries played a leading role in destroying some of the world's finest civilizations, including the Aztec, Polynesian, Chinese (Manchu), and Indian (Mogul). In most cases, those civilizations had reached their zenith when Christian missionaries appeared, as was the case in India, and were toppling from their own imperfections and rigidity.

The Carey that we know endured great hardships and deprivations, including the death of his first wife Dorothy and a child Peter, in separating himself for life from England and using his considerable talents in Asia for the enlightenment and salvation of the Indian people. He embraced the languages of India, including Sanskrit and Hindi, and almost certainly contributed to the viability of Indian culture by translating portions of the Scripture into thirty-four Indian languages.

Despite modern awe for the splendor of Hindu culture and civilization and the grandeur and pomp of the Muslim-dominated empire of the Moguls (that began in 1526 with Baber of Kabul and subsided with British rule in the nineteenth century)[,1] there were intolerable flaws in those cultures, including near-starvation for the masses. Only enlightenment from abroad and the Christian light could avail, although some might see in this an advocacy of Western imperialism. Carey, who founded Serampore College, threw his strength against the dark side of the culture, including widow-burning (suttee), the murder of infants, and the cruelty of the entrenched caste system. This simple man, who gave all tribute to Jesus Christ for his achievements in this foreign post, was the embodiment of the Christian consumed by a heavenly fire.

William Carey, despite his fertile career, was not the first Baptist foreign missionary laboring in the late 1700s. The black ex-slave George Leile (Lisle), in fleeing colonial America, established the Baptist faith in Jamaica at the end of the American Revolution. He probably influenced the flow of black missionaries to Africa after 1815, as sponsored by the African Baptist Missionary Society.[2]

Carey's most productive work proceeded in 1800 at Serampore, India. His career and his supporting organization, the British Missionary Society, provided inspiration to hundreds of missionaries of various denominations, which in turn led to the converting of hundreds of thousands of non-Christians on every continent. It is not surprising that a great host of people believe that Carey, who struggled against great odds, is the greatest Christian missionary of the modern period.

In the first half of the eighteenth century, there occurred a cataclysmic decline in the evangelical fervor in England that threatened both the General Baptists and the Particular Baptists, the latter the sponsoring body of Carey. The General Baptists, Arminian in theology, drew support from the poorer classes and were led by a largely-uneducated clergy, themselves sapped by the requirements to undertake both religious activities and secular work to support themselves. The General Baptists fell prey but did not finally succumb to Unitarian Christology and extreme liberalism, as proclaimed by Joseph Priestly and Matthew Caffyn. However, through the ministry of Dan Taylor, a former-Methodist-turned-Baptist, the "New Connection" movement of 1770 brought about a temporary conservative reaction. Taylor's energetic, inspired preaching and organization probably saved the General Baptists from extinction. However, despite the infusion of sound doctrine by Taylor, the General Baptists at the end of the eighteenth century faced obliteration as their leading revivalist leaders died.[3]

The death-lure for the Particular Baptists, long aligned with the doctrines of John Calvin (the group to which William Carey was attached) was the adverse influence of Hyper-Calvinism. The doctrine of Hyper-Calvinism (Antinomianism) could go so far as to kill all interest in evangelism. The extreme Calvinist argument was that God would save whom He would save or even frustrate efforts to ward off sin. The doctrine maintained that the "Saved" under all circumstances were doing only what God willed them to do. The chief philosophers of this bizarre ultra-Calvinism were Tobias Crisp, an Anglican, and a Baptist, John Gill, father of "Gillism."

Baptists further were handicapped in eighteenth-century England by legal expulsion from the major English universities. Also, the saints that had led the Particular Baptists through their trials in the eighteenth century had either retired or were dead: Hanserd Knollys, Thomas Collier, William Kiffin, Benjamin Keach, and Thomas Grantham. These great men, who had provided a reasonable balance between Calvinism and evangelism, had built beautiful churches, some with "baptisterions" for total immersion, and written confessions of faith. The positive message of these pioneers was replaced in the first fifty years of the eighteenth century by a cold retrograde philosophy, creating "the glacial epoch in English Baptist history."[4] Particular Baptist churches in England fell in number from 220 (1715) to 146 (1750) and General Baptist churches diminished from 146 (1715) to 65 (1750). In the case of the Particular Baptists, the decline was largely attributable to the doctrine of Hyper-Calvinism.[5]

However, in this dismal period, new trends would appear and change the course of Baptist history. John and Charles Wesley, from a wealthy and influential high-church Anglican family, helped reverse the rationalist surge and created a broad evangelistic movement in England and America. Their contemporary Andrew Fuller, perhaps the greatest English Baptist theologian, launched a more evangelical form of Calvinism, known today as "Fullerism." Meanwhile, in colonial America there was born an immense revival movement, the First Great Awakening, whose optimism was coupled to the vastness and almost limitless possibilities of a new nation. In the midst of the Particular Baptist recovery in England, William Carey in 1792 inspired the formation of the Baptist Missionary Society.[6]

His Early Life

Carey was born in 1761 in Paulerspury, eleven miles south of Northampton. As the son of a village schoolmaster and parish clerk, he was raised in the traditions of the Church of England. His interest was in gardening, but his sensitive skin and susceptibility to sun poisoning largely compelled him to work indoors. An early influence was his soldier uncle, Peter Carey, who regaled his nephew with intriguing tales of his life in Canada. William Carey also read with relish *Captain Cook's Voyages*, and his comrades appropriately nicknamed this mesmerized young man "Columbus." He also became acquainted with *Guthrie's Geographical Grammar* and memorized *Dyche's Latin Vocabulary*.[7]

When Carey was age fourteen, he was apprenticed to a cobbler, Clarke Nichols, in the neighboring village of Piddington. His fellow worker, senior apprentice John Warr, a religious Dissenter, persuaded Carey to attend a worship service, during which a Baptist minister preached the sermon. In 1779, at age eighteen, young Carey accepted Jesus as his Savior and attended the Hackleton Independent Church, but he did not immediately become baptized. However, Carey was persuaded to become a Baptist through his reading of the Scriptures, the preaching of a Particular Baptist minister, the Reverend John Hornsey,[8] and a study of Robert Hall's treatise, "Help to Zion's Travelers." Carey was baptized in the River Nen by the young

Baptist preacher John Ryland of Northampton on October 5, 1783. Ryland wrote in his diary, "Baptized today poor journeyman shoe cobbler."[9]

Carey began his faltering steps into adult life. Far from presenting a distinguished image, he was ineffectual in his speech, average to slight in build, prematurely bald, and sometimes wore on his head a poorly-fitted red wig. In 1781 he married Dorothy Plackett, more than five years his senior, from a well-known Puritan family, but a girl so ignorant that she could not sign her name. Dorothy possessed a strong will and would fiercely resist Carey's future mission trip to India.[10] While a member of the Hackleton congregation, Carey ministered as lay leader at Earls Barton and Paulerspury.[11]

Although he was persuaded that God wanted him to preach, his efforts to others appeared almost ludicrous. In 1785 he was discomfited by the church he attended at Olney, under Baptist pastor John Sutcliff. Carey's preaching was so unpolished and poorly constructed that Olney's parishioners refused to recommend him for ordination. One of his sermons was described as being "as weak and crude as anything ever called a sermon." Persistent in his quest, Carey pestered the reluctant church until in August 1786 it recommended that he be ordained to "preach wherever God in his providence might call him," the church bargaining perhaps that God might want to send him anywhere but to Olney. Miss Tressler, a leading church member, was appointed by the Baptist church to solicit church members for money to buy Carey an appropriate black suit for ordination. Later, Carey was called to become the pastor of the church at Moulton.[12]

At Moulton he would live four and one-half years, baptize his wife Dorothy, and witness the birth of three sons. In disregard for the Anglican Church practice of utilizing state-paid priests, Baptist pastors of this epoch, including Carey, sought or developed gainful employment. Carey continued his occupation as shoemaker. After Carey became a journeyman cobblerr (subordinate to his future brother-in-law, Thomas Old of Hackleton), kindly master Old suddenly died. Then after paying Mrs. Old for the time remaining for his training, Carey embarked on work for himself. Carey taught at a small school he began at Piddington and in other ways scrounged with his scant earnings to make a living.[13] His family knew poverty well and on occasion may have known hunger.

The shoemaker-minister had an extraordinary thirst for knowledge. He assiduously studied, with his books propped up close to the cobbler's bench. As Carey said of himself, "Give me credit for diligence and you will do me justice. Anything more will be untrue. But I can plod and persevere. To do this I owe everything."[14] This is an incredibly modest statement by a tenacious Christian saint, whose achievements would astound the world.

The most remarkable facet of Carey was his facility for learning languages. He mastered Latin, ancient Greek (for translating the New Testament), and, by age twenty, ancient Hebrew (for translating the Old Testament), and then Dutch, French, and Italian. In later years, and almost incomprehensibly, he would learn Sanskrit, Bengali, Hindi, Oriya, Marathi, Assamese, Punjabi, Pashot, Kashmiri, Telegu, and Konkani.[15] Carey did not attribute his success in language to brilliance, rather giving the credit to doggedness in his studies.[16] In this self-assessment, he was almost certainly in error. In linguistics, the man was a genius.

In teaching his geography classes at Piddington, Carey often used a globe made of leather, with the continents tinted in different colors, that he had fashioned in his cobbler's shop. As he viewed the miniature world he would become concerned about the ignorance of the world concerning Christ; then he would say to himself, as if in reproach: "Pagan! Pagan!" The conversion of the planet became his obsession.[17] On a larger world map he had made for himself on paper, he marked out information in each area on population, language, customs, and religion.[18]

When he had no preaching assignments on Sunday, Carey tramped many miles to Olney to hear the Reverend Thomas Scott. Scott was an evangelically-minded Anglican minister. Carey later wrote, "If there be any thing of the work of God in my soul, I owe much of it to Mr. Scott's preaching." Scott said in return that Carey would prove to be "no ordinary character."[19]

The most important men in Carey's pre-missionary life were Dr. John Ryland the younger, who baptized him; Andrew Fuller, Sr., who modified stifling Calvinism into a theology that accepted evangelism and missionary ventures; and perhaps, in a personal way, the kindly shoe merchant Gotch. After Carey had worked a few month's at Moulton, Gotch, who was a deacon in Andrew Fuller's Church said, "Let me see, Mr. Carey, how much do you earn a week by your shoemaking?" "About nine or ten shillings, sir," answered Carey. Then Gotch said, "Well now, I've a secret for you. I don't mean you to spoil any more of my leather, but get on as fast as you can with your Latin, Hebrew and Greek and I'll allow you from my private purse weekly ten shillings."[20] In a struggling society in the middle of the surges and problems of the Industrial Revolution, this was extraordinary generosity. But Gotch could see that his fellow-Christian Carey had abilities far removed from cobbling shoes, that could unlock God's mysteries to mankind.

The Struggle for Mission Support

In a mysterious way, certainly fueled by his studies of the Bible, his interest in languages, and the romantic embellished tales of adventures and traders, Carey became a missions enthusiast. However, in the philosophy of missions, he was a Trailblazer breasting a strong tide. As has been stated, the Regular Baptists of England, of which he was a member, were verging toward extinction because of the suffocating doctrine of Hyper-Calvinism, which deadened evangelical initiatives.

Fortunately, there were theologians of that time who challenged the rigid Calvinist assumptions. In 1752 Particular Baptist pastor Alvery Jackson of Yorkshire wrote a book discrediting extreme Calvinism. Also, the Reverend Abraham Booth of Nottinghamshire migrated from the General Baptists (Arminian in doctrine) to the

Particular Baptists and their Calvinist views. But in his book *The Reign of Grace* (1768), he called on Christians to evangelize sinners and those "ready to perish."[21] Booth was active in the missionary society of the 1790s, the founding of the Itinerant Society in 1797, and was one of the principals involved in the creation of Stepney College. Booth, although not formally educated, was a careful student of the Scriptures.[22] Then another shot against Antinomianism (Hyper-Calvinism) was fired by the Northamptonshire (Baptist) Association in a 1770 circular letter: ". . . every soul that comes to Christ to be saved from hell and sin by him, is to be encouraged— The coming soul need not fear that he is not elected."[23] But it was mainly the Reverend Andrew Fuller's preaching and his book *The Gospel Worthy of All-Acceptation* (1785) that turned the tide against Hyper-Calvinism and made possible the missionary efforts of William Carey.

Carey's next step was to publicly express his irrepressible desires to evangelize the world. As a minister, he and a colleague in 1787 were asked by Dr. John Ryland the elder to suggest topics of discussion for the Ministers Fraternal of the Northampton Particular Baptist Association. After much hesitation, Carey gave this theme: "Whether the command given to the apostles to preach the Gospel to all nations was not binding on all succeeding ministers to the end of the world." This was audacious, and Dr. Ryland frowned and then sprang to his feet. "Young man, sit down, sit down. You're an enthusiast [extremist]. When God pleases to convert the heathen, he'll do it without consulting you or me. Besides, sir, can you preach in Arabic, in Persian, in Hindustani, in Bengali? There must first be another Pentecostal gift of tongues."[24]

Momentarily stunned by the harsh retort, Carey was able to regain composure and strive once again to develop support for missions. In 1789 he left Moulton for Harvey Lane Chapel in Leicester, not an easy pastorate, for drunkenness was rife among its members and it became necessary to totally reorganize the Chapel.[25] At Leicester, in 1792, he wrote a remarkable eighty-seven-page book on missions: *An Enquiry into the Obligation of Christians to Use Means for the Conversion of the Heathen.*[26] This was no ordinary book, for it became the charter of the modern missionary movement, alluding to the successful mission work of Moravians and others. It remains a source book for every student of missions. A prominent Christian layman from Birmingham contributed ten pounds towards the publishing costs.[27]

Then, in May 1792, the former stumbling, almost incoherent churchman preached before the Baptist association meeting at Nottingham. His sermon produced tears in the congregation and, in time, electrified others throughout the world. His text was from Isaiah 54: 2: "Enlarge the place of thy tent, and let them stretch forth the curtains of thine habitations. Spare not, lengthen thy cords, and strengthen thy stakes; for those shalt break forth on the right hand and on the left; and Thy seed shall inherit the Gentiles, and make the desolate cities to be inhabited. Fear not." Carey's sermon had only two points: first, expect great things from God, and, second, attempt great things for God. This was the "deathless sermon" and the occasion was a pivotal point in Baptist history.[28]

The inspiring challenge had emotionally touched the messengers attending the meeting. Still, the Reverend Andrew Fuller, as the presiding official, had done nothing to initiate unified action to support missions. The next morning, when the conference was to end, William Carey in desperation seized the arm of Fuller and pled: "Is there nothing again to be done, Sir?" Then, Fuller the Calvinist, overcome with emotion, surrendered to the directives of his Lord, and led the assembly in creating the practical means to sustain a missions enterprise. The final resolution of the Baptist association read: "That against the next meeting of ministers at Kettering a plan should be made for the forming of a society for propagating the Gospel among the heathen."[29] As a consequence, fourteen persons met on October 2, 1792, at the home of widow Martha Wallace in Kettering, an active member of Fuller's church. This group voted, after prayer, to form the Particular Baptist Society for the Propagation of the Gospel among the Heathen," popularly known as the Baptist Missionary Society, or BMS. Immediately the Society collected 13 pounds, 2 shillings, and 6 pence, (about $58.30),[30] which sum was deposited in Fuller's snuffbox. Fuller was elected secretary and would give expert leadership and counsel for twenty-two years.[31] Carey was too poor at this time even to make a donation. The Executive Committee was composed of Dr. John Ryland the younger, Andrew Fuller, Reynold Hogg, John Sutcliff (the oldest of the group at age forty) and Carey.

The Baptist Missionary Society, nervous and fragile, with London churches unenthusiastic, began as an undertaking of a few Baptist churches in England's Midlands, but it still ventured to appoint its first missionary. However, this was not to be Carey. The appointee was an impossible blunderer, John Thomas, M.D., who after travel to India would in a few months waste a year's resources set aside by BMS for its missions support. As a ship's surgeon, earnest Christian, and licensed Baptist minister, with the gift of speaking Bengali, Thomas appeared to be an ideal choice as missionary. A committee reviewed Thomas's application on January 9, 1793, and disregarded his foot injury and his account of a heavy personal indebtedness of nearly five hundred pounds, and commissioned him to go as a missionary. Thomas desired an associate to accompany him, so Carey volunteered, and both men were charged together to go "to the East Indies preaching the gospel to the heathen." Fuller is reported to have said, "There is a gold mine in India but it seems almost as deep as the centre of the earth—who will venture to explore it?" Carey replied, "I will venture to go down but remember that you Fuller, Sutcliffe and Ryland must hold the ropes."[32]

The date of sailing for India was set before Carey's wife knew the details. She had three small children and was expecting another. Dorothy, a loving wife and mother, flatly refused to leave the Midlands for sultry India. Possibly, in five generations, no members of her family had ventured even forty miles beyond her birthplace. At times, she would think that Carey in his religious zeal may have become insane. Then William Carey, in desperation, went to join the transporting vessel with his oldest child, eight-year-old Felix, but the departure plans were changed. Even Carey's father was disturbed, and exclaimed, "Is William mad?"

Arrangements had been made to sail on the *Earl of Oxford*, on which Thomas had served as surgeon. The French Revolution was in progress and England was in a state of alert,[33] while Spain in 1793 joined an alliance with England and attacked France. The ship, meanwhile, had to wait at the Isle of Wight for a military convoy. On board was Carey and his son Felix and Thomas and his wife and daughter.[34] At the Isle of Wight, a letter from Dorothy informed Carey that his wife had given birth to a son Jabez, meaning Sorrowful. Dorothy asked about Carey's state of mind. He replied:

It is much as when I left you. If I had all the world, I would freely give it all to have you and my dear children with me, but the sense of duty is so strong as to overpower all other considerations; I could not turn back without guilt on my soul. . . . Trust in God. . . . Be assured I love you most affectionately.[35]

The powerful East India Company, organized in 1600, had a monopoly on trade with India and represented British authority there. This was no ordinary "company," for at its disposal it had its own private armies and navies and negotiated treaties with sultans and maharajahs. The ship's captain was warned by the India House in London that one of his passengers had no permit, and if this passenger was ejected by the authorities, the captain would lose his command. The result was that Mrs. Thomas and the daughter sailed away to India on board the *Earl of Oxford*, while Carey and Thomas found themselves forced to disembark.

However, with his maritime connections, Thomas found out that a Danish ship, *Kron Princessa Maria*, was surreptitiously sailing from Copenhagen to Calcutta and would lie off Dover within five days. Several unoccupied ship berths would go for 100 pounds for adults and 50 pounds for children. The little party was drastically short of funds, with only 150 pounds sterling returned by the captain of the

Earl of Oxford, and they now hoped to raise more. Carey also urgently wanted to visit his wife and try once more to gain her support for the India venture. After riding the stagecoach all night to Northampton and walking to Piddington, Thomas and Carey could not shake the determination of Dorothy to stay. Then a half-mile away, while exiting the Piddington area, Thomas turned around in the road and resolutely decided to confront Dorothy once more. Carey protested: "Well, do as you think proper, but I think we are losing time." When these pioneer Baptist missionaries reached the cottage, Thomas warned Mrs. Carey that her decision meant that "the family would be dispersed and divided, perhaps for ever," and that "she would repent of it as long as she lived."[36] This somber thought broke her resistance, and Dorothy agreed to sail if her sister Katherine Plackett would accompany her. After prayer about the decision, the plucky sister agreed to go to the end of the world.

This augmentation of the travel party by two women and four children increased the fare to seven hundred pounds. Warm-hearted Thomas worked out a scheme in which the steamship company, Smith and Company, would settle for three hundred pounds, provided that he and Katherine Plackett would travel as attendants, living and eating with the servants on the ship. The Careys, on the other hand, would have regular accommodations on the *Kron Princessa Maria*.[37] However, it was not finally necessary for Thomas and Katherine to become servants on the ship, for the English-born Captain Christmas invited the entire missionary group to live in good quarters and eat at the captain's table. The voyage, with strong contrary winds during the last month, took five months and the journey ended on 11 November 1793.[38]

Even as the party approached Calcutta via the Hooghly River on the northeast coast of India, Thomas gave lessons to Carey in Bengali, the language of the region. During the tedious trip, Thomas and Carey translated in crude fashion the book of Genesis. Carey wrote in his journal:

I am very desirous that my children may pursue the same works and now intend to bring up one in the study of Sanscrit, and another of Persian. O May God give them grace to fit them for the work![39]

Carey in India

The first six years of Carey's missionary life in India, 1794-1800, would be hard, disappointing, and a stiff learning experience. There would be multitudes who would not know Christ, with two hundred thousand prospects in Calcutta and twenty-five million in Bengal. But these hordes were trapped in a rigid caste system that produced persecution and even death for those who attempted to leave the traditional Hindu religion, or the other great faith, Islam. There would be some good counsel from Thomas's protegé Ram Ram Basu, the Christian language teacher and pundit. But it would be seven years before Carey would baptize his first convert, the carpenter Krishna Pal.[40]

John Thomas hastily sold the provisions reserved for the support of the missionaries for their first year. Then he recklessly spent their little treasury without consulting anyone. In three weeks, the total resources for the missions, valued at less than 150 pounds, were gone. Thomas then established his practice as a physician in Calcutta, which culminated in a life of relative luxury with many servants.

It is difficult to imagine that Carey did not explode over Thomas's profligacy. In Carey's journal are these gloomy words: "I am in a strange land alone, no Christian friends, a large family, and nothing to supply their wants."[41] Carey urgently was obliged to borrow money at a high rate of interest to travel to his mission station. Fortunately, he was able to secure free rent for three years on a tract of land at the village of Deharta (Debhetta) in the Sunderbuns. This village would be Carey's headquarters and a source of subsistence for his family and Christian nurture to his mission contacts, until the advent of the nineteenth century. His station was in a tiger-infested jungle area of the Ganges delta, southeast of Calcutta, that in 1794 was reachable only by three days of boat travel.[42]

Carey's first obligation was to provide food for his family. This he did by becoming at various times a planter, a manager for an indigo factory, and a professor at a new college. Although he was criticized for his self-support by the Baptist Missionary Society, which was sending him more advice than money, he was allowed to continue his lay work. Carey reported, "That after his family had obtained a bare allowance, his whole income goes for the purpose of the Gospel in supporting persons to assist in the translation of the scripture, in writing out copies of it and in teaching in school." During his tenure in India, Carey generously donated forty-six thousand British pounds to the furtherance of missions.[43]

The preaching from Deharta was frequent but the fruit was almost nonexistent. At first, the barrier was language, with Carey anxiously seeking to master Bengali and commence a translation of the Scriptures. However, the impediment was basically the caste system. Privileged Indians were born into one of the three "twice-born" castes: (1) Brahman (priest), (2) Kshatriya (warrior), or (3) Vaisya (merchant). These were twenty percent of the population—the educated, wealthy element, with special privileges in religion, economics, and government. The Sudra (servant) caste was comprised of the "once-born" workers that comprised fifty percent of the people. History scholars generally agree that caste (meaning Varna or color) was established in the early historical period, over a thousand years before, by the light-skinned Indo-Aryan conquerors (who took unto themselves the three highest castes) and conferred the lower caste structure (Sudra) on the conquered darker people. These castes fixed a person's employment for life, determined the rank of one's bride or groom, established how each person would be treated under the justice system, and in religion indicated what temples the casteholder would be allowed to enter. Even lower in the hierarchy, comprising thirty percent of the people, were the Non-Hindus and

Harijans (untouchables) who carried manure and handled cadavers and dead animals. It has been estimated that there were more than three thousand caste subdivisions, each of them cells imposing conformity, restrictions, and discipline.[44]

Then there was the question of Carey's wife Dorothy. She had not been insane before arriving in India, only miserable at leaving her English roots and being forced to struggle to feed and clothe her husband and four children on practically nothing. The jungle heat and humidity, the uncertainty, and the death of a five-year-old child in 1799 produced in her a depression and then insanity, which forced her to be locked in a padded room for her last thirteen years. Mercifully she died in 1807, a tragic reminder of the price missionaries often pay for their commitment.[45]

Then there were the barriers imposed by the British East Indies Company. This was a powerful trading company appointed by the king and Parliament, although it was the *de facto* government over a great part of India. The monopoly given to the East India Company for the sale of tea to the American colonials was to be one of the immediate causes of the American Revolution. Further, the company directors had no sympathy for Christian missionaries in their territory and excluded them from India, as potential agents of turmoil and divisiveness that the company could do without. These policies compelled Carey and other early missionaries to disguise their mission work, forcing them to take employment as clerks, traders, or teachers, and, where possible, to work from the safety of non-British enclaves governed by such countries as Portugal (Goa), or Denmark (Serampore). In retrospect, it is easy to understand the British East India Company's uneasiness about missionaries, for Bengal had been captured only about thirty-six years before Carey's arrival, and the decisive British victory in India over the French by Lord Clive (at the Battle of Plassey) had been attained only as recently as 1757.[46]

The history of Carey's work in India is also the unique story of the

Serampore "Triad," involving two other men besides Carey. In 1798, after Carey had purchased a wooden press in his determination to print translations of the Scriptures, he was joined by Baptist missionaries William Ward, a printer, and soon after by preacher John Marshman. These men and their families were strengthened by the Brunsdons, the Grants, and Miss Mary Tidd from England.[47] Now with the experiences gained, the preaching unrewarded, the disciples not obtained, and the disappointment of a wife's mind collapsing under the difficulties of missionary life, the situation would begin to be reversed. The three men comprising the Triad, aided by the others, would meld into an effective missionary team for disseminating the Gospel in many languages.

The Mudnabatty indigo plant had failed in 1799, but it had given employment when Carey needed it most, for three months in each year. In a twenty-square-mile district, containing two hundred villages, he had traveled by small boat to inspect the work of several hundred workers. His diversions from inspecting included making notes on the region's animal life, birds, flowers, and trees. After the failure of the indigo plant, Carey bought on credit a small indigo plant at Kidderpore, built on higher ground. He planned to establish there a Moravian-style mission compound, where the mission families each would have a house, but all would eat and work together.[48]

Carey reached the firm conclusion that the key to converting India to Christianity lay in translating the Gospel into the languages of India. There were some 845 languages and dialects in India, many of them variants of Hindi or Urdu,[49] and he would have to be selective. The classical language of Sanskrit, in which many ancient epics were written, was regarded by Carey to be the cornerstone for understanding Indian literature and languages. While his afternoons and evenings were spent entirely on mission activities, his primary focus was to continue translating the entire Bible into Bengali.

The prize convert of this period was Ignatius Fernandez, of Portuguese descent, a former Roman Catholic, who helped Carey organize a Baptist church at Dinajpur, and then became its pastor.[50]

The Refuge at Serampore

In January 1800 the whole party moved to the Danish enclave of Serampore, where the authority of the British East Indies Company had no effect. In Serampore the evangelical work would flower, seed, and cast an enduring influence over sub-continental India. The men of the mission almost daily preached in the neighboring villages, despite harassment and stones thrown at them. Carey (age thirty-eight), Marshman (age thirty-one), and Ward (age thirty) learned Bengali well and combined their formidable talents. Together they bought a large house for 758 pounds (U.S. $3,552) and pooled their resources to pay for a mission house and smaller buildings. Meals were taken together, although each family had its own living quarters. Each missionary, in turn, managed domestic affairs for one or more months.[51] In the 1930s a small party of Southern Baptist missionaries in Kowloon, Hong Kong would use some parts of this same format for eating and housing.

The "Moravian Concept" was followed in most matters except in finance. Carey persuaded the group to endorse the exception by tolerating a "house father, to whom the others should in love be subject." Already Carey had been named as the permanent treasurer. From now on, all incomes would go into a common fund. Each missionary would receive a small allowance for personal needs. When the plan was fully operational, Ward received twenty pounds per year, the Marshmans considerably more because of their larger family, and Carey the greatest amount.[52]

The institutions established by the group included a Baptist church, with Carey as pastor, and a number of schools, including a girls' school. Church services were conducted in English and Bengali, and often attended by the Danish governor, Bie, and other notables. In effect, the governor turned over the pulpit of his Lutheran church in Serampore to the Baptists. One of the boarding schools for English children proved to be a lucrative source of funds,[53] while at other schools the tuition was free. Ward's printing, largely devoted to producing Bibles and tracts, also brought in some revenue.[54]

Governor-General Lord Wellesley (the brother of the future Duke of Wellington) established Fort William College in 1801 in order to train British young men for service in India's administration. On the advice of two Anglican chaplains, who were aware that Carey was the foremost foreign master of Bengali and Sanskrit, he was offered its prime teaching position, the professorship of Bengali at the three-year training college. This was clearly a tack away from British hostility to Christian missions. However, Carey never lost sight of the fact that he was first a missionary, and for other professions he had a feeling of inadequacy. He once said, "I am not one of those who are strong and do exploits."[55] Carey accepted the post after consulting with his Baptist colleagues, who convinced him that it was important to grasp this opportunity to influence the future administrators of India.[56] The professorship was soon expanded to include two other languages, including Sanskrit, and the position was elevated to a full professorship at a salary of fifteen hundred pounds a year; all of this went into the mission fund at Serampore. In order to attend his classes, Carey was rowed on the river from Serampore each Tuesday and returned on Friday evening.[57] With this routine Carey could identify with the irony of man's actions and the strength of God's hand.

> Here again we see Providence guiding his ways. The East India Company had forbidden him to enter Bengal; had forced him to live in poor conditions for six years; was the cause that William Carey had to camouflage his work under the pretext of being a business man. Then the same Company forced his colleagues to stay on in Serampore. And now—after all these years of preparation, of moulding he is called to a college to fulfil a duty which was strongly forbidden by the Directors. So against the design of the Company he worked out his missionary plan, according to a higher plan: The Plan of the Lord.[58]

There were tragedies that hovered about the first converts. Thomas, not part of the Serampore group, brought to the mission compound in 1800 a Muslim inquirer about Christ, named Fukeer. He was accepted for baptism, but when he visited his family village he disappeared, probably the victim of foul play.[59] Then, a poor carpenter named Krishna Pal had his dislocated shoulder set by Thomas. He listened to religious instructions from Thomas and Carey, broke caste by eating with the missionaries, and was baptized by Carey on December 28, 1800, in the Hooghly River. Krishna's wife and a friend, Gokul, soon professed their faith and joined the group, but under threats from Hindus, fell away. Then Thomas, who had done so much to introduce Christian doctrine to Fukeer and Krishna, became insane and died in October 1801.[60] Despite the railings of the Brahmins and the threats of Hindu mobs, Krishna Pal would remain a faithful Christian, and Jaymani (his sister-in-law) would be the first Bengali woman baptized, followed by Krishna's wife and another woman.

The social break that occurred with conversion was formidable. In converting, the former Hindus broke caste, separated themselves from the social system, became outcasts, and were reviled by their relatives and friends. Also in Islam (which did not recognize caste), conversion was not accepted, converts became pariahs, and Christians were totally separated from their home village—the fountain of all Indian life. So, to be a Christian meant to be "born again" but left in isolation.[61] In 1803 there were thirteen baptized Bengalis, several of them from the higher castes and one of them a Brahmin.[62]

Despite his many activities, Carey's primary concern was his translation of the Bible. In March 1801 he began producing two thousand printed copies of the Bengali New Testament. It was the first book ever published in Bengali for the general reader, the product of seven and one-half years work by Carey.[63] Shortly after the publication of the New Testament, the Old Testament was printed in Bengali, and the whole Bible became available, as printed by William Ward. Astoundingly, Carey added nearly one language a year to his working knowledge. In time, Carey published the entire Bible in six languages of India, namely Bengali, Oriya, Hindi, Marathi, Sanskrit, and Assamese;[64] along with these, he prepared grammars for each language and parts of the Bible were printed in thirty other languages. Then, to assist his college students, he translated some classics. It is not to be suggested that Carey did all the translations in all the languages, remarkable as Carey was in linguistics. He was assisted by a corps of pundits and scholars that became increasingly expert in their skills. In the course of this work, Felix Carey, William's son, was commissioned by the Baptist Missionary Society to go as its missionary to Burma.[65]

The Sepoy Mutiny of Vellore began in 1806, involving the massacre of 114 army officers and men, and foreshadowing the "Great Mutiny" of 1857-58. The Vellore revolt was in response to religious pressure felt by Indian troops of the British East India Company. The impact of the mutiny on Carey and the Baptist work was to throttle down its evangelical momentum. Two young Baptist missionaries from England were ordered by the authorities to remain in Calcutta, pending possible return to the home country. But Carey had them transported to Danish Serampore, where Governor Krefting protected them. Then, on the authority of the British governor general, Sir George Barlow, other missionaries were ordered not to preach to the Indian people, nor distribute pamphlets, convert natives, or allow any of their believers to do those things.[66]

The enemies of Christian missions, many of them British military officers and English overseas administrators, were encouraged by the arrival of the new governor general, Lord Gilbert John Minto. There was absolutely no connection between the Vellore Mutiny and mission activity, but negative suppositions were made. Then there was a furor over a pamphlet in Persian from Serampore that described the Muslim prophet Muhammed as an "impostor" and "tyrant." Carey discovered that a Muslim convert had translated part of the Koran for Ward, and in doing so, inserted insulting terms. The missionaries apologized and withdrew the pamphlet. The British authorities continued to insist that no further efforts should be made to Christianize the Bengalis. Also, the mission press was ordered to be transferred to Calcutta, although such a change could unhinge the printing mission because of high rents and wages in Calcutta.

When Lord Minto was visited by Carey and Marshman, he could more accurately appraise the quality of their work and character. The missionaries informed him that one hundred Indians had been baptized, including twelve Brahmins and five Muslims. The missionaries were prepared to suffer, but they could not transfer their press. However, they would submit all future publications for the governor's approval. On this concession, the governor rescinded the previous bans that restricted the mission's work to Serampore and private houses in Calcutta.[67]

Carey's wife Dorothy, still mentally deranged, had physically attacked Carey on several occasions, and died in 1807. In 1808 Carey married Charlotte Rumohr, a Danish citizen, who suffered from a spinal malady and had come to India to recover. She left her Lutheran faith, became a Baptist, and was baptized by Carey. This marriage was particularly happy and lasted until 1821, when Charlotte died. In his letter to Ryland, Carey wrote: "My loss is irreparable. I am very lonely." In 1823 Carey would marry a widow, Grace Hughes, who cared for him tenderly and outlived him by one year.[68]

About five years before, plans had been made to establish mission stations outside of Serampore, and in 1810 that work began. A chapel was opened in Calcutta's notorious Lall Bazaar sector with good results. Then, in 1810, Carey appealed to his English supporters to send forty new missionaries,[69] and over the years the new recruits began to arrive.

Mission Fire

A disastrous fire in 1812 nearly destroyed half a lifetime's work, when the mission press burned to the ground. About sundown a fire broke out in the large printing plant, which was two hundred feet long. The fire was nearly snuffed out after Marshman and Ward closed all doors and windows. Then some foolish persons opened windows to throw water, and during the night the entire building was destroyed. When Carey arrived in the evening, the five printing presses had been carried to safety, but thousands of printed sheets for Bibles, manuscripts of Scripture translations, tracts, grammars, the classic Ramayana, also a polyglot dictionary based on Sanskrit, great stocks of printing paper, and twenty fonts of type in various languages were all lost. Fortunately, the paper mill and warehouse with printed books did not burn. From the ashes, Carey retrieved the undamaged punches and matrices, with which he could recast type. The loss was equivalent to at least ten thousand pounds.[70]

Here is where the character of Carey displayed itself, as clear as the sight of Excalibur to King Arthur, rising as it did from the lake. The news of the fire electrified England and markedly affected the Baptists, who responded promptly. Carey, sick at heart over the loss, wrote bravely to Fuller:

> We are able immediately to begin casting. In a fortnight we
> shall be able to begin printing again, in one language. Another
> month will enable us to begin in another and I trust that in six
> months our loss in Oriental type will be repaired.[71]

The fire revealed the dauntless faith of Marshman, Ward, and Carey (the "Triad"). The sympathy evoked overseas and in India overcame some of the principal barriers to their work. The Baptist Missionary Society in England pledged itself to raise ten thousand pounds. Even the Calcutta newspapers spoke of confidence in their future labors. By 1814 Carey had finished twenty-six versions of the Scriptures. In 1832 the Bible and other printings were completed in forty-two languages and dialects.[72] The honors and recognition that Carey had not sought began arriving. In 1807 he had been honored with the Doctor of Divinity degree by Brown University in Providence, Rhode Island,[73] the first Baptist College in North America.

The British Parliament at intervals of twenty years renewed the charter of the British East India Company, and was prepared to do so in 1813. Largely through the exertions of Fuller in England, many petitions were gathered that produced a revised charter, allowing Christian missionaries and evangelical activities in India for "benevolent designs" and "religious and moral improvements."[74]

Founding Serampore College

Carey's plans included not only the concept of schools attached to each mission station, but of the founding of Serampore College to influence the gifted young men of India's future government. Only through such Christian institutions, Carey believed, could India be won to Christ and then only by its own people.[75] After much discussion among his colleagues, the first prospectus was sent out in July 1818. There were no religious requirements, but dietary and other exceptions were made for those Indian students insisting on caste distinctions. All members of the Board of Trustees except one were to be Baptist. The Danish governor of Serampore received the honorary position of "first governor of the college," while Carey was named as the college principal. Lord Francis Moira (future Marquis of Hastings) became a generous supporter of the college. The college began with thirty-seven students, including nineteen Indian Christians, fourteen Hindus, and four students who professed neither religion nor caste. There was no separate theological college,[76] although a number of males were training for the ministry.

The king of Denmark granted a royal charter empowering the college to grant degrees. A large well-furnished building was erected for the college at a cost of fifteen thousand pounds. Serampore College then expanded to one hundred students, and in the late twentieth century accepted two thousand students. In 1994, with seventy persons enrolled in the theology department, the college was said to be the only institution in modern India that grants degrees in Christian theology.[77] A number of its graduates over the years have become influential in secular matters in India and abroad.[78]

Missionary life was and is far from being an idyllic bed of roses, although Carey maintained a five-acre flower garden, tending it with his hands. The Triad was advancing in years and these seniors were somewhat autocratic, particularly in the eyes of their junior partners. Younger missionaries that arrived challenged the "Moravian concept" of shared poverty. There was considerable opposition, both in

England and India, to Carey's educational programs. When dedicated missions advocate Andrew Fuller died in England in May 1815, only Ryland, now absorbed with work as principal of Bristol College, remained of Carey's old colleagues.[79] The questions of control and who should own property burst out into the open. John Dyer, Fuller's successor, wanted efficiency and had little understanding of the philosophy and style of work in India. The young men at Serampore finally left the older group and began their own mission. As a result, the Triad was forced to renounce the right and title to all property except the college, which they held jointly with the Trustees.[80]

The Managing Committee in London in 1817 demanded that all equipment, property, and expenditures should be controlled by an eight-member Board of Trustees (five of them in England). This was a clumsy administrative system, since two months was required for a letter to reach England from India. In 1827 Marshman in London turned over to the mission committee all the churches, missions, and properties at Serampore except the college and its campus.

Five new mission families, none over twenty-six years of age, separated themselves from Serampore and set up a rival mission in Calcutta, answerable only to London. These young rebels included Carey's nephew, Eustace Carey. They established their own printing press, schools, and chapels. The young missionaries were particularly disturbed by the attitudes of John Marshman. Carey answered their criticism by saying of Marshman, "I have not a single desire ungratified." He also added, "I wish I had half his piety, energy of mind, and zeal for the cause of God." But the damage was done, in part because of the meticulous concern for business by Carey, who like King Philip II of Spain (1556-98 A.D.) had to oversee too many small details—and, in Carey's case, never to return to England or take a vacation.[81]

In Carey's defense, his Serampore mission was largely self-supporting. If it had not been self-sustaining, the mission families on the basis of hunger alone would have been obliged to return to their Motherland. It has been estimated that during the entire life of Carey he was paid only six hundred pounds (beyond the ten thousand pounds restoration fund after the fire), while from his own earnings he gave to Baptist work in India about forty thousand pounds. Some persons in England heard the misleading rumors that the missionaries were living like princes. In their defense, and from its fragile beginning, the Serampore mission created and supported sixteen or more mission stations and churches.[82] And influenced by Carey's efforts, other mission work had developed in Java, Mauritius, Ceylon, Burma,[83] and elsewhere in Asia.

Despite his appreciation of Indian culture, particularly such classical literature as the *Ramayana* and *Mahabharata*, Carey was horrified by the killing of lepers and the practice of suttee (sati). Suttee was the tradition in India that impelled the widow, often a young girl, to throw herself on her husband's funeral pyre and to be burned to death. If the widow did not go willingly, she was tied to the bier, which was set on fire. Carey reported that in one year 430 women, in a radius of thiry miles from Calcutta, had died in this manner, which he regarded as a criminal offense. His research as official government translator proved that the practice was of recent origin, and, while considered meritorious as an Indian ideal of womanhood, it was not required by the ancient Hindu canons. When Governor General Lord William Bentinck approved Carey's recommendation to forbid the practice of suttee, Carey, on receiving a copy of the document, left his pulpit without preaching on December 6, 1829, to translate the order into Bengali. By that evening the mandate was dispatched throughout the provinces. The Brahmins made an uproar, but King George IV supported the new law and it remained.

Under the previous governor general, Lord Wellesley, Carey had been authorized to make an investigation of infanticide, in which small or sickly children were given as a sacrifice to the river goddess or left to die in the jungle. When Carey reported that the practice was not required by the Hindu sacred literature, Lord Wellesley declared infanticide to be murder and its practitioner's liable to the death penalty.[84]

This great Trailblazer had an ecumenical vision, believing that through a combined effort of various Christian traditions India could be won to Christ. Without any class pattern, after arriving in India he simply created a new structure, aided by Marshman and Ward. As a result, his example inspired the founding of a multitude of missionary societies throughout the world. Once he had decided to bear the Gospel, he knew no home on earth, neither England nor India. The "Great Commission," he asserted, laid on Christians "an obligation to disperse themselves into every country of the habitable globe, and preach to all inhabitants without exception or limitation."[85] Carey's Christian vision was on a universal scale, and he fired the hearts that led to the formation of the Congregationalist London Missionary Society and other mission organizations in England, Scotland, the Netherlands, Germany, Switzerland, and the United States.[86]

He thought in ecumenical terms and suggested to Fuller that international conferences on missions should be held every ten years. He conceived the dream of a first conference that could be held in 1810 at the Cape of Good Hope. While this concept did not become reality, a century later, in 1910, there was held a world missionary conference at Edinburgh, Scotland.[87]

After divesting himself of all church properties, except an interest in Serampore College, which would finally become independent, Carey found himself estranged and separated from London. The situation would be comparable to a scenario in which Moses, having led the Israelites to the borders of the Promised Land, would be repudiated by the Hebrews. It is more like the actual circumstances of the debasement of Maximilian Robespierre (1758-94), who, having been a leader of the French Revolution, would be guillotined by his colleagues.[88]

The separation of Carey from the Baptist Missionary Society he had founded would last for about seven years, following the 1827

Marshman trip to London. He lived in exile, sharing work with his esteemed co-worker Reverend John Marshman. William Ward had died many years before. Before this rupture the new business practices and standardized principles that characterized the new mission work had made almost unbridgeable the chasm that separated the older missionaries with their older styles from the new breed of workers. Still, Carey completed his final revision of the Bengali New Testament.[89]

In the summer of 1833, Carey wrote his sister that "this is the last letter you are likely to receive from me." However, he briefly recovered. As Carey in 1834 began to sink into a final struggle with his health, the illustrious leaders of India bade him farewell. Lord and Lady Bentinck visited him. The Anglican Bishop of Calcutta knelt at his bedside to receive his blessing. Young Alexander Duff, a missionary of the Church of Scotland, who had just prayed with Carey, was called back into the room. "Mr. Duff, you have been speaking about Dr. Carey, Dr. Carey. When I am gone, say nothing about Dr. Carey—speak about Dr. Carey's Saviour."[90]

William Carey died June 9, 1834, at the age of seventy-two. The Danish governor of Serampore stood beside his grave, where a gravestone would be placed bearing the words of Isaac Watts: "A wretched, poor and helpless worm, on thy kind arms I fall."

At the Paulerspury parish church in England, a tablet in the chancel would memorialize him. And the greatest honor would be conferred at Westminster Abbey, where an impressive lectern would bear Carey's immortal words:

Expect Great Things from God:
Attempt Great Things for God.

Carey, the inarticulate youth and stumbling pastor, had grown in his fellowship with God and had become the greatest linguist and translator in Baptist history, perhaps in all religious history. In his mission endeavors in India, he translated the entire Bible into six languages (including Sanskrit, Hindi, and Bengali) and key portions of the Scriptures into thirty-four languages. This work, assisted by Indian linguists, continued until the eve of Carey's death, when a revised Bengali New Testament was given to the world. Carey understood that the key to evangelizing India would require first the printing of God's Word in languages understood by the Indian people.

William Carey is foremost "the Father of modern missions." He arrived in a subcontinent hostile to Christian missions, from the standpoint of Hindu and Muslim believers and traditions and the exclusionary practices of the British East India Company. This Baptist pioneer was able to survive his first years through the generosity of the Danish governor general at Serampore, near Calcutta. At Serampore, he adopted the self-sufficiency of the "Moravian Concept," embodying the sharing of all resources, eating together, tilling the soil, and seeking employment to sustain the missionary community. Carey's professorship of Bengali and Sanskrit at Fort William College brought money to sustain the missionary work, but it also nurtured contacts and respect for missionaries among British officials and administrators.

One of the most effective innovations by Carey, at least for his first years, was his creation of schools to reach a caste-dominated Indian society. Closely affiliated to sixteen or more missions or churches begun by Carey's group, were a variety of schools at the mission stations, including a girls' school. All of this was capped by Serampore College, that among its other disciplines prepared students for the ministry. His concern for education would create misunderstandings between the Triad and the most recent London Trustees of the Baptist Missionary Society (BMS). The older methods, honed for years by the Triad, and a more autocratic style indulged in by the senior missionaries, would alienate the younger missionaries coming to India. The result was a crisis that would force Carey and John Marshman to separate themselves from the BMS in their final years.

Too little has been written of Carey's theology. He was a Particular Baptist, but he encouraged ecumenical cooperation and was a strong voice in modifying the doctrine of those who stressed Ultra-Calvinism and predestination, to the exclusion of man's choice. He believed that in imitation of Paul, Christian messengers must present the Gospel so God could add to His Kingdom. Carey's missionary calling and his insistence that the world should know that God sent his Son to save "whosoever believeth" was directly responsible for the creation of the Baptist Missionary Society. This, in turn, began a process influencing large numbers of British and American Baptists and other major denominations to promote missions as a vital portion of God's work. Carey also was deeply influenced by the pietism of Count Nikolaus Zinzendorf and the Moravians, and used their self-sustaining communities as his model in India.[91]

Then, translating his Christian zeal into social reform, Carey motivated the British government to condemn the murder of lepers and the sacrifice of invalids and young children to pagan gods. He had a splendid victory in virtually terminating the practice of suttee, in which a widow was compelled by custom to burn herself to death on her husband's funeral pyre.

William Carey was a great soul, freely exiling himself from England to minister to the "lost" multitudes of India. He never saw Europe again once he left those shores. His commitment to a Christlike vision was absolute, and he returned almost all his salary to the mission treasury to bring the Christian light to Asia. The translating and printing of the Scriptures in the major languages of India were herculean tasks, to which he devoted almost his entire life. Although a genius in linguistics and honored for his contributions in botany, under the gaze of the Lord whom he sought to serve with all his strength, he regarded himself as only a worm. However, in the appraisal of thousands who have read of his life, William Carey is the greatest missionary to follow in the steps of the Apostle Paul. The former cobbler of Paulerspury earned the accolade written in Romans 10:15, "How beautiful are the feet of them that preach the gospel of peace, and bring glad tidings of good things."

Luther Rice, age 34 (1817), Distributes Annual Report in Kentucky
(Artist's depiction based on a silhouette cut by Mrs. E. H. Goulding).

Chapter 11

Luther Rice
(1783-1836)

Visionary of Baptist Denominationalism

Luther Rice, a Baptist visionary shaped by his New England Congregational roots, was the dominant leader in leading hundreds of scattered congregations into the Triennial (Baptist) Convention. In 1814, largely through his perception and tenacity, the majority of mission-supporting Baptists in North America were brought together for the first time in a rudimentary Baptist denomination—as distinct from their ancient faith.

Before Rice, the Baptists in the colonies, having first begun in Providence, Rhode Island, were in small congregations and associations, largely unorganized and scattered, but—worthy of notice—comprising a vigorous, amorphous movement. By 1800 the Baptists had multiplied to become the most numerous Christians of any faith in America. So, influenced by Rice and his co-leaders, a large number of Baptists, especially those embraced by the Triennial Convention, would move cautiously, at other times impetuously, toward the concept of structural Baptist unity.

Rice, adept at combining the ideas of others with his own, did not create a denominational structure single-handedly, nor could he have done so, in view of the character of the independent, liberty-loving, and strong-willed Baptists that he normally encountered. In the formidable first task of organizing a network to support missions,

Rice consulted with and utilized the services of many servants of God, including a small army of distinguished Baptist ministers: William Staughton, graduate of Bristol (Baptist) College of England, corresponding secretary of the Triennial Convention, and head of the future Baptist Seminary in Philadelphia; Dr. Thomas Baldwin, pastor of Boston's Second Baptist Church, president of the Board, and probably the most influential Baptist in the North; Richard Furman, distinguished Charleston, South Carolina pastor, first president of the Triennial Convention, and perhaps the most powerful Baptist preacher in the South, whose administrative skills greatly assisted in achieving Rice's goals; Jesse Mercer of Georgia, a prominent preacher, advocate of missions and education, and editor from 1833 to 1840 of *The Christian Index*, (formerly *The Columbian Star*);[1] and W. Bullein Johnson of South Carolina, strong supporter of an educated clergy, who helped write the constitution of the Triennial Convention and became the advocate of a more centralized denomination, and who later was the first president of the Southern Baptist Convention.

The heaviest load in motivating Baptists for mission work and developing the framework of a denomination was borne by Luther Rice, the Yankee pastor from Massachusetts, who had embraced the Baptist faith after being nurtured in the Congregational Church. His crowning achievements would be the formidable progress he made in creating a missions network, bolstering the Triennial Convention (notably the first Baptist national union in North America) and later his inspiration to co-found a Baptist national college, Columbian College of Washington, D.C. (which became George Washington University).

The tragedy of his life would be the financial pressures, jealousies, and sectional pulls between Baptists in the North and the South that would disengage and then destroy much of his finest work for unity, and cause the forfeiture of George Washington University and the demise of the Triennial Convention. In the last ten years of his life, without a home of his own and owning little more than the clothes on his back, he would be accused by his colleagues of peculation and treated like a leper by some. Like William Carey in India, he would find himself shunned by the very faith to which he had brought honor, respect, and dignity, and for whose God he had given his entire life. This intrepid Trailblazer, despite his impetuosity and fiscal naiveté, laid the foundations for an educated clergy, the creation of seminaries and colleges, and a lively interest in home and foreign missions.

Rice's impact on Baptist structures and events was monumental. He was the preeminent founder of the Baptist denomination in the United States, although thousands of Baptists would follow their distinctive ways and not join in his dream for unity. It was church historian William Heth Whitsitt who, in praising him most effusively, said: "The coming of Luther Rice was the most important event in Baptist history in the nineteenth century."[2]

Luther Rice was born in Northborough, Massachusetts, on March 25, 1783, the ninth child and youngest of six sons of farmer and militia captain Amos Rice and Sarah Graves Rice. Despite their somewhat modest possessions, the Rices stemmed from an aristocratic lineage. They were direct descendants of William the Conqueror through the Duke of Cornwall and were near-kinsmen of President John Quincy Adams. Two cousins captured by the Iroquois Indians became chiefs; one of these Rice children was the Iroquois chief spokesman at a conference held during the American Revolution between British Lieutenant General John Burgoyne (who conceived the British strategy for the Battle of Saratoga) and the Indian chiefs of the Six Nations.

The Rice clan had large families, frequently numbering nine to nineteen children. The family members were long-lived, courageous, and had a reputation of being "pugnacious." Fifty Rices engaged in military actions during the American Revolution, including Luther's father, who defended "Breeds' Hill" in the so-called Battle of Bunker Hill.[3] Their neighbors regarded the Rices as gentry because of their land holdings.

Rice was raised in a comfortable Massachusetts two-story farm house a half-mile from Northborough, beside a brook and protected from storms by a wooded prominence. He was scarcely regarded as a *wunderkind* by his sturdy religious parents, who acknowledged no sense of uniqueness in the young man that foddered their cattle. However, from his earliest childhood he was "a rare combination of deep-seated seriousness and an unconquerable love of fun." Later on, this impish streak, which shriveled under the influence of Calvinism, would be called "levity," but the droll side of his nature never left him. As he developed, he had little sense of intellectual self-consciousness but he increasingly sought out intelligent people. He was a happy child, and misadventure could not overwhelm him.[4]

His father Amos was authoritarian in the customary role of a family head in Protestant New England, and Rice's first crisis was a confrontation with his father about the young man's religious awakening. He had a defining religious experience in 1803 when he was about twenty years old. He joined the Congregational Church and sought to establish family worship and to engage in religious conversation. This Christian activity infuriated an unregenerate Congregationalist father,[5] who could foresee the day when Luther, responding to religious influences, would abandon the home and farm of his old parents.

The religious "Damascus Road" experience of Luther Rice was recorded on February 25, 1803, in his diary:

> I will begin with relating a circumstance which happened last night [February 24]. I sat up till late, reading a book, the title, if I mistake not, is Religious Courtship, my mother setting up to hear it, my father also setting up in another room. When I left reading it, my mother left the room; I then took the bible, and after reading a chapter laid it away and sat down; after setting awhile, thinking of my wretched condition, I took again the bible, meaning to read, that chapter which contains the account of St. Paul's conversion, and pray, that I also might be convicted and converted. After having read the chapter, I laid

away the bible, and kneeling down prayed, that the same light which shone round Paul, might also shine round my heart, and that I might be struck down and convicted, at which time! something inexpressible! set me in the astonishingest maze and trembling! which, however, gradually subsided, and in a little time, I rose from my knees, and sat in a chair, not knowing what to do; but after awhile, I again kneeled down and endeavored to pray, after which, I went to bed!

As the youngest son in a family of ten, Luther was fully expected to remain on the farm for life. But the astute old militia captain, his father, sensed it would not be that way.

Luther Rice later wrote about his disappointment in his father's attitude:

When it pleased God to make me see, and feel, and manifest the reality and life of religion, he (my father) could not bear with it in me. This state of things effectively uprooted the fond anticipation I had indulged of possessing the home and taking care of my parents and thus what might have constituted a material barrier in the way of my devoting my life to the sacred service of the ministry was entirely removed![6]

Like the great Reformation leader Martin Luther, who sought God in desperation, with hairshirt and walking on his knees, Rice would be tormented for nearly three years in his search for God's purpose.[7] While cutting down a tree in 1804, a limb fell on his head, reminding him of the urgency of obtaining salvation. Unsure that God had forgiven his sins, he engaged in prayer and fasting and made a resolve to marry a Christian woman.[8] He spent long hours at night praying and meditating. As he dwelled on his spiritual condition, he became morose. Rice had begun to keep a diary in 1803 to "record the dispensations of Providence towards me." In this private record he reported on February 7, 1804, that "thoughts of death and eternity are almost constantly in my mind." In his bedroom he was repentant for his "levity" and amusements "too vain and too merry." Lightning and thunder became fearsome things to him.[9]

He was caught in a time-frame dominated by Calvinism, with God depicted as a severe "Potter," and mankind suffering in its total depravity. However, in the latter half of the eighteenth century the burdens of Calvinism would be lightened with the expanded acceptance of the teachings of Arminianism, that spoke of free choice in accepting God's grace.

His greatest release from guilt appeared to be in attending a nearby singing school. There he met a young woman who stirred his primitive passions, but whose character he did not esteem, and the relationship never flourished. Later, at Worchester, he discovered a pious young woman, for whose hand he begged the Lord's intervention. The prayer was unavailing.[10] In fact, it is one of the great mysteries of Luther Rice's life that, physically imposing at six feet in height, with a robust face, piercing eyes, a gregarious, animated personality, and a gentle temperament,[11] he had little success with women. He never married, although even in old age he sought a binding relationship.

The student life that would prepare Rice for his projected religious life would carry him from Leicester Academy, which he attended from 1803 to 1807, to Williams College in 1807, and finally to Andover Seminary in 1810. He had the firm backing of his mother, his faithful brother Asaph, an aunt, and his student friends in a journey that would transform him from a Northern farm boy into a Baptist dreamer and Trailblazer. He was not one to be ignored, and his neighbors would purchase his religious magazines to support his ministry. Rice also was an avid reader, both of religious and popular books, including Richard Baxter's *Saints Everlasting Rest*, John Newton's *Letters*, and the life of Mohammed.[12] In academia he was a serious student, earning good grades, and was elected to positions of campus leadership.[13]

Rice was multi-talented and articulate. He supported himself, in part as a schoolteacher, and displayed talent as a town song leader, reinforcing his style with a story or a song. He was an impressive public speaker, sensitive to the views and weaknesses of others. On one occasion he had a pleasant conversation with a Quaker, on another day debated with a Universalist, and then a third time rose with dignity to discuss the agenda in a church conference.[14] His charity failed him only infrequently, but it did so with a Shaker community, whose teachings exasperated him.

Rice, at this early period of spiritual development, had an immature faith, touched with fatalism, and flavored even with a propensity for divination in evoking God's favor. He believed God dealt directly with him through his opening the Bible to a particular passage. In another instance, in 1895, when he slept late and missed an opportunity to impress a committee seeking a teacher, he attributed the lapse to divine intervention. Rice also constantly berated himself for "baseness and stupidity."[15]

His spiritual decisive moment came on Sunday, September 14, 1805 (as recorded in his diary on September 15):

> Yesterday, in the morning, the thought came into my mind, whether I would be willing to give Deity a blank and let him fill up my future destiny as he would please! —After breakfast I retired, a second time, for prayer; but without any particular design of making such a solemn surrender unto God as I was enabled by his superabounding grace to do. I did then, on my bended knees, give up myself to the Eternal Jehovah, soul and body, for time and eternity to be dealt with as he should see fit . . .[16]

Then peace came to Luther Rice, after several years of agony and defeat. He discussed freely his religious struggles with his pastor, parents, and friends. Although he regarded himself as a "vile sinner before God," he now had the assurance that "Christ died for sinners."[17]

The strongest religious influence on Luther Rice while in college was the organization of young Congregational men who banded together as the "Brethren," led by Samuel Mills. In 1806, when Rice was attending Leicester Academy, five students of Congregational Williams College, led by Mills, committed themselves to missions during a thunderstorm. The little group had retreated from the storm to the protection of sheaves of hay, where they prayed together for the salvation of the heathen, in what has been celebrated as the "Haystack Prayer Meeting."[18] While Rice was not present at the haystack meeting, it was this meeting and Mills's influence that would ring an alarm bell for missions and awaken Yale and other colleges to its call. When Rice moved to Williams College in 1807, he became one of the Brethren, and when Mills graduated, Rice emerged as the leader. Rice collected funds, corresponded, and supervised the on-campus activities, that included enjoining a ban on marriage, soon to be broken. Rice was already known for his persuasive power and was quickly designated the group's orator. Attentive to his gifts, the Berkshire Mountain Association licensed Rice to preach during his last year at Williams.[19]

The final phase of Rice's theological training would be at Andover Seminary, which was established as a reaction to Harvard's perceived liberalism. There, Rice would have frequent contacts with most of the Brethren, as well as student leader and future celebrated Baptist missionary to Burma, Adoniram Judson. Judson had graduated from Brown, a Baptist university, and had completed his theological training at Andover before Rice arrived. They maintained their friendship through Brethren meetings, and both were on campus at Andover for months while awaiting Board action on their appointments as missionaries.[20]

Adoniram Judson exerted a dominant influence with the Brethren. In February 1810, deeply moved by a sermon, "Star in the East," that appealed for mission support in India, Judson knelt in the snow and dedicated himself to foreign missions.[21] Either at this time or later, Rice made a declaration of his calling: "I have deliberately made up my mind to preach the gospel to the heathen, and I do not know but it may be Asia."[22] Judson then persuaded the Congregational leaders in 1810 to form the American Board of Commissioners for Foreign Missions, the first organized foreign mission society in America.[23]

In its expansive mood, the American Board of Commissioners appointed Adoniram Judson and his wife, Ann Hasseltine Judson, and other colleagues from Andover to be missionaries to Asia. The appointees would be supported by Congregational and Presbyterian churches through the commissioners. Rice had not been included among the original selectees, with whom he had aggressively prayed and striven. But, audaciously, he persuaded a reluctant Board to include his name among the appointees; still, if he was to go, he would be compelled to raise his own support. He was to perform this daunting task in slightly less than one week.

In 1812 the intrepid young missionaries, including Rice, gathered for their solemn ordination service. Long before, in 1803, when almost twenty-two years old, Rice had begun his diary, and now at age twenty-eight, he entered [February 6, 1812] these meaningful words in that same journal:

> Received ordination together with Brothers Gordon Hall, Adoniram Judson, Jr., Samuel Newell, Samuel Nott, Jr., in Salem, Massachusetts, as a Missionary to the East Indies."
>
> The occasion was solemn and interesting; but worn down with fatigue and agitation of mind, I did not realize it so impressively. . . .[24]

It is no wonder that Rice felt exhausted, for in six days, as God's agent to the non-Christians, he had dashed from church to church in a frozen winter raising money to gain support for his voyage and sustenance abroad.[25]

Rice and Gordon Hall, his fellow appointee, raised money in Philadelphia, even among generous Presbyterians. At that bustling metropolis, he met the eminent Dr. William Staughton of the Sansom Street Baptist Church, who later organized a national Baptist seminary in his home.

At the ordination service for missionaries at Salem, Rice was "the tallest, the most athletic; energetic; gifted in speech and voice, a persuasive man but troubled in his thoughts this day as he wrote 'worn down with fatigue. . . ,'"[26] Rice's sweetheart, Rebecca Eton of Framington, was contributing to his fatigue with her own ambitions. Rebecca fully realized at last that Rice would not settle down in New England as a distinguished preacher, but was determined to go to Asia as a struggling missionary and live in an unfriendly milieu. Rebecca was appalled and refused both the romantic and the missions commitment.[27] Of Rice's companions at the ordination, both Hall and Newell died in India, while Nott returned to the United States in 1816 to teach. Judson left his Congregational roots and became a celebrated Baptist missionary in Burma, after which he died at sea.[28]

After his ordination, Rice bade goodbye to his brother Asaph and rode horseback almost the whole night. At one point, when his horse fell, with Rice's foot caught in the stirrup, he managed to extricate himself from danger.[29] He took the mail stage bound for Philadelphia. At New Haven he purchased passage on a packet bound for New York, collected money for foreign missions in that city, and next boarded a stage coach for Philadelphia, reaching that bustling city on February 14. Along the way he had met his family, friends, and missionaries Nott and Johns. The final trip began on February 18, 1812, first by a connecting packet that sailed down the Delaware River to New Castle, where the ship *Harmony* was anchored. The *Harmony* then sailed on February 20, on the long voyage, with stops at Cape Verde, Cape of Good Hope, Mauritius, Calcutta, and Serampore, India.[30]

Rice's trip to India aboard the *Harmony* was a voyage marred by seasickness, heat prostration, and anxiety. While striving to overcome his discomfort, he studied Hebrew, practiced French, and preached to the passengers and a disinterested crew. Among the travelers was an annoying and stubborn British Baptist missionary, William Johns, who persisted in presenting his theological views, particularly those relating to the meaning and form of baptism. This discussion motivated Luther to begin a study of key doctrines that separated Congregationalists and Baptists.

When the *Harmony* arrived at Mauritius (Isle de France) the missionaries were warned not to locate in Burma, India, or in any land areas under the jurisdiction of the British East India Company. At stake were the monopolistic interests of a powerful East India Company, the commercial priorities of the British colonial system, and the privileges accorded the Anglican Church. The new arrivals learned that the British governor stationed at Madras would allow no more missionaries to enter India and had forbidden preaching and the distribution of Bibles.[31] But Adoniram Judson, whose ultimate destination was Burma, had taken another ship and was already conferring with British missionaries in India.

Several weeks after leaving Mauritius, the new missionaries, including Luther Rice, landed at Calcutta on August 10, 1812; they were advised by the British Baptist pioneer missionary William Carey to seek another field because of the anti-mission state policy. Rice, meanwhile, found time to read *The History of Sumatra* (1783) by William Marsden and *Voyages to the East Indies* (1798) by J. Splinter Stavorinus.[32]

Adoniram Judson, the former student leader at Andover Seminary, was on the verge of leaving the Congregational faith and becoming a Baptist. Now, thanks to the tenacity of eccentric missionary William Johns, Luther also had studied thoroughly the available books on baptism. On August 28, 1812, the Judsons, Adoniram and Ann Hasseltine, announced that they had become Baptists. After Adoniram's conversion to the Baptist faith, his father, Adoniram, Sr., and mother Abigail traveled to Boston in 1817 and were immersed by Dr. Thomas Baldwin at the Second Baptist Church.[33] While sick in India for several weeks, Rice studied the Baptist position from borrowed books and consulted with Judson, Carey and others. Finally, William Ward baptized Rice by immersion on November 1, 1812, at William Carey's Lall Bazaar Chapel.[34]

The British colonial government at Calcutta was agitated by the flurry of evangelical activity, and, on November 18, 1812, informed missionaries Luther Rice, Gordon Hall, the Samuel Notts, and the

Judsons that they could not remain in India. Because of the War of 1812 with America, they would be deported to England in a convoy of the British Navy. In response, the missionaries hatched an ingenious plan to forestall the neutralization of their missionary goals. Rather than go unwillingly to England, Samuel and Roxanna Nott and Hall schemed to stow away on a ship bound for Bombay. Rice and the Judsons, on another ship, would sail together for Mauritius, and eventually the Judsons would reach their mission fields in Burma.

Rice and the Judsons were to spend seven weeks on a sea adventure that would forge a lifetime bond, for many years sustained by correspondence.[35] However, in spite of the David-Jonathan camaraderie between Luther Rice and Adoniram Judson, there were striking differences in appearance and personality that separated them. Adoniram was slight in stature, delicate, quiet, and dignified; he was basically a thinker, a rigid perfectionist, scholarly, introverted, and ascetic. In contrast, Luther was large-framed, impressive in appearance, little restrained, an activist, eloquent, and magnetic. With all this contrast, and never to meet again in Asia, Adoniram felt that Luther was "the best of all co-laborers."[36] These Christian soulmates had a "natural affinity," according to writer Evelyn Wingo Thompson, that blossomed even when they lived separately in America and Burma. "What happy days," recalled Adoniram, "we spent at Budgebudge and Fultah; what spiritual consolations and felicities we mutually imparted when chased about by the officers of the police. Have you ever seen happier?"[37]

Passage to Mauritius for the Judsons and Rice was on the ship *Creole*, with embarkation completed on November 22, 1812.[38] Rice relieved some of his misgivings and seasickness on board by playing his flute.[39] When Rice reached Mauritius, he was nearly thirty years old and suffering from hepatitis contracted in India; this illness may have been a major factor in his failure to return to the mission field. Dr. Felix Carey, son of William Carey, then urged the Judsons to go to Burma as missionaries, despite military unrest and unsafe living conditions there.[40]

Rice Pleads Case in America

In their discussions, the Judsons and Rice decided that Luther should return to the United States, primarily to inform the Congregational Board of their change of plans and to present the facts of their conversion to the Baptist faith. But, also, the Baptist churches in America were to be solicited for support of the overseas missionaries and to be informed of the reasons for opening a mission in Burma. The other reasons for Rice's return home, as rehearsed by this little knot of Christians, seem in retrospect to be somewhat far-fetched and impractical—Rice was to survey the countries of South America as potential mission fields and to study the languages of Burma in the United States.[41]

Rice returned to the United States on the ship *Donna Maria*, in a circuitous passage skirting South and Central America. A stop was made at St. Salvador, Brazil, where Rice was housed by a congenial American diplomat, Consul Henry Hill. Rice upset the diplomat by refusing to christen his children, since the practice was no longer acceptable to Rice.[42] After arriving on the American shore, he explained in September 1813 to the Congregational American Board of Commissioners for Foreign Missions why he had become a Baptist. The Board was understandably cool and asked for the return of funds expended. Rice refused the request and replied that the Board was interdenominational ("non-sectarian professions") in scope and that he had raised his own money for the missionary work.

Rice initiated his search for funds from Baptists and others to undergird the work in Asia of Adoniram Judson and his colleagues. In so doing, he and other missions enthusiasts, including Richard Furman and W. Bullein Johnson, knit together the widely-scattered churches and associations in a missions network. Not surprisingly, such cooperation also promoted the possibilities of a formal Baptist denomination. In 1813, few Baptist visionaries had even a foggy dream of Baptist unity, and there was no national Baptist structure of any kind. There was, as Rufus W. Weaver describes it, no denominational program, no convention, and no theological seminaries. There were two colleges, Brown University, organized in Rhode Island (in 1764), and Colby College, organized in Maine (in 1813), but no mission boards or Baptist evangelizing agencies. There were no national publishing houses and few religious periodicals. These were the circumstances when Rice returned from India in 1813. However, there would be a drastic increase of Baptist institutions before Rice died in 1836.[43]

As Weaver relates: "Luther Rice was the first to propose, to attempt, to outline and to promote a national Baptist program in which every feature of evangelical effort was given an appropriate place." The first stage of the new order, and that not clear to Rice at this time, would be achieved on a foundation of societies supported by separate churches.

Rice conceived the idea of a General Missionary Convention that resembled the Baptist Missionary Society in London. The concept was greeted with enthusiasm in the East, and delegates were chosen to attend a general meeting that would create the Triennial Convention in May 1814. This would be a great triumph for Luther Rice, and he was appointed the official agent of the Triennial Convention to organize local and regional groups and raise support for missionaries. He felt at this time that he would be in Asia as a missionary in about a year.[44] He was wrong in this conjecture and would never serve abroad in any capacity.

The few missionary societies in the United States were in the towns and were engaged in supporting the English Baptist Mission in India.[45] There were 115 Baptist associations in 1813, with a membership of 175,000, but only one Baptist state missionary society, that one in Massachusetts. Only a few associations cooperated in local missionary work. Baptist churches were scattered from Maine to Georgia, from the Atlantic Ocean to the Alleghenies, but there was no national structure.[46] There were three major Baptist centers in these first years of the American Republic, namely Boston, Philadelphia, and Charleston, with leading ministers in each center.

As early as 1707, Baptist churches near Philadelphia had joined together in the fraternal Philadelphia Baptist Association. Much later, in 1802, the Massachusetts Baptist Missionary Society was organized, contributing to the historical base through which the Boston Baptists "felt themselves to be the rightful leaders of the denomination," according to historian Rufus Weaver. The Massachusetts Missionary Society was organized in 1803. Later, the Massachusetts Baptist Education Society and the Massachusetts Evangelical Tract Society came into existence, but largely had a sectional importance only.[47]

Rice, after his return to America, appealed to the leaders of the Boston Baptist community. The major Baptist ministers clearly were pleased to learn that Rice and the Judsons had converted to the Baptist faith. Rice was given letters of introduction to the two leading Baptist ministers of Philadelphia—one, Dr. William Staughton, a famous pulpit orator and a member of the original English band that in 1792 supported William Carey, and, two, Dr. Henry Holcombe of Georgia, a man of commanding and imposing presence who had served as a cavalry officer in the American Revolution. Unfortunately, Staughton and Holcombe could barely endure each other, and their incivilities would cause much embarrassment to Luther Rice.

The other powerful figures were scarcely less formidable. Richard Furman, the dominant figure of South Carolina, was a man of great wealth and superior intellect whose dignity was enhanced by a gown he always wore when preaching. W. B. Johnson was the bearded and eminent pastor of the First Baptist Church of Savannah. Jesse Mercer, the leader of the Georgia Baptists, had become wealthy by marrying the widow of a Jew, Captain Simone.[48] Mercer, who took the lead in organizing the Powelton Baptist Society for Foreign Missions, attended the General Missionary Convention, and in 1820 and 1826 represented the Georgia Baptist Association at the Triennial Convention.[49]

Rice's Extensive Travels for Missions

Rice's travels in behalf of missions would take him by horseback, sulky, stage coach, steamboat, and foot from Massachusetts to Kentucky and Georgia. Prior to visiting churches and associations, he armed himself with credentials from the Board and letters of introduction. He always solicited an offering in support of foreign missions.[50] Rice attracted crowds, for he was the only missionary who had gone abroad and returned. Rice's eloquence persuaded the Reverend Thomas Baldwin of Boston's Second Church to form a mission society to support the Judsons. In this enterprise, the Massachusetts Missionary Society offered some help, and by 1813 seventeen Baptist organizations had agreed to support mission work.

Interest in missions was fanned by the preaching of Luther Rice. Next in importance to his influence was the lively correspondence of Ann Judson, wife of Adoniram. Mrs. Judson's letters were read in homes, churches, and published widely in religious papers. Her accounts of trials in Burma in support of her husband and the progress made in translation of the New Testament into Burmese brought widespread sympathy and support. Especially poignant to American women was Ann's remark that there were no English families in Rangoon and that "there is not a female in all of Burma with whom I can converse." Her early death brought tears to many families.[51]

Anti-Missions Reaction

Luther Rice's visit to Georgia in 1813 resulted in the organization of mission societies. It also was a catalyst that ignited opposition to missions and produced a storm of fierce debates, exclusions, and withdrawals. In 1784 the Georgia Baptist Association was formed, and by 1830 the anti-missions Ocmulgee Association withdrew from the state convention (now called the Georgia Baptist Convention). Every association in Georgia would either split or lose churches to the anti-missions Primitive Baptist movement.[52]

There were three principal leaders of the anti-missions reaction: Daniel Parker, John Taylor, and Alexander Campbell. Parker was a ranting, uncouth frontiersman and Hyper-Calvinist, known to missionary Baptists as "the notorious Daniel Parker." Particularly active in Tennessee, Illinois, and Texas, Parker was the father of an unusual branch of Baptists, the Two-Seed-in-the-Spirit Predestinarian Baptists. By 1945 this element of Baptists, once promoted with vigor, had dwindled to sixteen churches and 201 members. Parker's theology embraced a concept that two seeds were present in humanity, one good and one evil. No piety or prayer could change this condition. Missions were superfluous, since children born of the evil seed already were children of darkness, whereas children born of the divine seed were children of God. At an associational meeting, Rice preached and collected an offering for missions. Parker, who died unrepentant, refused at this time to give anything for missions and retorted that "he would not throw away good money for such an object."[53]

John Taylor, another antimissions leader, was an influential pioneer preacher in middle Kentucky. Taylor dubbed Luther Rice "a modern Tetzel," in reference to the Dominican friar who sold indulgences in Germany and inflamed Martin Luther to begin the Reformation. Taylor, after wreaking great harm to foreign missions, repented of his assaults.

Alexander Campbell may have done the greatest damage to missions. Initially a brilliant Presbyterian, he became superficially a Baptist, and then in later life organized the Disciples of Christ. Campbell taught the heresy that baptism would cause the remission of sins; he stole many Baptists away to the Disciples of Christ. Campbell, Taylor, and Parker generally opposed a paid ministry, Sunday School, theological training, and temperance societies. Campbell also argued that education and missionary societies were antiscriptural because they were man-made. Campbell claimed infallibility, and in 1823 published *The Christian Baptist* that attacked nearly all the work that Rice had promoted.[54]

Involved in this clamorous struggle were men susceptible to jealousy. John Taylor and other uneducated clergy were suspicious of Rice and home missionary John M. Peck, because they were educated Easterners and were paid for their work. Hypocrisy tainted the influence of the gadfly Alexander Campbell, whose prosperity was supported by black slaves tending a rich farm. One backwoods anti-missionary spoke the blunt truth about the prejudice concerning foreign missionaries at the Sagamore Association: "Well, if you must know, brother Moderator, you know the big trees in the woods overshadow the little ones, and these missionaries will be all great men, and the people will go where they preach, and we shall all be put down. That's the objection."[55]

The practical problem that confronted Rice was how to organize the scattered churches in a half-continent into a system or organization that could funnel financial support to the Judsons and other missions recruits. The solution to the problem would lead to the emergence of the Triennial Convention, that in all probability would not have come into existence without the vision and labor of Luther Rice. However, the immediate task for Rice was to develop a consciousness for foreign missions among Baptists, and he succeeded in obtaining a broad positive response, both in the North and South.[56]

Unifying Baptists North and South

Rice left Boston on September 29, 1813, traveled through New York, met with the Philadelphia Association, and played a major role in forming the Philadelphia Baptist Missionary Society. He then visited Baltimore, Washington, and Richmond and attended the Charleston Association in South Carolina. It was on the journey from Richmond to Petersburg, Virginia, that Rice began to formulate a plan for a General Convention of Baptists, linking state conventions, churches, missionary societies, and associations. In his half-formulated scheme, Baptist churches in every sector of the country would be invited to extend the work of the Kingdom of God.

The concept and reality of a general missionary convention was the work of Luther Rice, but there was an historical precedent in the Baptist Missionary Society of London. After a conference in Savannah, Georgia, with the Reverend W. Bullein Johnson, the decision was made by the pair to invite Baptist churches across America to form a convention. Rice wrote to all mission societies projecting his plans and received an enthusiastic response in the East.[57] Then the Philadelphia Missionary Society, inspired to organize by Rice, sent a formal invitation to the Baptist mission groups. Thus was founded and organized in May 18, 1814, through the work of thirty-three delegates, the General Convention of the Baptist Denomination in the United States. The creation of the organization was a personal triumph for Rice, and he was appointed agent to organize local and regional groups and obtain support for the work of the missionaries.

The name was unwieldy, and the organization, because of its routine of meeting every three years, became widely known as the Triennial Convention. Its purpose in behalf of world missions was to construct "a plan for eliciting, combining, and directing the energies of the whole denomination in one sacred effort, for sending the glad tidings of salvation to the heathen." Business was transacted between regular sessions by a board of Foreign Missions.[58] Thus the Triennial Convention came to exert great influence with Baptists, until May 1845, at Augusta, Georgia, when the Southern Baptist Convention was organized.[59]

Working for the Triennial Convention

The years 1814-1817 were Rice's busiest and happiest epoch. Largely on horseback and carriage, he traveled the corners of a huge new nation, between the Atlantic Ocean and the Mississippi River, enduring hardship but also receiving much fellowship. America was energetic and optimistic, with vast numbers of yeomen surging into the frontier in search of land. Baptists, now much more numerous than a hundred years before, poured in a flood into Kentucky and

Tennessee between 1790 and 1810. One-fourth of the Baptists of Virginia migrated to Kentucky, while North Carolina Baptists by the thousands crossed the mountains to Tennessee.[60] Rice hurled himself without hesitation into this bubbling cauldron, to knit Baptists together for foreign and home missions. But then he increasingly devoted himself to other sophisticated projects, such as the development of Christian literature, a seminary, a college, and the recruitment of Baptist teachers. He was in the very act of melding a Baptist denomination, with the help of other forward-looking ministers.

The first annual report of the Triennial Convention in 1815 contained information that Reverend Luther Rice would "continue his itinerant services" in the United States "for a reasonable time." As agent of the Board, he was able to raise one thousand dollars for Judson in India and only to receive eight dollars a week plus expenses for himself. However, Rice was not always able to collect his pay. His absence from the Burma mission field stretched from months into years, as the Board felt Rice could better serve the missions cause by raising funds for the overseas work. For not returning to Asia, Rice would be harshly assaulted by his critics, but for the first year the fault was not his.[61] Also, it may be surmised that his serious bout with hepatitis contracted in India eventually led him to ponder alternative ways to serve the Lord.

From time to time, Rice had strong impulses to return to Asia as a missionary. The following was recorded in his Journal on April 24, 1817: "Receive two letters—one from br. [brother] Judson in Rangoon. My feelings are strongly exercised whether to return to him soon or not. O Lord direct me! Attend a meeting of the Philadelphia Foreign Mission Society, having become a member of it . . ."[62]

For Rice, the impediments to returning as missionary included the necessity of overcoming cultural barriers, dangerous diseases, including hepatitis and dysentery, and the loneliness of separation from nation and friends. After his romance with Rebecca Eaton, and despite his gifts and handsome face, Rice had had no good fortune with women. And the reality in many mission fields was that life was nearly unendurable unless the hardships were surmounted by a married team.

The Board, through its failures and success, perfected the techniques of developing overseas missions. In 1814 Rice discovered George H. Hough, schoolteacher and printer, soon dispatched as a missionary candidate to join Adoniram Judson in Burma. Hough's wife Phoebe was permitted to go overseas, although at first she was not a church member.[63] Then arose the situation in 1815 of Charlotte H. White, who asked to be sent abroad to manage a mission school or to instruct native women in Christianity. Charlotte had a certain "pull" with the Board, since she had given fifty dollars in the first recorded contribution to the Triennial Convention. She then asked to lodge in Rangoon, Burma, with the newly-appointed Houghs. At this suggestion, missionaries Carey and Judson undoubtedly were upset. Attitudes about women in the formal societies of India and China were markedly different than those in America. Single adult women in such a setting would be suspected by many Asians of being in a polygamous relationship.

Fortunately for the Board and the missionary community, Miss White married the English Baptist missionary Joshua Rowe. Adoniram Judson pointedly commented in a letter: "We do not apprehend that the mission of single females to such a country as Burmah, is at all advisable."[64]

Rice was almost constantly on the move from 1815 to 1817. Often invisible and unnoticed, he was stitching together a denomination. He traveled to Ohio from his homebase in Pennsylvania, then to New York, New Jersey, New England, Virginia, North Carolina, South Carolina, Georgia, Kentucky, and Tennessee. In this three-year period, he reported that he had traveled over twenty thousand miles and received over thirteen thousand dollars. At Sandy Creek, North Carolina, and among Separate Baptists, in 1816, Luther Rice assisted the Separates in preparing ten "Principles of Faith" which were approved as a confession.[65] Even during his arduous duties on the road, he was attentive to record-keeping and financial management and gave regular accounting by statistics and reports to the Board.

His greatest relaxation sometimes coincided with his periods of illness, when his admirers would present him with food, clothing, socks, and, on one occasion, a horse and tack. When dehydrated by his travels, he relished stopping for tea or coffee; at one gathering at the Chowan Association, he astonished the ladies by drinking about seventeen small cups of tea.[66] On September 24, 1817, he preached on the text: "fell down and worshipped him."[67]

Horseback was his most common means of transportation. But he took the steamboat *Potomac* between Washington and Norfolk, and the *Connecticut* between Providence and New York. Turnpikes were coming into use, and he sometimes rode the regular stage between Boston and New York at three pence per mile and four miles per hour; the trip required four days.

Typical of his visits was the encounter at Sawyer's Creek meeting house near Elizabeth City, North Carolina. Rice appeared on his horse as a tall black-garbed figure and was asked to preach. The previous evening he had reached Norfolk, Virginia, traveling from Baltimore by boat, and during the night had ridden alone on horseback for sixty miles. His only stop was for breakfast at Sister Bushnell's house, about a mile from the church. After preaching on missions, he took an offering, and asked the association to appoint a person to distribute the Annual Report and forward the association proceedings to Dr. Staughton in Philadelphia.[68]

Rice spent the entire winter of 1815-16 in Kentucky, where missions support was generous, and he made his headquarters with Dean Benjamin Stout in Lexington.[69] A hostile anti-missions spokesman gave this account when in 1815 Rice visited the Elkhorn Baptist Association:

> When Luther rose up, the assembly of thousands, seemed stricken with his appearance. A tall, pale looking well-dressed young man, with all the solemn appearance of one who was

engaged in the work of the Lord, and perhaps he thought he was. He spoke some handsome things about the kingdom of Christ; but every stroke he gave seemed to men (sic) MONEY. He had the more pathos the nearer he came getting the money.[70]

The following partial itinerary of Rice in 1815 and 1816 will show the range of his contacts and travel.

March 28, 1815. Dined with Pres. Ashbel Green of Princeton College.

April 9, 1815. Preached to nearly 3,000 persons at baptismal service for Dr. Staughton at Philadelphia.

April 19, 1815. Bought books at $31.43 for Adoniram Judson & wrote letters to Dr. Carey and the Judsons.

August 19, 1815. Near Harrodsburg, Kentucky got lost in woods, while traveling 40 miles to the South District Association.

October 23, 1815. Collected .061/4 from "woman of colour" for foreign missions.

November 7, 1815. Visited Shakertown, near Lexington, Kentucky. Found Shakers deluded by "the scope & nature of their foolish errors & absurdities."

December 2, 1815. Met Isaac McCoy (1784-1846), who was recommended for missionary work among Indians in the Indiana Territory.

December 6, 1815. Slept on cold floor, surrounded by profane men at Madison Township, Indiana Territory.

On June 5, 1816, Rice visited John Jay, former governor of New York and former chief justice of the United States.[71]

In 1817 Rice diverted much of his resources and energy into home missions, working often with Native Americans on the frontier and occasionally with blacks. Prior to this the Philadelphia and Charleston associations had sent preachers to difficult areas. Under President Richard Furman, the Convention Board of Managers, prodded all the way by Rice, adopted in 1817 a provision for home (domestic) missions, and a further plan in 1818 for a collegiate and theological institution. All of this dovetailed into Rice's growing dream of a national Baptist organization, with a paid secretariat and a network of auxiliary societies.[72] Much of Rice's programmatic success would be due to Furman, a revolutionary war hero, prominent Charleston pastor, and first president of the Triennial Convention.[73]

Rice recruited the frontier preacher Isaac McCoy, blue-eyed, tall and thin, with two fingers missing, sometimes filled with self-pity, but rarely with self-blame. McCoy was stubborn and resourceful, and in the dead of winter swam his horses across the Maumee River and preached to a dozen hearers by candlelight.[74] This new home missionary had been distressed by trappers and traders plying the Indians with liquor and leaving Indian villages in squalor. He came to feel, with Oklahoma providing an exception, that the white man's influence was pervasively corrupting the Indians. McCoy headed the American Indian Mission Association, which was a factor in creating the cleavage between Northern and Southern Baptists.[75] McCoy also became the director of the Carey Station Indian Mission and involved Baptists in a matter of great controversy.

After his recruitment, McCoy badgered Rice to obtain a Baptist share of a ten-thousand-dollar annual federal allocation for Indian assistance, disbursed by the Secretary of War. Through an 1819 treaty, the United States Government undertook the reserving of lands for the education of Indian children. Indian families were to live at school sites where they could be fed and clothed. In time, educating and feeding Indians became an albatross, because each Indian mission would eventually cost as much as maintaining the entire missionary enterprise in Burma. In August 1819 Rice and the Board encouraged a Baptist delegation to meet with President James Monroe to obtain the funds dispensed through "Indian Reform." Out of this affair would come much confusion regarding Rice's involvement in money channeled to Isaac McCoy at Carey Station.[76]

The Triennial Convention was deeply interested in Indian mission work, but its Board members were horrified by the burgeoning expenses. McCoy badgered the Secretary of War, John C. Calhoun, for a miller for the Miami Indians, a teacher and blacksmith for the Pottawatomies, and a sizeable mission house, in addition to a share of the Indian Reform Fund. While McCoy was ardently pushing for Indian removal to reservations, he was rounding up more and more Indians to live at the school at the Board's expense.[77] As if Baptist resources were boundless, McCoy informed Rice that he intended to give a sow to the guardians of each Indian child and a cow for every ten students at the school. In 1824 McCoy refused Rice's instructions to channel through the Board offerings collected in Washington for Indian support. He also left an overdraft to be paid amounting to seventeen hundred dollars.[78] Still, the Indian missions projects continued to be matters of vital concern to Southerners and particularly to the Baptists of Kentucky.

Rice recruited two other young preachers, James Welch and John Mason Peck, who would provide invaluable service in the wilderness. Welch was contacted in Kentucky, where he was active as an itinerant preacher, and now felt called as a frontier missionary.[79] John Mason Peck, stemming from Congregational roots and a future pioneer Baptist missionary in the Illinois territory, was to become one of the greatest Baptist Trailblazers. He was the founder of Shurtleff College and various Bible societies, editor of a publication society, and an outstanding leader who helped the Baptists in various western states to confirm their Baptist beliefs.[80]

Peck and Luther Rice, both young men in 1815, met at the Warwick Association and spent the night talking about missions. In the end, Peck committed himself to home missions and to missionary work among people west of the Mississippi River. Probably influenced by Rice,[81] Peck, in January 1816, applied to receive theological training from Dr. William Staughton of the First Baptist Church, Philadelphia (then the corresponding secretary of the Triennial Convention). After study under Staughton, Peck and his wife made their way to St. Louis to begin their frontier religious work.[82]

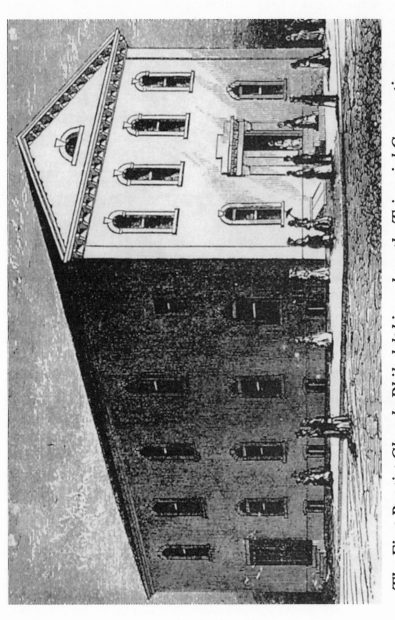

The First Baptist Church, Philadelphia, where the Triennial Convention was organized on May 18, 1814.

Home Missions

The home missions movement was never given a period of great peace. At each meeting of the Triennial Convention, there were conflicts between those who favored Convention-directed home missions and others who preferred locally-controlled mission societies. Many Easterners felt that the frontier churches should assume the initiative and expand their work into unchurched areas, and then money could be directed to Indian missions. Thus, in 1820, the Board voted to discontinue its work at St. Louis and instructed home missionary Peck to join Reverend McCoy in Indiana. Peck took Rice's suggestion, refused the assignment, remained at St. Louis, and on his own began an academy that became Shurtleff College. Peck had made his personal choice to educate Baptist clergy on the frontier, rather than expend his life preaching to bands of nomadic Indians.[83]

At the 1823 meeting in Washington, the committee on domestic missions strongly endorsed the concept that missions should be operated by the state organizations. Subsequently, home missions largely reverted to regional or state control, such as to the Massachusetts Missionary Society and the Mississippi Missionary Society.

America, in the nineteenth century, developed an appetite for missionary activities and stories. Sunday School (borrowed from the Methodists) stirred a demand for Bible literature and teachers' aids. In response, Rice and Staughton, the corresponding secretary of the Triennial Convention, made plans in 1814 to publish and mail the proceedings of the Convention.[84] In 1817 Rice suggested that the Board initiate a magazine comparable to the Massachusetts Baptist Missionary Magazine, which had limited circulation. At the September 1817 Board meeting, Rice was placed on a committee to supervise the General Convention's first publication; he upgraded the *Latter Day Luminary* that had been operating in Philadelphia as a quarterly missionary magazine and revived it in 1818 as a monthly publication to reflect Board actvities and missionary successes. *The*

Luminary, in Washington, D.C., with Rice as its founding editor, acquired a circulation of nearly eight thousand copies per month. Religious news was mirrored by several other private Baptist papers, including the *Columbian Star,* established in 1822 by Luther Rice; eventually the *Star,* devoted to promoting Columbian College and foreign missions, would become *The Christian Index* of Georgia.[85] Using his own funds, Rice purchased property and a printing office in Washington, D.C., to be used for the publication of *The Columbian Star,* which was printed as a religious weekly.

Ironically, the Boston clergy disregarded the publication of *The Luminary,* giving it little support, and continuing the publication of their own journal.[86] Rice hoped that *The Luminary* would become the voice of the Board, but Dr. Thomas Baldwin, very influential in the North and chairman of the Board, warned that linking *The Luminary* with missions had created "much uneasiness." Subsequently, the Board voted not to support the publication with Convention funds.[87] However, the establishment of two publications in Washington made an impact in unifying Baptists in support of common missionary and educational enterprises.

The Baptist General Tract Society was founded in 1824 through the efforts of eighteen men and seven women; while not the creation of Luther Rice, the Tract Society provided doctrinal and moral guidance, supported by a vigorous organization that published eighty-five thousand tracts in its first year. Rice, the Society's treasurer and agent, was to show great courage in resisting efforts in 1825-27 to move the Society from Washington to Philadelphia. Rice wanted Washington, D.C., to become the focus of Baptist strength, and the change of the Society's location was a great disappointment to him.[88]

Along with *The Luminary,* Rice received permission to distribute the Triennial Convention's *Annual Report.* Rice then undertook the initiative to arouse each Baptist association to appoint a secretary to receive the Board's literature and records and to correspond with Washington on local activities. He then sought the Board's approval to keep records of the names and numbers of the associations and their churches and the aggregate number of members. Thus, a design for denominational formation and strength became more than visionary.[89] After the first convention report was published in 1815, Rice drove in a wagon through New England, New York, and New Jersey, forming missionary societies and selling the reports.[90]

Rice stated in his *Second Annual Report* that Negroes, particularly those members attending Richmond's First Baptist Church, "want to give to an African mission." Two of the members of that church were the gifted free blacks, Lott Cary, manager of a large tobacco warehouse, and Collin Teague, harness maker. Inspired by Rice, Lott Cary organized "The Richmond African Baptist Missionary Society." In April 1819 the Board of the Baptist General Convention appointed Cary and Teague as missionaries to Africa, both reaching Sierra Leone in 1821.[91]

The indefatigable messenger Rice was constantly on the move in cities and towns, and as readily searching out Baptists on farms and in hamlets, and talking about a new college, Bible societies, and the Sunday School movement. Rice knew many anecdotes, tempered even serious talk with a flow of humor, and played the flute cheerfully.[92] He gathered children about him and told them of his adventures in India, Brazil, and the West, embellished with his encounters with wildcats, bears, and Indians. Never one to lose a good business opportunity, Rice, on a trip in New York, purchased a two-horse Dearborn wagon with a canvas top that he subsequently sold in Lexington, Kentucky, for one hundred dollars. On another occasion, he traded a mare and a gig for a horse and saddle.[93]

His hosts were of an amazing variety, including in Williamson County, near Nashville, Tennessee, black-haired elder Garner McConnico, who had a so-called "40-parson power" voice—sufficient, it was said, to carry across a swollen stream, and also an exaggerated reputation for casting out devils. In other more civilized communities, Rice, in Cincinnati, stayed with General Jonathan Gano, son of the famous Baptist frontier and New York preacher John Gano. In New York, he also obtained hospitality from Judge Talmadge.

In Madison County, Virginia, he would stay with President Madison's brother, General William Madison. In Georgia, his patron was Dr. Jesse Mercer, and in Charleston, Richard Furman. In Savannah, he often spent the winter months with the Dunnings.[94]

Columbian College (the future George Washington University)

The Charleston Association had a fund for ministerial education, established in 1757, and through this account financed a score of students at Brown University. In 1812 the Philadelphia Association, and in 1813-18 the Baptists of New York and New Jersey, gave modest support to the education of ministers. But for the southern students, Brown University was too distant. Further, there were more Baptists in Virginia than all of New England. In reviewing this knowledge, the Reverend W. B. Johnson spoke of a college geographically more accessible to students from the middle and southern states. Furman referred sadly to the little attention paid to "improvement" of the minds of "pious youth." Yet there were opportunities for ministerial education under Article 4 of the Triennial Convention Constitution of 1814, which if applied to missionaries allowed the Board to "take measures for the improvement of their qualifications."[95]

Luther Rice was the preeminent dreamer, and he had evolved a vision of a great unified Baptist denomination, with its center in Washington, D.C., equidistant from North and West. In the crude and dowdy town of Washington, but also the hub of an emerging empire, Rice wanted to forge a great Baptist seminary, a national denominational college, a publishing house, a center for missionary societies, and the infrastructure for a surging evangelical army. Captured by this vision, at least in part, were Dr. William Staughton of Philadelphia, W. Bullein Johnson of Savannah, Richard Furman of South Carolina, and for a time Dr. Thomas Baldwin of Boston. President Furman, in his 1817 Triennial address, convinced many Baptists of the importance of an educated clergy and laity. The burning brand igniting this conflagration for missions was the unstoppable Luther Rice. But then, in the first quarter of the nineteen century, he abruptly diverted his energies in another direction, to creating a seminary and a national Baptist institution, Columbian College.

Beginning in May 1818, Rice became absorbed in a tenacious resolve to bring Columbian College into being. The new initiative commenced when the Baptist Board for Foreign Missions (that acted for the Triennial Convention between sessions) approved a general scheme, conceived by Rice, Furman, and the Judsons, that would provide for an institution of collegiate and theological education. The first stage was the creation of a theological seminary in Philadelphia, to be housed initially in the home of Dr. William Staughton. Two committees of Philadelphians were appointed to arrange student boarding facilities and purchase books for the library. Some enlightened Baptists envisaged a "national institution" that would be theological and not literary.[96] Plans were then made for Staughton and the seminary to move to Washington. The move of Baptist institutions to Washington was originally the inspiration of Obadiah Brown, close friend of Luther Rice. Brown was the postmaster in the Capital, the chaplain to Congress, and also the pastor of the First Baptist Church of Washington. The next stage was the purchase of property and erection of buildings in Washington for a Baptist national college that would include a classical and theological department.[97]

At its 1817 and 1818 meetings, Board members of the Triennial Convention approved the concept of creating one or more theological seminaries if funds could be raised and if those monies would be separate from mission resources. This concept was overtaken by a companion "plan" conceived by Rice and the Board's select committee, projecting a Columbian College that would offer two years of classical studies. Eventually, as conceptualized, the college would give full preparation in medicine and law and two advanced years in theological studies.[98]

The Board, seized by its intoxicating vision, then plunged into a

series of extravagant ventures. By 1820 it had purchased forty-six
and one-half acres of prime land in Washington, about a mile from
the White House. However, the land purchase was virtually assured
in 1817, when a Literary Association purchased and held the property for the Convention.

The next phase was to construct a building and select the president and one professor. The Board selected Dr. Staughton as the
seminary "principal" and for its scholar-teacher Ira Chase, "a young
brother of piety, talents and learning," each to be paid six hundred
dollars per annum. Richard Furman of the Charleston Association,
and others, protested the myriad of projects, the haste, the dearth of
critical thinking, and the possibilities that the flimsy wax structure
could melt away under the sun's bright rays. Meanwhile, by 1820,
there was completed a five-story building, 117 by 47 feet, with dormitory facilities for one hundred students.[99] Agents scoured Europe
for equipment and the United States for sustaining funds, to support
the college and its new library.[100]

Wealthy and influential men, including George Washington, ardently supported the creation of the national university in the Capital. President John Quincy Adams was pleased to lend the college
twenty thousand dollars.[101] But most of the financial support would
come from the South. In 1820 the Triennial Convention passed a
resolution that the institution be located in Washington:

> Resolved, that the convention accept of the premises ten-
> dered to them for the site of an institution for the education of
> gospel ministers, and for a college, adjoining the city of Wash-
> ington; and that the Board be directed to take measures, as soon
> as convenient, for obtaining a legal title to the same. And that
> the Board be further directed, to keep the institution, already in
> a state of progress, first in view, and not to incur expenses be-
> yond the amount of funds which may be obtained for the estab-
> lishment of either of the institutions.[102]

Columbian College was beautifully situated on a Washington hill,
which provided a view of Georgetown and Alexandria and some-

times a glimpse of Mount Vernon. It had its own well and, within its first building, a small chapel. The seminary opened on September 1, 1821, while Columbian College began its classes in January 1822, with Dr. Staughton as president of the college.[103] There were lavish opening ceremonies that left the institution with new debts. By April 1824 the college was instructing ninety-three students from twenty-one states. Books and laboratory equipment had been purchased in Europe by Professor Alva Woods and James, the son of Dr. Staughton.[104] The growth was astounding, with a medical department established in 1825 and a law department in 1826. Through the assistance of Henry Clay and General John Gano of New York, the college obtained a charter and then amended it so that the students could be of any or no religion.[105]

Rice explained the complementary roles of the seminary and college, in his letter of January 6, 1823, to Adoniram Judson in Burma:

> In the progress of the business it became obvious that a Theological Institution was indispensably necessary to the attainment of the great objects contemplated, and after a while it was believed that a College would facilitate the purposes of the Theological Institution; and both these came at length to be combined in the Columbian College in the District of Columbia.

In order to support the expanding religious-academic complex, the country was divided into three geographical sectors, each with two fund-raisers. But Rice, authorized by the Board to obtain financial support for the twenty or more ministerial students, would be the most enthusiastic and raise most of the money.[106] Edward Kingsford wrote the following about Rice's resolute nature:

Nothing but absolute necessity ever prevented him from accomplishing any purpose which he had formed in his mind, or from fulfilling an engagement he had previously made. In his numerous journeys in the South, he had frequently to cross deep and rapid streams, yet he appeared never to have been disconcerted by the threatened impediment, or deterred from making the passage, however dangerous. At one time, on approaching a stream, he perceived by the turbid state of the water that it could not be forded without some danger; he left the horse and sulky on the bank and plunged into the river. Just as the water reached his neck, he found himself approaching the opposite shore; he then returned and with his horse and carriage, dashed through the foaming flood. At another time, on a similar occasion, discovering that he could not keep his books, papers, and other baggage dry, if he swam his horse and sulky through the water, he disengaged his horse from the vehicle, and with portions of his books, crossed the stream thirteen times, and then wet as he was, pursued his journey. Once, when he came to a very deep and rapid river on which stood a mill, he called to the miller to help him over. "Help you over?" said the man, with astonishment, "you will not be able to cross that river today." "Yes, I shall," said Rice, "if you will help me." Immediately alighting, he commenced operations. He first took one wheel off the sulky and carried it through the mill; he took off the other, and transported it in the same way. Afterwards, by the aid of the miller, he carried the body of the sulky through. By a number of successive trips, he conveyed over the harness and the baggage, then mounting his horse he swam him through the river, and then went on his way to secure the object to which he had devoted his life. . . ."[107]

President Staughton was not interested in financial matters, although optimistic about the college, and did not move to Washington until 1824. Customarily Staughton was in Washington only for two to three days at a time. He left almost everything to Rice, who was heavily burdened raising money for the college.[108]

Professor Ira Chase, who became head of the theological department,[109] arrived in Washington in 1824 after a search for laboratory equipment in Europe. His attitude quickly soured, for the promised faculty salaries could not be paid on time. He disagreed with Rice and Staughton about merging the theological seminary and the college, and disagreed with Staughton about the curriculum for the seminary. Then, not having Rice's vision of a denominational center, he felt that New England would be a better location for the seminary.[110] So the merger of the seminary and the college was not permanent.

Despite its dazzling start and the acclaim of dignitaries, including United States senators and representatives, the college from the beginning was in serious financial trouble. Between 1822 and 1825, Rice sought unsuccessfully to stabilize the college's finances, made critical by the withdrawal of promised support that shriveled under the impact of the financial panics of 1819 and the 1820s. Then Rice was unable to rally adequate support for the college within the Triennial Convention, in part because of strong anti-missionary feelings in the West and the Baptists disenchanted in New England. His own reputation was then placed in jeopardy.[111]

From the initial purchase of its campus site, and even before, three questions by Baptists would trouble the very existence of Columbian College. (1) Why had a missionary organization, the Triennial Convention, become an advocate for a Baptist College? (2) Why was the newly-formed Baptist seminary being moved from Philadelphia to Washington, D.C.? (3) Why was Luther Rice, ordained as a missionary, not serving with Adoniram Jordan in Burma?[112]

Despite the ebullience of its leading supporters, the college and the religious infrastructure so rapidly assembled in Washington was in peril. The financial structure supporting the college was like a delicate crosswork of jackstraws, feebly balanced and likely at any moment to disassemble. Not all the funds needed were at hand when campus construction began. After the first building was constructed, a second one, just as large, was imprudently begun. Loans and assurances provided the original impetus, but they would not be enough to sustain the growth. The mounting financial burdens became insurmountable.[113] When failures occurred, fingers would be pointed at Luther Rice, the hardest-working advocate.

Part of the attack on Rice's pattern of Baptist centralization in Washington, D.C., was the result of a preference by many Baptists in New England and the Middle Atlantic states for a loose societal "norm" (or decentralized convention) providing support for the missions-supporting organization. Such a "norm" or society in England had supported William Carey through the Baptist Missionary Society. Some Baptists of New England who had great influence on the leadership and expenditure of funds desired the financial institutions to be located in Boston or Philadelphia. Baptists in the Southern States, on the other hand, supported a tighter, more centralized structure, based on experience with the efficiency of the Southern plantation. Also, Southerners wanted the Baptist hub to be in close proximity to Washington D.C., where their friendly influence could be brought to bear.

Baptists in numbers felt that the primary, if not the exclusive, purpose of the Triennial Convention was support of foreign missions, and now many of them had concerns that the seminary would short-circuit this role. In his vigorous fight for the college, Rice disregarded the injunctions of the Convention, and, through desperation, took the lead in borrowing from foreign mission funds to support the seminary. In the summer of 1821, months before the seminary and college opened, Rice and the Education Committee requested a loan "not to exceed $10,000" from monies invested in United States stock. For this commitment, the Board was compelled to pay obligations in small amounts on twenty notes.

Rice Collapses

Rice rushed to New York and New England to raise funds. In his anxiety, in 1822-23, his health failed, and he narrowly escaped a nervous breakdown. Then vicious rumors arose, when Rice at the Triennial meeting did not produce an account of his collections.[114] Long before the critical 1826 Triennial meeting, Rice's friend Jonathan Going had warned Rice that the New England Baptists were disturbed about "a loan of certain Missionary Monies, to the Trustees of the College. . . . Unless the matter be adjusted . . . they are resolved . . . to secede from the Convention. . . ."[115]

Rice also endured numbers of nagging foes, who badgered him for years about his failure to return overseas as a missionary. Two of these tormentors in Philadelphia were three-hundred-pound Henry Holcombe, vice president of the Executive Board, and William J. Rogers, who addressed their complaints in a letter to Triennial president Richard Furman. They accused Rice of stalling on his missionary commitment to go to Burma, thereby costing the Baptists eight dollars a week for his salary.[116] In reply, Rice referred to a "liver complaint" [hepatitis] that would kill him if he returned to Asia, and also the lack of a missionary-wife to accompany him. Rogers also averred that Rice should not solicit funds, since he had not established himself as a Baptist after leaving the Congregational Church; he had not brought an accrediting letter from the Lall Bazaar Baptist Church at Calcutta. Furman was so disturbed by the friction generated by Rogers and Holcombe that he wrote to the Reverend Edmund Botsford, "there is a source of evil there, men working for the devil."[117] Holcombe was removed from the Board in 1817. But in ten years, the opponents of Rice, joined by others from New York and New England, would dominate the Board.[118]

Failure of the Baptist Unification Movement

In 1826 the roof fell in, both for Rice and the bright promises of Baptist unification that he had promoted. Rice was the catalyst who had brought Columbian College and many of the other agencies into existence. His efforts had been the principal means of their growth and maintenance.[119] Now he would be singled out as the prime villain. In expanding the college, too much money had been expended for the second building, the entertainment of distinguished guests, equipment, and faculty salaries. Tuition was fixed at sixteen dollars per student; however, many students had been given free lodging and tuition. But the primary cause for the disintegration of the Baptist dream of unity (nurtured by a minority) may have been the great ideological, economic, and social philosophies that separated the North from the South, and, thus, the Baptists of New England from the Baptists south of the Mason-Dixon Line.

The English Baptists, particularly the General Baptists, long had been wary of any control from clergy, associations, or societies, and shunned the style of church government fostered by state churches. The experience in North America of the intrusion into local church affairs by the co-associations of the Congregational Church were frightening. So, through experience and pragmatism, the Baptists in much of New England favored a weak "societal type" for a Baptist national structure, if there should be any national organization at all. This view of Baptist polity was the opposite of another option, "denominational connectionalism," that was favored by those Baptists, particularly Southerners, who valued more centralization in all phases of denominational life. While individuals cherished local congregational independence, denominational connectionalism allowed the centralization of powerful resources, money, and leadership in accomplishing the religious objectives impelled by a belief in Jesus Christ. Thus, leaders like Luther Rice and President Francis Wayland of Brown University encouraged unity of action through the Triennial Convention to promote home missions and educational activities.[120]

Lightning struck in 1826, when the General Convention completely severed its relations with Columbian College. The foreign mission board was transferred to Boston,[121] where it had avid supporters. Already, after 1824, the American Baptist General Tract Society, with Rice as its treasurer and agent, had become the unwilling pawn in the decentralization process, as the Society was transferred to Philadelphia, reportably because there was a stereotyping plant in the city. The Tract Society was transformed into the fruitful American Baptist Publication Society. The *Columbian Star*, the missions weekly given to the Convention by Rice, was moved to Philadelphia, to obtain more advertising. In Philadelphia, the *Star* would be used to print editorials against Rice and the other men who had created it.

The American Baptist Home Mission Society, organized in 1832, was assigned to New York City, ostensibly because it was near the Erie Canal, which would play a great commercial role in developing the West.

The Triennial Convention then took steps to extricate itself from home missions work, and most phases of the work were discontinued. But its activities with American Indians were sustained and supported by the Convention, and in 1865 mission work among the Indians was directed by the Home Mission Society.[122]

Baptists in North Re-Direct Triennial Convention

In 1826, sixty-three messengers attended the Triennial Convention in New York, of which twenty-three were from Massachusetts, and seventeen represented the New York churches. This put the convention in the hands of a challenging group of New Englanders and Easterners.[123] The Convention had been transformed into a favorable milieu for Baptists that approved the societal norm, and this element would now dominate and radically alter the direction of the denomination. In May 1826 the General Missionary Convention delivered the death-blow to Baptist support for Columbian College. The Convention voted to investigate Luther Rice, sever its affiliation with the College, and become a single-purpose missionary society.

As the price for being almost the sole manager of college funds, Rice was directly charged with peculation and dishonorable investments. His critics demanded that his Journal, the record of receipts and expenditures, be turned over to auditors. Rice was vulnerable, for despite his absolute honesty, he was an "untidy" fund-raiser and purchaser.[124] To the relief of his faithful friends, the Committee of Investigation found that Rice had committed "financial indiscretions" but that he was not guilty of great moral default. He was, however, discharged by the Board in 1826, for being "too loose in all his transactions."[125] For, against the instructions of the Convention and the wishes of Dr. Thomas Baldwin, spokesman for the North, Rice had stubbornly begun the college before the amassing of "competent and distinct funds."[126]

Some of his best friends now buckled or lost their zeal. William Staughton, the popular Baptist preacher of Philadelphia, had grown increasingly disenchanted with the financial practices in support of the college, from about 1924 to 1926. Richard Furman of South Carolina, strong advocate of an educated clergy and a friend of Luther Rice, had died in 1825. Of Rice's Northern friends, one of the most influential was Francis Wayland, who had changed his views, and by 1826 had become an advocate of the societal method in preference to a strong centralized denomination.[127]

The consequences of the upheaval in leadership and philosophy were profound. The Triennial Convention adopted new policies that pleased the New England states, but these were greeted less happily by the Baptists of the South. The Southerners, who had felt encouraged by the centralization promoted by Luther Rice, became disenchanted, as projects, leadership, and institutions now returned to the North or were placed under directives issued by leaders in the North. There was an uncertainty that had primitive origins, embracing even the old testy relations between Regular Baptists and General Baptists.

Some Baptists feared that the Convention might become strong enough to threaten a primal Baptist doctrine and practice—the independence of each church. Therefore, at the 1826 Triennial Convention, it was "Resolved . . . this Convention cannot exercise the least authority over the government of Churches."[128]

In an analysis by historian McBeth, the religious démarche of 1826, to use a diplomatic term, would bring many negative results. McBeth concluded that in the long reach of history, the vision of Rice in seeking a unified Baptist effort will be shown to be creative, intelligent, and broadly Christian. The return by the American

Baptists and others to a societal norm would, on the negative side, obstruct the integration of Baptists and compartmentalize their resources. The Judsons in Burma would be revered as saints, but Rice, remaining in America to unify the Baptists, would be vilified. While the final split between Northern and Southern Baptists in 1845 would be attributed to the slavery issue, the events of 1826 would make the rupture almost inevitable.[129]

Rice Dishonored

Stripped of titles and honor, Rice devoted his last ten years to saving the college he had founded. Almost a pauper, having no salary, he traveled incessantly and contributed every cent he could raise to paying off the debts of the college. His hope was to save Columbian College for the Baptists.[130] Robert B. Semple (1761-1831), principal leader of the Baptists in Virginia, had agreed in 1826 to become the chief agent of the college and president of its Board of Trustees. This brought Semple into contact with the volunteer traveling solicitor Luther Rice. But Rice often groused that Semple spent too much time at his estate "Mordington" and ignored the business of the college.[131]

In the end, Congress would bail out the college that many of its members had endorsed, but it would no longer be a Baptist institution. The college would become George Washington University, and, in 1904, sever its last links with the Baptists.[132] The great venture fell prey to a combination of factors, including the anti-intellectualism of many Baptists, the myopia of others, the hard times of the 1820s, and the drag of regional ties, all positioned against the heroic efforts of Luther Rice. Perhaps the creation of a great national Baptist university and the centralizing of Baptist interests, policies, and administration were designed prematurely. But, for the twinkling of an eye, the dream was exhilarating.

In the South, many Baptists now felt that its Board was an Eastern organization. Southerners grew restive and frustrated over the apparent unwillingness of the Board to expend resources south of the Mason-Dixon line. Even a plea to send missionaries to the Republic of Texas was not heeded. All this rejection revitalized an old anti-missions movement in the South. Those persons supporting missions began to ignore the Triennial Convention projects and chose instead to support causes and areas of local concern. Southerners complained increasingly that they had no control over the missionary funds that they had raised. Since the Convention met every three years, in the intervening years the Board, located in the North, controlled the active projects.

The absorption of Rice in developing Columbian College (beginning in 1818) probably had a short-term detrimental effect on missions, both foreign and domestic. The Board had plans in 1815 to expand mission work into Brazil and Africa, but those ventures did not take place. Between 1820 and 1823, no new missionaries were sent to Burma.[133] However, in 1832, after Rice's dismissal, the Baptists had a significant surge of activity with nineteen missionaries sent to Burma, or ready to embark. In 1835 (the year preceding Rice's death), there were 72 missionaries abroad. In 1844, there were 111 missionaries, of which 32 were in North America (engaged mainly in Indian work) and 63 in Asia.[134] While much of this productive work was not attributable to Rice, his early efforts had stirred the fire-coals and contributed to the missions surge.

By the time Rice left the scene, the Baptists, as a religious movement, had developed a high profile. By 1800 the Baptists made up the most numerous religious body in North America, and by 1844 they comprised 720,000 members and 9,385 churches.[135]

The Convention had lost faith in Rice's good judgment, but still he was permitted to raise money.[136] Working without pay and dependent on the charity of friends—such as William H. Turpin of Augusta, Georgia, and Archibald Thomas of Richmond, Virginia— he pled for support for the College. Then, plagued by diseases he contracted in India, he fell victim to a new crippling paralysis. He took comfort from his remaining friends, who remembered his old dynamism and urged him to moderate his work lest he die prematurely. Responding to the worries of his cronies, he answered: "I am ready [to die], but I would like to build up the college first.[137]

His Last Days

Even in his last year, he had goals. In January 1836 he wrote, "My plan is to read the Bible through systematically once a year . . . make a point to pray for every family where I tarry a night or call in the day. . . . I think this course tends to keep alive religion in the soul; to prevent lightness and other improprieties; to secure success to my efforts."[138]

Fatigued in body and soul, he began to fade at Elam, South Carolina, near Edgefield, after preaching his last sermon on August 28, 1836. Four weeks later, on September 25, probably suffering from appendicitis, he expired at the home of his friend, medical doctor R. G. Mays. He had no wife or children to comfort his last hours. Still, as his death approached, Luther Rice grew in grace as a Christ-imitator. And near the very end, he thought of his beloved college and begged his friends to sell his sulky and horse in support of the institution.[139] The Rice papers were found in his room at Columbian College, for he had no house of his own.[140]

His Legacy

Luther Rice, in reflection, was one of the Baptist faith's greatest Trailblazers. While John Smyth knew how to formulate Baptist core-beliefs, Rice mastered the techniques of educating Baptist clergy and laymen and the art of coalescing (at Washington, D.C.) publications, foreign missions, home missions, a college, and a seminary. His greatest achievements, but attained in collaboration with other great Baptist leaders in the North and South, were the Triennial Convention, the Seminary, and Columbian College.

He sought to mold the Triennial Convention into an expression of Baptist unity. His failure to achieve a great national Baptist denomination is probably attributable to a lack of precedent in this direction and the arching imperative for independence nurtured by separate Baptist churches and their members. Also, faulty public relations and great sectional differences undermined the leadership of Rice and the other Baptist leaders seeking a Baptist consensus. Later on, the slavery issue was a fatal flaw in the unifying process. The old leadership role of the North and traditional styles were never completely overcome by Rice, even when he was aided in his strategic aims by Staughton, Johnson, Furman, and Mercer; many of the New England Baptists strongly wanted institutions and leaders to be located in Boston and Philadelphia. Southerners, on the other hand, who had given generous support for foreign missions, wanted recognition of their sectional needs and sought recognition for new leaders in the growing South.

Rice, even as the discredited leader, was the tireless supporter of both missions and Columbian College. On horseback and in sulky, he crossed swamps, rivers, and the wilderness in the vastness of the continent to preach and solicit support for the institution in Washington. As an indication of his aggressive pace in evangelism, in 1816 he exceeded the circuit-riding record of Methodist missionary Francis Asbury, in traveling ninety miles in a day's journey in Carolina and Virginia. Luther Rice's remarkable travel gave him only ten hours of sleep during six days of preaching and deliberations at Baptist associations. In April 1818 Rice wrote Staughton that during the year he had traveled 9,359 miles and collected donations of $5,443.57.[141]

Working among the unsaved, Rice expounded the Scriptures as the Word of God. In his discourse both with the intelligentsia, as well as those who disdained the learned, he taught that men and women could love God with their intellects as well as their emotions. To the fragmented and independent Baptists, he formulated a plan that proved that through unity they could build foreign and domestic missions in a progressive and efficient way. In a developing Baptist faith, he showed his Christian supporters how to establish Baptist seminaries, colleges, and other elements of a great denomination.

His pioneer efforts were monumental, even in failure; for while the Seminary was removed, Columbian College was finally lost to secular education, and the Triennial Convention would be dissolved, in the minds of many believers were shown the vast potentialities when believers yoked themselves to God's purposes. And down through the ages, Baptists are inspired by the vision of the dreamer Luther Rice, riding his horse Columbus into the wilderness, with the Bible and *The Luminary* in his saddlebag.

*The Reverend John Gerhard Oncken Preaching at the
First Baptist Church in Hamburg, Germany (1852)*

Chapter 12

Johann Gerhard Oncken
(1800-1884)

Father of the Continental European Baptists

The German Baptist Trailblazer, Johann (John) Gerhardt Oncken, was by far the most dynamic and influential leader in the history of Baptist work in Continental Europe. His zeal, curiosity, restlessness, and driving evangelism took him from Hamburg, Germany, to Denmark, Switzerland, Sweden, Latvia, Russia, England, the Balkans, and America. His unwavering Christian drive impelled him to preach and organize churches, first in Germany, and then in northern, central, eastern and southern Europe; he sustained the work with a publishing ministry and through establishing the first German Baptist theological seminary at Hamburg.

Oncken and two Christian missionary colleagues, who largely pioneered Baptist work among German-speaking people on the Continental shelf, worked in close harmony, and were dubbed the *Kleeblatt* or cloverleaf. Oncken's collaborators were Julius Wilhelm Köbner (1806-84), son of a Danish rabbi and himself a prolific writer of hymns, and the energetic Gottfried Wilhelm Lehmann (1799-1882), who developed the Berlin church and helped organize churches in Hungary, Switzerland, and other countries.

Oncken was an inspired and autocratic Christian leader, spreading a conservative theology, heavily spiced with Calvinism. However, it was not on Calvinism that this dominant and forceful personality

would be challenged. Rather, Köbner and Lehmann would success-
fully battle in the 1870s for the autonomy of new churches, in preference to their becoming wards of the mother-church in Hamburg.
In German terminology, their struggle of wills was called the Hamburg *Streit* (debate). Oncken also would be confronted by his friend
Lehmann on the matter of sharing money within the German Baptist Union for non-European missions. Lehmann was unwavering as
he announced, "So long as I have two pfennigs, I will give one to our
mission and one to the heathen."[1] Thus, although clearly the dominant leader among the early German Baptists, Oncken would be
shaped and tested by his colleagues and also by his tormentors from
oppressing governments, as well as by the seismic economic and
political events that led to the revolutions of 1848 and the emergence in 1871 of the modern German state.

Johann Oncken was born on January 26, 1800, at Varel, in the
German state of Oldenburg. Prior to the downfall of Napoleon
Buonaparte at Waterloo in 1815, Oncken's father was involved in
political intrigue to overthrow Napoleonic dominance in the
Germanies. Because of the threat of arrest, the father was obliged to
take refuge in England, where he died after a few years. Meanwhile,
young Oncken was nurtured by a pious grandmother and confirmed
in the German Lutheran Church.[2]

The turning point in Oncken's life occurred after the famous Battle
of Leipzig (October 16-19, 1813), when Napoleon was first defeated
by an international army of Russians, Austrians, and Prussians.[3] A
Scottish merchant visited Varel, following the victory, to collect for
goods smuggled in contravention of Napoleon's Continental System
(erected to prevent British trade with the Continent). The foreign
businessman saw the potential of Oncken, although he was not fourteen years old, and invited him to Scotland to "make a man of him."[4]

Oncken agreed to the intriguing proposal, and in September 1813,
he and his patron reached Leith, near Edinburgh. Thereafter, Oncken
and his sponsor spent nine years on business trips that took them
through Scotland, England, France, and Germany. On those ven-

tures, he appears to have mastered three languages fluently.[5] His employer was a decent man, and while not a Bible reader, he purchased a Bible for his apprentice and introduced him to Presbyterian beliefs.[6]

The decisive religious experience for Oncken occurred in London, when he lodged with an Independent family at Blackheath. This household's worship and fervent prayers touched him profoundly. He was converted at a Methodist chapel, where the minister's sermon probed the text: "Therefore, there is now no condemnation for those who are in Christ Jesus" (Romans 8:1). Oncken at this time surrendered himself completely to the grace of God as manifested in Christ, and resolved at once to spread the message of salvation. His surrender was so complete that he began the distribution of religious tracts as his first service. He immediately undertook another act of self-sacrifice; instead of eating an adequate meal on his one-shilling allowance, he resolved to limit himself to a one-penny roll and apply the balance to purchase more Gospel tracts.[7]

Oncken was impelled by an inner compulsion to preach the Gospel among his fellow Germans. Conceivably the best-organized missionary society of that time to undertake that mission was the Continental Society, founded in London in 1819, with the broad purpose of spreading the evangelical faith in Europe. Oncken joined the Continental Society, and in 1823 was given the freedom to visit the northern German port cities of Hamburg and Bremen, where his missionary work was marked by great success. While many were converted, he had also aroused the apprehensions of the State Church, that would move to restrain and punish him.[8]

Oncken first began his German missionary labor in Hamburg in 1823, as a member of the English Reformed Church, while simultaneously an agent of the Continental Society. The Germanies, including the Freistadt of Hamburg, were composed of many separate kingdoms, states, and free cities, which would not be united until 1871. With the encouragement of Pastor Matthews, Oncken on January 4, 1824, delivered his first sermon to eighteen people in a private house. His first convert was C. F. Lange, who became one of his most valued assistants. As religious seekers began to inundate the tight quarters of the improvised chapel, the police closed the house to halt further preaching. The unstoppable Oncken then turned to preaching on street corners and rooms in restaurants. In order to avoid the real possibility of expulsion from Hamburg, he began a business venture in 1828 as a bookseller, and then, as further protection, registered as a citizen of Hamburg.[9]

After ten years of Continental evangelical work, he became an agent of the Edinburgh Bible Society, actively preaching and distributing Bibles and tracts. He also assisted the friendly minister of the parish of St. George in establishing the first Sunday School in Germany.

Oncken, up to this point, had had no contacts with Baptists, who on the Continent were only very few, and these hotly persecuted. According to historian Henry C. Vedder, the name of Baptist had been an epithet of scorn and contempt in Germany for centuries. This disdain for a brave people was undeserved and based on a misconception of Baptist beliefs and a misguided understanding of the Anabaptists and their practices. Upon the more ancient but closely-related Anabaptists—the so-called *Wiedertaufer*, great martyrs of the earliest Reformation period—were hurled the false accusations of being communists, polygamists, and wielders of the sword. The Germans often falsely attributed to the gallant Anabaptists (and by confusion, to the Baptists) the disorders and excesses of Mülhausen and Münster in the sixteenth century.[10] But there were few Anabaptists involved in those events, and no Baptists at all. The Anabaptists, unlike most Baptists, were pacifists, subscribed to no oaths, and excluded magistrates from their worship.

Oncken's first contacts with the Baptists occurred in 1826, when he visited Bremen. In that city he met Pastor Mallet, who was so impressed with Oncken that he offered to underwrite the young lay worker's education if he would undertake theological studies and formally prepare for the ministry. Oncken declined the generous offer, but now he was aware of people who shared similar beliefs on salvation and baptism. Oncken remarked later, "I already had doubts about infant baptism." He probed the Scriptures as he searchingly redefined his faith. A new spiritual Oncken was emerging, who refused to allow Lutheran prelates to christen his first daughter.[11]

During his work with the Continental Society, Oncken, through his studies of the Scriptures, became convinced that only the baptism of believers through immersion was practiced in Apostolic times. His study of the New Testament drew him close to Baptist beliefs, as revealed in his tract, "Triumphs of the Gospel":

> It was about this time [1828] that I became fully convinced from the study of the Scriptures (for I was entirely unacquainted with the sentiments of the Baptists) of the truth of believers' baptism and the nature of a Christian church. I and a few of the converts who had also seen the same truth now only waited for some one who, having himself followed the Lord in his ordinance, should be qualified to baptize us and form us into a church. But for this, we had to wait five long years, though we applied to both England and Scotland. . . .[12]

The man led by Providence to baptize Oncken in 1834 was an American Baptist clergyman, the Reverend Barnas Sears, professor at the Hamilton Literary Institution (later president of Newton Theological Institution and Brown University), who was studying in Germany.[13] Arriving in Germany in 1833, he found Baptists but no regular church. At Hamburg, situated on the Elbe River, he met Oncken, whom Sears recognized as having a "strong, acute mind." The American also saw a man "not liberally educated, very intelligent, possessed of much practical knowledge, and of amiable and winning manners."[14]

On April 22, 1834, Johann Gerhard Oncken, his wife, and five others were baptized by Sears in the Elbe near Hamburg. In the words of Oncken, the "little company of seven believers were rowed across our beautiful Elbe, in the dead hour of night, to a little island, and there descending into the waters, were buried with Christ in baptism. . . . The next day we were formed into a church [with the guidance of Sears], of which I was appointed the pastor."[15]

In receiving baptism through Barnas Sears, Oncken rejected the written advice of an "Independent Preacher of Edinburgh," probably James Haldane,[16] who counseled Oncken to follow the precedent of the Baptist Founding Father John Smyth and baptize himself. Although Oncken was decisive in matters of theology, on this matter he sought sound doctrine. The critical messenger in this event was Calvin Tubbs, a ship's master, who reported to the American Baptist Mission Society of Boston that on the Continent he met a German Christian [Oncken], who desired immersion. But after meeting Sears in 1833, Oncken for a while had to postpone the baptismal service until he returned from a scheduled trip to Poland.[17]

The Lutheran Church and the civic authorities exerted increasing pressure on the enthusiastic dissident Preacher. As early as 1829, fines were imposed on him, and because he was obstinate and refused to pay, his goods were seized. The punishments became more severe, as his association with Baptists became a matter of record. The evangelical society that he had served as secretary—the Neidersächsische Traktatgesellschaft (Lower Saxony Tract Society)—now disowned him. Also his ties were broken with the Independent Church. Even a school that he had co-founded repudiated him. However, the Hamburg chief of police, Hudtwalker, was a tolerant officer, and the law-enforcement agency under his authority was reluctant to prosecute. Badgered by the Lutheran clergy, Oncken reported his baptism, but the police made only a cursory report.[18]

More serious conflicts with the authorities were inevitable. The Lutheran church after the Reformation had become the State Church in many northern cities, such as Hamburg, but it was often formal and dormant. Especially irritating to the Lutheran clergy was the loss of adherents, who now were awakened by a "revival of spiritual religion." The Hamburg Baptist church had grown in two years from thirteen to sixty-eight members. Oncken, meanwhile, had accepted missionary support and become an agent of the American Baptists, through the Board of the Triennial Convention, while still maintaining his affiliation with the Edinburgh Bible Society.[19]

Oncken audaciously ventured far from Hamburg, to Bremen, Oldenburg, and towns along the German northern coast. At Bremen, the second commercial city in the region, fifty miles southwest of Hamburg, Oncken preached in that major center and among fourteen small satellite villages. Near Bremen, he found a considerable number of devout Christians with no preacher. These leaderless evangelicals held church services, and through "divine grace," attracted believers to their numbers.[20]

In September 1837 a religious crisis burst like a storm upon Hamburg. Baptist conversions had been unobtrusive and semi-private, and immersions were performed in the seclusion of the night. Now Oncken administered the ordinance of baptism boldly in the Elbe River in broad daylight, and the Lutheran clergy was enraged. A riot ensued that placed Oncken in grave danger. The meeting of Baptists in public was now forbidden, but, because of the indulgence of the police chief, was permitted to continue in private. To control congregational worship, tickets were issued by the authorities to church members. Despite this impediment, church membership at Hamburg increased to ninety-seven.[21]

The pressures on the Baptist flock mounted when Police Chief Hudtwalker died and his named successor was the formidable Dr. Binder. Appeals for toleration were directed to the Hamburg Senate, but Binder threatened to destroy the Baptists "root and branch." Oncken bravely replied that for his security he would trust in God, but he would not be silenced. On May 13, 1840, Oncken and his colleagues, Julius Köbner and Gottfried Lehmann, were arrested, with military troops assisting in breaking up the worship service. Oncken was given a month's imprisonment at the Winserbaum jail, while Köbner and Lange endured eight days of incarceration.[22] All of Oncken's household goods were sold to pay for the legal costs.[23]

As Benedict states, the imprisonment of Oncken introduced to the Germans the character of Baptists as a "quiet, virtuous and truely [*sic*] small christian denomination, entirely distinct from the old Anabaptists of that country."[24]

The resistance to German intolerance, and even the survival of the Hamburg church, was assisted through the expression of outrage by overseas English and American Christians. Even so, Oncken's family was reduced to desperate straits. He refused to leave Hamburg or to accept the Hamburg Senate's offer of a ticket to America, paid in part by the authorities. But the protests by clamoring Protestants abroad caused the Hamburg Senate once more to allow private worship.

The Hamburg Fire

A catastrophe in Hamburg finally provided the deliverance of the German Baptists. On May 5, 1842, the "Great Fire of Hamburg" destroyed a third of the city and left thousands of people without a home. Oncken offered the city authorities the use of the new church facilities. As a consequence, seventy refugees were sheltered, fed, and clothed by the Baptist community. In view of this generosity and the confirmation that the Baptists were among the bravest and most self-sacrificing citizens of Hamburg, serious persecution was no longer possible. There was a slight renewal of the old ways in 1843, when, at the instigation of the clergy, Oncken was imprisoned, but he served only four days instead of the declared sentence of four weeks. The Hamburg Senate even sent a letter of gratitude to Oncken. So, after a twenty-year fight, the Trailblazer and his church settled down to a period of "comparative" religious freedom.[25]

After the Hamburg fire and cessation of the crudest persecution, the Hamburg church grew rapidly. The record for baptisms was 273 in 1843, 322 in 1844, and 380 in 1845.[26]

As a consequence of the great Hamburg fire, young people, many seeking employment, came to Hamburg from outlying states and foreign countries. This enabled the Hamburg church to heighten its evangelical activities, including the distribution of tracts by church

German States and Austria until 1867

young people among the workers. While youthful evangelists were arrested and expelled by the police, some of these converts returned to their home cities with literature supplied by Oncken. Pastors were ordained, and small churches were established in such centers as Breslau, Stettin, Bremen, Elbing, Memel, Cassel, Marburg, Bitterfield, and Oldenburg.[27]

The increase in the numbers of inquirers revealed the need for a new building, and the practical Oncken procured a large granary on Second Market Street. The new sanctuary, opened in 1847, was equipped to serve as chapel, Sunday School, and bookstore.[28] The chief factors of growth, other than the leadership of Oncken, were the preaching, the appeal of Sunday School, and the persuasiveness of the books and tracts distributed.

The Cloverleaf (Kleeblatt)

Germans often describe the quality of Oncken's ministry by focusing on his cooperative partnership with Julius Wilhelm Köbner and Gottfried Wilhelm Lehmann. This missionary triumvirate of Oncken and his colleagues is well-known in Germany as the *Kleeblatt* or Cloverleaf. Köbner was born on June 11, 1806, at Odense, Fünen island, Denmark, the son of a Jewish rabbi. Dissatisfied with Judaism and attracted to the spiritual nature of Christianity, he found a guide in Pastor Geibel in Lübeck. Without any great spiritual awakening, Köbner declared himself a Christian in 1826.[29] Köbner, six years younger than Oncken, was an engraver and poet of remarkable intellectual and literary gifts; his hymns are still sung by German Baptists. He was a fervent preacher, the pioneer in evangelizing his homeland, Denmark.[30]

After his marriage, Köbner settled in Schleswig-Holstein, where he carried on his engraving trade but also wrote for the theatre. The Hamburg Senate offered prizes for essays on how to make orphan children productive, and Köbner's essay on straw-plaiting won first prize. When Köbner's wife was invited to Hamburg to demonstrate the art, Köbner accompanied her, and he, through curiosity, attended a Baptist service, having heard of Oncken as a remarkable orator. In the service, Köbner was gripped by the Holy Spirit and convicted of sin. On May 17, 1836, he was baptized by Oncken.[31] Köbner, as a vibrant Christian leader, was a man of extraordinary eloquence and imagination. For half a century he delighted Christians with his spiritual songs and literary works. He died in 1884 as a pastor in Berlin.

The second collegue was Gottfried Wilhelm Lehmann, who in Berlin became the Founding Father of the second Baptist church established in Germany. Lehmann was born in Hamburg on October 23, 1799, the son of a copper engraver, who moved to Berlin for better business opportunities. The Napoleonic wars shattered the family's dream of economic success. When young Lehmann moved to peaceful Friesland and the patronage of an uncle, he was led to the Lord through the influence of Mennonites and a circle of strong Christians. Finally, returning to Berlin, he learned the engraver's trade, and attended the Academy, becoming an avid student of music, literature, and languages.[32]

As a maturing scholar, Oncken maintained a keen interest in the Bible and, up to the point of his change of faith, remained a zealous Lutheran layman.[33] Lehmann's serious quest over the years for an understanding of the Scriptures led to correspondence with Johann Oncken and a friendship of great significance. Lehmann, three months older than Oncken, was disturbed by Oncken's baptism in the Elbe in 1834 and Oncken's decision to become a Baptist. After a brief estrangement, he closely queried Oncken, but finally was persuaded that his friend had acted on Biblical principles and sound theology in seeking believer's baptism through immersion.[34]

The ultimate decisions were made when Lehmann invited Oncken to Berlin to explain to a group of friends the New Testament concepts of church order and baptism. As a result, on May 13, 1837, Lehmann, his wife, and four others were baptized by Oncken in Rummelsburg Lake, outside Berlin. On the following day, the Baptist Church in Berlin was constituted, with Lehmann as its pastor. In Berlin, the first meetings were held in Lehmann's house. There was little progress for the congregation until the persecution subsided, after which a chapel was dedicated in 1848. As an intelligent and enthusiastic organizer with an immense capacity for work, Lehmann would travel widely over Europe to begin Baptist churches. He would die at his principal post in Berlin in 1882, while serving as pastor.[35]

Oncken the intrepid Christian and Trailblazer was stubbornly authoritarian. Through his strict and paternalistic outlook, he had molded the German Baptists to follow his leadership. He had little sympathy for church autonomy and of the need of the church structure to decentralize. He insisted on his authority, and a controversy developed with Köbner and Lehmann, who strongly felt that the churches they founded should not be branches of the Hamburg mother-church.[36]

Oncken's Work

Oncken's missionary travels carried him to East Prussia (including Memel), Oldenburg, Marburg, Stuttgart (capital of Württemberg), and Denmark, often starting churches in the cities. Köbner, on the other hand, was the chief catalyst responsible for evangelizing Denmark, where there were struggling small groups of dissenters. One religious fragment was led by Count Holstein of Holsteinborg, and a second flock, which adhered to the Lutheran Church but was uncomfortable with infant baptism, was directed by the engraver Peder C. Mønster in Copenhagen. In 1839 Köbner met Mønster in Denmark, for Kobner had undertaken work on the island of Langeland. Then, in October 1839, Oncken and Kobner traveled to Copenhagen, where eleven persons, including Mønster, were baptized by Oncken, with Mønster confirmed as the pastor. This small group comprised the nucleus of the first Danish Baptist church and, in fact, was the first such church in Scandinavia.[37] In a further effort to bolster the feeble Danish church, Oncken and Köbner, on another trip in 1840, baptized ten more converts, and later formed a church at Langeland with eight believers. The two missionaries, as a consequence, became *de facto* outlaws, with public rewards posted and their escape barely succeeding.[38]

The Danish Baptists immediately met severe opposition, with Mønster jailed for several weeks, after which he was ordered to leave the country. Oncken correctly predicted that the Baptists in Denmark would be charged with being Anabaptists. However, several preaching points around Copenhagen grew into active churches.

After Mønster's establishment of a third new church, at Aalborg, Jutland, he was arrested and imprisoned two times, under a strict code imposed by the absolute monarch, Christian V.[39] Oncken came to Mønster's rescue in September 1841 by arriving in Denmark with a delegation and a petition to the Danish king signed by four hundred English pastors. The Baptists refused an official offer to settle in a reserve once assigned to Huguenots. However, the Danes proclaimed a restrictive law: "That religion alone shall be allowed in the king's lands and realms which agrees with the Holy Scriptures, the Apostolic and Nicene creeds, the Athanasian creed, and the Augsburg Confession, and with Luther's Minor Catechism." Meanwhile, the Baptists were oppressed until 1850.

Köbner returned in 1865 as pastor of the Copenhagen church, which ultimately attained four hundred members. So, Oncken's co-worker continued to be a major contributor to Baptist church theology and practice. When Köbner left Denmark in 1879, his chief legacy was the first Danish Baptist hymnal, which he had compiled.

In 1849 the German and Danish Baptist churches joined together in the Union of Associated Churches of Baptized Christians in Germany and Denmark.[40] The principal objectives of the Union were to consider the feasibility of adopting a confession prepared by Oncken, Köbner, and Lehmann; to strengthen their fellowship and missionary activity; and to prepare statistics. The Union was divided into four Associations (later five): Prussia (Berlin), Northwest (Hamburg), Southcentral (Einbeck), and Denmark (Copenhagen). The various Associations (*Vereinigungen*) met yearly, while the Union convened every three years.[41]

The Prussian Baptist Association was founded by Lehmann in July 1848, when he summoned the churches of Prussia to a conference in Berlin. At this conference, the church representatives agreed that two-thirds of the total monetary contributions should be applied locally and one-third should be directed to foreign mission work through the American Board. Wilhelm Weist was appointed the first itinerant missionary in Prussia. The influence of this Association's missionary initiative would be felt in East Prussia, Silesia, Poland, and even Russia.[42]

Work in Sweden

Oncken helped spearhead Baptist beginnings in Sweden, sharing his leadership with Frederick O. Nilsson. Nilsson, the founder of Baptist work in his native Sweden, was converted in New York in 1834. He became a colporteur, a traveling evangelist that distributed tracts and Bibles. Nilsson was influenced by another Swedish sailor, Captain Gustav W. Schroeder, who told him about Baptist beliefs.[43] Schroeder then sent a group of Swedes to the New World, and they planted a Baptist church at New Sweden, in Aroostook County, Maine. On a return trip to Europe, in August 1847, Nilsson was baptized by Oncken in the Elbe near Hamburg. In September 1848 a small handful of Swedes, including Nilsson, were organized as the first Swedish church, at Varberg near Gothenburg, with the assistance of a Danish Baptist minister, the Reverend Mr. Förster. Nilsson was ordained by Oncken in 1849 in Oncken's "parish" in Hamburg and returned to Sweden to preach despite serious persecution.[44] Nilsson then was exiled from Sweden in 1851 and served as pastor at Copenhagen from 1851 until 1853.[45]

The successor to Nilsson in Sweden was Andrea Wiberg, a graduate of the University of Upsala, and at first a Lutheran minister.

Wiberg was disenchanted with the Lutheran practice of administering communion, both to the saved and the unsaved. He was led by Oncken to study the New Testament and to embrace the Baptist faith. On his way to the United States, Wiberg, on July 23, 1852, was baptized in the Baltic Sea by Nilsson. Wiberg returned to his native Sweden in 1855, as a colporteur of the American Baptist Publication Society. Since the press was uncensored in Sweden at that time, the Gospel truth was spread through tracts and books.[46]

Despite the persecution in Sweden, Baptists grew from nine churches in 1855 to 564 by the end of the century, and from 476 members to 40,750 members. This progress was noted by a second national German Baptist conference in 1858, attended by one hundred messengers including Oncken and Köbner. This Baptist growth was acknowledged in Sweden by further state fines and imprisonments. Captain Schroeder, who built a Baptist church at Gothenburg, was summoned by Lutheran Bishop Bjorck and fined fifty dollars. One Baptist pastor was shackled and imprisoned six times. Babies, immediately after birth, were forcibly taken from parents and christened in Lutheran churches. The costs for the rite were paid by seizing and publicly selling the personal property of the Baptist parents.[47]

In 1867 Swedish Baptists began to preach in Norway. The first Norwegian church was constituted in 1868. But by 1900 there were thirty-two Baptist churches in Norway with 2,671 members. Also, new ventures were undertaken in Finland in 1868 that produced thirty-one churches and 2,030 members by the twentieth century.[48]

The revolutionary year 1848 had great significance for German Baptists, for it introduced into German policy the concept of state tolerance. Severe persecution would follow this date, but the moral certainties that a State Church should be allowed to harm another church would be shaken and then shattered. Before 1848 there had been no freedom of press or assembly in Germany.[49] And it was only in 1858 that the first Baptist church in Germany, organized at Hamburg by Oncken, was recognized by the State.[50] Thus, in response to the reform mood, the Parliament of Berlin in 1847 demanded liberty of the press, and King Frederick William IV authorized a law separating the State and the State Church. Ultimately, by revolution and the constitutional documents of December 5, 1848, and January 31, 1850, the freedoms of religious confession and family and public worship were guaranteed in Prussia.[51] But, the other German states still continued their policies of repression, after a short period of flexibility.

After the exuberance of 1848, reactionary governments in the German states gained power and overthrew the new constitutions. Baptists again were driven to worship in woods and cellars for lack of permits. Rude mobs assaulted preachers and smashed meetinghouse furniture. Children of Baptists were snatched from their mothers' arms and forcibly christened, in accordance with German law.[52] Heavy penalties were imposed to enforce attendance at State churches, and to compel submission to Lutheran practice in rites, such as christenings and the Lord's Supper. In Hanover, the authorities refused to allow marriage ceremonies for Baptists. Arranging funerals became lengthy ordeals, and Baptists were frequently denied such simple procedures as an administered oath. This "baptism of blood" was most severe in the states of Mecklenburg, Schleswig, Hesse, and Bückeburg. In desperation, many believers were forced to emigrate to America. But, in general, the Baptist congregations reacted with heroism, patience, and forgiveness.[53]

The persecution in the German states aroused the anxieties of foreign governments and Protestant ministers. In 1853 the Evangelical Alliance in England and the Protestant Alliance sent a deputation to the Kirchentag Parliament in Berlin, with few positive results. In January 1855 Oncken and Lehmann were received in audience by King Frederick William IV, who promised assistance in obtaining recognition of the Baptist churches. After an Alliance presentation in Cologne, the king urged the other German states to consider lifting the religious restrictions. Legal recognition of Baptists in Prussia was achieved in 1858, and a degree of freedom was achieved in Saxony and Bavaria. Finally, in Prussia, the dominant German state, attacks on religious assemblies were forbidden and children were freed from religious instructions in schools.[54]

The new freedom energized the Baptists, who responded with aggressive missionary activity and a firmer organization of churches. In response to a revitalized church, Oncken said: "If hitherto we have needed grace to suffer and endure, we need it doubly now for joyous and full self-dedication to the work of spreading the Gospel." Friends from England and America augmented local resources and enabled new fields to be opened.[55]

Oncken and Lehmann made numerous trips to Memel, Denmark, and Switzerland to form new bands of Baptists and to strengthen older churches. A seaman's mission was established in Hamburg. Twenty thousand Bibles were distributed and a million tracts were circulated. In May 1848, the first regular journal, *Das Missionsblatt*, appeared in print.[56] A multi-faceted organization was being developed that would culminate in starting Oncken's seminary at Hamburg, which in 1876 would be attended by Russian pioneer V. G. Pavlov.[57] Great progress was made in the middle and northwest states and in Württemberg. Remarkable expansion also occurred in East Prussia after the founding in 1857 of a church in Königsberg. But, as a result of repression, Baptist expansion was stopped in Saxony, Bavaria, and Mecklenburg.

Within four years of his baptism, in 1838, Oncken had begun a private publishing house that established ties with the Scottish Bible Society. Finally, this enterprise was given by him to the German Baptist Union (Associated Churches of Baptist Christians).[58] Other institutions were established, including a charity endowment, *Invalidenkasse* (Fund for the Disabled) for the support of pastors, widows, and orphans of ministers.[59]

The idea of an educated clergy was slow to take hold in Germany. Baptists dreaded the ecclesiasticism that had tormented Baptists in every corner of Europe and feared particularly a caste of priests. Oncken, on the other hand, realized from the beginning that clergy and church members must be trained, and gradually this concept prevailed. The earliest students were called to Hamburg in the winter of 1849-50 for a course of elementary instructions. With few resources, the seminary consisted in some years only of six-month courses for its students. However, on October 1, 1880, a permanent seminary was opened in Hamburg, with a four-year curriculum. In time, there was a well-developed Sunday School, young people's work, and a deaconess movement.[60]

The growth of Baptists in the old German empire was spectacular. In 1838 there were only four Baptist churches in the German states.[61] By 1847 these had grown to twenty-six churches with 1,500 members.[62] In 1863 there were 11,275 German Baptist converts. In 1922 there were 55,770 members, 31,500 Sunday School students, 245 churches, and 390 ministers.[63] In 1963, in Germany, there were 96,000 church members.

Oncken was an indefatigable traveler for foreign missions. As a missionary, he visited Holland, Switzerland, Russia, Hungary, and the Balkans. He frequently reinforced the work in Great Britain, and in 1853 and 1854 paid prolonged visits to America, where he was held in high esteem.

Baptist Initiatives in the Baltic Area

In largely Roman Catholic Lithuania, Oncken played a major role with the few Baptists in that country. Because of the influence of the preacher Fröhlich, and sawmill worker William Edward Grimm of Memel, who had been baptized by affusion (sprinkling) in Switzerland, a small circle of Evangelical Christians was gathered in Memel and baptized by affusion by Grimm. When Grimm heard of a like-minded group of Baptists in Hamburg, he began corresponding with Oncken. Prior to the exchange of letters, Grimm had only heard of Baptists from Hague, an English resident in Memel. As a result of Grimm's successful labor, Oncken made a notable journey to Memel on October 3, 1841. There, Oncken immersed twenty-five members

Charles H. Spurgeon,
Eminent English Baptist Evangelist.

and constituted a church that became the most successful in converting Lithuanians.[64] Located in a disputed area, German-populated
Memel was transferred in 1923 to Lithuania as an autonomous region.[65]

In 1859 the Memel Baptist Church had among its members fourteen residents of the Libau District of Latvia. This motivated a
school teacher in the Windau District of Latvia in August 1860 to
lead seven men and a woman across the frontier to Memel in order
to be immersed.[66] On May 29, 1861, a second group of fourteen
persons sailed from Windau to Memel in a fishing boat to be baptized. They were intercepted, along with their store of Bibles and
hymnbooks as they sought to return. A third group of seven sailed
to Memel and were baptized, after surviving a fierce storm. The
seven, who included a sixteen-year-old girl, were sentenced upon
returning to Latvia to a flogging of thirty stripes each.[67]

Mission Projects Throughout Europe

The Baptist work in Holland was promoted through Oncken's
interest in the publications of Dutch minister J. E. Feisser, a clergyman of the Dutch Reformed Church. Feisser had developed serious
doubts about the validity of infant baptism and questioned the role
of his church on the basis of his own New Testament studies. His
personal life recently had gone through a series of crises, including
the loss of his young wife and two children. Feisser also suffered the
collapse of his health and blindness in the right eye. He was assaulted in body and soul. Tormented as he was, he began to doubt
some of the basic tenets of the Reformed faith, until in December
1843, he was stripped of his minister's office by the Reformed Church.
He sought to restore the church, "the body of Christ," to faithful
Christians, but, for his efforts, he was regarded as a "fanatic" by the
provincial Synod and even some of his relatives. As a result, he was
removed from two pastorates, one of them in the university city of
Franeker.[68]

After Dr. Feisser published his papers, Oncken sent Köbner to inquire further about Feisser's beliefs. Feisser, at this point, had never heard of Baptists or their doctrines. Then, Köbner persuaded Feisser that he must submit to believer's baptism, although he had been christened as an infant. On May 15, 1845, Feisser and six others were baptized by Köbner under the skies at Gasselte-Njveen, and they were formed into a church that Feissner served as pastor. In 1858 the minister of this church was E. Gerdes, from the village of Stadskanal. In only a few months, Gerdes was compelled to depart because he allowed unbaptized persons to participate in the Lord's Supper, the practice of John Bunyan in England.[69]

DeNeui, an evangelist trained by Oncken, organized at Franeker in April 1864 a church of forty members; in 1877 there were ninety-one members on the church roll. DeNeui founded four other Baptist churches in neighboring towns, but in 1871 he emigrated to America.[70]

In 1847 Oncken traveled to southern Germany and fortunately extended his tour to Switzerland. At Hochwart, Switzerland, he baptized a handful of people and organized a church. In 1849 the church at Zürich was constituted, and by 1856 there were fifty-two baptisms in the city. In 1859, with the encouragement of Oncken, two preachers, F. Meyer and I. Harnisch, were sent from Hamburg to Switzerland. The modest Baptist foothold was extended to include Bischofszell and Herisau, with some of the evangelical work attributable to the blind pastor Anton Haag. Severe persecution of Baptists occurred in Switzerland, but in 1858 the canton of Aargau legalized the marriages of Dissenters (including Baptists) and abolished compulsory State baptisms. Then, in 1874, the federal constitution was revised to allow freedom of religion.[71]

After the "Great Fire of 1842," Austrian Catholic workers flocked to Hamburg to find work. Many of them were received warmly by the Baptists there. Austrian Baptist converts Marschall and Hornung returned to Vienna, where they held religious meetings and distributed tracts, in the process winning a few believers. During Oncken's visit to Austria in October 1847, he baptized Wisotzky and his wife. In 1848 Oncken twice visited Vienna and preached to responsive seekers.

The Vienna Baptists frequently met in the home of ex-Catholic Karl Rauch. The revolutions of 1848 that swept Europe, not excluding Austria, produced a reaction in their wake, including a renewal of repression. Rauch's children were under pressure by the police to receive Catholic baptism. However, they narrowly avoided this injustice through a secret baptism at the hands of a Lutheran pastor, whose church was recognized by the Austrian state.[72]

In April 1850 Karl Rauch's home was raided by the authorities, and seventeen men and women were arrested. All non-Viennese were expelled from the city. Then, in 1851, an agent of the British and Foreign Bible Society, E. Millard, came to Vienna and offered his home as a refuge for the persecuted Protestants. Driven out of Vienna, Millard returned after about eleven years. His house was declared a Baptist church in 1869, with twenty members from various Austrian towns. Although the church and its members were harassed, the congregation continued to grow. Among its elders was Johann Rottmayer of the Bible Society and the manufacturer Josef Hoffman. However, religious freedom was not permanent in Austria, until after World War I, and enforcement of the "minority clauses" of the peace treaty.[73]

As J. H. Rushbrooke states it: "The Baptists of Hungary trace their spiritual pedigree to the modern apostle, J. G. Oncken, of Hamburg." Joseph Lehmann, Oncken's collaborator, tells a portion of the story in his *Geschicte Der Deutschen Baptisten (History of the German Baptists)*:

> Many young men, especially from Austria and Hungary, had been attracted to Hamburg by the opportunity to work offered by the rebuilding of the city after the Great Fire. They found there not only profitable occupation, but some of them the

salvation of their souls. The Hamburg Young Men's and Women's Unions decided to send out worthy young men and to support them in mission work. Accordingly in April, 1846, they despatched to Hungary the brethren Scharschmidt, Rottmayer, Voyka, and Lorders.— furthermore, they had received from Oncken some instruction with a view to preparation for their work.—— In all, these places [Budapest and Pecs] they endeavoured to secure a footing by distribution of tracts and Bibles,[74] and by holding meetings, but were obliged to act with the utmost prudence in view of the severity of the law. Later all united in Budapest; and as a consequence larger showers [of blessings] began to fall.——

F. Oncken remained in Budapest; Kruse journeyed to Pecs. From that time F. Oncken held regular meetings in Rottmayer's house, and the membership rose to nine persons. The work must needs be carried on as quietly as possible, since the Roman Catholic priesthood regarded it with hostility.——

In 1865, G. W. Lehmann of Berlin visited Budapest and baptized several persons.[75] The Hungarian congregations used the German language in their services, and it was not until about 1893 that, overcoming strong opposition, the first efforts were made to offer services in Hungarian.[76]

The first Baptist missionary to enter Romania was Karl Johann Scharschmidt, who in 1846 had been sent as a young evangelist to Hungary. Scharschmidt, a carpenter, was baptized by Oncken in 1845. He went to Bucharest as a colporteur in April 1846 and served with a co-worker, the English citizen Elizabeth Peacock Clarke. A handful of Baptists by 1863 were gathered at Bucharest. Oncken sent August Liebig as pastor to Romania, where Liebig conducted the first baptisms and served four years. After Oncken visited the Romanian church in 1869, Liebig went to serve as minister to the German colonists and Baptist migrants in the Turkish-ruled Danube delta, where a number of churches were organized.[77]

The Scope of Oncken's Work

"Without doubt, the greatest pioneer of the Baptist faith in [Continental] Europe was J. G. Oncken," the "Father" of the Continental Baptists.[78] When Oncken died in 1884, there were thirty-two thousand German Baptists in the German Baptist Union, a publication house in Hamburg,[79] and a theological seminary that had its origins in Oncken. However, his principal evangelical tools had been his personal witness, the employment of religious tracts, and the distribution of two million Bibles given out by 1879.

The extent of Oncken's ministry is awe-inspiring. His motto was: "every Baptist a missionary" (*Jeder Baptist ein Missionar*). Along with co-workers Julius Wilhelm Köbner and Gottfried Wilhelm Lehmann, he set a record in zeal, crossing the German states many times. With his heart aflame with Christian resolve, he made several journeys to Britain and America, but also numerous trips to Memel, Denmark, Sweden, Switzerland, Holland, Austria, Hungary, Romania, and Russia.

Oncken had long considered Russia to be a fertile ground for evangelism. But first he would attempt to gain a measure of toleration for his co-religionists. With remarkable temerity, he sought in 1864 an interview with the highest police authority in Russia, the minister of the Interior. He was able to have a conference with the vice president of the Ministry, to whom he declared:

> We believe that God has called us to preach the great truth of believer's baptism among Europe's millions, who have rejected revealed truth and who constitute a most dangerous element to any good government. If the Imperial Government tries forcibly to suppress the Baptists of Poland and Russia, they will discover that it is a very difficult thing to try and destroy a genuine religious movement.

The first Russian Baptist of Slavic descent, Nikita Voronin, was immersed in 1867 by Martin Kalweit, a German Baptist from Lithuania. The evangelical surge was reinforced when Oncken in

1869 visited the Ukraine and ordained the Mennonite Abraham Unger. Unger, in turn, baptized the blacksmith, Ivan G. Riaboshapka, the first native Ukrainian Baptist. In 1874, following a visit to England by Tsar Alexander II, Oncken arrived in London to intercede in behalf of the beleaguered Baptists in southern Russia. Through the intervention of an influential friend, Dean Stanley, who had friends in the Russian court, persecutions in that area ceased.[80]

In theology Oncken was conservative and an enlightened Calvinist, accepting the doctrine of predestination. After his visit to Russia in 1869, he published a confession of faith that was used by the Russian Baptist church. The confession appeared in 1872, first in the German language and then in a Russian-language translation. Among its major concepts was the viewpoint of original sin: "Since all men come from Adam's seed, they were made to partake of the same fallen and completely damaged nature, since they are conceived and born in sin."[81] The members of God's creation, he asserted, "are children of wrath, completely incapable of and not inclined to all that is good, but capable of and inclined to all that is evil."[82] Unfortunately, Oncken produced little in serious theological literature, other than his tracts and the journal *Das Missionsblatt*.[83] The printing enterprise of Oncken, known as the *Oncken Verlag*, would be converted by Philip Bickel and Oncken's son Karl into a major Baptist witness for Bible study and doctrine.[84]

Oncken was for the nineteenth century the great Baptist Apostle and Trailblazer, ceaseless in evangelizing, and following in fervor the great Apostle Paul. With inexhaustible energy, he began the Hamburg church, and, capable as an organizer, he melded a society of Baptist churches in the German states. He was an ardent missionary and established and nurtured Baptist churches and had a profound Christian influence in almost every country in Europe. With grace of manner, and a passion for souls, despite an authoritarian style, he left a permanent imprint as undoubtably the greatest Baptist builder in Continental Europe.[85]

Vasili Pavlov visits flock near Orenburg, Siberia (1893).

Chapter 13

Vasili Gurevich Pavlov
(1854-1924)

Russian Baptist Reformer and His Church

Nineteenth century imperial Russia was a powerful and absolutist nation, embracing over eight million square miles, nineteen major ethnic groups, and touched by twelve seas. Until the advent of minister Vasili G. Pavlov, the small presence of Russian Baptists was among the least of a myriad of national problems.

Russia in this epoch was dominated by a succession of autocratic tsars, a redoubtable, rigid, and intolerant Russian Orthodox Church, supported by an elite of nobility, wealthy boyars, and a growing middle class. This privileged society, living in luxury, contrasted sharply with millions of peasants, some of them land-bound serfs, living in rags and enduring a bare subsistence, most of them loyal to the State.

Barely tolerated in the 1860s and often persecuted were the precursors to the Baptists—the sectarian Kristovovers (New Israel), Dukhobors, and Molokans. Some of the practices of these groups were more pagan than Christian, but it would be the Molokans, most like the Baptists, from which a flow of new converts to the Baptist faith would be derived. Among the lesser so-called heretics, the Baptists numbered in the hundreds, but responding to missionary nurture and with heroism to affliction, largely imposed by the State Orthodox Church, Baptist growth would be measured in the millions in the twentieth century. The flowering in Russia of the

Baptist Church, without pope, bishop, or national hierarchy, is a veritable miracle, that spread from the Caucasus Mountains to Kiev and St. Petersburg, and ultimately to Vladivostok on the Sea of Japan.

The missionary V. G. Pavlov came from wealth and Molokan roots. His family, stemming from Tiflis (modern name, Tbilisi), Georgia, in the Caucasus Mountains, was prominent and financially successful. Valkevich wrote that "he [Pavlov] is indisputably the most prominent of the Baptist missionaries."[1]

The Baptist faith in Russia began in complete darkness on August 20, 1867. During that night, a German Baptist artisan from Kowno, Lithuania, Martin Kalweit, immersed Nikita Voronin in a creek close to Tiflis, near the Kura River, in the Caucasus region of southern Russia.[2] Nikita I. Voronin, a Russian merchant and representative of a Tiflis trading company, had emerged some time earlier as the first Baptist of Slavic descent in the Russian Empire but could find no one willing to risk imprisonment to baptize him.[3] Voronin became a prominent Baptist missionary and editor of *Golos Very* (*Voice of Truth*), a collection of spiritual songs. All of this is noteworthy, since on the date of the Battle of Waterloo, June 18, 1815, there was not a single Baptist church in continental Europe.

Under the influence of Voronin, V. G. Pavlov the Trailblazer trained as a Baptist worker, became a church steward. Pavlov soon developed a reputation in Baptist circles for his energy and theological clarity.[4] After a stay in Hamburg, Germany, for theological studies, in 1875, and a return to Russia in 1876, Pavlov challenged the leadership and business practices of Voronin.[5]

For centuries, there had been no Baptists or Evangelicals in Russia. The Protestant Reformation and its powerful reverberations, beginning in 1517 at Wittenberg Castle, Germany, and ending certainly by the proclamation of the English Toleration Act (1689), created a cataclysm in the religious, social, and political life of Europe and its colonies. In Russia, to the contrary, the Reformation scarcely caused a ripple. The beginning of Baptist life in Russia was closely tied, as McBeth states it, to four primary sources, all inter-connected: the Molokan sectarians, the Stundist movement in the Ukraine, the Russian Bible Society, and the Pashkovite movement from St. Petersburg. The Pietist movement in South Russia in the early nineteenth century prepared the ground for the Baptists, by asserting the authority of the Bible, the nearness of God, and the necessity of a personal conversion. This intimate Christian religious development contrasted sharply with the "cold confessionalism" of the Russian Orthodox Church.[6] Further, the Orthodox Church, a partner with the Tsarist government, had the power to suppress, condemn, imprison, and torture the so-called enemies of the Holy Church.

Even earlier, various sects, including the "Old Believers," had arisen out of discontent with the State Church or the misery of peasants and serfs who endured grinding poverty. However different these sects were from Apostolic Christians, their sufferings and travails enabled the Baptists to experience a degree of forbearance that permitted Baptists to gain a foothold in Russia.

Sectarians in Russia

When Nikita Voronin became the first Russian Baptist in 1867, there were at least three major dissenting sects in the Empire: the Khristovovers, the Dukhobors, and the Molokans.

The Khristovovers, or New Israel, began as a peasant sect in the seventeenth century and continued to persist into the twentieth century. Early in its history, this sect had a following of poor peasants and Cossacks, who increasingly rebelled against the liturgy and ceremonies of the Russian Orthodox Church. In some areas of Russia, the Khristovovers adopted communal living, stored grain together, jointly survived difficult times, and were led by authoritarian leaders. The first great leader was Perfil Petrovich Katasonov, who advocated celibacy, abolished ecstatic rites, and declared himself to be Christ.

Katasonov's followers, until his death in 1885,[7] saw themselves as the spiritually Elect, "living temples" of God, members of Israel, and united around their leader, the living Christ. Another leader, Vagilii Semenovich Lubkov, born in 1869 and exiled to the Transcaucasus, was recognized as the successor Christ. Lubkov divided Russia (the "kingdom of God") into seven "countries," each under an "archangel" appointed by him. Lubkov's supreme government consisted of seven archangels, four evangelists, twelve apostles, twelve prophets, and seventy-two men of apostolic rank appointed by him. Lubkov's High Council, "the heavenly inspectorate," traveled from place to place announcing the will of Christ to the followers. At the congregational level, elders led the flock, with activities directed by the so-called Christ.[8]

The Khristovovers had the leading place in sectarianism from the seventeenth to the mid-eighteenth century. But by the middle of the eighteenth century, Khristovovers were being hard-pressed by "Spiritual Christianity," and at the beginning of the nineteenth century by the Dukhobors. However, the Khristovovers were strong enough to seek reforms through a conference held in Rostov-on-Don in May 1905. In 1917 the Khristovovers probably numbered about forty thousand members.[9]

"Spiritual Christianity" began in the 1760s and 1770s as a restrained peasant revolt in Russia against the Russian Orthodox Church and the harsh obligatory services of the serfs. This quiet revolt involved and influenced the sects of Khristovovers, Dukhobors, and Molokans, some elements of the last sect similar to the Baptists. Spiritual Christianity sank deep roots in Voronezh, Tambov Province, and at Kozlov, where the serfs were about one-third of the taxable population.[10] This region between two borderlands, one formerly dominated by extensive serf-tilled agriculture and the other almost free of estates, allowed its peasants to dream of liberation.

Serfs were not liberated until 1861, under the reign of Alexander II. Spiritual Christians emerged about one hundred years before this date, to thunder against injustice and preach against such Russian Orthodox practices as icon worship, excessive ritual, veneration of holy objects, and a stifling liturgy. These religious revolutionaries often favored community ownership, as well as liberation of the serf and the return to apostolic Christianity.[11]

The Dukhobors, as a component of Spiritual Christianity, were branded by their accusers in the Orthodox Church as "fighters against the Holy Spirit." As early Christians had turned their appellation of ridicule into a name of honor, the Dukhobors bore their badge proudly, asserting that they were fighting for the Spirit that had left Russian Orthodoxy. Dukhobors based their views, not so much on the Bible, as on an "inner revelation." Their leader adopted the personification of Christ. As explained by P. V. Verigin, the Dukhobor concept of God was as follows: "God is life and participates in everything existing. . . . Understanding God as life itself, essential and the same in everything which appears, we should not fear bodily death...Man is part of one whole in the world. We also understand God as love, with whose help everything existing is maintained."[12] They were democratic but held views that were sometimes pantheistic and at variance with Christianity.[13]

Between the 1760s and the beginning of the nineteenth century, the Dukhobors had thousands of followers in Vornezh, Ekaterinoslav, Khar'kov, Tavriia, and in Astrakhan Province, Samara, Penza, and Riazan. In 1825, the Tsarist government reported that there were 23,207 registered Dukhobors, of which seventy-six percent were free and twenty-three percent serfs.[14]

The Dukhobors had become organized some ten years before the peasant and Cossack war of 1773-75, led by the Don Cossack Ye Melyan (Emilian) Ivanovich Pugachev, and they would absorb part of the consequences of the war. This insurrection, largely in southeastern Russia, was undertaken to depose Catherine the Great, and was most successful in the eastern part of the Empire.[15]

The Dukhobors were subjected to severe court restraints and persecution in the 1760s-70s. Then, the Russian government under Alexander I, during the period 1804-16, began moving the sectarians in increments to the fertile land of the Molochnaia River. The first emigrants, consisting of four thousand believers, preceded another group of twenty-three hundred, that settled in the Tiflis (Georgia) Guberniia.[16] In the Caucasus, the simplicity, leadership, and faith of the Dukhobors would undergo drastic changes.

At first, the Dukhobors, who preferred to farm, had a democratic structure, all adherents having a voice. At this stage, there was no religious or administrative hierarchy. In their religious meetings, they taught the Word of God to each other. Also, the rights of women were extensive. Each settlement had a guest house, where lay administrators were given free quarters. Two settlements of Dukhobors in Molochnye Vody based their life on collectivism and lived in large dormitories, sharing a common treasury and grain stores.[17] This simple life would change.

Later they would regard themselves not as Russians, or even as separated people, but as a nation,[18] and in the process many of them would become well-to-do, undemocratic, and submit themselves to autocratic leaders.

The restrictions on liberty were initiated by Savelii Kapustin, the son of Illarion Pobirokhin, who persuaded the congregation to adopt one-man rule; he had himself elevated to the rank of "Holy Leader." Then, Kapustin and the council of elders began to disburse the common funds at their discretion and exploit the ordinary believers. No marriages were allowed between Dukhobors and kindred sectarians. Many lost their zeal, and Dukhobors who were transplanted to the Caucasus in 1841-45 lost their will to proselytize.[19]

The Dukhobors advanced a capitalist entrepreneurial system of agriculture and technology into the Transcaucasus.[20] The richer parcels of grain-land in Georgia and Azerbaidjan tended to fall first into the hands of German colonists, and then to the Dukhobors, Molokans, and Baptists. The local native population, in contrast, was left poorer. The consequence for the Dukhobors was that co-religionists were hired as laborers, inequality became common, and the communal system was eroded. Although in times past all the brethren had eaten barley bread together, now the rich ate white bread, and, in the 1860s, the new vices of smoking tobacco and drinking alcohol, along with drunkenness, sapped the former stern virtues of the sect. The Dukhobor leaders did not hesitate to whip their poorer brothers for disciplinary reasons. Unlike the Baptists and Molokans, they were almost completely illiterate. No live sermons were preached, and children for disciplinary reasons learned the Psalms by rote.[21]

The powerful leader of the Dukhobors governed his "empire" from his seat at the village of Goreloe. So impressive was his strength that before 1886 he was visited by the viceroy of the Caucasus. In the period 1840-60s, the Dukhobors even created a military organization; the Dukhobor Cossacks, under local chiefs, and maintained mounted troops armed with sabers, daggers and revolvers.

The spiritual and material treasures of the Dukhobors were protected at the so-called Orphans Home, founded in the Tiflis Guberniia in the 1840s. This Orphans Home was modeled after another home at Molochnye Vody. The Orphans Home was essentially a treasury or bank, whose chief benefactors were large owners of cattle and grain. In 1886 the Orphans Home had a capital of a half-million rubles, in addition to ownership of land and a large number of horses, cattle, sheep, and goats. The basic source of its capital consisted of personal donations, conserved in a common fund under the direction of the Dukhobor leader. In periods of natural calamities, subsidies would be issued through its branches in various places.[22]

As well as a treasury, the two-story stone palace at Goreloe, known as the Orphans Home, was the center of the Dukhobor faith and its leader. In or about 1928 the Home was the residence of a kind of Dukhobor empress, Lukeria Kalmykova, who was surrounded by her retinue of elders and prince-courtiers. This little empire was sustained by poor Dukhobors and Muslims tending fertile fields and numerous livestock in support of an aristocracy. Their religious practices embraced prophesy, speaking in tongues, and experiences of ecstasy, including solo and group jumping, these expressions attributed to manifestations of the Holy Spirit. Their religion had become similar to that of the Pentecostals.[23]

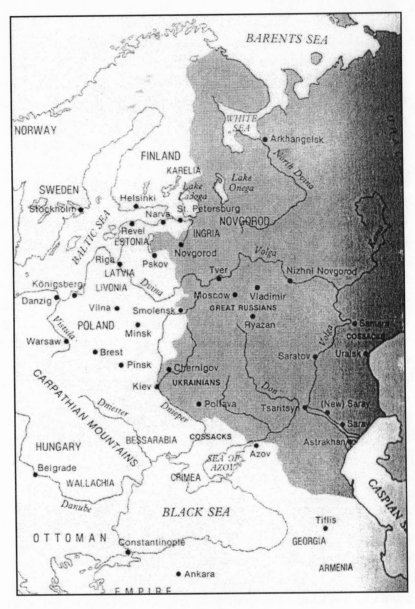

Russia in the Eighteenth Century

Molokans

The next sectarian element, the Molokans (or "milk drinkers"), as an offshoot of the Dukhobors would be a primal source and nurturer of the Baptist faith in Russia. Their religious order was based on work, brotherhood, and equality,[24] and because they placed less emphasis on social motifs, they were more successful than the Dukhobors. The Molokans arose in the 1760-70 period as a reaction to serfdom and the restraints of the Russian state and the State Church. The religious model of this sect was the early Christian church before the great Councils. The Molokans opposed the physical and spiritual bondage of serfdom,[25] and sought to achieve on earth the fulfillment of the "Kingdom of God." God, to them, was a force of love, and the Bible was the foundation for interpreting "spirit and truth," as applied to social conditions.

The early sources of the Molokans were in the central Chernozem Guberniias and Molochnye Vody (Milky Waters). Persecuted by the state, they would retreat to the Volga and borderlands of the country. They frequently referred to the teachings of the Gospels as "spiritual milk," and drank milk on fast days. These early Molokans followed the ideals of equality and holding of property in common.[26] Their progenitors had been the early Lutheran and Mennonite Germans who settled in southern Russia under the sponsorship of Peter the Great and Catherine II.[27]

Importantly, the peasant revolt of the 1760s-70s, which coincided with the birth of "Spiritual Christianity," would involve all three religious groups: the Khristovovers (Khlysty), Dukhobors, and the Molokans. Out of the Khlysty would come Siluan Kolesnikov and Illarion Pobirokhin, who preached a "Spiritual Christianity," which respectively laid the theological basis for the Dukhobor and Molokan movements. The early leader of the Dukhobors in the 1760s, Pobirokhin, would be succeeded by his reformist son-in-law, Semen Uklein.[28]

Molokanism arose as the result of a rift between Semen Uklein and his followers, on the one hand, and Illarion Pobirokhin and the Dukhobor believers, on the other hand. Uklein taught his Molokan followers to believe only in the Bible and to reject "everything that was not literally expressed in it."[29] Thus, on the basis of Biblical authority the Molokans moved, in this respect, to a position held from the beginning by the Baptists.

Despite the reliance of Dukhobors on an "inner revelation," there was much in common between the Dukhobors and Molokans. Both rejected serfdom, revered the Bible, and sought to establish equality and a community of property. On religious doctrine, the Molokans accepted the Orthodox as an arm of the Church and found themselves agreeing on many basics of that ancient Christian faith. Molokans taught that God was in three persons, Father, Son, and Holy Spirit; that the Son of God was conceived by the virgin Mary; and that the Bible was the sole authoritative written inspiration of faith. They also practiced praying for the dead in this epoch. However, on the concept of equality of property, the Molokans were not as strict as the Dukhobors.[30] Both Molokans and Baptists encouraged the development of literacy, but education was not of major concern to the Dukhobors.[31]

In contrast with the mysticism of the Khristovovers, and the inclination to seek utopias by the Dukhobors, the Molokans were moderate, sober, and loyal to the State. In some respects, like the Anabaptists in Switzerland and Holland in the sixteenth century, the Molokans in their earlier years were opposed to serfdom, oaths, wars, and military service.[32] Molokans in general had no Christs, such as prevailed among the Khristovovers and Dukhobors, but their believers reputedly acquired "spiritual wisdom."[33]

However, a different strain of Molokans settled among the Don Cossacks. They were pioneers in placing their Protestant-style evangelical church at the disposal of the Tsar's service. Some of the local leaders of the Don Molokans, in 1811, affirmed loyalty to the throne, expressed a willingness to take oaths, and approved the "necessity of the sacraments" embraced by the Orthodox church.[34] Much later, in 1905, major leaders and a congress of Molokans again would pledge loyalty to the Tsar. Their numbers had increased, and by about 1909 there were 91,500 Molokans spread over the empire.[35]

Expressing both Molokan vulnerability and its faithfulness to its simple Christian beliefs, a petition to the government was made in 1811 by the Samara Molokan leader, Akinfii Grachev:

> From ancient times, according to the legends of the ancestors, I have confessed the evangelical Christian faith—saying prayers to Our Lord Jesus Christ for His Imperial Majesty and his most holy house and the most holy ruling Synod according to the ritual of the early Christians and quietly and zealously fulfilling state obligations and public obligations for sixty years of my life—I have asked to be confirmed in our religion and to call our faith evangelical. . . .[36]

The Molokans changed markedly after the 1880-90s, as they adopted education and capitalism, while their internal structure crumbled. They had become more prosperous than many Orthodox, Khristovovers, and Dukhobors. Their economic superiority was remarkable on the Amur River in the Far East and in the villages in the Caucasus. But in a society that had become unequal, the majority of ordinary Molokans suffered from the economic disparity caused by fellow-believers. During the Russo-Japanese War (1904-05), many Molokan men became non-commissioned officers and, before World War I, army officers. This faith that was once pacifist, and against autocracy, serfdom, and Orthodoxy, now freely expressed loyal support to the Tsarist government.[37]

As early as 1908, at a missionary conference in Kiev, a warning had been given. A missionary stated: "Molokanism is a sect which is disintegrating and dying; whoever comes will take it; now the Shtundists [Baptists or near-Baptists] are coming with sermons to the Molokans and seducing them into their sect."[38]

The Molokans were tested severely in the 1820s and the 1830s. An upper stratum of wealthy Molokans turned away from their old democratic principles. This trend was resisted by the lower classes and believers from the Don River region. In the 1830s new prophets appeared proclaiming the end of the world. Among those preaching a chiliastic message was a Tambarov Molokan, Lukian Sokilov, who in 1836 warned his people to flee to the Ararat region to prepare for the end of the world. Throughout the Ukraine and Middle Volga in the 1830s and 1840s there were numerous riots against serfholders and landlords. Thousands of peasants fled to the Caucasus regions, joined by Molokans and by many Orthodox, who permanently left for the promise of a New Jerusalem and a new faith with the Molokans.[39]

In 1833 there reportedly was "an awesome phenomenon—a strong outpouring of the Holy Spirit." There also was a famine, during which the Molokans set up a common fund and a supply of food and clothing, distributing it according to need. Still, among the Molokans, there were supporters both of communalization and private farms. However, there was a growing antagonism to the bourgeois Molokans who nurtured serfdom.[40]

The right to worship without harassment or imprisonment, outside of Orthodoxy, was not easily acquired. The Tambov Molokans petitioned their governor on April 6, 1819, to allow the group to have official recognition and protection from those Russian Orthodox clergy who were interfering in their affairs.[41] Despite police and Orthodox surveillance, the Molokan preachers in a period of fifty years, beginning in the 1820s and including the reign of Alexander I, spread their faith from Tambov to Voronezh, Crimea, Samara, Saratov, Astrakhan, Tavriia, Siberia, Transcaucasus, Central Asia, and the eastern borders of the Russian state. By 1859 they settled in the Amur River region in the Far East.[42] But Molokan growth had excited the fear of the State Church, so that by March 15, 1847, the government had begun prohibiting the Molokans from working in Orthodox homes or even from hiring Orthodox persons.[43]

The basic equality of the Molokans continued to prevail, along with their professed loyalty to the tsar. However, by 1816 the Molokans had attracted a number of successful merchants and town people, some of them wealthy.[44] In the first half of the nineteenth century, there would occur a division between the upper-class Molokans (once characterized by their mystical motifs) and some of the lower ranks, the Prygun Molokans, who adopted Khristovover practices, including a Christ-figure as their leader.[45] These Prygun Molokans refused military service and military activities, while other Molokans would fight for the Tsarist government in World War I. And between 1901 and 1911, thirty-five hundred Pryguny Molokans would emigrate to California.[46]

The evangelical activities and the dissension in the Molokan ranks did not ease the vigilance of the national government. In 1870 the Don Cossack Molokan presbyter, A. I. Stoialov, wrote: "Why does not a beneficent government allow these Spiritual Christians [Molokans] to set up houses of prayer with tables for books and benches for sitting according to their simple teaching, so close to the simplicity of the Gospel?" And it was the inspiration of the Don Molokans to retain their moderate views and purge from their faith the false and exotic teachings derived from Semen Uklein.[47]

Baptists Attract the Molokans and Stundists

Within the Molokan movement, there had been groups almost identical to the Baptists. In the 1880s there developed a Neo-Molokanism called Christians of the Evangelical Faith, a Baptist-type of Molokanism. For a period their leader was Z. D. Zakharov, a rich property-owner and member of the Third State Duma, who lived in Astrakhanka, Tavriia. This group attracted many persons from the Don Branch in Tavriia.[48]

Zakharov's followers among the Neo-Molokans recognized the rites of water baptism, the Lord's Supper, marriage, and, strangely, extreme unction (a Roman Catholic and Orthodox practice). In their teachings on sin and justification, structure and organization, they were close to the Baptists and Evangelical Christians. Zakharov's group, in fact, joined the World Evangelical Union and founded a theological school for evangelists.[49]

The Christian zeal of the Molokans largely collapsed after 1890, and the Baptists, a Bible-nurtured faith, received Molokans in large numbers. The Molokan collapse was partly due to disillusionment over their economic exploitation by fellow-members. Also, their young people became indifferent to Christian teachings because of divided loyalties over the Russo-Japanese War (1904-05), the massacre of Armenians and Tatars, and scientific and rational explanations for the laws of nature, including the claims of Darwinism.[50] The Molokan religion was left increasingly with old men and women (estimates of their numbers ranging between two hundred thousand and one million in 1913), as their young people in the 1900s became infected with atheism and departed.[51]

The loss of militancy by the Molokans left them susceptible to conversion to a more vibrant Baptist faith. The modern Molokan does not proselytize (for, in faith, the new believer must convince himself), nor lay hands on their new ministers, nor even collect money during the worship service.[52] Such a quietist faith appeared not to be well-equipped to cope with a lively evangelical movement, stemming from either the Baptists or the Pentecostalists. And, like Baptists, modern Molokans go readily into military service. In the post-World War II period, Baptists and Molokans often jointly participated in prayer meetings, hymn-singing, and funeral services.[53]

My God Is Not an Icon

My God is not an icon with its smoky lamp,
my old mother bowing to it piously.
That painted face is silent, stiff,
powerless to warm the heart,
powerless to hear my weary prayers.

A man,
crushed in the struggle,

bends his lips and kisses it.
But it was made by men,
it has no life and cannot give life.
It is dead.
Turn, sorrowing, and leave it,
returning to the cold crowds of the streets.

My God
is not in temples under crosses,
incense and candles smoking,
but where hearts burn at his touch
and spirits burst in flame with love.

My God
is everywhere, alive in
town, village, fields, the endless woods,
capturing our hearts
and setting them free from sin.*

*Written by a Russian Baptist in the clandestine journal, *Herald of Salvation*, No. 1, 1966. Source: Michael Bourdeaux, *Faith on Trial In Russia*, 28-29.

Baptist Beginnings Among the Slavs

The emergence of the Baptist faith in Russia originally was achieved through German-speaking immigrants, some of them Mennonites, others Lutherans, in Transcaucasia, the Baltic Province, and the Ukraine (Kherson). The first probing initiatives of the Baptists built on: (1) Molokan spiritual dissatisfaction and transformation in the Caucasus Mountains, (2) Stundist Bible-study groups in the Ukraine, (3) The Russian Bible Society that penetrated the Russian Orthodox-dominated culture and reached into the pietist people in the autocratic nation, and (4) in a further development, the Spiritual Christians of Baptist or near-Baptist character, inspired by British

Lord Radstock (G.A.W. Waldgrave) and V. A. Pashkov, that began among the wealthy court officials and their servants of St. Petersburg and spread to the Ukraine.

Less than a decade in precedence to the founding of the Kherson (Ukraine) Baptist community, the Transcaucasian Baptists witnessed the growth of home missionary Vasili G. Pavlov. The early Christian mentor of Pavlov was the merchant-minister Nikita Voronin of Tiflis, Georgia, racially of Slavic roots and culturally of Molokan stock. Since forms of baptism were a common topic of conversation among the reformist Molokans, Voronin began searching the Scriptures for an answer. Through his study of the Bible, Voronin reached a theological position approximating that of the Baptists, in essence that he was a sinful man, redeemed by Christ's death on the cross. Voronin was determined now to seek New Testament baptism through immersion. His baptism, after years of waiting, was through the German, Martin Kalweit, whose early life was spent in Lithuania.[54]

Kalweit had been raised a Lutheran in Kowno, Lithuania. However, in seeking a more evangelical faith, he crossed the Russian frontier to visit a group of Baptists in East Prussia and was baptized in 1858. Four years later, Kalweit and his family settled in Tiflis, Georgia, then on the southern extremity of the Russian empire, where he gathered a small cluster of German Baptists. The evangelizing of adherents to the Russian Orthodox Church was illegal, and there were no Russians in Kalweit's congregation. However, when the Russian Nikita Voronin sought baptism, the courageous Kalweit baptized him, on August 20, 1867, in the dead of night. Voronin was, from the start, an energetic preacher, and by 1868 he had established in Georgia the first Russian Baptist church in the empire,[55] that attained forty members by 1875.

Voronin's remarkable success, despite church controversy and attacks on his character, produced a number of leading preachers and a Baptist church that grew rapidly for fifty years. His two greatest church builders in Georgia, both baptized in 1871, were V. G. Pavlov (1854-1924) the main personality in this account, and V. V. Ivanoff-

Klishnikoff (1846-1919). Both men worked with intense zeal among the Molokans, with Pavlov, only sixteen-seventeen years old, fervently striving under the guidance of the Tiflis church. Pavlov's Molokan father was Gury Grigorievich Pavlov (who died 1903), from Vorontsovka village near Tiflis, also the birthplace of Vasili G. Pavlov. Gury Grigorievich originally was vigorously opposed to the Baptist doctrine of his son.[56] Pavlov's friend, Ivanoff-Klishnikoff, beginning work when twenty-five years old, traveled throughout Transcaucasia and founded many Baptist churches from 1871 to 1876.[57]

Baptist Confession

Baptist pioneer and preacher Johann Oncken of Germany also had a profound impact on the Baptist faith in Russia. Not only did he visit Russia in 1869, when Pastor Voronin was struggling to give Baptists a toehold in Tiflis, but he probably composed the *Confession of Faith of the Baptist Christians,* written in the German language and published in 1872. The Russian version of the confession, likely translated into Russian by V. G. Pavlov, was *Tspovedanie Very Kristian-Baptisov.* Among the major dogmas contained in this declaration were the doctrines of predestination and original sin. "Since all men came from Adam's seed, they were made to partake of the same fallen and completely damaged nature, since they are conceived and born in sin."[58] The Russian translation contained these words: "[people] are children of wrath, completely incapable of and not inclined to all that is good, but capable of and inclined to all that is evil."[59]

This Baptist Confession of man's sinful nature and inability to earn salvation was a direct contradiction of the sectarian beliefs of some non-Baptists that attributed merit or even salvation to good deeds. Thus, the theology of the sinful nature of man had a major impact on those converts to the Baptists coming from the followers of Khristovoverie, Dukhoborism, and Molokanism.[60]

The Gospel message from another strain of Baptists located in the north, and proclaimed by British Lord Radstock, was received warmly by servants, aristocrats, and nobility at St. Petersburg. The theology of this branch, sometimes called Evangelical Christians or Pashkovites (from a leader, Count V. A. Pashkov), was similar in some respects to the General Baptists of Britain, who accepted the doctrine of Arminius, that God willed that all men be saved, and that they could be saved when they sought forgiveness of sins and salvation through the blood of Jesus Christ.

Oncken's confession, on the other hand, as influenced by the great Reformation leader John Calvin, spoke of predestination and of limited choice by man:

> . . . . those persons from the ruined race of man, who in the course of time really must acquire redemption, are also chosen by the Father—their names are written in Heaven and they themselves are given over into the hands of the Redeemer—as His people——These people are destined for eternal life in Jesus Christ——Such a divine determination is unchangeable and set forever—, so that those to whom it applies—the chosen ones—cannot be torn from the hands of Christ. . . .[61]

Thus, for most Baptists, but not the Evangelical Christians of Russia, the doctrines of election and predestination were core beliefs.

In 1875, when Pavlov was about twenty-one years of age, he traveled to Hamburg, Germany, to enroll in a six-month theological study presented by the eminent German pioneer Johann G. Oncken. Unfortunately, Pavlov's timing was not good, with Oncken's seminary closed, so he spent nearly a year studying under the supervision of a co-worker to Oncken, Herr P. Willraht. This training was to give Pavlov distinction and a leadership role in Russia and lead ultimately to reforms in the Russian Baptist churches. After Pavlov was ordained in 1876 by Oncken,[62] he and V. V. Ivanoff worked vigorously for ten years around Tiflis in establishing mission stations.

Eventually, their work moved to the north, and to the establishing of Baptist communities in distant places, such as Taurida, Samara, Astrakhan, and Mohilev.[63] Rushbrooke, a learned historian of the Russian church, refers to Pavlov and Ivanoff in these words: they "embody the character, the opinions, and even the very soul of the Baptists of Russia."[64]

Before 1875 Pavlov and his colleagues from Tiflis were totally ignorant of a sizable Baptist community growing separately in the Ukraine (Kherson).[65] However, after returning from Hamburg, Pavlov routed his return trip from Hamburg via Oseovo Village in the Ukraine, where he conferred with Baptist elders Ratuschny, Lassotsky, and Riaboschapka. Then Pavlov and Radionoff made a long missionary trip to Mount Ararat and the Caspian Sea, with many churches formed and dozens baptized.[66]

Thus, the second epochal Baptist growth in the Russian empire— but only fractionally behind the emergence of the church in Transcaucasia—occurred near Odessa in the Kherson (Ukraine). In 1876 Pavlov met with Baptist minister Michael Ratuschny (who had been baptized by Riaboschapka), probably linking for the first time the Baptists of Transcaucasia and the Ukraine.

The Baptist congregations in the Ukraine originally stemmed from German Mennonites or Stundists in the 1850s and the revivalist, Scripture-based teachings of Mennonite Pastor Wuest and Lutheran Preacher Bonnekempfer.[67] The term Stundist (often meaning Baptist) was derived from the German word *Stunde* or hour, that was spent in Bible study by seekers hungry for a personal faith. Thus, the German population element is important, since Germans in large numbers had migrated to Russia under Peter the Great, between 1689 and 1725, seeking religious freedom and land. Also, in the last part of the eighteenth century, Prussian Protestants flowed into southern Russia to escape military service and to secure the religious tolerance promised by the German-born empress, Catherine II ("the Great").[68]

Against the stern mandates of the Russian Imperial Government not to proselyte Russian Orthodox adherents, there evolved a percolating Biblical effect upon the masses. And so, on June 23, 1869, a former Mennonite, Abraham Unger, baptized Efim (Euphimius) Tsymbal (Zimbal), the first Stundist to embrace the Baptist faith in the Ukraine. It was forbidden to baptize Russians such as Tsymbal, but he managed to slip among thirty baptismal candidates awaiting baptism at the German Baptist church at Alt-Dantzig.[69] Next emerged the powerful Baptist peasant preacher Ivan Riaboschapka (Rjaboschapka)—baptized by Tsymbal—who stirred the people within the Kherson. Then, to mold these new converts in the Ukraine with Baptist discipline, came the great German pastor, J. G. Oncken.[70]

But there was a price to be paid for evangelizing in Russia. Under the Tsars, the Russians proclaimed freedom of religion, but the Orthodox Church was the State Church, and it would not tolerate any proselytizing of the Orthodox flock. No one must persuade an Orthodox Russian to join another church. He who did was guilty of high crimes and subject to banishment to Siberia. Further, any Russian who left the Orthodox Communion to become a Baptist was subject to the authority of the ecclesiastical courts. In such circumstances, guardians would be appointed for the children of the accused and an administrator for his estate until he returned to the Orthodox faith.[71]

The imperial state, ignoring its past mistreatments, imprisonments, seizures of property, and banishments, proclaimed its version of religious liberty before World War I:

> All the subjects of the Russian empire not belonging to the Established Church, both native Russians and those from abroad who are in the service of the State, are permitted at all times openly to confess their faith and practice their services in accordance with the rite. This freedom of faith is assured not only to Christians of foreign confessions, but also to the Jews, Mohammedans, and heathen, so that all the peoples in Russia may worship God, the Almighty, with different tongues, according to the laws and confessions of their fathers so that they may bless the government of the Russian tsar, and pray for his welfare to the Creator of the World.[72]

Despite the official warning, there were about twenty-five thousand Baptists in Russia in 1907, this number to increase to millions in the twentieth century.[73]

Struggles in the Early Church

Vasili Pavlov eventually was to face the intolerance of the Tsarist government, but his first trials were with Baptist archleaders Nikita I. Voronin and millionaire D. I. Mazaev (Masaeff). Pavlov was an eloquent intellectual and had his own vision for the Baptists, but he represented, in a sense, the newest stratum of leadership. After his return in 1876 from Germany, he became a preacher in the Tiflis congregation, where he distinguished himself for his energy and theological clarity.[74]

In December 1879, at a meeting of the Tiflis Baptist congregation, Pavlov accused Voronin the merchant-preacher and editor of *Golos Very* (*Voice of Truth*) of usury and hypocrisy. Voronin was challenged for being a shareholder of Kasumov and Company Trading House, in which he had invested one thousand rubles and served on a loan committee in a company making loans at high rates of interest. Pavlov confronted Voronin, since the latter reportedly had declared at several Baptist conferences that no one should be charged any interest. Voronin responded that he had invested in the company, not to receive interest, but to obtain profit from the trading operations.[75]

Pavlov achieved the excommunication of the powerful leader Voronin. But Voronin gathered his own supporters and formed a second Baptist congregation. Although Voronin's moral authority was shaken, with supporters from Vladikaukaz and several other churches, he forced Pavlov to review the decision and reinstate him. It was clear from the Pavlov-Voronin controversy that Baptists at some early period had agreed that usury was to be condemned. At Novo-Vassilievka (Taurida), on or about 1884, a Baptist conference took the position that only six percent interest could be charged in a business transaction.[76]

Less successful for Pavlov was his struggle with wealthy D. I. Mazaev (Masaeff), president of the All-Russian Baptist Union from 1885 to 1910. Mazaev was statesmanlike and the church's most eloquent speaker, with a great comprehension of the Baptist organization. In his complaints about Baptist autocratic leadership, Pavlov asserted his own foreign theological training and authority. In a letter to his successful fellow-missionary, V. V. Ivanoff, about 1873, Pavlov had insisted that there should be a critical appraisal of the decisions of the church and of the need for freedom of opinion. Pavlov wrote, that "the decision of the whole church should be tested in the same way as the opinion of one person."[77]

Missionaries directed by Mazaev attempted to absorb the near-Baptist Evangelical Christians, who existed in the Ukraine and St. Petersburg; members of this strain were often called Pashkovites after their organizer, the wealthy landholder and zealous evangelist, Colonel of the Guard Count Vasili Pashkov. This upper-class Pashkovite church element that began among noblemen at St. Petersburg included among its leaders Count M. M. Korff, Count Bobrinsky, and Princess Gagarina Lieven.[78] This near-Baptist element was Arminian in doctrine (whoever believes in Christ shall be saved), pietist in style, and influenced by the Plymouth Brethren beliefs of the founder, Lord Granville Radstock (G.A.W. Waldgrave). Then, in the remarkable setting of palatial homes in the Russian capital, peasants, civil servants, and nobility prayed and sang hymns together. Lord Radstock had been persuaded in 1870 to come to St. Petersburg by an aristocratic Russian lady, Mrs. E. S. (Yelena Ivanovna) Tchertkowa, a general's wife, whose twelve-year old son Misha died, vainly imploring his worldly mother to become a Christian. This lady of distinction subsequently became a seeker after Christ and traveled abroad, where she sought the assistance of the lay preacher, Lord Radstock.[79]

Blocking the efforts of Mazaev to absorb the Evangelical Christians (who sometimes partook of the Lord's Supper without being baptized) was the remarkable Baptist leader, Ivan S. Prokhanoff.[80]

Prokhanoff built on the initiative of the Baptist pioneer preacher I. V. Kargel, the founder of Baptist work in Bulgaria. Prokhanoff, a Baptist convert from the Caucasus region, migrated to St. Petersburg, led the Baptists there for thirty years, and eventually would forge a union of Evangelical Christians and Baptists and became a vice president of the Baptist World Alliance. In 1905 this "Pashkovite" movement of two elements united under the name Evangelical Christians-Baptists.

In 1890 Prokhanoff started the periodical "Besseda," in cooperation with editor Hermann Fast. When the publication was banned in Russia, Prokhanoff went abroad to study at England's Bristol (Baptist) College and attended the universities of Berlin and Paris. While overseas he continued to print "Besseda" and mailed it to Russia. He returned to Russia as an engineer and assistant professor and continued to serve the church as a lay Preacher. In 1902 he published the widely-used hymnbook "Gusli," accepted by Baptists and Evangelicals throughout Russia. In 1908 he founded The Union of Evangelical Christians, basically a Baptist group but containing non-immersed evangelicals; this Union had its first All-Russian Conference in 1909[81] and was headed by Prokhanoff in 1911. However, the organization held itself apart from the larger Baptist Union.

In time, Pavlov would seek an accord between the Baptists and the Evangelical Christians and their promoter, Ivan S. Prokhanoff. Pavlov always was generous to kindred confessions,[82] and it is known that Pavlov served as the preacher at the wedding in Georgia of a Molokan, Alexander S. Prokhanoff. However, in spite of internal conflicts, the All-Russian Baptist Union was formed in 1884 at Novo-Vassilievka (Taurida), and gradually the distinctions between the Baptists of South Russia and Transcaucasia began to vanish.[83]

Persecution

The assassination of Tsar Alexander II in 1881 marked the beginning of a severe persecution of Baptists. This period of trial occurred during the reign of Tsar Alexander III (ruling from 1881 to 1894) and his misguided wife Marie Feodorowna. Their agent for the suppression of non-Russian religions was K. P. Pobedonostsev, grey eminence and over-procurator of the Holy Synod, whose ideology focused on one tsar, one language (Russian), and one faith (Russian Orthodoxy).[84] In 1887 a more organized persecution would drive into exile V. G. Pavlov and Nikita Voronin, and, in 1894, Martin Kalweit, the baptizer of Voronin.[85]

An assault on Baptists and other religious and peaceful people— called "The Storm"—first broke out in an area north of the Black Sea and spread over the entire country. Baptists (frequently called Stundists) were transported to Siberia or forced into the army. Churches were closed and their pastors banished, even in Estonia, on the fringes of the Empire.[86]

Pobedonostsev was determined to eradicate the Stundists from the Ukraine.[87] Under his methodical directions, detailed security reports were submitted by provincial authorities. When the Governor of Kiev sent his report in 1881 on the growth of Stundists [Baptists], Tsar Alexander III wrote in reply: "A very serious question. Call to the attention of the Ministry of Internal Affairs [national police] and the over-procurator of the Holy Synod." The governor's report falsely reflected that the Stundists taught that natural wealth, including land, was regarded as common property and that Stundists refused to pay taxes, obligations and obedience to the authorities." The tsar wrote that this was "almost socialism."

Pobedonostsev forwarded erroneous reports from Kiev's Orthodox priests, associating Stundists with socialism. However, police reports from Odessa and Elisavetgrad reported that the Stundists did not practice doctrines of property equality (socialism) and treated their spiritual brothers as equals. Further, the police asserted that the Stundists circumspectly carried out the decrees of government, police, and village elders, even assuming obligations as police deputy and other rural jobs.[88]

Frequently imprisoned for preaching, Pavlov was twice exiled to Orenburg (later called Chkalov) in southeast Russia, close to the

Ural Mountains, where he was placed under police surveillance. As he left Tiflis in chains for Siberia, a thousand Baptists and friends followed him in tribute to the outskirts of the city.

After his first banishment, which began in 1887, an ordeal lasting four years, he did "amazing work" in Orenburg, despite winter temperatures that sometimes attained minus forty degrees centigrade. Strangely, the church at Tiflis remained strong and even increased, although always torn by dissension. After being given freedom to return to Tiflis in 1891, he began again to preach the Gospel; he was immediately exiled to Orenburg, again for four years. He lived in a friend's basement room while he was busy with his missionary work, helping to establish three new churches at Ufa and baptizing 150 persons. His success in evangelizing brought him to the attention of Orthodox priests, who challenged (virtually commanded) him to debate theology at their seminary. Pavlov accepted this opportunity to preach the Word. Tragically, in July 1892 he would lose his wife and three children to cholera, the result in part of scratching out a living with inadequate food and shelter. Sometime before, he had lost another daughter to drowning. The single child that remained was Paul, age nine, who was destined to become an international Baptist leader. In time, Paul became president of the All-Russian Baptist Union.[89]

When Pavlov returned to Tiflis in 1895, the persecution was so intense that he accepted a call to a Russo-German church at Tulcea, Romania, where he remained until 1901. There he preached to Romanians, Russians, Bulgarians, and Turks. There was a sizable Russian exile community in Tulcea, and a prayer hall seating six hundred people was filled on many Sundays. During his six years in Romania, he made some trips into Bulgaria and campaigned for human rights, letting the world know about the intolerable treatment of Protestants in Russia. Then, he returned once more to his native soil at Tiflis.[90]

In 1905 Pavlov went to London where he helped establish the Baptist World Alliance (his name was missing from the minutes), along with Ivanoff-Klishnikoff, G.I. Mazaev, and Baron Waldemar Uixhüll, who was pastor of a Baptist Church near his family castle in Estonia. Upon his return, Pavlov began a ministry on the Black Sea at Odessa.[91]

Much of Pavlov's wrestling with Voronin and some other Baptist leaders related to the perception of the insensitivity of rich and bourgeois Baptist leaders to their less fortunate brothers. As early as 1892, Pavlov wrote: "I have a very unfavorable opinion of the Tiflis congregation: with the acceptance of the rich many have begun to toady to them, and their voices prevail over all others in everything." Almost certainly, he was talking about Voronin, or the Mazaev family, or both. Even earlier, in November 1891, from Orenburg, he railed against the rich that fawned before the tsarist authorities, when the latter were persecuting Baptists and forbidding public prayer services. "Oh, where is the spirit of the first Christian martyrs!"[92]

The rift with Voronin was never fully healed. On July 26, 1903, Pavlov wrote the following note: "Voronin and his 10-men party broke away for good, and we decided to give them one fifth of the property—a total of 7 benches."[93] But Voronin had preached at the funeral of Gury Grigorievich, Pavlov's father, on July 17, 1903,[94] perhaps out of respect for the living leader. When news came from Vorontsovka a month later that an uncle had died, Pavlov found this an occasion to talk to villagers there about God and their immortal souls until late into the night.[95]

The Russian Revolution of 1905 was one of those rare moments in modern Russian history that loomed glowingly with hope. As Ernest Payne states of the situation, "No Baptist community had suffered more than the Russians," and only the Anabaptists in the sixteenth century had been so harried and persecuted. But the believers knew that "the Word of God cannot be bound and that the spirit of man is the candle of the Lord." Except after the years 1905-14, the "Golden Decade" of the 1920s, and perhaps during the 1950s, Baptists were seldom free from harassment by police or church authorities.[96]

As V. V. Ivanov wrote, "In Russia this large movement of Baptists began with 1905, when God granted us religious freedom.... With 1905 there began an era in the history of Baptism [Baptists] which we can call the era of open storm." This epoch resulted in many conversions among the Molokans and Orthodox.[97]

The exceptional fissure of freedom that opened in Russia in 1905 enabled Pavlov to travel abroad. Pavlov gave a graphic review of his life's work and tribulations at the Baptist Congress, held at Exeter Hall, London, that opened on June 28, 1905. When asked to speak extemporaneously, the bearded Russian rose and spoke from his heart:

> I am very glad to see you, but I must tell you that I have never tried to speak English in public. Although I have not prepared a speech, I hope to do without an interpreter. If I speak pigeon language, I ask you in advance to forgive me. I [am] now minister in Tiflis, Transcaucasia, and in Asia. Our work in Asia began thirty years ago. We built prayer houses but were persecuted, and I and many others were exiled to Siberia. When I returned from exile, police came and demanded that I would pledge not to preach any more. But I told them: I will not give you such a promise. Do you think I am scared? I am not and I am fully determined to go on preaching. My conscience did not let me do what police demanded from me, and I was exiled again for four years. I spent a total of eight years in exile, and when I was free, I went to Romania and preached there. When the time came, I returned to Russia, and now I minister in Tiflis. We have gone through much suffering for Christ and have been persecuted as criminals. We have been exiled and stripped of all our rights. But we are glad that our position in Russia has become far better. We have been given more freedom, but we are not completely free yet. There are up to 20,000 Baptists in Russia, all baptized in one faith according to the Bible.[98]

In 1907 Pavlov was authorized to guide the work in the Ukraine (Kherson), and he made Odessa his operational center. From this flourishing port of five hundred thousand, he began new work in Nicolaieff, Terespol, Bendery, and in Bessarabia. Divisions and novel practices had hurt church unity in that vast area, in part because of misinterpreting the Bible by uneducated leaders. His duty, then, was to enunciate the true doctrine. In his three-year ministry to the Ukraine, Pavlov baptized 240 believers.[99]

It was in the early years of the twentieth century that Pavlov gave so much time to representing the Russian Baptists abroad and to his writings. He attended World and European Baptist conferences from 1905 to 1911. Pavlov and M. Timoshenko also began a publishing house and issued the *Baptist Journal* from 1907 to 1910.[100] These were days of optimism for the Baptists. In 1909, at Rostov-on-Don, a Baptist congress established the All-Russian Union of Baptist Youth Circles.[101] From 1913 to 1917 Pavlov edited the *Slovo Istiny* journal, into which he inserted his writings. Also, he translated and published sermons received from such eminent clergymen as Charles Spurgeon of Britain (by then deceased).[102]

After the loss of his first wife (in 1892), he married again, at Orenburg, his new wife Alexandra Egorovna. Together, the Pavlovs in 1911 attended the Baptist World Alliance at Philadelphia. The couple traveled by way of the Cameroons, West Africa, London, and New York.[103] They were joined at Philadelphia by Russian delegates: I.S. Prokhanoff, Ivanoff-Klishnikoff, and William Andrew Fetler, whose father had been a missionary in Latvia.[104] Pavlov's son Paul wrote about the increasing prosperity of Baptists in Russia before World War I. In time, Paul became president of the All-Russian Baptist Union.[105]

In October 1917 the Bolshevik Revolution, led by Nikolai Lenin, a Marxian socialist, overthrew the provisional government and exiled Tsar Nicholas II and his family. Since the Russians were at war with Germany and Austria, they were compelled by desperate conditions to sign the humiliating Treaty of Brest-Litovsk. But the cessation of external hostilities and the radical change in government awakened the hopes of its mistreated peasants and Non-Conformists. In January 1918, the Red Government, which would expose so many "western imperial" secret treaties, now appealed to its own citizens by separating the Orthodox Church and the State.[106] As a consequence, Pavlov, along with M. D. Timoshenko, and I. S. Prokhanoff openly expressed confidence in the new administration. However, W. A. Fetler, suspicious of the new government on political and religious grounds, remained abroad.

In 1884 Colonel Vasili Pashkov and Count M. M. Korff tried to unite all Russian evangelicals at a national conference at St. Petersburg. This bold venture failed because the groups, including large numbers of Baptists, could not agree on an acceptable mode of baptism or even on whether they should take the Lord's Supper together. However, they were convinced that they belonged together.[107]

Then, in July 1921, the Evangelical Christians-Baptists, and their more numerous Calvinistic Baptist brethren, met in Moscow to try to forge a union once more. Among the dignitaries attending the conference was Vasili G. Pavlov, about sixty-seven years old and nearing death, and his son Paul. Included in the delegation of sixty were Baptist leader M. D. Timoshenko and Evangelical Christian patriarch Prokhanoff. But despite the favorable milieu, their accord signed at Moscow could not be implemented.[108] In 1923 I. S. Prokhanoff was elected vice president of the Baptist World Alliance at Stockholm.[109]

In the mid-1920s, Baptist publications were allowed to resume: *The Christian* in 1924 and *The Baptist* in 1925. The new *Baptist of the Ukraine* was founded in 1926. Two hymn books appeared: The *Voice of Truth* and *The Harp*.[110] Russian government toleration, of short duration, enabled the Baptists to publish at Leningrad in 1926 twenty-five thousand copies of the entire Bible, a New Testament (twenty-five thousand copies), and in 1928, a biblical concordance (ten thousand copies).[111]

The original growth of the Russian Baptist Church is far too complex and heroic to attribute to one or several persons. But Baltic Germans and Swedes were involved in the process.[112] When Baptist pioneer Vasili Pavlov died in 1924, a few months after the 1923 Baptist Congress in Moscow, reportedly there were five thousand Sunday Schools and three hundred thousand Baptist and Evangelical Christians, boys and girls, attending classes in Russia. Baptists and Evangelicals under a Communist government would be so daring as to propose (and be denied) their own communal "City of the Sun" at Evangelsk in Siberia. But under the seemingly non-threatening government, the ones correctly gauging the long-range political weather were twenty-one thousand Mennonites, who in the period 1923-27 emigrated from Russia to Canada.[113] After that period, millions of Russians would be murdered by Stalin's underlings.

Postword

As the result of the work of Pavlov and the gallant Russian Christian band, there were in Russia in 1974 about 550,000 Baptists linked in the All Union Council of Evangelical Christians—Baptists (AUCECB). This aggregation of Baptists compares in number with those in India (700,000) and the United States (over 33 million).[114] Other Russian Baptists, part of a formerly underground non-conforming church, are vigorous in their separate testimony. The Russian faithful represent strains from the amalgam of Baptists with Molokan, Stundist, Pietist, Mennonite, and Plymouth Brethren roots. However, more startling is the revelation of the 1954 Baptist publication *Fraternal Chronicle* (Bratsky Vestnik) that there are an estimated three million Russian and other Baptists in the old Soviet Union, embracing baptized believers in fifty-four hundred congregations.[115]

Of immeasurable value both to the Baptists and their brethren, the Radstock-Pashkovite Evangelical Christians, was the printing and distribution of Bibles and religious tracts. The translation of the Bible into Russian dates from the 1860s and 1870s on the initiative of estate owners, several centuries after Jan Hus and Martin Luther translated the Scriptures into Czech and German.[116] The Russian Branch of the Bible Society (1812-26) affiliated with the British and Foreign Bible Society (founded in 1804), produced fifteen editions of the Bible from 1817 to 1823. Old Testament books were printed but not allowed to circulate. In 1822 the Psalter (Psalms) was printed in Russian, one hundred thousand copies in two years. This occurred even when Church Slavonic, under Orthodox Church prohibitions, was not given wide distribution. Also, the London Missionary Society, from 1817, prepared a Mongolian Bible and undertook evangelical work among Buryats and Kalmucks, of Buddhist stock.[117]

During the reign of Nicholas I (ruler from 1825 to 1855) the Russian Bible Society was repressed and the Russian translation of the Pentateuch burned. However, during the "Russian Emancipation Period," 1860s-70s, the Old and New Testament again were published in Russia.[118]

The Marxist regime, lax toward religious minorities in its formative stages, now perfected its own cruelties and restraints. A strident anti-God campaign was enforced as new government policy. Even the Orthodox priesthood was compelled to support the militant Godless doctrine. Despite this, in 1928, ten thousand copies of a biblical concordance were published. There was even a short-lived Baptist seminary, opened in 1927 at Moscow, with Ivanoff-Klishnikoff as rector. But by 1929 the seminary closed, with the rector and Preacher Nikolai Odintsov sent as prisoners to Central Asia.[119]

The Legacy

How can we weigh the impact of Vasili G. Pavlov? His life was not in any sense that of an ascetic, contemplative philosopher, or docile prelate avoiding controversy. Far from the quietist role, his life was portrayed through the restless career of activist, builder, missionary, and religious controversialist. He was complex, intelligent, and fired of the Holy Spirit. He was primarily the messenger-preacher, but also the theologian-challenger, church historian, and Christian journalist. As co-founder of the Baptist Church (Slavic phase) in Russia, he shares honors with Nikita Voronin, V. V. Ivanoff-Klishnikoff, Ivan S. Prokhanoff, and others. Yet even he built on the spearhead work of others, many of them Germans.

His fearless commitment to Christ and his tireless efforts in organizing churches resulted in his imprisonment ten times and two exiles to Siberia and once to Romania.[120] He sought to unite the Evangelical Christians and the Baptists, and, thus, he assisted the work of denominational unification. As a founding father, he helped begin the church in Georgia. He pioneered in the Ukraine, where he clarified for the Baptists their basic doctrines. As an evangelist, he glorified his Lord by suffering imprisonment in Siberia, while expanding the preaching centers in that vast area. He died, even as he lived, giving his exceptional talents to the task of bringing the lost to his Savior, Jesus Christ. Pavlov, like the great German pioneer Johann Oncken, was among the greatest Baptist Trailblazers in Europe.

Chapter 14

Philip P. Bliss
(1838-1876)

Meteor in the Musical Sky

In the composition of hymns (hymnology), Baptists have no composers equal in prestige to the Lutherans Paul Gerhardt and Johann Sebastian Bach, "high priest of church music." However, in hymnody, which means both the writing and the singing of hymns, the Baptists throughout the world may provide in their congregations and choirs literally multitudes of full-throated, Spirit-filled enthusiasts and singers. The Baptists embody a faith that sings to God on all occasions and does it with enthusiasm. Conceivably, the most accepted twentieth-century gospel song writer to many Baptists in America, and much of the world, was blind hymn writer Fanny Crosby, a Methodist. And among the leading gospel song writers of the Crosby era (1820-1915) was the Baptist hymn composer and writer, Philip P. Bliss (1838-76), whose young life ended in tragedy.

Bliss was not only notable in hymnology, often writing both music and lyrics, but was a "Founding Father" of the Gospel Song Movement, along with evangelist-singer Ira D. Sankey. Bliss was among the most prominent Trailblazers in writing children's songs and hymns. Also, he was a pioneer in Sunday School music and in 1873 published his collection *Sunshine for Sunday School.*[1]

Bliss often is remembered in connection with music publisher George F. Root and evangelists Dwight L. Moody, Major Daniel

Philip P. Bliss (1876) Studying His Latest Work

W. Whittle, and singer-evangelist Ira D. Sankey. The preaching-singing crusades of those religious figures, often including Bliss in the 1870s, carried them to every corner of America, England, and Scotland, where gospel music was warmly received. Bliss, as the first editor of the hymnbook *Gospel Hymns* (1871), along with co-publisher Sankey, had a powerful influence on the direction of religious music and hymnody in the American post-Civil War period. In some denominations, this hymnbook displaced the official songbooks.[2] Bliss in 1874 published another collection of hymns under the title *Gospel Songs* that continued a trend in gospel song writing and publishing.[3]

The remarkable facet of Bliss is that without formal training in music he became a proficient musician and composer of many of Christendom's best-loved hymns. Ultimately, he became a master of music with a special devotion to gospel hymns.

It can always be debated as to who is the paramount hymn writer and composer among Baptists. That select circle of candidates certainly would include Bliss and his contemporaries, William B. Bradbury (1816-68), Robert Lowry (1826-99), and William H. Doane (1832-1915), the latter the closest collaborator of Fanny Crosby. In the years that include the twenty-first century, attention also must be directed to that prolific author-producer of texts and tunes, B. B. McKinney. In all such appraisals the questions arise of the quality, taste, and timelessness of the music, and the spirituality, clarity, and beauty of the text. Although the work of Bliss is loved by thousands, perhaps millions, of hymn singers, his products are not regarded by all music scholars to have earned him a niche among the foremost hymn writers. His critics include E. E. Ryden, who appreciates the emotional quality of Blisss' hymns but does not find great merit or depth in his texts or music.[4]

Despite the short life of this imaginative song writer, the trends initiated in part by him, and the popularity of his hymns, which include "Let the Lower Lights Be Burning" and "Wonderful Words of Life," probably will give him enduring stature wherever gospel music is loved. Certainly he has tapped a wellspring more typical of Baptist tastes and temperament in the modern period than Gerhardt's staid and somber songs of worship, including the mournful if great medieval transition hymn, "O Sacred Head Now Wounded." Throughout the ages, hymn singing for Baptists has become a vital and increasingly precious expression of worship, sometimes prayerful and reflective but more often in the Bliss mode, vibrant, lively, and emotion-gathering.

Sometimes the quality of the religious song writer is judged on the basis of whether the product is a true hymn. One critic, Harvey B. Marks, concludes that most gospel songs written by Bliss should not be classified as hymns. Hymns, Marks states, are defined as the most difficult poetry to write, and must express praise to God through singing. Therefore, a "hymn is a sacred poem expressive of devotion, spiritual experience or religious truth, fitted to be sung by an assembly of people." In contrast, a gospel song, Marks asserts, is a "religious exhortation to fellow man." Simple words, clear language, and honest emotions are obligatory for a good hymn.

An example of an early English religious song that depicts the crudity of language and imagery to be shunned is the following:

> A filthy dog I am by sin,
> A furious dog, dear Lord, I've been,
> A greedy dog in evil ways,
> And a dumb dog to all Thy praise.[5]

Ancient Developments in Church Music

The traditions of hymn writing and singing are ancient practices stemming in part from Jewish worship and exultation. Moses and Miriam the prophetess composed triumphant songs. David, the warrior, sometimes the pursuer, and often the pursued, wrote most of the Psalms and is the greatest poet of the Old Testament period. In the Christian era, the Apostle Paul sang hymns to God while chained in prison.

Under the threat of torture and martyrdom in Germany and Switzerland, the sixteenth-century Anabaptists, faithful servants of Jesus, wrote their songs of praise to God, some of them contained in Wackernagel's celebrated work, *German Hymnology*.[6]

In 1527 scholarly Felix Mantz of Zurich, Switzerland, an Anabaptist opposing infant baptism and other state religious practices, was executed by drowning. Before his death, he write the following hymn:

> With rapture I will sing,
> Grateful to God for breath,
> The strong, almighty King
> Who saves my soul from death,
> The death that has no end.
> Thee, too, O Christ, I praise,
> Who dost thine own defend.[7]

Until the Reformation, beginning in 1517 in the half-world of Europe, the Middle East, and North Africa, the Christian religion was dominated by Roman Catholic authority and forms in the West, and Greek Orthodox influence and practices in the East. Only a few dissidents confronted the Established Churches and stood apart: the hardy Arians, Albigenses, Waldensians, Hussites, and other heretics. The music and much of the tone of the Roman Catholic Church tradition centered on the Mass, and through this celebration much of its music would be expressed.

For nearly fourteen centuries, little congregational singing was heard in Roman Catholic churches in Europe, except rarely during Masses celebrated at Easter. However, church music in Europe developed from tenth-century Gregorian plainsong into the polyphony or many-voiced music of the sixteenth century.[8] Such church music differed markedly from secular folksong, but that certainly is not the case with much of North American church music as the world enters the twenty-first century. The Flemish genius Josquin Des Prés (1445-1521) mastered polyphony and developed a music style of greater simplicity, flowing melody, and harmonic richness. Josquin died in 1522, the year following the excommunication of Martin Luther by Pope Leo X. In such progression there evolved the development of music for the Eucharist with five parts, culminating in a masterpiece, the "B Minor Mass" by the Lutheran Johann Sebastian Bach.[9] Then, Giovanni P. Palestrina, illustrious Catholic composer and master of the Julian Choir at St. Peters, attempted in his own work to eliminate all secular themes.[10]

England produced one masterly polyphonic composer, John Taverner, who wrote eight Masses and many motets before the Reformation. Unfortunately for the Catholic faith, he joined the Protestants and assisted Oliver Cromwell in the destruction of Catholic monasteries. Later, Taverner "repented very muche that he had made songs to popish ditties."[11]

During the Protestant Reformation and the Catholic Counter-Reformation, spiritual, physical, and intellectual battles of immense proportions surged back and forth in Europe. These struggles affected and altered beliefs and practices in Germany, the Low Countries, Switzerland, Bohemia, Sweden, France, Italy, England, and even rigid Spain. During the great religious struggle, old forms, intellectual concepts, institutions, orders, and communities would be revised, reformed, or swept away.

The new expressions included variations of church music, which in the Roman Catholic Church revolved around the Mass, but in the Protestant churches focused on Psalm singing or, eventually, congregational singing directed toward praise of God. Music as a church practice would be embellished or changed in response to the dynamics of a religious revolution. The Swedish Protestants that marched into battle in 1632 under Gustavus Adolphus sang hymns to God, while their key victory at Luetzen shattered the Imperial Catholic forces and saved the Protestant cause.[12] By the end of the Thirty Years War, which lasted from 1618 to 1648, both the map of Europe and religious worship through music would be drastically changed.

The revival of hymn singing, of vast importance to the Protestants, began in Germany when Martin Luther wrote for his stirred countrymen the religious battle hymn, "A Mighty Fortress is Our God." Luther's interest in congregational singing produced a flood of hymnbooks in the German language that set all German princedoms singing. The practice of singing hymns was contagious, and soon the Catholics were producing hymnbooks written in the vernacular.[13]

Changes of Musical Style in England

Striking changes would greatly alter the rites and ceremonies in the Church of England (once the Catholic church in England) as the Reformation was received gladly by many and opposed as strenuously by strong apponents. But changes would occur under the directives of Henry VIII, Elizabeth II, and Edward VI, and through strictures imposed by the English Parliament. Also, religious forms would be modified through the pressures exerted by Protestant squires and a pious middle class. Under Edward VI, and possibly expressing the shadow of Geneva and John Calvin, the English sang virtually no religious songs that were not paraphrases of the Bible during church services in the sixteenth century. They abandoned even the most beautiful Latin hymns.[14]

The Catholic Church in England found itself increasingly impotent against Protestant reformers, many of them middle class believers of sturdy roots and pride, who identified with the Bible, the ancient Magna Carta (1215), and the independence of the House of Commons. Against the changes, the "Old Order" often could only mutter and endure.

In the words of a supporter of the Old Order: "The central body of Catholic-minded bishops and clergy, who were willing enough for reform, but did not want a revolution, were soon drowned in the clamour of extreme men goaded on by the extravagance of foreign divines [undoubtedly, Lutherans and Calvinists] and the shamelessness of rapacious politicians." Already, the Latin church service had been proscribed, with English serving as the liturgical language. The choral Eucharist also had practically disappeared in 1625, replaced in the English church by observing the sacraments without music.[15]

Latin was abandoned as the church vernacular, and the English tongue became its replacement. In 1544 Archbishop Cranmer permitted the litanies that enhanced the church processions to be sung in English instead of Latin.[16] Under Protestant King Edward VI, a complete English Mass was sung in simplified plainsong for the opening of Parliament.[17]

As a further development, English Psalmody would emerge amid the chaos and become a direct influence in New England. The bishop of Exeter, Miles Coverdale, published in 1538 a metrical version of fifteen Psalms, named the *Goastly Psalms and Spirituall Songs, drawn out of the Holy Scripture*. Later, Thomas Sternhold's organ playing and singing delighted Edward VI. Then, with John Hopkins, he produced in 1562 a hymnbook of Psalms, called the *Old Version*. Subsequently, John Knox, pastor of an exiled knot of Protestants fleeing from "Bloody" Mary and living in Frankfurt, Germany, and then Geneva, adopted the Psalms of Sternhold and Hopkins, including that revered tune, "Old Hundredth."[18] These pristine attempts to implant congregational singing foreshadowed in early America the *Bay Psalm Book* (1640), largely the work of Richard Mather, Thomas Welde, and John Eliot.[19]

Singing, where it existed in Great Britain in seventeenth-century Protestant churches, consisted primarily of Psalms ponderously sung or droned by the congregations. After a leader read one or two lines, the church body would follow in chant fashion. Some of the paraphrased Psalms were atrociously rendered:

> Ye monsters of the bubbling deep,
> your Master's praises spout;
> Up from the sands ye coddlings peep,
> and wag your tails about.[20]

Both in English and colonial churches, the texts of Psalms used in singing were derived from the Sternhold-Hopkins Psalter (Old

Version), known for its faithfulness to the original Hebrew but still unpalatable to many congregations. King William III, who arrived in England from the Netherlands in 1688, gave royal approval to a new Psalter for the church of England—the New Version—that was prepared by two Irishmen, Nahum Tate and Nicholas Brady. The phrasing was more fitting to English literary tastes, but still it met with widespread resistance. However, the New Version, aside from the metrical Psalms, contained sixteen original hymns, one of them to become a classic entitled "While Shepherds Watched Their Flocks."[21]

Baptist Hymns

In England the Baptists existed as a harried, brave minority that experimented with and then adopted singing. Congregational singing was introduced to Baptists and all English churches by Baptists Benjamin Keach, Anna Trapnell, Hanserd Knollys, and Katherine Sutton. In 1664, Keach wrote a *Children's Primer* that contained songs for children. Keach also in 1673 persuaded the Baptist church at Horsleydown to sing a hymn after celebrating the Lord's Supper. But the effort to introduce music was costly, with some members leaving Keach's church, while twenty years were required to gain general acceptance for singing. Initially, in many churches, only males and children were permitted to sing. John Bunyan wrote songs for children, but his adult congregation refused to sing. Finally, in 1689, the Particular Baptists of England allowed each church to accept or reject congregational singing.[22]

While Baptist composers have not received the recognition they deserve, two British hymn writers, Non-Conformist and Calvinist Isaac Watts (1674-1788), the "father of English Hymnody," and Charles Wesley (1708-88), a high clergyman of the Church of England, but still an Arminian (believing God's grace opened the door for many to be saved), gained acceptance for modern lyric poetry and freed the church to sing original music and lyrics. Almost everywhere, Psalmody long has been regarded as a suitable vehicle of divine praise.

Productive Isaac Watts, while not the first to create modern hymns, gave a "distinct impetus" to original songs and rooted them permanently in the structure of church worship. Then Charles Wesley proceeded to write six thousand hymns of praise in a new style for regular worship. Watts had cut a road through a forest, which Wesley now widened and made accessible to all.[23] The hymn-writing style of Charles Wesley and his brother John, who concentrated on Psalmody, was modified permanently on a trip to colonial Georgia. Through their contact with a devout Moravian in America, Peter Boehler, they were instructed in the stirring music of German hymnody.[24] Thus the German influence in modern hymnody that began with Luther would be strengthened through another German believer in America.

Then, the Baptists would assert their influence again. By 1808, Baptist Anne Steele had written fifty-seven hymns, all of them published in an Episcopal hymnbook authorized by Trinity Church of Boston.[25]

Life of Bliss

Philip (originally two p's) P. Bliss, the gospel song Trailblazer, and among the greatest song writers of his genre, was born in Cleveland County, Pennsylvania, on July 9, 1838. His parents were desperately poor. Bliss's youthful days were spent on farms and in lumber camps in a milieu of oppressive poverty. As he grew into puberty, he was described as an overgrown boy, large and awkward. In 1850, about ten years before the commencement of the American Civil War, when he was twelve years old, he accepted Christ and joined the Cherry Flats Baptist Church, Tioga County, Pennsylvania.[26]

His hidden talent was his astonishing understanding of melody and verse, and this deprived urchin "loved music like a bird." At age ten, as if under a hypnotic spell, he followed the sound of music into a private home, where a young woman was playing a piano. He had never heard the instrument before. In innocence he burst in on her, imploring: "O lady, play some more." Instead, the disturbed lady ordered the young barefoot intruder into the streets. Like other poor aspiring artists, Bliss would have to struggle hard to develop his natural talents and attain his musical goals.

At the age of twenty-six, he had the confidence to send a self-composed song to Dr. George F. Root, a well-known composer and a principal partner in a leading publishing house, the Root and Cady Music Company. If the music was acceptable, young Bliss asked only that he be paid with a flute, which he did receive for his work. Bliss's first song, "Lora Vale," had a popular reception.[27] Far more than that, he began an association lasting ten years as evangelist and musician with Root and Ira D. Sankey, the well-known gospel revivalist.

After the flute incident, Bliss moved with his family from Pennsylvania to Chicago, and as the representative for the Root and Cady Company, he conducted music conventions and training institutes throughout the Midwest. It was during this time that the self-taught musician, without any formal training in music, was maturing into a knowledgeable and proficient master. He developed talents as gospel singer, song leader, and writer that would impress evangelist Dwight L. Moody.[28]

Bliss, possessing nearly perfect physical features, and standing six feet tall, was a splendid specimen of a man. One admirer described him as "one of the handsomest men I ever met." With a deep singing voice, he became extremely popular as a song leader. He had a baritone voice of extraordinary range and evenness, and often accompanied himself. In character, he was modest and gentle and sang without ostentation. His gifts as singer and leader were only a little less than those of his prowess as hymn writer.[29] It would have been difficult at mid-life to recall that in his pre-teen years he was once a poor, ungainly duckling.

This talented man had the uncanny ability of writing original hymns, often quickly composing both melody and text together. He found in dramatic, heroic, or epic struggles the framework for his hymn writing. In 1870 he rapidly wrote the vigorous words and music of "Hold the Fort." His inspiration was the desperate plight in the Civil War of Union troops at Allatoona Pass, Georgia, where an outnumbered force guarded a great quantity of supplies. Confederate General French, menacing the isolated Northern garrison, ordered the frightened Union soldiers to surrender. The game appeared to be over, but miles away, by semaphore or heliograph on a hill, General William Tecumseh Sherman, the Union field commander, signaled: "Hold the fort, I am coming. W. T. Sherman." The war story, narrated by Major Whittle, generated in Bliss the impulse to compose his famous hymn, introduced at a Young Men's Christian Association service, but it was not considered by Bliss to be among his best creations. "Hold the Fort," however, was a great favorite of the Moody-Sankey evangelical team as it toured the United States and Great Britain.[30] Despite its appeal, "Hold the Fort" is not regarded as a proper hymn by Harvey B. Marks, who maintains that a hymn must be restrained and essentially be an ode of praise to God.[31]

Bliss often got his inspiration while listening to sermons. His writing of the hymn "Let the Lower Lights Be Burning" is illustrative of the dramatic quality found in his hymns. In composing this hymn, he built on the story told by Evangelist Dwight L. Moody, while the two were traveling together on a preaching campaign.

On a dark stormy night, when the waves rolled like mountains and not a star was to be seen, a boat, rocking and plunging, neared the Cleveland harbor.

"Are you sure this is Cleveland?" asked the Captain, seeing only light from the lighthouse.

"Quite sure, sir," replied the pilot.

"Where are the lower lights?"

"Gone out, sir!"

"Can you make the harbor?"

"We must, or perish, sir."

With a strong hand and a brave heart, the old pilot turned the wheel, but alas, in the darkness he missed the channel, and with a crash upon the rocks, the boat was slivered and many a life lost in a watery grave.

"Brethren," concluded Mr. Moody," the Master will take care of the great lighthouse. Let us keep the lower lights burning."

"Let the Lower Lights Be Burning" first appeared in 1871 in Bliss's earliest songbook, *The Charm*, and later, in *Gospel Hymns*, published by Sankey and Bliss in the same year.[32]

Incidents with dramatic features would suggest the combat of the Christian against evil adversaries or a struggle for salvation. In one precedent used to formulate a hymn, Bliss heard of a desperate effort to save the crew of a shipwrecked vessel. The captain realizing that only drastic measures could rescue his men, ordered his sailors to exert their utmost as they began to "pull for the shore." Immediately, Bliss wrote the memorable words in the refrain that became part of a widely-known song.[33]

In a night sermon on another occasion, a preacher completed his message with words that inspired the writing of the hymn "Almost Persuaded." The minister said in closing: "He who is almost persuaded is almost saved, but to be almost saved is to be entirely lost." The hymn, "Almost Persuaded," reportedly brought more souls to Christ than any other work produced by Bliss.[34]

Working with Moody

Bliss first met the Reverend D. L. Moody in Chicago in the summer of 1869, but he was not engaged in full-time evangelistic work with Moody until 1873 and only for two years. The employment was terminated by Bliss's death.[35] He became the lead singer for evangelical campaigns directed by evangelists Moody and Major Daniel W. Whittle. The impression made by Bliss's singing and the potential of his musical interpretations for soul-winning made a deep impression on Moody, a non-singer, who was searching about for talent that would enlarge his evangelistic ministry. Moody left this account of his evaluation of the value of religious music:

> I feel sure that the great majority of people do like singing. It helps to build up audience—even if you preach a dry sermon. If you have singing that reaches the heart, it will fill the church every time. There is more said in the Bible about praise than prayer, and music and song have not only accompanied all scriptural revivals, but are essential in deepening spiritual life. Singing does at least as much as preaching to impress the Word of God upon people's minds. Ever since God first called me, the importance of praise expressed in song has grown upon me.[36]

In 1874 Bliss compiled a small hymn collection, entitled *Gospel Songs,* and it is by the appellation "gospel" that subsequently all songs of this genre were called. Then Bliss joined forces with Ira D. Sankey in publishing many gospel collections. These two innovators then became recognized as the Founding Fathers of the Gospel Song Movement in the United States. In sum, what Stephen Foster did for secular folksongs, Ira Sankey and Philip Bliss did as convincingly for sacred music, at least of the gospel type.[37]

No hymnbook in America from 1865 to 1900 exceeded the influence of *Gospel Hymns*, which was issued in six editions and in some cases became more popular than the official denominational hymnbooks. Philip Bliss was the first editor of *Gospel Hymns*, and was joined in 1875 by the renowned gospel singer Ira D. Sankey in publishing *Gospel Hymns No. 1*, the first of two editions. Sankey had initially gained worldwide fame as the singing partner for the evangelistic campaigns of Moody.[38] The popularity of *Gospel Hymns* found imitators, one of them Will Lamartine Thompson, who wrote the hymn "Softly and Tenderly Jesus is Calling." Thompson sold his hymns throughout Ohio from a wagon pulled by horses. Both Moody and Sankey employed Thompson's songs in their revivals.[39]

While the wealthy could obtain a fine education, there was no education for four out of five English children in the late 1800s. The

Sunday School became the key to modern Baptist training for children, young adults, and senior adults. Largely the gift of Methodists in England, the techniques of Bible study, literacy training, and hymn singing were adopted by other denominations, and fervently so by the Baptists in Great Britain and the new United States. One of the most important agents of this movement was Robert Raikes (1736-1811), "founder of the Modern Sunday School." Raikes was born in Gloucester, England, of a middle-class family and devoted much of his career, beyond his responsibilities as town newspaper editor, to the amelioration of the poor and their unchurched, illiterate children. [40]

In England, after the American Revolution, the Methodist followers of John and Charles Wesley began establishing Sunday Schools. And, in the United States, in 1824 they began the American Sunday School Union. One of the brilliant prizes of this movement was the specialized music for children. Foremost in the creation of children's music were Philip Bliss, Fanny Crosby, Ira Sankey, George Root, and Charles Gabriel. They wrote simple songs that children could understand and enjoy, and this, in turn, was an important factor in the Gospel Song Movement that prevailed in the last part of the nineteenth century.[41]

Bliss wrote the entirety of the hymn "Jesus Loves Even Me" after attending a meeting where "O How I Love Jesus" was often sung. He reflected on the thought that, rather than consider his own pathetic love for Jesus, he would rather dwell on Jesus' "great love for me." The hymn "Jesus Loves Even Me" became one of the all-time favorite children's hymns.[42]

Bliss wrote the words and music for the hymn "Once for All," given credit by the noted song writer George C. Stebbins as the cleanest statement in hymnody expressing the doctrine of Grace, as differing from obedience through law. This hymn, by report, had more to do with breaking down Scotch Presbyterian prejudice against American gospel hymns than any other musical composition.

The Scottish clergy prided itself on Biblical scholarship and purity. In 1873 Moody and Sankey made their first evangelical visit to Scotland in a historic area where only the Psalms were sung, and that without accompaniment. Ira Sankey was apprehensive about how to proceed when he saw in the audience the noted Scottish composer, Horatius Bonar, who to Sankey was "my ideal hymn writer." But even Bonar ministered in a church that employed only Psalms and no gospel songs. When "with fear and trembling" Sankey sang Bliss's hymn, which contained the words "Free from the Law, O Happy Condition," the ice was broken. Dr. Bonar congratulated Sankey, for "you sang the gospel tonight." Thus, the way was opened to extend the ministry of sacred songs into Scotland.[43]

Bliss had written the text after meditating on the truth of Hebrews 10:10: "By the which will we are sanctified through the offering of the body of Jesus Christ once for all." "Once for All" first appeared in Bliss's *Sunshine for Sunday School* collection (1873) and again in his *Gospel Songs* (1875).[44]

Frances Ridley Havergal, "hymnody's sweetest voice," daughter of a Church of England minister, was saintly and frail. While studying in Dusseldorf, Germany, she was fascinated by Sternberg's portrayal of Christ standing before Pilate with a crown of thorns, entitled "Ecce Homo." Beneath the painting are the words: "This have I done for thee; what hast thou done for Me?" Mrs. Havergal, profoundly moved, quickly wrote the words for "I Gave My Life for Thee." Later in England, thinking that her lines were poorly written, she tossed the text into the fire, but the paper floated out and was rescued by her father. Later Bliss composed the well-known tune that made the hymn complete.[45]

There is a depiction of tragedy overcome by redemption in the poignant story of the lyric "It is Well With My Soul." The music was written by Bliss and published in 1876 in the Sankey-Bliss hymnal, *Gospel Hymns No. 2.* This possibly was Bliss's last composition before his sudden death. The author of the poetic words was Presbyterian attorney Horatio B. Spafford of the Chicago British campaign, who had volunteered to assist Moody and Sankey in their British revival.

Spafford in rapid succession lost a son through death, lost expensive real estate holdings on Lake Michigan in the Chicago fire of 1871, and suffered the drowning deaths of four daughters in 1874 in a ship-to-ship collision off the coast of Ireland. At the last minute, Spafford had been obliged to forego the sea voyage on the French ship *Ville De Havre* and remained in Chicago. His grief-stricken wife cabled from Cardiff, Wales: "Saved Alone." Spafford left by ship to join his wife. He is believed to have pinned the impressive lines, "When sorrows like sea billows roll," on ship board and near the deep seas where his daughters died. However, the lines did not dwell on life's sorrows but rather on the redemptive work of Christ and his glorious second coming.[46] Spafford, in late life, became deranged and died in 1888 in the Holy Land, where he went with Mrs. Spafford to await in Jerusalem the expected return of the Lord.[47]

Tragic Death

The great Baptist hymn Trailblazer, Philip P. Bliss, died in 1876 when he was only thirty-eight years old. Both he and his wife were the victims of a catastrophic railroad accident that killed one hundred persons near Ashtabula, Ohio. The couple were on the train during the Christmas season, traveling from Pennsylvania to Chicago. A railroad bridge collapsed and the train plunged into a ravine sixty feet below. Then a fire ignited the cars and created an even worse disaster. Bliss perished by fire when he re-entered the mangled train to rescue his wife. His sudden death, terminating a promising career, saddened the country.[48]

In his trunk, which escaped damage, was found the text of "I Will Sing of My Redeemer." James McGranaham, Bliss's replacement as song leader for Major Whittle, wrote the music for the triumphant hymn, first introduced at a large tabernacle audience in Chicago.[49] This hymn and a monument erected at his childhood home in Rome, Pennsylvania, are Bliss's permanent memorials.

The Anglo-Catholics, in their hymnbook *The English Hymnal*

(1906), gave one of the final tributes to Bliss. The *English Hymnal*, which was rejected by the evangelical wing of the Church of England, contained the works of only eleven Americans, but it included one hymn by Philip Bliss. The other writers are among America's most illustrious poets and composers, including John Greenleaf Whittier and William Cullen Bryant.[50] Also his hymn "More Holiness Give Me" was included in the Church of Sweden's 1937 *Psalmbook*.

Music authority E. E. Ryden does not hold in great favor much of Bliss's work, perhaps the majority of his hymns. While Ryden attests to the hymns' imaginative, picturesque, and emotional quality, he disputes their literary merit. He finds that Bliss's tunes analyzed by him possessed lilt and movement but lacked the depth of character and the rich harmony found in the better hymn tunes and chorales.[51] While his vision is that Christian denominations are seeking "a higher standard of hymnody," a major trend in Baptist and Evangelical church music at the advent of the twenty-first century favors simple lyrics and lively tunes, and embraces the choices of the masses, rather than selections made by the elite and traditional musicologists.

An Appraisal

An analysis of the contribution of Baptist composer and lyricist Philip P. Bliss necessarily includes also an appraisal of what is merit or quality in hymn writing. While classical music applied to hymnody may well be regarded as a higher standard of music, it is not necessarily always the most effective in reaching the hearts of persons seeking answers from God, expressing praise, or even as an aid to worshipers trying to understand themselves. Despite variety in musical education, there is no rule that mandates that one must love classical opera to the exclusion of folksongs, gospel hymns, jazz, or even rock and roll—just as in literature, a reader might simultaneously have a taste for Shakespeare, Scott, and Whittier. That which appeals to the heart is evasive and mysterious, having much to do with experience, feeling, time, and the magical aura of words, sounds, meter, rhythm, and rhyme. Probably for the millions that love the gospel hymns of Bliss, there is a link with the ancient folk songs of the Scots, Irish, and English that evoke a forgotten time and memory. Therefore, there is a certain futility in harshly judging gospel music, for to many that is the music that grips their soul.

The permanent legacy of Philip Bliss is that, along with Ira D. Sankey, he is the Father of the Gospel Song Movement. He wrote over twenty hymns that have endured and are sung daily throughout the world. Two of his hymns that may touch the faithful until the end of time are "I Gave My Life for Thee" and "Wonderful Words of Life." In his evangelistic work with Major Daniel Whittle, Ira Sankey, and D. L. Moody, he was a major musical presence, commanding attention through his voice, stature, physique, and an expressive public personality.[52] He also is one of the most prominent writers of songs for children and the Sunday School.

George C. Stebbins, the noted hymn writer, gave this incisive description of the great musical Trailblazer:

> He occupied a preeminence that still stands unrivaled. There has been no writer since his time who has shown such a grasp of the fundamental truths of the gospel, nor such a gift for putting them into poetic and singable form as he. In all of his hymns, there was manifest a happy blending of the poet and musician, and along with it a rare judgment and deep spiritual insight into the needs of presenting the saving truths of Scripture in clear and singable form.[53]

The meteor, Philip P. Bliss, streaked across the musical sky and then disappeared, but his emanations very probably made a permanent change in the character of modern hymnody.

He left an unforgettable legacy in the following well-known gospel songs:

Hold the Fort (both words and music)

I Gave My Life for Thee (music only)
It is Well With My Soul (music only)
Let the Lower Lights Be Burning (both words and music)
Once for All (both words and music)
Jesus Loves Even Me (both words and music)
Man of Sorrows, What a Name (both words and music)
Wonderful Words of Life (both words and music)
Hallelujah, What a Savior (both words and music)
Almost Persuaded (both words and music)
Whosoever Will (both words and music)
Free from the Law, O Happy Condition (both words
    and music)
I Gave My Life for Thee (music only)
I Will Sing of My Redeemer (words only)
The Light of the World is Jesus (both words and music)
More Holiness Give Me
Whosoever Will (Same as Whosoever Heareth)
Whosoever Heareth
Shout, Shout the Sound (both words and music)
I Am So Glad That Our Father in Heaven
There's a Light in the Valley
Down Life's Dark Vale We Wander
Where Hast Thou Gleaned Today
When Peace Like a River (music only)

The legacy of Philip Bliss is the gladsome light he directed to the love of God, the redemption purchased by Jesus, and the buoyant freedom of the true believer. His songs were joyous and the Light he praised was unquenchable.

Chapter 15

Lottie (Charlotte) Moon
(1841-1912)

Martyr for World Missions

In the early stages of the life of Charlotte Diggs Moon (called "Lottie"), few people could envisage that this wealthy daughter of Virginia, full of irreverent jokes and destined to be among the best educated women in America, would in time become perhaps the most famous North American Baptist missionary of the pre-World War I era. In Christianity, she had ancient predecessors born into wealth: Saint Augustine (354-430 A.D.), born in Numidia, North Africa, and Francis of Assisi (1182-1226), born in Central Italy, and others. Like these early "Fathers of the Church," she would renounce comfort and family fortune for a life of Christian sacrifice, but in her case, largely among Chinese villagers, small merchants, toilers, and farmers, leading them to Christ.

Despite her acquired fame as a missionary in Asia, she was never on a higher pinnacle than William Carey of India nor Adoniram Judson of Burma. She was not the first Southern Baptist missionary sent to China. Nor was she the first single Baptist woman appointed to Shantung Province, China; that honor went to her sister, Edmonia Moon, who arrived in the city of Tengchow in 1872, but shortly thereafter suffered a mental collapse. Lottie Moon would serve in China for mission work, while the issue of sending single women

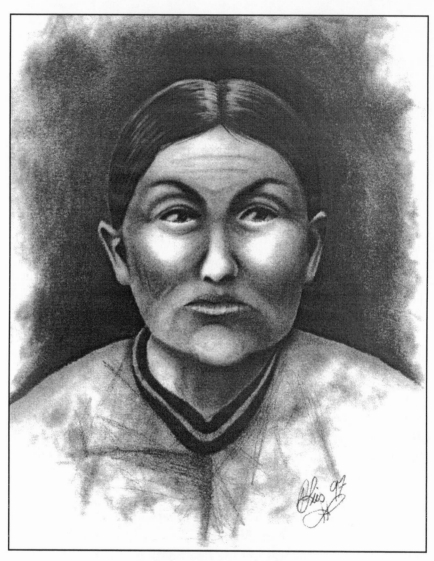

Portrait of Lottie Moon

abroad as missionaries was still debated among the Baptists in America.

Her influence on future Southern Baptist missions strategy was formidable: Lottie Moon insisted that women missionaries in North China should be allowed to vote and propose measures in business meetings, rather than quietly knitting in the corner. Her high intelligence, doggedness, and industry in firing a volley of correspondence to the Foreign Mission Board, the Woman's Missionary Union, and mite supporters in a myriad of churches gave her far more leverage than exceptional women of that period could expect. Through her correspondence, she exerted a major influence on missionary policies and the operations of the Foreign Mission Board. Her lasting contribution was her proposal to the WMU corresponding secretary, Annie Armstrong, that resulted in creating the Lottie Moon Christmas Offering for Foreign Missions.

Beginning of Missions

The Nestorians plying the Silk Route along the Gobi Desert in the thirteenth century were the first Christian missionaries to work in China. As camel herders, merchants, and traders, they would diminish in influence, along with their converts, after their suppression by the Manchus in the sixteenth century. However, there were about a million Nestorians at their zenith, long after their doctrine was defined by Bar-Soma in the Persian Church in the fifth century. In thirteenth century China, the Nestorians under the patriarch of Baghdad built churches at Chenkiang, Yangchou, and Hangchou. After an *entente* was negotiated between the Nestorian and Roman churches, John of Montecorvino was the first of several Roman missionaries sent to China in the period 1294 to 1328.[1]

On the other side of the world, newly-established America scarcely thought of China at all—until the building of its western railroads by Chinese coolies—except in terms of silks, tea, and demands by China's upper classes for beaver and otter skins from the American interior. The Christian foreign missionary movement was slow to develop in the United States and gathered steam only about twenty-five years before the Civil War. In the haste to bring salvation to the world, the Presbyterians beat the Baptists to China, during China's precipitous decline under the Ch'ing Dynasty.

In North America, Baptist missions began with Mary "Polly" Webb, who was confined for life to a wheelchair. Undaunted, Polly Webb founded the Boston Female Society for Missionary Purposes in 1800, and served as its secretary-treasurer for more than fifty years. She was encouraged by her pastor, the Reverend Thomas C. Baldwin, who in 1802 headed the Massachusetts Baptist Missionary Society, the first state missionary organization in North America.[2] In 1836 the Baptists sent Jehu Lewis Shuck and his wife Henrietta Hall Shuck to China; Henrietta thereby became the first American Protestant woman missionary sent to China.[3]

The foreign missions commitment in continental America arose among small bands of Baptist and Congregationalist women that prayed together. Their search for means to support missionaries resulted in the formation of Female Cent Societies, Mite Societies, Female Praying Societies, and Dorcas Societies. Among the first recipients of financial support from these benevolent groups was Luther Rice, missionary to India, who arrived in India in 1812 but endured only a three-month stay because of the anti-missionary policies of the British East India Company.[4] Other early recipients of financial support were Adoniram and Ann Hasseltine Judson, first Baptist missionaries to Burma, who followed in the trail of the English Baptist pioneer in India, William Carey. Rice and the Judsons were appointed as Congregational missionaries, but after searching the Bible they became Baptists soon after their arrival in India; they were baptized by Carey's associate William Ward.[5]

Lottie's Early Life

Lottie Moon was born into the extremely wealthy and privileged Virginia society of the pre-Civil War family of Edward Harris Moon. Her ancestry was distinguished and contained a mixture of English gentlemen, colonial governors, and American Revolution notables. She shared as a child the beneficence of her foster grandfather, Captain John Harris, the richest man in prosperous Albemarle County, Virginia, and a powerful figure in the cotton markets of Memphis and New Orleans. In the immediate vicinity of his mansion were the estates of former presidents Thomas Jefferson and James Monroe. Lottie Moon as a child enjoyed residence in Viewmont, the two-storied wooden mansion built by her grandfather, from which he once ruled three thousand aces of fine real estate and 160 slaves. Viewmont had eight rooms, fifteen beds, and exquisite hand-carved paneling in the parlors.[6] However, John Harris's total holdings were much more extensive and included eight estates, five thousand acres, and eight hundred slaves.

Lottie, even as a child, was energetic, forceful, and impish. She was petite, never exceeding four feet three inches in height, with deep blue eyes, dark black-brown hair, and a prominent chin. During her entire life, she had only one male admirer and was never described as beautiful. But above all, she was bright, gifted, and audacious, and seldom if ever nurtured self-doubt. Her voice was musical, rich, and deep.[7]

Lottie's handsome father, Edward Harris Moon (born February 14, 1805, died January 26, 1853), married on October 16, 1830, his stunningly pretty fiancée, Orianna Maria Barclay, from a highly respected family. The couple had two sons: Thomas B., who became a physician and died of yellow fever,[8] and Isaac ("Ike") Anderson, who managed the reduced Viewmont estate through the Civil War. There were five daughters born to the pair: Orianna Russell, Charlotte Diggs (Lottie), Sarah Coleman (Sallie or Colie), Mary E. (Mollie), and Edmonia (Eddie),[9] the last preceding Lottie as a missionary to China.

Lottie's parents, Edward Harris Moon and Orianna Maria (more often called Anna Maria) were devout Christians, he a Presbyterian, she a soul-seeking Baptist. After reading a book to gain an insight into the success of Alexander Campbell (founder of the Disciples of

Christ), whose work was creating havoc among the Baptists, Edward
Moon became a Baptist, was ordained a deacon, and headed a
movement to establish a brick Baptist church and Sunday School in
Scottsville. At home, Mrs. Moon read to Lottie and the other children about the intriguing struggles of lonely Ann Judson, first Baptist woman missionary sent to Burma from the United States.[10]

The five daughters of Edward Harris Moon and Anna Maria
were a special breed and, if spoiled by wealth, would rise far above
it. Orianna ("Orie") Russell, the second child, was trained as a doctor
in Pennsylvania and Paris. Orie was a plucky woman and, while
traveling in the Middle East before the Civil War, had leveled a
pistol on an Arab chief intent on adding her to his harem.[11] Later,
during the war, she was given a real or honorary commission as
medical captain in the Confederate Army and was placed in charge
of a hospital ward at the University of Virginia. It was there that
Captain Orianna tended the first wounded soldiers of the Civil War,
routed to Charlottesville from the Battle of Bull Run.

In view of the affluence of the Moon family, only the finest tutors
stayed at Viewmont, to teach classics, music, and French to the
children. Available at the estate was their father's fine library and a
mother steadfast to impart knowledge. Despite Anna Maria's enthusiasm for the Baptist faith, the children often remained at home
instead of worshiping at church; some of this strange laxness was due
to confusion caused by the teachings of Alexander Campbell and the
Disciples of Christ. But there also was the likelihood that the children simply were overindulged.[12]

The fortunes of the family changed drastically a few years before
the outbreak of the Civil War. Lottie's father, Edward Harris Moon,
died suddenly on January 26, 1853, on a river bank while suffering
a heart attack or stroke. The steamboat *James Robb*, on which he was
a passenger, was stricken by fire, and he overtaxed his body as he
struggled to gain the shore with a heavy money trunk. Thus, with his
death, an illustrious father, with a church leadership position, fifty-
two slaves, tobacco land in Virginia, and other properties in Missis-

sippi, abruptly thrust the responsibilities of estate management on an overburdened widow. The seven children were given equal shares with their mother in the property. Lottie Moon was only thirteen years old and Edmonia not two years old, when, with the family's survival at stake, the mother assumed firm control of Viewmont.[13]

Her mother was faithful to Christian principles and, in keeping with the stern standards of the Baptist faith, allowed no cooking on Sunday after breakfast. Lottie, on the other hand, was mischievous to the core and on one occasion contrived to have her widowed mother and the slaves attend church at Scottsville, nine miles away. Meanwhile, she and the other children busily prepared a dinner in the outside kitchen building. Her mother was not amused when, upon her return home, she found that the strict Sabbath rule had been violated.[14]

Lottie in 1854 was sent to a school financed by leading Virginia Baptists, Virginia Female Seminary at Botetourt Springs. She made good marks in arithmetic, English, and Latin during the two-year college program. In French she had perfect grades for two quarters. But her professors noted that in natural science she was at first "very deficient," later only "tolerable." After Lottie returned in fall 1855 for her second year, the school had become Hollins Institute (later Hollins College). She maintained superior grades in French, good grades in Latin, but barely passed mathematics. Despite the mixed results, her spunky sense of humor and wit gained her a reputation among the students as an intellect.[15]

Lottie nurtured her development as an independent-minded and eager scholar. She joined the Euzelian Society, a literary club, and became co-editor of the college paper. She graduated from Hollins on July 3, 1856, crisply attired, as were the other girls, in a white dress with a blue sash.[16]

Inspired by a startling new concept, that women should obtain the same quality of education as men, Virginia Baptists organized the Albemarle Female Institute in Charlottesville, near the all-male University of Virginia. This emerging college was conceived by A. E.

Dickinson, associate editor of the *Religious Herald*, and John A. Broadus, pastor of the Charlottesville Baptist Church. In courses, examinations, and degrees, Albemarle Female Institute was meant to be and largely became the female counterpart of the University of Virginia. So Lottie Moon and her roommate, Cary Ann Coleman, enrolled at Albemarle in its second class that began September 1857.[17]

While attending the Albemarle Female Institute, Lottie abandoned her carefree attitude, but not soon nor predictably. The principal of A.F.I. was John Hart and his assistant was Crawford Howell Toy, the latter to maintain an intriguing, long-lasting friendship with Lottie. Professor Toy was seemingly fascinated by this vivacious young woman, who was regarded by her friends as a "brain" and a skeptic, possibly even a heretic. She excelled in English composition and Greek,[18] her reading of the ancient text the most fluent ever heard from a student by her language professor at Albemarle.[19] But there was ever-present the frolicsome, turbulent scholar, who two years earlier, on April Fool's Day, 1855, had climbed the bell tower at Hollins Institute to muffle the school bell with bed sheets; this would cause her deportment grade at Hollins to decline to "tolerable."[20]

The spiritual change came dramatically. The Reverend Mr. Broadus led evangelistic services in December 1858, during which time the students held a sunrise prayer vigil. Among those on the prayer list for the unsaved was Lottie Moon. Then, to the surprise of the prayer circle, Lottie made her appearance and engaged Broadus in an earnest conversation about her salvation. Lottie made her confession of faith on December 21 at the Charlottesville Baptist Church and then publicly explained, on December 22, that she came to a religious service to scoff at religion but left to pray all night. In the account of a schoolmate, this roguish and irreverent student became overnight submissive, meek, and eager to do the Master's will.[21]

Next came a call to the mission field. The Reverend Mr. Broadus frequently appealed to the young men of the student body to dedicate their lives as ministers and missionaries. As Allen states it, young women were not "called" to anything, but to Lottie no stream was unbridgeable and she was listening attentively. Two young men, John L. Johnson and Crawford Toy, dedicated themselves to mission work, and in 1859 both were appointed by the Foreign Mission Board of the Southern Baptist Commission to be its first missionaries assigned to Japan. The ship that was chosen to carry them to the Orient left its home port with other missionaries, then it mysteriously disappeared into the ocean vastness, leaving behind no trace of its fate. Johnson, who had contracted typhoid and measles, had been too sick to travel. The life of Professor Toy also was spared when he missed the ship, probably because of a lack of money. However, the "Call," unspeakably soft, had permeated the solitude of Lottie Moon's inward consciousness; from those days she felt an inescapable commitment to foreign missions and believed that Japan would be her field.[22]

Impact of Civil War

The most determinative event of mid-nineteenth-century North America history, the American Civil War, then appeared and altered ruthlessly the dreams, aspirations, and destinies of its warring people. While this event was both shocking and stirring, particularly in Virginia, Lottie and four other women extended their studies to 1861-62, one year beyond the standard three-year course, earning probably the first post-graduate degrees for women in the South. Lottie and her friends were awarded the Master of Arts degree by Albemarle Female Institute, and immediately they became an elite group, comprised of the most highly trained women in the divided nation. Professor Hart recorded that Lottie's Moral Philosophy examination was the best he had ever seen.[23] Also, Professor John A. Broadus, later a professor at the Southern Baptist Theological Seminary, proudly referred to Lottie as "the most educated woman in the South."[24]

The Moon family became almost totally involved in the burgeoning war between the States. Some of the male members joined Mosby's Rangers in harassing the Northern forces. Cynthia and Virginia Moon, close relatives, sought work as washer women with the Union armies in order to gather military intelligence. Orianna, as a medical doctor, quickly joined Confederate medical units in Richmond to lend vital assistance. But to Lottie fell the drab life of largely remaining at home, to look after Edmonia the youngest child, to whom she was devoted.[25]

The Civil War would produce severe hardships for the Moon family, but in the beginning phase of the struggle Anna Maria and her son Ike managed the estate well. Tradition holds that Lottie and her sisters Sarah Coleman ("Colie") and Mary ("Mollie") visited Charlottesville to nurse wounded soldiers. A Confederate chaplain, reportedly Crawford Howell Toy (who would create a minor scandal at the Southern Baptist Seminary in Greenville, South Carolina, by embracing the evolutionary doctrine of Charles Darwin) stopped by Viewmont in 1861 to visit Lottie, possibly to propose. But if there was ever a romantic spark between Crawford Toy and Lottie, it never had the intensity to produce a flame.

Lottie filled her free time with a new passion for language study, beginning with ancient Greek and Latin and venturing into scholarly books in German, French, Spanish, and Italian. She shared her new language studies with eager student Edmonia. In addition, in 1862, Lottie transferred her church membership from Charlottesville to the Pine Grove Church, which held its services at Hardware Meeting House. In her new church home, Lottie taught Sunday School to a mixed class of white and black children. Despite the increasing trials of the war, with slaves slipping away and the mounting anxieties produced by a lost cause, she asserted to her friends, "we ought to be just as thankful for sorrows as for joys."[26]

As Robert E. Lee's once-mighty army began to collapse, and the Virginia countryside was menaced by Northern irregulars and raiders, the family made a decision to save its valuables. Lottie was assigned, along with a trustworthy slave, Uncle Jacob, to hide the family silver and jewels in an orchard twenty miles away. The matter became alarming when it was rumored that foragers were approaching Viewmont. Lottie and the faithful servant raced a loaded wagon to the selected hiding place, and the valuables were shoveled into the ground; most of the silver would never be recovered.[27]

As the Civil War ended in 1865, Anna Maria, Lottie's mother, was compelled to sell or lease hundreds of acres. Viewmont was reduced to a fraction of its former value, and the Moon estate proper was now reduced to the house, the orchards, and the cemetery. Anna Maria, once among the wealthiest widows in Virginia, now was compelled to live on one-third of the crop raised on her land. The family's resources were severely restricted; even so, Edmonia ("Eddie") and Mary E. ("Mollie") were sent to Richmond Female Institute, but with the knowledge that there would be no funds to bring them home on holidays. Lottie's sister, Dr. Orianna, had married and with her own family migrated to northern Alabama.[28]

In periods between 1863 and 1866, in order to augment her meager financial resources and to relieve her boredom, Lottie served as private tutor or governess to several families in Alabama, Bishopville, South Carolina, and Farmington, Georgia. With her sharp sense of humor, Lottie recounted that when she paid the young son of a Georgia planter five cents for driving cackling geese away from her window, the boy then arranged every day thereafter to have other geese standing by her quarters to generate further earnings.[29]

Around September 1866, with the family in straits because of widespread economic and political changes of enormous magnitude, Lottie began teaching at the Danville Female Academy of Danville, Kentucky. The Academy was operated by the First Baptist Church of Danville in order to give free education to the daughters of Baptist ministers made destitute by the Civil War. In 1869-70, the Academy merged with another school and became the Presbyterian-managed Caldwell Institute. In the meantime, in 1868-69, Lottie was joined by her sister Mary ("Mollie").[30]

In April 1868 Lottie moved her church membership from the

Pine Grove Church at Hardware to the First Baptist Church of Danville. She also served as the pastor's assistant and taught a Sunday School class of teenagers. During this time, she was greatly influenced by former Southern Baptist missionary to China, Dr. G. W. Burton. Dr. Burton generously sent funds to his stranded co-workers in China, who endured with little support while the Southern fiscal economy largely collapsed because of the Civil War.[31]

Lottie's sister Edmonia ("Eddie") became a Baptist, and in 1870 she expressed an interest in becoming a missionary to China. However, the SBC Foreign Mission Board at that time was surviving only through prayer and grit; it barely averted bankruptcy, and that because of the generosity of supporters in the border states of Maryland and Kentucky. So there was no commissioning of new missionaries for several years and no thought, for a time, of contracting single women bent on bringing salvation to China.

The year 1870 would have a major impact on the Moon family but drastically so for the destiny of Lottie. Anna Maria, her mother, died on June 21, 1870. Before her death, Lottie's sisters, Mary E. ("Mollie") and Sarah Coleman ("Colie"), influenced by their handsome music teacher, had become Catholics, a move that saddened the old lady. Lottie wrote to the family members urging toleration.[32]

During the summer of 1870, Lottie returned to teach for one more year at the Caldwell Institute in Danville. Lottie agreed for the year 1870-71 to teach history, grammar, rhetoric, and literature. At the school for girls she developed a close friendship with fellow teacher Anna Cunningham Safford, an intelligent Presbyterian lady from Georgia. With nearly a quarter of a million Southern men killed in the recent war, probably both women, no longer young, had given up on marriage and both seriously considered foreign missions and evangelism as their future life work.[33]

In pursuit of a new start, she and Anna Safford in 1871 traveled by train to Cartersville, Georgia, to help open a school for girls; this venture was the concept of prominent men including Lottie's cousin Pleasant Moon. The Cartersville Female High School was established in an old cannery, with classrooms in one large and two small rooms. Placed in charge of the primary department, Lottie assisted in opening the school on July 3, 1871. By the 1872-73 school year, there were more than one hundred students.[34] Lottie found religious work in the Cartersville Baptist Church, where she taught a Sunday School class for young women and spent long hours visiting poor families on behalf of the church.[35]

However, neither Kentucky nor Georgia would be more than milestones for a maturing Lottie, who began to visualize the Far East as her Promised Land. Lottie was drawn to books that depicted the Chinese as having an advanced culture and highly developed religions, which while non-Christian, nevertheless contained lofty ethical teachings. Her sister Orianna had stimulated this consciousness by lending her books on the Orient, including China. As Hyatt describes it, Lottie, at age thirty-two, was an incurable "romantic" but one who was Christian to the core and tempered by training and adversity to be a solid and, possibly in time, great missionary. She had put her gifts, resolve, and spiritual dedication together "as though," said a friend, "she was going home."[36]

The question of single women in religious vocations was being debated, as women sought specialized religious work. In anticipation of the discussion on the value of women in the mission field, at an 1872 meeting of the Southern Baptist Convention in Raleigh, North Carolina, Dr. J. W.N. Williams proposed to the messengers (delegates) "his hope and faith in woman's agency, and urged the propriety of sending unmarried women to foreign fields." His proposal was not received favorably. However, before the year ended, eight missionaries were commissioned for foreign service at the Eutaw Place Baptist Church in Baltimore, including two unmarried women, Edmonia Moon of Virginia and Lula Whilden of South Carolina, both appointed to North China.[37]

The Woman's Missionary Society of Richmond, Virginia, supported by about four hundred women, was organized in 1872 to provide support for Edmonia. In its first year, the Society collected

$1,260 through its mite boxes in various churches. Later the women of Georgia and Virginia would give $2,382.63 to build a home in China for Edmonia and Lottie Moon.[38]

The dominant influence that overpowered Lottie's desire to teach in the South was in all probability the SBC missionary appointment to China, on April 9, 1872, of Edmonia ("Eddie"), nearly fourteen years younger than Lottie. Eddie's salary of four hundred dollars per year was supported by pledges from five Richmond churches. Lottie's sister then departed for China and the mission field in the middle of the 1872-73 school year.[39] The inspiration of and correspondence with Southern Baptist missionaries Tarleton Perry Crawford and his wife Martha Foster, serving since 1863 in the north China port of Tengchow, Shantung Province, had played a leading role in Edmonia's future. Mrs. Crawford's school in Tengchow was supported in part, in 1871, by a thirty-dollar contribution from Eddie and a fifteen-dollar gift from Lottie. Lottie also sent an anonymous gift to maintain a Baptist chapel in Rome.[40] Lottie, who would prove to be an indefatigable correspondent, already was writing to James B. Taylor, corresponding secretary of the Southern Baptist Convention Foreign Mission Board.

Call to China

Lottie was preparing to make an irreversible decision. In 1873 Lottie and her bosom friend Anna Cunningham Safford startled their students and school supporters by announcing that the Cartersville school would be given up, and both women were going overseas as missionaries, one as a Presbyterian, the other as a Baptist.[41] The final catalyst had been a sermon by the Reverend R. B. Headden in Cartersville in February 1873 that caused Lottie to pray all afternoon. She reported to others that her call to China was "as clear as a bell."[42] Some adults resented the difficulties imposed by the teachers leaving the Cartersville high school so abruptly, while others were only saddened. In support of Lottie's decision, the Cartersville

Baptist Church organized perhaps the first woman's missionary society among the Georgia Baptists.[43]

Lottie had first contemplated a missionary life to be spent in Japan, but letters from Edmonia, who had reached China in 1872, gradually won Lottie over to service in China. By January 1873 Lottie was exchanging letters with Dr. H. A. Tupper, who had become Secretary of the SBC Foreign Mission Board. Dr. Tupper was confronted with the problem of numbers of missionaries seeking appointment to foreign countries, but he had almost no money to supply them. He issued instructions that each state Central Committee could organize missionary societies within the state, and that these societies could then raise the funds necessary for missionary support.[44]

On July 7, 1873, Lottie was officially appointed a missionary to China by the Foreign Mission Board. She first made a side trip to Lauderdale County, Alabama to visit her sister Orianna ("Orie"), a practicing doctor. Then, beginning on August 15, she scheduled a circuitous train trip from Florence, Alabama, to New York and cross-country to San Francisco, toward her destination in China. Before turning toward the West Coast, Lottie stopped briefly in Albemarle County, Virginia, to bid farewell to her family, and in Baltimore, to confer with the Baptist women that gave vigorous support to missions.[45]

A friend in San Francisco, who had known her in Danville, sent this descriptive message to Virginia:

> Miss Moon was once a member of my family, and a most devoted and successful teacher. . . . It has been a cherished purpose with Miss Moon, for years past, to be a missionary to the heathen; and now that her desires in this regard are about to be gratified, she is quite happy, and says that in going to China to join her sister, she feels as if she were going home. A lady of fine intellect, of rare culture, and of splendid social gifts, she lays herself on the altar of sacrifice to glorify him who

purchased her with his precious blood. Virginia never served a truer, nobler woman. May heaven abundantly bless her in her noble mission.[46]

Lottie sailed aboard the *Costa Rica* from San Francisco on September 1, 1873, bound for the Orient. She landed at Yokohama, Japan, on September 25, where she experienced her first ricksha ride. She also toured Kobe and Nagasaki. Then in a frightful misfortune, the new missionary nearly lost her life on the voyage from Nagasaki to Shanghai, when a typhoon struck the ship. The storm ripped away parts of the ship, including the ship's rudder. The passengers, sensing that their life was over, gulped down large quantities of alcohol. Lottie, however, remained calm, and prophesied that God would send a celestial messenger to appear above the towering waves. When the storm abated, the ship limped back to Nagasaki, where she talked with Dutch Reformed missionaries and prayed in an Anglican church for the reigning British monarch, Queen Victoria.[47]

At Shanghai, the bustling trade port, Lottie was greeted on October 7 by distinguished Southern Baptist missionary Matthew T. Yates of the city, and from Tengchow, her destination, the Reverend and Mrs. Tarleton Perry Crawford. Both missionary families were regarded as venerable, each having survived many years in China. The older missionaries spoke approvingly of Lottie's sister, Eddie, the pretty young woman in Tengchow. Eddie, during her short time in China, had declined a proposal of marriage, was teaching a newly-organized Sunday School, and was mastering the Chinese language at a prodigious rate.[48]

Shantung Province, projecting like a spearhead into the China Sea, was the next objective of Lottie. The Province was rich with history, as the ancient land of Confucius (Kung Fu Tzu). Since the Opium Wars (1839-42 and 1856-60), extraterritorial treaties had placed western nationals, including Americans, under their separate laws, courts, and authority, and permitted trade, travel, and mission work in designated ports and far inland. Christianity was protected,

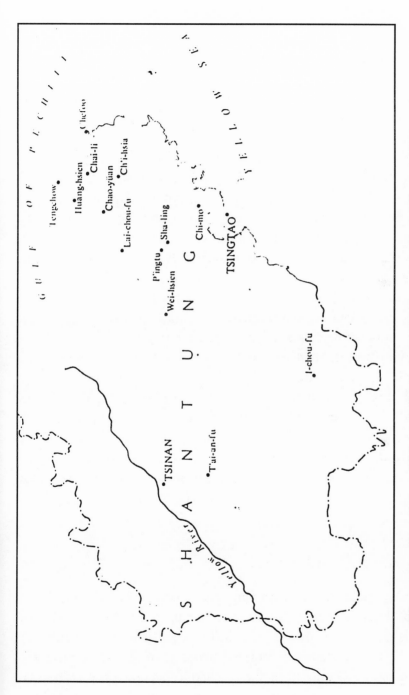

Shantung Province, China, Missionary Stations in the Nineteenth Century

and China, as a defeated nation, was obliged to shield the missionaries. But as history would prove, treaty obligations did not always
restrain hostile mobs or prevent hordes of bandits from menacing
the countryside. In 1858, invoking the treaties, the Western powers
opened Tengchow and Chefoo as treaty ports, after which an American Consul was stationed at Chefoo. Into the mounting maelstrom,
and through the chief Shantung port of Chefoo, ventured Lottie
Moon, this time surviving a final voyage involving a fierce typhoon.[49]

At Chefoo, she first met veteran Southern Baptist missionary
Jesse Boardman Hartwell, his second wife, and their children. Unfortunately, Mrs. Hartwell had been sick since arriving in China in
1872, in company with Edmonia Moon. Reverend Hartwell, from
Darlington, South Carolina, had been on the mission field since
1861, and at Tengchow, fifty-five miles away, he began a school and
the North Street Baptist Church (which attained sixty members).
When supporting funds failed to arrive during the American Civil
War, Hartwell in 1864-65 was compelled to work as an interpreter
for the Shanghai Municipal Council. In the absence of Hartwell, the
North Street Church was guided by the Chinese pastor Woo Tswan
Chao.[50] Thus, we are introduced to elements of the crippling quarrel
between James Hartwell and his missionary associate, Tarleton Perry
Crawford, that generated into a schism and a short-lived Gospel
Mission Movement. Lottie would hear of this ugly controversy for
thirty-nine years of her missionary career but remain friends to both
families.

Tengchow as Gospel Center

Lottie made the overland trip to her mission assignment in the
city of Tengchow in a *shentze*, a carrier made of a large basket or
howdah, and borne by one mule in front, and one mule in the rear.
Such bone-shaking travel required two days of discomfort and was
completed by Lottie when she reached Tengchow on October 25,
1873.[51] Lottie, having reached her battle-front at age thirty-three,
and eager to serve her Master but contemptuous of many things

Chinese, would be compelled in time to revise many of her early views and methods.

Tengchow (now called Pèng-Lai) was a treaty port open to foreigners, but the harbor was silted and not navigable for large vessels. In that city of one-story houses with thatched and tile roofs the dominant feature was the Chee Monument, its ancient oriental gate. Many of the Chinese were sullen, even outraged, because of foreign intrusions into the city, including the erection of a two-story American missionary house and an American-style Baptist church with steeple, Monument Street Baptist Church; these structures were built by T. P. Crawford and his wife Martha Foster Crawford with three thousand dollars in personal funds. Crawford then cooly requested reimbursement for his expenditures from the Southern Baptist Convention.[52]

Tengchow has ancient roots, and two illustrious Chinese emperors had an impact on it: Ch'in Shih Huang-Ti (221-210 B.C.) who built a portion of the Great Wall of China, and Han Wu Ti (141-87 B.C.) who visited the area. Ch'in Shih Huang-Ti was said to have sent three thousand young men and women from Pèng-Lai to the Japanese islands, where reportedly they competed with Japan's original inhabitants, the Ainu.

In Tengchow, but serving an extensive Shantung mission field, there were only a small cluster of Northern Presbyterians and six Southern Baptists: Lottie Moon, her sister Edmonia, T. P. and Martha Crawford, Sally J. Holmes (a widow), and her young son Landrum. They would be joined later by the Reverend and Mrs. J. B. Hartwell.

As the original pioneers in North China, Sally Holmes and her husband had worked before 1860 in Chefoo and Tengchow. After her husband was murdered by a Chinese robber band, Mrs. Holmes operated a girls boarding school and a boys day school. In 1860 J. B. Hartwell arrived and agreed to undertake the Tengchow work, while the Holmes pair consented to minister in Chefoo. The peaceful division and administration of missionary work would take a different tack after the arrival in 1863 of T. P. Crawford and Martha Foster

Crawford. The impetuous, decisive, and bold character of T. P. Crawford would be defined after his missionary appointment, when he galloped by horseback to Martha Foster's home in Alabama, where he would make a successful proposal of marriage to a deeply religious woman he had never seen before.[53]

When Lottie arrived in Tengchow in 1873, she found her sister Edmonia living in the Crawford compound, but outside his extensive house, in damp and spartan quarters whose dimensions were eleven feet by thirteen feet.[54] Edmonia was teaching in a small boys day school started by Sally Holmes.[55] Crawford wanted both Lottie and Edmonia to live in his compound that contained his thirty-six-room house, and where his powerful personality could direct them. He shrewdly constructed a two-story addition to his house, so Edmonia and Lottie each had an upstairs bedroom and a downstairs study.

The Chinese, who already resented the acquisition of land by "foreign devils" (the Crawfords and Hartwells), now gathered in mob force to protect themselves from the American "intruders." The Chinese believed that the Americans, from a high vantage point, would be observing their women. In order to prevent being attacked and overrun, the missionaries pulled out their firearms, until some order was restored.[56]

Lottie wisely saw no reason for all Baptist work to be centralized under Tarleton P. Crawford, and this meant moving their quarters. Promptly after arriving in Tengchow, she wrote to Foreign Mission Board secretary H. A. Tupper that she and Eddie wanted a new house for themselves. The sisters also confided that they planned to start a boarding house for girls.[57] Lottie's friend from Cartersville, Georgia, Anna Cunningham Safford, was now attached to her Presbyterian missionary labors in Soochow, where she founded the periodical *Woman's Work in China*. In Hyatt's words, Lottie's friend "became a fierce businesswoman and journalist who never forgot anything and never made a mistake."[58]

The study by missionaries of Mandarin, the language of Peking,

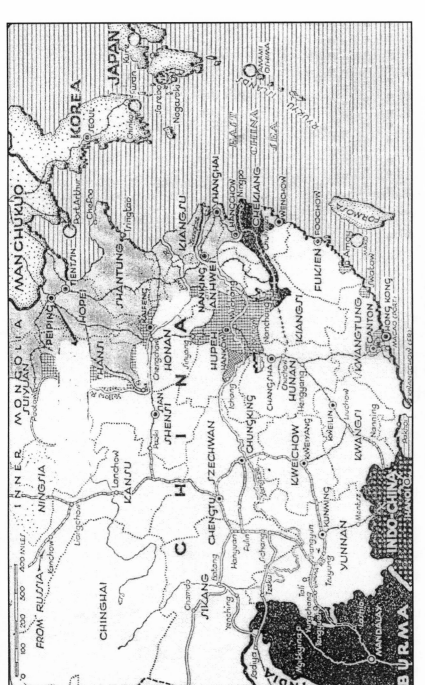

China in the Twentieth Century

usually requires a two or three year course of instruction to obtain working knowledge, and traditionally is undertaken with a personal Chinese instructor. Chinese is difficult both because of its written characters that must be memorized and the intricate tonal qualities of the language that must be mastered. Lottie's sister Eddie proved to be a language expert, and within a year of study was teaching Sunday School in Mandarin. Lottie, while not as competent, plowed ahead in her studies, and found mastery of the written language to be the easier side. If help was needed, Lottie and Eddie could call on Mrs. Holmes and Mrs. Crawford, both of whom were adept in Chinese.[59]

The senior missionaries were impressed with Lottie, and, noting her dignity, toughness, and intelligence, reported that she was a model missionary. Mr. Crawford wrote the Foreign Mission Board that Lottie "will prove a true missionary." Martha Crawford was even more adulatory in stating: "Miss L. Moon is a highly cultivated, very pious, self-sacrificing woman."[60] By March 1874, assisted by Bible-woman Mrs. Mung, she was bold enough to venture into the city to make evangelical calls. The Chinese women, pressing about her, asked her about her marital status and how she stood with her mother-in-law. She learned to humorously quip: "No [I'm not married, because] I'm afraid she [mother-in-law]" will beat me."[61] Lottie took time to relax. At Tengchow she walked on the city wall, rode sidesaddle on a donkey, embroidered, collected seashells, and swam in the sea.[62]

The Baptist missionaries in Tengchow were at first perplexed, then confounded, by the degenerating condition of Edmonia. She was a very young lady, only twenty in 1874, but manifesting some strange symptoms. The Crawfords, without warning of her arrival, had given her inadequate quarters, probably an outside servant cell, cold and miserable, and subsequently were mystified when Eddie became rude, gossipy, and fault-finding. Edmonia was increasingly subject to seizures, nerves, and difficulty with her throat, lungs, and eyes, sometimes professing to be "crazy." Martha Crawford, not at all enchanted, thought Eddie was a hypochondriac. Today, her collapse might be viewed as the understandable nervous breakdown of an immature young woman facing enormous challenges. Her deterioration would be a disquieting factor to the mission school close to Tengchow, where she and Lottie taught.[63]

Lottie, in contrast, emerged as a prolific and imaginative correspondent, who could stir the feelings and missionary zeal of her supporters back home. She soon became the best-known single missionary woman in Baptist circles. Secretary H. A. Tupper developed a warm friendship with Lottie, but also exploited the growing attachment to Lottie by mite circles, to create additional missionary societies. Tupper then stimulated a friendly rivalry between missionary circles in Virginia (pledged to support Edmonia) and societies in Georgia (pledged to Lottie) to raise twenty-five hundred dollars for the Moon House Fund. Lottie and Eddie then reduced their own salaries, so that the savings could provide the final amount to construct their own house in Tengchow.[64] An emergency would cause the funds to be used in quite a different way than planned.

Financial Crisis in America

A serious financial crisis arose in the United States in 1875 that had drastic implications for mission work. The Foreign Mission Board in Richmond again had no money to send overseas, and the missionaries in North China ran out of credit. Tupper raised the grim possibility that all Baptist missionaries could be recalled. However, by urgently appealing to Baptist congregations and mission societies to overcome the crisis, he forestalled the closing down of denominational missions support. Responding to Tupper's appeals, thousands of Baptist women, through their mite boxes and mission societies, reversed the tide and restored the Foreign Mission Board to solvency.[65]

The physical problems relating to Eddie were now almost out of control. By 1875, only Lottie was teaching at their school and was spending much time nursing her sister.[66] Hartwell was in America, and the two sisters were living in Hartwell's house. Despite the scarcity of money in the mission coffers, there was a desperate need to return Eddie to Virginia for recuperation. As a consequence, Lottie and Eddie sailed for America via Japan, where Eddie had a mental collapse; one doctor there diagnosed her as "hysterical, not crazy." The abrupt voyage of the Moon sisters from China to America ended on December 22, 1876.[67] Although this unexpected return to the homeland was an act of mercy for Eddie, Lottie used the return to generate mission support. In New York, heading back to China, she visited with the famous women's leader, Mrs. T. C. Doremus of the Woman's Union Missionary Society.[68]

On the circuitous return from the United States, Lottie first stopped in Shanghai, where she conferred with senior missionaries Matthew and Eliza Yates. Her steamer disembarked at Chefoo, in the middle of a raging snowstorm. Then, again, she headed for Tengchow, bouncing and bucking in a mule-borne shentze. The time was not propitious, for Shantung Province was experiencing a famine, usually an occasion for thousands to die from hunger. The Foreign Mission Board could not give much help, and, in its desperation, the Board sent to Lottie some pathetic little gifts: $5.50 in cash, an earring, and some stamps.[69]

After her second trip to China, in 1877, Lottie resumed serious language study. But this time in Tengchow, she was isolated and lonely. She wrote the Foreign Mission Board: "I especially am bored to death living alone. I don't find my own society either agreeable or edifying . . . I really think a few more winters like the one just past would put an end to me. This is no joke, but dead earnest. Verbum Sat."[70]

Professor Crawford Howell Toy, brilliant linguist and theologian, wrote Lottie from the Southern Baptist Theological Seminary at Greenville, South Carolina. Historian McBeth states that Toy and Lottie considered marriage in two different periods, sixteen years apart, 1861 and 1877.[71] Toy's acceptance of Charles Darwin and deviant concepts of Old Testament history and inspiration were creating problems that would force him to leave the seminary. It was typical of Lottie Moon, the intellectual, that she made a thorough study of the evolutionary theory in relationship to Biblical studies. She rejected evolution but concluded that Darwin was "the gentlest and wisest of heathens." Eventually, about 1880, Professor Toy married, joined the Unitarian Church, and taught Hebrew and other Semitic languages at Harvard. The depth of his feelings for Lottie remains a mystery,[72] but the separate way chosen by Lottie marked her own final commitment to China in the service of her Lord.

The native-born women of China, over-worked, often abused, but even in China exerting great power in family decisions, were to be Lottie Moon's great focus. She set her course to establish a girls boarding school, to attract the women of the higher classes. This would give her an opportunity to present the Gospel and penetrate Chinese social barriers. In 1878 the school opened, and soon there were thirteen pupils. Parents were required to pay for students' clothing, even if this meant paying a few hard-earned coppers. The school provided teachers, books, lodging, food, and medicine. Courses included reading, arithmetic, and geography. The texts embraced a one-hundred-page (*Hsiao Wen-Ta*) by Mrs. Crawford, a hymnbook by Mr. Crawford, a primer *Peep of Day*, and a book of Bible stories by Mrs. Holmes.[73]

The Hartwell-Crawford Controversy

One of the most contentious issues facing Lottie and all Baptists in Shantung Province was the quarrel between veteran missionaries Tarleton Perry Crawford and Jesse Boardman Hartwell. Beyond personal disagreements, the issues would crescendo into Crawford's Landmarkism and an anti-convention philosophy that would wrack the missionary meetings, and, then in the United States, beset the Southern Baptist Convention (SBC) because of the Gospel Mission Movement.

The dispute began over financial support for missionaries, and, from Crawford's view, opposition to the Southern Baptist Convention sending funds to local Chinese churches. The two missionary families had not gotten along well, while living under the same roof in 1865 in Tengchow. But the original problems stemmed basically from the business ties of both men, who had to work in Shanghai, when the Foreign Mission Board could send no salaries because of the American Civil War. Hartwell, absent from Tengchow from 1864-1865, supported himself as an interpreter in Shanghai. Crawford, on his part, in 1862-63, made a fine living of U. S. $6,600 in Shanghai real estate and continued his business ventures, until he returned in 1863 to missionary activities in Tengchow. Crawford continued to make loans and business deals with Chinese Christians in Hartwell's church, the North Street Baptist Church.[74] Crawford, with help from American Consul E. T. Sandford, then founded Monument Street Baptist Church.[75]

The two missionaries and their wives quarreled over order of worship and whether foreign mission money should be used to pay Chinese pastors and teachers. Finally, the Foreign Mission Board dealt with the two men separately, as if each was head of missions in a separate country.[76]

Hartwell returned briefly to the homeland, where his wife died. However, he maintained control of the Tengchow North Street Baptist Church, with Lottie Moon as a member. But she remained neutral in the feud, while feeling greater sympathy for the Crawfords. After Hartwell returned to Tengchow with a second wife, the leading financial supporter in Hartwell's North Street Church sued Crawford in a consular court. However, the court ruled that Crawford was due a considerable sum of money, and if the Chinese churchman did not pay the assessment in one year his property would be forfeited. The Chinese litigant then went berserk and prepared to kill Crawford. Crawford believed that his co-missionary Hartwell was involved in a plot, particularly so when after asking Hartwell and the North Street Church to censure its enraged members, the church instead censured Crawford. Crawford then denounced Hartwell "as a heathen and publican" and presented his accusations of Hartwell to the Foreign Mission Board. The situation was out of control. When venerated Baptist missionary Matthew T. Yates was mandated to unify the two Baptist churches in Tengchow, he was helpless to do anything in that direction.[77]

Crawford's ideas affected other missionaries as they came into the field, and his concepts ripened into the Gospel Mission Movement (1893-94), when Crawford defected with ten Baptist missionaries to Taiyuanfu, China's sacred mountain. Part of the concern of the defectors was the drift of the Southern Baptists to central leadership and greater bureaucracy, particularly as it related to the Foreign Mission Board. Crawford preferred direct support from individual American churches for missions and did not believe in leadership training for Chinese workers. Crawford's followers wore Chinese clothing and endured their exertions cheerfully but won few converts.

In the United States, Crawford's doctrines influenced about fifty anti-missionary churches that left the Southern Baptist Convention. His chief follower in China was newly-arrived red-bearded ultra-fundamentalist missionary, George P. Bostick, who urged Crawford to take the Gospel Mission to Szechwan Province in the far west.[78] The controversy came to a head in November 1885, when the Foreign Mission Board convened a meeting with veteran missionaries present. The Board rejected the notions projected by Crawford that every Baptist missionary should be a free agent to receive supporting funds and that the formal "missions" structure be abolished. The Foreign Mission Board, instead, adopted policies that private business on the mission field should be abolished and that there should not be any more drawing at will from the mission treasury.[79]

Most of the defecting missionaries eventually returned to the Foreign Mission Board. Crawford was dropped from the SBC roll by 1900, followed in 1902 by his death, and by 1910 the Gospel Mission Movement was only a historical footnote. In 1893, the Board returned J. B. Hartwell to China to head the Shantung work.[80]

Finding Peace of Mind

Lottie's decisive moment came around 1880, when she was about forty years old. She had come to terms with her missionary commitment, made her final refusal to marry Professor Crawford Howell Toy, and adopted a tolerant attitude toward the Gospel Mission Movement. Years later, when asked if she ever had a love affair, she said: "Yes, but God had first claim on my life, and since the two conflicted, there could be no question about the result." Although many times lonely, she was free from the added restrictions of nursing Edmonia, who had been left in America in 1877 to mend.

Lottie in the beginning of her work had hated the pressing crowds in China, the lack of privacy in a woman's life, the spying through the waxed paper windows, the spitting on the floor, the cruelty of binding feet. She followed in the steps of kindly Martha Foster Crawford and Sally J. Holmes in riding rickshaws, shentzes, and donkeys to visit her Chinese women or inviting peasant women to live for a few days in her borrowed North Street compound. She would spend hours explaining the Gospel or discussing American dress and habits, while reclining on a low Chinese flue-heated *kang*. Whereas she had begun her Bible-preaching in American garb, she was now knotting her hair in a severe style and dressing more frequently in Chinese garb. She was determined to lose all vanity but was still defensive about her small stature; she seldom stood in a crowd. She was determined not to waste her time, and by expanding her efforts beyond Tengchow sought to reach into the Chinese masses. She envisaged frontier mission stations that extended clear across the Shantung peninsula. When Tarlton Crawford was absent, she established beyond Tengchow the Hwanghsien mission and could already see the possibility of penetrating to P'Ingtu, 120 miles from the North Street Church.[81]

Lottie Moon concluded that Chinese peasant women had "minds utterly blank," except a minority "of intelligence, eager to learn." She admired the Chinese female tongue and temper as necessary tools. But her preference in Chinese went to the rural people, with whom evangelistic prospects were better, as contrasted with the "hatred and cold distrust" of the Tengchow city dwellers.

Interpreting Chinese city and country by ancient *yin* and *yang* rules, Lottie saw Tengchow's silted harbor, beggars, and decaying homes as evidence of timidity (*yin*). She then saw the country, exemplifying poverty but also family loyalty and vitality, as expressing virility (*yang*). These two features in her mind were bound together by the Confucian principle of filiality, passing from the village to the emperor himself.[82]

The reality was that Lottie, with all her devotion and talents, was moving toward maturity and peace as a missionary. In her missionary trips to the countryside, she countered the Chinese who frequently called her "foreign devil" to her face. "Why do you curse me?" she would quickly retort. In correspondence with her friend Secretary H. A. Tupper, she asked the FMB to be more modern and humane, instead of expecting Southern Baptist missionaries to die in the field. She reminded Richmond that other denominations had five-year or seven-year terms of service, relieved by furloughs. She asked the Foreign Mission Board to adopt a policy of granting a furlough after ten years of service. Lottie apparently was motivated by the plight of the Crawfords, who had been in the field for many years, interrupted by a trip to Japan in 1876.[83] In other letters, she berated the one million Southern Baptists for augmenting the missionary army with one man and three women only, when they were expected to convert thirty millions souls in Shantung.[84]

At times angry, at other times self-pitying, she revealed the depth of her attachment to service: "As I wander from village to village, I feel it no idle fancy that the Master walks beside me. . . ." In order to gain greater spiritual insight, she requested the magazine "The Way of Holiness," while undertaking a deeper study of the Bible and religious literature.[85] Still, at times, the little rebel of pranks and jokes would emerge to lighten her narratives. She had learned a little of the "nu speling" being promoted by Crawford Howell Toy, who was president of the American Philological Society. In a letter written to

Tupper in 1879, she quipped, "Hav yu eny rules for speling in the Fr J? I ask bekaus I hav adopted the fonetic style of speling. . . ."

Jesse Boardman Hartwell, veteran missionary, was in America but resigned his missionary commission in 1879. He performed notable service in behalf of the Chinese in San Francisco from 1878 to 1884, during which time he organized the First Chinese Baptist Church in the Bay area.[86] Hartwell was not happy when Lottie and Edmonia had occupied his North Street house in Tengchow, instead of using the Moon House Fund to construct new quarters. The sisters had employed some of the money, instead, to travel to the United States.[87]

In Tengchow, Martha Foster Crawford's school was making good progress, along with the Presbyterian boys school, and the two were merging into a college. But this successful development aroused the jealousy of missionary Tarleton Crawford, who had a physical break-down in 1878. Tarleton Crawford, in order to rectify a marriage drifting toward the rocks, demanded the termination of the school. Then, alone, he went on leave to the United States. Mrs. Crawford, horrified by the school closure request, likened it to "amputating all my limbs." After returning from overseas, Reverend Crawford asked his wife to give up a large medical practice. Martha Crawford was a teacher, not a surgeon, but through necessity persevered with the medical work, and now discarded all medical assistance except aid to students and church members.

The girders of mutual support in remote Tengchow seemed to be collapsing. In 1881, Mrs. Crawford in turmoil about her school, marriage, and health, announced that she could no longer remain in China. Brokenhearted, she left separately on a furlough, seeking her own medical treatment.[88] She was joined by Mrs. Holmes, the widow, who could bear no further separation from her son. This would leave Lottie Moon behind in 1882 to preserve twenty years of Baptist work. Lottie was indignant that so much responsibility had been thrust upon her, and she threatened in correspondence to the For-eign Mission Board to take a professorship at Harvard. Lottie was understandably miffed that in Shantung the work was left short of workers, but soon she regained her composure.[89]

"Little Cross Roads"

Lottie had acquired a routine but not one she completely relished. But she was inspired in 1881 to move into a modest house in town, which she called Little Crossroads (Hsiao Shih-Tzu Ko). In repose, she could read spiritual books, study the Chinese language, and grow flowers from Virginia seed. There, she occasionally saw T. P. Crawford and received Chinese friends in a separate house.[90]

On the other hand, Tarleton Crawford's capacity for creating chaos was almost boundless. Martha Foster returned to Tengchow after an absence of almost two years. Crawford in 1883 made his most serious attempt to scrap his wife's flourishing school. However, this effort was forestalled by the votes of two newly appointed missionaries, H. Weston Halcomb and Cicero Washington Pruitt, both of whom had arrived in Tengchow in January 1882. When the Reverend Mr. Crawford, at his own expense, went to the United States and preached on the "folly of schools" and self-support for missions, Lottie intervened through correspondence. In letters to Secretary Tupper, she rebutted Crawford's assertions that his policies gave "perfect freedom to all parties."[91] Still, by 1890, Crawford's influence had increased, with the assistance of George P. Bostick, to the extent of obtaining a vote prohibiting any spending by Americans on the "natives" for salaries of the Chinese or their Christian work; this measure went against the grain of Lottie and missionary C. W. Pruitt. Crawford wanted the Chinese to support their own preachers, evangelists, schools, and students.

About 1885 Lottie wrote in the *Woman's Work in China* (created by her friend Anna Cunningham Safford) that women missionaries teaching in an elementary school was "the greatest folly of modern missions." She continued: "Can we wonder at the mortal weariness and disgust, the sense of wasted powers and the conviction that her life is a failure that comes over a woman, when, instead of the ever-broadening activities she had planned, she finds herself tied down to the petty work of teaching a few girls."[92]

On the trend favored by some missionaries to adopt Chinese clothes and hairstyles, including trailing queues, she examined all sides of the question in an article written for *Woman's Work in China*. She was probably influenced by missionary C. W. Pruitt, who experimented with Chinese dress. However, Pruitt had a Chinese deride him, with: "See, the devil is pretending to be a man."[93] At first, Lottie thought that missionaries dressed in Chinese attire would appear ridiculous to the Chinese.[94] On the other hand, recruits of the China Inland Mission went about their work with shaven heads and Chinese padded garments. Later she would dress almost exclusively in Chinese garments.

In 1885, a committee studying woman's work for the Foreign Mission Board reported on an article by Lottie Moon in the Woman's Work in China. Lottie had classified single women missionaries in three categories:

a) Serious grievances and want reforms;
b) Satisfied but use indirect methods; and
c) Rights secured but want others to share.

When Lottie concluded that in Richmond she had been identified with Category A (serious grievances), she felt insulted, and in a letter to H. A. Tupper she offered to resign. Lottie saw herself as belonging to Category C (rights secured). Secretary Tupper wisely let the matter cool down, and it was soon forgotten.[95]

In 1879 Lottie and Sally Holmes traveled in mid-winter snow and cold winds to hamlets five to ten miles (twenty to thirty li) from Tengchow. She preached from six to eleven times a day. Not at all positioning herself to be a martyr, she wrote: "if anyone thinks all this is agreeable—I differ."[96] Lottie on this trip was still learning and absorbing. She regarded the villagers as the "Great Unwashed," an opinion on the absence of Chinese hygiene supported by the travel writer Harry A. Franck.[97] Lottie was rattled by a crowd of youth that assembled outside of the house where she was staying, tore out the paper windows, and climbed inside to stand on a table. Lottie wrote in exasperation: "O! the torture of human eyes upon you; scanning every feature. . . ." The hostess replied in the Chinese manner: "You see," she explained, "We have never seen any heavenly people [Americans] before."[98]

Beginning in 1883, Lottie spent two and one-half years visiting villagers south and west of Tengchow. She was probing toward P'Ingtu, where there was a readiness to receive missionaries.[99] She also was absorbing the logic of a Presbyterian minister, who said: "If experience teaches anything in China, it is that the Gospel succeeds much better in the country than in the cities. Preaching in a city chapel has a fine sound and looks like work. In point of fact, it is the easiest and least productive kind of missionary work."[100]

Living in P'Ingtu

In 1884 Lottie pondered whether to return to the States. The problem again was T. P. Crawford, the only male in the Tengchow Baptist Community, who was engaged in annoying Lottie and others by enforcing "peculiar rules." Crawford had an ingenious record for stirring up fights. Instead of returning to America, Lottie chose to fulfill her vision and moved to rural P'Ingtu Chou (department), a relatively prosperous area, 115 miles west of Tengchow. There were only a few converts, and they were derived from Presbyterian work that had been abandoned and an unknown number of Nestorians. She planned to live in a peasant milieu, after arriving in the city, conveyed by a mule-borne shentze on a trip requiring four miserable days of bouncing and swaying.[101]

P'Ingtu was a prosperous walled city, more affluent than Tengchow, but with no foreign resident official present and very few foreign visitors. There were possibilities for the mission, for there were many Buddhist, Muslim, and vegetarian sects, some of whose adherents were seeking "the unknown god." In order to get a start, there also was the potential of employing two Christians of the Tengchow Baptist community, including Mrs. Chao, the Crawford's Christian servant.[102]

Her intended action was drastic, for no Southern Baptist woman had begun a new outpost in such a rugged environment, in particular, to live in smelly rat-and-bug-infected stables and mud-floor inns, patronized only by muleteers and the wretched poor.[103] This move amazed almost everyone and was confronted by T. P. Crawford, Congregationalist missionary Arthur H. Smith, and Lottie's Baptist friends in America. Crawford prophesied that terrible things would occur if she left for P'Ingtu. Lottie, not reluctant to fire back, made it clear to the Foreign Mission Board that she abhorred Crawford's "plantation slavery," with his control of budgets, and that she preferred not to work under a "dictator." "What is there for me to fear if God be with me?" she pluckily asked Crawford.[104]

In the autumn of 1885, Lottie made an initial trip to P'Ingtu in a swaying shentze,[105] despite the admonition of the American Consul against women traveling in the interior. But Mrs. Crawford promised to join her later, as did Presbyterian missionary C. W. Mateer and Baptist missionary C. W. Pruitt. So, in December 1885, she left Tengchow and the Little Crossroads house for a five-year stay in P'Ingtu until 1890. Mr. Chao and his wife accompanied her to cook and perform household chores. The following essentials were loaded on mules for the journey: a mattress, bedding, winter underwear, medicine, Chinese literature, basic foods, books and magazines, and a Chinese trunk.[106]

Her new residence (rented for twenty-four dollars a year) was a four-room house with dirt floor near the West Gate; her landlord was an opium eater. She designated rooms for kitchen, storeroom, passageway, and reception-sleeping quarters. Her few western possessions were a cookstove, table, and two chairs. She made radical changes in her style of living, adopting the exclusive use of the Chinese mud-brick-heated bed (the *k'ang*) and, later, Chinese clothing.[107] Arriving in American dress, she quickly changed to a quilted

Chinese coat extending below her knees, triple-size sleeves, and a robe of deep blue cotton, the attire of an average Chinese woman. Her hair was parted down the middle in a severe style. Thus attired, she sat cross-legged on the *k'ang* by day, meeting her Chinese visitors and sleeping on the same *k'ang* by night.[108] Jesting like a sad clown, Lottie wrote: "I tried to bring down my style of living as nearly to the level of my respectable middle-class neighbors as possible."[109]

Hyatt concludes that Lottie's decision to move to P'Ingtu probably was a mistake, joined to other wrong decisions; she had "miscalculated at every turn" he asserts. Her intent was to convert the heathen, but there was not one conversion of a Chinese female. When an attempt was made to convert the males, that limited success was attributed largely to her co-workers in Sha-Ling. Her austere life, he states, did nothing to attract the Chinese to Christian beliefs.[110]

In her first six months, nevertheless, she showed great dedication throughout the P'Ingtu valley, by visiting 122 city homes and several hundred houses in thirty-three villages nearby. Lottie wrote the Foreign Mission Board, "I am more and more impressed by the belief that to win these people to God, we must first win them to ourselves. We need to go out and live among them. . . ."[111]

She wrote the Foreign Mission Board that it should establish a permanent station at P'Ingtu by renting a cluster of small houses. She advised that the work could be sustained by missionary families, and by single women (at least two) supporting each other. In order to serve as a retreat for stressed women missionaries, she offered her Little Crossroads house in Tengchow.[112] At Tengchow, to which she retreated from time to time, she would teach and relax with gardening and read the *Atlantic Monthly, Edinburgh Review,* and *Littel's Magazine.*[113]

Lottie's lure with Chinese women was always to allow herself to be sought. In some instances, she placed plates of cookies at the doorway. Through this enticement, she met the mothers and told them how things were done in America. However, the extreme variance in cultures could produce a volatile situation. In 1890 she was followed by a rabble crying, "devil, devil!" Her procedure was to act deliberately on such occasions, and the tension would soon die.[114]

She found country women to be ill-tempered without exception and ingenious at reviling each other. But she also found them to be intelligent, hospitable, and religious. Through force of will and bad temper, Chinese women often ruled their husbands. Lottie was determined to bolster women in a society that emphasized the family, especially its males. She acknowledged that in China she had expected to touch millions; instead, as in Cartersville, she found herself tied down to the petty work of "teaching a few girls." In a country that practiced infanticide, wife beating, and foot binding, she discovered that severe mothers-in-law were a necessity.[115]

The Chinese were suspicious in their expectation that an extra adult female in a Western household sometimes should be viewed as a second or third wife, a mistress, or a concubine. When Baptist missionary C. W. Pruitt arrived in P'Ingtu, Lottie circumspectly would not publicly approach him, walk with him in the streets, or even shake his hand.[116]

During the period 1886-88, dozens of letters from Lottie were published in the *Foreign Mission Journal, The Religious Herald* (Virginia) and the *Christian Index* (Georgia). In one of these letters (January 1886), she wrote about the "disgustingly filthy" practice of polygamy in P'Ingtu. She described a visit to a Mandarin's house, where the discarded first wife lived in rags under the same roof with a favored second wife, the latter lounging in luxury and surrounded by servants.[117]

The W.M.U. and Lottie Moon Offering

In order to reinforce the work in China, Lottie alluded to "wonderful progress" that could be made if more Christian workers could be provided. In September 16, 1887, Lottie wrote glowingly of the work of the Southern Methodist Church, that at a crucial moment had been in a state of collapse until women came to the rescue. The Southern Baptist situation was in similar straits, but it could be reversed by appealing to the women. First, Lottie noted, there must be organization and then a massive effort to collect funds. As a practical measure, she suggested a week of prayer and collective giving for mission work in 1888 during the Christmas season, the effort to be controlled by the Baptist women.[118] Her letter, published in the *Foreign Mission Journal* will go down in Southern Baptist history as a foundational pillar of foreign missions and for the creation of the organization to support it. Her letter read in part:

> Some years ago the Southern Methodist Mission in China had run down to the lowest watermark; the rising of the tide seems to have begun with the enlisting of the women of the church in the cause of missions. The previously unexampled increase in missionary zeal and activity in the Northern Presbyterian Church is attributed to the same reason—the thorough awakening of the women of the church upon the subject of missions. In like manner, until the women of our Southern Baptist churches are thoroughly aroused, we shall continue to go on in our present hand-to-mouth system. We shall continue to see mission stations so poorly manned that missionaries break down from overwork, loneliness, and isolation; we shall continue to see promising fields unentered and old stations languishing; and we shall continue to see other denominations no richer and no better educated than ours, outstripping us in the race. . . . I am convinced that one of the chief reasons our Southern Baptist women do so little is the lack of organization.[119]

The contents of this letter became part of the agenda of the Southern Baptist Convention and the Baptist women's meeting of 1888.[120]

This was the torrential Lottie Moon, lashing out and unstoppable, in her quest to goad Baptists to follow the Great Commission and bring Christ to the world. This also was her supreme moment in the history of saints, to be a catalyst rather than expecting to be a martyr;

she sought to stir and create rather than to serve as an exemplar of piety and suffering, although these also were her companions. She also was proposing an effective more centralized structure for the woman's missionary organization. In 1887 she had written:

> In seeking organization we do not need to adopt plans or methods unsuitable to the view, or repugnant to the tastes of our brethren. What we want is not power, but simply combination in order to elicit the largest possible giving. Power of appointment and of disbursing funds should be left, as heretofore, in the hands of the Foreign Mission Board. Separate organization is undesirable, and would do harm; but organization in subordination to the Board is the imperative need of the hour.[121]

Another letter from Lottie, in the spring of 1888, appearing in the *Foreign Mission Journal*, made a major impact on some Baptist churches in America; she was involved at the time in itinerant work in the village of Sha-Ling, Lottie made a bold request that American helpers should "come down and live among the natives" with no frills, expecting no more costly foreign houses in a "pleasant foreign community." Instead, missionary recruits should anticipate "making themselves part and parcel of the native society around them."[122] Events would prove that even Lottie, a formidable warrior, could not live completely isolated and bereft of comfort, nor long exist on the level of a Chinese peasant.

In Touch With Headquarters

Contemporary with Lottie's correspondence from P'Ingtu, there was only a skeletal Foreign Mission Board, its impetus provided Secretary H. A. Tupper. In May 1888, the Woman's Missionary Union (WMU) began to organize as an auxiliary to the Southern Baptist Convention; however, even earlier, there existed a woman's missionary "clearing house," headed by Annie W. Armstrong, as the first Secretary of the WMU in Baltimore. As the national organization took form, Annie Armstrong from 1888 to 1906 served as the

WMU Corresponding Secretary. Miss Armstrong, while sometimes frosty and arrogant, quickly won recognition, both for her quick temper and efficiency. She worked closely with H. A. Tupper and brought to the new organization crisp leadership and a fervor for missions.[123]

Dr. Tupper wrote Annie Armstrong from Richmond on July 24, 1888:

> Dear Miss Armstrong:
>
> I send you a letter from Miss [Lottie] Moon of China. There is force in it that must be felt by every appreciative reader. Her proposition to send several woman workers of the right sort to the region of P'Ingtu is important, wise and I believe practicable. It has occurred to me that your Executive Committee might give special attention to this matter, until it should be accomplished. What do you think? Here is a clear work for Woman's Mission to Woman. The only hope of China is through the women. Might this not be successfully pressed? After using this letter at pleasure it may be returned.
>
> H. A. Tupper
>
> P.S. This letter is suggested by your kind offer to present to the women of the country some special work of our Board. H.A.T."[124]

Following this suggestion of Lottie from December 1887, Miss Armstrong solicited a special 1888 Christmas offering, with a goal of $2,000 to support two new women workers assigned to China, a project approved by the Executive Board. The Baltimore organization mailed literature, urging women to pray and support the Christmas offering. The results were immensely gratifying, amounting to $3,315.26, enough to commission three missionaries for P'Ingtu, instead of two: Misses F. S. Knight (North Carolina), L. G. Barton (Texas), and N. J. Thornton (Alabama). The offering touched Lottie, who was enabled to travel for rest to the United States, and while in the homeland to help shape the mission program. In January 9, 1889, Lottie advised the new appointees through Annie Armstrong to come to China with an "abundance of heavy flannel underclothing" and "rejoicing to suffer."[125]

In late 1887 a local publication reported that of new missionaries to North China, after Lottie Moon's arrival, three were dead, three had physical or medical problems and had left the field, and one missionary, N. W. Halcomb, had resigned because of doctrinal matters. Lottie, for a month, pled with Halcomb to remain.[126] In P'Ingtu, besides Lottie, only C. W. Pruitt remained, and in 1888 he married Anna Seward, a Presbyterian missionary. The Foreign Mission Board was not amused when it was obliged to purchase Miss Seward's outfit and to reimburse the Presbyterians for her travel expenses. Pruitt moved with his bride to Hwanghsien, to continue the work that had felled seven of his predecessors. Martha Foster Crawford was recuperating in America, while T. P. Crawford was succumbing to a variety of problems.[127] When civil unrest occurred in September 1887, Lottie fled to P'Ingtu, ignoring an American warship that had been ordered to Tengchow to protect Americans there.[128]

Teaching Vegetarians at Sha-Ling

Lottie, in 1887, planned a furlough in the United States for the ensuing year, the request only reluctantly granted by the Foreign Mission Board. She was eager to visit Eddie, who was teaching school in America but was not physically well. The Viewmont estate had been sold, but Lottie was longing to see Scottsville, Virginia, where she and Edmonia had purchased twenty acres of land.[129]

These plans would evaporate when three men from Sha-ling, a small village ten miles from P'Ingtu, knocked on her door in P'Ingtu in 1887. The visitors had been sent by Chinese leader Dan Ho Bang to seek out "the new doctrine woman" (Lottie Moon) and invite her to Sha-ling to teach and live in his house. Dan Ho Bang had heard the preaching of T. P. Crawford and was the leader of forty members of a vegetarian sect who were willing to listen to teachings about Jesus. Lottie saw an opportunity and visited Sha-Ling, where she found two families seeking God, and moved in with the family of Dan Ho Bang. She slept native-style on a mud-brick *k`ang* with her hostess. Then she hurriedly summoned Martha Crawford from Tengchow to join her.[130]

The American women found that Sha-Ling had two dominant religious groups: (a) Confucianists, led by Li Shou Ting, a schoolmaster, who felt Christianity was "not so deep or complete" as the doctrine of Confucius, and (b) Vegetarians (present or former members) of the Venerable Heaven Sect (*Lao-Tien Hui*), a "truth seeker" cult. The leader of the Lao-Tien Hui was Dan Ho Bang, who would follow a solitary road, after repudiation by the majority of his group Dan became a serious enquirer, and then matured as a Christian evangelist in nearby Li-Tzu-Yuan village.[131]

The two Americans lived at the home of Dan Ho Bang for a week and worked twelve-hour shifts while teaching primarily women but also men from several hamlets. Martha Crawford mainly taught Bible classes. Lottie taught learners to memorize the Scriptures and such hymns as "Jesus Loves Me" and "The Father Surely Will Watch Over Me." Men turned their heads to listen from the adjoining room. When Lottie preached on Sunday evenings, half-converted men would lead the singing and read the Scriptures.[132] The Sha-Ling extension work undertaken by Lottie eventually embraced about twenty families out of the fifty families that lived there. This included about thirty persons who were participants in the four weekly services. But she also evangelized in their homes. Even a community of Buddhist nuns permitted her to present the Christian message.[133]

She wrote H. A. Tupper and Annie Armstrong to send new workers expeditiously to P'Ingtu, so she could train them. In her appeals for self-sacrificing candidates, she wrote: "They must be men and women of absolute self-consecration, ready to come down and live among the natives, to wear the Chinese dress and live in Chinese houses . . . ." Lottie herself was adopting the Chinese village lifestyle, even more, preaching in barnyards, and eating noodles with chopsticks.[134] However, this "going native" style offended Tarleton Crawford.

C. W. Pruitt and George P. Bostick (the latter to enthusiastically join Tarleton Crawford in his ill-fated Gospel Mission Movement) began the process of constituting a church at Sha-Ling. Pruitt baptized four men and two women from the families of Dan and Yuan in a village pool. These new converts and missionary Miss Fannie Knight (later Mrs. W. D. King) became the Sha-Ling Baptist Church, fourth Southern Baptist Church in North China and the first church in P'Ingtu Chou. In view of the strong anti-foreign feelings throughout the country, all of the converts, but especially the women, were laying their lives on the line. One brave young Christian woman, soon to marry, told her groom and her mother-in-law that she would not worship the groom's ancestors nor bow before his ancestral tablets.[135]

After the humiliating Treaty of Nanking (1842) and the demoralizing Chinese concessions of territories and power to Japan, England, France, and the other Western powers, China was overrun from time to time by Chinese hordes venting anti-foreign violence and protests. The most notable of these manifestations were the Taiping Rebellion (1848-65), during which twenty million Chinese died, and the Boxer Rebellion (1900-01). Such violent anti-foreign manifestation on a lesser scale would occur in Shantung Province in 1890, when Lottie was begining to gather her effects for a furlough in America.

Extra-territorial rights gave advantages to American citizens in treaty ports, such as Tengchow, including physical protection afforded by American warships. Lottie, however, had turned against such treaty protection, for Chinese Christians tended to cluster in the treaty ports with the foreign missionaries, and she wanted the Christians to be strengthened by bearing the burdens of their witness. Her philosophy would be tested in Sha-Ling during the 1890 riots, when she would be threatened with death by an anti-Christian mob leader during the Chinese New Year celebrations.[136] Instead of sending a messenger to the American Consul for help, she faced the mob and said, "If you attempt to destroy this church, you will have to kill me first. Jesus gave himself for us Christians. Now I am ready to die for him."[137]

During a six-month period, the Sha-Ling church faced pandemonium and persecution. Young girl enquirers were married against their will to "disgusting" nonbelievers. Services were disrupted and all foreign missionaries were asked to leave. In her personal copy of *The Imitation of Christ* by Thomas A`Kempis, Lottie scribbled that she expected to die during the disorders. After several days of turmoil, she assented to the request of church members who begged her to leave Sha-Ling to assure the safety of all.[138] However, the Sha-Ling church, tested by its persecution, would become the strongest and most evangelistic of the Shantung churches.[139]

Out of the Sha-Ling community would emerge some of China's greatest Christians: Li Shou Ting, the schoolmaster, perhaps the pre-eminent evangelist of North China, and his companion, evangelist Dan Ho Bang. Because of the persecution, Mr. Li, for refusing to worship ancestral tablets, would lose his teaching job, suffer beatings, and have his scalp torn from his head. Mr. Li first had been taught by Lottie, then nurtured by Tarleton Crawford, and finally examined by Pruitt. During his lifetime, Li Shou Ting would baptize at least fourteen hundred converts.[140] Don Ho Bang, the former vegetarian leader, rather than renounce his Christian faith, was strung on a pole during the mob demonstration, his feet and hands bound, and beaten before his ancestral tablets. He endured this torture, and because of it, an old man (one hundred miles away in Tengchow), hearing of his faith, became a believer.[141]

The year 1900 was a watermark in multiple ways. Missions were thriving in Tengchow, P'Ingtu, and Sha-Ling, despite the anti-foreign riots. In contrast to the drying-up of financial resources in Richmond, the American women supporting missions had developed an enthusiastic *esprit de corps*. Lottie's positive reports on the work at Sha-Ling had buoyed with hope the Women's Mission Union. Lottie had now completed an apprenticeship that had lasted seventeen years, which she had mastered with optimism and balance.[142]

Tarleton P. Crawford's obsessions had led him to create disaffection, then to wage open warfare against the Foreign Mission Board. Eventually, he would be separated from its service. While Lottie did not join Crawford's followers at Taishan, she clearly had been influenced by some of Crawford's views and the discussions on indigenous autonomy. Living in P'Ingtu, Lottie wrote in *Woman's Work in the Far East* about her desire "to keep the movement as free of foreign interference as possible. . . ." Then, in the *Foreign Mission Journal*, she wrote in the same vein: "God grant us faith and courage to keep hands off," to allow the church to "grow naturally in China, without forcing the process."[143]

In 1890 Crawford, while still an accredited Southern Baptist missionary, was able to get a favorable vote from his Shantung colleagues on his "Articles of Agreement," an action that disturbed the Foreign Mission Board. The Articles stated that missionaries first would be evangelistic and would use no mission money beyond personal and itenerating expenses. George P. Bostick, an ardent Crawford follower, added: "We also deem it unwise for us to become pastors, schoolteachers, charity vendors, or meddlers in Chinese lawsuits." These expressions were supported by the Pruitts, Mrs. Crawford, and, not surprisingly, Lottie Moon. Lottie added: "I do not think this [self-help] ideal is best attained by bearing their pecuniary burdens for them and building their churches and establishing their schools. . . ."[144]

The Mature Years

Lottie was beginning to dread her drab, earthy existence spent in P'Ingtu and Sha-Ling. Especially illuminating is a letter written after a vacation in Chinkiang, in which she expressed distaste for returning to Sha-Ling and doubts that she had the "strength of body and soul to plunge again into that burial alive." This was in contrast with other letters speaking of the potentiality of "thousands of inquirers and converts" and a vision of mission stations extending from

P'Ingtu to Chinkiang on the Yangtze River.[145] Desperate for home scenes, familiar people, and relaxation, Lottie in mid-1891 sailed with the Pruitts for America on board the *Empress of Japan*. She had not seen Virginia for fourteen years, and would not return to China until early 1894.[146]

During her furlough, and while speaking in 1892 before the Atlanta Convention of the WMU, she appealed for help to start medical missions in North China. Her petition was answered by Dr. Thomas W. Ayers of Alabama, who established a hospital at Huang-Hsien.[147]

When Lottie moon returned to Shantung Province, she lived in Tengchow and the Little Crossroads house for twenty years until her death. She never returned to P'Ingtu, although the P'Ingtu mission became the greatest evangelistic center in China during her lifetime.

Something mysterious and yet foreseeable had changed her temperament as she entered her last two decades in China. She was less adventurous and more passive. The Chinese were no longer quite so dull and stupid, and she was not so astute nor better than the city-dwellers and villagers with whom she worked. Certainly she was not physically nor mentally as tough as before, and her inability to again endure the "noise, publicity, filth, and confusion" of Chinese rural life probably accounted for her failure to stay in P'Ingtu. Her experiments over the years had given her an austere life but not quite a common bond with the villagers. But overriding these considerations was her inward peace; Lottie's dwindling years probably were the happiest of her entire life. Her sense of well-being was bolstered by the return to China of white-bearded Jesse Boardman Hartwell, now as spiritual head of the Baptist mission in North China.[148]

In 1894-95, the Sino-Japanese War was fought and won by the Japanese, resulting in an independent Korea and the acquisition of Formosa (Taiwan) by Japan. One of the major military engagements, the naval battle of Weihaiwei, involved the Weihaiwei forts in Shantung, manned by the Japanese army.[149] In Tengchow, unruly Chinese troops were menacing foreigners in the streets, while Japanese warships passed close to the harbor. The Chinese authorities, in a confusing situation, demanded that foreigners in the city remain in place as pawns for the protection of the Chinese, but at the same time accused them of being spies. Some missionaries fled for protection to the U.S. warship *Yorktown*. The Japanese bombarded Tengchow on January 16, 1895, while Lottie was striving to make her way over snow-covered roads and through desperate crowds to spend Christmas in P'Ingtu. Returning, she found that a Japanese shell had destroyed the wall and damaged the veranda at her Little Crossroads home. Frightened upper-class Chinese of Tengchow, having ignored her for thirty years, now came calling on Lottie, asking her to remain for their protection. When missionary James B. Hartwell returned to the city, unprecedented numbers of people swarmed to attend the services at the North Street Baptist Church.[150]

During the Chinese-Japanese conflict, Lottie visited 118 villages and later apologized that the rains and a throat ailment prevented her from attaining her goal of teaching in 200 villages. Things were going well, the Chinese were making heavy financial contributions, and during the war there had been fifty-three baptisms. At the Baptist association annual meeting, there was an open discussion on education and the cruel practice of foot-binding.[151] Customarily in China, the feet of young girls were deformed by wrapping or else the foot bones were broken to make them small and beautiful in the eyes of their future husbands.[152] This primitive custom began to decline around the period of the Chinese Nationalist Revolution in 1911.

Lottie was only fifty-six years old in 1896 when her health began to fade. She was never known as a pretty woman, but it was a sad blow when she lost her teeth and immediately looked old.[153] The Chinese countryside was plagued by bandits, sometimes in bands numbering in the hundreds, many of them penniless, disbanded soldiers. During 1896-97, Lottie's house in Tengchow was invaded by thieves, who stole her Chinese clothes and other articles from the kitchen and storeroom.

Despite such normal impediments in the China missions life, Lottie taught a Sunday School class of young men under the bell tower of the Tengchow church and also a New Testament class of illiterate males. The elderly Hartwells weakened and then departed for San Francisco, leaving behind their daughter Anna Hartwell and Lottie Moon to shoulder the burdens of the mission station.[154]

Meanwhile, the Little Crossroads house became a playground for children. The cook doled out cookies from a bottomless jar. Dogs roamed freely in the yard. Little children peering through the window were invited in. A single child picking Lottie's favorite flowers was admonished, then told to pick all he wanted. When a youngster died after falling from her crepe myrtle tree, she had the tree trimmed sharply, almost as a reprimand. She apologized abjectly to the boy's mother.[155]

The Russo-Japanese War (1904-05) was notably the first modern war in which a European power (Russia) was defeated by a non-Western foe (Japan). Its economic effect on China was to deny Manchuria as a labor frontier to the thousands of starving Shantung families, who needed a new food source. Consequently, between 1905 and 1909, the cost of living in Shantung rose fifty percent. Malnutrition exacted its toll, as plague and smallpox ravaged the population.[156]

Lottie had already lost her brother Isaac, who for years had guarded the family estate before its sale. Then came the tragic news that her devoted sister Edmonia, living in Starke, Florida, had committed suicide. Eddie, on November 19, 1908, despondent from her illness, had pulled the covers over her head and with a gun had ended her life.[157]

A tribute was paid to Lottie by Mrs. T. O. Hearn, a missions promoter from America, who visited Lottie for three days in 1909.

> Her home and manner of living is plain and it seemed to me unsuited to a lady of such rare intellect, education, and refinement—like a diamond in a setting of silver. And yet, as I noted with interest the gentle dignity with which she performed her daily duties, and the pleasure she took, I realized that although she is a woman of rare attainments and would be an ornament to society in America, she is not out of place in China. The love

of Christ which fills her heart makes her well fitted to live among her less enlightened sisters and lead them out of their narrow groove into the broader life of light and happiness in a Savior's love.[158]

Despite her earlier distaste for the confining strictures of teaching a few girls, and believing herself competent to assume other major areas of responsibility, she now found pleasure in guiding five or six girls schools, three of which met in her compound. Her greatest delight however, was the successful Memorial School, composed of men and boys of the upper classes, taught by three excellent teachers. Showing her special preparation for this school, she insisted that the curriculum should include Chinese classics, along with Christian and Western academic courses. Even in 1910, while slowing down, she advised young missionaries, made her parochial visits every afternoon, and surveyed the work in eighteen nearby villages.[159]

The curtains were coming down on the first generation that created the Southern Baptist North China Mission. Tarleton Perry Crawford and Martha Foster were gone by 1900, dropped from the list of Southern Baptist missionaries.[160] Lottie had a particular fondness for Martha Foster and genuinely missed her. By 1912 veteran J. B. Hartwell died; he had been Lottie's only contemporary in China. As he lay dying, he greeted by name a missionary and a Chinese deacon, both later determined to have died recently. Lottie also was running out of time.[161]

As Lottie was finishing her last days, there was emerging through a revolution in 1911-12 a new republican China, shaped by the doctrines of Dr. Sun Yat Sen. As the disorders mounted, Lottie joined a number of missionaries evacuated to Chefoo. There she and Chinese friends organized a Red Cross unit. She also initiated a binational Baptist organization, the Woman's Missionary Union of North China, to assist with famine relief. This organization was deemed necessary, since the Foreign Mission Board, overcome with its own financial difficulties, could not help.[162]

Lottie could summon strength that was almost mythical. When she heard of a desperate starving Chinese woman, who became mortally injured after throwing herself from a bridge to a stony riverbank, Lottie went into action. The filthy crippled creature was bandaged and placed on a scrubbed *k'ang*, her eyes anointed, and her hair washed and combed by Lottie. For weeks, the suffering woman heard the Gospel story and shared the finest hospitality Lottie could afford.[163]

Lottie was emotionally stricken by the severe famine that littered the roads with corpses and induced mothers to hang themselves. Suffering from senility and melancholia, that surged from mid-1912, she gave away to the famine relief fund her small savings in a Shanghai bank. She wrote as the last entry in her account book: "I pray that no missionary will ever be as lonely as I have been."[164]

She developed a cranial abscess and began to hallucinate. Lottie's frailty became severe when she decided not to eat, her resolve motivated by sympathy for the suffering P'Ingtu Christians. When a Baptist physician confirmed that she was suffering from self-afflicted starvation, her missionary colleagues decided to send her home. After being informed of her plight, the Foreign Mission Board requested nurse Cynthia Miller to escort Lottie home via Japan.[165] Lottie was placed on a ship that sailed from China on December 20, and she died shortly thereafter in Japan's Kobe harbor, on December 24, 1912. She passed away while appearing to talk to Chinese friends who had died long before. Then her body was cremated in accordance with Japanese law. The ashes were buried later in her brother Isaac's plot near Crewe, Virginia, fifty miles west of Richmond.[166]

Her Legacy

Lottie Moon, a complex person, is more difficult to analyze than venturesome Baptist men such as John Smyth, John Bunyan, or Billy Graham; she, nevertheless, emerges as a true Trailblazer. She never hesitated to fully use her brilliant intellect and pliant Christian spirit to prompt the Foreign Mission Board to modernize procedures for its workers, resulting in scheduled and more frequent furloughs, and to give more latitude to its women missionaries. Lottie exercised a pioneering Christian zest to venture alone deep into the Shantung backcountry of P'Ingtu and Sha-Ling. She insisted on attending mission business meetings in Tengchow and elsewhere as an equal with her male Baptist colleagues and was determined to offer her proposals, instead of quietly knitting as had been the expectation. Thus, she set the pace for Southern Baptists to make effective use of the remarkable talents of Christian women, which in her case exceeded on occasions that of her male co-workers. It was not a coarse joke but reality that impelled *The Foreign Mission Journal*, after her death, to cite her as *"the best man among our missionaries."*[167]

What made her unique was not her longevity of seventy-two years, nor her thirty-nine years of service, but her courageous experimentation that involved: (1) study and absorption of Chinese language, culture and classics; (2) her full immersion into the Chinese village milieu, adopting Chinese friends, clothing, and customs; and (3) the confirmation that Christian schools were a powerful tool to shape both males and females, and to be used as effective means to befriend and influence the upper classes, as well as the peasants.

Lottie was a persuasive and prolific letter writer, and through her correspondence she helped shape the recommendations of FMB secretary H. A. Tupper and WMU corresponding secretary Annie Armstrong. While Lottie Moon was not the inspiration for the founding of the Woman's Missionary Union (WMU), she contributed mightily to its growth, as its most visible ambassador abroad. Lottie's 1887 letter inspired Annie Armstrong and the WMU to collect funds to support two new missionaries for the China work. The new venture grew into the annual "Lottie Moon Christmas Offering," which collects more than twenty million dollars annually for the support of world missions.[168]

While the Gospel Mission Movement, spearheaded by Tarleton Perry Crawford, was a painful episode to Southern Baptists, Lottie agreed with some elements of its indigenous self-support philosophy. The policies of the Chinese government in the last quarter of the twentieth century to limit foreign influence with regard to Chinese Christians, gives considerable support to some of Crawford's ideals but not his disruptive behavior. Lottie, however, was not in agreement with Crawford's anarchic dream of the dissolution of the Foreign Mission Board, his disavowal of educating Chinese workers, and refusal to pay American money for the support of Chinese churches. However, Lottie's frustration but also her fond attachment was to the cluster of Christian schools at Tengchow. She also planted the idea of a Southern Baptist hospital at Huang-Hsien, supporting the concept that doctors and medical personnel are necessary adjuncts for spreading the Gospel story.

Lottie Moon's struggles and successes as a missionary, published and read widely, sustain powerfully the momentum of Southern Baptist foreign missions. The term Woman's Missionary Union (WMU), it should be noted, was derived from a basement prayer meeting at Austin, Texas, in 1880, at which time the Texas WMU was created. A WMU "open" meeting in Maryland (1879) and a Virginia Central Committee meeting (1881) were aspects of a growing movement that would help overcome the skepticism about women's missionary activities. The turning point for the WMU seems to have occurred in May 1883, at the Southern Baptist Convention at Waco, Texas, when the women met together, with Mrs. Sallie Rochester Ford presiding. Mrs. Ford, an accomplished writer, convinced the gathering that Southern Baptist women should organize to support the struggling Home and Foreign Mission boards.[169]

Mary Webb was the first woman to arouse American Baptist women to missions, but Lottie Moon was its greatest sustainer. In McBeth's words: "Lottie Moon had done more to inspire, encourage, and channel the energies of Southern Baptist women than any other person."[170] That would be her "noble" legacy.

The Rev. B. H. Carroll addresses theological students in Texas.

Chapter 16

Benajah Harvey Carroll

(1843-1914)

The Giant That Shook Texas

The life of a poor but brilliant farm boy, B. H. Carroll, was marked by its major impact on the new frontier state of Texas and on the expansion and progress of the Southern Baptist Convention. Texas recently had gone through a number of cataclysmic changes, when the Carroll family arrived in Burleson County by ox wagon and horse in 1858; the Republic of Texas had won in 1836 a war with Mexico, merged into the United States in 1845 as the Lone Star State, and then served as the center of gravity for the Mexican War, which defined the borders of the state in 1848 through the Treaty of Guadalupe Hidalgo. A more terrible war in young Carroll's lifetime, the American Civil War (1861-65) would align Texas with the Confederate States and leave the young man wounded, impoverished, and bitter.

Texas was immense, in places unsettled, and over seven hundred miles wide from the Sabine River to El Paso. This was an era when the Cheyenne, Sioux, Comanche, and Apache nations were still unconquered, and the youthful Carroll hunted buffalo in the Panhandle. Baptists, such as his father and mother, were adept at overcoming adversity in the backwoods and the horizonless prairie in North America. Whether in Rhode Island, New York, North Carolina, or Texas, other Baptist yeomen hacked and plowed their way through the American frontier. The simplicity and intensity of the hymn-singing, Bible-reading Baptists made their faith almost the perfect one for the great wilderness. They were democratic and could adapt. The Baptists would become the dominant faith of Texas for decades because of their zeal and piety, and would only lose their numerical dominance to Catholics in 1998, because of immigration.

The transition of B. H. Carroll from reviler of preachers and skeptic of the Bible to conservative upholder of the Word, while sensational and incredible, is supported by sound research. He would rapidly assume a leading role in Texas in bolstering scholarship and religious education, as powerful factors for the Baptist clergy and laity. He would encourage the development of sophistication in young preachers through careful study. His remarkable career is mirrored by his commitment to Baylor University, where he was both trustee and professor; by his service to Southwestern Baptist Theological Seminary, of which he was the founder; and again by his tenure as pastor of the First Baptist Church of Waco for twenty-eight years. He was a powerful counselor and leader in the Southern Baptist Convention, but simultaneously was the defender of the country pastor and the small-church preacher.

B. H. Carroll (known in childhood as Harvey) was born on December 27, 1843 on a farm near Carrolton, Mississippi, the land worked by his parents, Benajah and Mary Eliza Carroll. Carroll's father was a self-educated country farmer and small-town preacher, scratching hard to feed and shelter a family of twelve children. The father's bivocation was a common feature of Baptist ministers in the nineteenth century. His mother was a devout and humble Christian woman. The Carrolls, in an astounding example of charity and faith, adopted twelve orphans, and, around 1850, the augmented family moved to Drew County, Arkansas. There Harvey demonstrated to his schoolmates a remarkable prowess in debate.[1]

In the fall of 1858, about three years before the Civil War, the Carroll clan migrated to Texas and settled near Caldwell, Burleson County. The journey involved a caravan made up of an ox wagon, a horse wagon, a hack, and a buggy. Harvey rode the point on a mule for the major part of the trip, but amused himself by reading while jogging along. Then, around the fire at night, he gave himself to books that he would read for hours, sometimes until dawn. His brother J. M. Carroll and other members of the family reported that the young Trailblazer often read three hundred pages a day, in the span of twenty to twenty-four hours. This absorption in books was one of B.H.'s enduring characteristics for sixty of his seventy-one years,[2] and the scope of his omnivorous appetite for knowledge included books by Hume, Rousseau, Voltaire, Calvin, and Gibbon.[3]

Arriving in Texas, over six feet tall but not yet fifteen years old, he enrolled in the school of T. K. Crittenden, two miles from Caldwell. After Carroll experienced one year of tutelage under Crittenden, the schoolmaster said, "Harvey, I can't teach you any further; you know more now than I do." Carroll then taught the elementary subjects at home to the younger siblings.[4]

This maturing prodigy kept religion at bay, at least until the trials of war wracked his life. In a family of a devout preacher and Christian kinsmen, he was a dedicated pagan and infidel. His exclusion of Christianity had come from his own skepticism and not because of ready access to anti-religious literature. He did not doubt the existence of God and angels, or the immortality of the soul. He was never an atheist, pantheist, or materialist. But he was dubious of the truth of Christianity when only thirteen years old.[5]

While the family was living in Arkansas, and he was age thirteen, he attended a revival, and responding to the urgings of the minister submitted like a robot to immersion. He became an unsaved member of a Baptist church. Mature for his years and stubborn in his fidelity to truth, he then requested the Arkansas church to withdraw his name, since he acknowledged that he was not converted. But this request was refused, since the church felt he was only depressed. However, he continued to read the Bible, finishing it many times in unbelief.[6]

This impasse with God was explained by Carroll in his advanced years:

> My answers had been educational. I did not believe that the Bible was God's revelation. I did not believe its miracles and doctrines. I did not believe, in any true sense, in the divinity or vicarious sufferings of Jesus. I had no confidence in professed conversion and regeneration. I had not felt lost nor did I feel saved. There was no perceptible, radical change in my disposition or affections. What I once loved, I still loved; what I once hated, I still hated.[7]

Baylor University

In 1859 Carroll was enrolled in Baylor, a Baptist institution (that would move to Waco and become a university) at Independence, Texas, where he joined the student body of 275 students. However, after the examination of his qualifications by President Rufus C. Burleson, he was enrolled at age sixteen as a junior because of his learning and high intellect.

During his two years at Baylor, he debated twice each week and soon won the distinction as the best debater at the school.[8] On a debate regarding the doctrines of Alexander Campbell, founder of the Disciples of Christ, he won on the affirmative side; then, reversing himself, he won on the negative side. Among the eight ministerial students present at Baylor was W. W. "Spurgeon" Harris, an eloquent debater, who, after the Civil War, would baptize Carroll a second time.[9]

The Civil War (1861-65)

The Civil War came abruptly, but discerning persons knew for decades that political and economic events had been building toward a crisis. When the war erupted, Texas, Louisiana, and Arkansas became the Confederate guardians on the western flank of the

Mississippi River and were suppliers of men and munitions to the Southern cause. On April 10, 1861, Carroll began active service on the Confederate side by joining McCullough's Texas Rangers; he rode with them for two hundred miles from Caldwell to the San Antonio frontier. His detachment consisted of twelve volunteers, including Carroll and his brother Andrew Fuller.[10]

In 1862 Carroll was transferred to the regular CSA army and assigned, with his brother Laban, to the Seventeenth Regiment of Texas Infantry. His courage and military discipline were notable and drew praise from the colonel in command. His principal military actions were at Perkins Landing (April 30, 1863), Milliken's Bend (June 7, 1863), and Mansfield (April 8, 1864). At Milliken's Bend, he led a daredevil charge through a half-mile of open field against the Northern breastworks. Finally, at the battle of Mansfield, Louisiana, his thigh was pierced by a Minie ball. His brother Laban, a Samson of two hundred pounds and six feet four and one-half inches in height, found him on the battlefield and carried him two miles to safety. But Carroll would suffer from this wound for the rest of his life.[11]

Carroll was realistic concerning the long-range effects of the war. Perhaps because he had such a good reputation as a fighter, in fire-light debates he was allowed to challenge the theories of his fellow-soldiers. In 1862 he spoke of the four "delusions of the South": (1) that Northern troops were cowardly; (2) that the South would win the war speedily; (3) that Northern Democrats were reliable allies of the South; and (4) that European countries would intervene in the struggle.[12] Despite his doubts that the South would be victorious in a final resurgence, he remained loyal until 1865, when the last CSA corps surrendered.[13]

Two tragedies marred his life during the earliest phase of the war. Carroll's father was severely injured in a farm accident that culminated in his death. Then, occurred a quick romance with a woman of shallow character in November 1861, while Carroll was on furlough. He married the woman on December 13, 1861, but because

of suspected fornication attributed to his new bride, the marriage
was terminated by jury on November 9, 1863. Later, in his famous
sermon, "My Infidelity and What Became of It," Carroll asserted
that the divorce "came from no sin on my part."

This misfortune literally blew apart Carroll's desire to live or have
respect for formal religion, although he was never blamed for the
unfortunate situation. In his fury and disillusionment, he sought to
dissolve his church connection, to reject "every semblance of Bible
belief," and on the battlefield to risk it all.[14] In 1862 the bitter soldier
said, "In seeking the field of war I seek death."[15] Tormented as he
was, Carroll would marry twice again in his lifetime, to pretty Ellen
Bell in 1866[16] and to his lifelong friend, Hallie Harrison, in 1899,[17]
after Ellen's death.

Meanwhile, serving in the Southern Army, he picked up the use
of tobacco, including smoking cigars, a habit he never abandoned.
His sharp wit and ridicule were increasingly directed against the
preachers that ministered to the half-fed troops, their wounded and
the dying.[18]

As the end of the war approached, conditions were desperate for
the large and hungry Carroll family. Remunerative work was scarce,
but the crippled B. H. Carroll assumed the financial obligations of
providing for his widowed mother and the younger children. His
first venture for one year was to direct a new school at Yellow Prairie,
about five miles from the Carroll farm. Then he moved to the town
of Caldwell, and it was there in 1865 that he heard with sorrow that
the gallant Southern commander Robert E. Lee had surrendered his
dwindling forces at Appomattox Courthouse.[19]

His mastery of the teachings of Epicurus, Zeno, Voltaire, Huxley,
and Darwin were now turning sour. As Carroll later explained in a
famous sermon: "I had turned my back on Christianity and had
found nothing in infidelity; happiness was gone, and death would
not come. The Civil War had left me a wounded cripple on crutches,
utterly poverty stricken and loaded with debt." The philosophies he

loved to quote, he found to be negations, and in his hour of need they were as consoling as pitiless pillows of granite.[20]

While twenty-one years old, the war still enduring in the fall 1865, his mother persuaded him to attend a Methodist camp meeting at Caldwell. When challenged by the preacher, he went to the altar to test God's Word, but he explained to bystanders that his heart was as cold as ice. Then, he recounted, "I did not see Jesus with my eye, but I seemed to see him—looking reproachfully and tenderly and pleadingly—I went once and forever, casting myself unreservedly—at Christ's feet, and—the rest came, indescribable and unspeakable and it has remained from that day until now."[21]

When Carroll reached home, he walked to his bedroom on his crutches, lay on the bed, and covered his face with his hands. His mother pulled his hands away and said, "My son, you have found the Lord." He spent the night beside her bed reading Bunyan's *Pilgrim's Progress*. "My soul was filled with such rapture," wrote Carroll. "I knew then as well as I know now that I would preach; that it would be my lifework; that I would have no other work."[22]

B. H. Carroll was baptized on May 27, 1866, in Davidson Creek by W. W. "Spurgeon" Harris, his Baylor schoolmate, and he became a member of the Caldwell church.[23] His ordination would be solemnized within a few weeks at the hands of a presbytery of three ministers, who would lay their hands on him. He would preach his first sermon at Caldwell; the occasion was a revival, where Carroll assisted but was not the principal evangelist. He addressed the veterans in the congregation, who had fought with the Second Texas Regiment at Corinth and Shiloh, asking them to give their souls to God. The result was that all of the soldiers present pressed forward to make their profession of faith.[24]

While his life had been turned inside-out, his full happiness would return with his pursuit of the lovely Ellen Bell. After the cessation of war, the Bell family had moved from Mississippi to Caldwell. Ellen, a Methodist, with no college training, but very pretty at age seventeen, completely captivated the young preacher, now twenty-three. She was quick and caustic, optimistic and good humored, and with determination to acquire a liberal education—just the qualities to snare the untried preacher. In their future marriage, she would be the realist, while Carroll would be the "star dwelling idealist."[25]

Carroll rode horseback for nearly ninety miles to Waco to obtain the consent of Baylor College president, Rufus C. Burleson, to officiate at the wedding. The couple's only possession would be a feather bed, and Carroll dressed himself in a borrowed coat. Despite his poverty and a limp from his war wound, Carroll—with posture as straight as an arrow, six feet, four inches tall, florid face, and eyes that were gray and animated—was regarded by many men and women as the most startlingly handsome man they had ever seen. At maturity and for most of his life, he would have a full brown beard. The couple was married at the Caldwell church on December 28, 1866,[26] and the couple would be blessed with nine children.

During one of Carroll's first revivals, Ellen professed her faith at home, where "the light had burst into her heart," and she immediately joined the Baptist church.[27]

Despite the inward peace of Carroll and his young bride, the countryside was in turmoil. At the end of the Civil War, Texas experienced cultural, economic, and moral collapse. Lawlessness became general. Even Governor Pendleton Murrah and other state officers were compelled to flee for safety to Mexico. The struggling preacher undertook the burden of supporting his wife, mother, and the younger siblings in the family. He also shouldered debts of seven thousand dollars, of which four thousand were not his legal burden.

In a personal struggle lasting about three years, Carroll taught school during the week and preached on Saturdays and Sundays in Burleson County, Texas, at churches that paid almost nothing. When the school and churches could not give him even produce to keep his family alive, he tried farming to keep afloat. The weather worked against him, and the rains drowned out his efforts to grow corn and cotton. Still, after revivals in small churches, three members of his family were baptized.[28]

The Gifted Preacher

Carroll's success as a preacher was mounting. He was approved as the moderator of a church conference and a messenger-delegate to the Sunday School Convention at Plantersville.[29] He reported in the January 16, 1867, edition of the *Texas Baptist Herald*, that he led services in which there were seventeen professions of faith, followed by baptisms. Then, he inserted in the *Herald* (August 2, 1868 edition) that at Spring Hill, ten miles from Waco, he led a revival that produced twenty-six candidates for baptism, with a new church constituted. Then, he raised eight hundred dollars to begin the New Hope Church, which later he would serve as pastor.[30]

As he gained experience, he made steady strides in conquering his major liabilities. Carroll had two basic faults: a violent temper and, because of his intrinsic kindness, poor judgment in appraising men; this defect followed him to his grave. He failed to consider that men are not always ruled by conscience and high principles. As his brother J. M. Carroll reflected, B. H. Carroll was "fearfully quick tempered." This candid brother then added, "Grace did more for Harvey Carroll than for any other man I have ever known. Never was a life more thoroughly made over."[31]

In an incredible stroke of good fortune, the twenty-five-year-old preacher was invited by President Burleson to deliver the commencement address at Waco University. The service, held on July 17, 1869, stirred the crowd, with Carroll giving a graphic description of the Jewish people witnessing Christ's crucifixion. Some of the founding members of the New Hope Church attending the service invited Carroll to spend a week with them and there to consider becoming the pastor of their new church, at a salary of five hundred dollars a year. This offer was a God-send, since at Masterville, in route to Waco, Carroll had lost to a thief all the money he had, a twenty-dollar gold piece.[32]

After his decision to accept the new pastorate, Carroll made the three-day trip to New Hope in a borrowed wagon, bearing Ellen his

bride and B. H., Jr. Behind, the family left an infant daughter buried
in the cemetery and some precious books given to friends. Their new
abode was in comfortable quarters on the plantation of General
James Harrison.[33] But this stay in New Hope would pass fleetingly.

The God-blessed fortunes of Carroll would be embellished suddenly like the passing of a meteor. The most distinguished Baptist
church in Texas was the First Baptist Church of Waco, and in 1869
that church lost its minister. Normally, it would be beyond the realm
of possibility that a young rawbone preacher could fill that position.
Dr. Rufus C. Burleson, president of Waco University, reluctantly
consented to preach two Sundays a month at Waco to supply, but he
did not desire to serve as full-time pastor at Waco because of his
academic duties.

In order to relieve Dr. Burleson, Carroll was asked by the college
president if he would reduce his duties at New Hope and become its
half-time minister and, then, for two weeks in the month, serve the
First Baptist Church at Waco. Carroll was awed by the proposal that
would give him such prominence and was reluctant at first to take
the position. He would later write: "I greatly distrusted my fitness
for the important position. I was young and inexperienced."[34] However, in 1870, both men agreed to serve together the three-hundred-
member Waco church, and at the close of the year, Carroll was
persuaded to become the full-time pastor at Waco, with a salary of
fifteen hundred dollars a year. Thus began a commitment of twenty-
eight years by Carroll as the spiritual leader of the Waco church.[35]

The process had already begun in the Trailblazer, with prayer and
Bible-study, that would give him greater maturity and seasoning.
Remarkable changes would be wrought in a person once ultra-sen-
sitive, with trigger-quick temper, bitter wit, and cynicism; now, with
newly acquired humility, he boarded needy young preachers without
finances, such as Jeff D. Ray and George W. Truett. He rarely left
his Waco pulpit except to preach at a revival, to promote missions,
or to bolster the forces of Prohibition.

Carroll made it clear to all that preaching was the knightliest, most appealing, and noblest task that man ever undertook; this embrace included both the city pastor and the country vicar. He once said, "there is something about preaching which affects me even more than the approach of death."[36] Despite this bizarre statement about his calling, B. H. Carroll was a stern disciplinarian. During his tenure, a number of the "movers and shakers" of Waco would be arraigned before the church for immoral conduct or heresy, and, despite this, some would embrace him as their closest friend.

The style of Carroll's preaching was direct and practical, with frequent reference to history and classical writers. He was a near-genius in his retentive ability, sometimes able to recall the exact page of a reference or to quote long passages of poetry. He preached with an expressive face and eyes. His posture throughout his ministry was always erect, and his full brown beard gave him the aura of a prophet. At age forty, he was already one of the outstanding orators of the Southern Baptist Convention.[37]

As to the critical character of preaching in his life, there is a quotation from his sermon "I Magnify My Office" (Romans 11: 13):

> I magnify my office, O my God, as I get nearer home. I can say more truthfully every year, I thank God that He put me in this office; I thank Him that He would not let me have any other; that He shut me up to this glorious work; and when I get home among the blessed on the bank of the everlasting deliverance and look back toward time and all of its clouds and sorrows, and pains, and privations, I expect to stand up and shout for joy that down there in the fog and mists, down there in the dust and struggle, God let me be a preacher. I magnify my office in life; I magnify it in death; I magnify it in heaven; I magnify it, whether poor, or rich, whether sick or well, whether strong or weak, anywhere, everywhere, among all people, in any crowd. Lord God, I am glad that I am a preacher, that I am a preacher of the glorious gospel of Jesus Christ.[3]

This preacher had an enormous vocabulary. Although he knew no Hebrew, he was a master in Latin, had a working knowledge in ancient Greek, and was an expert in English. He was a voracious reader of biography, science, poetry, and romance, and possessed an astounding grasp of history.[39] But in harmony with this erudition, he accepted the whole Bible as the inspired Word of God and yielded fully to the authority expressed in it.[40]

Carroll was the prime leader and innovator in supporting the Waco (Baptist) Association and promoted such varied activities as orphanages, old ministers' relief, Christian education, and missions. His impact on home missions was remarkable. Pastor Carroll was preeminent in founding mission stations and chapels around Waco. The First Baptist Church of Waco under his guidance led the state in gifts to missions, and the Mission Board of the General Association made Waco its center. Carroll's church not only supplied numbers of foreign mission volunteers, but this single church donated one-third of all the home, state, and foreign missions support given by Texas Baptists.[41]

In this period of long cattle drives and mule-drawn wagons, and little excitement in the towns, it was not uncommon for ministers of various denominations to publicly debate the Biblical soundness of their respective faiths. Although Carroll was a superb debater, he never believed that debate was the premier way to promote the truth.

However, in 1872 Carroll was drawn into a great debate at Davilla, Texas, with the Methodist star-preacher, Dr. Fisher, on the topic of baptism. Fisher, an accomplished orator, challenged the Waco Baptists to produce a champion, and Dr. Burleson requested the twenty-nine-year-old Carroll to represent the Baptists well. Carroll not only prepared to vigorously assert the Baptist doctrinal view, but anticipated expertly before the debate almost every conceivable point to be made by his opponent. Dr. Fisher was vanquished and never sought a return bout. As Carroll stated: "God [never] commanded or authorized any man to sprinkle water and just water upon any person, place or thing."[42]

The tender side of Carroll was manifest as he served other ministers. Brother Hurt, an uneducated missionary from the Texas frontier, would arrive in a rickety old buggy to spend time at the Carroll house. Early in the morning, after one of these unannounced visits, Carroll was seen polishing the old man's worn boots. When asked what he was doing, Carroll replied with a twinkle, "I am washing a saint's feet."[43]

On another occasion, Jeff D. Ray, a Waco University student destined to be a well-known Baptist minister, fell sick for weeks from typhoid fever. Dr. Carroll ministered to the student, who was unable to stand, and bathed him from head to foot, rubbed him down, and carried him back to the bed.[44]

An exceptional revival meeting organized by the First Baptist Church of Waco began on September 13, 1893, and lasted eight weeks. There was a momentous impact on every church in the city, and hundreds were converted. Carroll preached two sermons a day, and young George W. Truett, later a national leader, preached for three days when Carroll became sick. The revival produced 173 additions to the church.[45]

The Great Waco Fire

On Sunday, February 22, 1877, in the seventh year of Carroll's pastoral service in Waco, a spectacular fire consumed the Baptist church. First it destroyed the beautiful City Market Opera House, spread to an adjoining private residence, and then crossed over to the church. After the initial shock dissipated, Pastor Carroll proposed that a new church be built but that the construction costs be paid as the work progressed. The financial cloud was lifted, since Carroll's personal credit was so good in Waco that he could borrow thousands of dollars on his plain note.[46]

The ground floor of the church was completed in 1880 and was immediately utilized for Sunday School and preaching services. Prior to that, the church had conducted its activities at the courthouse, the chapel of Waco University, and the men's dormitory. Despite the severe problems it faced, the church cooperated with other congregations, supported home and foreign missions, and increased the pastor's salary, already the highest in Texas. The membership rejoiced when the church edifice was completed in 1883.[47]

At a period in history when Baptists detested the terms "to organize," as suggestive of outside control, Carroll was the consummate organizer. Under Carroll, the First Baptist Church set new standards for church efficiency and organization. The church expansion and activities included plans for a church library, a choir, a Sunday School that utilized literature published by the Sunday School Board, and a formal church budget—anticipating by several decades the budget pattern of Southern Baptists.[48]

In 1883, after the fire, the Southern Baptist Convention accepted Carroll's invitation to conduct the Convention's annual meeting in the new church building. However, the unexpected massive surge of messengers into Waco came close to inundating the newly-constructed church and its supporters. The messengers were to be lodged for five days in the houses of church members. But, instead of one thousand delegates, the Baptist messengers became part of the largest congregation ever hosted to that period by a Southern Baptist Convention. The local church supporters were staggered when they discovered that they would feed and house 3000 to 3500 delegates— a record number.[49] Still, the convention was warmly hosted and praised for its success.

Carroll was direct and bluntly honest on civic issues, and he directed his mobilized army with integrity. He wrote a tract against dancing and was well-known for his aversion to dirty stories and speech. In 1873, he led his congregation to include in the church covenant an article "to abstain from the use of or traffic in intoxicating liquor as a beverage." This was in an historical period when many preachers and church members drank liquor, but generally in moderation. His bold stand made Carroll, in 1887, state chairman in support of the prohibition initiative in the state referendum. His stand against the use of liquor was so absolute that a supporting preacher said: "That man [Carroll] would live on corn cobs and stump water the rest of his life rather than to turn Texas over to the whiskey whelps."[50]

He became a protagonist in another famous debate held in Waco in 1887, on the topic of liquor traffic. Dr. Carroll, leader of the Texas Prohibition forces, faced his opponent, the respected U. S. Senator Roger Q. Mills. The issue was contentious and volatile. A huge crowd, boisterous and vocal, many of them onlookers from outlying cities and towns, chortled and applauded as the debate played for three hours. Carroll lost the battle at the polls, but years later he won the debate, when Texas elected to become dry. Carroll's brilliant campaigns, which included the debate, determined that public sale of liquor would be prohibited.[51]

The two preachers whose beliefs affected Carroll most were John A. Broadus, president of the Southern Baptists, and Charles H. Spurgeon, the great London minister who fought against liberalism in the Downgrade Controversy. When Spurgeon died in 1892, Carroll praised him in a laudatory sermon. Carroll met Broadus in 1874, and declared that Dr. Broadus had a greater influence over his life "than all other men put together." Broadus was president of the Southern Baptist Theological Seminary at Louisville when Professor C. H. Toy, who had studied in Germany, embraced "Higher Criticism," and then at the Seminary began to assert the evolutionist doctrines of Charles Darwin. Broadus felt that Darwin's views compromised the Baptist tenet on the inspiration of the Scriptures. As a consequence, Dr. Toy, a friend of missionary Lottie Moon, was fired in 1871 for his liberal views.[52]

In a broad sense, Southern Baptist attitudes on Darwin's theories were reflected by SBC President George W. McDaniel in a 1926 speech: "This Convention accepts Genesis as teaching that man was the special creation of God, and rejects every theory, evolution or other, which teaches that man originated in, or came by way of, a lower animal ancestry." By agreement, it was moved [and affirmed] that the statement of the president was the sentiment of the Convention.

The Hayden Affair

In 1894 Carroll became involved in the Hayden affair, one of the most acrimonious church fights in Baptist history. In 1853, because of reasons involving education, a large Baptist element, including the Waco Church, withdrew from the Texas State Convention; in 1868 the new group became the Baptist General Association of Texas (BGAT). In 1871 Carroll became chairman of its Committee for Schools and Education. The leading figure of the General Association (and often its president or vice president between 1871 and 1884) was R. C. Burleson, but after 1874 Carroll became its foremost spokesman.[53]

The oldest Southern Baptist seminary, the Southern Baptist Theological Seminary (SBTS) was founded at Furman University in 1859 in Greenville, South Carolina. In 1877, the Southern Baptist Seminary moved to its permanent home, Louisville, Kentucky.[54] This mother-seminary was regarded with pride and sentiment throughout the South, but geographically it was too distant from Texas, especially for ministerial students with little money.

Then, some enlightened Baptists on both sides of the Mason-Dixon Line began discussions on cooperation in developing model Baptist colleges and schools. Among Southern leaders striving to promote Christian education were the brothers B. H. and James M. Carroll, John A. Broadus, J. B. Gambrell, and T. T. Eaton. Their hope was that Baptists in the North and South would jointly provide quality education to Baptist colleges. Thus the American Baptist Education Society (ABES), composed of various shades of Baptists, was formed in 1888 to promote "under Baptist auspices" Christian education in North America.[55]

However, these efforts floundered when too many resources and too much money were concentrated on developing the University of Chicago. The Baptists lost denominational control of that promising university, despite the vast fortune of John D. Rockefeller, Sr., and the acumen of President William Rainey Harper. However, in 1891,

B. H. Carroll was exulting that the American Baptist Education Society "knows no North, no South, no East, no West."[56]

Until 1900 Baptist schools in Southern states were under the influence of Baptist associations, state conventions, and occasionally the Southern Baptist Convention. New and more sophisticated schools were urgently needed in Texas, since between 1860 and 1900 the population had increased 404%, while the number of Baptists in that state catapulted by 1,643%.[57]

A charter was issued to Baylor University at Waco on August 7, 1886, this move consolidating Waco University and Baylor, the latter having previously been maintained at Independence, Texas.[58] The consolidated institution also included the new Baylor College for Women at Belton. B. H. Carroll, in the years before this development, probably the dominant figure in Baptist education in Texas, was elected president of the trustees and held this post until 1907. The new university president was Dr. Rufus C. Burleson, who was the same educator-preacher who had invited Carroll to the First Baptist Church.[59]

Baylor University ventured forward on faith and constructed two new multi-storied buildings, Burleson Hall and Old Main. The financing of the edifices and university operations were considered sound in 1890, even when free tuition was provided for twenty-six preacher students and twenty of their children.[60]

In 1891 Carroll reported that the gifted young minister, George W. Truett, had been enlisted to raise money to retire Baylor's debts, in response to standards set by the American Baptist Education Society. Truett who labored for seven months, raised thirty-seven thousand dollars in cash, lands, and pledges. The campaign was successful, and by 1893 not a single cent was owed by the university for grounds or buildings.

In 1893 a Department of Bible Teaching was initiated at Baylor University, with B. H. Carroll as dean. Carroll held the chair of exegesis and systematic theology, while Dr. Burleson held the chair of pastoral duties, and J. H. Luther, the chair of homiletics. There were seventy-five students enrolled. In 1897, there was added a chair of Hebrew and Greek, to be filled by John S. Tanner, that greatly strengthened the curriculum.[61]

In the 1890s thirteen Baptist colleges in Texas, not established by the Baptist State Convention, were suffering financial distress and in danger of collapse. However, Baylor University, chartered by the Baptist Convention, was fiscally solvent and its future support was a separate issue. In order to render life-saving assistance to the distressed colleges, the Texas Baptist Convention referred the matter to a committee of thirteen that evolved into the Texas Baptist Education Commission (TBEC),[62] with J. M. Carroll as its financial manager.

The concept of a united campaign to eliminate the debts of all Baptist schools in Texas was at first the vision of state mission secretary, J. B. Gambrell, and then of James M. Carroll, financial manager of Baylor Female College at Belton. The colleges were "federated" under Texas law and then their debts were referred to the Education Commission (TBEC). Baylor University was without debt, but a special campaign for a $250,000 endowment was included in the unified effort.[63]

James Carroll was convinced that his brother B. H. Carroll, pastor of the First Baptist Church for nearly three decades, should be the chairman of the combined effort. A tragedy would intervene to force the issue. On November 6, 1897, Carroll's beloved wife Ellen Bell died. His life drastically changed, and, from that time he became instantly a lonely old man.[64]

After close friends guaranteed Carroll's salary for one year to enable him to pursue the financial campaign, he resigned in December 1898 his pastorate of the Waco church. Only fifty-five years old but despondent, often ill, and almost totally deaf, he now lived for "the general cause of Christian education." While it was presumed that he would resume his teachings at Baylor University at some stage, it was clear that he was not thinking of organizing a theological seminary. What became manifest was that Carroll, despite his profound sorrow and his physical impairments, was a Trailblazer of tremendous faith.[65] His goal, as future chairman of the Baptist campaign to rescue its colleges, would be to raise half a million dollars.[66]

B. H. Carroll took office on January 1, 1899, with the Texas Baptist Education Commission. J. M. Carroll, his brother, served as his principal assistant. Within the year, some portion of the $60,109 that was raised was used to salvage Decatur and Howard Payne colleges. The campaign extended into 1901, and in that year the goal of $100,000 was raised despite the continuing illness of B. H. Carroll.[67] The aging patriarch, now with white hair and an impressive beard, still bore his huge body with no slouching. His eloquence, prestige, and vision had persuaded influential friends to save their Baptist schools, some of which could have been lost forever. But the principal reward probably was the denominational unity shaped by the rescue campaign.[68]

The great progress made in Texas in ministerial education was manifested between 1901 and 1908. This achievement should be ascribed in large part to Carroll, and marked by Carroll's return by 1902 to theological teaching at Baylor University. His faculty salary in 1902 of $1,950 for nine months was underwritten by generous friends.[69] At Waco, he continued to support ministerial education by soliciting new donations.

In 1899 Oscar H. Cooper became president of Baylor University in place of the eminent Rufus C. Burleson. Then in 1901 Cooper joined Carroll in creating the new Theological Department. The Baylor theological faculty was strengthened by adding to the faculty Professor Albert Henry Newman, recently of McMaster University, Toronto.[70]

Carroll, as long-time chairman of Baylor's trustees, had announced in 1901 the new theological department and predictably made the annual report on Baylor to the Baptist state convention. He would confront a man of sturdier mettle than its past president, when S. P. Brooks became president of Baylor University in 1902. Brooks was embarrassed to find himself beholden to one of his faculty members

[Carroll] who taught Bible. Brooks had a notable background, as an A. B. graduate of Baylor and an M.A. from Yale, and had served as an excellent teacher of economics and history. Between 1901 and 1904, he would nurture 80 to 101 ministerial students. Beginning in 1902, Brooks asserted his prerogative, as the chief college administrator, to take from Carroll the annual report to the Baptist convention.[71] Historical documents, unfortunately, do not adequately reflect the intensity and tenor of the meetings when Brooks carved out his partial independence in a confrontation with B. H. Carroll.

Engaging the Great Controversies

Carroll was a distinguished church statesman, not only as the pastor of the most influential Texas church, the First Baptist of Waco, but as a committed educator in its most promising school, Baylor University. He was a leader or member of numerous committees, serving the SBC Convention, the Texas State Convention, and the Waco Association. He dominated work in the Waco Association for about twenty years. He also served as president of its Mission Board from 1874 to 1888, and again from 1889 to 1892. His duties involved visiting each church in the association during the year, holding meetings, and instructing on missions.[72] Not only was Carroll deeply involved in almost every aspect of Baptist politics and progress, he had an irresistible attraction to contentious issues and loved a good fight. If there arose a major denominational issue, it was almost a certainty that in some way Carroll would become involved and bring along his wisdom and perceptions.

The fountainhead of the most corrosive issues to Texas Baptist and most Southern Baptists in this epoch was the problem of Landmarkism. However, Baptists North and South would be compelled to discuss territories, cooperation, and monetary resources. Then, there was the possibility that Baptists might unite with the Disciples of Christ. Carroll served on a SBC committee to determine if union on a scriptural basis was feasible; it wasn't. Carroll attended his first Southern Baptist Convention in 1874, when it met at Jefferson, Texas. He was an ardent supporter of such denominational conventions, attending twenty-two sessions in all.[73] Including the issue of the Disciples of Christ, Carroll was in the thick of problems, such as the "Whitsitt Affair"; on this question he was consulted in Chattanooga (1896) and Wilmington (1897). He participated in conferences on young people's work in the South and in discussions on whether to establish a SBC Sunday School Board. Then, for a long time, Carroll would grapple with the Landmark issue.

Landmarkism Becomes Major Issue

According to McBeth, since the hundred or more references to "church" (*Ecclesia*) in the New Testament refer to one local congregation, this designation to Landmarkers was remarkably significant. Thus, in the decentralized Baptist structure, other bodies such as associations and conventions were regarded only as "religious societies" and had no Biblical church functions.[74]

Since "church" and "kingdom" are synonymous in the New Testament, and only Baptist churches (under a variety of names) comprise that "kingdom," then only Baptists (according to the Landmarkers) had the authority from God to preach, baptize, and celebrate the Lord's Supper. However, Graves denied numerous times that he believed that only Baptists could be saved.[75]

Landmarkism, which intruded as a corrosive doctrine, would plague the Southern Baptists and Texas Baptists for years. It was the creation of J. R. Graves, the editor of the *Tennessee Baptist*. Landmarkism opposed the existence of the Southern Baptist Convention (as an expression of centralism), emphasized the importance of each church as a holy succession, was suspicious of higher education, and sought to limit missionaries to those called through local churches.

The Landmark doctrine became a nagging force throughout the nation, but particularly in the South and in Texas, in its short-term

George W. Truett Preaching at the National Capitol (1920)

effect on missions contributions. Graves was a native of Vermont, a former Congregationalist, and his state Baptist paper, the *Tennessee Baptist*, would rank high in popularity in Texas. While Landmarkism emphasized the autonomy and authority of the local church, church autonomy has been a key tenet of the Baptist faith from its earliest days to the present; it served as a basic doctrine to protect the local church from abuse of power.

The advocacy of Landmarkism in Texas was led by Samuel A. Hayden, editor in Dallas of the *Texas Baptist and Herald*, who was frequently in written conflict with J. B. Cranfill, editor in Waco of the *Baptist Standard*.[76] While there were many Landmark supporters in Texas, Hayden's most prestigious ally was Baylor President Rufus C. Burleson, and the controversy would strain the longtime friendship of Burleson and Carroll.[77]

In 1894 Hayden circulated a letter and attacked the Baptist state Mission Board for allowing mission work to deteriorate, accused it of financial extravagance, and warned that a crippling deficit was impending. Basically, the issue was the Landmark doctrine, although the quarrel also involved clashing personalities, the costs of sustaining a religious bureaucracy, and the financial burden borne by the state mission board.[78] When the Texas Convention rejected the Landmark measures prepared by Hayden as remedies, Hayden then directed his assaults against the Baptist state leaders. Carroll, while not intimidated, was determined that the state mission board would not have a financial deficit as predicted by Hayden.[79]

With the assistance of his young assistant, George W. Truett (who had vigorously spearheaded the fight to eliminate Baylor's debts), Carroll now sprang into the fray. He took leave from the Waco church and solicited gifts throughout Texas to sustain missions. As a result, Carroll became the chief target of abusive attacks by Hayden. These insults continued, even when a surplus for missions was achieved by the campaign.[80]

The complex struggle would go on until 1899 and became involved with the stifling Gospel Mission Movement of Lottie Moon's colleague, T. P. Crawford, and the hounding and forced resignation of President William H. Whitsitt of the Southern Baptist Theological Seminary, Louisville, for truthfully asserting that Baptists originally did not immerse and had their origin in the religious revolution in the seventeenth century.

This acrimony so wracked Carroll and his allies, that in 1896 the Texas Convention (since 1886 united, and bearing the name Baptist General Convention of Texas, BGCT) accused Hayden of "undermining the mission work." In 1897 and 1898 Hayden was denied a seat at the State Convention, and he sued the convention for $100,000.[81] He was disqualified as an independent messenger (delegate), and not because he was a representative of a church or association; this is a fine point of Baptist logic, since the "messenger" represents himself only and not his church. Hayden's followers were largely discredited by 1899, and the Landmark defectors organized the Baptist Missionary Association (BMA), while the other Landmarkers scattered to their various churches.[82]

At this stage, B. H. Carroll, between 1883 and 1886, played a major role in consolidating five associations in Texas into one, the Baptist General Convention of Texas. The two Sunday School Conventions were joined and the two newspapers, *The Texas Baptist Herald* and *The Texas Baptists*, were merged. After this monumental achievement, Carroll commented: "—Let every feeling of sectionalism and alienation be buried beneath the Cross. Let unity, fraternity, and loyalty to our Lord characterize every step of our advance.—"[83]

Out of the exclusivism of Landmarkism thrived such practices as "closed communion" (with non-Baptists excluded), opposition to mission boards and structure (including the SBC Foreign Mission Board), and opposition to strengthening the Southern Baptist Convention. Even immersion, as sometime practiced by Congregationalists, Presbyterians, and Methodists, was referred to by Landmarkers as "alien immersion." Some Baptist historians have characterized B. H. Carroll as a Landmarker because of his defense of the local church and his part in the resignation of President William H.

Whitsitt of the Southern Baptist Theological Seminary.[84] But Carroll was a complex figure that must be examined with probity, and certainly he was no Landmarker, since he fought that doctrine, as promoted by Samuel A. Hayden, and helped defeat the expansion into Texas of the Gospel Mission Movement, as led by T. P. Crawford of China.

Through the travails produced by Landmarkism—and its ultimate rejection by the vast majority of Baptists—the definition as to the meaning of Baptist faith was refined. The Baptists in North America tended to regard themselves as a unique people, quite able to nurture the Good News in a pure form.[85]

The Whitsitt Controversy

The Whitsitt affair of 1896-97 divided Baptists in America and shocked even the religious leaders who had been fed a legend that Baptists originated in unbroken line from the days of John the Baptist. The legend was not true, and the scholarly Baptist academician, President William H. Whitsitt of the Southern Baptist Theological Seminary in Louisville, who revealed the truth, would be reviled and forced to leave his position. The move to dismiss him was particularly strong in Texas, and would prevail, despite the attempt by Carroll to reach a reasoned and moderate assessment.

Dr. Whitsitt at the Louisville seminary had been the chairman of its Church History Department in 1872, became its president in 1895, and was probably the best technical scholar among the Southern Baptists. Whitsitt, in an ironical occurrence, had been ordained by a presbytery that included J. R. Graves, the founder of Landmarkism (and an early advocate of the false teaching of church succession of Baptists from Apostolic days). However, after his visit to Europe and study in 1880 in Great Britain, Leipzig, and Berlin,[86] Whitsitt adopted the modern scientific method of history and discarded the notion of Baptist "historical succession." He also discarded the view that Baptists had always immersed new converts.

Through his research, Whitsitt concluded that before adopting immersion around 1641, Baptists in England and America baptized by sprinkling and pouring.[87]

The reaction was intense when Whitsitt published his findings, first anonymously as editorials in 1880 in a New York Congregationalist weekly; this was followed by an open article in 1895 for Johnson's *Universal Cyclopaedia.* Many professors of the Southern Baptist seminary and Baptist editors from the Eastern seaboard supported him. Generally, inland and western Baptists, particularly those influenced by the views of J. R. Graves and Landmarkism, attacked him. Whitsitt's findings also were opposed in 1895 by T. T. Eaton, editor of the *Western Recorder,* and violently so by J. H. Spencer.[88] The matter was volatile and would require intensive discussion by the Southern Baptist Convention.

The Baptists in Texas almost *in toto* opposed the findings of Whitsitt, and various spokesmen clamored to cut support for the Louisville seminary or require the resignation of its entire faculty. Opposing editors, S. A. Hayden and J. B. Cranfill, joined in the attack on the Whitsitt doctrine. Texans were also inflamed when it was learned that Whitsitt gave his sister approval to join a Presbyterian church.[89]

In Carroll's considered opinion, the seminary trustees, a self-perpetuating board not under the authority of the SBC, would have to sit in judgment on its faculty.[90] This would directly involve Carroll, since he had been a trustee of the Louisville Seminary from 1894 to 1911. Carroll was cautioned by distinguished SBTS scholar John R. Sampey, professor of Old Testament, to be temperate. In May 7, 1896, Carroll wrote to the *Baptist Standard:*

> I love the seminary. I love it much. I don't want to hurt that. And I do deeply love Dr. Whitsitt. Let us keep cool, brethren, and get before us all the facts. The foundation of God standeth sure. Hear Davy Crockett. Be sure you are right—then go ahead.[91]

Carroll's calm attitude was in sharp contrast to the strident calls by many Texans to withdraw support from the vulnerable seminary or else remove its faculty. At Wilmington, North Carolina, May 6-7, 1897, the seminary trustees debated the issue that was greatly undermining the financial support in the Southwest for the Louisville theological school. Carroll presented a motion that the trustees determine "our best judgment of the facts and merits of the case."[92]

Then, Professor Whitsitt, unlike Gallileo who bent his knee to his inquisitors, made this courageous statement:

> That on the historical question involved in the discussion I find myself out of agreement with some honored historians; but what I have written is the outcome of patient and honest research and I can do no otherwise than to reaffirm my convictions and maintain my position. But if in the future it shall ever be made to appear that I have erred in my conclusions I would promptly and cheerfully say so. I am a searcher after truth and will gladly hail every helper in my work.[93]

Now the truth was out, and the Landmarkers circled their prey, knowing he would fall.

In 1897 Carroll had reached the conclusion that the Whitsitt Affair placed the Southern Baptist Convention in jeopardy. He became convinced that the Seminary, if necessary, should sever its narrow connections that bound it to the Southern Baptist Convention. He openly stated that "You cannot hold Southern Baptists in alignment for the Seminary with Dr. Whitsitt as President." While Carroll could not prove or disprove historical succession, he was certain that the Convention was worth more than the seminary. Therefore, the sacrificial lamb must go. The Landmark fury abated and the crisis ended, when on July 13, 1898, W. H. Whitsitt resigned as president of the seminary.[94] In retrospect, the motives of Carroll on this issue can be understood, but perhaps more admiration should be given to Dr. William Whitsitt, in this instance, for his pure intellectual courage.

The Gospel Mission Movement had peculiar roots that intertwined with the Landmark and Hayden issues. Gospel Mission was the creature of Southern Baptist missionary to China Tarleton Perry Crawford. Crawford, from his base in Shantung Province, North China, entered into a fierce debate over how to promote missions, partly with his colleagues but principally with veteran China missionary Jesse Boardman Hartwell. Crawford, in an extension of Landmark philosophy, wanted missionaries to be supported by individual churches, and opposed the directions of the Foreign Mission Board. He would become more radical, and, in 1893-94, he defected from the SBC with ten Baptist missionaries, advocates of the Gospel Mission Movement. Crawford, while in America, induced about fifty anti-missionary churches to leave the Southern Baptist Convention.

For years, Carroll was a member of the SBC Foreign Mission Board. From that vantage point, it became apparent that the Gospel Mission Movement was not only hostile to the Foreign Mission Board but wanted no mission boards of any kind. Under the logic of the movement, if someone wanted to be a missionary, he went abroad freely, and had faith that the Holy Spirit would send funds. In contradiction, most Baptist missionaries were more practical and generally sought financial support from a cluster of churches (societal mode) or by a Convention (centralized mode). Seeing mission support dry up, Carroll in 1894 asked the Waco Baptist Church to grant him summer leave to fight both Samuel A. Hayden and his Landmark message and to obtain funds to block the Gospel Mission Movement. In Texas, as a consequence, Gospel Mission was stopped in its tracks.[95]

The problems faced by the Texas Baptists were almost unending. Intruding into the decades from the 1860s to the 1880s was the persisting issue between the Northern Home Mission Society and the Southern Home Mission Board regarding territorial jurisdiction in the appointment of home missionaries. During the Civil War and into the 1880s, the American Baptist Home Mission Society of New

York asserted its right to appoint missionaries anywhere in North America and to send missionaries and teachers into the South, where the Southern Baptist Convention was engaged.[96] Since there were many Northern missionaries in Texas, there was a great need for support money.

In the 1880's, the struggle culminated on the basis of a movement to commit Texas Baptists to joint cooperation with the Society of New York and the Home Mission Board of the SBC. Texas was financially desperate in the post-Civil War period, since the Southern economy was in ruins and there was an army of Northern Baptists in Texas, with a horde of their Texas supporters. In this hard battle, Carroll threw himself boldly on the side of solidarity of Texas work under Southern Baptist Home Missions.[97] He believed that joint cooperation with the New York society would lead to confusion and strife in the Texas work. In this assessment, Carroll displayed great foresight in swinging his fellow Baptists into support of the Southern Board.[98]

When the issue of whether the SBC Home Mission Board should be abolished—a conclusion that would have pleased the Landmarkers—Carroll maintained that the Board was a valuable asset and fought to preserve it. Carroll took the stance that the Home Board needed to expand its ministry into the frontiers of Texas, Oklahoma Indian Territory, and New Mexico. Against well-respected leaders of the opposition, he spoke on the question at Richmond in 1888, at the Southern Baptist Convention. Not surprisingly, Carroll won the day, with his address on "The Necessity of Home Missions in Texas."[99]

Many years later, at Chattanooga (1906), Carroll supported the evangelism initiatives of the Home Mission Board. His victory encouraged evangelism throughout the South and inspired him to create a Chair of Evangelism (unheard of at the time) at Southwestern Theological Seminary.[100]

As Baker recounts it, Carroll attended his first Southern Baptist Convention in 1874, when it met in Jefferson, Texas. He was an enthusiastic supporter of the denominational convention, attending twenty-two sessions in all. In 1878, at age thirty-five, Carroll preached the Convention sermon in Nashville and later delivered other ser-mons—at Richmond (1888), Atlanta (1892), Washington (1895), Hot Springs (1900), Chattanooga (1906), and Hot Springs (1908).[101]

The Sunday School has been one of the most dynamic features of Baptist religious training in twentieth century America, even though derived from Methodist practice. Still, its organized form in the South was slow to take shape. In 1845 there probably were fewer than five hundred Baptist churches with Sunday Schools in the South, so the support base was not strong. The first SBC Sunday School Board was established in 1863, but it failed in its efforts to create a permanent printing program, a vital aspect of Sunday School work. As a consequence, many churches in the South purchased their Sunday School materials from the American Baptist Publica-tion Society in Philadelphia, and many Baptists wished this coop-eration to continue.[102]

The next attempt to create a SBC Sunday School Board would be successful. In 1890, at Fort Worth, a SBC committee met to con-sider the matter. The feasibility of a Board was seriously debated and produced a majority report (favoring a new Board) and also a minor-ity report. With Carroll backing the majority, the Sunday School Board became a reality. The second SBC Sunday School Board took form in May 1891 and was approved in Texas by a resolution made by Carroll.[103]

A third North-South dispute broke out and required a solution, namely on the subject of organizing Baptist youth. In 1891 the Northern Baptists formed the Baptist Young People's Union of America (BYPU), a successful youth program, and expanded it into the South, with the hope of uniting all Baptist young people in the nation. In 1893 this initiative was sharply criticized in the Southern Baptist Convention, because the Southern leaders feared the loss of Southern Baptist youth. The proposed solution was to adopt the organization without Northern control, and in 1895 the BYPU in the South was made an auxiliary of the Southern Baptist Convention. B. H. Carroll continued to participate in matters of North-South interests, and, in 1894, at Fortress Monroe, Virginia, he attended the first committee meeting between Northern and Southern Baptists.[104]

In response to attacks by volatile preacher J. Frank Norris and to quell the agitation created by a host of religious issues (including the published theories of Charles Darwin), and, importantly, to maintain a common doctrinal front with European Baptists, the Southern Baptists issued a basic confession of faith: *The Baptist Faith and Message* (the "Memphis Articles") adopted by the Southern Baptist Convention in 1925 at Memphis. This pivotal work was drawn up by Professor E. Y. Mullins and a committee in reply to a 1919 resolution at the Southern Baptist Convention. This Confession of Faith has been held in utmost respect by most Baptists of conservative and moderate backgrounds, at least until 1998, when a disputed new article, not acceptable to many moderates, on the relationship of husband and wife, was added to the Confession. The 1925 Confession contained no article on evolution but asserted from Genesis the teaching that "man was a special creation of God."[105]

Founding Southwestern Baptist Theological Seminary (SWBTS)

The creativity and versatility of Carroll was legendary, even when he was wracked with pain at age sixty-two. He had left the pastorate of the distinguished First Baptist Church at Waco in January 1899 and resumed his theological teaching at Baylor University's Theological Department, but he was deeply involved in a beehive of Baptist business, whether local, state or national in scope. As a trustee at Baylor, he would make that university the matrix of Southwestern Baptist Theological Seminary.

His visions continued to drive him forward. In 1905, on a train in the Panhandle bound for Amarillo, and because of his deafness not talking to strangers, he was given the inspiration to found the theological seminary. He was traveling across the very plains where as a boy he had hunted buffalo. And then, as he wrote,

> I saw multitudes of our preachers with very limited educa-
> tion, with few books and with small skill in using to the best
> advantage even the books they had—I saw here in the South-
> west many institutions for the professional training of the young
> teacher, the young lawyer, the young doctor, the young nurse
> and the young farmer, but not a single institution dedicated to
> the specific training of the young Baptist preacher. It weighed
> upon my soul like the earth on the shoulders of Atlas.[106]
> — from that hour I knew—that God would plant a great
> school here in the Southwest for the training of our young
> Baptist preachers.[107]

Carroll believed that Christ had spoken to him, and when his faculties again were under control, he found himself gripping the seat in front. He knew from that moment that God would begin a great school in the Southwest. That night in Amarillo, he made a list of one hundred friends that would be asked to donate one hundred dollars a year for three years, as a fund to launch the seminary. He had persuasiveness, and ninety-nine of the listed one hundred eventually sent the money requested.[108] Thus, even before reaching Waco in 1905, he set a goal of raising thirty thousand dollars to provide the salaries and expenses of a seminary staff for three years. By the end of summer, he would raise twenty-two thousand dollars in pledges and cash.[109]

The audacity of Carroll was astounding. Although he was uniquely a faculty member and chairman of Baylor's trustees for more than twenty years,[110] he was changing the structure of Baylor without consulting the trustees, Baylor President S. P. Brooks, or the Baptist General Convention of Texas. Since President Brooks was in Europe, it is impossible to believe that he was not flabbergasted when he received word that one member of the Baylor faculty, although distinguished, was busily detaching one of Baylor's departments and redesigning it as a separate institution. Further, it is difficult to think of any man, other than Carroll, that would have had the audacity to undertake the venture.[111]

In explaining his actions and the need for the new seminary, Carroll wrote in the *Baptist Standard* (May 4, 1905) the following statement:

> About one-fifteenth of the Baptists in the world are here in Texas. As the Great Northern Lakes are the nesting place of all migratory fowls, so is Texas the breeding place of preachers. From the timbered sections of East Texas; from the prairies and plains of the West; from red lands, black lands, and white lands; from wheat fields; cornfields, rice fields, cane fields, cotton patches, and ranches they heard and heed the moaning prayer of a destitute world: "Laborers, more laborers, Lord." They hear the Master's inquiry: "Whom shall I send" and they respond, each for himself, "Lord, send me." They ask no question of the thither. Anywhere in the world where needed. The missionary nestling prepares for migratory flight to any destitute field in the wide world. They go flight by flight. First to some country church; thence to a town pastorate; thence over the Texas border to some city pastorate in the older states; thence by a longer flight, they light on foreign shores, Mexico, Cuba, Brazil, Europe, Africa, Asia, the islands of the sea. In the meantime, as they swarm they fill a thousand mission fields and three thousand pastorates in Texas.[112]

Carroll stressed the practical value of training preachers for Texas. In the *Baptist Standard* (11 May 1905), Carroll stated that his greatest concern was to train adequate numbers of pastors, evangelists, missionaries, and Sunday School teachers, rather than scholars. He bolstered his agreement with: "The graduates this year [1905] from all the theological seminaries of the world would not suffice in number to supply the Baptist churches of Texas, if all were Baptists and acceptable." For the year 1905, Baylor's Theological Department had enrolled only 138 students, of whom 118 were preachers, 11 were laymen, and 7 were women.[113]

Carroll made his decisive move to legally register the seminary on August 31, 1905, when he presented his dreams to the trustees of Baylor. Eight trustees, including future Baylor President Pat M. Neff, approved the action and passed the following resolution:

> Dr. Carroll offered the following resolution: Resolved, that Baylor University now make the Theological Department a complete School of Divinity—teaching all the courses and conferring all the degrees of a regular first class theological seminary, provided that no debt on the university is contracted in prosecuting this work—the resolution was adopted."[114]
>
> Then, a further resolution was adopted:
>
> Moved: That B. H. Carroll be authorized to raise, without cost to Baylor University, funds with which to pay the salaries of the teachers employed in the Theological Department of Baylor University for the three scholastic years 1905-6, 1906-7, 1907-8. Said funds, as raised, to be deposited with the Treasurer of Baylor University and to be known as the "Theological Teachers Salary Fund" and to be so entered on his book. This fund to be used exclusively and to be the only authorized fund, for the payment of salaries of said teachers for the three scholastic years designated.[115]

The trustees were stunned as they considered Carroll's grand design, but were driven to fully accept what they regarded as an imperative from God. Judge W. H. Jenkins, a trustee, recognized that Carroll "had a vision from God" and moved for acceptance of the concept.[116] The astonished President S. P. Brooks might have had other ideas, conceivably that the school of divinity was born of earthly ambition. When he returned from Europe, he discovered that without his authority a virtual seminary, now the Baylor Theological Seminary, was being surgically removed from the mother institution. Still, it was true that the premier Baptist Seminary at Louisville did not have the facilities to provide training for an additional 250-500 ministers annually required to augment the 3000 Texas preachers. Therefore, a vibrant new Seminary arguably was needed to address the needs of an expansive West and to confront the threat of divisive doctrines such as Landmarkism and the Gospel Mission Movement.[117] At the end of 1905, the Divinity School was a functioning component of Baylor, with four teachers and B. H. Carroll as teacher and dean.[118]

The Seminary at Waco offered three degrees in 1905-06: the Bachelor of Theology (Th. B.) after two years of study (entailing such subjects as English New Testament, Systematic Theology, Church History, Hebrew, and New Testament Greek); the Master of Theology (Th. M), offered after three years of study; and, the Doctor of Theology (Th.D.), based on the candidate having a B.A. or B.Ph., a working knowledge of German and French, and further studies embracing a major and two minors.[119] Such a curriculum, more demanding than some other seminaries, attracted as students 140 young preachers, and a score of men and women interested in other religious avocations.[120]

It was clear by 1906 that Carroll sought the clean separation of the Seminary from Baylor, and that he was conceptualizing its removal to another city. If this were the president of a large corporation, we might perceive Carroll as ruthless, wily, or rampant. But as a religious leader, a more appropriate description might emerge that he was a clear-headed visionary. In 1907 he requested the trustees to clarify with a definite plan the future relations between Baylor University and the seminary. Carroll, probably to his delight, was named chairman of the reporting committee. Carroll's report suggested that the Seminary "ultimately" would be obliged to have "its own distinct habitat," and that "separate from any other institution."[121]

Again, caught off balance during a critical maneuver, President Brooks, while occupied at Shreveport, Louisiana, responded on June 26, 1907, in a crisp manner: "I regret to dissent from the conclusions. . . ." However, influenced by J. B. Gambrell, who considered as necessary the separation of the seminary and Baylor, and the seminary's change of location as far-sighted, Dr. Brooks between June and September 1907 became reconciled to the impending changes.[122] In a final harmonious mood, Brooks, on September 19, 1907, wrote Carroll: "In every fact you and I believe in absolute and complete separation. Let us work together to attain it."[123]

Strong signals augured a successful advent for the future Southwestern Baptist Seminary. B. H. Carroll had raised an endowment of $61,011, including four hundred acres of land. There was reason to be optimistic in college year 1906-07, when about 153 preachers registered as students from several foreign countries and a variety of states.[124]

On November 9, 1907, at the Baptist General Convention of Texas, meeting in San Antonio, the decisive actions were taken. The seminary was separated from Baylor University, to be guided by twenty-five new trustees and a charter, and authorized to seek a campus of its own.[125]

Under a charter filed on March 14, 1908, with the Texas secretary of state, a new seminary emerged with the name Southwestern Baptist Theological Seminary (SBTS). Carroll seemingly fashioned the seminary after Charles H. Spurgeon's Pastors' College in London. The seminary, Carroll said, was "to be mainly for the promotion of theological education, but to be responsible for the instruction of a Woman's Training School for special Christian service, and such other instruction as may be needful to equip preachers for their life's work."[126] Twenty-six women were enrolled in school year 1907-08 at the seminary, in Waco,[127] with classes to convene at the First Baptist Church Waco. The Seminary's first graduating class was approved by the trustees in May 1908.[128]

The seminary was owned and operated by the Baptist General Convention of Texas, from 1908 until 1925, after which it became the property of the Southern Baptist Convention.[129]

The seminary faculty of four was small but of fine quality. This teaching staff was enlarged in 1908 to include Lee R. Scarborough to teach evangelism and Jefferson D. Ray to teach homiletics. Lee Scarborough, the eighth of nine children born to a Baptist minister, graduated from Baylor, and then, aspiring to be a lawyer, studied at

Yale. His decision to become a preacher brought him back to Texas in 1896 and influenced him to study for one year at the Southern Baptist Theological Seminary. The other new professor, Jeff Ray, a master of journalism and elocution, had graduated from Baylor, studied at the Southern Baptist Theological Seminary, and then served as pastor of Seventh and James Baptist Church, Waco. Carroll was occupied by constantly raising money for the seminary, preaching almost every Sunday, but somehow finding time to lecture in Texas, New Mexico, Louisiana, Illinois, and Arkansas.[130]

The faculty of the seminary were required to be members of a "regular Baptist church" and to subscribe to the New Hampshire Confession of Faith.[131]

On November 14, 1908, Carroll as seminary president reported to the Baptist General Convention of Texas that, in the first year of the seminary at Waco, 190 ministerial students had matriculated, and other laymen and women had been trained. The Seminary had taught, *in toto*, 215 persons from eleven states and territories and four foreign countries. Meanwhile, President Carroll had incurred a serious fall at Eureka Springs, and, in early 1809, he was unable to descend the stairs in his house. Still, while recuperating, he was soliciting money for the seminary.[132]

A small impressive ceremony in the seminary's second year would become inordinately significant. The second commencement was observed on May 28, 1909, in the Carroll Chapel of Baylor University, with nine students receiving degrees. While Carroll delivered the baccalaureate, the charge was given by the editor of the *Baptist Standard*, J. Frank Norris, and the commencement sermon by brilliant young preacher George W. Truett. Carroll was so impressed by the persona and oratory of Norris that he recommended him to be pastor of the First Baptist Church, Fort Worth. It is well to recall at this point that the great weakness of Carroll—perhaps his greatest vulnerability—was to take men at face-value. After assuming the pastorate at Fort Worth, Norris then would persuade Carroll and the trustees to move the seminary there. Few of the Baptist intelligentsia would have guessed at this stage that Norris would become the greatest nemesis and persecutor of the seminary for a half-century.[133]

J. Frank Norris—Firebrand

Between 1907 and 1910, until its move to Fort Worth, Southwestern Baptist Seminary remained at Baylor University, its teaching staff utilizing the facilities of the First Baptist Church at Waco. J. Frank Norris, a magnetic speaker who could attract large crowds, served on the SWTS Board of Trustees from 1909 to 1915. It was Norris that was most responsible for bringing the seminary to Fort Worth, and in the early days he was a friend of B. H Carroll. However, by 1925, he would become engaged in a bitter controversy with ardent Baptists, including pastor George W. Truett and SWTS president L. R. Scarborough (the successor of B. H. Carroll), and turn into an implacable enemy of the seminary. His relentless attacks against Scarborough continued, even while President Scarborough was leading the fund-raising "Seventy Five Million Campaign."[134]

Norris, a gifted writer and preacher, purchased in 1907 a controlling interest in the Dallas-printed periodical *Baptist Standard*. In 1909, on the recommendation of B. H. Carroll, he became the pastor of the First Baptist Church, Fort Worth; this church would pledge forty-five thousand dollars to bring the Seminary to Fort Worth.[135]

Then, in 1911, there developed a startling change in the Norris personality. Some attributed this aberration to his sharp disappointment in not receiving a call to the First Baptist Church, Waco, after Carroll, its pastor, had resigned in 1899. The estrangement with the Southern Baptist Convention began in 1911, when he announced to his wife by telephone from Owensboro, Kentucky: "You have a new husband. He has been saved tonight, he is starting home and we are going to start life over again and kick the tar out of that crowd and build the biggest church in the world."[136] Then, in his effort to make the Fort Worth church a "great soul-winning station," a ruthless side emerged. Norris practically eliminated the standing committees in the church, the Woman's Missionary Union, and other church organizations that could threaten his control. Meanwhile, his church was packed with believers as he inveighed against sin.[137]

The controversies that hovered around Norris merely increased his following. However, violence began to overshadow the volatile preacher, including shots fired at him, two attempts to burn his house, and an arson attack against the church.[138] Still, his church in Fort Worth became too small for the crowds that joined him, and the church in 1912 mysteriously burned down. When Norris was charged with arson, the jury acquitted him. Then, a Fort Worth citizen, D. E. Chipps, at odds with Norris, was shot dead in Norris's office, with Norris alleging that he fired his pistol in self-defense. When the jury acquitted Norris, his followers began a revival service in the courtroom.[139]

The trial, after Chipps's death in 1926, and Norris's inflammatory sermons, produced a split in the First Baptist Church, Fort Worth. Some of the faculty of the Southwestern Baptist Seminary, including B. H. Carroll,[140] who had been aligned with Norris's church since 1910, severed their membership.

Norris, sometimes called the "religious hunting dog of the Baptists," had ambitions almost without limits. Beginning in 1923, he began a systematic campaign to take over the direction of both the Texas Baptist Convention and the Southern Baptist Convention. At every annual meeting of the Southern Baptist Convention, Norris held a rival convention in the same city. His chief associates were W. B. Riley and T. T. Shields, and together they organized in 1923 the Baptist Bible Union of America. After separating themselves from their northern fundamentalist colleagues by 1927, the triumvirate established in 1938 a seminary in Fort Worth, the Fundamentalist Baptist Bible Institute (under Reverend G. Beauchamp Vick of Detroit); even earlier, in 1934, they had created a missions organization, the Premillennial Baptist Missionary Fellowship, and in 1947, it became the World Baptist Missionary Fellowship.[141]

In 1935 Norris was pastor of both the First Baptist Church in Fort Worth and Temple Baptist Church in Detroit, commuting to his churches by plane. His associate pastor in Detroit was Dr. Vick, who had developed Temple Church as the largest Baptist congregation in Detroit. Then, Vick was persuaded to head the seminary in Fort Worth, and, against the wishes of Norris, tried to separate the finances of the seminary from those of the First Baptist Church of Fort Worth.[142]

Intemperate actions and bellicose language were often the companions of Norris. When the outstanding Waco pastor, Dr. Joseph Dawson, cooperated with Methodists and Episcopalians for religious discussions or requested the Congregationalist congressman, Walter H. Judd, to give a speech, the outcry by Norris in his publication *Searchlight* was incredible.[143] He also attacked Baylor University for Darwinism (a false charge) and the seminaries at Louisville and Fort Worth for "secret cabals" against the Scriptures.

In 1948 Norris's mental health deteriorated; like Russian dictator Joseph Stalin in his last days, he attacked as "traitors" his closest colleagues, and charged them with disloyalty and fiscal mismanagement. On May 23, 1950, 150 pastors and laymen broke away from Norris to organize "Bible Baptist Fellowship," a fundamentalist and premillennialist religious body. This organization is still thriving, with over sixteen hundred churches, about a million and a half members, and five hundred missionaries (1979). This denomination sponsors in Springfield, Missouri, the Baptist Bible College, and a publication, the *Baptist Bible Tribune*.[144]

The Seminary Moves to Fort Worth

Determined to move the seminary to a permanent location, Carroll inserted an article in the *Baptist Standard* (April 2, 1908) inviting Texas cities to compete as the host city to the seminary. Before a group of Fort Worth pastors, Carroll discussed on April 5 at the pastorless First Baptist Church, Fort Worth, the future of the seminary. From the pastors, there was a clamor for the seminary to be relocated at Fort Worth. A friendly resolution presented by Baptist deacon and Fort Worth mayor W. D. Harris, and endorsed by eight wealthy laymen, promised moral and financial support if Fort Worth was selected for the seminary. Competing bids came from Dallas, the denominational center of Texas Baptists, and other Texas communities.[145]

At another meeting in September 1909, attended by Fort Worth businessmen and clergy, Carroll alarmed the participants with his prolonged absence during the break. As the worried friends peered over the transom of his bedroom, they heard his prayer, while he was lying prostrate: "Oh, God, they don't have any idea about what needs to be done. Their dream is not big enough." The aging Carroll was partially deaf and used a hearing horn but was acutely aware that the city fathers had offered for the seminary only a small area downtown.[146]

As sentiment grew in Fort Worth for the seminary, Carroll agreed to place it there if the Fort Worth pastors and citizens would raise one hundred thousand dollars for building purposes and would provide an adequate site. The city already was involved in raising large sums for an interurban train connecting Dallas and Fort Worth, besides assisting manufacturing companies, burned churches, and Polytechnic College. Carroll assigned Professor Lee Scarborough as his agent in Fort Worth, to raise commitments in thirty days for a hundred-thousand-dollar bonus, or else the search would continue elsewhere.[147]

But the needed funds were oversubscribed in time, and a site was found on a suitable unforested high ground several miles from the city limits. The land had no water line and was not served by a streetcar, but it was accessible to the Santa Fe Railroad. The land acquisitions procured by Scarborough in ten added days were worth an additional hundred thousand dollars. And so, on November 2, 1909, the decision was made that the Southwestern Seminary would relocate to its new home. Fort Worth, sometimes called Old Panther City, that had been established in 1849 for defense against marauding Indians. By 1910 the city had about seventy-five thousand people, including five thousand Baptists and fourteen churches.[148]

At the meeting of the trustees, on November 12, 1909, at Dallas, Carroll was reelected president of the Seminary, and the faculty was reelected for one year. Scarborough was assigned to stay in Fort Worth to supervise the construction of the first new building, Fort Worth Hall, while Carroll returned to Waco. The other buildings, to be constructed when funds were available, included an administration building in the center of the campus, a Woman's Missionary Training School, and a gymnasium. The contract for $105,000 for the construction of Fort Worth Hall was signed on March 2, 1910, but did not provide for wiring, heating, and plumbing. Anticipating that work would be completed by May 10, 1910, the faculty members borrowed money in order to build their homes on the new campus.[149]

The first Doctor of Theology degree was conferred on William T. Rouse in spring 1910. Despite these optimistic harbingers, the seminary had been going through a period of crisis as crops failed in Texas and commitments for support were withdrawn. As Carroll testified:

> There came a drought which dried up our water courses, burned up our grain fields, cut off our cotton crop and parched our stock ranges until thousands of our cattle miserably perished. As it grew in intensity it extended from fields and cattle to the faith of men. In the case of thousands great faith became little faith and subscribers to benevolent funds began to "say before the angel our vow was in error." It withered emergency subscriptions behind us, it melted away present endowment pledges so that they lost the name of action; it sealed up once freely flowing fountains of benevolence ahead of us and even as we considered, behold! Israel was in a desert crying out for rock-smiters who would bring forth water.[150]

Under conditions that would have challenged pioneers on the Oregon Trail, the seminary opened on October 3, 1910. Poor as many of the students were, they hardly could expect that they would live through winter in a half-finished, unheated building at Seminary Hill, Fort Worth, on a thirty-acre campus, and an adjoining wild three hundred acres (fifty percent owned by the Seminary).[151]

The conditions for the first-year classes were not short of miserable; they were miserable. There were 126 students, some of them living in unfinished Fort Worth Hall, surviving on a campus of Johnson grass and few trees. The stark, ugly environs were scarcely distinguishable from the surrounding fields. Ultimately, explosives would be required to blow the rocky ground apart for young trees to have a footing. "The whole campus presented a most bedraggled and despondent appearance." One outstanding student recalled his sacrifice at selling his farm and then at Seminary Hill to endure cold winters and hot summers.[152]

The campus was isolated, a mile and a half across the prairie to the Bolt Works, the nearest streetcar connection, and six miles away to downtown Fort Worth. Students wishing to commute walked to the streetcar stop. Others, more patient, availed themselves of the horse and buggy provided by faculty member Dr. A. H. Newman, or fruitlessly discussed the one old "tin lizzy" automobile so seldom on the scene.[153]

There was only one building, Fort Worth Hall, that was even barely completed before Dr. Carroll's death in 1914. Thus, in a sense, it was the seminary, for within those walls were held classes, chapel, offices, administration, and faculty quarters. The temperature inside was oppressive, and water seeped in when it rained. Students and faculty froze there in the winter and spring. There was no roof to the building, and the only cover was the concrete flooring above the first and second floors. There was no heating plant nor even a sewerage system for five years. Also, there was an inadequate water system, with water pumped from an old ranch well.[154]

Until his move to Fort Worth in 1910, Carroll lived for forty years in a comfortable spacious home. Now with only four years left, and nearly deaf, he would begin again in a faculty house near Fort Worth. Two of these last years, he would be largely confined to his bed. President Carroll wrote in November 1910:

> My own house was to be ready by September 1. So I boxed and shipped all seminary records with my private library and household goods late in August and rented my Waco house. To this day all these goods, books and papers are stored in Fort Worth. It may be yet a month before I can get at them. I expressed to a Fort Worth bank the files of the seminary pledges, notes and deeds, and carried only my cash book in my suit-case.[155]

The financial situation for the new seminary was precarious. Therefore, Carroll was constantly engaged in soliciting funds. Carroll wrote one pastor: "I am up a tree. Can you and your fine men help me?" The pastor replied, "I'm in a hole. How can a man in a hole help a man up a tree?" Carroll replied: "When you come up the tree to help me down, you will be out of your hole."[156]

The total cost of finishing Fort Worth Hall had inflated in four years to about $175,000, while only $73,000 was collected from the $100,000 pledged by Fort Worth citizens. Then there was an illogical dream—to augment the resources with the sale of lots—but the sales proceeded slowly. Pressed by financial needs, Carroll often could not sleep peacefully. Carroll spoke of desperately praying with his wife for $60,000 from a St. Louis banking corporation:

> And on our knees, with our arms about each other, we prostrated ourselves in prayer and she led the prayer—a prayer the like of which I have rarely heard in my life. My own faith was strengthened and my hopes were revitalized and I tried to pray—came struggling along in supplication after the lead of this faithful heroine. When we got up from our knees, she said: "God has answered and we will get the money."[157] The loan was granted in three days.

The number of seminary employees in 1910-11 was twenty-three, including eight professors and one teacher for the Woman's Training School. The impact of the seminary on the community was soon felt in the Tarrant County Association, which supplied the churches with pastors trained by the seminary.[158]

Despite the cold classrooms and the hard floors for sleeping, the enrollment increased by fall 1911 to 104 ministers, 10 laymen, and 51 women, for a total student body of 165. By 1913-114, enrollment would be 208.[159] Scarborough reported that assets had increased from $184,000 in 1910 to $800,000 in 1913.

But finally the plans were beginning to cohere. On January 9, 1913, the trustees approved a contract for $12,000 to complete the third floor of Fort Worth Hall. Other contracts were authorized to provide plumbing, heating, and an elevator.[160]

While Carroll was physically unable to perform because of illness, Scarborough served as acting president and did much of the fund raising, and Professor Jeff D. Ray headed the drive for the Student Aid Fund. From several directions, matters began to coalesce and succeed: the third floor of Fort Worth Hall was completed in November 1913, and new water mains and a water tower were installed. The Woman's Missionary Training School, with quarters for 112 students on the campus, was nearly completed by October 1914. Even a "Seminary Hill Street Railway Company" emerged under Scarborough's directorship to haul students to Fort Worth.[161]

The Twilight Hours

In his last two years, Carroll suffered greatly from heart trouble and impaired breathing. One of his students built a board fan above his head, so that ropes could be pulled back and forth to cool him. In 1911-12, he was so weak he could lecture only once a day. His lectures to other classes were dictated and then distributed following their reproduction.[162]

Carroll was ill for the major portion of 1912, and in the spring of 1913 he fell into a coma. When he rallied, he learned that Dean A. H. Newman and Professor J. J. Reeve were planning to dismantle his Department of English Bible, since he was unable to lecture. Both academicians were summarily fired. Then Carroll consulted the trustees and gained their approval to name L. R. Scarborough as his assistant and the chief administrative officer of the seminary.

During his entire life as a minister, Carroll was impressive as he prayed, sometimes managing to incite awe or even to intimidate. As he approached his final days, he badly frightened his wife Hallie, as he prayed: "O Lord, you know that I don't mind dying. I am ready to go. But I worry so much about Hallie and my family. What will they do after I am gone? I hate to go and leave them in this wicked world, so Lord, I pray that you will take Hallie and my family before I go, so that I can go in peace." Mrs. Carroll, visibly unsettled, asked the doctor to change the prescription.[163]

Carroll had amassed a large library and always read prodigiously. Shortly before his death, he read one thousand pages a day for ten days.[164] His collection included seventeen volumes of exegetical publications, *The Interpretation of the English Bible*; eighteen volumes of sermons; five volumes of addresses; three volumes of debates and discussions; one volume of questions and answers; one volume on the Church and Articles of Faith; and four volumes of miscellaneous writings.[165]

After days in a coma, Carroll died on November 11, 1914, having almost bridged the period between the War with Mexico and World War I. His last words to L. R. Scarborough, his successor as president of Southwestern Baptist Theological Seminary, were reportedly the following:

> Lee, keep the Seminary lashed to the cross. If heresy ever comes in the teaching, take it to the faculty. If they will not hear you and take prompt action, take it to the trustees of the Seminary. If they will not hear you, take it to the Convention that appoints the Board of Trustees, and if they will not hear you

take it to the great common people of our churches. You will not fail to get a hearing there.[166]

Dr. Scarborough then delivered his final eulogy of Carroll's worth to the Seminary: "He planned it, nurtured it, formed its ideals, set its standards, projected its endowment, and contributed most largely to its spirit. It was born in his loving heart. . . ."[167]

Thus passed away a physical, intellectual, and spiritual giant that molded the Baptist character in definable ways. Self-taught as a skeptic, and learned in the Greek and Roman classics, he was humbled by giving his life to Christ in a born-again experience. His solid-rock Christian faith then bound itself tenaciously to the Holy Bible.

Although he served as the pastor of the First Baptist Church of Waco, Texas for twenty-eight years, preeminently he was the leading Baptist educator in Texas. In the crucial years following the Civil War, this gifted man was able to inflame Texas to financially preserve their numerous colleges. Then, as chairman of trustees, he was able to join Rufus C. Burleson and William Carey Crane to make Baylor University the crown jewel of the Southern Baptist Convention.

Baptists may be the world's most liberated men and women and, thus, they are much given to disputes over religious freedom and theology. Many of the controversies held in the Texas hinterland were important; the issues included slavery, the evolutionary doctrines of Charles Darwin, Landmarkism, the Gospel Mission Movement, the Whitsitt Affair, the Hayden controversy, and Northern-Southern missions and youth activities. In all of these contentions, Carroll was deeply involved and his decisions were pivotal. Only in the case of the resignation of President William H. Whitsitt of the Southern Baptist Theological Seminary is there an aspect of diminished honor, for, in the long run, the dishonored Whitsitt was proven correct. However, as a Christian advocate, stable force, visionary, and inordinately judicious and kind leader, Carroll was of incalculable value in moving forward the banner of the Southern Baptists.

Arguably, the greatest achievement of Carroll was his vision of the Southwestern Baptist Theological Seminary, that was nurtured at

Baylor University, Waco. The re-structuring of the seminary at Fort Worth, with new buildings and an ample campus, allowed it to become the largest seminary, perhaps the greatest of its kind in the world. Its inspired genius and builder was the deaf and pain-ridden Carroll, who would live only about four years after his arrival in 1910 at Fort Worth.

The mystery of this unusual man is that, having done so much before the age of sixty-two, he felt compelled by God to establish a new life and fulfill with his last breath a new vision. Benajah Harvey Carroll was not the Biblical Abraham, but there were parallels with that patriarch. However, the river that beckoned Carroll forward was not the renowned Jordan, but the obscure Trinity, and close by, he would build his city on the hill, the Southwestern Baptist Theological Seminary.

Chapter 17

Walter Rauschenbusch
(1861-1918)

Father of the Social Gospel

Walter Rauschenbusch, born in upstate New York, was a German-speaking Baptist social revolutionary, who distressed many mainline conservative Baptists by his radical views. But by the time of his death, he left the religious landscape in America irreversibly changed, with many religious leaders having accepted his principal doctrines. He was at various times a Christian Socialist, pacifist, reformer, civic leader, intellectual, writer, and Baptist leader. His formidable impact on society marks him as one of the greatest Trailblazers in Baptist history and, undeniably, one of the most remarkable religious leaders of North America.

The destiny of this articulate, tall, and distinguished pastor with the trim moustache and fashionably-cut clothes was nurtured in an obscure and almost unknown following of German-speaking Baptists, the North American Baptist General Conference. This little society originated as an extra bounty from the 5,425,208 Germans that flooded into the United States between 1855 and 1890, many of them from Russia's Mennonite stock or refugees from Prussia's surging militarism.[1]

Walter's father, Augustus, arrived in America in 1846, slightly ahead of the flood, as a Lutheran missionary to the United States

Walter Rauschenbusch (1861-1918)

and Canada from Altena, Westphalia (a German state), as a first-generation immigrant to North America and a member of the Landenberger Society for German Emigrants in America. The Rauschenbusch family in Germany took pride in a distinguished line of Lutheran pastors and was much distressed when, in 1850, Augustus was immersed as a Baptist convert in the Mississippi River in Illinois (near St. Louis), by the Reverend Sigismund Kuepfer of Newark, New Jersey.[2]

Augustus was academically well prepared for his life's work—the years that he would serve as professor at the Baptist Theological Seminary at Rochester, New York—since he had studied theology in Berlin and devoted two other years to classes at Bonn. His indoctrination for the New World began in Canada, where he organized and served as the pastor of the Bridgeport (Ontario) Baptist Church.

However, the life of Augustus often was in turmoil. Beginning his religious migration in the German states as a strict Lutheran pastor, he had aroused opposition by specifying individual sins and proclaiming temperance to a beer-drinking society. Then, at Mt. Sterling, Missouri, he wrote a book, *The Night of the West*—some portions of which he was obliged to retract—that was highly critical of the life of Lutheran and Methodist churches. In 1854, when thirty-eight years old, he married in Germany a twenty-six-year old Christian cleaning woman, the incredibly backward Karoline Rump, who had to be trained in the graces by a tutor. Karoline produced such havoc in his life between 1870 and 1888, with her yelling and "shabby treatment," that eventually he enjoyed her absence more than her presence.[3] Still, the wife, on her part, had borne the pressures stemming from an easily offended saint, much set in his ways, with a stern, oppressive outlook on life.[4] Nevertheless, this unhappy union produced five children, including Walter, the gifted fourth child.

The family problems do not overshadow the achievements of Walter's father, who in 1857 began an accomplished career at Rochester Baptist Seminary, where he earned renown for his scholarship, served as a founding leader of the German Baptists in the United

States, and compiled two German-language hymnals, *Die Pilgerharfe* and *Die Glauben Stimme*. Augustus accepted a modified Calvinistic view of salvation. At Rochester Theological Seminary, Augustus was respected as its professor of theology and organizer of the German Department. He was a prolific writer and a lecturer on baptism, closed communion, foot washing, foreign missions, and Sunday observance. His death in Hamburg on 5 December 1899, which was attributed to alcoholism, was a further tragedy for a pastor who had fervently preached on temperance. Still, he was eighty-three years old at his passing, and he had witnessed a considerable growth of the German Baptists in his lifetime and an expansion overseas of the conference mission effort.[5]

The German Baptists in America, represented by Augustus and his son Walter, were an audacious band. The first German Baptist church in America was organized by Pastor Konrad Anton Fleischmann in 1843 at Philadelphia as the Meeting House of the Baptist Church (*Versammlungs Haus Der Getauften Gemeinde*). Reverend Fleischmann had been confirmed as a Lutheran in Germany, but became a Swiss Separatist and was immersed near Basel, Switzerland. His Philadelphia church joined the Philadelphia Baptist Association in 1848. The Second German Baptist Church was founded in New York City by John Eschmann, who was born in Zurich Canton, Switzerland. Some of the thirty-three charter members had been baptized in Germany by the great missionary J. G. Oncken.[6] Other prominent German Baptist leaders included ex-Prussian army officer Alexander von Puttkammer, a relative of Prince Otto von Bismarck. In 1847 the Reverend Wilhelm Grimm led his persecuted flock of fourteen to Milwaukee, Wisconsin, from Memel, East Prussia.[7] Thus, the elements that would form the North American Baptist General Conference began to coalesce.

Early Life of Walter Rauschenbusch

As we have mentioned, Walter Rauschenbusch was born on October 4, 1861, in Rochester, New York, to German-speaking immigrant parents on a missionary quest. Rochester, his birth place, had an astonishing growth, from a village of three hundred (1815) to a flour-milling and commercial city of nearly twenty thousand (1830) on the Erie Canal.[8] Walter's life would span the Civil War, which had begun six months before his birth, almost to the end of World War I in 1918,[9] and his life would leave a social imprint on the expanding industrial society of the United States shaped by those great wars.

Walter's scholarly father Augustus and his untutored mother Karoline would influence most of their children to marry into good German Baptist stock. Daughter Frieda, born September 5, 1855, married Professor George Fetzer, who taught at the German Baptist Seminary at Hamburg, Germany. Emma, another daughter, born August 2, 1859, would earn a doctorate, serve in India as a missionary, and then go to Vienna to meet her future husband, Baptist missionary to India Dr. John E. Clough, twenty-eight years her senior. Son Winfried, born on April 24, 1857, died in early life.[10] Walter, as the fourth child, would mature as a prodigy and marry a sensitive, caring woman of German extraction. The details about the fifth child are obscure.

The stern molding of young Rauschenbusch in a pastoral household consisted of a routine of daily Bible reading, prayer, and devotions. The religious training of the lad obviously "took," for Walter told visitors in their home that he aspired to be a new "John the Baptist." The precocious youth easily mastered not only German and English but also French, Greek, and Hebrew. Whether he was aware of it, the parameters of his Baptist faith were defined by the New Hampshire Confession of Faith, adopted in 1871 by the Third General Conference, held in New York.[11]

While Walter was still young, his father Augustus remained at his post as professor at Rochester (New York) Baptist Seminary, but sent the rest of the family to Germany for a German cultural immersion. Walter would remain for three years of instruction at the Guestersloh Gymnasium (equivalent to America's junior colleges) in Westphalia. He surprised his father at Christmas with a letter written in ancient

Greek.[12] When Professor Rauschenbusch joined his family for a summer vacation, he pointed to a spot on the Rhine River where a cousin had drowned; Walter, to prove that he had no fear, peeled off his clothes, swam to the shallows on the river's farther shore, and then back, without once touching bottom. This lack of fear would characterize Walter's entire life.[13]

The decisive branding-iron Christian experience came to Walter Rauschenbusch when he was seventeen years old and left him with the lifelong conviction that spiritual rebirth is essential to salvation. Alluding to the Prodigal Son, he wrote: "I felt I was in a far country and I wanted to come back to my own country. I did not want to tend hogs any longer. This experience influenced my soul down to its depths." This born-again experience and its recollection became his answer in later years to those who feared that his Social Gospel had displaced the need for repentance and the personal acceptance of Christ as Savior. On the basis of his experience, he chose to become a minister, as had been his father and five fathers before him.[14]

Walter, who was fluent both in German and English, completed his studies at Rochester Theological Seminary, largely as an understudy to his father. His majors were completed in the German Department, under the tutelage of his father, and then in the English Department.[15] Both at the seminary and later, Walter experimented with unorthodox ideas about Christian social responsibility that set him apart from other preachers and other men.[16]

Walter confided to a fellow academician at the seminary: "I want to do hard work for God—I want to be a pastor, powerful with men, preaching to them Christ as the man in whom their affections and energies can find the satisfaction for which mankind is groaning. And if I do become anything but a pastor, you may believe that I have sunk to a lower ideal or that there was a very unmistakable call to duty in that direction."[17]

After graduating from the seminary, at the behest of the German Baptist congregation, he spent the summer of 1885 trying to rejuvenate a run-down church in Louisville, Kentucky. He noted that,

Augustus Rauschenbusch (father of Walter) as professor at the Baptist Theological Seminary of Rochester, New York.

"The sins of pastors and sins of members had created distrust within and contempt among outsiders." The effort to change the spirit of the congregation almost overwhelmed him, and he wanted other work. But, after three months labor, the congregation almost doubled, and the church invited him to return for the following summer.[18]

His confidence would be shaken by rejections of his applications to several religious positions. When Walter's sister Emma departed for India to serve as a missionary among the Telugus, he felt a call to serve the Lord in that distant land.[19] After he asked for an appointment, the American Baptist Foreign Mission Society recommended him to be president of the Telugu Theological Seminary at Ramapatnam in South India. Eager to go, the young preacher made his preparations. However, the professor of Old Testament at Rochester expressed his doubts about Walter's "doctrinal soundness," and the offer was withdrawn. Also, the First Baptist Church of Springfield, Illinois, that had requested Walter to be its pastor, now lost interest. These rebuffs came after his open statement that Christian people should apply Christian solutions to social problems. Being turned down by a promising church and the foreign mission board of his faith left his morale badly battered.[20]

New York's Hell's Kitchen

Then, Walter Rauschenbusch discovered gold by choosing the perfect milieu for his inquisitive mind and probing social consciousness. He responded positively to an offer to become the pastor, at age twenty-four, of the Second Baptist Church at West 43rd Street in Hell's Kitchen, in the middle of the "disreputable" West Side of New York. This would place him in a maelstrom of immigrants, working blue-collar stock, prostitutes, peddlers, pushcart hawkers, and steamy laborers. Walter would pastor his flock in this boiling crucible for eleven years, 1886-97. The 125 church members would struggle to give him a meager nine-hundred-dollar-a-year salary, three hundred of which paid the rent on a five-room flat. The church building was an ugly, old, and graceless building.[21] It was merciful that in these desolate quarters that Walter was a bachelor—until April 12, 1893, when to the surprise of many, he married a school teacher in Milwaukee, Wisconsin, the patient and comforting Pauline E. Rother (or Rather).[22]

In his tawdry vicarate of wretched apartments and distressed wage earners, Walter would preach, labor, and lobby for social reforms. This was a tough, hard-drinking war zone. Still, within three years, the church membership had risen to 213 members. After his arrival in New York, he wrote to a friend: "God knows I have a little desire to be useful to my fellowmen and these few weeks have again taught me that I can do so best by bringing them into living and personal relations with our Lord Jesus Christ."[23]

The seamy side of New York's Hell's Kitchen had little in common with the physical side of the handsome Baptist pastor. He was six feet tall, elegantly dressed and sporty, with red hair, hazel eyes, a trimmed moustache, and a Van Dyke beard. Beyond the dress, he was highly educated, articulate, positive, dignified, and convincing,[24] someone to boldly challenge the Establishment.

Among his first projects, Walter made a meticulous personal survey of the West Side, noting the condition of the population, the economic possibilities, the sanitation standards, and the moral environment around him. He took a sharp look at the crime-ridden, crowded slum area, assaulted by fetid air and disease. He observed first-hand the barriers to the newly arrived immigrants, many of them German-born, borne down by malnutrition, insecurity, and unemployment. Then he took note of the neglected children and the causes for their waywardness and "youthful wickedness." At the Second Baptist Church, he began to preach that the Kingdom of God begins with a personal faith but it extends further to include seeking justice for the working family. From that core message, his ministry embraced the sick and imprisoned non-worshipers, and the dying, over whom he prayed.[25]

In 1887 Walter found it necessary to enlist allies in his social reform efforts; he organized an informal three-man prayer band, the Brotherhood of the Kingdom, that included Nathaniel Schmidt, pastor of a Swedish Baptist congregation, and Leighton Williams, pastor of Amity Baptist Church. This little corps appears to have been formed in emulation of the *Kleeblatt* (cloverleaf), the three-man band formed by the great German Baptist missionary to Europe, Johann G. Oncken, in collaboration with his colleagues Julius W. Köbner and Gottfried W. Lehmann.

Walter Rauschenbusch's *Brotherhood of the Kingdom* had as its purpose the striving for "the ethical and spiritual principles of Jesus, both in their individual and social aspects, in their own lives and work." After several informal meetings, the Brotherhood organized in December 1892 in conjunction with meetings of Baptist missionary societies. The news media reported on the follow-up meeting in August 1893, held at the Williams's summer home in Marlboro, New York: "A group of Baptist clergymen had met who have organized for the study of Christianity in its social aspects, for the promulgation of more just views of the Kingdom of God, and the application of the principles of the Gospel to the social and industrial systems of the world."[26]

The Brotherhood became international in scope as a promoter of social Christianity.[27] Aside from Marlboro, there were chapters of the Brotherhood in Rochester and Boston. Annual meetings were held in the summer. The fellowship group, despite its name, involved women and spread overseas. One of its prime achievements was the influence exerted by the Brotherhood with regard to the social direction of the Northern Baptist Convention, after it organized in 1908.[28]

In New York City, Walter battled for tenement sanitation facilities, safety inspections, fresh-air centers, and sandpiles for children's playgrounds. Often he got his way with the authorities, since he was a persistent and highly-respected advocate.[29]

However, some Baptist preachers were apprehensive, and even alarmed by his message. The Social Gospel, not easily understood, was viewed by many with suspicion and animosity. In return, Walter preached about the social gospel of Amos the Tekoa prophet and herdsman. He also referred to the Lord's Prayer: "Thy kingdom come, thy will be done on earth." A butcher in Walter's congregation proclaimed: "We have found in Pastor Rauschenbusch more that is Christlike than in any human being we have ever met."[30]

In 1888 occurred two events that would affect his life forever: while in bed with a violent influenza, called Russian grippe, he left the parsonage against doctor's orders to assist a church family; the result was that the disease had a recurrence, and he would become completely deaf for life.[31] Perhaps his physical impairment had some influence on his decision in 1893 to marry school teacher Miss Pauline E. Rother, who would become his most faithful assistant. She would mitigate the effects of his deafness and attend closely to his needs on the third floor of the church house that served as pastorium. This happy marriage was blessed with five children.[32]

The second major event of 1888 was the resignation of Walter's father from the Rochester Baptist Seminary and his departure for Germany, which he hoped to make his retirement home. Walter was asked to fill the teaching vacancy at Rochester Seminary, but he refused the post because he did not relish the working conditions or the cold climate at Rochester. In addition, he did not want to abandon his pastorate at the Second Baptist Church at Hell's Kitchen, since he had served there only two years. Therefore, his father Augustus felt obliged to continue the instruction of his worried seminary students at Rochester, and returned to the seminary for one more year, before permanently retiring in June 1890 in Germany.[33] Karoline, Augustus's irascible wife, would eventually join him in Europe, for better or worse.

Despite his refusal to fill the prestigious seminary post, Walter at the denominational Ninth General Conference was elected to the School Committee for the Seminary. Also, although not thirty years old, he was chosen by the Conference to be one of its two secretaries and its Sunday morning Conference preacher.[34]

The Hell's Gate church congregation had grown and required new facilities. The old building on West 43rd Street was sold after

Walter had preached there for three years. On October 19, 1889, the cornerstone was laid for a new church with greater accommodations at a price of twenty-five thousand dollars, part of this sum offset by the sale of the old property. Walter eked out an existence, with his thrifty instincts, despite his pathetic salary. However, in 1892 he made a bold financial plunge and purchased a typewriter, so he could formulate his theology and innovative concepts, to be printed in *For the Right*, a weekly paper that attracted the favorable attention of the *New York Times*.

In pursuing religious writing, Walter was following in the tradition of other learned German Baptist leaders; these pioneers had employed their publications, including the weekly journal *Der Sendbote* (from 1865) and its editor Philip Bickel,[35] to rail against public support for Roman Catholic parochial schools, to denounce the doctrine of Papal Infallibility (proclaimed in Rome on July 21, 1870), and to give support to the temperance movement. The German Baptist General Conference, in 1877, going against the grain of a German drinking society, passed a resolution against the habitual use of beer and alcohol. However, wine continued to be used for the Lord's Supper.[36]

The energy and creativity of Walter Rauschenbusch was able to give life to new causes. The fastest growth of German Baptist youth organizations began in 1889 with the launching of its denomination youth paper *Der Jugend-Herold (Youth Herald)* that enjoyed a one-hundred-percent growth in four years, beginning in 1892. Walter Rauschenbusch, from November 1892 until May 1897, in his final years at Hell's Kitchen, was commissioned by the General Conference to be the editor on a part-time basis of the *Jugend-Herold*; his editorship lasted four years, with subscriptions ranging in the best years from about 3,122 to 2,500, although the paper sometimes lost money.[37]

This growth was remarkable, since in 1875 (thirty-two years after the founding of the German Baptist Church in North America) there was not in existence a single German Baptist young people's society. In 1879 there were three such societies; in 1895 there were

129 societies with a total of 4,069 members, composed of young single and married persons, ranging in age from twenty to forty.[38]

He was an ardent speaker in support of youth and, as an orator in 1892, upheld young Christians in his speech, "Our Young People and Baptist Principles." Then, in 1893, as editor of the *Jugend-Herold*, he urged at the Eastern Conference the organizing of the General Young People's Union; this concept, while not gaining unanimous assent, was accepted in 1895 at Dayton. As a result, the General Young People's Union held a convocation in July 18-19, 1898, in Buffalo, New York, with Walter as one of its featured speakers.

After his resignation as editor of the *Jugend-Herold* in 1897, the youth organization began to decline until 1913, but even so William Kuhn introduced the concept of *synzygus* (yokefellow) to the young people.[39]

Der Sendbote, from its first edition in 1853,[40] was the major German Baptist publication, and, before the death of editor J. C. Haselhuhn, the Publication Committee requested Walter to assume the new position of associate editor, possibly as the trainee and editor-designate. Walter declined the position because of his attachment to his Hell's Kitchen church, while heeding the urgings of fellow-pastors for him to remain in New York City. The committee then filled the position of associate editor by naming Gottlob Fetzer, a pastor in Berlin, Ontario, and promoted as editor J. C. Grimmel. Before voting in favor of Grimmel, the General Conference disregarded Walter's protests and for three ballots allowed the voters to include the name of Walter Rauschenbusch along with other candidates.[41] Then ironically, much later in 1901-02, Walter would serve as a member of the Publication Committee when Grimmell would be removed as editor of *Der Sendbote*.[42]

The lyrical talents of Walter Rauschenbusch surfaced in 1892, when he and world-famous evangelist-musician Ira D. Sankey jointly published a German-language hymnal *Evangeliums Lieder (Gospel Songs)*, a collection of sacred songs, many of them translated superbly from English by Walter. Essentially, this hymnal was a translation of

Ira Sankey's *Gospel Hymns.* The work was popular, both with German Baptists and other German-speaking groups.[43]

In 1916, there appeared a new hymnal, the *Neue Glauben Sharfe (New Harp of Faith),* produced by Sankey and Rauschenbusch. This work included about one hundred German translations of English hymns. Walter's translations of beloved songs included the following: "Holy, Holy, Holy," "Come, Thou Almighty King," "In the Cross of Christ I Glory," "When I Survey the Wondrous Cross," "Guide Me, O Thou Great Jehovah," and "My Country, 'Tis of Thee." However, the major credit for publishing this hymnal should be given to Herman Von Berge.[44]

Looking Into His Soul

Walter far surpassed his fellow Baptist ministers in his ecumenical spirit. In explaining his generous open hand, he stated:

> Baptists, in tying to the New Testament, have hitched their chariot to a star, and they will have to keep moving— We are not a perfect denomination. We are capable of being just as narrow and small as anybody. There are fine qualities in which other denominations surpass us. I do not want to foster Baptist self-deceit, because thereby I should grieve the spirit of Christ. I do not want to make Baptists shut themselves up in their little clam shells and be indifferent to the ocean outside of them. I am a Baptist, but I am more than a Baptist. All things are mine; whether Francis of Assisi, or Luther, or Knox, or Wesley; all are mine because I am Christ's. The old Adam is a strict denominationalist; the new Adam is just a Christian.[45]

In referring to narrowness, could Rauchenbusch have been alluding in one sense to the restrictions of "closed communion" practiced by his father Augustus? In 1853 the small number of German Baptists had their peace fractured by a religious dispute over whether to allow baptized (immersed) Christians to participate in taking the Lord's Supper when they were not members of the local Baptist church. Prominent German Baptists that were opposed to such "closed communion" included the Reverend Konrad Anton Fleischmann, first publisher of *Der Sendbote*, and Reverend E. S. Kuepfer. Fleischmann in his church baptized converts and then allowed them to join in the Lord's Supper, whether members or not.[46] Today, "open communion" is practiced widely in Baptist churches.

Walter Rauschenbusch was committed to prayer as his lifeblood and considered it vital for the nation's future. He prayed often and eloquently, and said of prayer:

> Perhaps the secret of the decline and fall of nations, or of their rise and power, could more truly be sought in that direction than in wars and trade balances. Perhaps the future of our nation, the future of the white race, the future of humanity is largely contained in the future of prayer. To some extent it depends on the question whether you and I pray. The duty of prayer may be the real "white man's burden."[47]

He relied on prayer, and prayer was the force that drove him in concern to appear at the shabby apartments, jails, and shops. Walter made it his habit to regularly visit the inmates in prison, the mentally ill, the elderly, the unemployed, and the saddened. He identified himself with friendliness to individuals. Because of his sensitivity, he then tackled the evil social order—rampant, uncontrolled capitalism—that was oppressing society. His consuming concern for the individual person induced him to crusade for a society where the person could achieve his or her full potential as God's creature. Thus, his mission was simultaneously social and personal Christianity.[48]

The depth of Walter's spirituality can be glimpsed with this note inserted in 1909 in the visitor's book of the Brotherhood of the Kingdom:

> Only where mind touches mind does the mind do its best work. Where love and confidence draw the bars and bolts of caution and distrust, thought passes easily from heart to heart, and finds ready lodgment. So we grow — God bless this hilltop temple of the spirit — may it do for others in the future what it did for me in the past.[49]

He was like a foreign substance—a *sabot* or wooden shoe—thrust into the noisy industrial complex, and he hated liquor as the specific enemy of the working man. His "Prayer for Alcoholics" was used extensively in churches and homes. The intensity of his convictions would be sharpened by the death of his father, Professor August Rauschenbusch, who died an alcoholic.[50]

This articulate and neatly dressed pastor, his immaculate English defined by a German accent, discussed topics before polite church circles, heretofore considered offbounds; he used as illustrations "fallen girls" and unwed mothers. In Hell's Kitchen, on the West Side, he was both praised as a hero and despised as a fanatic. In 1886 he appeared before New York City councilmen to plead for sandboxes and safe areas for children to play. He argued there and before fellow Ministers that to escape tuberculosis the children must have play areas with adequate sunshine and fresh air. The minors, he asserted, must be given recreational facilities as buffers to give them a chance to avoid a life of stealing and delinquency.[51]

Leading the Christian Revolution

Rauschenbusch as a good Baptist did not believe that man could be saved by good works. He believed, in contrast, that salvation only came through the grace of God. However, he was the Trailblazer in asserting that the church must remove itself from its isolation and address the problems of the Industrial Age, such as occurred through slums, unemployment, crime, and poverty. He was not alone in his thinking. One of his allies was Methodist preacher Harry F. Ward, writer of *The New Social Order*.[52] The church for centuries, Rauschenbusch insisted, had concentrated on ecclesiastical interests and had paid little attention to child labor, prostitution, or predatory landlords. He cut away the thorns and bushes to demonstrate what Christ had taught, that faith without works was void.[53]

Walter alerted some people but scared many others, when he referred to Jesus Christ as a "revolutionary" and spoke of Christianity as engaged in a "revolution."

Christianity is in its nature revolutionary. Its revolutionary character is apparent from the spiritual ancestry to which it traces its lineage. Jesus was the successor of the Old Testament prophets. The common people of his day discerned this kinship and whispered that he must be Elijah or Jeremiah or some other of the prophets. (Luke 9: 19)[54]

The prophets were the revolutionists of their age. They were dreamers of Utopias. They pictured an ideal state of society in which the poor should be judged with equity and the cry of the oppressed should no longer be heard; a time in which men would beat their idle swords into ploughshares and their spears into pruning hooks, for then the nations would learn war no more. (Isaiah 2: 4) No slight amelioration contented them, nothing but a change so radical that they dared to represent it as a repealing of the ancient and hallowed covenant and the construction of a new one. . . .[55]

Nor were the prophets mere impractical dreamers and declaimers. They were men of action. They overthrew dynasties. They were popular agitators, tribunes of the people. They rebuked to their faces kings who had robbed the plain man of his wife or tricked him out of his ancestral holding.

These were the men whose successor Christ professed to be. . . .[56]

When, in the synagogue at Nazareth, Jesus chose for his test the passage of Isaiah which tells of glad tidings to the poor, of release to the captives, of liberty to the bruised, and of the acceptable year of the Lord, "the eyes of all in the synagogue were fastened upon him." The people were ready to follow Jesus as king when he raised the standard of revolt.[57]

Rauschenbusch regarded himself as the enemy of rampant capitalism, that is capitalism lusting supremely for profits and possessing no conscience. He was the Christian advocate, proclaiming the Gospel, but also railing against savage competition in industry. In his war, he sought the cooperation of fellow ministers to fight monopolies.

He also thrust needles into the slumbering church: "Its theology is silent or stammers where we most need a ringing and dogmatic message. It has no adequate answer to the fundamental moral questions of our day—Its hymns, its ritual, its prayers of devotion, are so devoid of social thought that the most thrilling passions of our generation lie in us half stifled for lack of religious utterance."[58]

Rauschenbusch referred to himself as a "Christian Socialist," when the term "socialist" was odious to most North American Christians. However, his application of Socialism had specific reference to his belief in public ownership of such utilities as gas, water, electricity power, roads, and telegraph and telephone lines. For a while—although he abandoned the idea later—he accepted the single-tax concept of Henry George, who proposed making property the basis for all taxes.[59]

At an historical period of strong prejudice against organized labor in America, he protested against the dehumanizing of the laborer; the worker must be regarded as more than a "thing," engaged in producing products at high speed. "It is the function of religion to teach the individual to value his soul more than his body, and his moral integrity more than his income," argued Rauschenbusch. Thus, he was in harmony with social leaders, such as Congregational minister Washington Gladden and Catholic advocate James Cardinal Gibbons (1834-1921), in pleading that machinery and industry existed for the benefit of man, instead of being their masters.[60]

At the site of employment, he favored a safe and healthy work environment for the skilled and unskilled laborer, restricted labor for women, and prevention of child labor. He cooperated with Jacob Riis and others to initiate reforms that resonated in municipal, state, and national assemblies.[61] In order to ameliorate the cultural conditions, he proposed improvements in education, libraries, parks, playgrounds, and museums.

Armstrong notes that Walter Rauschenbusch, while brilliant, was not quite the all-perceiving Socrates of industry; he failed to foresee that capitalism could be pressured and induced to be more humane and balanced by the influence of stockholders, cooperatives, and the forced distribution of profits by government taxes.[62]

The depressions of 1873 and 1893 caused many immigrant families to suffer intensely. Walter, in part because of these tragedies, supported the laboring man in his claim for higher wages and the right to strike. He justified the strikes of 1890 to establish the eight-hour working day. The pastor then denounced some tenement owners for their avarice in allowing rental property to deteriorate but the rent to remain high. The hard times of 1893-94 forced many members of Rauschenbusch's church to move uptown or across the East River to obtain cheaper flats. Also, he backed in 1895 the streetcar employees in Brooklyn who struck for higher wages.[63]

Rauschenbusch wrote:

> When I saw how men toiled all their life long, hard, toilsome lives, and at the end had almost nothing to show for it; hard strong men begged for work and could not get it in hard times; how little children died—oh, the children's funerals! They gripped my heart.[64]

The spectrum of the disadvantaged was broad and of immediate interest to Walter. He felt that Jesus Christ was concerned about the right use of company money in paying workers a living wage. Likewise, the slum pastor felt compassion for the plight of the aged, handicapped, sick, and unemployed. He enjoined the Hell's Kitchen church to attend to public needs, in these words:

> Our business is to make over an antiquated and immoral economic system; to get rid of laws, customs, maxims, and philosophies inherited from an evil and despotic past; to create just and brotherly relations between great groups and classes of society; and thus to lay a social foundation on which modern men individually can live and work in a fashion that will not outrage all the elements in them.[65]

Teaching at Rochester Theological Seminary

Rochester Theological Seminary, from which developed a Northern Baptist institution, the Colgate-Rochester Divinity School, began in 1850 in an old hotel building. In this early period, there were only eight German Baptist churches in America. The first German-American theological students were dirt-poor, sometimes going hungry, and initially paying board costing only $1.50 per week. There was a scholarship for needy students, of $70 per year, but the fund was inadequate. In the German Department, well underway in 1869, German students were taught Biblical literature and theology. The first graduating exercise for the German Department was held in 1855, with Phillip Bickel obtaining his degree, and nine students continuing in the Department.

Walter's father faithfully served the seminary for thirty years, partially engaged in seeking support funds for his students. During his tenure, Augustus supervised 190 men students, with 177 of them entering the Ministry.[66]

In 1897 the life of Walter Rauschenbusch would be altered once more, when he accepted the call to teach church history at the Rochester Theological Seminary; there, he would give the Seminary a "forward look."[67] He had served as the pastor of Hell's Gate Second German Baptist Church, where he projected the Social Gospel vision. Now, at Rochester, he would teach and formulate his revolutionary doctrines in widely-read and disturbing volumes: *Christianity and the Social Crisis* (1907), *Christianizing the Social Order* (1912),[68] and *A Theology for the Social Gospel* (1917). These three dynamic volumes would be read world-wide, raise eyebrows, produce anger and dismay, dominate seminary discussions, and modify for the foreseeable future the moral thinking and actions of many, but certainly not all religious leaders.

Following the death of Professor H. M. Schaeffer, the outstanding New Testament scholar in the German Department at Rochester, Walter accepted the call to serve as professor at the seminary. He was almost certainly aware that Professor Schaeffer had played the leading role in raising funds to construct Rochester Seminary's first building in 1874, another new building in 1890, and had died while strenuously exerting himself in raising sixty-four thousand dollars toward a one-hundred-thousand-dollar endowment fund (finally completed in 1913).[69]

Walter's commitment to the Second German Baptist Church in Hell's Kitchen had lasted for eleven years, and despite the clamor and turmoil of the work, he did not find it easy to leave. He was influenced in part to assume the seminary position by a desire to train a new generation of German-American pastors.[70] His words in accepting the new challenge included the following: "I can think of no more rewarding task than that of interpreting the New Testament and that of leading the brethren, through the gate of the Word, into the temple of the spirit." His tenure in the Seminary's German department would last only five years.

In the fall of 1902, Walter resigned from the German Department, organized by his father Augustus, and transferred to the English Department, where he would assume the post of professor of church history. There, he would be lauded for his "exceptional gifts and teaching ability." Despite its scholarship, this was a small seminary, and he would teach English, natural sciences, civics, zoology, and New Testament interpretation. As late as 1902-03, there were only thirteen students in the seminary's theology unit. Simultaneously, while teaching, he was the pastor of a small German Baptist church supported by immigrants.

In the twenty-one years that began in 1897, in which Walter Rauschenbusch would serve as professor at Rochester Theological Seminary, he would live to see the transition of German-speaking churches to bilingual and then to predominantly English-speaking German Baptist churches.[71] While remaining active in the German Conference, he would become a national religious leader and attain an international renown. In 1916, at the General Conference in Detroit, he delivered the principal speech at the morning service and was selected as the speaker for the patriotic service on Labor Day.[72]

In contrast to his father Augustus, Walter's teaching was both daring and amusing. On labor conditions, he stressed factors affecting health, wages, and safe working conditions, but also the necessity of time for workers' self-improvement and leisure. Both Walter and his students were amused when he offered a new course on the Devil. His students queried each other over whether Professor Rauschenbusch would take them on a field trip to view the Devil. Despite his deafness, while serving as party host for his students, he was the life of the party. Even after bruising events off campus, he was good natured. In one such incident, when a streetcar knocked him down at a busy intersection, he jumped up, brushed off his pants, then apologized to the conductor and mailed the streetcar company a five-dollar bill as compensation for colliding with their vehicle.[73]

Disposing of Baggage from the Past

While every child bears burdens left from the past by the forefathers, it is not surprising that Walter was left with residual baggage. He faced his heritage in the company of the German Baptists, bearing the disproportionate name of North American Baptist General Conference. The cultural tie that German Baptists clearly loved was not only the cultural links to the German traditions but also a visceral tie to the German language. And the German tongue would be spoken in their churches until their society's very survival was threatened.

The key factor was that millions of German immigrants in the late nineteenth century legally had entered the United States, but by 1907 the stream had narrowed to 37,807 arrivals. The source stream was drying up.[74] Further, many of the German immigrants—contrary to public knowledge—were cold to religion and wanted to master English and meld into the American mainstream. In 1846 the German Baptists in America numbered sixteen thousand and only slowly forged ahead to thirty-four thousand in 1931 and nearly thirty-nine thousand in 1946. However, the numbers of German Baptist churches fell from 289 in 1918 to 266 in 1946.[75] One of the obstacles to growth among the German Baptist churches was their refusal to abandon the German language in church services.

In the generation of Augustus Rauschenbusch, there co-existed with him the pioneer German Baptist church builder, Alexander von Puttkammer, an officer of the Union army and possibly the first German Baptist ordained in the United States. Of Puttkammer's attachment to the use of German language in church services, he wrote:

> I plead with you, dear young pastors: do not serve American [English-speaking] churches, but remain faithful to the German work. The biggest mistake that I ever made was that I left the German work. What a joy it was for me, after twenty-eight years, once again to preach in German at the First German Baptist Church in New York! O that I was sixty-five instead of eighty-five, in order to be able to serve the German work![76]

In the development of the German Baptist church body, there were two active conferences: the Eastern (formed in 1851) and the Western (established in 1859). However, a new trend for unification occurred with the convening of the first General Conference that was held in Wilmot, Ontario, in 1865.[77] In the beginning of the German missionary undertaking in North America, corresponding to the period of Augustus Rauschenbusch, the employment of the German language was believed by some to be a temporary phenomenon. American Baptists in the North felt that eventually the German cultural fellowship would diminish, and that as the believers became fluent in English, they would transfer their membership to the English-speaking churches and associations of the American Baptists . However, after years of observation, American Baptists, particularly in the North, felt that the process was moving too slowly, and surmised with good reason that the German churches were perpetuating the German language and culture while retaining their English-speaking members. In fact, there was an aggressive bid by many German-speaking Baptist churches to continue church services and Sunday School in German, until the beginning of World

War I; also, they fostered the teaching of German language to children in their homes.[78]

The intricacies of the language/cultural identity of the German Baptists were well known to Walter Rauschenbusch. However, as long as a liberal immigration policy guaranteed a flow of new German-Americans, German Baptists felt they should train pastors and provide churches and Sunday schools taught in German.

The mood of the American Baptists (organized as the Northern Baptist Convention in 1908), American Baptist Convention (1950), and American Baptist Churches in the USA (1972), who had worked fraternally with the German Baptists, was increasingly impatient. In a letter to Walter Rauschenbusch, Dr. T. J. Morgan, secretary of the American Baptist Home Mission Society, prompted the German Baptists to "ultimately" discontinue use of the German language. After all, he wrote: "This is America and not Germany, or Ireland or Italy or France." In response, one of the leading German Baptist pastors, Dr. J. C. Grimmell, responded that Americanization should not be as important as evangelicization. Further, he argued, twenty thousand German Baptists had given as much for evangelizing ten million Germans as one and one-half million English Baptists in the North.[79] However, by the end of World War I, the Americanization of the German Baptists had become a serious goal.[80]

The United States had become a world power and the country was intoxicated by its industrialization, new status, and potential. In the church General Conference of 1928, the membership demanded greater use of English in its services. In 1937, at Portland, Oregon, the business sessions were conducted largely in English. Then a special development occurred; in 1940, at the General Conference, hosted by the Oak Street Baptist Church of Burlington, Iowa, this church insisted that the conference be conducted entirely in English. Thereafter, the conference programs were predominantly addressed in English, as were the local conferences.[81]

During the existence of the Rochester Seminary, there was a shortage of trained pastors. Still, local churches were warned not to ordain without the advice of a Baptist ordination council and not to unfrock a pastor without the lead of a council. Churches were admonished to take precautions against preachers that practiced intemperance and lived ungodly lives.[82]

Baptist Monasteries

Roman Catholics and others1 have long maintained monasteries for celibate monks and nuns, but the practice was limited in the world of the Baptists. However, about 1950, the author was startled to see a dying Baptist monastery of a Seventh-Day Baptist group at Ephrata, Lancaster County, Pennsylvania—this one under pragmatic rules (as Baptists are inclined), with separate dormitories for married couples, single men, and single women. There were only three survivors of the old ways.

In 1869 the German Baptist Church of Cincinnati, Ohio, nurtured in its organization a cluster of deaconesses. Their duties included conducting sewing schools, teaching Sunday School, and visiting house to house.[83]

The German Baptists experimented with several homes for women in New York and Chicago in the Rauschenbusch period. A local board of directors operated from 1896 a Girl's Home or *Maedchenheim* at Sutton Place, New York City. Then in 1903 it bought new property, a brownstone house, that served several thousand guests.

Of greater interest was the abortive effort to found a permanent Chicago deaconess society. In Germany, both Lutherans and Baptists sponsored deaconess societies, a kind of Protestant equivalent of Roman Catholic sisters. One of the requirements of the Chicago order was that the deaconesses commit themselves to remain unmarried. Many of them served as nurses. In 1897 a Chicago deaconess society was constituted to support their hospital, with 150 charter members. In Europe, a deaconess society would have a mother house, with a variant of mother superior, and a central office. The Chicago experiment did not succeed in the fast-moving American climate, and the property eventually became a Girl's Home.[84]

German Missions in Africa

A favorite mission field of German Baptists in Germany and America was the Cameroon(s) (*Kamerun*) in West Africa. In 1884 Germany, lagging behind in the international race for colonies, began annexing Cameroon territory. By 1889 the Cameroon became a German colony, with its capital at Buea. British Baptists maintained a main station at Victoria, but the work was so discouraging that in 1886 they sold their facilities to the Reformed Basel Mission. The stranded Baptists in the Cameroon then appealed to the Baptists of Germany, and as a consequence there arose a semi-independent organization under the supervision of the Reverend Mr. Scheve of Berlin.

The first missionaries to the Cameroon under this new administration were the Americans, Mr. and Mrs. August Steffens; they had been invited in 1890 to apply for support by Professor Augustus Rauschenbusch on his last assignment at Rochester, New York. Young preacher Steffens boarded the *SS Prince Bismark* bound for Germany and a final conference in Berlin with Scheve and the Berlin Committee. Steffens then was joined overseas by his fianceé, Miss Anna Kappel, and after their marriage, they proceeded to the Cameroon, arriving there on December 8, 1891. They were partially supported by the German Baptist General Missionary Committee in Buffalo.[85]

As other young German-speaking missionaries were appointed for overseas work through the American Baptists (Northern Baptist Foreign Missionary Society), the German-American churches became major financial contributors. These missionary appointees maintained a lively contact with the German constituency in America. Missionaries were sent to India, China, Philippines, and other countries. In the beginning, Home Mission work was supported by local congregations, dependent on the American Baptist Home Mission

Society. Later, the German Baptists resorted to their General Missionary Society.[86]

As America prospered in the period before World War I, European Baptists frequently visited the United States to obtain financial support for their programs. But this tendency disturbed the German-American Baptists, who were hard pressed to find support for their seminary, the Publication Society, and church extension work. The General Missionary Committee requested solicitors from Europe to obtain advance approval for such trips to America. When overseas German fundraisers came, despite this advice, the financial results would be meager. A notable example was the trip to America by J. G. Fetzer, the son-in-law of Augustus Rauschenbusch, who was able to obtain only $440 from German-American Baptists in support of a seminary in Hamburg.[87]

On public issues, the German Baptist churches were dismayed that Roman Catholics sought public funds for the support of parochial schools. In their ideological debates, Catholics assailed the practice of permitting Bible reading and prayer in classrooms in public schools in Cincinnati, Buffalo, and Newark.[88]

The cooperation between the German Baptists and the Northern Baptists had been close for years, particularly in the areas of foreign and home missions. This partnership was particularly fruitful, when it involved the American Baptist Home Missionary Society's work among German immigrants.[89] It came as no surprise when in 1940 the Northern Baptist Convention extended to the (German-American) General Conference an invitation to enter into an "associate relation," not abridging the General Conference independence or involving financial obligations. The German Baptists rejected this proposal in order to maintain their separate culture and quality of worship. If the action had been approved, fifty-one German Baptist churches would not have accepted their loss of identity.

There were other strong reasons for non-acceptance that went beyond the language question; the German Baptists had developed a strong cohesive organization and now wished to carry the Gospel

to non-Germans as well as Germans. Further, the General Conference was an orthodox Christian body, with real fears about the liberal
trends originating from such schools as Colgate-Rochester, Crozier,
the University of Chicago, and Andover-Newton. The conservatives, comprising the vast majority of the German church, simply did
not want any closer ties with the Northern Baptist Convention.[90]

During World War I, Walter Rauschenbusch became an implacable pacifist, but his views were not typical of the German Baptists.
In that "war to end all wars" (1914-18), German-Americans bought
Liberty Bonds and volunteered for military service—forty-two servicemen, for example, from the Baptist church in Burlington, Iowa,
and thirty-two servicemen from Temple Church of Pittsburgh. With
the forced suppression of such terms as sauerkraut, given by public
pressure the new name of "Liberty Cabbage," and the induced
anglicization of German surnames in the frenzy of the times, Germans abandoned their private language instructions. However, the
Baptist German language press did not have to close down, as was
feared.[91]

This was another stage in the German-American struggle to remain loyal to their fundamental traditions, while trying hard to be
good American citizens. In the Franco-German War (1870-71), the
German-American press had blamed Napoleon III for the war, and
Augustus Rauschenbusch justified Prussia's taking of Alsace-Lorraine
as a prize after the victory at Sedan.[92] In the Spanish-American War
(1898), despite the fact that the Kaiser's family was related by blood
to the Spanish royal line and that Germans in Europe sided with
Spain, Walter Rauschenbusch threw his support to the American
side, in a letter he wrote to the *Frankfurter Zeitung* as a professor
from the German department at Rochester Theological Seminary.[93]

World War I was a wrenching experience for the German Baptists. They pled through their publication *Der Sendbote* for American
non-involvement and the original neutralist position of President
Woodrow Wilson. German-Americans could predict the disaster
that awaited both Germany, where many were born, and their newly

adopted homeland. When the United States began to supply the Western Allies with munitions, the German-Americans could quickly understand the consequences of the reversal in national policy. Following in the track of the protest of J. G. Fetzer (the husband of Walter's sister Frieda), Walter joined his signature to 1,035,696 others who sought an embargo on shipping munitions to all combatants. However, President Wilson's decision to rescue France and the United Kingdom, and to retaliate against German submarine warfare, nullified the efforts to be neutral.[94]

Walter Rauschenbusch the Christian Socialist became the Christian pacifist during World War I. As a student of history and *real politik*, he developed a profound hatred of war. As the conflict broke out in Europe in August 1914, after the assassination of Austrian Crown Prince Francis Ferdinand, he was grieved and dismayed. He felt a special pain that the German leader, Kaiser Wilhelm II, should so provocatively align Germany with Austria-Hungary and make general war inevitable.

Rauschenbusch, in his dismay, pinned a black crepe ribbon on his coat, an emblem of grief, and wore it until the day of his death to signify his disdain of war as an extension of foreign policy.[95] During the war years, Walter wrote a study course, "The 49 Social Principles of Jesus." This course, printed in twenty thousand copies, was distributed by the YMCA to soldiers in the trenches and camps in France.[96]

His Concepts and Writings

At the Seminary in Rochester, Walter perfected the concepts of his Social Gospel and wracked many a pulpit with the publication of his revolutionary doctrines. He was challenged by others as to whether he remained a true Baptist. He wrote in reply to the inquiry: "I do believe that we Baptists have a magnificent body of truth—free, vital, honest, spiritual, and wholly in line with the noblest tendencies of our age." The primary reason for his remaining a Baptist was that: "The Christian faith as Baptists hold it sets spiritual experience boldly to the front as the one great thing in religion. It aims at experimental religion. We are an evangelistic body. We summon all men to conscious repentance from sin, to conscious prayer for forgiveness. If anyone desires to enter our churches we ask for evidence of such experience and we ask for nothing else."[97]

His further reason for being a Baptist was its social expression of the Christian faith. "Our Baptist organization, though it is faulty in many ways and though it creaks and groans as it works along, is built on very noble Christian lives and therefore is dear to me." This Baptist faith is unique, comprised of churches with no priestly caste or hierarchy, thereby serving as local Christian democracies, with home rule and "declining all alliances with the state."

Then, he loved his Baptist affiliation because of the Baptist mode of worship. He commented: "In our common worship we shall come closest to the spirit of true Christianity if every act is full of joy in God and his fellowship, love for one another, hatred for all evil, and an honest desire to live a right life in the sight of Christ."[98]

Walter's ideas and principles, as noted by the Armstrongs, were embraced by a multitude of people. They also evoked a hurricane of fierce opposition from fellow Baptists and evangelicals. After his first article in *Der Sendbote* (July 1890) on social reform, he was branded a "revolutionary" and "dangerous radical."[99] These mainline opponents feared that his social ideas diluted, if they did not ignore, the doctrine of salvation through the grace of God. Paul's admonition to the Romans had been: "Not by works lest any man should boast." But some Baptist clergy felt that the Social Gospel would fill churches with persons striving to earn entrance into Heaven on the basis of good works. The premillenial belief of other Baptists presumed that the world was getting worse, and only the Lord's return would bring an end to the moral decline.

If the world was approaching Armageddon and the second coming of Christ, the impetus of the church should be in fleeing from the Lord's judgment, a call for repentance, and the preaching of salvation. The Saved should then follow the injunction: "Come ye apart from them."[100]

While considering himself a Teddy Roosevelt Republican, Rauschenbusch brashly barged into forbidden territory and proclaimed himself a "Christian Socialist," at a historical period when socialists were identified with anarchists, nihilists, and atheists. Still, he repudiated all kinship with the materialism and atheism of Karl Marx and Communism, and boldly asserted that: "Religion is the only power which can make socialism succeed if it is established." Probably referring to the "godless movement" in the Soviet Union, he added: "[Socialism] cannot work in an irreligious country." Despite his disclaimers, his publicized remarks sounded ominous to many Christians who feared Marxism almost as much as the Anti-Christ.[101]

In Gaustad's study of Rauschenbusch, he asserts that in all probability Walter was the preeminent Protestant leader of Christians seeking to apply Christian principles to social problems. Wherever it took him, Walter battled monopolistic cartels and industry's rapacious methods. He assailed the materialism and mammonism of the period; he made among his primary commitments the eradication of capitalism's injustices.[102]

In his book *A Theology for the Social Gospel*, he wrote:

> If a man sacrifices his human dignity, and self-respect to increase his income, or stunts his intellectual growth and his human affections to swell his bank account, he is to that extent serving mammon and denying God. Likewise if he uses up and injures the life of his fellow-men to make money for himself, he serves mammon and denies God. But our industrial order does both. It makes property the end, and man the means to produce it.

Man is treated as a *thing* to produce more things: Men are hired as hands and not as men. They are paid only enough to maintain their working capacity and not enough to develop their manhood.

When their working force is exhausted, they are flung aside without consideration of their human needs. Jesus asked, "Is not a man more than a sheep?" Our industry says "No." It is careful of its livestock and machinery and careless of its human working force. It keeps its electrical engines immaculate in burnished cleanliness and lets its human dynamos sicken in dirt. . . .[103]

Writing with Conviction

Walter Rauschenbusch was a prolific writer, but his message was seldom moderate. He spoke for causes, and the causes spoke for urgency. In 1902 he had become a professor in the English Department of Rochester Theological Seminary, transferring from the German Department, and this change facilitated his literary efforts. His best-known publications were the three volumes on the Social Gospel, but he also wrote expansively on a wide variety of religious, social, and political topics. One of his most popular books was *Dare We Be Christians*. Then, from 1909 to 1911, in each issue of *The American Magazine*, under the heading "Prayers for the Social Awakening," he wrote a separate prayer.[104]

The Social Gospel was intricately described in Walter's book *Christianity and the Social Crisis*. Aware that his book would stir up controversy, in 1906 he left his manuscript with a publisher and departed for a year's study in Germany. He was astonished to learn that while he was vigorously condemned, there were other Christians that were hailing him as a prophet. His prime example was Jesus Christ, who ministered both to the spiritual and physical needs of a troubled people, poor, sick, diseased, and hungry. Walter's challenge was so insistent that it almost jumped from the pages:

> The first apostolate of Christianity was born from a deep fellow-feeling for social misery and from the consciousness of a great historical opportunity. Jesus saw the peasantry of Galilee

following him about with their poverty and their diseases, like shepherdless sheep that have been scattered and harried by beasts of prey, and his heart had compassion on them. He felt that the harvest was ripe, but there were few to reap it. Past history had come to its culmination; but there were few who understood the situation and were prepared to cope with it. He bade his disciples to pray for laborers for the harvest, and then made them answer their own prayers by sending them out two by two to proclaim the kingdom of God. That was the beginning of the worldwide mission of Christianity.[105]

The situation is repeated on a vaster scale today. If Jesus stood today amid our modern life, with that outlook on the condition of all humanity which observation and travel and the press would spread before him, he would create a new apostolate to meet the new needs in a new harvest time of history.[106]

The remarkable period in which Rauschenbusch was trumpeting his call for reform was one of the rawest epochs of capitalism, during which the American infrastructure ultimately would become the mightiest capital force in the world. But as the United States became a world contender, there would intervene the dark forces of World War I to crumble empires, deplete their finest men, and mobilize and then break the back of many of the most aggressive world cartels. During the industrialization of America, there was a period when twenty percent of the country's wealth was in the hands of 4,047 millionaires, such as Henry Ford, J. P. Morgan, and John D. Rockefeller. Only slowly were labor unions emerging, with men, women, and small children receiving pitiful rewards, in many cases, under harsh conditions. Having no adequate protectors, in some situations the unemployed organized marches and protests such as the march on Washington and the Chicago Pullman riots.[107]

On exploiting labor forces, Walter wrote:

> Men are first of all men, folks, members of our human family. To view them first of all as labor force is civilized barbarism. It is the attitude of the exploiter. — Our commercialization has

tainted our sense of fundamental human verities and values. We measure our national prosperity by pig-iron and steel instead of by the welfare of the people. . . .[108]

He then continued his discourse into the role of religion as the teacher of values to an industrial society:

> It is the function of religion to teach the individual to value his soul more than his body, and his moral integrity more than his income. In the same way it is the function of religion to teach society to value human life more than property, and to value property only in so far as it forms the material basis for the higher development of human life. . . . When commercialism in its headlong greed deteriorates the mass of human life, it defeats its own covetousness by killing the goose that lays the golden egg. Humanity is that goose—in more senses than one. —Religious men have been carved by the prevailing materialism and arrogant selfishness of our business world. They should have the courage of religious faith and assert that "man liveth not by bread alone," but by doing the will of God, and that the life of a nation "consisteth not in the abundance of things" which it produces, but in the way men live justly with one another and humbly with their God."[109]

The Curtain Falls

As the shadows began to creep toward Rauschenbusch in the decade marked by the first Great War, his concepts were powerful, both to his friends and foes. He was stone-deaf but comprehending much, and he had become an ardent pacifist, hating the World War that began in 1914.[110] He died of stomach cancer on July 25, 1918, only a few months before the acclaimed Armistice ending the Great War and signed in Paris on November 11. He had been one of the few American Christian intellectuals admired around the world.[111] His books were translated into French, German, Norwegian, Finnish, Swedish, Russian, Chinese, and Japanese.[112]

Among his staunch supporters were Chicago theologian Shailer Mathews and brilliant writer and preacher Harry Emerson Fosdick, both of these preachers widely accused of being extremely liberal. Although calling himself a Baptist, Fosdick was nearly tried for heresy by the Presbyterians in 1922, while he was serving as pastor of New York's First Presbyterian Church. Fosdick maintained that full immersion and the virginity of Mary, mother of Jesus, were not critical issues for Christianity and that there was no necessity for a Christian doctrine that Jesus' death is a substitutionary atonement for mankind's sins. Supported by millionaire John D. Rockefeller, Fosdick served many years as pastor of the non-denominational Riverside Church in New York City.[113]

One of his scholarly admirers acclaimed Walter Rauschenbusch as among the three greatest contributors in America to the "Thought of the Christian Church," the other two being Horace Bushnell and Jonathan Edwards.[114]

Summary

As Father of the Social Gospel, Walter Rauschenbusch is the author of three books that turned the religious world on its ear. These works were *Christianity and the Social Crisis* (1907), *Christianity and the Social Gospel*, and *A Theology for the Social Gospel* (1917. He also wrote *Dare We Be Christians* and composed prayers for "The American Magazine." His versatility extended to new hymnals written in German and co-authored with evangelist Ira D. Sankey: *Evangeliums Lieder* (*Gospel Songs*), published in 1892, *Evangeliums Saenger*, published in 1910, and *Glaubensharfe* (*New Harp of Faith*), published in 1916.

Rauschenbusch was an unexpected nugget discovered in the soil of a microscopic organization with an unlikely name, the North American Baptist General Conference. The first Baptist church of this obscure German-speaking band was organized in Philadelphia in 1843, and even as late as 1977 the German Baptist congregations consisted of a combined membership of fifty-seven thousand souls. Still, that little matrix in mysterious ways influenced Rauschenbusch to become a radical Christian, while he invited enemies by calling himself a Christian Socialist. The German Baptists, his flock, were conservative missionary Baptists, but some of them had been pietists and persecuted in Germany, and nearly all struggled from day to day enduring shabby housing and an oppressive working environment.

He gladly chose to launch his crusade from his urban Galilee, the Second German Baptist Church, situated in New York City's notorious "Hell's Kitchen." He sharpened his tools of the Social Gospel for eleven years in a blighted neighborhood of struggling immigrants, while living on a meager salary of nine hundred dollars a year. Still, his personality and outward appearance were deceptive, for he was handsome, nurtured a bright sense of humor, favored a trim moustache, and sometimes wore a natty suit. He could have been a *bon vivant*, but this young preacher was dead-serious and his message was often harsh. Walter Rauschenbusch's motivator was Jesus Christ the Revolutionary, the same Christ who cleansed the temple. Rauschenbusch would rip into the industrial world and tear it apart, if necessary, until the great capitalists, monopolists, and managers became sensitive to housing, industrial safety, and fair wages for the male, female, and child workers and their distressed families.

Thus, in American industry's transcendent period—the epoch between the Civil War and World War I—the worker's prophet of Hell's Kitchen ignited the fire of the Social Gospel. Even as Jesus hated the hypocrisy of the Pharisees, Rauschenbusch scourged the capitalists, cartelists, and monopolists, not because they aspired to become rich but because in the process they often oppressed their laborers and cared little for their welfare. His concerns were often focused on protection of sick workers, education, recreation, children's health, pollution, and assistance for workers forced to abandon their houses. He favored unions and the strike as practical means for protection against abuse. He supported the right of labor to protest in the hard times of 1893-94 and to strike in Brooklyn in 1895. As a self-called Christian Socialist, he spoke for cleaning out the anti-quated labor laws and instituting new norms.

Despite his radicalism, Rauschenbusch proclaimed that salvation could be attained only through grace provided by the blood of Christ. Although a Christian Socialist, he was not stalking the streets to destroy the churches and demolish the Ten Commandments. But he would have concluded with the Apostle Paul that faith without works is dead.

He was deeply involved in the ideological struggle in the North between fundamentalists and liberals that some dated to the founding of the University of Chicago in 1890[115] and that reached its apex in the 1920s. One of the principal personalities of this controversy was the University of Chicago theological professor George B. Foster, who appeared to question the reliability of the Scriptures and to attribute to Paul more than Jesus the founding of the Christian church. Some conservatives felt that liberal clergymen were attempting to deliver the Baptist Faith to the Unitarians. The struggle caused 225 Northern Baptist churches in southern Illinois to defect to the Southern Baptist Convention.

Rauschenbusch was in the middle of the fray, accusing the churches of forsaking the message of Jesus about the coming Kingdom of God and doling out a mild Greek sop about the goodness of Jesus. He wanted a church of prophets, but the church was producing only priests.[116] But he did not question the Bible, salvation by grace, the messiahship of Christ, immersion, or the democratic concept at the heart of Baptist choice.

As World War I was terminating in 1918 (the struggle having killed a million men at Verdun alone) the deaf revolutionary Walter Rauschenbusch died in the saddle. Until almost the signing of the terms of peace, he had been an avowed pacifist, hating the war that had killed 293,000 Americans and had impoverished the German empire.

Out of the steadiness and vision of the German Baptists that sustained Walter Rauschenbusch there came a surge of inspiration. The German branch, now called North American Baptist Conference (NABC), has grown in numbers and employs mainly English in its services. It established its organizational headquarters at Oakbrook Terrace, Illinois, and moved its seminary from Rochester to Sioux Falls, South Dakota. These moves were to strengthen ties with traditional cultural German-American communities in Canada and the West. Rauschenbusch, the Christian optimist, the product of immigration and industrial change, probably would have welcomed all of these providential trends.

The exceptional legacy of Walter Rauschenbusch was the carving of the new path of the Social Gospel to be expanded by Baptists and Christians of all denominations. His ingenuity was to leave to all generations in modern terms Jesus' injunction: "Love your neighbor as yourself."

Chapter 18

Martin Luther King, Jr.
(1929-1968)

Black Champion and the Civil Rights Revolution

The Civil Rights avalanche in America that enveloped its black minority and changed forever its white majority, began almost noiselessly during the Korean War, gathered force in the 1950s, and then thundered to unimagined power during the Eisenhower, Kennedy, and Johnson presidencies. The movement escalated as an unstoppable force, and its young leader, Baptist preacher Martin Luther King, Jr., the black Moses, assumed a legendary place in history.

In a sense, the struggle had begun in 1877, when the northern Republicans forsook their unhappy Reconstruction mandate for the South and left the fate of the former slaves to their old slavemasters. The Negro, in cruel abandonment, both in the North and the South, was generally to be "grandfathered," not properly educated, given the most menial work, and treated socially as inferior. Negro soldiers returning home from World War II were angry and sullen when turned away from hotels and restaurants and obliged to drink from "colored only" drinking fountains.

The "grandfather clauses" perpetuated white political control. This was a foxy concept in the Southern states, which allowed otherwise unqualified whites to vote if their grandfathers had voted.

President Harry S. Truman, by executive order in 1948, signaled

Martin Luther King, Jr.,
the Christian Visionary (1929-1968)

a new direction by ordering the integration of all segregated military units, just prior to the Korean War. Also, an epochal change in education was initiated in May 1954 by the U. S. Supreme Court, with its decision in *Brown v Board of Education of Topeka, Kansas.* This decision nullified the doctrine of "separate but equal" education, as enunciated in the case of *Plessy v Ferguson.* Then, to underline the commitment of the government to continued reform in civil rights, there was added the Johnson Civil Rights Act of 1957; however, its inadequate measures convinced many blacks that to attain equal rights they must rely on themselves alone.

Into this maelstrom of dangerous social change would step its leader, a highly-educated twenty-seven-year-old inexperienced Southern intellect from a privileged Negro Baptist minister's family. His post-graduate seminary education was derived from liberal institutions in the North, and he became a dabbler in the teachings of Protestant theologians Paul Tillich and Reinhold Niebuhr, Baptist social gospeler Walter Rauschenbusch, and (from the Orient) Mahatma Gandhi. In his intellectual world, he sampled a diverse menu, even Marxist dogma and philosophy, but he never embraced Communist materialism. Perhaps, in his final choice of doctrine, he was pragmatically drawn to Reinhold Niebuhr, who reminded his readers that injustice was due, not to innocence, but to "predatory self-interest." It was the same Niebuhr that charged "the liberal world of being in full flight from the Christian doctrine of sin."

Martin Luther King differed from thousands of disturbed people and many civil rights leaders by his consistent advocacy of nonviolence. In view of his prominence in the Civil Rights struggle, had he not urged nonviolence repeatedly his leadership role conceivably could have been snatched by violent men, including those who directed the Black Muslims. Any appeal to force also would have given justification to dangerous whites, outraged by their social displacement, and a multitude of peaceful persons black and white might have paid the price. King's proclivity for peace should have flowed naturally from a minister of Jesus Christ. In that context, it is not always remembered that Martin Luther King was a close friend of Baptist evangelist Billy Graham, and it is a certainty that Graham would have advised him to remain peaceful in his tactics. Then, much attention has been given to the 1959 trip of King to visit India and confer with Nehru and other associates of deceased Hindu saint Mahatma Gandhi. While King remained fascinated for years by Gandhi-inspired Satyagraha, or Soul Force, action that embodied nonviolence, his inspiration for practicing nonviolence preceded by years the trip to Asia.

As leader of the Montgomery bus boycott and the Birmingham demonstrations, his willingness to endure jailing and abuse without bitterness, to accept peril to his family and the bombing of his home, Martin Luther King became an institution, the symbol of the black man's struggle for equality. In 1963 King was selected "Man of the Year" by *Time* magazine. His accomplishments were numerous: he had headed the Montgomery Improvement Association (MIA), had been a major organizer of the Southern Christian Leadership Conference (SCLC), and had shone brilliantly as speaker at the March on Washington in 1963. His fame was not only national but international, and whether in Ghana or India, he was mobbed and entertained lavishly. He was received at the White House by Presidents Dwight D. Eisenhower and John Kennedy and hosted on a world trip by Vice President Richard Nixon. But, as in a Chinese fabric or rug, there were hidden flaws, and they were in the privacy of his personal life.

Then, on April 4, 1968, when only thirty-nine years of age, Martin Luther King was assassinated in Memphis, Tennessee, and, as is the case too often, the man of peace who would not hate was removed by hate. But that could not erase his sacrificial life and lofty ideals nor rob him of the acclaim due to him as one of the great men of history.

Martin Luther King (Trailblazer) was born on January 15, 1929, in the house of his maternal grandfather A. D. Williams in Atlanta. The Trailblazer's father was "Big Mike," a struggling Negro Baptist minister, soon to be pastor of Atlanta's prominent Ebenezer Baptist Church, who would name his child Michael Luther King, Jr. However, this child of destiny and protagonist of this chapter, for most of his life, would be called "M. L." or "Little Mike." For good fortune or bad, M. L. was the middle child subsisting between sister Christine, sixteen months older, and brother A. D., seventeen months younger.[1]

The Great Depression of the 1920s-1930s had wreaked devastation across America. Ebenezer Church was reduced to two hundred members, and the church was on the threshold of foreclosure when in March 1931 the old pastor, the Reverend A. D. Williams, president of the Atlanta Baptist (Negro) Ministers Union, passed away. The staunch widow, Jennie, with imposing prestige and chutzpah, forthwith declared that Big Mike (M. L.'s father) would be the minister at Ebenezer, although he had pastored only small country churches. In order to align themselves properly, the Ebenezer deacons reversed themselves and elected Big Mike pastor of the church, although the bank's padlocks still closed the portals of the sanctuary.[2]

The mother of M. L. King was Alberta, daughter of the Reverend A. D. Williams, in an earlier period a homely, shy, and rarely noticed child. In time, she would become the organist at Ebenezer Church, and an organizer and tower of strength. Her professional education was partially gained at Spelman College, Atlanta, her mother's alma mater.[3]

The story of M. L.'s grandfather A. D. Williams embodied a remarkable demonstration of social ascent. A. D., son of a slave, ran away to Atlanta and was "called" to become a Baptist minister. In the days of slavery, blacks flocked joyfully to the plain uncluttered Baptist churches, because there was much freedom there. Elder Wilson Thompson relates in his biography that in Missouri Green's household, a slave named Dick risked a severe beating and loss of privileges by insisting that he be baptized. A white elder, Pastor Thomson, also risked imprisonment by immersing the resolute Negro Dick—who defied his infidel master and won his respect by persevering in the baptism.[4]

In 1894, A. D. became the pastor of the tiny Ebenezer Baptist Church, with its heavy mortgage and only thirteen members. But there were remarkable potentialities in this young preacher, for he attended Morehouse College in Atlanta, married Miss Jennie Parks, increased the church membership to over one hundred members, and absorbed another larger church.[5] A. D., through real estate transactions, religious leadership, and civic action, would become known as one of the nation's leading black ministers. His honors included serving as national treasurer of the National Baptist Convention, while a member of foreign and home mission boards. In 1914 Morehouse College conferred an honorary doctorate on him.[6]

In this post-Reconstruction period, even "good" whites from the North and South often ignored the fate of the black worker, deprived him of any voting role, prevented him from serving in the legislatures, and conspired to break up black coalitions. Northerners also regarded racial confrontation like leprosy, fearing such outbreaks would harm business and obstruct reform legislation. President Theodore Roosevelt (president 1901-09) invited black educator Booker T. Washington to the White House, and for his generosity Roosevelt was denounced severely.[7]

A violent outbreak in this repressive period occurred in 1906, when news stories of alleged insults and rape of white women in Atlanta resulted in white mobs killing nearly fifty blacks. The Atlanta race riot in 1906 caused many wealthy whites to flee from downtown Atlanta. However, this had a bright side for urban Negroes. The Reverend A. D. Williams, as a consequence, was then able to buy for himself at a bargain price on Auburn Avenue a two-story, five-bedroom Victorian mansion, with twelve-foot ceilings. The Williams family accepted boarders, whose monthly payments helped reduce the mortgage.[8]

As a youth, M. L.'s father "Big Mike" was a country yokel, raw and unkempt, but bursting with ambition. Even when he traveled to Atlanta to earn a college education, he was only an ignorant bumpkin, with grammar-school skills. His acceptance into college and his remarkable courtship of the elitist Miss Alberta Williams were both in the order of semi-miracles.

Mike King, the father of M. L., born in December 1899, the second in a line of ten children, was conceived on a sharecropper's farm near Stockbridge, Georgia. His father James was a heavy drinker and wife-beater. After a brutal fight between James and fourteen-year-old Mike, who was trying to protect his mother Delia, his father swore repeatedly that he would kill the young man. Delia somehow managed to sell a portion of the family livestock so that her son could buy an old car and escape to Atlanta. At an early age, he had felt called to be a Baptist preacher. The Ford enabled him to travel before he was twenty years old and minister to several churches as a circuit preacher. His most dependable source of financial support, however, was his work in an Atlanta tire plant.[9]

As an untutored preacher, Big Mike attended local Atlanta conferences sponsored by the large National Baptist (Negro) Convention. It was there that he heard about Alberta Williams, daughter of the Reverend A. D. Williams, the Convention's national treasurer. Before he had glimpsed her form or spoken a word to her, he bragged to his laughing, disbelieving friends that he would marry the lady. Meanwhile, not knowing what God would deliver, Alberta Williams was confined to a strict regimen at her Spelman College dormitory or busily organizing a new choir at Ebenezer, her father's church.[10]

Baptist Spelman College was not quite a reformatory, even in the 1920s, but the rules were almost as tough. Visits between boys and girls were limited to one Saturday per month, the full tryst to last twenty minutes and no more. But Big Mike found a way to his target, and it was through her misfortune. Alberta had broken her ankle and was recuperating at the Williams home, where Big Mike's sister was boarding. They spoke only once, but Mike told her he was a Baptist minister. Mike was twenty years old, and the gulf between him and the college girl he planned to marry seemed unbridgeable. His education was pathetic, and in humiliation he began his upward climb from a fifth-grade class in a Negro school filled with minor children.[11]

However, the unlikely suitor had the courage of a tiger. He met Alberta again walking home from Spelman for an overnight stay. He sputtered in his feeling of inadequacy. "Oh," she said, "I couldn't forget meeting a preacher. My father wouldn't allow it." When he asked her to begin a courtship, she said she would request her father's permission. Thus, began a relationship of six years, filled with teas, socials, and rides in the Model-T Ford.[12]

Big Mike was blustery in telling Alberta about his ambitions. Someday he would pastor an imposing church, like new Ebenezer Baptist (the construction begun by Williams and finished in 1922). Also, he would attain management rank in the new Citizens Trust Company. In his stride, he predicted that he would live in a prestigious brick mansion, like those near Atlanta's Morris Brown College. However, perhaps aspiring for more for his daughter, the Reverend A. D. Williams refused permission for the couple to marry. Apparently, the backward, ambitious Mike was just not in the same league as the eminent Williams family.[13]

Then, seeking to vindicate himself, Mike took a battery of tests to enter Morehouse College, regarded by many male blacks as their Princeton. He failed the tests miserably; then he was insulted by the registrar, who informed him that he was "just not college material." Exploding with frustration, he rushed into the president's office. The kindly president, John Hope, seeing some potential in the youth, overruled his staff, and issued special orders to admit Big Mike to the college.[14]

Mike King and Alberta were married at Ebenezer Baptist Church on Thanksgiving Day, 1926. The couple moved into an upstairs bedroom in the Williams home on Auburn Avenue. Like John D. Rockefeller, their Baptist college benefactor who lived with his wife's family, Mike would dwell with his in-laws until the senior Williams died.[15]

After Big Mike's succession in 1931 as pastor to Ebenezer, expedited by his mother-in-law Mrs. Jennie Williams, his native abilities began to emerge. He signaled his leadership by purchasing a Wurlitzer organ with two thousand pipes. Then he developed a rivalry lasting forty years with the Wheat Street Baptist Church's polished pastor, the Reverend William Holmes Borders. Borders, as a faculty member of Morehouse, began an ambitious radio program and then the expansion of his church. Big Mike, on the other hand, was soon in trouble with the black Atlanta Baptist Ministers Union. When the epic film *Gone With the Wind* (1939) had its gala opening in Atlanta's City Auditorium, along with its alcoholic refreshments, dancing, and a segregated crowd at the reception, trouble was brewing among Atlanta's blacks. Mike Sr. (Big Mike) was the only Negro preacher there to listen as the Ebenezer choir sang under the direction of Mrs. King.[16]

Mike King's progress was phenomenal. Not only did he become known as one of North America's best-known Negro pastors, he was elected a trustee both of the Citizens Trust Bank and Morehouse College. After the death of his mother-in-law, "Mama," he bought a yellow brick house on Bishop's Row, fulfilling his earlier promise to Alberta. Mike Sr. became a principal local organizer, when in 1939 the international organization the Baptist World Alliance, thirty-five thousand faithful strong, met in Atlanta's Ponce de Leon Park. The highlight of the occasion was the address given by the Reverend J. H. Jackson, pastor of the largest Negro Baptist church in the United States, Olivet Baptist Church in Chicago. While in Atlanta, Jackson was a guest in the King home, where he would meet and be adored by the son, young Mike (M. L.). Much later, the rival visions and programs of J. H. Jackson and Young Mike would create an enmity and an unbridgeable canyon of distrust.[17]

Mike King was not a great theologian, but he was an organizer and man of action. He was practical, plainspoken, and loyal to his congregation. With the severe financial depression hurting the whole population, he induced his flock to support each other financially and spiritually. Finances were centralized in the church. He created twelve clubs, one for each month, that competed in giving church gifts. Each club had its own officers and social events. Church members who were barbers had exclusive calls for business, while insurance agents in the church monopolized that business. Because of this church-wide cooperation and the friendly competition, Mike King could proudly say that he rescued Ebenezer from bankruptcy. Soon, it could be said that he was the highest paid Negro minister in Atlanta, with four thousand members in the congregation.[18]

Early Life of M. L. King

Sandwiched between his sister Christine, an excellent student, and A. D., a rock thrower, M. L. was a placid middle child. As a youngster, M. L. did very little complaining, even when spanked. He was a stoic, taking his punishment and bearing no grudges. When he was attacked, he did not strike back.[19]

In 1934, after only two years as pastor of Ebenezer, Mike King (Big Daddy) made a trip to the Holy Land and on to the Baptist World Alliance meeting in Berlin. He toured the sites where the German monk Martin Luther defied Pope Leo X and Emperor Charles V, and where the Anabaptists withstood Martin Luther and the princes. After returning to Atlanta to compelling headlines, Mike changed his name to Martin Luther King and the name of his young son, five years old, to Martin Luther King, Jr.[20] To family friends, the pastor was called Big Mike or Daddy King, while the son used the moniker of Little Mike or M. L.

M. L.'s first formal Christian act was to follow his sister Christine in 1934 to the front row of Ebenezer Church and there to affirm his willingness to be baptized. Later, he would confess that he had no idea of the significance of his action. He was immersed, but by his own words he became a church member without being "born-again" in Christ.[21]

During his attendance at the grammar school, the black middle class was leaving Auburn Avenue and moving into Atlanta's Hunter Hill, now called the West Side. This was in contrast to the stark conditions and long breadlines of the poor black class and the reality that about sixty-six percent of black males in Atlanta were unemployed. In M. L.'s privileged environment, the Congregational Church was at the apex of black society. Young M. L. attended the elitist Lab School and was thrown into the company of the Hunter Hill crowd. Young Martin described his own Auburn Avenue neighborhood as "a wholesome community, notwithstanding the fact that none of us were even considered member[s] of the upper, upper class."[22]

The youngster M. L. was given the name "Tweedie," since choosing to be a dandy, he was well-groomed in his tweed suits. He doted on Victorian love poetry, large words, and a grandiose style. But his mastery of this affectation was so impressive that he was not ridiculed. Thus he was accepted, along with other neighborhood characters such as "Shag," "Rooster," "Sack," and "Mole."

The Atlanta University Laboratory School had been created to prove that high-quality teachers could turn out Negro graduates as skilled as white ones. World War II destroyed this experiment, as the student body was absorbed into the military services. M. L. then entered the only Negro public high school on Atlanta's West Side, riding to classes on a public bus. As a thirteen-year-old, an achiever leading his class, he was transferred in the fall of 1942 to the tenth grade at Booker T. Washington High School. Despite his prowess, Negro schools in general were deficient in equipment, scholarship, and properly trained teachers. And young M. L. eventually came face to face with truth; at age fifteen he sought admission to prestigious Morehouse College and discovered that he could read no better than a junior high school eighth grader.[23]

Morehouse president "Buck Benny" Mays was desperate because the college was nearly bankrupt. The United States was engaged in World War II, involved in fierce combat with Germany and Japan, and the young college men were going off to war. In order to salvage the declining fortunes of Morehouse, President Mays lowered the standards and accepted freshmen that normally should have been attending high school classes. During the heady war years, young M. L. at Morehouse found friendship with students rebelling against their fathers, who were pushing them into preaching careers. His closest comrades included opera aspirant Bob Williams (an Army veteran), fifteen-year-old Samuel Cook, and college barber and part-time preacher Walter McCall.[24]

It was Walter "Mac" McCall who became his closest companion, and the pair were known on the campus as "Mac and Mike," but this friendship developed only after a wild wrestling match. McCall was the campus hair stylist and when M. L. was unable to pay his dime fee, a fight broke out on the campus. Although lighter in weight, M. L. won, and the two became inseparable, after young Martin paid for his haircut. The two would go to church, sitting in the balcony, but Mac detested sermons about heaven and the cross. Serious doubts about the validity of Christianity began to assail M. L., and by his sophomore year he began to dislike the idea of going to church. Young King had entered Morehouse planning to become a medical doctor, but when he found the biological sciences too tough, he switched his program to train as an attorney.[25]

In his deepening skepticism, the college boy mulled the words of faith from his grandmother "Mama," with whom he shared a tight bond, and he recalled (as he defined them) the insufficient and fraudulent preachments on race by his father Big Mike. His father usually avoided confrontation on matters of race and felt that, while racism was wrong, the perverse actions of some white people was to be answered by God alone. However, when a shoe clerk tried to fit shoes for Big Mike and M. L. in a "black-only" nook, the two customers marched out. In contrast, sociology professor Walter Chivers described racism in terms shaped by Marxist dialectics.[26]

At this stage in his life, no one could believe that Mike would become a preacher. At Morehouse he wrote: "the shackles of fundamentalism were removed from my body." He and McCall began experimenting with dancing and card-playing, both minor sins on the Baptist list. Also, Professor Gladstone Chandler taught him word-games. In answer to the question "How are you?" young Mike would reply, "I surmise that my physical equilibrium is organically quiescent."[27]

In 1945, Vice President Harry S. Truman, a Baptist from Missouri, became the thirty-third president of the United States, succeeding the deceased New Deal president, Franklin Delano Roosevelt.[28] It was Truman who would sign the executive order ending segregated military units in the armed forces. President Truman soon appointed a special commission to recommend social legislation, after he learned about two couples murdered by hooded men near Monroe, Georgia. In the aftermath of this development, Mike's college friend Samuel Cook helped organize a chapter of the NAACP (National Association for the Advancement of Colored People).[29]

The Western Alliance, which had achieved the ending of World War II in 1945, would find itself split into two camps; the Soviet Union and its Warsaw Pact allies would engage in a deadly standoff with the North Atlantic Treaty Organization (NATO). Meanwhile, the Soviet Union was breaking its promises on holding free elections in Soviet-occupied East Germany, Poland, and Czechoslovakia, hesitated to retire from Austria, and refused as promised to give Poland a free choice of governments. There was great unrest abroad, as the old colonial powers, Great Britain, France, Netherlands, and Portugal, sought to restore their empires and snuff out the independence movements in the colonies. Negro troops returning to the United States after combat in World War II demanded political and economic equality with whites, but were met with indifference or defiance.[30]

During the summer of 1946, young Mike quit his job as a laborer with the Atlanta Railway Express Company, after the foreman repeatedly called him "nigger." Whites were using the term more frequently, as tensions mounted. There was a resurgence of mob violence, particularly in the South, and in one week six Negro war veterans were killed.[31]

Young King and his friends Larry Williams and Walter McCall did not involve themselves in the campus agitation that was becoming commonplace in the nation. Instead, they were frequently crowded together on the balcony of the Wheat Street Baptist Church studying the style and secrets of the Reverend William Holmes Borders. Martin Luther King, Sr., was offended when he heard that Larry Williams had offered himself as an understudy to Borders, but M. L. refused to end his friendship with Williams. While M. L. by his junior year had given up his ambition to become a lawyer, he was clearly looking for something in a Christian career beyond his father's fundamentalism.[32]

In Atlanta, young Mike told his father that he had been "called by God to the pulpit" and that he intended to enter the ministry. So, to his father's delight, at age eighteen, he delivered his trial sermon— one borrowed from Baptist preacher Harry Emerson Fosdick—before a home crowd at Ebenezer. Soon he was ordained and became Ebenezer's assistant pastor under the patriarchal guidance of his father. He shared the responsibilities of officiating at marriages, funerals, and ceremonies with Larry Williams, now the assistant pastor under the Reverend Mr. Borders.[33]

In M. L.'s last year at Morehouse, President Harry Truman addressed the NAACP national convention, and in response to its report, the President appointed the Commission on Civil Rights; he asked Congress for a federal anti-lynching law. Concern over civil rights continued nationally to percolate as an issue, and NAACP's Walter White and *Atlanta Constitution's* editor Ralph McGill, both liberals, began a lively exchange of views.[34]

Attending Crozier

The stifling control of young Mike's thought processes and development at the hands of his father was becoming unendurable. The final example of parental interference was the apology demanded of M. L. by Mike, Sr., to be made before the Ebenezer congregation for attending a YMCA dance with Larry Williams. In order to obtain an advanced degree—but also to get away from his father and Atlanta—young Mike decided in 1948 to attend liberal, largely-white Crozier Theological Seminary in Chester, Pennsylvania. M. L.'s best friend, Walter McCall, would join him there. This was an epochal year, both on the national and international stage, for in it Truman gained his startling unexpected political victory over Republican presidential candidate Thomas Dewey, and the Soviet Union initiated the Berlin blockade, seeking to drive the Western allies from Berlin.[35]

Crozier was a citadel of free-thinking. One of its leading professors of New Testament, M. Scott Enslin, observed neither Christmas nor Easter. M. L.'s favorite instructor, however, was Professor George W. Davis, an admirer both of Walter Rauschenbusch's Social Gospel and of Mahatma Gandhi. M. L. felt reasonably comfortable at the seminary, for one-third of the members of his thirty-two-man class were blacks.[36]

At Crozier, M. L. won a reputation for his eloquence in presenting his practice sermons. When he was scheduled to deliver a sermon, his fellow seminarians packed the chapel. The economic success of his father relieved him of any requirement to work for a living. Thus, he could give full attention to his studies and the poetry of James Russell Lowell and William Cullen Bryant. Both M. L. and Walter McCall were fighting Negro stereotypes, and young Mike was described as "too carefully dressed." However, in the racial tension that penetrated even Crozier, M. L. asserted his belief that love and reason would transcend racial hatreds.[37]

In 1949 in Atlanta, while home for the Christmas holiday, and alerted by the Alger Hiss trial in New York, he spent hours studying the political views of Karl Marx. During this period, the Reverend Harry Emerson Fosdick, the much-imitated Baptist preacher, had presented a widely-discussed sermon proclaiming that the Communists had stolen the psychology of conversion and the commitment to the oppressed. In his analysis of Marxism, King took note that moral forces had no value to Communism. He rejected both historical materialism and ethical relativism and their homage to economic forces.[38]

In his last year at Crozier, Mike was deeply affected by the theological teachings of Reinhold Niebuhr, while the Social Gospel of Walter Rauschenbusch had lost much of its magnetism.[39] Niebuhr, through his book *Moral Man and Immoral Society*, ridiculed John Dewey's thesis that injustice was principally attributable to ignorance. Instead, stated Niebuhr, injustice was due to "predatory self-interest." Niebuhr also assailed the liberal world for running away from the Christian doctrine of sin.[40] Niebuhr maintained that only laws of force, not persuasion, would achieve equal rights for the Negro. Niebuhr also attacked the Marxists for deluding the masses, pretending to have discovered a science of history.[41] However, it was evident that religious conservatives, such as Big Mike, would not embrace a scholar [Reinhold Niebuhr] who found President Franklin Roosevelt too rightist and questioned the literal truth of the Bible.

Some biographers of Martin Luther King have ascribed supreme importance to the influence of Mahatma Gandhi on M. L.'s civil actions and beliefs. However, it may be more logical to attribute this influence to Niebuhr, who favored the linkage of religion and politics as a weapon for minorities seeking equality. But Niebuhr did believe that Gandhi's nonviolent techniques could be adapted to American conditions and employed in a protracted campaign. As a consequence, M. L. purchased a half-dozen books about Gandhi and adopted nonviolence as his strategy for power.[42]

On November 25, 1950, while King was taking his final examination in American church history at Crozier, 180,000 Communist Chinese crossed the Yalu River into Korea to attack the American troops there.[43] General Douglas MacArthur, the allied commander, had misinterpreted Chinese intentions in the area, and President Harry Truman was visibly upset by the failure of his intelligence sources. Secretary of State Dean Acheson then sought a criminal trial for eighty-two-year old black NAACP leader W.E.B. Dubois for distributing a peace petition. However, the books and sentiments of DuBois had circulated among black troops since World War II, and the charges were dismissed.[44]

As he closed out his days at Crozier, Martin Luther King, Jr., had already decided, by September 1951, to seek a Ph.D. at Boston University. This further venture left Big Mike unhappy, for Ph.D. attainers tended to teach in universities rather than to preach. But eventually relenting, the father gave his son a green Chevrolet as the prize for being the top achiever in his Crozier class. M. L. had selected Boston University in part because Crozier professor George W. Davis was an admirer of Boston University's Professor Edgar S. Brightman, who advanced the "Theology of Personalism" about the personal God of the Scriptures. Meanwhile, on the Boston campus, theologians Karl Barth and Paul Tillich were referring to God in such vague impersonal terms as "wholly other" and "something of supreme value."[45]

At Boston University

In September 1951, at age twenty-two, young Mike headed from Atlanta to Boston. President Harry Truman was confronting the knotty problem of overcoming the bloody stalemate of the Korean conflict. King was given the singular honor of preaching at one of the largest Baptist churches in the world, Gardner Taylor's Concord Baptist Church in Brooklyn, which was in a friendly rivalry with Adam Clayton Powell's Abyssinian Baptist Church.[46]

At Boston University, King took ten courses from professors L. Harold DeWolf and Edgar Brightman and became a favorite student of the latter Personalist specialist. At this time, Martin Luther King was a little below average height, with an oblong face.[47] He smoked a pipe, had a proper look of distraction, and wore tailored suits. M. L. shared an apartment with student Philip Lenud, who did the cooking, while M. L. washed the dishes. He was active in the graduate discussion group, called the "Dialectical Society" or "Philosophical Club."[48] The twenty-odd blacks at the graduate school met once a week for supper and discussions. M. L. once startled the senior students by asserting that he had just buried "Jim." "Jim who?" They laughed when he replied, "Jim Crow."[49]

King enjoyed the company of women and contrived a code to rank them: "Doctor" for attractive ladies, "Constitution" for hardy ones willing to go on an adventure. He stumbled into an encounter with his future wife, Miss Coretta Scott, who was earning her living as a maid while attending Boston's New England Conservatory of Music. Coretta was the daughter of a fairly successful black farmer in rural Alabama—the owner of a fine house and several hundred acres of cotton. Coretta as a young woman had picked cotton with her sisters, scrubbed clothes in Obadiah Scott's household, attended a Congregational school, and then ventured to Antioch College. In his grandiose style upon meeting Coretta, M. L. referred to himself as Napoleon facing his Waterloo. He continued: "I'm on my knees." Coretta snapped crisply, "That's absurd. You don't even know me." After the verbal fencing, Miss Scott agreed to have lunch with him the next day. She eventually revealed that her ambition was to be a classical singer, but in order to attain this goal she worked at her boarding house as a simple maid among a group of Irish maids.[50]

Coretta had a different style than the other girls of the young King crowd. She was almost two years older than M. L., wouldn't jitterbug, loved classical music, and admired hoop-skirted formal gowns, tastes that did not endear her to Walter McCall. But the attraction was mutual, and although the intelligent, strong-willed Coretta was treated coolly by the King family in Atlanta, who wanted their son to marry into the Georgia black royalty, M. L. firmly announced his intentions.[51]

Martin Luther King, Jr., and Coretta were married on June 18, 1953, in a grand wedding near Selma, Alabama. Coretta was strong enough to remove from the marriage vow the promise to obey her husband. Their wedding night was spent in a funeral parlor owned by friends. On the following Sunday, she became a Baptist and was immersed in the baptistry at Ebenezer Church by Daddy King, who also arranged for her to get a teller's position at Citizens Trust Bank.[52]

In the summer of 1953, an historic meeting was held in Miami of the black National Baptist Convention. Blind President D. V. Jemison had directed the Convention for many years, but this year saw two formidable challengers: the Reverend William Holmes Borders of Atlanta and the outstanding Chicago orator, the Reverend J. H. Jackson (with Daddy King as his floor manager and young M. L. as rally leader). With ten thousand preachers cheering, the contingent from Crozier Seminary overturned the odds, and the Reverend J. H. Jackson was elected the new president.[53] But the alliance would not last, and in time young Martin and the family friend J. H. Jackson would become estranged contenders.

At Boston University, M. L. had one more year of course work, and was seriously pursuing his Ph.D requirements at the School of Theology. His advisor, Professor DeWolf, unveiled the life of St. Augustine and the pertinent lessons in pride, reverence, and sensuality to Martin and his classmates.[54] Martin wrote his doctoral dissertation on the perceptions of God as seen through the writings of Harvard theologian Paul Tillich and University of Chicago professor Henry Nelson Wieman, both of them Transcendentalists. His original intent was to criticize Tillich and Wieman for their liberal theology, evidencing teachings too arid and speculative to satisfy human yearnings.[55]

Pastor at Montgomery

On September 5, 1954, the aspiring scholar M. L. King, Jr., on the recommendation of his powerful father, became the pastor of the prestigious Dexter Avenue Baptist Church in Montgomery, Alabama. Dexter was a rarity, a middle-class Negro church of three hundred members in central Montgomery, within walking distance of the white Capitol building.[56] It was a stiff, even stuffy church, with shouting frowned upon, an organist that refused to accompany spiritual songs, and no night services. This was a "white-collar" black church dominated by powerful deacons, who expected their intellectual pastor to tow the line. Young M. L. King knew the trap he was stepping into, and he contrived to smash his way to freedom in his first weeks at Dexter.[57]

The previous pastor was the Reverend Vernon Johns, brilliant and eccentric, who sometimes wore mismatched socks. He was a graduate of Oberlin College and had received his graduate theological training at the University of Chicago. In his lofty position, Johns sometimes excoriated long-absent members, and when Dr. H. C. Trenholm, president of Alabama State, finally arrived, Johns admonished him: "I want to pause here in the service until Dr. Trenholm can get himself seated here on his semi-annual visit to the church." Dr. Trenholm never returned to Dexter. On another occasion, he identified a doctor in his congregation facing a trial as a "murderer."[58]

The Reverend Mr. Johns, amid the racial tensions in the South, could be both resolute and brave. At the Montgomery police station, he protested in vain the alleged rape of two black women, one of them by six white police officers. Then, in a "whites only" restaurant, his drink was deliberately poured on the counter top, and he was chased away by white patrons that went to their cars for guns.[59]

Justice was meted out in uneven measures in Alabama, and its importance was measured by whether the subject was white or black. On July 26, 1948, President Harry Truman issued an executive order that effectively ended military segregation at two airbases, Maxwell and Gunther, that annually channeled fifty million dollars to the merchants of Montgomery. On the other hand, in the courts of Alabama, a judge and jury sentenced a black man to death for stealing $1.95 from a white woman—the sentence ultimately commuted by Governor Folsom.

In the spring of 1951, sixteen-year-old Barbara Johns, niece of the Reverend Vernon Johns, led a strike in Prince Edward County, Virginia, against policies that allowed tar shack schools for Negroes, cold classrooms, broken-down buses, and teachers forced to gather firewood. The hesitant NAACP lawyers were pushed by inflamed students and parents into filing the suit of May 23, 1951, that escalated into the classic case of *Brown v. Board of Education of Topeka*, which ended separate but equal education.[60]

Despite his erudition and daring, Johns could be absolutely peculiar, particularly in dealing with his educated and refined congregation. After presenting a remarkable sermon, he would leave the church to sell cabbages and tomatoes to the members of the Dexter congregation, who were clothed in their best suits.

In political philosophy Johns steered a "middle course" between the doctrines of Booker T. Washington, who advocated hard manual work in the basic trades, and W. E. B. DuBois, who called for an educated black elite to claim leadership positions in the American society. Johns felt that blacks should build an "economic base," and he ridiculed Alabama State business professors who would not dirty their hands by engaging in farming and business.[61]

The congregation of Johns had ceased to be intimidated after his several threats to resign, and some parishioners were beginning to anticipate his departure. The final crisis came after he posted in the out-of-doors bulletin case the title of his next sermon: "It's Safe to Murder Negroes in Montgomery." The Ku Klux Klan replied by burning a cross on the Dexter Church lawn. Then the leading church women became indignant after he sold watermelons on the campus of Alabama State College.[62] The congregation accepted—to his surprise—his tendered resignation, but for nearly a year he refused to leave the parsonage. The deacons then were forced to disconnect the utilities, but he fought the siege by carrying his own water and reading by candlelight.[63] In December 1952 he had departed to Farmville, Virginia, where dogged white opponents to integration would close down the entire public school system for five years.[64]

Before assuming the pastorate at Montgomery, Alabama, M. L. had to win debates both with Coretta and his father Big Mike. Everything had not gone his way, for his first choice in churches had been the First Baptist Church of Chattanooga, which had not tendered an invitation. However, after a trial sermon at Dexter, he was offered a salary of forty-two hundred dollars a year, which would make him the highest paid Negro minister in Alabama. The struggle with Coretta was intense, since this bright woman had fallen in love with Boston, its symphonies and choirs, and was determined not to return to Alabama. Taking his clues from Daddy King, he reminded Coretta that biblical authority made him the head of the house and conferred on him the right to make the decision.[65]

Daddy King pointedly reminded him that not only must he serve as a scholarly leader at Dexter, but also he must manage its finances, personnel, and committees. Terribly upset that M. L. would not be his successor at Atlanta's Ebenezer Baptist Church, Big Daddy warned M. L. that soon enough the "Barons at Dexter" would strip him of power and humiliate him. Young Martin's response was: "I'm going to be pastor, and I'm going to run that church."[66] And so the green pastor, twenty-five years old, would be molded by the crucible in ways he never could have foretold.

Beyond Alabama, the world plates of external and internal politics were grinding against each other with groans and shudders. In 1954 the French commander had surrendered at Dien Bien Phu in French Indo-China. Then, in ten days, with Baptist Chief Justice Earl Warren presiding, the Supreme Court of the United States struck down school segregation as unconstitutional. The decision, 8-0 in the *Brown* case, would radically change American mores and life.[67]

Early in his pastorate at Dexter, M. L. distributed copies of his "Recommendations" and informed the church that his authority originated with God and that the agreement was confirmed by the "unconditional willingness of the people to accept the pastor's leadership." He then presented to the church thirty-four specific recommendations with the aim of mobilizing its financial and organizational resources. All church members would be assigned to one of twelve clubs, according to the month of his or her birth. Each club would make special donations to the church. New committees, boards, and councils would be formed, and a Political Action Committee would support the NAACP. All adult church members had to be registered voters.[68] Henceforth, there would be no anonymous giving, *ad hoc* rallies, or special collections. Each deacon would shepherd twenty-five members whom the deacon would instruct on financial support. He named specific people to the various committees. M. L.

felt that he was in control, and he proudly sent his plan to other pastors.[69]

Martin settled into a routine, partially academic and partially church-nurturing. He arose at 5:30 A.M. to work on his dissertation for three hours, devoted more time to research and writing, and then he returned late at night. In between, he went to church to preach at funerals or to socialize with the youth and fellow pastors. In such circumstances, he wore his fedora, impressed with his employment of big words, and projected a manner that was aristocratic but genteel.[70]

In addition, in his first year at Dexter, he made two student trips to Boston, delivered twenty addresses between Louisiana and New York, attended ten conclaves of the National Baptist Convention, read twenty-six books, and preached forty-six sermons at his church. On one Sunday, the collection was twenty-one hundred dollars (half of M. L.'s annual salary), an amazing achievement for his congregation.[71]

In the beginning of his ministry, some older members of his church complained that Martin Luther was "not a God man," meaning that his primary focus was not on salvation. In fact, he laced his sermons with classical quotations, including some from Paul Tillich. His ideas electrified his congregation, even though his voice never became a shout. After preaching, he asked his members *how* they were doing, not *what* they were doing. Daddy King, still trying to maintain control over his son, sent M. L. his checkbook carefully balanced. But the youthful minister was already becoming a celebrity, and in November 1954 was invited to preach at Atlanta's Friendship Baptist Church.[72]

After finishing his doctorate, M. L. was tempted by an offer to become dean at Dillard University at New Orleans and also preacher at the new Lawless Memorial Chapel. But his program at Dexter was progressing, and the church had paid off its debt of nearly five thousand dollars. Still, little advance was made in members, and M. L. baptized only twelve persons in his first year. In contrast, Daddy King had expanded a church of two hundred into a mega-church of four thousand. But it was clear that if M. L. had tried to lead his flock in his father's direction, the conservative congregation would have opposed him.[73]

In his second year at Dexter, M. L.'s wife gave birth to a baby girl, Yolanda Denise, that Martin called "Yoki." Then, M. L. announced he had considered running for president of the local NAACP chapter. However, he backed away when E. D. Nixon, the Montgomery leader, said he favored another candidate.[74]

Among Martin's closest friends was the Reverend Ralph Abernathy ("Mr. Rough"), pastor of Montgomery's First Baptist Church, who often shared church functions with M. L. ("Mr. Smooth"). They found a common bond with one of the few white liberals in Montgomery, the Reverend Robert Graetz, pastor of Trinity Lutheran Church. Graetz, shunned by many whites, found unity with blacks by attending movies upstairs in the cinemas.[75] The friendship between these men had all kinds of incongruities, for while Martin enjoyed great opera, including *Lucia di Lammermoor*, he also loved to chomp on a pigs-ear sandwich.[76] M. L. King, as pastor of Dexter, was a sturdy man, weighing 166 pounds, but in height fairly short, at five feet six inches.[77]

Ralph Abernathy, M. L.'s close friend, referred to the difference between First Baptist that he pastored and Martin's Dexter church, with an illustration that at First Church a preacher could with ease talk and preach about Jesus, while at the Dexter Church the congregation would tolerate only a brief and subdued mention of Jesus, but would welcome a discourse on Plato or Socrates. In return, Dexter members sometimes spoke of First Baptist as a "shouting congregation," but this simply was not so.[78]

Montgomery Bus Boycott

The event that would thrust Martin onto the national stage was the Montgomery bus boycott, initiated by a polite, undistinguished Negro woman, Mrs. Rosa Parks. Rosa Parks, a Methodist and seamstress at a Montgomery department store, and also the secretary of the local chapter of the NAACP, was a quiet, tireless worker, known for giving to the world more than she extracted.[79] On December 1, 1955, Mrs. Parks tried to ride home on her regular bus, with twenty-two black riders in the rear, and fourteen white riders in the front. The driver J. P. Blake asked four blacks in the neutral area to move for a single white man, in which case the four vacated seats became a "white area" under local regulations. Mrs. Parks, tired from her day's work, simply refused to move, and was taken to the police station where she was fingerprinted and jailed. NAACP official E. D. Nixon then telephoned white lawyer Clifford Durr, and the incident grew into a national event.[80]

Durr felt that Rosa Parks's respectability would make the incident a good test case to attack segregation policies, but Mrs. Parks would have to remain steadfast to endure the legal fight. Her husband was exasperated: "The white folks will kill you, Rosa." Then, Alabama State English professor Jo Ann Robinson and her friends joined the movement and issued an appeal that on the following Monday (December 5) every Negro should refuse to ride the buses, in defiance of the arrest.[81]

Then, Martin Luther King and about fifty Negro leaders, organized by train porter E. D. Nixon, met at Dexter Baptist Church and decided to collectively refuse bus transportation on December 5. The boycott became an instant success, and M. L. noted with exhilaration that buses on Monday were guarded by officers in police cars with shotguns and helmets, but the buses were transporting no blacks. At the courthouse five hundred blacks crowded the corridors as Rosa Parks posted bond.[82]

The initiative to protest segregated busing gained strength, along with the Montgomery Improvement Association (MIA), of which M. L. King was surprisingly elected president, instead of the volatile porter E. D. Nixon. At the Holt Street Church, an immense crowd of about five thousand stretched into the street, which M. L. rallied with these poetic words: "There comes a time when people get tired of being pushed out of the glittering sunlight of life's July, and left standing amidst the piercing chill of an Alpine November."[83] Differentiating his movement from Klan activities, he said, "There will be no crosses burned at any bus stops in Montgomery. . . . There will be no white persons pulled out of their homes and taken out on some distant road and murdered. There will be nobody among us who will stand up and defy the Constitution of this nation."[84]

Martin then added further pressure: "Love is one of the principal parts of the Christian faith. There is another side called justice—justice is love correcting that which would work against love." M. L., with his persuasive speech, had become a public figure, to some a prophet, and the masses pressed to touch him. At age twenty-six, he was racing on an uncertain road.[85] The Reverend Ralph Abernathy remained behind in Montgomery as his lieutenant.

The greatest hardship during the boycott that stretched into weeks was borne by the Negro working class, the maids and day laborers that had to find transportation to their daily jobs. The MIA made its principal demand the elimination of the bus "reserved section." Then, M. L. telephoned T. J. Jemison, secretary of the National Baptist Convention, who had led a bus boycott in Baton Rouge, seeking advice on how to mobilize cars and drivers into a Montgomery car pool and how to bus black workers to their jobs. Spontaneously, 150 car owners transformed their cars into transports and with thirty to forty thousand workers commuting daily, the bus companies faced bankruptcy.[86]

M. L. put little trust in "emotional bosh" but much faith in the virtue of love. In urging blacks to boycott he stressed the futility of violence:

> Agape is understanding, creative, redemptive goodwill for all men, it is the love of God operating in the human heart. It is an overflowing love which seeks nothing in return—Love is a willingness to go the second mile in order to restore the broken community. Yes, love is even a willingness to die on a cross in order that others may live.[87]

Even in the struggle for justice on bus inequities, Martin was forging his views on more complex economic and social problems. While pastor at Dexter and as a guest speaker at the United Church of Christ, he sounded his beliefs:

> Any religion that professes to be concerned about the souls of men and is not concerned about the economic conditions that damn the soul, the social conditions that corrupt men, and the city governments that cripple them, is a dry, dead, do-nothing religion in need of new blood.[88]

In a 1955 radio sermon on "Paul's Letters to the American Christians," Martin criticized Christians for selfishness and failures of brotherhood.[89] He was on sound ground, for in the Montgomery work force more than fifty percent of blacks were laborers and domestic workers, while the segment of black professionals was extremely small. Sales clerk jobs were thirty to one in favor of white residents. For fifty thousand blacks, there were only three doctors and one dentist to serve them, while the same number of whites had their health protected by 144 doctors and 43 dentists.[90]

The white merchants during the Christmas season were mildly hurt by reduced purchases by blacks, but the City Bus Lines was facing collapse. M. L. had suggested to his church followers that money for Christmas presents could be routed during the boycott to savings accounts, charity, and the MIA.[91] The *Montgomery Advertiser's* reporter Tom Johnson verified that King was the real boycott boss and respected by the older ministers, despite his inclination to pontificate about Paul Tillich, Immanuel Kant, and Friedrich Nietzsche.[92]

When a false rumor was spread that the boycott was over, King spoke brusquely to his task force, including many preachers, to spread the truth into Negro night clubs and country dives. Twenty thousand daily riders had to be transported, so the honky-tonk dance music was stopped and the message delivered. Montgomery police, at first polite, now issued a flurry of tickets for faulty windshield wipers, unadjusted headlights, slow traffic, and fast traffic. M. L., carrying several passengers, was arrested for speeding thirty miles an hour in a twenty-five mile zone and confined in the Montgomery City Jail with other supporters of the boycott. He was badly frightened on the patrol ride, his body shaking severely, believing that the ride might be his last. But then, as he was to be released on his recognizance, a large crowd of blacks besieged the jail.[93] Hereafter, as a precaution, M. L. would be protected by a special corps of black drivers and bodyguards.

King had his first major religious experience after an incident of terror inflicted by hostile whites. His sleep was shattered by a violent phone call in the evening. He admitted that his defenses were obliterated: "I've come to the point where I can't face it alone." Then, he had the comfort of an "inner voice" that urged him to do the right thing, and while he did not call on God, he had a feeling of peace.[94] Although at this time Martin was an accomplished pastor of a respected church, it must be recalled that at baptism in his childhood, in his own words, he did not reconcile himself to God through Jesus Christ.

MIA members voted to proceed through federal courts to bring down bus segregation. The bus boycott, on the other hand, was another matter that required intricate management. For protection, MIA records were transferred to Pastor Ralph D. Abernathy's First Baptist Church, while MIA headquarters was moved to a building owned by the Negro Bricklayers Union.[95]

While participating in a MIA meeting at First Baptist, with two thousand persons present, Martin was quietly informed that his house had been burned. He rushed home and found Coretta in her bathrobe and his daughter Yoki, both of them unharmed. A crowd of outraged blacks, some brandishing knives and guns, jammed the street outside. Martin addressed the unsettled crowd of blacks:

> If you have weapons, take them home. He who lives by the sword will perish by the sword. Remember that is what Jesus said. We are not advocating violence. We want to love our enemies. I want you to love our enemies. Be good to them. This is what we must live by. We must meet hate with love.[96]

Martin refused Big Daddy's advice to return to Atlanta, where he could be a live dog, rather than die as a brave lion in Montgomery.[97]

Now, in the third month of the unrest, there arrived in Montgomery to help the cause—and expose Martin to false accusations of being a Marxist—Bayard Rustin, a talented Negro pacifist and Greenwich Village philosopher from West Chester, Pennsylvania. Although a Quaker, Rustin at one time reportedly dressed like a hobo. He had great ability as an organizer and writer. In reckless disregard for his reputation in later years, Martin would solicit Rustin to be his SCLC publicist. During Martin's rise to prominence, Communists or fellow-travelers would flock to the SCLC banner, including Wyatt Tee Walker (alleged former member of the Young Communist League) from New Jersey, and M. L.'s closest white friend and steadfast supporter, Stanley Levison, an alleged financial supporter of the Communist Party and the leftist American Jewish Congress. Despite rumors to the contrary, M. L. King never embraced the doctrines of the Communist Party nor gave credence to the distortions of history propagandized by Karl Marx, Friedrich Engels, and Nikolai Lenin. Still, the Reverend Adam Clayton Powell, preacher-politician of New York, thoroughly disliked Martin's new lieutenant Bayard Rustin.[98]

Before arriving at Alabama's capital, Rustin had in 1941 resigned his Communist membership, joined forces with union leader A. Philip Randolph, and had become the youth secretary for the Fellowship of Reconciliation (FOR) a non-violent anti-colonialist organization. He and James Farmer worked together in behalf of FOR and with the Congress of Racial Equality (CORE), organized during World War II. Rustin became a follower of Gandhi's disciple Krishnalal Shridharani, who wrote *War Without Violence*, which became the doctrinal book for CORE. For refusing a military draft call, Rustin spent time in Lewisburg Penitentiary.[99]

The rumor was circulated while Martin was in Nashville, that 115 or so Montgomery boycott leaders had been indicted. Among them was E. D. Nixon, who walked freely into the county courthouse. M.

L. sheltered his wife and daughter in Atlanta, and on the advice of Ralph Abernathy and Bayard Rustin determined bravely to return to Montgomery to assume leadership and face trial and imprisonment. Against this impending move, Daddy King had assembled a half-dozen of the leading black clerics in Atlanta, and also the editor of the *Atlanta Daily World*, to persuade M. L. to cautiously wait in Atlanta. M. L.'s reply was that his friends were being arrested at that moment and hauled off to jail. His final decision was that as the permanent boycott leader, "I must go back to Montgomery." At the Montgomery courthouse, with Daddy King supporting him, Martin Luther King became the twenty-fourth minister to be booked.[100]

A huge demonstration against the arrests assembled at the Reverend Ralph Abernathy's church, with a crowd that included thirty-five reporters from across the country and ninety persons who had been arrested. Rushing to support the boycott were two unique whites, Lutheran minister Robert Graetz, and from Texas, Methodist minister and pacifist Glenn Smiley.[101]

The Montgomery authorities chose to make King's arrest a test case, while eighty-nine indictments against others were held in abeyance. As the trial opened on 19 March 1956, M. L. was defended by eight lawyers. The judge, who taught a Sunday School class close to the Dexter Church, sentenced M. L. to a five hundred dollar fine or to one year at hard labor. King emerged from the courtroom to announce that the boycott would continue. Before a huge crowd that night on Holt Street, he was introduced as a man "nailed to the cross for you and me." Then he was acknowledged by *Jet* magazine ("Alabama's Modern Moses"), *The New York Times*, and black prophet W.E.B. DuBois. Martin Luther King became an epic figure, and ten thousand people attended his fund-raiser at New York's Concord Baptist Church.[102] Still, there was a legal injunction against the carpools, so the boycott continued.[103] As the Negro action in Montgomery was extended, the MIA became wealthier than the older organization, the national NAACP,[104] and jealousies arose. Martin went to considerable efforts to assuage the venerable longer-lived

NAACP and its director Roy Wilkins, but he was not about to leave the fray.

The National Association for the Advancement of Colored People (NAACP) was founded in the aftermath of the Atlanta race riot (1906) and the Springfield, Illinois, riot (1908), and pursued its goals largely through court actions.[105] In 1934 the NAACP split in a struggle between W.E.B. DuBois, editor of its magazine *The Crisis*, who proposed living with voluntary segregation, and Walter White, its elected leader; White reached the conclusion that DuBois was too eccentric and ineffective to lead the organization in its battles against lynchings and white supremacy.[106] Finally, DuBois abandoned the top leadership role to teach at Atlanta University.

After King had publicly criticized the NAACP for ignoring the boycott, the NAACP made a financial contribution through Roy Wilkins, but NAACP's relationship with the MIA, and, later with its successor the Southern Christian Leadership Conference (SCLC), never approached cordiality.[107] Meanwhile, the MIA, through national publicity and an effective organization, was receiving greater financial support than the national NAACP (that from the beginning had not accepted the tactics of the mass boycott). But the NAACP assumed all costs for the attorneys representing King and the other defendants in the Montgomery trial, the Rosa Parks case, and the MIA-initiated case against bus segregation. After the multiple arrests, King and Roy Wilkins engaged in a long quarrel over money, with King accusing the NAACP of funneling money to its organization under the cover of the boycott. Wilkins defended his actions, since the NAACP required funds for its legal actions.[108]

The court cases were not passively received by the Alabama state officials, and on June 1, 1956, Alabama attorney general John Patterson obtained a court order banning the NAACP within Alabama from soliciting new members, collecting dues, or raising funds. It required eight years for the NAACP to overcome these restrictions.[109] Then, a sweet victory came to the boycott leaders on June 4, 1956, when a federal judicial panel ruled two to one to strike down as unconstitutional Montgomery's bus segregation ordinances. The judges in the case were white jurists, and the effect of the ruling was to raise the expectation that the U. S. Supreme Court in the months ahead would rule favorably in other cases for the black minority.[110]

When M. L. flew to San Francisco to address the 47th NAACP convention, he met Mississippi NAACP field secretary Medgar Evers. King's proposals favoring only non-violent means to desegregate schools were noted by reporters. However, he ran into the stiff opposition of Wilkins and Thurgood Marshall on the non-violent methods conceived for the bus boycott in Montgomery. In order to preserve harmony, NAACP's Wilkins gave notice that the Montgomery model, as managed by King, would be evaluated by its Executive Committee.[111]

After seeking advance approval from Roy Wilkins, King testified before the platform committee of the Democratic National Convention meeting in Chicago. On August 25, two or three sticks of dynamite exploded in the Montgomery front yard of the Reverend Robert Graetz, effecting minor damage. Two days later, King wrote to President Dwight D. Eisenhower that Montgomery Negroes were "without protection of law."[112]

In the national electoral campaign Adlai Stevenson was criticized for being not involved with Negro voters. On the other hand, Eisenhower's popularity ratings soared when he got the endorsement of Democrat Adam Clayton Powell, Jr. The Negro issue was eventually submerged amid the international issues of the Soviets snuffing out the Hungarian revolt and the surprise seizure of the Suez Canal by Israel, Great Britain, and France. The canal possessors were forced ignobly to disgorge their conquest.[113]

It should have been a moment of supreme confidence for blacks everywhere, when the U. S. Supreme Court issued its finding that Alabama's state and local laws enforcing bus segregation were unconstitutional. Still, until the Supreme Court decision was implemented—a long process—the injunction banning the carpool was enforced. In celebration of the Supreme Court victory, King prolonged the euphoria by organizing a week of church programs and seminars. Invited as speakers to the celebrations were reporter Carl Rowan and Atlanta pastor William Holmes Borders.[114] In his analysis of the struggle, M. L. listed as gains the achievement of leadership and unity, the instilling of church militancy, and the "discovery" of nonviolence. While M. L. was now in the learning-phase of race struggles, six years later at Birmingham he would be a veteran of tactics and strategies.[115]

Martin Luther King was now more prominent than even his father Big Mike. The Reverend J. H. Jackson signaled the new status quo by inviting Coretta King to give a recital at his church in Chicago, although Jackson had never publicly endorsed the boycott. Thus, M. L. joined the royalty of Negro Baptists, which included Jackson, Gardner Taylor, the Jemisons, and Adam Clayton Powell, Jr.[116]

Launching the Southern Christian Leadership Conference (SCLC)

After the astounding victory at the Supreme Court, violent attacks in the South were launched mainly on prominent blacks by infuriated whites. On Christmas eve, a fifteen-year-old Negro girl at a bus stop in Montgomery was beaten by five men. In Birmingham, Fred Shuttlesworth, preparing to lead a black action group to the front of public buses, was nearly killed when fifteen sticks of dynamite destroyed his house. At King's invitation, sixty preachers from the South arrived at Atlanta's Ebenezer Church in January 1957 to attend the first Negro Leaders Conference on Nonviolent Integration. The conference leaders included Bayard Rustin, Fred Shuttlesworth of Birmingham, C. K. Steele of Tallahassee, Florida, and William Holmes Borders of Atlanta.[117]

On January 10, 1957, the day of the promising Atlanta conference, the porch and front room of the Montgomery home of the Reverend Ralph Abernathy were destroyed by explosives. Then, a series of assaults were made on two houses and four black churches, including Abernathy's First Baptist. Abernathy and King hurriedly left their assembly for a quick survey of damaged property in Montgomery. Upon their return to Atlanta, the conference inaugurated the Southern Christian Leadership Conference (SCLC), with King elected as president in February in New Orleans. But no newly-formed civil rights organization would succeed in prodding the national government into drastic reforms. Still, U. S. Attorney General Brownell did promise an investigation of the bombings and attacks, but presidential advisor Sherman Adams informed King that President Eisenhower would not make a major speech against violence in the South as requested by King.[118]

The founding of the SCLC on January 10-11, 1957, brought together powerful preachers from the Southern states. The organization was concerned in the beginning mainly with segregation of transportation facilities and voter registration.[119] SCLC was designed to be a national organization, based on a consortium of churches and civic groups, thus intending not to give offense to the NAACP, but it failed in this attempt. In the 1960s it maintained an office in Atlanta. One of the most promising aspects of SCLC was its training facility, Dorchester Center at McIntosh, Georgia, where instructions were given to teach reading to illiterates, voter registration, and practical methods to help petitioners applying for government benefits.[120]

After failing in his attempt to induce President Eisenhower to make a speech in the South, M. L. then tried to persuade Vice President Richard Nixon and Attorney General Herbert Brownwell to make a statement on race, but the requests were politely declined.

As the boycott began to fade into the background, the Montgomery airport was selected as the next target for desegregation. But the fertile mind of King was searching for a means to convert the momentum into something like the Great Awakening of the 1740s. Meanwhile, his vision embraced general plans to register millions of new Negro voters, organize the clergy for action, and obtain the blessings of leading whites on the nonviolent army surging forward.[121]

Feeling remorse over the disunity in the local movement, smarting from the increasing hostility of Montgomery organizer E. D. Nixon, and sensing the vulnerability of some leaders, M. L. released his feelings in a prayer at the First Baptist Church on January 15, 1956:

> Lord, I hope no one will have to die as a result of our struggle for freedom in Montgomery. Certainly I don't want to die. But if anyone has to die, let it be me.

He was so paralyzed by his emotions, two ministers helped him to a seat.[122] Two weeks later, a terrified M. L. bolted from his bed to gain refuge in another house. Several hours later, an explosion occurred near the parsonage, crushing the house front. Then, twelve sticks of dynamite were found on the porch of the King-occupied parsonage, although Coretta and daughter Yoki had been sent earlier to Atlanta. In the near-riot that followed, M. L. arrived to quiet the crowd of Negroes. Two whites accused of involvement in unlawful acts were acquitted by the jury.

On a technicality [missing the filing date], the Alabama Supreme Court ruled against King on the appeal from the illegal boycott conviction, and he was assessed a five hundred dollar fine. King, who had sought a judgment on the legality of the case, was pointedly disappointed. The eighty-nine black boycotters had their cases dismissed.[123]

The prominence attained by King in the Montgomery struggle influenced Claire Boothe Luce, ambassador to Italy, to write to him: "No man has ever waged the battle for equality under our law in a more lawful and Christian way than you have." Then *Time* magazine in February 1957 featured his portrait and life story.[124] In 1964, he would be awarded the Nobel Peace Prize.

In April 1957, Martin Luther King and Vice President Richard Nixon conferred in Africa, both of them celebrating with charismatic leader Nkrumah the advent of the new Subsaharan country of Ghana. Later, before Dexter Church, he recounted that Nkrumah attended the celebrations in his prison garb and that, in contrast, the

Church of England from its high office at Westminster Abbey was not moved to renounce colonialism. However, the contact with Nixon was encouraging, for M. L. was invited to Washington for talks on civil rights.[125]

King carefully rehearsed a speech to be given before a huge audience that would gather at the Lincoln Memorial in Washington for the national Prayer Pilgrimage for Freedom. The Pilgrimage (in support of the Voting Rights Bill) was held on May 17, 1957, third anniversary of the Brown decision, with about thirty-seven thousand persons attending, including three thousand whites. M. L. and Roy Wilkins, the co-organizers, were joined by such notables as preacher-politician Adam Clayton Powell, singer Mahalia Jackson, actor Sidney Poitier, baseball player Jackie Robinson, entertainer Harry Belafonte, and performer Sammy Davis, Jr.[126] Again King used this major event to advocate reform with peaceful methods: "We must meet hate with love, physical force with soul force."

On June 23, 1958, in a carefully orchestrated meeting, King, along with NAACP leader Roy Wilkins, unionist A. Philip Randolph, and ex-director of the Urban League Lester Granger, met with President Dwight Eisenhower. This meeting was delicate, even though Daddy King and most of the powerful preachers at the National Baptist Convention at this stage were long-term Republicans.[127] While Eisenhower believed in controlled reform, he had long felt it inadvisable to make any major statement on race relations, and M. L. attributed to Eisenhower's reticence a major cause of the impasse in race relations.[128] In defense of Eisenhower, he had supported the *Brown* case and the Civil Rights Act of 1957, and had caused the desegregation of the public facilities in Washington, D.C.[129] At the meeting, Eisenhower was unhappy with talk about Negro bitterness, as expressed by Granger. King made his remarks on moral leadership. Then, in a consensus of sorts, the participants agreed that voting rights legislation was needed.[130]

The attitude of Eisenhower on social legislation was reflected in a remark he made in 1957: "You can't legislate morality." This brought a response from a frustrated King, that "A law may not make a man love me, but it can stop him from lynching me."[131]

Outside of the Civil Rights debate, the United States was stunned and humiliated when the Soviet satellite Sputnik began its orbits on October 4, 1957.

Attempt on His Life

The Trailblazer Martin Luther King, Jr., barely escaped death on September 20, 1958, in a New York department store. While promoting his book *Stride Toward Freedom* at Blumstein's, he was attacked by a disturbed black woman from Adrian, Georgia; she was Izola Ware Curry, who was armed with a letter opener. She drove the blade into his chest, between his heart and lung. As King sat down, he calmly said, "Everything is going to be all right." If King had acted compulsively and pulled out the blade he would almost certainly have died immediately, for the letter opener was close to the aorta. Surgeons removed the blade but also two ribs and a portion of his breastbone. During his recovery, until 1960, he made few if any more speeches, except at Dexter. During this time, he would analyze his programs and redefine his goals and strategies.[132] King felt that God had spared him for a special mission.

In seeking new techniques to give momentum to the civil rights movement, M. L. adopted at first the methods of Baptist revivalist Billy Graham. In cities mobilized by the Graham team, lists of organizers were assembled, supporting groups were trained, and publicity was directed. Graham and King had a cordial relationship; in fact, M. L. said the prayer at the 1957 Madison Square Garden Crusade. Graham and the black leader he called "Mr. Mike" then held three strategy meetings, preparing for an untried approach. Then, in October 18, 1957, M. L. at a board meeting of the SCLC presented his Crusade for Citizenship, based on Billy Graham's style.[133]

Billy Graham had among his New York black supporters Gardner

Taylor, pastor of Brooklyn's Concord Baptist Church, and Thomas Kilgore, who also were his close friends. King hoped with the nucleus from Billy Graham's Crusade supporters to commence a series of Graham-King crusades. The original plans were to begin in the Northern states and then move gradually into the Deep South. But Graham opposed the intrusion of politics into the religious revival activities, and the scheme died early. Graham and King remained good friends, and during the Kennedy Administration, at the Baptist World Alliance in Rio de Janeiro, the Reverend Billy Graham hosted a banquet in honor of King.[134]

Power Plays in the Church

Then King, in what many would call naked opportunitism, sought to turn the black National Baptist Convention with its five million members and over ten thousand preachers into a reform mechanism. The key to this gigantic venture was the promise by powerful Chicago preacher J. H. Jackson to step down as its leader in September 1957. Some four years before, in the summer of 1953, M. L.'s father Big Daddy, with help from M. L., had outmaneuvered the Reverend William Holmes Borders and managed the election of J. H. Jackson to become the head of the National Baptist Convention.[135] Even prior to that, in 1939, when J. H. Jackson gave the highlight address at the Baptist World Alliance convening at Ponce de Leon Park, Atlanta, Jackson, staying as guest at the King residence, was idolized by young Mike.[136] Now, in late 1957, the orator Jackson, called by some the "Negro Pope," had decided that he did not wish to vacate the key position in the Negro Baptist hierarchy. He also had taken a firm stand against the Convention becoming directly involved in the Civil Rights struggle.[137]

In 1960 King's further strategy was to win control of the 80th National Baptist Convention and make the Southern Christian Leadership Conference (SCLC) a virtual auxiliary of the Convention. This would pit the Reverend Gardner Taylor of Brooklyn, M.

L.'s ally and powerful Baptist leader, against J. H. Jackson. After the messengers voted, there was a whirlwind of noise, confusion, and disorder, with Jackson claiming victory and refusing to leave the rostrum. Unverified reports circulated that Taylor had received 1,864 votes to Jackson's 536. In the aftermath, there was a flood of litigation, but it was clear that M. L.'s hopes to utilize the Convention as his vessel to advance the civil rights revolution had been thwarted. The assembly dissolved two days early, with Jackson clearly in control.[138]

The acrimony that ensued from this struggle culminated in the defection from the Convention of Martin Luther King, Gardner Taylor, Benjamin Mays (president of Morehouse College), and about two thousand pastors.[139]

King admitted to the Dexter faithful that he had neglected the congregation with his work for civil rights. His second child, Martin Luther King, III, was born and that signaled that King was entering an early mid-life[140]—but that omen was misleading, for tragedy was stalking King and would strike him down before his thirty-ninth birthday.

Martin Luther had admired, emulated, and adapted to the life and practice of the Hindu ascetic Mahatma Gandhi—but to a far less degree than his beliefs and acknowledgments of his great master Jesus Christ. King's style was American, not Indian; his non-retaliatory tactics were more of Christ than of Vishnu or Shiva; his quoted words were from the Holy Bible, not from the *Mahabharata* or the *Bhaghavad Ghita*. However, his quest had led him to study extensively regarding the non-violent methods used by Gandhi in his struggle with the British *raj*.

Around February 8, 1959, M. L. began a four-week study-tour in India, on the invitation of Indian prime minister Jawaharlal Nehru, and paid for by the SCLC and a Quaker organization. Between Delhi and New Delhi, he laid a wreath on Gandhi's tomb. One of the vacation places reminded him of the training camp for American civil rights workers, the Highlander Folk School, near Monteagle, Tennessee.[141]

Martin Luther King at close range was able to study "Satyagraha" (Soul Force), Gandhi's concept of nonviolence, and "Sarvodaya," a pacific socialism utilized by him that involved cooperatives and commitment to social service. Also, M. L. learned of the discipline of the "Shanti Sena," the Gandhian non-violent army that dressed in white homespun Khadi cloth.[142] He visited the Ashram on the Sabarmati River in South India, where Gandhi in 1930 marched to the sea in defiance of the British to collect untaxed salt. M. L. was clearly inspired by the courage and perception of Gandhi's disciple Nehru, whose vision he felt surpassed that of many American politicians.[143] However, despite the fascination of Gandhi's experiments to Martin Luther King, Bayard Rustin, and to a lesser extent Ralph D. Abernathy, there was uncertainty as to how Gandhi's techniques could be applied to the American culture.[144]

Back to Ebenezer

The news of Martin Luther's resignation from the staid Dexter Church in November 1959 jolted the Montgomery congregation, but the pastor would delay until January 1960 his departure for Atlanta and the Ebenezer Church; he would serve in a new capacity under his father M. L. King, Sr. There were compelling needs for a change, for in three years the SCLC had not flourished as expected, and King wanted a full-scale assault on segregation; the constant work and travel had converted M. L. into a "physical and psychological wreck." While, M. L. disliked the stifling control of his father, his salary was elevated to a hefty six thousand dollars. On hearing the news of his latest taxpayer's arrival, the governor of Georgia, Ernest Vandiver, proclaimed, "He is not welcome."[145] In the same vein, the *Atlanta Constitution's* editor Ralph McGill, writing of M. L.'s return to Georgia, reflected that whites welcomed him like medieval cities welcomed the plague.[146]

Also, successful black businessmen and some of the powerful black preachers were dismayed by Martin Luther's new "humble life-style." King was riding about the city in an old 1954 Pontiac and was seriously considering the purchase of a house in the "barely respectable" Vine City area.[147] While this was not a new King, it was one tacking to a different wind, mellowed by experience, and tuned to lead with example. In that same attitude years before, he had blistered the brothers of the Negro fraternity Omega Psi Phi, then meeting in Baltimore, for consuming in one week a volume of liquor valued at five hundred thousand dollars. That expenditure, he reminded the celebrating middle-class fraternity blacks, exceeded all the money given in one year to the United Negro College Fund and the NAACP by sixteen million Negroes. For his candor, he was lustily cheered.[148]

Freedom Riders and Protesters

Nationwide, the fat was in the fire, and the years 1960-61 would crackle with sit-ins and freedom riders, spreading across the country. First, there were sit-ins in sixteen U.S. cities. Then, there was a sit-down protest by four black college students at the Greensboro, North Carolina, Woolworth's store, with white students from Greensboro College choosing to join them, followed by sit-ins in Raleigh, Durham, and Winston-Salem.[149] M. L. stopped at Durham to encourage the activities: "Men are tired of being trampled over by the iron feet of oppression." Then he added, "Let us not fear going to jail"—and with that comment, the non-violent crusade appeared to have swelled into a revolution.[150]

As a formidable ally in the student sit-ins—and performing a huge share of the work—the Student Nonviolent Coordinating Committee (SNCC) lived in the public relations shadow, while M. L.'s SCLC got most of the money and the greatest publicity. SNCC was organized in 1960 by students from about forty communities and it engaged in selective-buying programs and boycotts, while bearing the heaviest burdens in the most unbending parts of the South. The civil disobedience tactics of SNCC, accompanied by sit-ins and jail-ins, was adopted by King, and he became SNCC's patron saint and the black symbol, although the specific actions were often student-driven.[151]

Most of the direct action in Louisiana and much of the non-violent work in Florida and Mississippi and the stunning Freedom Ride of 1961 to Florida and Mississippi were done by another or-ganization—the Congress of Racial Equality (CORE), founded in 1942. From CORE and A. Philip Randolph, King borrowed some of their nonviolent mass action tactics.[152] CORE then offered the office of CORE National Director to M. L. King, and when he declined, it then conferred the title on James Farmer, who had trained in Harlem.[153]

The trend was set for the civil rights unrest to spread, particularly throughout the South, and as the whites reacted the confrontation tended to become more violent. In 1960 M. L. joined a student sit-in in Atlanta, while in 1961 a freedom bus burned near Anniston, Alabama, and new freedom riders reached Montgomery. Martin Luther would experience in the ensuing years a failure of peaceful integration in the following communities: Albany, Georgia, Danville, Virginia, Birmingham, Alabama, and St. Augustine, Florida, but each failure would increase his stature and enhance his renown. His emotional scars received at Birmingham would produce the Federal Civil Rights Act.[154]

Perhaps the most demeaning blows were those aimed at Martin Luther's financial integrity. After a speech in Durham, North Caro-lina, he was arrested at the behest of Alabama officials for felony tax evasion and non-payment of income taxes, and arraigned at Atlanta's county courthouse. In his humiliation, M. L. sought to get an im-partial panel, to include the head of the National Council of Churches and the president of the Southern Baptist Convention, to examine his records, but this effort was unavailing.[155] Defended by NAACP lawyers in Montgomery, and bolstered by funds raised by Bayard

Rustin in New York, M. L. was uneasy about using civil rights money in his defense. Finally, M. L. was released on a four thousand dollar bond. Then, his colleague, Ralph Abernathy, tried to lead a protest march to the Alabama Capitol, but it was stopped by a picket line of police and firemen.[156]

After a meticulous examination of M. L.'s financial transactions, he was found to be absolutely and impeccably honest. Martin Luther King had proven to be careless and inefficient with money, but he had evinced no greed. His only records were personal diaries from an old trunk in Atlanta, and following their examination, and after tens of thousands of dollars, loosely controlled, had flowed through his hands, the remaining discrepancy was a trifling $368.00. It was obvious that he had been an honest steward. However, the local forces had gone hungry, while the funds went to the gorged SCLC.[157]

Kennedy and M. L. King

In 1960, Martin Luther King and his father would play pivotal roles in the election of President John F. Kennedy. Kennedy was an Irish-American Roman Catholic, and there was a profound apprehension throughout the predominantly-Protestant American nation as to whether any Catholic president could separate his religion from national policies. At the beginning of the pre-electoral skirmishes between the Republican Richard Nixon and Democrat Kennedy, most of the leading black pastors of the National Baptist Convention, U.S.A., Inc., had voted in favor of Republican Dwight D. Eisenhower and were inclined initially to favor as his successor Vice President Richard Nixon.[158] The contest was hotly fought, both contestants excelling in debate, and this situation gave the Negro leaders more leverage than in past elections.

Although M. L. was openly nonpartisan, he verged beyond neutrality under the prodding of Congressman Chester Bowles (chairman of the Platform Committee of the Democratic Convention), Bayard Rustin, and white supporter Harris Wofford, who attended

Yale Law School; this panel secretly worked on a civil rights plank for the Democratic Party platform. Then, in a meeting between King and Senator Kennedy, M. L. worked at the session but came to the conclusion that the senator was under-educated in civil rights matters. Nevertheless, the adroit Kennedy, influenced by black baseball player Jackie Robinson, released a letter promising full support for Negro rights.[159] Noted singer Harry Belafonte also persuaded Senator Kennedy to telephone King and to maintain close relations with him. Meanwhile, in South Africa sixty-nine blacks protesting apartheid were killed by police and Francis Gary Powers and his spy plane were shot down by the Soviets,[160] throwing U.S.-Soviet relations into a period of great tension.

During this time, M. L. was entangled in at least four legal suits originating in Alabama, including a defamation suit filed by Montgomery police Commissioner L. B. Sullivan (awarding him at least five hundred thousand dollars) and Alabama's Governor Patterson (claiming one million dollars in damages) for a New York advertisement placed by supporters of M. L. King.[161]

Then occurred one of those trifling things which unpredictably expand and then move mountains, but in this case leveraged a young Catholic Democrat into the White House.[162] At Rich's Complex in Atlanta, King's student group provoked an incident at a snack bar on Forsyth Street. With M. L. proclaiming, "I had to practice what I preached," he was arrested with thirty-five demonstrators and conveyed to the county jail. There, he refused to pay the five hundred dollar bond. The students were released but M. L. was retained on a second charge, driving without a license, the hearing to be held in DeKalb County. That Friday, eighty-five million Americans watched the final debate between contenders Kennedy and Nixon on foreign policy, with little or no thought given to a black revolution in progress.[163]

King was transferred to the court in handcuffs and leg shackles. During the trial two hundred King supporters, including four college presidents, heard in disbelief Judge Mitchell sentence M. L.

King to four months of hard labor as punishment for a minor offense. The courtroom was thrown into uncontrollable turmoil, and Coretta, six months pregnant, could not be consoled. Some supporters believed that while he was working out his punishment, state road gangs would contrive to kill the black leader. On this occasion, King was calm: "I think we must prepare ourselves for the fact that I am going to have to serve this time."[164] In the aftermath of the trial, King was transferred at night to the maximum security prison at Reidsville, in south Georgia, well on the way to coastal Savannah.[165]

From prison, wearing striped convict garb, M. L. wrote:

> —— but as I said to you yesterday this is the cross that we must bear for the freedom of our people. —— I have the faith to believe that this excessive suffering that is now coming to our family will in some little way serve to make Atlanta a better city, Georgia a better state, and America a better country. —— If I am correct then our suffering is not in vain.[166]

The excessive and unjust sentence meted out to King was the "minor incident" that arguably clinched the national election for John Kennedy and denied an almost certain victory to Richard Nixon. The students at the Rich's Complex had set the charge, and M. L.'s audacious persistence had caused the judge to over-react, and to tilt the black perception of temperance, equity, and justice. The national election was a "white knuckle affair," with Kennedy receiving 34,221,463 votes and Nixon 34,108,582 votes. The winner John Kennedy had bested his opponent in a heavily-populated country by the startlingly slim edge of 112,881 votes, or a popular margin of two-tenths of one percent. Negroes, however, voted for the Democratic candidate by a margin of seventy percent versus thirty percent for the Republican candidate.[167]

What had induced the black Eisenhower supporters, many of them Baptists, to desert the Republicans and vote for a Democrat from New England? The answer was in two telephone calls made when King was languishing in his prison cell: one, a sympathetic call from Senator John Kennedy to Coretta, and, two, a telephone call from the candidate's brother, Robert Kennedy, to Judge Mitchell. These calls were probably cynically political, but whether engineered by Sargent Shriver or others, the effect was telling. Daddy King broke ranks with the Reverend William Holmes Borders and Atlanta's Baptist elder statesmen and announced that he would vote for Kennedy.[168] In a change of strategy, Judge Mitchell, before the national vote, released M. L. from jail on a two thousand dollar bond.[169] The election result was a razor-thin victory for Kennedy—but it was a beginning for a new generation and the birth of fresh ideas on racial equality.

The new administration was nurturing little gratitude, and Martin Luther King was not invited to the Kennedy inauguration, nor even for a private meeting with the president-elect. President Kennedy, in his inaugural address, did not make any reference to race, civil rights, or segregation. However, the popular singer Frank Sinatra organized a tribute to King at New York's Carnegie Hall and raised fifty thousand dollars for the SCLC. Soon after, Coretta gave birth to their third child Dexter.[170]

Boycotts, Sit-ins, and Demonstrations

In his groping toward an overall strategy of civic action, Martin Luther King faced the reality that some progress had been made since the passing of the Civil Rights Act of 1957 but there had evolved little integration. In so-called "integrated-schools," there were often only a handful of black students, shunned by the white students. The muscular Southern white-power structure, often polite, had learned to express its strength in subtle ways, while repudiating the crude extremism of the Ku Klux Klan.

Giving open support to mass marches and demonstrations, M. L. on one occasion had said:

> There is more power in socially organized masses on the march than there is in guns in the hands of a few desperate men—our enemies would prefer to deal with a small armed group than with a huge, unarmed but resolute mass of people.

. . . Our powerful weapons are the voices, the feet, and the bodies of dedicated, united, people moving without rest toward a just goal. Greater tyrants than Southern segregationists have been subdued and defeated by this form of struggle.[171]

His strategy in each city was to cooperate with the local leader— often in an engagement long in progress—and face the dogs, tear gas, fire hoses, jails, and brutality. In his final years, M. L. would steer his goals more toward national programs, federal legislation, and self-directed civic actions. Meanwhile, he would engage where the situation was promising, and if a white judge barred him from marching, then the movement would be strengthened by a second cause, the right to protest peacefully.[172]

Albany—The Battle Ground

The right target appeared to loom in the community of Albany, Georgia, and a torrid social battle would be engaged from December 1961 until spring 1962. Albany, on the Flint River, was a medium-size city of fifty-eight thousand people in old plantation country, in extreme southwest Georgia close to the Alabama line. It was a trade and edible nut center, but was far more than a provincial town sustained by a state college and nearby Turner Air Force Base. This civil rights engagement would be unusual since, at least in the beginning, both the whites and blacks would be nonviolent.

The Student Nonviolent Coordinating Committee (SNCC)— financed in part by the SCLC—launched freedom rides into Albany to integrate its facilities. This immediately placed M. L. at odds with the policy of the NAACP. Despite this outside friction, Albany Negroes were mobilized and led by King and local physician Dr. G. T. Anderson. Some whites and eleven hundred blacks marched, were arrested, and deliberately clogged the jail. King's words were: "Get on your walking shoes; walk together, children and don't cha get weary." If the goal was to bring down the walls of separation, the effort was a spectacular failure. In contravention, twenty percent of the maids and cooks lost their jobs.[173]

Many blacks across the country harshly accused M. L. King of being "chicken" when he found an avenue of escape from prison. Initially, he was on a course to spend forty-five days in jail with the others, rather than pay the $178 fine. Then, in a conflict of facts—whether to escort from the jail a mentally-ill "Jesus figure," or else to accept the clever ploy of Albany's mayor to pay the fine—M. L. walked out of prison. He was roundly criticized by a host of blacks for "blowing it."[174]

Mississippi was realistically viewed by many black leaders as the most dangerous and difficult racial territory to be transformed. Therefore, in October 1962, many observers were fascinated as black student James Meredith sought to enroll at the University of Mississippi ("Ole Miss"). White mobs crowded the streets in violent protests. During the Cuban Missile Crisis, involving Russian Premier Kruschev, with the world tottering on the edge of a nuclear holocaust, Kennedy was obliged to give some attention to the internal crisis. On October 2, 1962, about three thousand U.S. troops with armed vehicles were employed in Oxford, Mississippi, to take control, seize two hundred demonstrators, and register at the state university one black man, James Meredith. In the savage confrontation, in an all-night riot, three observers were killed, twenty-eight U.S. marshals were shot, and 160 marshals were injured; this was the same day that President Kennedy announced a peaceful resolution of the issue and the university's integration. At the finale, the U.S. government held hearings in New Orleans and brought contempt charges against Mississippi governor Ross Barnett, but little was accomplished in those legal battles.[175]

Birmingham: Opposition from Black Leaders

Birmingham, Alabama, site of another confrontation, would prove to be a massive wall to surmount, tragic for small children, and a setback to M. L. King. Birmingham, an important business, industrial and cultural center, had a large population, thirty-seven percent of it Negro. It was in this Southern city that M. L. decided to adopt more aggressive tactics, in the extension of the philosophy of "unmerited suffering" as employed by SNCC.[176]

The Kennedy administration had done little to change racial job patterns other than to refer to the minimal wages of the moppers and sweepers at the Post Office and the Veterans Administration; of the two thousand federal jobs in the city, only twenty were held by blacks. In 1963, at the Army Ordnance Plant and the regional Treasury Department Disbursing Office, there was not one Negro worker.[177]

Long before Martin Luther King arrived on the scene, his friend, the Reverend Fred Shuttlesworth, had led a contingent against the tough, much-publicized police official, Eugene T. "Bull" Connor. Before entering the fray and finding himself in jail for an eight-day stay, beginning on April 12, 1963, King had made difficult decisions with ten associates in a planning session at Savannah. From now on, he would take the initiative, try not to lose the momentum to conservative allies, and choose his own battlefields, in this instance Birmingham. He would try to maintain the forward action and utilize any openings provided by the Kennedy Administration,[178] knowing that the President would not vigorously intrude into Birmingham. Even some of his SCLC colleagues informed King that nonviolent tactics were dead.[179]

Savannah, that tranquil period-piece of history, noted for its good manners and attachment to the past, would not go untouched in the revolution. There, Hosea Williams, King's "wild man" would lead five hundred Negroes to jail and incite a Negro doorman to unlock the great doors of the Manger Hotel for a sit-in. In order to restore order, Savannians returned to Civil War laws, while M. L. King in his silk tie joined longshoremen for beer and a game of billiards.[180]

Martin Luther faced in Birmingham the open opposition of the vast majority of black preachers. Three-fourths of Birmingham's four hundred Negro pastors voted against any nonviolent demonstration in the city. After he was behind the bars of a Birmingham jail, Martin wrote his famous voluminous "Letter from the Birmingham

Jail," in response to eight ministers, priests, and rabbis who urged other Negroes to withdraw their support of the demonstrations.[181] He replied with courage: "We will reach the goal of freedom in Birmingham and all over the nation, because the goal of America is freedom. Abused and scorned though we may be, our duty is tied up with the destiny of America."[182]

Also, he prophesied about the country's ultimate destiny:

> One day the South will know that when these disinherited children of God sat down at lunch counters, they were in reality standing up for what is best in the American dream and for the most sacred values in our Judaeo-Christian heritage, thereby bringing our nation back to those great wells of democracy—[183]

Discouraged by the non-involvement of white moderates,[184] repudiated by most Birmingham black preachers, and losing in the streets, M. L. then utilized school children to assist the cause. Those young recruits, that numbered over one thousand, trampled down the locked gates of Parker High School, then found themselves facing police dogs that bit them and fire hoses that knocked them flat. The result was tragic, for, at the Sixteenth Street Baptist Church, four adolescent girls rehearsing for a Youth Day program were killed in a man-set explosion. Later, Martin Luther King, preaching at a funeral with three caskets, told the mourners, "We must not lose faith in our white brothers."[185] In Nashville, white Southern Baptist leaders responded with condolences and financial support, but took no formal action. The situation became ugly, as blacks retaliated and hurled rocks and bottles toward the police lines. Twenty-five hundred demonstrators found themselves in the Birmingham jail.[186]

In the aftermath, Birmingham Negroes turned against M. L. King. But there were gains, one of them being an invitation for M. L. and his Birmingham lieutenants to confer with President Kennedy, who was beginning to understand the need for a national standard of law.[187] National interest in Birmingham also created support for federal legislation outlawing segregation in interstate commerce.[188]

As the Birmingham story faded, in the ten weeks that followed May 10, 1963, there were 14,733 arrests in 186 American communities and 758 racial demonstrations. But the city editors had turned their attention to the Muslim trial in Los Angeles and the Selma, Alabama, racial demonstrations.[189]

The Muslims and King

While in the Birmingham jail, Martin Luther King had warned moderate whites that if they did not value peaceful protests, then the Black Muslim doctrine of violence might direct the black revolution.[190] The phenomenon of Black Muslim militancy made its appearance after World War II among the inmates of the federal prison at Lorton, Virginia, near the national capital. Black Muslims, as the followers of Elijah Muhammad's Nation of Islam were called, talked passionately of their hatred for whites but maintained a tight discipline. Followers became an army that did not drink alcohol nor eat pork, but took Arabic names, bathed at least once a day, and kept their houses immaculately clean. They were gaining national recognition for practicing martial arts, but also pursuing personal lives of sexual purity and racial separation.[191]

King made it clear that the Nation of Islam repudiated not only white people, but also Christianity and democracy.[192] In 1959 the Black Muslim sub-leader Malcolm X (once known as Malcolm Little) had taunted M. L. King for replying with peaceful tactics against the "blue-eyed devils," after the lynching by hooded men of Negro Mack Parker in Poplarville, Mississippi. Then, during the Birmingham campaign, Elijah Muhammad told the *Los Angeles Times* that by using school children King was "making a fool of himself." Malcolm X stiffened this position by declaring on television that "any man who puts his women and children on the front lines is a chump, not a champ!"[193]

The Los Angeles Muslim trial on May 30 was about a complex shootout involving Muslims, their local leader John X Morris, and the Los Angeles police. The final verdict brought an acquittal for Morris and a conviction for eleven Muslims. M. L., having raised $150,000 on a tour that took him to Los Angeles, did not want to add anything to a volatile situation.[194]

Motivated by a growing disrespect for his absolute leader, Malcolm X began disregarding the commands of Elijah Muhammad not to mingle with M. L. King's supporters, nor to march, petition, or even vote. However, Malcolm X (until his pilgrimage to Mecca) held that the black man was the "original man" and the white man was a "snake" or a devil.[195] He inveighed against the U. S. government's treatment of dark people and its questionable and sometimes duplicitous involvement with Patrice Lumumba of the Congo (later called Zaire) and President Ngo Dinh Diem of South Vietnam. Eventually, on March 26, 1964, Malcolm X would meet one time with M. L. King.[196]

In the faithful Muslim ranks, it became known that Malcolm X mixed with King's SNCC supporters at the Statler Hilton Hotel in Washington, D.C. Then, in violation of orders not to promote activism in the "white world," he directed a shopping boycott in Queens, New York. When reports circulated in the Philadelphia FBI that Malcolm would be shot by gunmen, he made an alliance with Wallace Muhammad, Elijah's son. This did not save him, and in the Newark area, Muslim assassins with shotguns and pistols murdered Malcolm X as he addressed his supporters.[197]

In the flurry after the Los Angeles Muslim trials, M. L. King, on May 30, sent a telegram to President Kennedy asking for a conference to clarify Kennedy's civil rights goals. Martin needed assurances, for the Negro middle-class was wary or even offended by his activism, and the NAACP had taken measures not to be overpowered by the King forces in the South.[198]

Then, in August 28, 1963, the Trailblazer King made his unforgettable "I Have a Dream" speech before 250,000 black and white persons at the Lincoln Memorial in Washington, D.C. The "March on Washington" had been planned by Bayard Rustin, and for the occasion M. L. wore his "Black is Beautiful" button and dressed in overalls, a garb he seldom if ever wore as an adult. On hearing about plans for the March, Muslim leader Malcolm X said, "it wont solve the problems of the black people."[199]

The U. S. Government manifested nervousness about the forthcoming Washington event and the potential that one hundred thousand militants might go on a rampage. The Pentagon readied nineteen thousand troops and placed them on alert to rush to the capital's assistance. Plans also were made to interrupt the public address system, if needed. In the end, millions of people, including President Kennedy, heard on television M. L. King's full address that spoke to "all God's children, black men and white men, Jews and Gentiles, Protestants and Catholics."[200]

Despised by many after Birmingham, King's popularity soared before the Washington March. A *Newsweek* magazine poll of the acceptance rate of Negro leaders, registered eighty-eight percent favoring King, sixty-eight percent for Roy Wilkins, and fifty-one percent for Adam Clayton Powell.[201] Always eager to find openings for his cause, M. L. then made himself available on June 10, 1964, in St. Augustine, Florida, to encourage the pickets in that besieged city.

The Bridge at Selma

Selma, in south central Alabama, half way between Demopolis and Montgomery, had a population of about twenty-eight thousand, and during the Civil War had maintained one of the few important foundries of the Confederacy. There were thousands of blacks, but ninety-nine percent of the Selma voters were white. In some of the surrounding counties, there was not a single black voter. Selma would be catapulted to fame or infamy by the attempt by King's supporters to radically change the city's racial customs. In this time-frame, Attorney General Robert Kennedy and the director of the FBI, J. Edgar Hoover, conferred about the placement of wire taps and electronic "bugs" to ferret information from King's Atlanta home and SCLC offices in Atlanta and New York; the FBI had identified King as "the most dangerous Negro of the future in the nation," an assessment based in part on M. L.'s Communist friends.[202]

The "battle" for Selma roughly extended from the summer of 1964 to about 15 March 1965, during which time M. L. was jailed and released. In this campaign, King did not always remain in Selma, and responding to the lack of progress called on outside white clergy and rabbis to assist him, with 450 of them responding to the call. In a tactical sense, the Selma campaign was a turning point, for many of the student activists no longer believed in nonviolence and turned against the white liberals who were giving them limited support. M. L.'s peaceful reactions brought on a crisis with SNCC and CORE protesters: SNCC had been active in Selma for two years with little publicity, and now King was getting most of the attention.[203] However, in one of the most startling developments of the campaign, two hundred black youth knelt and prayed for the opposing leader, hefty James "Jim" Clark, "the best dressed sheriff in the Black Belt."[204]

On Bloody Sunday, March 7, 1965, an orderly march led by John Lewis and Hosea Williams for voter rights was turned into a scene of blood by state troopers and Sheriff Jim Clark and his fifty deputies, wielding clubs from horses. Women and children, as well as men and college students, were tear-gassed and beaten to the ground.[205] King had escalated the contest in Selma step by step, first gathering potential voters at the Selma courthouse, then courting arrests by illegal marches, causing his own arrest and confinement in jail, demonstrating in surrounding counties, then initiating night marches.[206]

The second major effort was to assemble Tuesday, March 9, at the Browne Chapel A.M.E., converge at the Edmund Pettus Bridge, and then to march to confront Governor George Wallace fifty-four miles away in Montgomery. At the Browne Chapel, before three thousand people, Martin Luther King said: "I have made my choice. I have got to march—but I would rather die on the highways of Alabama than make a butchery of my conscience."[207]

On the orders of Judge Frank M. Johnson, only three hundred

marchers were authorized to begin the trek. Beyond the Pettus Bridge, King faced with a line of state police, infuriated his enemies and saddened his friends by turning back, instead of taking the blows. Then Lyndon Johnson, who had assumed the presidency after President Kennedy was assassinated in November 1963, sent federal troops to protect the marchers venturing from Selma to Montgomery. In the third phase, from March 21 to 25, the quest to Montgomery sometimes involved eight thousand people, later perhaps thirty thousand. M. L. returned to walk the last three miles;[208] some cheered his decision, while others muttered in disdain. While Selma was not his finest hour, he was a human being with human frailties, who had been consistent in his nonviolent mission, and while his life was in constant danger, had remained the revolution's paramount leader.[209] He may have felt at this time that further violence would cause the loss of the white middle class.

The confrontation in Selma had far-reaching effects, generating mass meetings in Washington, D.C., and the arrival in Alabama of Protestant, Unitarian, Catholic, and Jewish leaders. President Lyndon Johnson, watching the violence on television, made up his mind on civil rights, and taking the issue to Congress, he requested passage of the Voting Rights Act, which became law in August 1965.[210]

The Revolution Moves North

Following the massive black rampage in the Los Angeles enclave of Watts, which left thirty-four Negroes dead and entire blocks of the community burned down, King and Rustin on August 19, 1965, viewed the blackened ruins. Sickened by the spectacle, M. L. was reminded that he had not considered designing a program for Northern ghetto youth.[211]

The racial situation in the North was volatile. The War in Vietnam (or its American phase) had realistically begun in 1966, or more likely in the period when President Kennedy had sent "military advisors" to assist South Vietnam. In response to racial and social friction, the black communities of the North were troubled and agitated. Half of Black America was in the North, and the civil rights movement had ignored them. The white Northern element, feeling itself safe at first, responded to rising restlessness with its own brand of racism and bigotry.[212]

With his stripe of asceticism, Martin Luther King, on January 22, 1966, installed himself in "Lawndale," a Chicago slum tenement, to commence his "Chicago Movement." He lightened this oppressive work with the condition that he spend three days of the week in Atlanta as the co-pastor of Ebenezer Church. His mission at Lawndale was to instruct people about slums, to organize a slum-dwellers union, and to mobilize the tenants as demonstrators. His formidable financial goal was to increase the income of Chicago blacks by fifty million dollars. Partly in response to his efforts, the federal government, about May 1966, granted a loan for the purpose of renovating five hundred Chicago apartments.[213]

In order to relieve the tedium, King sometimes returned to famil-iar forms of relaxation, drinking a beer or two and playing pool with the hustlers. And where he encountered a worthy opponent, he ar-gued against the Frantz Fanon thesis that "violence is the only thing that will bring about liberation."[214]

In 1968, the divisive Vietnam War, which would split America into two camps, was in full operation. Not only so, but President Johnson and the American government were deeply involved in the sinister business of replacing the South Vietnamese president. By November, secret cables alerted the White House to an anti-govern-ment coup that was proceeding in Saigon, and that President Dgo Dinh Diem and his brother Nhu had been hacked to death by machete-wielding South Vietnamese plotters.[215]

At New York's Riverside Church, built by Baptist philanthropist John D. Rockefeller, Martin Luther King had made a scathing de-nunciation of the United States involvement in the war in Vietnam. In some circles, he became as unpopular as actress Jane Fonda, who denounced America from Hanoi, while American war prisoners were being held in "tiger cages" and tortured to death. M. L. did not flinch in his opposition to the war, which he decried as "the greatest purveyor of violence in the world today."[216] His anti-war sentiments, expressed while the United States was rotating over five hundred thousand troops to South Vietnam, was a source of embarrassment to the national leaders of the Southern Christian Leadership Conference. Rattled by the patriotic backfire, the SCLC National Board voted that if King spoke on the Vietnam War, he must do so as a private citizen.[217]

The Killer Strikes

The civil rights revolution produced an abundant bloody harvest of martyrs, black and white, that included President John F. Kennedy, Attorney General Robert Kennedy, Mississippi NAACP organizer Medgar Evers, three student activists (Andrew Goodman, James Chaney, and Michael Schwerner) in Neshoba County, Mississippi, and now the great Trailblazer Martin Luther King, Jr. He would die assisting the lonely garbage collectors of Memphis, Tennessee.

The garbage personnel of Memphis, ninety-five percent of them black, had been on strike for weeks for higher wages. Since the first march involved violence, the local judge enjoined Martin Luther King, invited by the strikers to reinforce them, not to participate in the marches. M. L. regarded this instruction as an illegal order and he intended to disregard it.[218]

At Mason Temple in Memphis, King spoke with emotion about threats to his life, possibly mobilizing his personal resources to disregard the injunction. "Longevity has its place," he said, "but I'm not concerned about that now. I just want to do God's will. And He's allowed me to go up to the mountain. And I've looked over, and I've seen the Promised Land."[219]

Martin Luther had arrived in Memphis on April 1, 1968, and by 6:00 P.M. on April 4 at the Negro-owned Lorraine Hotel he would be breathing his last. He was on the balcony of the Lorraine talking to rally leader Jesse Jackson, standing in the courtyard below.[220] Slightly more than 205 feet away, a white man that had registered in a seedy nearby hotel as John Willard (later identified as James Earl Ray), focused his binoculars, loaded a high powered 30.06 rifle with telescope, and allegedly fired a shot into Martin Luther King.[221] King's earthly work was finished.

After the funeral, in violence and grief, blacks in 125 cities burned and looted stores and shops, fighting the police in many instances. In order to subdue the outburst, sixty-eight thousand troops were employed. By April 11, forty-six people were dead, thirty-five thousand injured, and twenty thousand in jail. Blacks viewed with open contempt and as cheap showmanship the ostentatious mourning by some whites. The 1968 Civil Rights Act, designed to outlaw discrimination in the sale and rental of housing, was passed on April 10, but the specifics were hard to enforce. The civil rights provisions relating to intimidation and murder were simply four years too late.[222]

The Dream That Did Not Die

Martin Luther King, Jr., may have achieved more by his death than he did by his life. He had collected and would earn a formidable array of honors. Among his principal accolades were the Nobel Peace Prize (1964), *Time* magazine "Man of the Year" (1963), the Solomon Schecter award, and by Congressional action an annual national Martin Luther King, Jr., Day (first celebrated in 1986).[223]

The real memorial to King is that he served as paramount leader of the social-racial revolution in America, extending from 1956 to 1978, which would change favorably and forever the lives of blacks, Spanish, Native Americans, and, perhaps most drastically, the white majority. Because of King, the United States today is arguably more tolerant, more obedient to its own democratic principles, and the nation possibly more durable and secure.

Without M. L. King and his Christ-determined tactics of nonviolence, the inevitable struggle would certainly have been far more violent and bloody. There were dangerous black and white agitators, needing only perceived authority to murder those who stood in their way. The Black Muslims, with their small armies and code of hatred, ached for the chance to turn the revolution into a blood bath. But M. L. King stood steady and talked earnestly about black and white brothers, about the lesser significance of skin color, about hope and character, and the Promised Land. He might not get there, but his brothers would.

What kind of Baptist leader was this? What manner of hero? He played a little pool, and had human defects, which were far outweighed by the stunning fact that he changed history—for an infinite good. This was no Oliver Cromwell with absolute assurance, nor a Prime Minster Neville Chamberlain floundering in illusions. In a different milieu, he was realistic and stubborn even when fanatics sought his life. He was frightened for his wife and child when the side of his house was shattered, and sometimes his knees buckled when once more he faced police dogs and jolting blows. Still, he endured and persevered, and pressed forward whatever the cost, because the Bible was the engine that drove Martin Luther King, Jr., to his fantastic dream.[224]

By challenging the Christian Church—its elements both black and white—he gave the ministry a stern sense of social purpose and restored its prophetic voice.[225] As the supreme orator and mobilizer of people, he drove a sharp wedge into the old institutions and gained access for a neglected minority to the vote, public services, schools, and better jobs, to which they were entitled. Martin Luther King, Jr., as foretold by Emerson, was one of those heroic souls, who "forgets himself into immortality."[226]

Jimmy Carter, President of the United States

Chapter 19

Jimmy Carter
(1924-)

Born-Again Statesman

Baptists worldwide, during the twentieth and twenty-first centuries, have had their share of economic power brokers—but none richer than Baptist John D. Rockefeller, Sr. Baptists also have been honored through the fidelity of an array of statesmen of renown: the United Kingdom's prime minister, David Lloyd George (1863-1945); Canada's prime minister, John George Diefenbaker (1895-1979); Liberia's president, William V. S. Tubman (his fifth term, 1963); and a chief justice of the U.S. Supreme Court, Charles Evans Hughes (1862-1948). In addition, there have been, by the beginning of the twenty-first century, four presidents of the United States who have declared themselves to be Baptists: Warren G. Harding (1865-1923), Harry S. Truman (1884-1972), Jimmy Carter (1924-), and Bill Clinton (1946-).

Because most of his life has been focused on biblical principles, and because he has sought earnestly to follow the example of Jesus Christ, the story of Jimmy Carter is unique. At least three factors make Carter worthy of inclusion among the other illustrious Baptist Trailblazers cited in *The Origins and Growth of Baptist Faith*: (1) his steady Christian testimony through a multitude of activities, as a servant of Christ; (2) his integrity and courage in taking a stand on racism and asserting boldly that his church—the Plains Baptist

Church—should be open to African-Americans; and (3) finally, his profound faith in declaring himself a "born-again Christian," a term not understood by many non-Baptists in the United States or by non-Christians elsewhere.

The Carter presidency (1977-1981) was in difficulties from its beginning day. Carter, coming from the Georgia agricultural whistle-stop of Plains, had few dependable friends and connections in Washington, D.C., other than the Georgia partisans he brought with him to the Capital. With his moral scruples he was not always conciliatory, and Congress returned the favor by blocking many of his favorite programs, including Salt II. Since he changed his mind on some issues, his leadership was viewed by many Americans as weak and erratic. Personally, he was brilliant, a hard-worker, and sensitive to social problems, although his administration was besieged by ravaging inflation and a sapping energy crisis. Then there were the factors of his own defects, for on occasions he was hampered by his own stubbornness and a Georgia small-town perception. Carter had come from political near-obscurity and was borne up by a meteoric ascendancy, but his political collapse in four years would be devastating and apparently complete. No one would have expected a Phoenix to crawl from the ashes, but the experts would be wrong again.

The Carter presidency in profile is not viewed by a host of observers as an outstanding legacy; the Camp David Accords that brought peace to Israel and Egypt will most probably remain the crowning achievement of his administration. Even so, the *Chicago Tribune* in 1982 ranked Carter number twenty-sixth in effectiveness out of thirty-eight presidents,[1] immediately ahead of Calvin Coolidge. Then, a poll of historians in February 2000 ranked the leadership of Carter twenty-second out of forty-one presidents, immediately ahead of Gerald Ford.[2] However, Jimmy and Rosalynn Carter, after leaving Washington, refused to close the door on their legacy and began to assert a new Christian dynamism devoted to international mediation and good works that would brush aside mediocrity and lay bare the character of Carter as an aggressive peace-maker and an exceptional Christian leader.

His Early Years

James Earl Carter, Jr. ("Jimmy") was born at the Wise Hospital on October 1, 1924, in the small, plain country town of Plains, Georgia (population about 572), close to Americus, where the greatest event of the day might be the noisy arrival and departure of the huffing freight train. Jimmy's great-grandfather, Littleberry Walker Carter, a Confederate veteran, reportedly was killed in a dispute with his partner over the earnings from a merry-go-round. His paternal grandfather, William A. "Billy" Carter, also was tragically killed, this time to settle the ownership of a desk.

Things fared better with his other immediate kinsmen. His maternal grandfather, Jim Jack Gordy, postmaster at Richland, apparently originated the concept of rural free delivery and died peacefully. James Earl Carter, Sr. (1894-1953), Jimmy's father, sold insurance and founded the Carter peanut warehouse business in Plains. Eventually, James Earl owned four thousand acres of farmland, worked by two hundred black tenant farmers. Politically, the elder Carter was a conservative Democrat, and during the Great Depression was opposed to venturesome President Franklin D. Roosevelt. The father of Jimmy served on the Sumter County School Board and in 1952 was elected to the Georgia legislature. He embodied a mixture of moral uprightness and old Southern conservatism; he refused to join the powerful and popular Ku Klux Klan, but reportedly felt impelled to leave the house when his wife entertained a black guest.[3]

The Trailblazer's mother was (Bessie) Lillian Gordy Carter (1898-1983), a registered nurse, whose Christ-inspired enlightened views incited severe criticism from her white neighbors; Bessie's unforgivable sin was that she served as a midwife for poor, black sharecropper mothers. She instilled in young Carter the compulsions to read well and to seek a fine education. At Auburn University she worked as a fraternity house mother and later became a co-chairman in Americus, Georgia, for a political group supporting presidential aspirant Lyndon Johnson. Then, for two years, she volunteered her services in the Peace Corps and was assigned to work with the Marathis of India, at the village of Vikroli. In February 1977 she was the United States representative at the funeral of Indian President Fakhruddin Ali Ahmed.[4]

When Jimmy Carter was four years old, the family moved from Plains to a farm at neighboring Archery, a largely black community, where he spent the remainder of his childhood. Jimmy is the oldest of four children. His older sister became Mrs. Gloria Spann; his second sister was evangelist Mrs. Ruth Carter Stapleton, who wrote *The Gift of Inner Healing*; and his brother Billy Carter made his living as a peanut broker and gas station owner. Young Jimmy attended the public elementary school and high school at Plains. He was well behaved in school and eager to learn, excelling in history and literature and competing in sports as a member of the high school basketball team.[5]

The early Carter home was fervently Christian, with Jimmy shaped by ardent prayers and Bible reading. His acquaintances recall that the youthful Jimmy threw himself with intensity into churchgoing. After Jimmy was immersed at age eleven and had become a member of the Plains Baptist Church, he borrowed on Sunday his mother's old black Plymouth and would sweep the backroads for boys of his age and bring them to church. His social life had twin epicenters: first the Plains Baptist Church, and later the Sumter County School Board. Following the directives of the Bible as a good Baptist, he knew as an adolescent that sexual intercourse outside of marriage was sinful.[6]

After graduating from high school, Jimmy attended Georgia Southwestern College at Americus, about ten miles from the site of Andersonville Confederate Cemetery and its sad memories of starved Civil War prisoners. In the midst of World War II and its Pacific offensive against Japan, Jimmy in 1942 took mathematics courses at

Atlanta's Georgia Institute of Technology. He was preparing for an appointment to the U.S. Naval Academy, which admitted him in 1943.[7] At the Naval Academy at Annapolis, Carter, with Christian commitment, taught a Bible class for young girls.[8]

Surviving at the Academy, "Hot" Carter, as he was dubbed, was treated roughly by upper-classmen, eager to modify the Southerner's drawl and to wipe away the ever-present grin on his face. As a tribute to his character, he took some brutal beatings but refused to sing General Sherman's insulting Civil War conquest hymn, "Marching Through Georgia." In his undergraduate classes, Carter proved adept in gunnery, electronics, and naval tactics. His exposure to practical seamanship was tested in 1944, with a training tour aboard the USS *New York*; his assignment was to clean the latrines. He graduated 59th out of a class of 820 midshipmen, but his discreet ambition was to rise to become the chief of Naval Operations.

As an ensign, at age twenty-one, Jimmy Carter on July 7, 1946, married (Eleanor) Rosalynn Smith, age eighteen, at the Plains Methodist Church. She was born on August 18, 1927, in Plains. Rosalynn, an extraordinarily strong character, was the daughter of a staunch Methodist and teetotaler Edgar Smith, a garage mechanic and schoolbus driver, and Allie Murray Smith. Rosalynn experienced a desperately hard young life; she was thirteen years old when her father died of leukemia. Before his death, Smith sold his farmland to the Carters. Rosalynn's mother existed on a meager income as a postal clerk and part-time seamstress. Rosalynn also found employment through sewing and work at the local beauty parlor. Despite the austerity forced on the family, she was an excellent scholar and class spokesman, the valedictorian of her high school class.[9]

Rosalynn attended Georgia Southwestern College for two years, planning for a career as an interior decorator or a secretary. Otherwise, she was a normal smalltown girl, who read books, shuffled cards, and in high school played basketball. She was always impeccably neat. Although Rosalynn's father was not one of life's great winners, he left some money for his children's education. On home leave from Annapolis, Carter asked his sister Ruth to arrange a date with pretty, curly-haired Rosalynn, Ruth's best friend. Jimmy took his date to a movie and informed his mother afterwards that this was the girl he would marry. His mother's response was: "Jimmy, she's just a little girl! She's Ruth's friend."[10] By their second date, Carter and Rosalynn were in love, and soon they scheduled a date to marry, after Jimmy's graduation at Annapolis. Carter would later affirm that Rosalynn is the only woman that he ever loved;[11] and their destinies—political, cultural, intellectual, and religious—would be inseparable.

Life in the Navy

After their marriage, the Carters moved to a small apartment at Norfolk, Virginia, while the ensign took his position aboard the USS *Wyoming*. The short military career would embrace their cycles of togetherness and separation. Their life, more than that of many couples, bonded firmly as they studied books together, read the Bible, memorized Shakespeare, and listened to musical classics, including Rachmaninoff.[12] The couple would raise three boys: John William ("Jack"), later a lawyer, born at Portsmouth, Virginia, in July 1947; James Earl ("Chip"), to become the director of a consulting firm, born in Hawaii in 1950; and (Donnell) Jeffrey, who trained to become a computer consultant, born at New London, Connecticut, in 1952. Also they were parents to a daughter, Amy Lynn Carter, a sometime student activist who opposed CIA recruiting and fought apartheid in South Africa. Meanwhile, potential careers in the peacetime navy shrank, as that force diminished from three million to one million men.[13]

In June 1948, after his rejection for a Rhodes scholarship, Carter won a berth at the submarine school at New London, Connecticut. He would spend five years aboard four conventional submarines and less than one year in the training and applications of the brand-new program on nuclear propulsion. Despite misleading stories, Carter never served as a nuclear submarine commander; he had left the U.S. Navy sixteen months before the first nuclear submarine put out to sea.[14]

Carter was assigned in December 1948 to the submarine USS *Pomfret*, berthed in Hawaii. On its maiden cruise, he became terribly seasick, and while he was standing watch topside an enormous wave bounced him thirty feet aft, before he could gain his feet. He had nearly been swept overboard. His instant reaction was that God had protected him. He later said: "I don't have any fear at all of death."

This young officer was of a distinct breed, intense, ever-smiling, but different from the rest. While others were playing poker, he was reading manuals or solving a problem.[15] His superiors regarded Carter as an outstanding officer, low-key but confident, sometimes introverted. He was dedicated, self-sufficient, hard-working, and congenial. He enjoyed the physical and masculine closeness of the crew and the demands for perfection.[16]

While Carter was an officer in the Navy, the British officials at Nassau gave a party for the American crew. A U.S. black sailor was not invited to the gala event, so none of the white submariners would attend the reception. But when Lieutenant Carter, on leave, tried to explain the situation to his father, the traditional old-line Southerner, he simply could not understand the crew's reaction.[17]

On February 1, 1951, Carter arrived at New London, Connecticut, and became the engineering officer (later, as second in command, the executive officer) of the submarine K-1. This type of small submersible served as a submarine killer, lying in ambush for its prey along the submarine lanes. Carter's superior, Lieutenant Commander Frank Andrews, described his colleague as "smart as hell," but beyond that there were no legends of close friendships or mirthful sea stories. Carter was utterly unobtrusive but knew his job better than anybody.[18]

After service on the submarine K-1, Carter was interviewed in 1952 by no-nonsense Admiral Hyman Rickover, as a candidate for work on the Navy's prototype atomic submarine *Sea Wolf*. The interview lasted two hours, and Carter was accepted. In changing his assignment, Carter submitted to the curbing perfectionist style of Rickover, much like he bowed to the strictures of his father, Mr. Earl. Rickover, the detailist, read every duplicate "pink sheet," and Jimmy Carter, later as president, would copy that style and read every line of every bill. Carter's future micro-management style would be much like that of the sixteenth-century Spanish ruler Philip II, who reportedly examined every bill of one hundred florins or more. Only twenty-eight years old, Carter would serve for eleven months under Rickover. However, when Jimmy's father died in 1953, it would require the strong arm of Georgia Senator Richard Russell to wrench him free from the Navy. Admiral Rickover would gruffly denounce Carter's separation as a "breach of loyalty."[19]

Return to Plains

In 1953 Jimmy's father, James Earl, Sr., lay dying of cancer. The family farms and business had declined as the older Carter was sinking under the weight of his adverse health. There was a stabbing loneliness in Carter's heart, since he felt that the father he so ardently loved and admired had not returned to him an equal measure of affection.[20] So the submarine officer made the quick, painful decision to assume the role of tribal elder and return to Plains in order to improve the family estate. However, that about-face was a powerfully disturbing retreat for his wife Rosalynn, who had shaken off the drabness of Plains and was thoroughly enjoying the freedom of a Navy officer's wife. The confrontation of the couple over the matter was so severe that even the possibility of divorce was lurking somewhere amid their angry words.[21] Unmoved, Jimmy Carter related the biblical words that the husband is the head of the household and that his decision in such matters must be honored. In submitting, Rosalynn undoubtedly passed the severest test of a marriage that seemed made in Heaven.

By 1979 Jimmy Carter would become a millionaire from the agricultural proceeds earned from the land. Carter Sr. owned thirty parcels of land, worked by two hundred tenants, and altogether fiteen hundred persons, including dependent wives and children, were getting their livelihood from the Carter enterprises. In town, there was an affiliated seed and fertilizer business. Also, Jimmy's father was a banker of sorts, granting loans and credit for seed peanuts and seed cotton. In 1953 the family's worth may have been fifty thousand dollars in cash and forty thousand dollars in credits.[22]

However, the primary lure that brought Jimmy back to Plains was the emotional tie to his father. At Mr. Earl's deathbed, as the powerful man wasted away, the two talked for hours about old times. The senior man's workers and tenant farmers were grateful for his support in hard times, when he supplied clothes and sometimes support for education. Now, as to a medieval lord, they left gifts at his door: flowers, a cooked quail, a fresh loaf of bread. When he died in 1953, Jimmy broke down in tears and declared that he wished "to be a man like my father."[23]

The Jimmy Carters and their three young sons moved into a new "white only" housing project in Plains, paying thirty dollars monthly rent. Jimmy was heir to the farming and peanut brokerage business, but his training was in abstemious living. Rosalynn took a correspondence course in accounting and became the bookkeeper for the Carter peanut business.[24] In the first year, Carter sold two thousand tons of fertilizer, but after a devastating drought his debtors could not pay. He sometimes worked sixteen hours a day loading fertilizer bags. He searched for productive methods through science, devoured agricultural manuals, and for advice sought out the county agent and the Plains Agricultural Experiment Station. In the 1960s-1970s, farms might not survive that did not produce two or three tons of peanuts per acre. Still, this was no longer a marginal crop, and with modern changes, the crop was on the edge of take-off. And in the 1970s peanuts became Georgia's leading cash crop.[25]

At this stage, the Carters were scarcely self-denying Puritans. In company with several couples, the Carters found pleasure in dancing and in stock car races on Georgia's seacoast. In one instance, the Carters and their friends lost all their money while gambling. Then, as religion and politics again became more pivotal in their lives, Jimmy and Rosalynn began to revert back to basic beliefs. In the mid-1950s, Jimmy followed in the tracks of his father and became a Sunday School teacher at the Plains Baptist Church.[26] Sunday School teachers at a Southern Baptist Church are considered qualified if they are active church members, attend a Bible class, know the Bible expertly, and, on occasions, undertake specialized training. Jimmy from long experience became an accomplished Bible scholar and a skilled lay preacher. In a progression toward religious maturity, he was ordained as a deacon, and then became leader of the Royal Ambassadors, a Baptist children's organization on Boy Scout lines, that employs an array of religious retreats and camping trips.[27]

As a social activist Carter joined the library board, supported plans to build a swimming pool, and for six years was a member of the Sumter County School Board, finally becoming its chairman. This was an era of racial controversy and inequality, and white students rode buses to their school classes while black students walked. Carter had arrived at this social level two years after the Supreme Court's decision in *Brown v. Board of Education*, which terminated the doctrine of separate but equal education. This decision was cataclysmic and would have to be enforced in the nation at each state and county level. The era was a tumultuous period, particularly in the South, and old mores would be shaken loose, and traditional leaders would be tried by fire and sometimes broken. Not always perceiving it as such, the United States was in the midst of a Civil Rights Revolution that would last for two decades, from 1956 to 1976, from the Eisenhower presidency to the Ford presidency. And the moral-social foundations of the South, but also the North, would be tested in ways that were unimaginable.[28]

As a Southerner, Carter acted on the whole with moderation and courage, but this independence placed him at odds with many of his neighbors. Jim Crow, with its multitude of uneven and demeaning laws thwarting black progress, had ruled the schools, hospitals, courts, and even churches. At this early period, Carter believed in separate education for the races, but he migrated to the position that blacks should be given buses for school transportation. He supported sick pay and pay raises for white teachers, but did not push these privileges for black teachers. He made a proposal that the Sumter black and white schools be consolidated and then joined to the Americus community system (while leaving them separate), but this measure stood no chance. He was earning some enmity, and his cousin Hugh Carter gave him the poisonous appellation—an "integrationist."[29]

Penetrated as they were by the Federal Bureau of Investigation (FBI), the White Knights of the Ku Klux Klan kept a low profile. In the 1950-1960 period, the Plains police chief and the railroad agent together asked Carter to join the new chapter of the White Citizens Council. James Earl, Sr., had rejected the Ku Klux Klan (a courageous act for a rural politician in Georgia) and now Jimmy would rebuff the entreaties of its blood brothers because he did not respect their authority. In a few days the invitation was renewed, with the warning that failure to join would result in a boycott of the Carter enterprises. Jimmy's reply was that he would rather leave Plains than join the organization.[30] This was a remarkable stance in this period for a Southerner seeking political office in the Deep South.

As America began to confront its racial inequities in the early 1950s, an unusual Christian commune, "Koinonia," made its appearance in Sumter County, about seven miles from Plains. On its four-teen-hundred-acre farm, the commune raised cotton and peanuts. This settlement, which contained mostly whites but a few blacks, was founded by Christian pacifist Clarence Jordan, a Baptist minister and Greek scholar; he was a Ph.D. educated theologically at the Southern Baptist Theological Seminary in Louisville, Kentucky. The racial mixing advanced at Koinonia was an aberration, and a radical departure from the mores of the nation.

After Jordan assisted two black students to enroll at Georgia State

College of Business in Atlanta in 1956, the commune was attacked. Not only was it assailed by a boycott, its fences were destroyed, its corn stolen, bullets fired, and explosives wrecked a building. A grand jury investigating the turmoil could find no person to accuse. When a member of the commune, Jack Singletary, lost his child to leukemia, no preacher could be found to bury the child. Upset by this lack of charity, Rosalynn Carter boldly badgered a preacher (frightened that he would be ostracized) into conducting the funeral rites.[31]

Carter in Politics

Following in his father's footsteps, Jimmy was elected in 1962 as a Georgia state senator; his victory came in the general election, but only after Carter unveiled the voter fraud that had given his opponent a temporary victory. Carter served as state senator from 1963 to 1966. As a conscientious legislator, he promoted educational reforms and literally read every word of hundreds of bills.[32]

In 1966 Carter entered the gubernatorial primary but ran third behind Lester Maddox and Ellis Arnall.[33] After his defeat in the governor's race, the despondent Carter spoke to his sister, ardent Christian evangelist Ruth Carter Stapleton; she in turn challenged him to live with the total commitment demanded by Christ, and the ambitious politician submitted and became a "born-again Christian." He later said, "I formed a very close, intimate personal relationship with God, through Christ, that has given me a great deal of peace, equanimity, and the ability to accept difficulty without unnecessarily being disturbed." After this, he volunteered for Baptist missionary work among New York's poor.[34]

The Civil Rights Revolution intruded as another huge cloud. Now black leaders Martin Luther King and Andrew Young were encouraging blacks to intensify civic action by participating in "pray-ins" at white churches. The pastor and eleven deacons of the Plains Baptist Church voted that black demonstrators should be barred from entering the church on Sundays. Prior to this time, on special occasions, blacks had attended weddings, funerals, and some baptisms.

Carter, the twelfth deacon, had been on a trip to Atlanta when the deacons were to make the final recommendation to the church on the demonstrator issue. Advised by his friend, casket manufacturer John Pope, not to become involved in an issue that could hurt his political future, Carter replied that there was "no way" he would miss the vote by the church members. On Sunday morning, about two hundred persons heard Jimmy Carter urge the congregation to reject the deacons' proposal. In a stirring speech, Carter reminded the assembled members that the church was God's house and did not belong to its members. But in the vote that followed, only six persons voted to keep the service open: one non-Carter, Jimmy, Lillian, Rosalynn, and the two Carter sons. About fifty members, in the majority, voted with the deacons.[35]

A decade later, in 1976, the pastor, the Reverend Bruce Edwards, and Carter gathered a majority at the church and rescinded the prior vote on admittance. However, the dialogue was bruising, and the deacons fired their minister. One faction of the church, supporters of Edwards, resigned from the Plains Church and formed a new church, Maranatha Baptist Church. On the vote on the racial issue, Mazlish concluded that afterwards Carter pondered reflectively and theorized: (1) the majority of people are decent but need courageous moral leadership and (2) even people taking a hard line against change have some justification for their viewpoints, and, therefore, have a special need for justice. The elder Earl Carter, Sr., according to his lights, had cleared some of the obstacles, and now Jimmy Carter would push other racial barriers away.[36]

In 1970 Carter ran for governor of Georgia against a moderate, former Governor Carl E. Sanders. Carter took a stand opposing school busing to establish racial balance. Also, he invited an arch segregationist, Alabama Governor George Wallace, to campaign for him. Carter won points with the rural farmers by criticizing the well-dressed Sanders as "Cufflinks Carl." After his victory over Sanders, he defeated in the general election the Republican challenger, television newsman Hal Suit. Carter after his victory was hailed as a new stripe of Southern governor, and he said in his January 1971 inaugural address, "the time for racial discrimination is over."[37]

As governor, Carter promoted a social-progressive program. He equalized school funding for poor and rich districts, increased black state employees by forty percent, and appointed dozens of blacks to state boards. He streamlined state agencies, improved educational facilities for prison inmates, established centers for the mentally retarded, and supported measures to protect the environment. On national issues, he approved of the Vietnam War. While nation-wide Jimmy Carter was almost unknown, in a few vital sectors of Democratic politics he was influential; in 1972 he nominated Senator Henry Jackson of Washington to be chairman of the Democratic National Campaign, and in 1974 Carter became head of the Democratic National Campaign Committee.[38]

As the governor's wife, Rosalynn learned much about gracious entertainment from the German consul's wife in Atlanta. The shy lady from Plains learned to jog with her husband, and upgraded her appearance by wearing wigs. In public life, the Carters were openly affectionate, let their knees touch in church, and kissed and hugged in public view.[39]

Battling to Become President

As a "dark horse," with two terms in the Georgia Senate and only a single term (1971-1975) as governor of Georgia, Carter astounded a number of veteran politicians by declaring in 1976 his intention to seek the Democratic nomination for president. In 218 B.C. the Carthaginian general Hannibal had shocked the Romans by audaciously crossing the Alps with elephants,[40] and now Carter in 1976 A.D. would "cross the Alps" before his hesitant Democratic rivals were awake and get the jump in the early primaries. In a fortunate conjunction, Carter's book *Why Not the Best* (1976), appeared at bookstores to amplify his moderate views. Carter expressed personal regret for the injustices of segregation and his failure to respond to them at an earlier period. However, Carter felt that in the existing fluctuating stage of racial adjustment, private schools in the South served as safety valves.[41] When Carter finally told his mother he intended to run for president, she did not comprehend: "president of what?" she inquired.[42]

Presenting himself in the aftermath of the Watergate scandals as a forthright, convivial, and honest steward, Carter stole the march on his opponents by winning in the Iowa caucus and the New Hampshire primary. Then, one after the other, he outstripped his major rivals: (1) Alabama Governor George Wallace (in Florida), (2) U.S. Representative Morris Udall (in Wisconsin), and (3) Senator Henry Jackson (in Pennsylvania). Governor Jerry Brown of California won the California and Maryland primaries but could not stop the Carter momentum.[43]

At the July national Democratic Convention in New York, Carter was nominated with 2,238+ votes as opposed to his closest contender Udall's 329+ votes. Alabama governor George Wallace and Coretta Scott King, wife of the martyred black leader, then joined him on the victory platform. In accepting the nomination, Carter said, "It is time to honor and strengthen our families and our neighborhoods and our diverse cultures and customs." The Democratic platform expressed opposition to an anti-abortion initiative, approved national health insurance, endorsed a Panama Canal treaty, and approved busing, but only as a last-ditch measure, for racial balance.[44]

The Gerald Ford administration, still leading the government, was seriously vulnerable on two counts: (1) the pardon Ford had given President Richard Nixon for Nixon's involvement in the Watergate incident, and (2) an inflation, increasing at an average of six percent each year.[45] Ford, attending the Republican National Convention at Kansas City, Missouri, in August 1976, had narrowly survived the surge by presidential aspirant, California Governor

Ronald Reagan. The Republican platform favored a tax cut, retention of the Panama Canal, busing to achieve racial integration, and a constitutional amendment to bar abortion. Also opposed were gun control measures and national health insurance.[46]

Running far behind Carter in the polls, the Republican candidate Ford challenged Carter to debate their differences. During three debates in 1976, Ford made a sensational *faux pas* by declaring that Eastern Europe was free of Soviet domination. Carter quickly reminded Ford that Poland was struggling to become free. Then, Carter stumbled in a *Playboy Magazine* interview by admitting to having sinful thoughts about women, which for weeks provided talk-show hosts with material for a myriad of ribald jokes.[47] But Carter was confident of victory. He said before the balloting, "I know ministers, teachers, blacks, Jews. I have consulted the best minds on every subject. I am as well prepared as anyone has been, including Roosevelt back in the 30's. I draw my strength from my personal relationship with the American people." And it must be surmised that this confidence came from his inner strength and self-reliance, rather than from intellectual power, with which he was well endowed.[48]

Rosalynn had shed the timid profile, and for the presidential race she became a gladiator. She was tough and untiring, and, beginning in 1975 lobbied in thirty states. Against Gerald Ford, she traveled by Lear Jet to one hundred cities, remaining awake at times for eighteen hours. One reporter called Rosalynn "a Sherman tank in a field of clover." When Rosalynn heard that Carter admitted that he lusted in his heart for other women, her reply was: "Jimmy talks too much but at least people know he is honest."

Jimmy Carter, President (January 20, 1977—January 20, 1981)

Carter narrowly won in the presidential elections of November 2, 1976. The popular vote was: for Carter, 40,825,000 votes, and for Ford, 39,147,000 votes. The key electoral votes were 297 for Carter and 240 for Ford. Carter had attracted strength from the South, the industrial North, and organized support from blacks, whites, and labor. He was the first winner from the Deep South since Zachary Taylor in 1848.[49] Carter, beyond the negative shadow of Watergate that shackled Gerald Ford, had won in 1976 because he gained the confidence of people concerned about competency, national responsiveness, and the size of its government.[50]

It was a humble Jimmy Carter that addressed the nation in his inaugural address of January 20, 1977:

> You have given me a great responsibility—to stay close to you, to be worthy of you, and to exemplify what you are. Let us create together a new national spirit of unity and trust. Your strength can compensate for my weakness, and your wisdom can help to minimize my mistakes.

After the inauguration, the Carters walked in egalité down Pennsylvania Avenue.[51]

The move to the White House brought sea changes in style, tastes, and protocol. His closest staff supporter was Vice President Walter F. Mondale, a Methodist minister's son. Some of the key Cabinet members were: Secretary of State Cyrus R. Vance (soon to be succeeded by Edmund S. Muskie), long an advocate of *détente* with the Soviet Union; Secretary of Defense Harold Brown; Attorney General Griffin B. Bell of Georgia; and, Secretary of Housing and Urban Development (a black woman) Patricia R. Harris, former ambassador to Luxembourg.[52]

Rosalynn blossomed as "First Lady," even attending Cabinet meetings. Her advice was sought by the president. She became an effective speaker and spoke against abortion and for the Equal Rights Amendment (written to enforce equality for women) and promoted mental health.[53] Amy Carter, Jimmy and Rosalynn's daughter, was sent to a public school in Washington, D.C. Amy added to the White House as residents the "First Family Cat" ("Misty Malarky Ying-Yang") and "Executive Dog" ("Grits").[54]

Carter continued his simple tastes in Washington, even carried some of his luggage for flights on the presidential plane Airforce One. He dressed casually, preferred sweaters, and in music listened to Bob Dylan, Paul Simon, and the Allman Brothers. He read rapidly at two thousand words per minute, and completed three or four books a week. He was especially fond of fishing, but indulged also in jogging, hiking, bicycling, tennis, skiing, and bowling. In most of these activities, Rosalynn would be his partner. He exhibited few bad habits but drank Scotch moderately and occasionally smoked a cigar.[55] As president, Carter had sandy hair, hazel eyes, and a medium frame, his height five feet nine and one-half inches, and his weight 155 pounds. He lived with a bad knee from a cotton gin accident, a permanently bent finger, and a soft contact lens over his right eye. When working, he preferred his "lucky" red tie, and blue denim "peanut clothes."[56]

If what a man reads turns a spotlight on a man's soul, then Carter's reading list is revealing. He was fascinated with the writings of Paul Tillich, who suggested that the soul's search for God cannot be satisfied. As president, Jimmy Carter was continuously searching for God's will, and he and the First Lady nightly took turns reading the Bible to each other in bed. He also taught a Bible class at the First Baptist Church in Washington.[57]

Carter through much of his life was attracted to the writings of Reinhold Niebuhr, who wrote *Moral Man and Immoral Society* (1932), with its reflection of man's fallen state. Society, which as Niebuhr points out is unable to achieve perfection, must aim for realistic goals and limited justice. Physical and cultural endowments can never be equal, and neither love nor rationality can lead mankind to Utopia, according to Niebuhr. But, on the other hand, Niebuhr argues, men must fight continuously and non-violently for justice. The Negro, for example, must wage war for equality, not expecting it to be delivered by the goodness of man. But since man is part of nature, he should utilize for good the strength of nature, rather than discarding it.[58]

Carter's taste in poetry led him to the bohemian Welshman Dylan Thomas: "Rage, rage against the dying of the light." Despite his predilection for things morally straight, as the senior of the White House staff, he did not channel their expression of tastes or censor their personal lives. He was publicly more cordial than austere, and following a revered Southern tradition, he was constantly greeting with hugs, kisses, pats, and squeezes.[59]

The Agenda

The Carters, both Jimmy and Rosalynn, came to Washington with the conviction that they would have a major impact on America and the world. They had not reckoned with the strength of their opposition, and the Carter administration would be stymied on many fronts. As noble a man as Carter was in Washington, he was a "newcomer," to some a Georgia provincial, almost a foreign element, unwilling to compromise and supported by too few allies. His programs would take a battering. However, the timid governor's wife (now changed into a lioness) was determined to be his co-leader. She would spearhead in areas of mental health, older Americans, and inner-city problems, and became the spokeswoman for passage of the Equal Rights Amendment for Women. She was also the honorary chairman of the Mental Health initiative. In the words of Margaret Truman, Rosalynn was almost a coequal in the White House, more so than any First Lady except Hillary Rodham Clinton.[60] But her appearance at Cabinet meetings as the president's wife would infuriate many of her fellow citizens, particularly the males.

Within nine months of his taking office, inflation was rampant and Carter's administration appeared to be in disarray. His advisor and closest friend, Thomas Bertram (Bert) Lance, banker, and devout Methodist, was disgraced. Many on his inner staff were regarded as second-rate and ineffective. His energy program was getting nowhere, and the welfare renovations were on a sidetrack.

Carter was hammered by enormous economic problems, including the public's losing its purchasing power because of expanding inflation; this inflation would double during the Carter administration to twelve percent.[61] Then, the country suffered an energy crisis. In one year (1979) the Organization of Petroleum Exporting Countries (OPEC) doubled oil prices from fourteen to twenty-eight dollars a barrel. With long lines at the pumps, most states introduced gas rationing. People bought fewer American-manufactured automobiles and turned to smaller fuel-efficient Japanese cars. As a consequence, about three hundred thousand American auto workers lost their jobs. Carter sought to fashion a national energy bill, but the effort consumed eighteen months and the bill which passed in November 1978 was much too weak. This was ironic, since the Democrats in 1977-79 had an advantage over the Republicans and Independents of 22 seats in the Senate and 145 seats in the House. This advantage was only slightly less in 1979-81, of 16 Democratic seats in the Senate and 117 seats in the House. But Carter did not work well with Congress and rarely got his way.[62]

The attempt to pass the Equal Rights Amendment (ERA) for women was a massive effort that appeared to be successful, until it was stopped cold by a counter-attack launched by a Mormon woman activist Phyllis Schlafly and a coalition of traditional women and men. The ERA proclaimed, "Equality of rights under the law shall not be denied or abridged . . . on account of sex." In an attempt in 1972 to incorporate ERA into the Constitution, a brisk battle took place. Mrs. Schlafly, fearing that the traditional role of women in the home was threatened, boldly fought with her supporters against the National Organization of Women (NOW) and the other avant-garde groups. Time ran out on the ratification process in 1978, after thirty-five of a required thirty-eight states had ratified it.[63] Rosalynn Carter had lost, after having fought tirelessly for passage of the proposed amendment.

In a comparison with other presidents, including Lyndon B. Johnson, Carter may have been the most successful president in advancing the public careers of women. Before the Carter administration only three women had held Cabinet rank; to these, Carter added two more. His principles were involved, for Carter had pledged in 1976: "I am going to do for women what Lyndon B. Johnson did for blacks." In an assessment of top presidential appointees, more than one in ten under Carter were women. Also, blacks were given positions of real authority. This president did not unravel all the mysteries of Washington, but he brought to those marble monuments hard work and integrity, and integrated solidly the Deep South and the Federal Establishment.[64]

As a moderate, Carter promoted human rights as the cornerstone of his foreign policy. He demonstrated courage in extending a presidential pardon to ten thousand American draft evaders from the Vietnam War period; this action angered the powerful Veterans of Foreign Wars (VFW), but the pardon did not protect deserters.[65] In upholding human rights, Carter suspended foreign aid to some repressive governments. He denounced the Soviet Union for its inhumanity for placing on trial the social advocates Anatoly Shcharansky and Alexander Ginsburg. Traveling to Warsaw in 1977, he championed the struggles of Eastern Europeans to free themselves from the grip of Communism. He condemned racism in South Africa and supported the struggle by blacks to gain majority rule in Southern Rhodesia (later Zimbabwe). Carter openly decried the cruel and restrictive regimes of Idi Amin in Uganda and Fidel Castro in Cuba.[66]

As a peanut farmer, Carter had powerful impulses to protect the environment. In 1977 he signed into law a ban on dumping raw sewage into the ocean. In other actions, protective measures were assured through the Strip Mining Control and Reclamation Act (1977) and the Alaska Land Act (1980), that set aside 104 million acres of national park, wilderness, and wildlife refuges.[67]

Camp David Accords (September 17, 1978)

The brightest achievement of the Carter administration was the intricate fashioning of a peace treaty between Israel and Egypt, key players in the Middle East. The Middle East peace process began in 1977 with Egyptian President Anwar el-Sadat's visit to Jerusalem but was stalled by September 1978. President Carter then invited el-Sadat and Israel's prime minister, Menachem Begin, to Carter's presidential Catoctin Mountain retreat, Camp David. There, after thirteen days of personal talks, two documents were signed: (1) a Framework for Peace in the Middle East, and (2) a Framework for the Conclusion of a Peace Treaty Between Egypt and Israel. This concerted effort led to a peace treaty in March 1979, ending the thirty-one year state of war between Egypt and Israel, and the return of the Sinai Peninsula to Egypt.[68] This commitment was costly, involving billions of dollars to be paid by the United States as guarantor, and heavy arms shipments to both countries.[69]

Diplomatic Activities

The shift of policy by the United States that affected both Communist-ruled China and its prosperous runaway province of Taiwan involved some risk-taking. Pursuant to Carter's lead and the State Department's advisories in 1979, the United States withdrew its military forces from Taiwan and established formal diplomatic relations with China. Given the improved development, China's Deputy Premier Teng Hsiao-ping in 1979 became the first Communist Chinese leader to visit the United States. Thus, Peking received official recognition as the legitimate government of China. Taiwan, on the other hand, while still benefitting from trade and cultural exchanges, lost its status with the United States as a state. That island-nation, in view of its increased vulnerability to the threats of military invasion by a well-armed mainland China, increased its own security measures.[70]

A major initiative of the president, the Salt II Treaty, was defeated in 1979. Still, Carter supported the Nixon commitment to *détente* with the Soviet Union. In June 1979 President Carter and Soviet Premier Leonid Brezhnev signed the second treaty negotiated at the Strategic Arms Limitation Talks. However, this treaty was vigorously opposed by U.S. Senate leaders, who felt that the treaty placed the United States at a disadvantage. The treaty opponents included Democratic Senator Sam Nunn (Georgia), Democratic Senator Henry Jackson (Washington), and Republican Senator John Tower (Texas). All possibilities for acceptance of the treaty were lost when the Soviet Union, in December 1979, invaded Afghanistan to engage in a Vietnam-style war. The Salt II Treaty was never brought to the Senate floor for a vote, and a grain embargo was declared against the Soviet Union.[71]

Afghanistan, an isolated Muslim Asian nation, proved to be a quagmire for the Soviet Union, but also a turning point in American relations with Moscow. In 1979 U.S. Ambassador Adolph Dubs was murdered in Kabul. President Carter quickly cut all relations, except humanitarian aid. The Soviets, bolstering the regime of Babrak Karmal, invaded Afghanistan to crush the insurgents, whose intent was to defeat Moscow's ally, Karmal. This Russian incursion marked the beginning of a nine-year war by the Soviet Union to control Afghan internal politics. Like the U.S. involvement in the Vietnam War, there would be disillusionment for the Soviets.

Carter was enraged by the rash Soviet intrusion into Afghanistan and mobilized a global protest. Subsequently, in 1980, the United States suspended the sale of grain and high-technology equipment to the Soviets. In the United Nations General Assembly, the United States won approval for a resolution demanding that all foreign troops be removed from Afghanistan. Then, in a remarkable action, the United States joined sixty-three nations to boycott the Olympic games held in Moscow. The Afghan War would cost the Soviet Union thirteen thousand dead and thirty-five thousand men wounded, and would cause that nation to leave in defeat in 1988-1989. President Ronald Reagan would then lift the grain embargo in 1981.[72]

In the 1970s, some Americans began to oppose the construction of nuclear plants. As concern mounted in May 1977, fifteen hundred demonstrators were arrested trying to stop construction of a plant at Seabrook, New Hampshire. Then, in March 1979, a hair-raising major accident occurred at Three Mile Island near Harrisburg, Pennsylvania. In the aftermath of that incident, in May 1979 at Washington, D.C., sixty-five thousand people protested the expansion of nuclear power facilities, while the Carter-led government was seeking to develop a balanced fuel policy. This demonstration was followed by a No Nukes Rally in New York City, involving two hundred thousand protesters. Widespread protests then called for a halt to further construction of nuclear plants and to demand greater safety measures at existing facilities.[73]

American Hostages in Iran (1979-1981)

An Islamic revolution in 1979 toppled the U.S.-supported Iranian government, and its monarch fled abroad. Later, on November 4, 1979, Iranian students stormed the American Embassy in Teheran and captured more than sixty American hostages. In reply, President Carter froze all Iranian assets in the United States and suspended oil imports from Iran. The captors proposed that the Americans would be released if the traditional Iranian ruler, Shah Mohammad Reza Pahlavi, who was in the United States, were released to the revolutionaries. The Shah was undergoing medical treatment for cancer in New York, and the United States authorities would not expel him for a trial in his country. In retaliation, the Iranians held as prisoners for more than a year fifty-two Americans, while releasing as a gesture one ill person, the black civil servants, and most of the women. The Carter administration continued a series of diplomatic and economic measures to accelerate the release of the Americans.[74]

In December 1979 the U.N. Security Council, under pressure, demanded the immediate release of the prisoners, and Carter expelled all 183 Iranian diplomats in the United States. Tightening the screws, but also wary of interference by the Soviet Union, Carter carefully crafted his State of the Union address, delivered in January 1980. Carter warned the Soviet Union not to take advantage of unrest in Afghanistan and Iran by seizing a warm-water port. The Carter Doctrine was expressed in blunt language:

Any attempt by an outside force to gain control of the Persian Gulf region will be regarded as an assault on the vital interests of the United States. It will be repelled by the use of any means necessary including military force.

Carter then imposed in April 1980 more economic sanctions and banned all travel to Iran.[75] But all of this maneuvering was not enough.

Obsession nearly verged into desperation. Determined to do something positive, Carter on April 24 ordered a military rescue mission to secure the prisoners. Events would stamp this attempt as a terrible blunder: of the American rescue force, three helicopters would be crippled by the sand-filled air of Iran, and two aircraft (a helicopter and a transport plane) would collide, killing eight servicemen. The Iranians then scattered their American hostages throughout their country, to make another rescue attempt futile. Secretary of State Cyrus Vance, who had opposed the rescue operation, resigned in protest.[76]

The Shah died in Cairo, Egypt; still, the Iranian fundamentalist cleric Ayatollah Khomeini imposed more rigid conditions as the price for freeing the prisoners. Meanwhile, the hostage situation took a backseat in Teheran as a war broke out between Iran and Iraq. In November 1980 the Iranian revolutionaries made a decision to release the captive Americans, and, on January 20, 1981, after 444 days of captivity, the prisoners were released to their fellow citizens.[77] But the delay in releasing the prisoners, whether deliberate or by chance, may have cost Carter the national elections and given the Republican Ronald Reagan a victory. On his first day of retirement from office, Carter was at a military hospital in West Germany welcoming the freed hostages.[78]

An Analysis of the Carter Style

Margaret Truman, daughter of Baptist President Harry Truman, made a sage assessment of the Carter failures: success in the White

House, she wrote, comes not from wielding naked power but through powerful connections, both inside and outside Washington. Carter lacked those connections and during his presidency did not master the technique of working within the intricate national political system.[79]

By doing what he considered right while in the White House, Carter alienated to some degree many of his early supporters. His commitment to fiscal conservatism and a balanced budget lost him the liberals. Then, despite the peace achieved by the Camp David Accords and the neutralization of the Egyptians as a military threat to Israel, American Jews flocked to the Republican Party, fearing a re-elected Carter would exact more concessions from Israel. He also lost the "Big Business" element that had formerly supported him but which now was nervous concerning the high interest rates and the growing inflation.[80]

The basis of Carter's foreign policy was human rights. Carter believed that it was immoral to support governments that abused the people, even if they were anti-Communist governments. As a consequence, he cut off aid to Anastasio Somoza Debayle in Nicaragua and other military dictatorships in Argentina, Ethiopia, and Uruguay. In a strange twist, Carter gave immediate financial support in July 1979 to the Nicaraguan pro-Communist Sandinista government. Then, his initiative to return the Panama Canal Zone by 1999 to a Panama led by Omar Torrinos became a disturbing event to millions of Americans. The treaty was barely endorsed over strong opposition, sixty-eight to thirty-two in the Senate, only one vote more than the two-thirds required for ratification.[81]

Conservative Christians, after years of ignoring pressure politics, now joined others of the political right to form the "Moral Majority" in support of candidate Ronald Reagan. Ironically, after Reagan became the president, he was described by historian Henry Steele Commanger as "the least religious president in American history."[82] Some conservatives abandoned Carter because of his promotion of women and blacks, his concern for Third World nations, his emphasis on human rights, and cuts in the defense systems. Also, the Carter non-belligerent foreign policy was viewed by his opponents as weak and ineffective. Consequently, Carter was forced to rely on the loyalty of Democratic governors and mayors, but they could not rally a winning force for the national elections.[83]

Carter's advisors had taken for granted the loyalty of born-again Christians, many of them Baptists; these advisors were wrong, and conservative Christians flocked in large numbers to the Republican party candidate Ronald Reagan, endorsed by the Moral Majority leaders. Although, the Protestant religious picture is not monolithic, some forty percent of Americans consider themselves to be born-again Christians and these were among the first to abandon Carter. While many Baptists are "fundamentalists" and gave support to the Moral Majority, there also is a large minority element of "moderates," the latter often unpredictable, their choices influenced by good education and business success. Fundamentalists, however, are prominent not only in Baptist ranks but also thrive in large numbers among Methodists, Presbyterians, Holiness bodies, and the Church of Christ.[84]

Carter, an evangelical Christian, frequently refers to himself as a "born-again" Christian, but not a fundamentalist. He believes in the Bible as the ultimate authoritative guide for the Christian. But he does not consider the Holy Scriptures in all of its aspects—in distinction from the fundamentalist orientation—as the literal word of God. Therefore, the president who reads his Bible in daily exercises, increased the members of minority civil servants, and actively strove to elevate the status of blacks was rejected in large numbers by his fellow white Christians.[85]

The kiss of death was given to the Carter style in 1980 by former Secretary of State Henry Kissinger, who opined:

> The Carter administration has managed the extraordinary feat of having, at one and the same time, the worst relations with our allies, the worst relations with our adversaries, and the

most serious upheavals in the developing world since the end of the Second World War.[86]

However, in what appeared to be a political corpse there would be manifest such vigorous surges of life and energy as to astound the world. The new life-form would speak with one voice but through two bodies, those of Jimmy and Rosalynn Carter, the latter who in her first year at the White House visited twenty-one U.S. cities and sixteen nations.[87] Then, there was the dynamo Jimmy Carter—"unlike anyone" else, according to his friend Peter G. Bourne. This was "a man of extremes. He was tenacious, disciplined, physically and psychologically strong; committed to self-improvement, to living up to his religious beliefs; to not wasting a moment of his life; and more driven than anyone I [Bourne] had ever known to make the world a better place."[88]

Carter Phase II

The Resurgent Carter: Leaving the White House Behind

From the beginning of the re-election campaign (before 1980), President Carter was in trouble: (1) Inflation was depressing the value of money; (2) soaring interest rates made borrowing expensive; (3) the Iranian hostage crisis projected (falsely) the President as weak; and (4) he was facing the "tough hombre" image of sixty-nine-year-old cowboy-actor Ronald Wilson Reagan. In the Democratic primary, Senator Edward Kennedy, Carter's major opponent, was weakened by the disclosures of the Chappaquiddick bridge incident, and the untimely death of Democratic staff worker Mary Jo Kopechne, and was beaten. But the close in-fighting involving Kennedy disrupted the Democratic Party, and Carter would lose support.[89]

After the failure by the American military helicopter team to rescue American prisoners held by the Iranian leader Ayatollah Khomeini, Carter's last chances for a political victory vanished.[90]

The termination of the Carter presidency, bitterly disappointing to the Carters, was especially wounding to Rosalynn; still, it regenerated inner resources in a man driven by principles. The fired-up social engineer and Trailblazer Carter would cut new roads where conventional ways had often failed and been frustrated. After his defeat by Republican actor-politician Ronald Reagan, who became the fortieth president of the United States, Carter retired to Plains, Georgia; he learned that the family peanut enterprise, held in a blind trust during his presidency, was heavily in debt. Resolutely driven by an optimistic impulse, he began plans for the Carter Presidential Center in Atlanta, which eventually would be directed toward solving international health and social-political issues.[91]

Habitat for Humanity

Beginning about October 16, 1982, the "retired" Carters developed an interest in Habitat for Humanity. Habitat was founded by Millard Fuller, a wealthy mail-order partner, who in the 1960s was overcome by personal problems and a crisis of conscience. This led him, as a deeply religious man, to Koinonia near Plains and the influence of Clarence Jordan. Fuller and his wife Linda decided to lavishly dispose of their money to provide shelter for impoverished people. In Africa, at Mbandaka, Zaire, Fuller built for indigenous people a total of 162 houses. Then, in 1976, the Fullers returned to Americus, Georgia, where they founded Habitat for Humanity.[92]

Jimmy Carter, on October 16, 1982, spoke to Habitat personnel about refugees in Indo-China and Haiti and disclosed his admiration for the organization. This led to his raising funds for Habitat from February 1984, and then serving as its director. Carter contributed a day's labor in Americus and then organized a team of volunteers from the (Plains) Maranatha Baptist Church to construct houses in the slums of New York in July 1985 and further work on the Lower East Side. On his first visit, Carter, a skilled carpenter, and Rosalynn slept in bunks at the Metropolitan Baptist Church. It was the call to Christian service that drew the Carters for their week of volunteer work every June. However, the publicity generated for Humanity by the Carters was instrumental in spreading the organization to 171 U.S. communities and seventeen foreign nations.[93] The former president also lectured on political science topics at Emory University.[94]

Carter then scheduled a series of visits and consultations with Latin American diplomats and officials—initiatives that often were disquieting to the U.S. State Department. In mid-1984, Carter visited Argentina, Brazil, and Peru. The U.S. Embassy spokesmen warned the Carters not to include Argentina in their itinerary. But they came anyway—uninvited—and in Buenos Aires, President Alfonsin welcomed them, and a crowd of thousands cheered the Carters when they spoke against the military dictatorship. In Peru, Carter reached the conclusion that fair elections demanded the presence of teams of international observers;[95] this was only the beginning of the diplomatic offensives developed by the Carter team. In the summer of 1986, the Carters made a multi-nation preliminary circuit in preparation for two conferences on the Debt Crisis and Democracy in Inter-America. The Carters then traveled to Costa Rica, El Salvador, Nicaragua, and Mexico. From the information gleaned about the volatile politics in that wide region, an organization was established to monitor national elections. But in Mexico, American Ambassador Gavin reportedly was so angry about his exclusion from talks between Carter and the Mexican president that he canceled the scheduled U.S. Embassy reception for the Carters.[96]

The Carters focused much of their energy on world health problems. So personal was their involvement that Jimmy and Rosalynn largely ceased eating red meat, adopted an exercise schedule, and engaged in a strict diet regimen.[97] As a Georgia governor, Carter had launched a program called "Cripplers and Killers." Then in 1979, under President Carter's administration, Surgeon General Julius Richmond had published a national report on "Healthy People." Carter also supported a successful immunization drive against measles, with the goal of inoculating ninety percent of American children; this effort was eminently successful.[98]

The Carter Center, a long-range dream, was finally dedicated near Emory University in Atlanta on October 1, 1986. However, Carter in May 1986 was already organizing a program for the eradication of the Guinea Worm, the cause of a parasitic disease transmitted through impure drinking water. This disease afflicts ten million people in India, Pakistan, and Middle Africa. An older campaign to provide clean drinking water to protect people from cholera, typhoid fever, and infant diarrhea was now directed to fight the Guinea Worm disease. This effort would involve drilling wells, filtering water, and maintaining a clean source of water. Carter's interest in the project led him to inspect the health conditions in interior Ghana and to view while touring with President Jerry Rawlings the terrible sights of Guinea Worm abscesses on people.

Other major activities initiated by Carter were the promotion of peace-making, and operating a *de facto* citizen-directed diplomatic agency from the Carter Center; for this, the ex-President should have expected and did receive heavy flak from official agencies. In 1990, a year of accomplishments, the Carters had considerable success in bringing peace and creating peaceful initiatives in Nicaragua, Haiti, and the Dominican Republic. In addition, on the Mexican-U.S. border, Habitat created its own "miracle." But disappointments also occurred in 1991, when Carter attacked the Bush administration for promoting the Gulf War allegedly to save American oil interests and Kuwait, and defeats were suffered on civil rights, welfare policies, and pro-gun legislation.[99]

In international developments, the Carter positions in 1991 were faring badly: Aristide's government in Haiti (favored by Carter) was too weak to consolidate power; Yasser Arafat's Palestine Liberation Organization (PLO) backed the Iraq invasion of Kuwait (led by Saddam Hussein); and, the Palestine Liberation Organization (PLO) was excluded from peace talks in Madrid.[100]

However, there also were encouraging developments: Habitat for Humanity in 1991 was being praised and Carter's contributions were prominently mentioned. By 1995, Habitat, joined by ex-President Gerald Ford and comedian Bob Hope, had nurtured 900 groups and

350 college chapters. When Habitat's prime mover Millard Fuller was accused of sexual harassment and stripped of leadership responsibilities, Carter rushed to his defense and had his authority restored. Habitat, once treated as a socialist experiment, built seven thousand houses by 1992 and was almost totally accepted by the American public.

Mediation with the Koreans

The Korean Peninsula was divided after World War II, on September 3, 1945, between a Communist state in the north and a prowestern patriarchal, autocratic state in the south. The tension between these states would remain volatile and dangerous for decades. The first prominent leaders were Kim Il Sung in North Korea and Syngman Rhee in South Korea. Providing its junior partner Kim with ideology, arms, and fighter pilots, the Soviet Union did not block the North from invading the South on June 25, 1950. A rapid response by President Harry Truman resulted in the massing of a United Nations force, predominantly American and South Korean, that wrested from the North Koreans and their Chinese ally much of their conquered territory. Until the signing of a cease-fire on July 27, 1953, an estimated 33,651 Americans would be killed. The so-called "Korean Incident" was in fact a major international war, involving more than a million Communist troops from the North and six hundred thousand United Nations troops in the South.[101]

Against the advice of his key foreign policy experts, Carter advocated for several years the withdrawal of all U.S. ground troops from Korea. His objective was to lay the groundwork for a united nuclear-free Korea, but his main doctrinal supporter, not surprisingly, was the Communist dictator Kim Il Sung. The animosity between the two Koreas was seemingly insurmountable, although during his administration Carter tried to reconcile President Park Chung Hee of South Korea and the North's Kim Il Sung. Then Carter, in June

1979, traveled to Seoul on an almost hopeless mission, and effected a limited success by reducing the number of U.S. nuclear weapons in that theater from 700 to about 250. The accord signed by the two Koreas in December 1991, which set a goal of a nuclear-free Korea, was a macabre joke; North Korea, with Chinese assistance, was at that precise time assembling an assortment of missile-borne nuclear devices.

In January 1992 Carter again was eager to meet Kim in Pyongyang, but the Bush administration considered it inadvisable. The Central Intelligence Agency (CIA) already had prepared detailed reports that affirmed that North Korea had accumulated sufficient plutonium for one or two bombs at its facility at Yongbyon. Later Carter proposed another summit meeting to include both countries, with South Korea having a clear economic advantage, since its Gross National Product (GNP) was about fifteen times greater than the North.[102]

The Korean Communist-North was viewed by much of the world as a renegade state. While North Korea, in December 1985, was a signator of the Nuclear Nonproliferation-Treaty, that government announced on March 12, 1993, its intention to withdraw from the treaty.[103] Then, Reverend Billy Graham, Southern Baptist evangelist, was sent to Pyongyang by President Clinton in January 1994 with a tough message, that North Korea was expected to fall in line on the nuclear issue. When the nuclear stand-off became increasingly disturbing, Clinton held military maneuvers in South Korea with U.S. troops, then sent Patriot missiles to the peninsula, and pushed the U.N. Security Council to invoke sanctions. Now Carter, invited to Pyongyang by the Communist government, and personally worried by the crisis, was given authorization by the Clinton administration to visit Kim in a "private" capacity.[104]

With tension high in North Korea and fifty-one percent of Americans favoring a military strike to destroy the Yongbyon facility, Jimmy and Rosalynn Carter arrived in Seoul on June 13, 1994. War was clearly possible, but, instead, an agreement was signed on a nuclear freeze. In the aftermath, observers marveled at the friendly relations created between Kim and Carter, which in turn led to a further agreement by Kim Il Sung to engage in a peace summit with South Korean President Kim Young Sam.[105] However, a withdrawal of U.S. troops from South Korea was not achieved.

The completion of the Carter Korean mission produced political embarrassment. President Clinton had been upstaged, the State Department calls for sanctions had been bypassed, and, in consequence, Carter was shunned at the White House as persona non grata. Carter then boldly appeared in Washington at the White House, but found there no president, no vice president, and no Cabinet members. Then, leading diplomats and journalists lampooned Carter as a new Neville Chamberlain, as if he had bargained with Hitler. In reply, Carter, teaching his Sunday School class at Plains, had kinder words for the North Korean dictator than for U.S. President Clinton.[106] Carter heard of Kim Il Sung's death from a heart attack, after the American ex-president climbed the 12,388-foot slopes of Japan's Mount Fujiyama. The North Korean leader would be succeeded, after a three-year mourning period, by his son Kim Jong Il. Later, there would evolve a new respect in the State Department for Carter's Korean mission.[107]

There were two fascinating Christian contacts made in negotiations with the Koreans. When Carter, on a mission in South America, sought out in that region the arrogant and immoral South Korean leader Park Chung Hee in June 1979, he tried to instruct him about Christ. Later, he sent Baptist evangelist Chang Hwan (Billy) Kim to explain the Christian faith to Park. After hearing the Gospel message from Billy Kim, Park was assassinated by the head of his intelligence agency.[108] Later, in 1994, Kim Il Sung, the North Korean leader, disclosed to Carter that he was saved from death by a Christian pastor, when held by Japanese authorities in China. This discussion may have generated Kim's invitation to the Reverend Billy Graham to lead a crusade in North Korea.[109]

The Haitian Crisis

On December 16, 1990, Roman Catholic priest Jean-Bertrand Aristide became president of Haiti, its first elected president in a 190-year history. This followed the ejection in 1986 of dictator Jean-Claude Duvalier. However, civil tranquility was not established, and President Aristide, on September 30, 1991, after a seven-month administration, was deposed by his military leaders. Haiti's newly declared leader was Lieutenant General Raoul Cedras. In retaliation for the assault on the democratic process, President George Bush banned trade with Haiti, while the Organization of American States (OAS) declared a trade embargo. Meanwhile, Aristide sought refuge and supporters in the United States.

Carter had acquired much experience in dealing with Haiti. Not only had he visited Haiti seven times since 1987, but in 1990 he had chaired the delegation that monitored the brief victory of Aristide. Now he regularly faced an Aristide who was disenchanted with the Bush-initiated and Carter-backed embargo, while Aristide in exile made the Carter Center his base of operations. But Aristide was no longer being treated as a hero by all who knew him. In fact, some reports circulated that he was a demagogue and psychopath, who had allowed some of his enemies to be killed by placing fiery tires around their necks—"necklacing." Carter was more interested in implanting democracy in Haiti, but made a case of restoring Aristide, whose claim to be an altruist was dubious.[110]

As repression mounted in Haiti, refugees began fleeing Haiti in rickety boats bound for the Florida Keys. The Bush administration in power took the conservative line that the refugees were seeking economic, not political, betterment, and, therefore, should be returned. Jimmy Carter, on the other hand, saw Haiti as a "basket case," and by returning the desperate immigrants the United States was affronting its own laws, violating mandates in the Bible, as well as the U.N. refugee protocols. He cited the severe problems of Haiti: prevalence of AIDS, unemployment, high-density population, and a country almost awash in sewage. Joining the logic of the Congressional Black Caucus, he attacked as "racist" the Bush policy toward Haiti. The Bush administration, however, adhered doggedly to its format of returning uncertified immigrants. In February 1992, during one month, 381 refugees were confined at U.S.-governed Guantanamo in Cuba. Then, Carter struck hard at the President in power: "Bush acted as if the Haitians weren't people."[111]

Beginning in December 1991, the Democratic candidate for president, Bill Clinton, made speeches that may have caused Haitian refugees to believe that the United States would accept them en masse on a legal basis. On the other hand, Carter asserted that the main solution for the refugees lay in restoring Aristide to his elected position. However, the Clinton administration was becoming leery of "Carter mediation," when it learned that Carter allegedly had been in telephone contact with Fidel Castro about refugee problems. President Clinton then ordered the State Department and the National Security Council to keep Carter out of Cuban Policy.[112]

The American ambassador to the United Nations, Madeleine Albright, persuaded the U.N. Security Council to sanction force to restore constitutional government to Haiti. Next, thirty thousand American troops were placed on alert for a possible invasion of the island. Clinton warned General Cedras, "Your time is up." Meanwhile, Carter in his self-generated appointments was in contact by phone with Cedras, trying to persuade him to leave Haiti gracefully. The culminating act was the Clinton appointment of an extraordinary three-man diplomatic mission to Cedras, consisting of Senator Sam Nunn of Georgia, former chief of the joint chiefs of staff, Colin L. Powell, and Jimmy Carter. This mission reached Port-au-Prince, and it arranged an agreement for Cedras to step down and U.S. troops to arrive peacefully.[113]

A tense moment in the negotiations occurred when Haitian Brigadier General Philippe Biamby burst into the conference room with a submachine gun. Carter exploded: "You must accept this agreement right now, or your children will be killed. Your country will be burned." General Powell was amazed at Carter's determination. When the Haitian government surrendered, through its provisional-president Emile Jonassaint, it was necessary to call back American war planes on their way from Fort Bragg.[114]

Thousands of U.S. troops landed in Haiti on September 19, 1994, and were greeted by the Haitians as liberators. Without congressional endorsement or the backing of all of his advisors, the Clinton-ordered incursion was generally approved by the U.S. public. Carter in his after-action critique praised General Cedras for his courage but denounced the State Department for its ineptness. At the White House, Carter berated President Clinton for endangering the lives of the American delegation at Port-au-Prince by engaging in an armed invasion while negotiations were in progress.

Saving Bosnia from the Contenders

Yugoslavia in the Balkans was formed as a nation after World War I to coalesce a conglomeration of incompatible Slavic ethnic groups. The dominant elements were the Serbs and the Croatians, followed by the Slovenians, Muslims, Macedonians, and Albanians (Kosovars). After World War II, the Communist Croatian dictator Josip Broz (Tito) held this multi-ethnic land together for thirty-five years. But after Tito's death in 1992, the country dissolved, as Slovenia and Macedonia got their freedom, and the Serbs, Croatians, and Muslims fought it out for the remainder of the land, with heavy losses suffered everywhere. On February 5, 1994, sixty-eight civilians died after a Serb mortar attack on the city of Serajevo. Mounting protests from the Americans induced President Clinton and the North Atlantic Treaty Organization (NATO) to take measures to protect the Bosnians (Muslims) by means of "safe havens." Even Congressional Republicans favored providing weapons to the Yugoslav Muslims, so that they could defend themselves against the Serbs. While NATO was unable to stop the slaughter, by April its jet planes were hitting Serbian ground targets at Gorazde.[115]

The Serbs held most of the contested territory in Bosnia-

Herzegovina, after a thirty-two month conflict; there had been two hundred persons killed or wounded. However, Carter carefully refrained from blaming either side. Instead, and in the process infuriating the State Department, in mid-December he accepted an invitation from the Bosnian Serb leader Radovan Karadzic to negotiate peace. This effort would be among Carter's most daring ventures. He adopted the Contact Group Plan that would divide Bosnia into sectors of land, that gave forty-nine percent to the Serbs and about fifty-one percent to the Muslim-Croatian Federation. Karadzic offered as a negotiating site his mountaintop headquarters at Pale, twenty miles southeast of Serajevo. So, the Carter team left Atlanta on December 17, resisting heavy pressure from American authorities not to intervene. Jimmy Carter and Rosalynn began the mission by sleeping on army cots in the ruined Bosnian capital of Serajevo and at the U.N. military headquarters of British General Sir Michael Rose.[116]

With sniping from the Clinton staff for his mispronouncing of difficult Slavic words and for wearing inappropriate apparel—his turtleneck sweaters—Carter began the process.[117] Journalist John Pomfret encapsulated the importance of the occasion: " a commitment to silence Bosnia's guns by tomorrow and the first negotiation between Serbs and Muslims since a breakdown in talks this summer led to a nasty autumn of intensified warfare." Peace was short-lived, but it gave all parties some breathing space;[118] the intense effort gained a four-month cease-fire. President Clinton then appeared before the Senate Armed Services Committee on June 14, 1995, to testify after the Serbs had taken hostage several hundred U.N. peace-keepers.[119]

Subsequent to the Carter negotiations, Srebrenica and Zepa fell to the Serbs and thousands of Muslim civilians were killed. Then, following a Bosnian Serb attack on Serajevo, NATO (mainly U.S. forces) counter-attacked with devastating air strikes. Carter was again engaged to convince Karadzic to remove the artillery which was hammering Serajevo, but this venture failed. After a succession of false hopes, peace was arranged at Dayton, Ohio, at Wright Patterson Air Force Base. This allowed Assistant Secretary of State Richard C. Holbrooke to consult with Carter, while the working parties, including Serb leader Slobadan Milosevic, met in Dayton to broker a peace. To guarantee the peace, the United States committed twenty thousand U.S. troops to the NATO Implementation Force (IFOR) to collaborate with forty thousand other NATO troops. Carter was proud of the earlier peace efforts in December 1994: "I'm sure the cease-fire saved lives." In reviewing the Balkan campaigns of 1994-1995, other Balkan experts would join to applaud the peacemaking role of Carter.

The Man with the World-Soul

Jimmy Carter's soul-seeking, diplomacy, and humanitarian missions over the years took him to far-flung mountains, deserts, tropics, and fertile and temperate lands. He was greatly influenced by his mother Lillian, who in her prime went as a Peace Corps volunteer to India; she admitted loving blacks so much that, before her death on October 30, 1983, she fantasized about being one, and as a mature lady she served the African-Americans near Plains as a midwife. Jimmy's father was not a traveler, nor a great intellect, but he was no Georgia "cracker"; he, instead, was a land-holder politician who loved the Lord, treated his black plowmen with respect and even tenderness, and rejected firmly the offers to join the White Citizens Council.

However, the critical Christian influence in Carter's life may have been his beloved sister Ruth Stapleton Carter, who died when fifty-four years old on September 26, 1983. After his defeat in 1966 in the Georgia governor's race, Carter was jolted by his pastor at the Plains Baptist Church; the clergyman desired to know if his parishioners bore in their character enough Christian commitment to cause their arrest, if a hostile world turned against them. In autumn 1966, in this valley of his depression, Ruth Stapleton asked Carter if he would give up everything, including his political ambitions, as a sacrifice to Christ. If he could not surrender his political goals, she said, he would never find peace. At this point, Jimmy Carter broke down, cried, and changed dramatically.[120]

Some psychologists attribute Carter's "born-again" experience to his middle-age emptiness, his sense of failure, or even narcissism.[121] However, the stability and permanence of Carter's new character make a creditable case that Carter was not merely trying to measure up to his deceased father James Earl Carter, but that God was working through him. While the psychologist William James might have speculated about the "mind-cure movement," and mental adaptations, Carter would be off again in a cloud of dust to solve another problem.

Shortly after this religious experience, Carter gave himself for a year to lay missions work in the states of Massachusetts and Pennsylvania. At Lock Haven, Pennsylvania, in May 1967, he worked among one hundred families of listed unbelievers. His partner was Milo Pennington, a peanut farmer from Texas, who won fifteen to twenty families to Christ, despite his lack of education. The sense of awe that swept over Carter, as he worked for God, completely inundated him. After he phoned his wife one night, she replied, "Jimmy, you sound almost like you're intoxicated." "Well, in a way I am," he replied. His goals had been reversed, from working with and using people, to assisting and nurturing them.[122]

Jimmy Carter, during most of his life, was closely identified with the Southern Baptist Convention. In October 2000, he left that Convention because of his perception that it had become increasingly rigid, and because of changes made in the doctrinal statement, the Baptist Faith and Message. Carter's church, the Maranatha Baptist Church, is affiliated with the Cooperative Baptist Fellowship.

International Involvement

The scope of Carter's international involvement is breathtaking. With former Presidents Gerald Ford and George Bush, he was present in Washington on September 14, 1993, when President Clinton signed the North American Free Trade Agreement (NAFTA). But, in May 6-9, 1994, he was overseas again, monitoring the elections in Panama.

In January 1986, Carter, humanitarian Norman Borlaug, and Japanese philanthropist Ryoichi Sasakawa took a tour of Ghana, Sudan, Tanzania, and Zambia. Then, Carter revisited the Sudan in October 1986, and, again in June 1995. On the latter occasion, Carter was seeking to extend a ceasefire in a civil war in Southern Sudan and to further his campaign to eradicate the Guinea Worm.[123] In 1995 he visited Nigeria to become an honorary tribal chief for his fight against the Guinea Worm, and, then in November, to view the horror of a massacre site in Rwanda. On 19 January 1996, the day before the Palestine election, he had talks with Chairman Yasser Arafat. His commitment to peace and the latitude of his playing field seemed boundless.

Somehow in all the flurry of his intensely-lived career, Carter found time up to 1988 to write four books. These were:

Why Not The Best (1976)
Keeping Faith: Memoirs of a President (1982)
Everything to Gain: Making the Most Out of the Rest of Your Life (with Rosalynn Carter, 1987)
An Outdoor Journal (1988)

Jimmy Carter—the Legend

At this writing, in December 2000, Carter is vigorous, alert, healthy, and expressing himself through the gifts God has given him. Much of the world has submerged the view once held that Carter the president was a vacillating, sometimes lucky, and good-natured country politician, but way out of his depth in Washington. That is no longer the dominant perception, and his former decriers and opponents, hundreds of thousands of them Republicans that voted for Ronald Reagan, now boldly acclaim him for his good works, as the forgiver of past wrongs, a hewer of new paths, an ardent disease fighter, a man of peace, and a Trailblazer for world harmony. The legend of Jimmy Carter among his countrymen in the twenty-first century is that he is almost certainly the greatest ex-president to embellish the character of the United States. He probably now exceeds, as a citizen-patriot, the reputation *as ex-president* of even the noble George Washington.

His single epic attainment from the political viewpoint was setting the stage for the Camp David Accords, that established peace between Israel and Egypt, and from that to nurture the harmony that allowed those documents to be signed by Menachem Begin and Anwar el-Sadat. In this prospect, we see at work the fine Carter characteristics identified by Degregorio: "He is industrious and self-disciplined and believes strongly in the power of positive thinking." But his greatest strength (as admitted by Carter) is "an inner peace."[124]

However, it was typical of Carter to attribute to another president, Lyndon Johnson, the most fruitful civil rights work in the South: passage of the Civil Rights Act of 1964, the Voting Rights Act of 1965, and the Civil Rights Act of 1968.[125] It was about these mores-changing bills that Carter said: "The passage of the civil rights acts during the 1960s was the greatest thing to happen to the South in my lifetime. It lifted a burden from the whites as well as the blacks."[126]

Carter was serious about enhancing the roles of women. He appointed two women to his cabinet and named forty-one women as federal judges.[127] He encouraged Rosalynn Carter to attend cabinet meetings—inciting widespread American male disgust—and empowered her to attend the funeral of Pope Paul VI, inspect refugee camps in Cambodia, and visit sixteen or more nations abroad. When newly arrived in Washington, Carter sent Rosalynn as roving ambassador to seven South American countries, leaving the State Department apoplectic and the macho Latinos responding with insults.[128] Such failures and successes on the part of Carter stirred in U.S. Representative (later Speaker) Newt Gingrich the following analysis:

I think Jimmy means well, but he doesn't understand the world. He has an enormous willingness to put himself on the line and a good work ethic. Those are his strengths. And he is technically smart. His weaknesses are that the world is organic, it is not mechanical. The good intentions are the beginning, they are not the result. Carter's worldview is clearly an amalgam of a very small town and an Atlas.[129]

Carter, with his post-administration "track two" diplomacy was someone anachronistic but compelling. He was more directed toward alleviating present and future suffering and less inclined to play the "blame game." He had observed the tendency in the American government to "select a favorite side in a dispute, and that side [became] angelic and the other side [became] satanic." The written and spoken styles of Carter in showing respect to adversaries and then bringing about stability and justice, rather than retribution, was in the beginning gobbledygook to the Clinton administration. And yet in many instances, this approach worked. He appears to have gained the trust of Fidel Castro in Cuba, Yasser Arafat in Palestine, Hafiz el-Assad in Syria, and Kim Il Sung in North Korea. And while Secretary of State Warren Christopher in the Clinton Cabinet tried to keep him out of State Department activities in foreign lands, Jimmy Carter, in all likelihood because of his friendly hand, was the "most admired living American."[130]

In health activities, Carter as president prodded agencies to inoculate ninety percent of American children against measles. Then, as ex-president, he waged a war against unhealthy drinking water and the Guinea Worm, so dangerous in Africa and many Third World countries.

His pioneering in placing black Americans in meaningful and important public jobs extended from his governorship to the presidency. This achievement was not cheap window dressing, but a true expression of his Christian character.

In Korea, Haiti, and Bosnia, Jimmy and Rosalynn Carter made heroic efforts to promote peace with opposing factions and work with negotiators that were not always sincere. Still, the results of their mediation were impressive: in Haiti, a civil war was averted; in Korea, an American pre-emptive attack was forestalled; in Bosnia in mid-December, a deadly war was shortened and peace enforced. While the Carters cannot be given all the credit for the peaceful results, they deserve high praise for making negotiations possible.

Nothing has created brotherly good will more extensively than Carter's work under the auspices of Habitat for Humanity. His support of the work of Millard Fuller led him to build houses in the New York slums and then to help expand Habitat to seventeen other countries. He and Rosalynn are not symbolic royalty of this Good Samaritan enterprise; they physically plied hammers and saws and devoted long hours of work without fanfare.

Then, in counterpoise, the Carter failures are stark. He opposed the Gulf War. But without the American intervention led by President George Bush, Iraq's Saddam Hussein could have become the grey eminence of the Middle East. Carter's hopeful efforts to bring peace to the two Koreas—and forestall North Korea's missile and nuclear expansion—were only limited short-range successes. The friendly talks, however, may have set the stage for an eventual reconciliation of North and South Korea, the most promising efforts beginning in the year 2000. The fuel shortages in the United States, high interest rates, and inflation plaguing the Carter administration were never brought under control by a president possessed of a quick scientific mind; and for Carter, who had aspirations for a second term as president, there was the heart-break of Iran. As the politician with good fortune as governor and the audacity to run for president, he projected an image (false, as it was) as a weak leader, when he could not extricate from Tehran the American diplomats held as prisoners by the Iranians. Still, Carter is not culpable for the failure of the Nuclear Test Ban Treaty, the collapse occurring when the Soviet Union invaded Afghanistan.

The character of Jimmy Carter has been probed and tested by a legion of experts, one of the most astute being former Democratic Speaker Thomas P. "Tip" O'Neill. In 1987 he wrote:

> When it came to understanding the issues of the day, Jimmy Carter was the smartest public official I've ever known. The range and extent of his knowledge were astounding; he could speak with authority about energy, the nuclear issue, space travel, the Middle East, Latin America, human rights, American history, and just about any other topic that came up.[131]

However, the most enduring aspect of Jimmy Carter is not his intellect nor a devotion to shuttle diplomacy for peace. It is the way he dignifies every child of God, male, female, minority, power mover or servant, treating each with kindness and respect. He openly testifies that he is a born-again Christian, unashamed to teach and witness about Christ. He is an unpretentious Baptist, affirming the values that George Leile and John Leland taught: the primary truth of the priesthood of the believer. If we viewed in toto all his works in world-encircling flights to Nicaragua, Panama, Bosnia, and North Korea, these images would be eclipsed by a living man hammering nails for humanity and building a poor man's house in inner-city America. It is not illogical to believe that if a Carpenter's Son from Nazareth arrived suddenly from Glory, he would quickly hear of a great man, once rejected by his countrymen, that humbled himself to build them homes and work without pause for world peace. At this writing, ex-President Carter is alive and highly esteemed by his grateful countrymen.

William Franklin Graham, Jr. (b. 1918),
God's Messenger to the World

Chapter 20

William Franklin Graham, Jr.
(1918-)

God's Messenger to the World

The Baptist global evangelist Billy Graham debatably is the most influential preacher in the world. By 1999, through his television ministry alone, he had preached to 180 million persons, and his television sermons had been viewed in eighty or more countries.

Graham has traveled the world from Canada to Australia, from India to Ghana, to Central America, and the Gospel message he preaches bears the imprimatur of Jesus the Messiah. Graham believes ardently that the Bible is the supreme written authority, divinely inspired, and that trust must be given to the living Christ. Also, he proclaims the doctrine of atonement, the virgin birth, miracles, bodily resurrection of the Saints, the need for converts to be born-again, and the certainty of Christ's second coming.[1] While his vision is tempered by a church ecumenical, he unashamedly preaches a doctrine rooted firmly in his evangelical Southern Baptist beliefs.

This once-raw, half-educated young college preacher from a red dirt farm of North Carolina glued himself to God's message of repentance, reconciliation, and love. Thus, his eloquence is not that of poetic words and clever phrases but an expression of profound sincerity fixed firmly to God's Word. Consequently, he found his way to counsel and confer with notables of the age: Prime Minister

Winston Churchill, President Dwight Eisenhower, Generalissimo Chiang Kai-shek in Taiwan, President Syngman Rhee in South Korea, Dr. Martin Luther King, Jr., in Brazil, publisher William Randolph Hearst, and many others.

Although universally loved, Graham also has an array of enemies, some of them liberals, who distrust his attachment to the New Testament and its proclamation of blood atonement, and other conservative beliefs. On the right, he is detested by ultra-conservatives, who hate his flamboyant style, his cooperation with the World Council of Churches, and his charitable attitude toward the Catholic Church, Muslims, and non-believers. In this respect, he acts under the shadow of Christ, who conversed and lingered with harlots, tax collectors, lepers, senators, Romans, and, on the cross, possibly murderers.

The impact and influence of Graham, the gray-haired, tall, but physically-slowing church-statesman, now eighty years old, is so great that any moral misstep by him would have disastrous effects. Other Christ-followers have been shattered by evangelists misusing money or tempted by power or women, and a slip by Billy Graham probably would cause an earthquake of disillusionment—perhaps disaffection from Christianity by hundreds of thousands.

His protector is the Lord Jesus, to whom he daily prays, pouring out his heart in humble petitions. Then, he immerses himself in the Bible, reading through a Gospel each week, and studying five Psalms and a chapter of Proverbs every day. Sometimes, when he cannot sleep, he prays to God under the stars.[2]

In his unlikely transition, from pleadings in a circus tent to Bible-centered lectures on television or humbly serving as a social observer, Graham is following in the footsteps of an array of world preachers. His theological predecessors were the monk Martin Luther, the ex-Catholic priest John Calvin, the high-church Episcopalian evangelist John Wesley, and the stirring soul-mover John Whitefield. In his early ministry, he emulated a number of revered revivalists: Jonathan Edwards of New England, Dwight L. Moody, Billy Sunday, who shook Chicago, and positive thinker-psychologist Norman Vincent

Peale. But Billy Graham did not and does not follow the Modernist trend of producing positive feelings about amoral action, and then disregarding guilt for sins. The John the Baptist message—and its Billy Graham echo—is: "Repent, repent—then come to the Fountain and be washed of your sins." This has been the consistent cry of Graham's message to the world.

His Early Life

The story of William Franklin Graham, Jr. (known as Billy Frank), is that of a farm boy who knew he did not want to farm. Billy Graham was born on November 7, 1918, in a white frame house on a dairy farm outside of Charlotte, North Carolina, four days before the ending of World War I.[3] The grandfather, William Crook Graham, had been a hard-cursing Confederate veteran, tempered by his wife Maggie McCall, a God-fearing tutor to eight daughters and three sons.[4]

Billy Frank, a matrilineal descendant of President James K. Polk, was the son of Morrow Coffey and farmer William Franklin Graham. The parents, strict Scottish Presbyterians, had married in 1916. Billy Graham's father was six feet two inches in height, hated liquor, suspected Yankees, and scrutinized any stranger not a Presbyterian, Baptist, or Methodist.[5] The elder Franklin was level-straight in his business dealings, and relaxed with a big cigar. Still, despite the Great Depression of 1929 and the shutting down of the Farmers and Merchants Bank in Charlotte, the neighbors would gather at the farm to hear the irrepressible farmer's dry jokes.[6]

Surviving with his siblings in the poor South, Billy Frank's education was as poor as that of youthful Abraham Lincoln. Two or three of his teachers at Sharon High School had not been to college, and the public education was barebones. However, there were other compensations. He engaged in an array of pranks with his sister Catherine and his brother Melvin, but refrained from tough play with his infant sister Jean, fourteen years younger than Billy.[7] In adolescence, Billy Frank engaged in reckless whooping car rides through Charlotte, often with a girl close by, sometimes drag-racing with bootleggers. He was full of country-style jokes, greeting his friends with an electric shock-buzzer in the palm. However, in the things that matter to a Presbyterian family, he was circumspect; he did not smoke, drink, or utter coarse language, not even common slang.[8]

On the day the county voted in beer and wine, the astute father brought home a case of beer; he compelled Billy and Catherine to drink bottle after bottle of beer until they vomited. Some years later, at a high school class party, Billy drank wine and acted foolishly in an episode that embarrassed him. Still, he did not regard himself as an "oddball," until forced one Sunday afternoon to milk the cows. He began then to detest the uniformity and drabness of farm labor.[9]

Growing into young manhood, he had feelings of being buried alive "on that little farm, in that little community, I understood little, and resented my parents, my teachers, my humdrum life as a farm-hand and a high-school student." He turned to literature and began to devour history books, one hundred volumes before he was fifteen years old, including Gibbon's *Decline and Fall of the Roman Empire*. Like his cloistered farm-bound mother Morrow, he dreamed of living in Paris, Rome, and other faraway places. But the school classes rarely were touched with romance, and the young student faltered in poetry, French, and algebra. At intervals, he forgot the classes when he accelerated his father's Plymouth on the back roads, racing with his friends, and taking the curves on two wheels.[10]

He was a handsome young man, with a high brow, blond hair, and nice clothes, well liked by the girls—and that aspect was truly exhilarating. He was also described as "tall and awkward and good looking." Billy Frank was constantly in love, sometimes dating two girls on the same night. He, in turn, was proud of being a good kisser. As an adult, Graham reflected: "Those were years when I had tendencies to become wild and go with pretty girls, but somehow I never engaged in sexual immorality. For some reason, God kept me clean.

I never touched a girl in the wrong way. . . . This restraint was because my parents expected us to be clean."[11]

He had a prolonged infatuation with Pauline Presson, a young lady with extravagant brown eyes. Pauline recalls that "he wore clothes like a prince," white jacket, navy slacks, white shoes. "He was the best looking thing around." But Pauline related later that he never discussed religion with her.[12]

Billy Graham found salvation in November 1934, in a crude revival setting, on an empty lot in Charlotte near the Seaboard Railway. The fiery evangelist was Dr. Mordecai Ham—a tall strapping figure with moustache and pince-nez spectacles " who had allegedly discovered—fornication at Central High School. Graham, age sixteen, was curious about the rumor of sexual misconduct, so he and his friend Grady Wilson sat behind Ham in the choir during the second night of the revival. In this way, the evangelist could not point his accusing fingers at the young friends, who had mingled with the two thousand participants.

Graham and Wilson went forward on the altar call: I willed to seek Christ . . . it was partly intellect, partly emotion, but primarily will."[13]

> I remember that I felt very little emotion. I had a deep sense of peace and joy, but I shed no tears and I was not at all certain what was happening. In fact when I saw that others had tears in their eyes, I felt like a hypocrite, and this disturbed me.[14]

At home, young Graham threw his arms around his mother: I'm saved, Mother, I got saved.[15]

He began preaching to all who knew him, first to the tenants' offspring, then to the cook's black children, and finally to everyone and no one on a city corner in the cold winter. At a Charlotte garage, while having an automobile tire patched, he saw the mechanic hit his thumb and yell "Christ." Billy Graham glowered and warned him, "Sir, don't do that. I'm a Christian. Don't you ever take the Lord's name in vain again."[16]

After he graduated from Sharon High School in 1936, Billy was hired as a door-to-door Fuller Brush salesman. Some of those salesmen were organized into teams that moved from town to town across the tobacco and cotton South. At night they rested in dollar-per-night boarding houses. Tired of salesmen ringing her bell, one woman dumped a pitcher of water on Graham. At the end of the summer, Graham was informed that he was the leading salesman of his group.[17]

Bob Jones College

At the insistence of his mother, in fall 1935, and the recommendation of his sidekick Jimmie Jordan—Billy was enrolled in Bob Jones College, a Christian school, located in Cleveland, Tennessee (later Greenville, South Carolina). Bob Jones was not exactly a Disney World, and was described by non-admirers as a glacial Christian institution, that chaperoned its dating parlors, fostered strict curfews, permitted no holding hands, and tolerated no inter-racial dating. Its high-Calvinistic regimen was enforced by a no-nonsense former Methodist evangelist Bob Jones, who ran his school like boot camp. The redeeming factor was that Billy, a totally liberated youth, had entered the college with his lively friend, evangelist Jimmie Johnson.[18]

As academia, for a youth in suspension, the experiment at Bob Jones was a disaster. Billy's grades were poor, but only partial blame could be laid on his high school in North Carolina that had been weak in science and mathematics.[19] His dormitory room, shared with Jimmie Johnson, was an absolute mess, with peanut shells and fruit rinds lying in the corner. But Billy had charisma and wandered about with a swarm of friends. Town boys, for their own amusement, would invade the campus to throw firecrackers from time to time, and on one occasion were met by Billy's patrol, who pelted their car windows with rocks.[20]

But Bob Jones College was relentlessly driving Billy Graham to distraction. He was a normal, sometimes uninhibited, social being, imprisoned in a school that allowed no loitering in the halls, no speaking to girls, and grudgingly donated fifteen minutes per week in separated chairs for male-female discourse. Once in an open assembly, he admitted to an astonished President Bob Jones that since arriving, his spiritual life had diminished.[21]

This free-soul was thirsting for another milieu, like a prisoner seeking liberation from Devil's Island.

Liberation at Florida Bible Institute

On Christmas leave, while sick with flu, he heard beckoning words from a friend who had transferred to Florida Bible Institute, a small religious school in a setting of palms near Tampa. Billy persuaded his father to take a vacation trip in their new green Plymouth to Orlando, Florida. Billy was stunned by the panorama of Florida sunsets, flowers, and oranges.[22]

Then, he was compelled to confront the Bob Jones president, who couldn't believe his ears. The president exclaimed:

> Look here, if you're a misfit at Bob Jones College, you'll be a misfit anywhere, Billy. You leave and throw away your life at a little country school like that down there, chances are you'll never be heard of again. Best you'll ever amount to is a poor country preacher somewhere out in the sticks.[23]

The arguments were too late and futile; Graham was determined to go.

When young Graham left for classes in Florida, he also left behind the girl with whom he had a deep infatuation, Pauline Presson. But Pauline had no desire to be a preacher's wife, and went on to a life sustained by Cal-Tex Oil in places like Singapore and Kuala Lumpur.[24]

Graham arrived in February 1937 at Florida Bible Institute (F.B.I.), a Bible academy of seventy-five souls set in the orange grove community of Temple Terrace, several miles from Tampa. The organizer of the Institute, evangelist W. T. Watson, had stumbled on a financial gold mine, and purchased the property—a furnished hotel—for sixty thousand dollars, but no principle or interest was due for a ten-year period. The property was embellished on one side with a golf course.

Billy Graham, in brogans and chartreuse trousers and recently liberated from Bob Jones College, was nearly ecstatic. He was not a great scholar, but he dipped into a variety of courses: Doctrine (7:00 a.m.), Chapel (11:00 a.m.), Bible History, Life of Christ, Bible Customs. In this languorous atmosphere, he was receptive to friendly guidance and remained open-hearted and somewhat naive, according to school dean Reverend John Minder. In the clothes he wore, he was outstanding: a friend said, "Billy was always turned out sharp as a tack."[25]

It was no phenomenon for young Graham to fall in love, or, for that matter, to be rejected. But his rejection by beautiful Emily Cavanaugh, with the coal-black hair but also a spiritual nature, produced in him a profound despair. He wandered late in the autumn night onto the golf links, his eyes blurred with tears of disappointment. In his own Gethsemane, Graham surrendered himself to God. He spoke: "All right, Lord! If you want me, you've got me. If I'm never to get Emily, I'm going to follow you. No girl or anything else will ever come first in my life again. You can have all of me from now on. I'm going to follow you at all cost." It was an authentic commitment and the making of the spiritual man. He stood, walked back to his dormitory, and gathered a fervent knot of young men, who prayed with him through the night.[26]

In the rapture of his new relationship with God, Graham released himself to preach at broken-down missions, street corners, and trailer courts. He was venturing on the bases of emotion and little experience. At the north Florida village of Bostwick, amid palmettos and scrub pines, he telescoped four sermons into eight minutes of delivery. His parishioners were sawmill hands and cattle farmers. He faced dangers he had never before encountered; in a swamp settlement, he talked a gang of toughs in coveralls out of beating him up. "Harm me," he said, "and God will strike you dead."[27] On another occasion, he fired a shot through a dwelling-house door to discourage a disoriented drunk, who was referring to himself as Billy Graham. In downtown Tampa, where he continued to entreat saloon customers, a group of rowdies proceeded to push his face into the mire.[28]

Graham, during his life, was baptized three times. He was sprinkled in 1919 at Chalmers Memorial Church at the behest of his Presbyterian parents.[29] Long after the visit of Mordecai Ham in 1934, he was immersed by the pastor of Tampa Gospel Tabernacle and Florida Bible Institute, Dean John Minder. Now, with his parents approval, to satisfy his Southern Baptist leanings and in response to his prayerful search, he was baptized by immersion on December 4, 1938, by Reverend Cecil Underwood in Silver Lake near Palatka, Florida, with church members as witnesses.[30] Then, in 1939, Cecil Underwood, pastor at Peniel Baptist Church near Palatka, called together four or five neighboring pastors of St. Johns Association, to form a Southern Baptist ordination council. Graham, after the doctrinal questioning, knelt on a little platform, was blessed by the hands of the encircling preachers, and was ordained at night in the Peniel church under the cedars.[31] He was now a Southern Baptist preacher with full credentials.

Graham, after his religious experiences, had an obsession to do some great thing. As a rural boy, he was fascinated by the leading revivalists, with their high collars, string ties, and plumes of hair. Those wandering evangelists included Gypsy Smith, Homer Rodeheaver from the Billy Sunday entourage, and William Evans, associated with Dwight L. Moody. Graham was captured by their grandiose style and he was eager to serve them in any way.[32]

When Pastor John Minder departed for a six-week stay in California, he left Billy Graham, as the assistant pastor, in charge of Tampa Gospel Tabernacle. Like St. Francis of Assisi, his parishioners were jailbirds at the Tampa Stockade, trailer park residents, and the very poor. At another chapel, a former meat market in Venice, Florida, he prayed for a full afternoon, entreating the presence of the Holy Spirit. That evening, with one hundred persons pressing against each other, thirty-two young men and women came forward. The amazed Sunday School superintendent proclaimed, "There's a young man who is going to be known around the world." In order to enliven his sermons, he read the newspapers and purchased a discarded set of encyclopedias for about four dollars.[33]

The novice preacher would practice his sermons in strange places. At times, he was thundering his pronouncements late at night to gasoline cans and mowers in the school garage. Then he paddled a canoe across the Hillsboro River to convict frogs and alligators in a loud untrained voice. Even in his apprenticeship Graham had a premonition, perhaps an inspiration, that someday he would stir the hearts of thousands.[34]

By the summer of 1940, far more than frogs and egrets were startled, since Nazi Germany had invaded Poland and France. He was occupied as president of his Florida Bible Institute class, editor of the yearbook, and he was hoping to continue his education at a more advanced and academically reputable religious school, Wheaton College near Chicago.[35]

Billy Graham had a stroke of good fortune that would permit him to enter Wheaton College. During the fall of 1940, two Christian businessmen for whom Graham had caddied on the golf links at Temple Terrace, offered to finance him for one year at conservative, staid Wheaton College. After first arriving on the campus, he felt completely out of place.[36] Graham was so unseasoned after his move that when he saw the aurora borealis over the Illinois sky for the first time, he thought he was experiencing the Second Coming. His reaction was to throw himself on the ground in fervent prayer.

Since his father did not financially support him, he worked for fifty cents an hour in afternoons as a mover and driver of a battered yellow truck. While lifting furniture into a boarding house, he met his future wife, Ruth Bell; she was set apart because of her deep-set hazel brown eyes, a pretty face, a lithe form, and the maturity of a second-year student at Wheaton. Ruth would not be an easy catch, for she wanted to prepare herself for spinster missionary work in Tibet. She arose before dawn each day for a two-hour devotional and was described as the "most devout girl on the campus."[37] After they attended a Sunday glee-club concert together, a two-year courtship followed; their romance consisted mainly of attending religious services togther, and Ruth admitted that she was almost bored by the lack of excitement and intimacy.[38]

Ruth Bell was born in provincial Tsing Kingpu, northeastern China, her father Presbyterian medical missionary Nelson Bell. As a serious child, she had prayed nightly that the Lord would allow her to be captured by bandits and beheaded for Jesus' sake. Nelson Bell, from Waynesboro, Virginia, permitted his family to read the Bible, and only such classics as Joel Chandler Harris's *Uncle Remus*, Walter Scott's *Little Lord Fauntleroy*, and Charles Dickens's *David Copperfield*. In the style of the times, the family and other Southern missionaries entertained themselves with black-faced minstrel shows.[39]

Eventually the love of art and literature, so strongly borne by Ruth and her world vision, would influence Billy Graham in broadening his concept of Christian witness.[40]

In 1941, Billy proposed: Graham informed Ruth that she was not meant to go to Tibet as a single woman. She was not certain that she loved him, but could feel the leading of the Lord, and accepted.[41] In outlining their plans, Graham reminded his future wife that the Bible teaches that the husband is head of the wife, and she conceded.[42] The couple then waited for their joint graduation at Wheaton in the summer of 1943.

The Grahams were married on Friday, August 13, 1943, at Montreat, a Presbyterian conference center in the mountains of North Carolina (close to the Southern Baptist Center at Ridgecrest). Their honeymoon was spent in a cottage at two dollars a day, at Blowing Rock in the Blue Ridge Mountains. During their first night together, he remembered a lesson from an Indian chief and slept a portion of the evening on the hard wood floor. Ruth, after studying the Bible, refused his suggestions to be immersed. She was boldly independent and encouraged Billy Graham to go without her to many crusades and church rallies. Like numerous youthful marriages, theirs required some adjustments.

The couple chose to return to Western Springs, a middle-class suburb of Chicago. He became pastor of The Village Church, with its little congregation of thirty-five souls, located in the basement of an unfurnished church. The chairman of the deacons was youthful Robert Van Kampen, president of Hitchcock Publishing Company, who cooperated with Graham to attract the attention of a devotional club. As a consequence, the three hundred men of the club, meeting at the Spinning Wheel, became part of a dinner prayer ministry.

The Village Church in October 1943 was scarcely bloated in its treasury, receiving donations of only $86.50 a week. Graham was given an offer to take over Torrey Johnson's broadcasts, called "Songs in the Night." This transfer involved a contract of thirteen weeks and expenditures of $100 weekly. Each segment of broadcasting would be consumed with forty-five minutes of preaching and singing. The church accepted the challenge, and the Canadian-born bass-baritone George Beverly Shea (formerly featured on the ABC network's "Club Time") joined the broadcast team. The program came on the air, beginning January 1944, from the Western Springs suburban church.[43]

With World War II being fought with deadly ferocity, Graham was hoping to become a chaplain. Advanced plans had been made by the Allied forces for a cross-channel invasion of the Normandy Peninsula on June 6, 1944, and by September 1944, Army infantry and Marines would be bloodily engaged with the Japanese on the rocky Pacific island of Peleliu.[44] The concern Graham had for the thousands of servicemen on leave in Chicago led him to Torrey Johnson, professor of New Testament Greek at the Northern Baptist Seminary, and the Youth for Christ ministry.[45]

In the fall of 1944, when Graham was afflicted for six weeks with mumps, he left Ruth with her parents at Montreat, North Carolina, and went for recovery to Florida. Graham's companion and host was Reverend Torrey Johnson, then engaged in the Youth for Christ expansion. After organizing a Youth for Christ rally at Chicago's Orchestra Hall, adjoining the USO Center, Johnson invited Billy Graham to be the preacher for the opening rally. To the shock of Graham, twenty-eight hundred people attended. Forty-two persons came forward in response to the invitation. Then, in Detroit, Graham became the substitute preacher for Johnson.[46] Much later, the Youth for Christ rally would be attended by a large crowd, in a stadium that could seat twenty thousand people.[47]

Youth for Christ, operating from Torrey Johnson's sparsely decorated office on North Wells Street, Chicago spread its operations over the entire world. Its messengers were a corps of handsome, fresh revivalists. Two of these became inseparably linked, Charles Templeton and Billy Graham—called the Gold Dust Twins. As he traveled, Graham took with him his Bible Concordance, and secular books by James Michener and John Steinbeck, that were intended to give his sermons breadth. Another factor would give buoyancy to Youth for Christ; Graham had attracted the attention of prominent news publisher William Randolph Hearst.[48]

Between 1946 and 1949, Graham made six trips to Europe for Youth for Christ, traveling about 750,000 miles. When the youth team first landed in war-ravaged London, it was attired in white shoes and bow ties. Their suits were tinted in pastel colors or sometimes pink. In response to the economic scarcity of the post-war days, at Monte Carlo, Graham paid with nylon stockings for his room and board.[49]

In the British Isles, between 1946 and March 1947, Graham and Billie Barrows spoke at 370 meetings in twenty-seven communities.[50] These were hard times for Graham, despite the friendly involvement of British industrialist Alfred Owen. London in 1947 experienced its worse weather in a hundred years, with Graham sick for two weeks. He ran out of money in Dublin, Ireland, and made a desperate call to Texas millionaire R. G. LeTourneau, who responded with funds. But despite the travels, the British religious ice pack began to break up.[51]

Near the Welsh mines that have given to America its surplus population and some of its singing-religious ardor, Graham was charged with hope. He acquired a surge of spirituality after praying, fasting, and rejoicing with Welsh pastor Stephen Olford, from the mining town of Pontypridd. The two men grappled with the power of God after Olford prayed on the theme: "Be ye not drunk with wine ... but filled with the Spirit." In a stone hostel in late October, the two men lost track of time, and for two days they became mesmerized in prayer, praise, and wrestling with the Lord.[52]

Graham always had more fear of an empty stadium than of some bizarre embellishment to his preaching. This became evident in 1947, at his hometown of Charlotte, North Carolina. In a warehouse-like quasi-stadium that seated five thousand persons, he was afraid of the numbers that would not attend. For his support, he brought along several soloists and a xylophone player. Then, as star guest performer, he presented mile-runner Gil Dodds, who sprinted six laps on a temporary track against an athlete from the University of North Carolina.[53]

Graham preached over a vast area that included Canada and almost every state. He spent only two to three months in each year resting in the small North Carolina cabin, across the street from the Bells. The Grahams took their long separations in stride, but found time to be with their daughter Virginia "Gigi," and newly-born son William Franklin, Jr. Ruth then began assembling a new mountain home out of logs retrieved from abandoned country stores and houses. She moved in 1956 to the new site, with five children, one maid, and a caretaker, and prettied it with flagstones and ivy. They kept company with family dogs Peter and Belshazzar. Meanwhile, Billy roamed to New Delhi, Nairobi, and Seoul.[54]

Presidency of Northwestern Schools

Billy Graham had considered on occasions the undertaking of graduate studies at Princeton or in the United Kingdom, but he never expected to be a college administrator. When his path converged with that of Dr. William Bill Riley, circumstances would modify his career. Dr. Riley was the pastor of the First Baptist Church of Minneapolis and founder of the interdenominational Northwestern Bible Training Institute (NBTI). Northwestern was augmented by a seminary, and enlarged in 1944 with a liberal arts college to become Northwestern Schools.

In the summer of 1947, Dr. Riley was dying and desperately seeking a successor. Riley had been a fired-up evangelist in the tradition of Gerald L. K. Smith; he had fought modernism, Catholic power, and Jewish hypocrites. Billy Graham, at age twenty-eight or twenty-nine, succumbed to Riley's pronouncement that God had anointed Graham to be head of the Northwestern Schools. The real flashes of lightning that Riley saw, appeared to be God's endorsement of Billy Graham, and awed by Dr. Riley's vision, Graham consented to assume the presidency if Riley should die within a ten month span.[55]

But almost from the beginning, the presidency, added to the Youth for Christ responsibilities, soon became too taxing a burden. Graham became largely an in absentia president, and the academic responsibilities were often laid on associates. The pageant of succession to the old warrior Riley might have been Elijah passing his mantel to Elisha, but to Graham, the symbol passed to him might have been more like an anvil. Affronted by the schools locked-in, outmoded beliefs, and fearful of the influence of Midwest ultraconservatism, Graham found too frequently a reason to travel and preach off the campus.[56]

The new president of Northwestern Schools was different, only a kid scarcely older than his charges, and not a professional educator. He never drew his salary. Graham's associate, T. W. Wilson, became the vice president. The combined schools enrolled 739 students and

200 in night courses. For the faculty and students, there had been a lazy relationship within the facility, but with strangers now administering, it was not the same. This change became startling, when the new president wrote a "Dear Gang" memo to his faculty.[57]

Although Graham had quick reflexes and a sense of command, he was not fully aware that in academe jealousies are not far away and policies often move slowly. His vision was to forge a new Wheaton College. But to accomplish that goal, he was thwarted and spent far too many days away from Northwestern. His priority clearly remained in evangelism. Still, under his administration, enrollment increased, new buildings were erected, and a two-wave radio station opened. In addition, the college publication *Northwestern Pilot* reached a circulation of thirty-five thousand.[58] All of these accomplishments, however, could not divert him from his primary concentration on evangelistic crusades, and in 1953 he resigned the presidency of Northwestern Schools.

During his presidency of Northwestern Schools, Graham experienced a personal hard struggle with the Bible's authenticity. The struggle was generated by differences with his friend, the Reverend Charles Templeton, pastor of an independent Toronto church. Templeton joined Youth for Christ, collaborated with Graham in Europe, and engaged in a running debate with Graham over Higher Criticism. The heart of the mini-debates was on the question of the dependability and veracity of the Bible.

At Montreat, North Carolina, Templeton tried to persuade Billy to attend Princeton University for graduate studies. In that suggestion was the consideration of Bible authenticity. At one point in the debate, Graham responded: "the Biblical record can be completely trusted." With the re-affirmation by Graham of the Bible as the reliable Word of the Lord, and other matters of orthodoxy, Templeton accused Graham of taking a position that was intellectual suicide. At a Presbyterian rally in the San Bernandino Mountains, California, Graham cried out: "O Lord, help me. I don't have the knowledge." And lifting his Bible on that starlit night, he declared with his soul,

"Come what may, without question or falter, I believe this is your holy word."[59]

After Graham made his final assessment of the Bible's reliability, he clenched his fist and asserted: "It gave me a lasting, unassailable strength." From that moment, Graham was a theological rock, resting his solidity and preaching on the assurance that the preacher is only the messenger, not the author of the message. It is the Book speaking, not he; it is God speaking, not the speaker. "I never wavered," Billy Graham declared, "from that moment to this."[60]

In the year 2000, the evangelist Graham was conservative in his dress and style, but it had not always been so. Formerly, he liked to dress with a splash of color. In his preaching at Albuquerque, he wore a twill suit with cowboy belt and silver buckles; in San Francisco, he was attired in blue suede shoes and a ten-gallon sombrero. "Slovenliness," he said, is one of the deadly sins."[61]

Typically, he awakens in darkness or early dawn, shaves, sips a cup of coffee, and then returns to bed for thirty minutes of prayer or sleep. "I've noticed," he says, "that if I get up in the morning and, for some reason don't spend time in prayer, get busy with something else first, nothing seems to go right the rest of the day." After breakfast, he watches the news on television, and scans through five or six newspapers, sometimes a book. Immaculately hygienic, he takes four or five showers a day.[62] He concentrates intently on a subject or future sermon topic.

He is aware of his deficiencies: "I have read the reports in the press, and I thoroughly agree that I am a very ordinary speaker." He then added: "I have severe intellectual limitations."[63]

Mingling with leaders overseas, he is friendly and open. Contrary to reports, he is not a teetotaler, and in company with overseas clergymen, he will drink a glass or two of wine. But before he preaches, Graham will not eat or drink anything except a light soup or tea. After returning from an overseas trip, he sometimes arrives by train at Black Mountain, North Carolina, and for lunch fixes himself Vienna sausages or a can of pork and beans, or Irish potatoes cooked in the hearth. Sometimes he relaxes by pacing his secluded yard in pajamas and baseball hat. While growing up, his young children charged five cents each for photos of the house or its illustrious family.[64]

Los Angeles Campaign

The Los Angeles Youth for Christ campaign in 1949 was extended to last an incredible eight weeks. Billy Graham, then thirty years old, was a lively but obscure young evangelist. Invited by a group of Christian businessmen, he was depicted in the newspaper heading as "America's Sensational Young Evangelist." The services were to be held in a triple-spired circus tent in a downtown district, with sawdust on the floor, and rows of wooden chairs.[65]

In the emotional meteor-trail of President Harry Truman's gloomy announcement that the Soviet Union had detonated an atomic bomb, Graham's message was somber: "Judgment is coming just as sure as I'm standing here! . . . The world is divided into two camps! On the one side, we see Communism. On the other, we see so-called Western culture, and its fruit had its foundation in the Bible, the Word of God, and in the revivals of the seventeenth and eighteenth centuries. Communism, on the other hand, has declared war against God, against Christ, against the Bible, and against all religion. . . . Unless the Western world has an old-fashioned revival, we cannot last!"[66]

Graham, in his first major city as an evangelist, saw in Los Angeles his date with destiny. The Los Angeles organizing committee saw Graham as only their next evangelist. Still, he narrowly persuaded them to expand the budget to twenty-five thousand dollars. He said, "I want to see God sweep in [for the] repercussions would sweep across the entire world."[67] And the excitement and techniques of that campaign set the pattern for his future role. The Los Angeles revival, with the Youth of Christ managing, brought 350,000 people to the meetings with 4,200 coming forward to be counseled.[68]

Among the converts were long-distance Olympic runner Louis Zamperini (who at the Olympics in 1936 tore down the Swastika), Jim Vaus, a gangster linked with Mickey Cohen, and radio personality Stuart Hamblen (who after his conversion wrote the song, "It Is No Secret What God Can Do.") Hamblen was the son of a Methodist preacher, but the radio singer was leading a double-life as a hunter, gambler, and heavy drinker. Reluctantly, he attended the revival with his Christian wife Suzy. After the crowds departed, Hamblen at 2:00 a.m. insisted on an intimate talk with Grady Wilson and Billy Graham at their apartment hotel. There, Stuart Hamblen, his wife Suzy, Wilson, and Graham talked and prayed until 5:00 in the morning. Hamblen then told his radio audience bluntly that he had given his life to Christ, and he immediately sloughed away his horse racing, drinking, and smoking.[69] Jim Vans, cynically amused at hearing that Hamblen had been saved, went to attend the service, was saved and uttered the words: Lord, I believe."[70]

After preaching, Graham retreated to his North Carolina seclusion. For there were three concentric circles that comprised the Graham cosmos: (1) the evangelistic universe, (2) the Billy Graham Evangelistic Association, and (3) the small protective world near Montreat, North Carolina. There, in isolation, he enjoyed the counsel and friendship of his father-in-law, Dr. Lemuel Nelson Bell. Dr. Bell, a fundamentalist Presbyterian doctor, had operated on Graham and was influential enough in later years to dissuade Billy from running for the U. S. Senate.[71]

Graham's marriage to Ruth has been secure and peaceful. About her, Graham says, "She has my cup of coffee right there every morning. I've never seen her moody. . . . I've never known her to lie down in the daytime. . . . She's wonderful." Like high school sweethearts, they embrace, joke, and banter.[72]

In 1956 Billy, Ruth, and their five children moved further up the mountain to a retreat protected by several guards, fierce dogs, and an eight-foot fence. This was not security enough to prevent a demented youth from encroaching; the intrusion was halted by Graham, who felled the invader. In this enclave, no neighbor's house was in sight and few children came to the little fortress. Sundays were reserved for Bible games and stories, but also were the only days for candy, gum, and soft drinks—but no television. The children could attend football games but no high school dances. Even so, son Franklin, a hulking youth, loved to swig a few beers and race over back roads.[73]

Organizing the Billy Graham Evangelistic Association

The Billy Graham Evangelistic Association (BGEA) became a reality in the summer of 1950, during the Portland, Oregon, Crusade. Fiscal matters had to be resolved at the Portland Crusade, because a large sum of money had been collected for establishing a radio broadcasting program, and there were no procedures in place for handling the funds. On the insistence of George Wilson, the business manager at Northwestern Schools, an organization was incorporated under the name Billy Graham Evangelistic Association (BGEA). The purpose was "to spread and propagate the Gospel of the Lord Christ by any and all . . . means." The first directors were Graham, Cliff Barrows, Grady Wilson, George Wilson, later George Beverly Shea. Then, after the successful crusade in Atlanta, at the invitation of 135 churches, and heeding the advice of Dr. Jesse M. Bader, formerly of the Federal Council of Churches, Billy Graham agreed to become a salaried employee of the BGEA.[74] This action was to forestall any misgivings by the faithful regarding the sizeable funds received by the organization.

The organization's senior staff included personalities soon to be known throughout the world: Cliff Barrows, the song leader, who "jumps about like someone plugged into a 220-volt socket"; George Beverly Shea, painfully shy, the bass-baritone soloist who was plucked from the Chicago radio devotional program "Club Time"; Grady Wilson, the practical organizer and planner, who walks about as "unpretentious as a turnip" and was ordained near Charlotte. Wilson is the evangelist's closest friend—and described as Graham's Sancho Panza. Ted Smith, pianist, from Toronto's Royal Conservatory, has been the most obscure.[75]

It was at Atlanta's Ponce DeLeon Park on November 5, 1950, that Graham began his radio program "Hour of Decision," which was carried by 150 stations and expanded by 1954 to an audience of fifteen million.[76]

When the American Broadcasting Company offered Graham the opening for a Sunday afternoon radio program, he had hesitated because of the twenty-five-thousand-dollar stake required. He fell to his knees and made a bargain with the Lord, the proof of God's affirmation to be twenty-five thousand dollars by midnight tonight. When he explained the situation to the evening congregation gathered in Portland, Oregon, almost the entire amount—twenty-three thousand dollars—was collected in a shoe box. The remainder was received in two envelopes delivered to the hotel.[77]

The Graham team was becoming more astute in using mass media. At the Fort Worth crusade in February-March 1951, he produced a Christian Western film, *Mr. Texas*, that cost twenty-five thousand dollars. This venture was mildly audacious, for some evangelicals regarded fiction films to be the work of the devil. With movie magnate Cecil B. de Mille present at the debut at the Hollywood Bowl, the projector broke down—but the film resumed after a short prayer by Graham. The film, although panned as amateurish, became an effective missions tool.[78]

By 1952, Graham and his team adopted the term "crusade," and abandoned the words "campaign" and "revival." Personal workers became counselors, and that title was adopted by the religious world. No invitation for a Crusade would be accepted, unless the tender came from a substantial number of churches, and only after a full discussion and then approval by Graham and his colleagues.[79]

In the course of his experience, Graham found three areas of vulnerability that could damage or even destroy an evangelical organization: (1) money poorly handled, (2) pride foolishly displayed, and (3) morals—potentially related to contacts with women—not alertly guarded.

The security rules adopted by the Graham team, formal or informal, included the following: a public disclosure of financial support, and team members to be paid through a budgeted salary. By 1952 Graham would not stay in a hotel unless a male associate was nearby who could account for his company and the lodging of each team member.[80] Graham's rules required a reliable male to check his hotel room before he entered. He also chose never to be alone with a woman, nor to walk or ride with one, not even with his secretary.

All of this prudence did not protect Graham from attacks, left and right, for being a conservative antediluvian or for being a left-wing ecumenicist. His opponents included at various times scholar Dr. William G. McLoughlin, Jr., and conservatives Dr. John R. Rice and Dr. Carl McIntyre; the latter two accused him of nurturing a relationship with modernists and the National Council of Churches and also of rejecting the fundamentals of Christianity, including atonement, and not supporting salient beliefs from the Bible. While lauding him for his preaching, his critics accused him of immature homiletics and ignoring the sacraments and old-fashioned theology.[81]

Graham spent many hours mingling and talking with clergymen. In the words of Cliff Barrows, "He genuinely loves them. I've never once heard him publicly say one derogatory remark about any minister."[82]

In response to his conservative critics, he said:

> I would like to make myself clear. I intend to go anywhere, sponsored by anybody, to preach the gospel of Christ, if there are not strings attached to my message. I am sponsored by civic clubs, universities, ministerial associations, and councils of churches all over the world. I intend to continue. The one badge of Christian discipleship is not orthodoxy, but love. . . . Christians are not limited to any church. The only question is: "Are you committed to Christ?"[83]

Despite Graham's flashy style in his beginnings as a preacher, there was a deep chasm between him and insincere, turncoat evangelists. In the period when Graham first ventured out, in Los Angeles, mass evangelism largely had lost the nation's respect. This decline in interest had been noted after the death of D. L. Moody in 1899, and even during the career of the fireball Billy Sunday, who preached in Charlotte in 1924; the influence of these revivalists could not reverse the downward trend.[84]

The team analyzed the deficiencies of shady or careless evangelists in November 1948 at Modesto, California. The defects that were most apparent were: (1) too much of their time was spent in raising finances and love offerings, (2) money raised was not honestly accounted for tax purposes, or even properly recorded, (3) sensationalism or over-emotionalism, (4) digression to prophecy, (5) controversy, (6) anti-intellectualism. Then, the focus was on the defects of evangelists becoming anti-church and not following up on their recent converts and contacts.[85]

Strong feelings were shown by Graham about tainted evangelists, who instead of proclaiming Christ, won easy popularity by assailing modernism and the local clergy. The irony is that Graham adopted extensively from leading old-time preachers. From Willis Haymaker, he borrowed the term crusade; from D. L. Moody, he took advance publicity, advertisement, mobilization of churches, and mass evangelism; from Billy Sunday, he borrowed businessmen's luncheons specialized committees, mobilized clergymen, mass choirs, celebrities, and prayer groups.

Fortunately, in part because of the assistance of William Randolph Hearst, there developed a symbiosis between Billy Graham and the news media. Beginning in December 1952, Graham reached fifteen million readers through his daily news column "My Answer." This commentary appeared in seventy-three newspapers, including the *New York News* and the *Chicago Tribune.*[86]

The dynamic young preacher had exploded on the American scene through radio, films, television, articles, and then books. In Novem-

ber 1953, Graham published his book *Peace with God*, which clarified the Gospel in simple terms; the profit was channeled into a trust
fund for children's education. In three months, 125,000 copies were
sold, and this number vaulted to 1.25 million copies sold by 1965.[87]

By February 1966, his book *World Aflame* had been purchased in
440,000 copies. Then, he released another film, *The Restless*, based
on teenage problems, and reviewed by large audiences in America
and Great Britain.[88]

The Nation Embraces Him

The status of Graham was elevated by two events in 1952: (1) a
crusade in Washington, D.C., and (2) a Christmas trip to Japan and
Korea. At the National Guard Armory at the District of Columbia,
he talked to national leaders and congressmen, but also to clerks,
African-Americans, and housewives. On February 3, in the presence
of Speaker Sam Rayburn, he addressed millions on television and
radio from the steps of the Capitol. The young Graham, thirty-three
years old, for a Day of Humiliation and Prayer, read Lincoln's 1863
proclamation. The Washington Crusade brought Graham praise from
leaders of both parties and the friendship of Senator Richard M.
Nixon and Senator Lyndon B. Johnson.[89]

Then, in 1952, during the third winter of a savage war in Korea,
he visited that torn country. The front lines had been stabilized, but
the American dead stood at twenty-one thousand. Washington at
first had denied authorization for the visit; then under pressure from
friends in power the trip was allowed. Ruth Graham pulled one of
her jokes on the travelers by substituting for sleeping pills other
capsules filled with mustard powder; the one to suffer most in this
troublesome exchange was Grady Wilson. Christmas Day was spent
on the front line, with the sounds of gunfire. Graham visited the
wounded, including one soldier with bullets lodged in his spine.[90]

While in Korea, Graham was almost paralyzed with emotion after he examined reprints of a freedom testimony from captured North Koreans and Chinese held by the allied forces. The prisoners had submitted their petition to remain under allied control, in what was called *A Book Signed in Blood*. In the book, several hundred North Korean and Chinese prisoners, who vowed not to return alive to their communist countries, had stamped their fingerprints in blood. Graham sent a copy of the book to President Eisenhower.[91]

The Korean episode deepened Graham's concern for overseas missions. Returning to the United States in January 1953, he talked for a half hour with President Eisenhower. Later, the nation was surprised when Eisenhower closed his inauguration with prayer.[92]

Forty-two years later, in 1994, Graham carried a message from President Bill Clinton to North Korean leader Kim Il Sung on the nuclear issue. Kim Il Sung responded by shouting and clenching his fist, when Graham met him for about thirty minutes. Fortunately, during this brief encounter, Graham convinced Kim that the message of President Clinton was sincere. In only a few short weeks, Kim agreed to permit international inspectors to visit the North Korean nuclear testing sites.[93]

The Graham Message

The preaching of Billy Graham over the years has had an apocalyptic overtone, but the message mellows as time passes. In Los Angeles (1949) he declared: "Unless the Western world has an old-fashioned revival we cannot last." In 1951 he said: "We seem to be moving toward a climactic battle which will settle the destiny, if not the annihilation of the human race." In 1961 he declared: "This Christmas is the most precarious in history. The world hangs on the edge of an abyss."[94]

The international crises and times of urgency gave an edge to his preaching. One of his friends said: "Unless there was a crisis somewhere, Billy couldn't preach." Before beginning a European tour, he commented: "This year, weapons for mass destruction will reach the peak of perfection. We have reached the point of no return in our destructive philosophy and strategy."[95]

He outlines sins that are particularly offensive to him. In 1969 he railed against the bartender who sells beer to minors, the barbiturate peddler, and the drug pusher who infests campuses, the income-tax chiseler, the insurance faker, the college graduate whose diploma is won by cribbing rather than cramming, the professor who allows himself to be intimidated into giving superior grades to inferior students.[96]

During his training in Florida, Graham had practiced his style of preaching amid frogs and swamp alligators. While his stock of sermons was small, he rehearsed until he was drained. "I had one passion," he related, "to win souls. I didn't have a passion to be a great preacher." Since he was not in a league with Harry Emerson Fosdick, he copied the style of famous evangelical preachers.[97]

He believed in a vigorous, sturdy Christ—"a real he-man," with square jaws and strong shoulders: not for him any anemic, fragile, wilting Jesus in a Renaissance painting. "I think a Christian ought to look like a Christian," he stated in 1958.

His mind was constantly directed toward unsaved men and women, but especially toward the youth who would carry forward the Christian banner. This vision was ever-present in his crusades. In 1960, near the Reichstag in West Berlin, he thundered out: "The young people of this generation who cannot remember much about the war [World War II] are searching for a flag to follow, a leader to believe in. Let that flag be the Christian flag! Let that leader be Christ!" The interpreter compressed the message into: "Lasst Christus Euer Führer Sein" ("Let Christ be your führer [leader]").

His sermons nearly always crest in an awesome moment. All present in the vast arenas are told that to reject Christ is to die in the Pit apart from the Savior, while those who repent and accept Christ join the family of God and the great celestial choir. The music softens as he reminds his immense audience that even the famous and productive celebrities like Bertrand Russell and George Bernard Shaw had to face God on Judgment Day.[98]

And the moved and newly saved stream forward to be fortified and counseled by Graham's helpers. The final prayer is always preceded by the majestic, searching, poignant hymn sung by the great choirs: "Just as I am, without one plea, but that Thy blood was shed for me."

Despite the numbers won to Christ or revitalized by Graham's message, not all the Christian notables were applauding. An adverse reaction to Graham's preaching came from Canon Stanley Evans of London's Southwark Cathedral, who said: "It is not the Gospel at all. It never speaks of anything other than a sentimental relationship between the individual and God. . . . The mind and the will are left out of this completely. This is not the Gospel, this is the Gospel degutted and individualized."[99]

London Crusade (1954)

Billy Graham's Greater London Crusade in 1954 ran into tough sailing on its first days. The English press reacted adversely. The *London Evening Press* referred to Graham as an American "hot gospel specialist who was actor-manager of the show'." He was portrayed as "like a Biblical Baedeker; he takes his listeners strolling down Pavements of Gold, introduces them to a rippling-muscled Christ (who resembles Charles Atlas with a halo), then drops them abruptly into the Lake of Fire for a sample scalding."[100]

At the Harringay Stadium in the dingiest corner of north London, he was wretched in spirit and almost overcome with dark forebodings. Approaching the arena with Ruth at night, from the side opposite to the main entrance, he saw only a few people; he feared the negative pull of the press had dampened all possibilities. But Graham said to Ruth, "Honey, let's just go and face it and believe God had a purpose in it." But the shock factor came with a glimpse through the main entrance—for the arena was packed and the crowd was enormous.[101]

At the stadium, he was greeted by Anglican bishops, members of Parliament, and the Archbishop of Canterbury. Among his converts was Sir John Hunt, leader of Sir Edmund Hillary's successful attempt to conquer Mount Everest. The British were won over by the less-garish trappings of the reworked crusade, and the unpretentious style of Graham.[102]

The *Daily Mail* reflected that he was the first preacher many British had seen who took the Bible and preached it with simplicity, clarity, and urgency. The *Daily Mail* mirrored this view: "He has no magic, no magnetism, he makes no appeal to the emotions. . . . He punches home the facts—the facts that he reads out from the Bible in his hand."[103]

Soon the crusade was moved to the more spacious Wembley Stadium, where he preached to audiences of 185,000 people—the largest crowds in English religious history. Including those who heard Graham by wire, his audience nearly reached 400,000 listeners.[104] When 2,000 people at Wembley Stadium responded to Graham's invitation, the Archbishop of Canterbury said to Graham's colleague Grady Wilson, "We'll never see a sight like that again until we get to heaven."[105] The success of the London Crusade should be attributed in no small part to the Bishop of Barking, who said to the evangelist: If you've been made to appear a fool for Christ's sake, then I'm happy to appear a fool with you."[106]

That confirmation of Christian support had been given after major errors were made by the Graham team and before their arrival in England. The promotional brochure misspelled the names of eight prominent Britons and referred to the evils of British socialism. Billy, sailing on the liner *United States*, informed the *London Daily Herald* that the correct word was secularism, not socialism. However, in his "Hour of Decision" broadcast in the United States, Graham had said, after his arrival in England, he might challenge Marxian socialism. In England, he would clarify his views by asserting: "I am not anti-Socialist, anti-Liberal or anti-Conservative. I am completely neutral in politics."[107]

Some British did not turn out for a love-feast, since a number of divines and writers disliked the presence of the evangelist. A religious writer, the Reverend Frank Martin, wrote in the *Sunday Graphic*: "This Billy Graham line just won't do! . . . Just pelting us with texts will never convert British sinners. The whole thing is (and I say it in all charity) too spiritually bouncy, and immature."[108]

Dr. Donald Soper, president of the Methodist Conference, was unhinged by Graham's theology and Graham's disdain of socialism and pacifism; he refused to meet Graham. Also Graham found himself not favored by a Presbyterian leader, The Very Reverend (later Lord) George MacLeod, who preferred texts built on social reform.[109]

After twelve weeks of arduous preaching, Graham had lost twelve pounds. He had endured, although afflicted by a myriad of problems: hernia, tumors, polyps, headaches, nausea, and jaw abscesses.[110]

But his triumph was to be dined at the House of Commons and given audiences with the Queen Mother and Prime Minister Winston Churchhill.

When a British chaplain asked Graham if his converts stick, Queen Elizabeth II, who had received him, replied quick as a flash: "Sir, of course they stick." Billy Graham's organization studied that question in 1988, and found that seventy-five percent of those confessing at the crusades remained Christians.[111]

His two-sided relationship with the British would be revisited again in 1959 in London. He had just returned from New Zealand and Australia. The British press howled when he told reporters: "It looks as though your parks have been turned into bedrooms."[112]

Somehow, in 1954, Graham and his father-in-law, Dr. Nelson Bell, found time to start the popular evangelical magazine *Christianity Today*. Graham, after a sleepless night, announced: "God has given me a vision." He shared his ideas with Dr. Wilbur Smith of Fuller Theological Seminary, Pasadena, California, philanthropist J. Howard Pew, chairman, Sun Oil Company, and Baptist layman

Maxey Jarman of Nashville, Tennessee. With Carl F. H. Henry as editor, 285,000 copies rolled off the presses at Dayton on October 10, 1956. The purpose of the paper, professionally fulfilled, was that evangelical Christianity needs a clear voice to speak with conviction and love.[113]

Then efforts were directed to a magazine to help ordinary Christians in their witness and daily walk, and this became *Decision Magazine*, which began at San Francisco in 1958. The first editor was Sherwood Wirt, a Ph.D. from the University of Edinburgh. The initial print run was 299,000 copies; by 1962 circulation was over one million, then rose to four million. Often copies were deliberately used as wrappings for gifts to Iron Curtain nationals, who read their Christian messages. In time, several foreign-language editions were added to the standard English editions.[114]

The All-Scotland Crusade in 1955, unlike the London counterpart, was borne along in a flood of good will. At Kelvin Hall more than half of the attendees stemmed from remote corners of Scotland. They were responding to Graham's presence and the Tell Scotland movement.[115] After the campaign a letter arrived from a laborer, whose life had been changed. He spoke to a disfigured man about going to church. "I couldn't go," the marred man said, because his face was distorted by terrible scars. "Why, Charlie, his friend replied, "we follow a Man who had worse scars than you."[116]

On Good Friday, Graham spoke on television to the United Kingdom before an audience only second in size to the Coronation crowd. It was heard in Buckingham Palace, public houses, and tenement rooms—the greatest audience for a preacher in Britain's history.[117]

Honored and praised in Scotland, Graham persisted in joining Ruth in London for a short second London Crusade. He was entertained by the Duke of Hamilton, Lord High Commissioner to the Church of Scotland. At Holyrood House, he met one distinguished lord after another. Meeting one more person in formal attire, he greeted him: "How do you do, my lord." The man stuttered: "I'm sorry, sir, I'm your waiter."[118]

Then, Graham led the BGEA team to the Far East, including India. After visiting with Gandhi's successor in India, Jawaharlal Nehru, he was greeted by larger crowds than those swarming Soviet visitor Premier Nikita Khrushchev. In the city of Palamcottah, five to six thousand people jammed the cathedral when he was in attendance. An English missionary reported that the crowds fell down around him, greeting him like a god.[119]

The New York Crusade (1957)

In a grueling crusade lasting into a fourth month, in which he would lose thirty pounds, Graham imbedded himself in possibly his most audacious venture, the New York Manhattan Crusade.[120] The preparations for this formidable religious confrontation began at least a year earlier; Graham did his planning in Montreat, where he was planting lawns, plowing his garden, and strengthening himself with calisthenics.

The advance team of Jerry Beavan and twenty-five assistants at Times Square were preparing the ground through a highly-developed strategy that included interviews at local offices and preachers assigned to church pulpits. Everything was massive or detailed: mailings to four hundred campuses and ten thousand prayer cells established. Counselors were carefully selected, and instructed to use mints for breath and deodorants to sweeten active bodies. Counselors would be matched by race, sex, and age, so as to be compatible with the inquirers coming to the front during the crusades. In the great metropolitan area, notices were posted on about 650 billboards; forty thousand bumper stickers were distributed; and two thousand people were trained for the choir. In Frady's words, the organization was not unlike a Watermelon swarmed by wasps.[121]

At the Hotel New Yorker, the team knelt in solemn prayer: Graham, Barrows, Grady Wilson, and Beverly Shea. They would then be prepared to face the crowds at Madison Square Garden and Times Square.

As Graham took the stage, it was instantly clear that his God was no jocular, waffling Man Upstairs:

> He is not a jolly fellow like Santa Claus. He is the Great Bookkeeper. And He is keeping the book on you! . . . I am a Western Union boy! I have a death message! I must tell you plainly—you are going to Hell! You listen! Don't you trifle with God! Don't you think you can barter! You are a sinner! You have come short of God's requirements! Your punishment is sure![122]

The text he read from Isaiah would stop a man in his forward stride, and, in fact, hushed the great crowd:

> Ah, sinful nation; a people laden with iniquity, a seed of evildoers, children that are corrupters. . . . Your country is desolate, your cities are burned with fire: Your land, strangers devour it in your presence. . . . Hear the word of the Lord, ye rulers of Sodom; give ear unto the law of our God, ye people of Gomorrah. . . . If ye be willing and obedient, ye shall eat the good of the land: But if ye refuse and rebel, ye shall be devoured with the sword: for the mouth of the Lord hath spoken it.[123]

During the crusade, two million people had heard the message, and some responded to the call for repentance and to the commitment that Graham affirmed "you make with your will, not your mind, not your emotions." But the *New York Times* published that sixty-four percent of those who came forward were already members of churches. Billy Graham then verified that forty to seventy-five percent of all decisions were former church members or members of sponsoring churches, described by some critics as weightless popcorn Christians. Those coming forward were given a "salvation kit" containing Gospel verses, memorization lessons, and a letter from Graham.

Notables were given special attention and seated in a celebrity section of Madison Square Garden; those guests included singer Pearl Bailey, actress Dale Evans, actress Gene Tierney, ice skater Sonja Henjie, impresario Ed Sullivan, and columnist Walter Winchell.

The most distinguished guest may have been Vice President Richard Nixon, who heard Billy Graham declare that one hundred thousand people were gathered together because of God, and not because of him.[124]

On July 20, the final day, the rally was held at Yankee Stadium, with 100,000 to 125,000 people filling every cranny; he preached with fire and frankness in a stadium with oven-heat temperature, reaching 105 degrees. He proclaimed the Gospel as God's warrior— unafraid, unintimidated, and unconquered, but terribly exhausted. The crusade, including the television outlay, had cost $2.5 million.[125]

This did not stop his critics. Religious scholar William G. McLoughlin said that if revivalism is to be successful: revivalism must be commercial in its advertising, exploitive in its mechanics, literal in its theology, bland in its pietism, statistical in its measure-ment.[126] Graham also was attacked by ultra-conservatives Carl McIntyre, John R. Rice, and the elder Dr. Bob Jones, who reviled Graham for support given by modernists. In the actual situation, the New York Crusade was sponsored by fifteen men who shared Graham's philosophy. The philosophical lines were so boldly drawn that no Bob Jones University student was permitted to pray in a prayer meeting for Billy Graham preaching in New York.[127]

Graham, twelve years later, led a new crusade in the burgeoning eight-million-person New York metropolitan area. This religious revival was characterized by well-drilled teams and supported by professional media devices. Invoking God's blessing, Graham preached to more people in an evening than the Apostle Paul reached in a lifetime. However, the people of New York largely remained cool to direct evangelism.[128]

Melbourne and the other large Australian cities offered to host a 1959 crusade, sharing the preaching with New Zealand. Graham visited the sister Australian centers of Sydney, Brisbane, Canberra, Perth and Hobart. While the Australian-New Zealand crusade was considered eminently successful, writer William G. McLoughlin, Jr., spoke disparagingly of the campaign and predicted that revivals had lost their luster.

Facing the Social Issues

The two greatest social ordeals in Graham's life were the Civil Rights Revolution and the Vietnam War. Also, in the decades between the founding of the Billy Graham Evangelistic Association (BGEA) at Portland in 1950 and Graham's 1970 television address from Dortmund, Germany, the world community faced two major wars in Korea and Vietnam. The United Nations had been directly involved in the Korean War that erupted in 1950. Then the world watched the United States confront the problems caused by the divisive Vietnam War, and at the same time be confounded by a turbulent internal Civil Rights Revolution. The Civil Rights struggle was climaxed by the murder of its Baptist black leader Martin Luther King, Jr., on April 1, 1968, in Memphis.

The Civil Rights Revolution

As in other aspects of his life, Graham would modify the immature concepts of his youth, and swayed by his loyal attachment to the Bible and by association with respected leaders, he would become wiser and more accommodating in his views of race.

When a teenager, Graham refused to have his hair cut in a Negro-operated barber shop in Charlotte;[129] he was not unlike hundreds of thousands of white youth across the country. At Wheaton (1940-1943), a conservative Christian school, Billy Graham was mentored by Alexander Grigolia, an anthropology professor in his major field. Grigolia advised him that there was no validity to arguments of Negro inferiority. Still unpersuaded, on a trip to Florida, Graham was unmoved when the black driver was fed separately from a trap window at the rear of the cafe. Graham reminded the protesting

Welsh preacher Stephen Olford who accompanied him that Ham and all Negroes had been cursed by God to be servants.[130]

However, long after Wheaton, and the social experience acquired on the road, he would declare in 1952 that: Of all people, Christians should be the most active in reaching out to those of other races.[131]

Graham's great leap forward occurred in 1953, when he made the climactic decision not to preach again to segregated audiences. On March 15, 1953, at Chattanooga, he physically tore down the ropes separating blacks from whites, and he informed the Crusade committee that blacks could sit anywhere in the auditorium.[132] He was adamant: Either these ropes stay down, or you can go on and have this revival without me.[133] While adhering to the change, Graham did not believe at that time that forced integration could ever be successful. While he lost friends, he supported the Supreme Court's decision, and asserted that the Bible did not teach segregation.[134]

By 1956 Graham, and seemingly the leading Protestant ministers, felt that segregation should end in restaurants, hotels, railroads, and bus stations. While Graham believed that school integration would eventually be achieved, he did not feel that the country was ready for it; at this time the South was in a period marked by tense civil confrontations. When South Carolina governor (1958) George Bill Timmerman protested Graham's scheduled use of the state capitol lawn and the probability of race mixing, the religious service was moved to the Fort Jackson parade ground.[135]

The national racial changes during 1956 occurred in part because President Eisenhower, never moving at meteoric speed, had requested Graham to use his influence to dampen down the racial tension. And Graham's bravest service was to hold his preaching as a cross-cultural communion with God.

However, by 1960, his migration on race had reached another plateau. In explaining why he omitted South Africa from his African tour, he stated:

> To keep the races in total separation is a policy that won't work and is immoral and un-Christian. The segregated churches

and church institutions in America are becoming known to people all over the world. They cannot believe it. They can't take it in. They're astonished to hear that Christian institutions bar a man on the basis of color. The greatest need in the South today is contact between the races and the church in the South should lead the way toward bettering racial relationships.

Not the Supreme Court, but gestures of good will, love, and understanding would result in the greatest racial good and the least social harm. In 1961 Graham felt that black and white Freedom Riders demonstrating in the South had made their point; now, having created in most white southerners a sizzling reaction, the danger point had been reached. At a 1961 Baptist Convention in Atlantic City, he declared that the church is not for one [white] race only. He also asserted in another statement that civil rights demonstrations may have gone too far. In 1964 he added: "The greatest racial tension is really in the North, but those conflicts are put on the back pages."[136]

In April 1964 Billy Graham escaped briefly from the escalating racial tension. The Billy Graham Pavilion opened with the beginning of the New York World's Fair at Flushing Meadow. There had been skepticism from Graham in 1963 as to whether an evangelistic center would draw the crowds. It was necessary to install equipment to present a twenty-eight-minute film in Todd-AO called *Man in the Fifth Dimension*. Five million visitors from 125 countries visited the 117-foot tower gracing the pavilion. After each showing of the film, counselors had personal talks with the inquirers.[137]

On the invitation of President Lyndon Johnson, Graham in April 1965 visited Alabama and Governor George Wallace. He also advised the Ku Klux Klan to quiet down, the civil rights leaders to give Alabama time to adjust to new federal laws, and the politicians to be restrained. President Johnson wrote to Graham, "You are doing a brave and fine thing for your country in your courageous effort to contribute to the understanding and brotherhood of the Americans in the South. In this instance, I am praying for your success and want you to know I am very proud of you."[138]

There were two cooks in the kitchen, one (Martin Luther King,

Jr.) turning up the heat, and the second (Billy Graham) adjusting the burners down. Both of them would remain friendly, respectful, and gracious, but working with their different roles and perspectives. King was followed by preachers, student leaders and a coterie of fellow-travelers, and even Communists. FBI Director Hoover would give alarming reports to Graham based on his wire taps of King. In 1963, at the Lincoln Memorial, King made his immortal speech, "I Have a Dream": "I have a dream that my four little children one day will live in a nation where they will not be judged by the color of their skin, but by the content of their character." Graham's reply was, "Only when Christ comes again will the little white children of Alabama walk hand in hand with little black children."[139]

But these two great Baptist Trailblazers had a continuing amiable relationship. Graham refused to join the Freedom Marchers that raised the tempo of social change in the 1960s. While many Northern churchmen joined black demonstrators in the South, Graham had no part with them. However, when the Sixteenth Street Baptist Church in Birmingham, Alabama was bombed in September 1963 and four Negro children killed, he agreed to serve on a four-man interfaith committee with Harry Truman. Graham, showing great courage, brought his team and preached in 1964 on Easter Day at the Legion Field Stadium at Birmingham. Opposition came from the segregationist Citizens Council and the Black Muslims; despite the possibility of trouble, thirty thousand people, equally black and white, gathered together in the name of Jesus Christ. Graham spoke of earthly troubles, but those not so formidable, when standing in the shadow of the cross. "Father, forgive them, for they know not what they do." The national press was stunned as blacks and whites streamed forward at the invitation.[140]

For years, Graham had been a lone voice on race among American white preachers. M. L. King had been with Graham in New York for two days during the 1951 Manhattan Crusade and had delivered a prayer there.[141] Now some of those who railed against him felt he should march with the demonstrators; this was reaching an unbearable intensity for Graham, who was known for his emphasis on integrating worship services. Billy Graham's views were expressed in his article, published in August 1960, in the *Readers Digest*: "Why Don't the Churches Practice the Brotherhood They Preach?" Things were changing, however, in Birmingham, for in April 1965 one-third of the members of the rain-soaked congregation were black; they were welcomed by the Ministerial Alliance and encouraged by President Johnson.[142]

In 1960, after running into M. L. King at the Miami airport, the two leaders decided to vacation in Puerto Rico for a "wonderful two days of fellowship and discussion." M. L. King told him there: "You know, I just can't preach the gospel any longer. Something's left me." During the Baptist World Alliance in Brazil, Graham gave a party for King at the Copacabana in Rio de Janeiro.[143] In 1965 Graham publicly appealed to King to arrange a moratorium on demonstrations until the country could digest the new Civil Rights Act.[144] He said of King: "I thought he was a man filled with as much charisma mixed with intellect as any man I'd ever met."

Born and bred a Southerner, Graham never could understand segregation in the church. While in the early days the seating was left to the local committee, he insisted always that whites and blacks should come forward together on the invitation. As he would say: There's no racial distinction here. Here are white and colored alike, standing before the cross of Christ. The ground is level at the foot of the cross.[145]

Working for Reconciliation

Billy Graham did more for racial advancement than the Northern social engineers, who pointed accusing fingers at the South and ignored the beams in their own eyes. Although a Southern Baptist, he was far ahead of the SBC position on race relations. In spring 1956, he discussed the topic with President Dwight D. Eisenhower at the White House, and then affirmed on June 4, 1956, that he had conferred on racial matters with Negro universities and Protestant conferences. His recommendation was, "if the Supreme Court will go along slowly and the extremists on both sides will quiet down, we can have a peaceful social readjustment over the next ten years."

Graham's consistent position was that the root of the racial problem was spiritual. Integration, Graham stated, must advance in love, hand in hand with conciliation. The psychological and moral adaptation takes place in a man who receives Christ, and he forgets all about race when he's giving his life to Christ. He projected this view in an article for *Life Magazine* (October 1, 1956). As the consequence of his example, other Southern churchmen were compelled to face the race situation. But, since he displayed even-handedness in the racial struggle, he was attacked as a foot-dragging conservative by some and as a traitor to the South by others. However, his conciliatory stance emboldened pastors in the middle and won the praise of the Negro-managed magazines *Ebony* and *Jet-Age*.[146]

Support and Opposition to the Vietnam War

In the aftermath of the French failure to restore their control of French Indo-China after World War II, as climaxed by their military defeat at Dienbien Phu (20 November 1953—7 May 1954), the United States was increasingly drawn into the affairs of Southeast Asia.[147]

The involvement of the United States in the war in Vietnam (1961-1975) produced across America widespread protests, divisiveness, and acrimony, for this was probably the least popular war in the nation's history. Billy Graham, many Southerners, and probably the vast majority of Americans regarded the War in Vietnam as an extension of the global war against Communism, although many observers would regard the Vietnam struggle as an anti-colonial uprising and in many ways a civil war.

Graham first heard of Vietnam at the Seminole Golf Club from Senator John Kennedy, who had not been inaugurated as president. Graham was impressed with the politician's words: "We've just got to do something about Vietnam." President Kennedy, acting on his own words, sent General Maxwell Taylor to bolster the South Vietnam defense against Communist Viet Cong guerilla attacks. He then pledged assistance to President Ngo Dinh Diem, and, by February 1962 had established a U.S. Military Assistance Command in South Vietnam. Graham was a loyal American throughout and preached at the Pentagon, West Point, and Annapolis; he maintained that America must remain the strongest military establishment on earth.[148]

In 1965 the two religious giants in America had a minor quarrel. The Negro leader, Martin Luther King, Jr., firmly opposed to the war in Vietnam, warned the public: "I'm not going to sit by and see war escalated." Graham responded: that King's message was "an affront to the thousands of loyal Negro troops."[149]

Then, in 1966, in his sympathy for American combatants in Vietnam, Graham went to visit the troops. The invitation to go abroad stemmed from his close relationship with President Lyndon B. Johnson and at the urging of General William C. Westmoreland. As the consequence, Graham spoke to ten thousand troops holding candles on Christmas eve at An Khe and five thousand at Long Binh.[150]

Graham seemed fascinated with the apocalyptic overtones of Vietnam, a war that continued as a bloody, long-lasting confrontation between the Communist hordes in Asia and their foes, the Christian armies of the West. He reminded his listeners in 1968 that Christ once said: "I didn't come to bring peace, I came to bring a sword." Even if war is sinful, Graham reminded his listeners, until Christ comes again, we're going to have convulsions and wars. On other occasions, such as the student demonstrations at UCLA, he conceded: "Vietnam is difficult, confused, complex, and perplexing . . . [but] we should see it through to a satisfactory conclusion."

Investigation of the My Lai tragedy revealed that American troops attacked a hostile Vietnamese village and retaliated for its sniping at the soldiers by killing its people, including children and old people. Graham said: "We have all had our My Lais in one way or another . . . with a thoughtless word, an arrogant act, or a selfish deed."[151]

The war was long, most of its years fought without an end in sight.

When Nixon launched the bombing attacks on North Vietnam during Christmas 1972, Graham was now having doubts. He said: ". . . all through this period, I have not been sure whether our involvement was right or wrong. . . . I don't want to get involved on either side." However, he refused the request by prominent clergymen to advise Nixon to stop the bombing; Nixon had informed him privately that the B-52 air strikes were meant to show America's resolution, preparatory to achieving a just peace.[152]

Again, in 1973, he stated: "I have avoided expressions as to who was right and who was wrong. . . . During all this time, though, I have repeatedly indicated my hope for a proud and just peace in Southeast Asia. . . ."[153]

In a letter to the *Christian Century*, in answer to criticism of his support of the war in Vietnam, he replied: "I have been extremely careful not to be drawn into the moral implications of the Vietnam war." At this point, Billy Graham appeared to be veering away from his former patriotic, anti-Communist, and supportive rhetoric on the war in Vietnam; this was in stark contrast with the bold aggressiveness of Roman Catholic Cardinal Francis Joseph Spellman, who in 1972 told Vice President Lyndon Johnson: "Bomb them! Just bomb them."[154]

Graham was accused by some critics of forgetting his support for an American commitment to the Vietnam War. This view was amplified by a writer to include this remark: "I think that [Graham's changing perspective] is the political reality Graham actually lives in." The final comment was made by Graham after the 1972 Paris accords: We should never have gotten into a no-win land war in Asia."[155]

The Crusades Are Carried On

In 1960 Billy Graham's work carried him through Israel. He was on a world tour, with the major contacts in Africa and Western Europe. Prime Minister David Ben-Gurion wired from the United States that there would be flexibility as to the arrangements in Israel so long as Graham refrained from mentioning Jesus Christ before a Jewish audience. Graham knew how to confront that restriction. At the King David Hotel, he told the press: "I am going to address only Christian audiences. I have no intention of proselyting. In fact, I must be grateful to you for proselyting me. For Jesus Christ was a Jew, all his apostles were Jews, and the whole early church was Jewish." It was perceivable to the Israelis that their chief influence might lie with the Christians in America.[156]

The itinerary in Africa, beginning in Dakar, Senegal, in 1960 would require nine weeks and involve fourteen thousand miles of travel. In Ghana, he faced the strange situation of Prime Minister Nkrumah presenting himself as the redeemer and his mother receiving the respect of an African Virgin Mary ("Blessed art thou among women").[157]

With Muslim leaders, he was challenged to match their healing powers with sick patients. At Victoria Falls, he was reminded of the exploits of Presbyterian missionary David Livingstone. In Abyssinia, he exchanged greetings with the Copts, who have practiced an ancient strain of Christianity for sixteen hundred years. Graham then visited greater Nigeria and Rwanda-Burundi, the latter home to the Tutsi's and Hutu's.[158]

The Manchester, England, Crusade in 1961 was a frustrating experience. The American leaders made a bad decision in selecting the cotton manufacturing center of Manchester for the crusade, rather than designating Liverpool. Some advisors of the Manchester Council of Churches felt that the industrial workers prevailing in the city could not be reached by mass evangelism. Following this line, Bishop Ted Wickham of Middleton forcefully told Graham that the workers wanted to hear of social righteousness, not personal mercy. In other words, the advice was that Graham should forget the preaching of a plain New Testament message. Also, the physical facilities were depressing—comprised as they were of a bleak, steep outdoor stadium. Then, Graham was sick for a week, and under leaden skies that poured rain and chilled with bitter cold, doughty Leighton Ford served as the substitute preacher.

Despite these adversities, Graham, still sick, arrived to preach during the second week. The nightly attendance was encouraging, totaling about thirty thousand persons per session.[159] Billy Graham, near the end of one sermon, stopped suddenly and said: "I have been criticized for emotional appeal, for choir singing softly and for artificially urging people to come forward. Tonight the choir will not sing. As a consequence, you may have to stand twenty minutes in the deluge." An Anglican clergyman was amazed as twelve hundred persons came forward; his words were: "I went away convinced that here was only one power—that of the Holy Spirit."[160]

Lausanne (1974) and Amsterdam (1983)

The International Congress of World Evangelization met in Lausanne, Switzerland (1974). Partially in continuation of the evangelical Berlin Congress (1962), it was sponsored by *Christianity Today*, attended by twelve hundred delegates from one hundred churches[161] and addressed by the emperor of Ethiopia, Haile Selassie I. At this Congress of World Evangelization, generated by Graham, a debate arose over the meaning of evangelism, because in 1973 in Bangkok, the World Council of Churches had speakers that spread the heresy that Christ had already given salvation to every person. This false belief—an essence of universalism—would probably block from all humans any need to repent for sins or to believe in Christ for salvation.[162]

In contrast to Bangkok, the Lausanne Congress was another matter, and was well attended with 2,473 official delegates from 150 countries.[163]

The most significant contribution of this evangelical congress was its Lausanne Covenant (quoted in part below) and signed by Billy Graham:

> To evangelize is to spread the good news that Jesus Christ

died for our sins and was raised from the dead according to the Scriptures, and that as the reigning Lord he now offers the forgiveness of sins and the liberating gift of the Spirit to all who repent and believe. . . . The results of evangelism include obedience to Christ, incorporation into his church and responsible service in the world.

In response to the inspiration generated from countless anonymous evangelists, there was created the International Conference for Itinerant Evangelists (ICIE), to assist the foot soldiers of evangelism. The initial main effort was to find thousands of obscure men and women evangelists, mainly from the third world.[164] The location of this conference was to be Amsterdam's RAI Center (Zuidhal). On the opening of this conference, on July 12, 1983, there were four thousand evangelists, and twelve hundred guests, all representing 133 nations. The largest number came from India, Nigeria, and Brazil. Some delegates arrived barefoot, one African youth-preacher walked sixteen hundred miles from Zambia to Malawi. Samaritan's Purse, Franklin Graham's charity outlet, provided five hundred tons of clothes for those who needed a change. Two hundred workshops dealt with such topics as reaching political leaders or organizing a crusade. In 1986 in Amsterdam there would be other conferences of the Itinerant Evangelists (ICIE).[165]

Graham's perceptions and leadership matured through stages of tent evangelism, mass organizations, radio broadcasting, and, later, television sermons. In 1969, at Madison Square Garden, a closed-circuit television had relayed his message to a nearby audience. Then, in 1970, from Dortmund, Germany, he spoke by television to ten nations, that included Great Britain, Norway, and Yugoslavia; his audience totaled 840,000 persons, of which 15,813 were converted. Meanwhile, at Wheaton College, there began the building of a fourteen-million-dollar Billy Graham Center and a library that aspired to touch the lives of millions.[166]

In 1982 Graham hesitantly attended a Moscow peace conference sponsored by the Communist-infiltrated Russian Orthodox Church.

The U.S. ambassador opposed the visit, but Richard Nixon, the former president, advised him to go despite the risks. Billy Graham's knowledge of the Soviet Union was limited; in his unsophisticated way, he concluded that the gold crosses surmounting church museums (confiscated churches) manifested some Christian spirit in the Kremlin.[167]

Graham accepted the invitation to Moscow, provided that he attend as an observer, was permitted to speak only on biblical topics, and authorized to address two Moscow churches. When Graham was asked why he did not intervene in the case of two Pentecostal families that had taken refuge for four years in the American Embassy, Graham said:

> I knew that if I publicly castigated the Soviet Government for its policies, I would never have another chance to meet privately with the only people—the leaders—who could bring about change.[168]

This, however, was not the first time Graham had visited Russia. In the 1950s he slipped into Russia and found that outwardly the citizens were morally clean. He said at that time:

> In the Moscow Parks, I saw thousands of young people but I did not see one locked in an embrace. I hate Communism, but I love the Russian people and the moral purity I found among the Muscovites.[169]

Powerful Men He Influenced

There is no doubt that Graham enjoyed the company and confidences of the world's leaders, even those with blood on their hands. He was the friend of President Dwight D. Eisenhower, Lyndon B. Johnson, Gerald Ford, George Bush, and Bill Clinton, and cherished a special fraternal bond with Richard Nixon. He, in turn, could not be trusted by President Jimmy Carter and was thoroughly disliked by President Harry F. Truman, both of the latter fellow Southern

Baptists. Then, beyond these, there were a host of political leaders, idealists, revolutionaries, theologians, and pace-setters who had such confidence in Graham's sincerity, principles, and integrity that they would set aside their normal constraints to confide in him. Graham's basic goodness and openness sometimes, unfortunately, impelled him to take risks by accepting the word of schemers and rascals.

The London Crusade (1954) left such an impact in England that at its conclusion Graham was honored with a thirty-minute conference with Prime Minister Winston Churchill.[170]

The converts that went forward at the crusade included the First Sea Lord and Chief of the Naval Staff, and also Sir John Hunt, who was the leader of the 1953 expedition that supported Sir Edmund Hillary in reaching the summit of Mount Everest.[171]

At times, he could be badly hoodwinked. In 1956 he described Methodist Syngman Rhee of South Korea as every inch a Christian. Also he lauded Generalissimo and Madame Chiang Kai-shek in Taiwan with: "I doubt if there are two statesmen in the world today that are more dedicated to Christ and His cause than Generalissimo Chiang Kai-shek and his wife." Observers of the Chinese political leader would have scoffed at that characterization. In another circumstance, the Chinese couple were described by Graham as "spiritually-minded Christians," who arise and pray every morning at five o'clock.[172]

A key factor in Graham's universal success was the attention he received from the American news magnates William Randolph Hearst and Henry R. Luce. When Hearst learned about young Graham's evangelistic style, he instructed his staff to keep Graham in their sights; as a consequence, Graham became a familiar figure to the American public.[173]

Luce, as the editor of *Time* and *Life* magazines, was drawn to Graham through Franklin Roosevelt's Jewish friend and confidante, Bernard Baruch; this new contact was established when Baruch was impressed with a speech delivered by Graham on February 1950 before the South Carolina legislature. Graham was to begin his

Crusade on February 19, 1950, at the state capitol in Columbia, before four thousand people. He considered changing his chosen topic, on Judgment and Hell, when he knew Luce would be present. Then he steadied himself and preached the truth, as he felt God was leading him, and 256 people came forward to confess Christ. Graham was invited to stay at the governor's mansion. There he talked with Luce and they became close friends.[174]

On one occasion, Graham asked Luce to send sympathetic reporters to his Crusades, rather than secularists, since he (Luce) would not send a dress designer to cover a ball game. Luce quickly agreed.[175]

His powerful friends had their own agendas and were not always reticent in using him as their conduit. Before embarking for India in 1956, he was invited to consult in Washington with Secretary of State John Foster Dulles, a devout Presbyterian and exponent of massive retaliation—the response, should there arise a threat to the United States of nuclear war. Dulles confessed that the most important message of the age was to proclaim Christian discipline to the world's masses.[176]

This format almost certainly was conceived on the premise that lack of discipline could cause the world's destruction through a nuclear war. Then, in 1964, Texas millionaire H. L. Hunt offered to financially support Graham if he would become a candidate for president, to run against Lyndon B. Johnson.[177] Graham quickly declined the offer.

While often called to Washington, D.C., for prayer and an exchange of confidences with the president in power, the relationship with President Harry S. Truman was brief and unfriendly. After Graham and his colleagues Barrows and Grady met with Truman at the White House, they then knelt on the White House lawn for photographers and talked about the personal meeting to reporters. Truman was infuriated and never again invited Graham to the Executive Mansion. Truman, following that pattern, did not attend the 1952 five-week crusade at the National Guard Armory in Washington, D.C.[178]

Truman said about the event:

> Graham has gone off the beam. He's ... well, I hadn't ought
> to say this, but he's one of those counterfeits I was telling you
> about. He claims he's a friend of all the presidents, but he was
> never a friend of mine when I was president. I just don't go for
> people like that. All he's interested in is getting his name in the
> paper.[179]

Although a traditional Democrat, Graham frequently alluded to
his neutrality in politics. His preferences, however, were often tele-
graphed by his friendships and side remarks. In 1952, he wrote a
letter and otherwise influenced General Dwight Eisenhower to run
for president.[180] However, Eisenhower was formal and never invited
Graham to his private quarters in the White House. Still, in 1957,
before sending the 101st Airborne to Little Rock to enforce the
integration of the public schools, Eisenhower conferred by phone
with Graham, who was conducting the Madison Square Garden
Crusade. Graham said that "the Arkansas situation is out of hand
and the time has come to stop it."[181]

In the election campaign of 1960, there was inserted a new element—a wealthy, vibrant Roman Catholic candidate, John (Jack)
Kennedy. While Billy Graham states that he was not concerned
about the candidate's religion, many Protestants and Baptists in large
numbers were seriously concerned that through a Catholic president, the Vatican would exert unwanted influence.[182] Graham refused to endorse Kennedy, not because of religious feelings, but
largelybecause of Graham's friendship with Vice President Richard
Nixon. He also was concerned that his endorsement would limit his
acceptance and outreach among the world's diverse groups (despite
an appeal to support Nixon raised by Dr. Norman Vincent Peale,
pastor of New York's Marble Collegiate Church).[183] Later, his warm
relationship with the Kennedys was nurtured through conversations
and golf matches. Graham, after President Kennedy's assassination,
would be seated with the president's family at the funeral in
Washington's St. Matthew's Cathedral.[184]

Graham had a close relationship with Lyndon B. Johnson. Johnson was a rough-hewn but liberal politician, in some ways like frontiersman Andrew Jackson. Graham stayed overnight at the White House and at the Texas ranch on the Pedernales River. Johnson cut moral corners in his rural travels—but also the two, Graham and Johnson, would kneel on the floor and pray. Graham was among the first to know that Johnson, frustrated by the War in Vietnam, would not run for a second term.[185] Billy Graham preached at President Johnson's burial in Austin, Texas in 1973.[186]

President Gerald Ford inherited one of the worse political situations, following Nixon's involvement in Watergate. Ford, while an active member of the Reformed Church, was accused of selling out when he gave an absolute pardon to Richard Nixon. Graham asked Ford by telephone to save Nixon's life with a pardon, but also to free the Ford administration from a formidable barrier to success. After the pardon, a furor descended, and Ford's popularity fell by twenty-five percent.[187] Graham in 1977 at Charlotte played golf with Ford, and while Ford was apprehensive about Graham's preaching in Communist Romania, he relented when he heard that the Christian faith was awakened there by Graham's message.[188]

As previously noted, the relationship was testy for a time between Graham and fellow Baptist, President Jimmy Carter. Graham said of Carter: "I would rather have a man in office who is highly qualified to be president who didn't make much of a religious profession than to have a man who had no qualifications."[189] Carter was stung and replied: "I think what people should look out for is people like Billy Graham, who go around telling people how to live their lives."[190] In 1966, as state senator, Carter had served as outreach leader for a Graham film project in Americus, Georgia, and, then, while Georgia governor was honorary Georgia state chairman of the Atlanta Crusade in 1971.[191] Later, Carter and the Grahams had infrequent personal contacts and the Grahams on one occasion were guests at the White House. In 1994, with amicable relations restored, Carter agreed to serve as honorary chairman of the Atlanta Crusade.[192]

President George A. Bush, in January 1991, invited the Grahams to the Green Room at the White House to pray and watch on television the unfolding developments of the Gulf War with Iraq.[193] This type of invitation was becoming almost normal life for the Grahams, since Billy Graham had given the prayers during Bush's 1989 inauguration. Later, the pair would share a state dinner with Russian Prime Minister Mikhail Gorbachev.[194] Graham's most celebrated assistance to President Bush may have been his suggestion to return Hungary's ancient crown, in the custody of the United States at Fort Knox; as the result, the crown was restored to Hungary during the height of the Cold War as a gesture of good will.

On January 29, 1994, Graham delivered a message from President Bill Clinton to Kim Il Sung, Communist dictator of North Korea. Later, the president and Graham developed a cordial relationship, that included sessions of prayer during Clinton's period of crisis.[195]

Graham for many years was the close friend of Richard Nixon and remained his friend until the end. Nixon had been a U.S. representative and later a senator from California, selected to serve under Eisenhower as vice president, and then was elected as president for two terms. Nixon's threatened impeachment, relating to the Watergate affair, crescendoed into a national crisis and produced his resignation during the second term.

Graham and Richard Nixon first met in 1952 in Washington, D.C.—creating between them a rapt synergy. At that time, while Nixon was boundlessly ambitious, as a Quaker he appeared to be morally clean. In 1959, prior to Nixon's presidential candidacy, after an interlude of golf, Graham reported to a church gathering at Indianapolis that "Mr. Nixon is probably the best-trained man for president in American history, and he is certainly every inch a Christian gentleman."[196] Those two, the evangelist to the world and the political aspirant, hit it off smoothly. In 1956 at Asheville, Nixon declared: "No man has done more for the cause of good will and brotherhood throughout the world than Billy Graham."[197]

Graham tried to have a calming effect on Protestant-Roman

Catholic issues and disagreements, particularly as they occurred in Latin America.[198] But, during the Kennedy-Nixon face-off for the presidency in 1960, Graham said that religion is an issue, since the Roman Catholic Church is not only religious but also secular, with its own ministers and ambassadors.[199]

Graham publicly hinted broadly that he would support Nixon in the elections. He delivered the invocation at a rally for Nixon in Columbia, South Carolina. After Nixon then lost, Graham showed his flexibility by accepting an invitation to play golf with Jack Kennedy at Palm Beach.[200] In this period of despondency for Nixon, Nixon and Graham continued to meet for dinner, golf, and brain sessions, sometimes Graham encouraging Nixon to run again for the presidency. Graham also attended the Republican Convention in Miami.

In 1968, Hubert Humphrey, vice president under Lyndon Johnson, ran for the presidency, against the rebounding Richard Nixon. Four days before the election, Billy Graham announced that he had voted for Nixon by absentee ballot. Subsequently, he delivered the inaugural prayer for Nixon's governance at the monumental hour.[201] Above all, Graham considered his gifted friend to be a man with a deep religious commitment and personal honesty.[202]

The Watergate inquiry brought shocking revelations of Nixon's desperate conniving to protect his administration, and a series of sickening tapes that disclosed obscenities and treachery. In November 1973, after the Senate hearings, Graham was certain that the scandal would probably make him [Nixon] a stronger man and a better President.[203] In 1974, Graham kept repeating, after the startling disclosures contained in Nixon's tapes: "Those tapes revealed a man I never knew; I never saw that side of him."[204]

Crushed by the disclosures, Graham wept and revealed his own thoughts: "I have a real love for him—there's a reason why so many people were loyal to him. . . . I'd thought he was a man of such great integrity. I really believed. The facts were laid open, and the faith of the public quickly eroded; Graham was sick for an afternoon.[205]

When his legal case became hopeless, Nixon boarded his plane and departed the Capitol. After Nixon returned to San Clemente, California, Graham released his own reflections: "I feel sorry for President Nixon and his family. . . . I shall always consider him a personal friend. His personal suffering must be almost unbearable. He deserves the prayers of even those who feel betrayed and let down. . . . We should let President Nixon and his family have some privacy now."[206]

After the blight of Watergate—and without any national election—Gerald Ford became the president of the United States. Graham read the Bible and prayed with Ford regarding his awesome duties, and then rode with the new president to a reception for the Liberian president.[207] The tone for reconciliation was exemplified by Billy Graham, who in one of his sermons told of a Negro who felt freed, after the Civil War. The ex-slave, in a fashionable church, went forward and knelt at the altar. The church rustled with shock and disdain. But then Robert E. Lee went forward and knelt beside the black man. The congregation became quiet and followed in humility.[208]

The Legacy of Graham

Billy Graham is followed by millions of the faithful because he obeys the words of Christ the Master in simplicity and love. His life, above reproach, sets the standards in moral purity for a host of pastors, priests, and laymen. While his clean lines of conduct, advocacy of biblical judgments, and his own Baptist evangelical salvation style cause some to mistrust him, he is consistent in adhering to scriptural standards, and warm in the mode of Jesus in his approach to men and women.

Some have accused him of mixing with sinners, favoring the powerful (Lyndon B. Johnson, Kim Il Sung, Richard Nixon), cooperating with the liberals (World Council of Churches), playing golf with the rich (John Kennedy, Gerald Ford, Bob Hope); still, he is at heart a plain man, direct and as honest as the mountains of North Carolina. Although he is forgetful, he is not duplicitous, and his forward social steps, as in his openness to blacks and friendship to a variety of world religious leaders, have been by incremental advances. He nurtures a personal relationship to the worldly and unsaved, to whom he can be "uncritical, unchallenging, unquestioning."[209]

The apprentice preacher who once rehearsed his sermons at night with an audience of Florida frogs in a swamp now addresses millions of listeners, readers, and watchers throughout the world on radio, television, and through literature. As of the year 2000, Billy Graham has written twenty-four books, including *Calling Youth to Christ* (1947) and *Just As I Am* (1998). In Amsterdam in 1983, he addressed four thousand evangelists and twelve hundred guests from 133 nations.[210] His impact is formidable, for Graham beginning in 1952 reached fifteen million readers in his daily column "My Answer," which became a feature of the *Chicago Tribune* and the *New York Daily News*.[211] In his crusade at Yankee Stadium in July 20, 1957, there were one hundred thousand people in the stadium and another twenty thousand outside the gates.[212] At the Los Angeles Coliseum in 1963, 134,254 persons were pressed against each other to hear the evangelist preach about his Lord.[213] By Billy Graham's eightieth birth date, in 1999, he had visited eighty countries and preached to some 180 million persons.

His honors are extensive, and he is regarded by millions as the premier preacher of the world. He has been received for private audiences by the Queen Mother of England, Winston Churchill, Pope John Paul II, and the foremost statesmen of the world. On May 2, 1996, Billy and Ruth Graham were presented the Congressional Gold Medal, the highest honor of the United States Congress. The ceremony was attended by Vice President Al Gore, Speaker of the House Newt Gingrich, and Senate Majority Leader Bob Dole.[214] His greatest service is as true messenger of the Lord, faithfully interpreting the Holy Word, affirming the redemption by Jesus Christ, and the reality of miracles, the existence of Heaven and Hell, the eternal reign of the Heavenly Father, and the power of the Holy Spirit.

He is, in a sense, an expatriate, who has given his life to the multitudes and strangers for Christ's sake. His separation from Ruth and their children over the years has taken its toll. This cost probably contributed to the early waywardness of son Franklin, who after his experimentations returned to basic Baptist beliefs; Franklin was subsequently anointed by Billy Graham as the successor-leader of BGEA. This separation of Graham and his team from America for long periods of time has had its own rewards: a participation in ecumenicity, an enlarging comprehension of world values, and a realization of the vastness of and opportunities for God's earthly kingdom. Billy Graham is the closest prototype of a world preacher and while not sparsely clothed in camel's hide nor eating locusts he brings to the crowds the message of John the Baptist—repent, repent, believe, and be saved. He has become the sophisticate—but with the plainness of a Puritan or a modern Baptist, he repeats endlessly the old story of Christ redeeming the nations with His death on the cross. The world may be swept by self-indulgence and many false gods—but Billy Graham with gray hair and unsteady body, thrusts his jaw forward to challenge the earth's carnality and asserts Christ's apocalyptical words:

"I [Jesus] am the way, and the truth, and the life. No one comes to the Father, except through me" (John 14: 6).

Epilogue

What Makes a Baptist a Baptist

After nearly four hundred years, against daunting odds, the Baptist Faith—stemming from Anabaptist and Independent roots—has become the leading Evangelical voice in the New World. From obscurity and then persecution in England and Colonial America, this rugged faith has thrived, despite seizure of goods, beatings, and imprisonment of its adherents, to become vigorous, first in Great Britain. Then, in the United States by 1800, the Baptists, after years of persecution, became the fastest growing religious body in the new country, and by 2000 A.D. it embraced the largest number of Evangelicals in North America.

The Baptist Faith has given proof that it was uniquely prepared to be the natural Faith to solace the oppressed and to accept with open arms those seeking God in the rugged and dangerous frontiers of early America. The small congregations confronted the wilderness in their isolation, the community sharing hardships and emotions—finding in extended preaching, open prayers, congregational singing and their self-governing deliberative sessions an outlet for community diversion and faith.

Baptist administrative practice—when true to its church history—is a nearly complete congregational democracy. In its traditional form, the pastor is the spiritual and congregational leader, and the deacons are the church servants and crisis managers (both levels of leadership sharing to meet the demands of long-range plans, finances, and discipline). But the congregation in equality at its busi-

675

ness meetings is the clearest expression of Christian democracy—
and there the ordinary church members cast the determining vote on
church policy, procedures, discipline, or change of a pastor. This
egalitarian quality of Baptist government was captured in the writings of Thomas Jefferson, James Madison, and Patrick Henry—who
closely associated with the Baptists of Virginia—and found in the
Baptist model an example to be followed in the newlyproclaimed
country.

Today, the Baptists of the world, regardless of nationality, share
the joy of being a unique people. Stemming directly from biblical
inspiration, they have given to the world some of religion's greatest
and most advanced concepts. Few if any people, other than the
Anabaptists, have so upheld as sacred principles, the inviolability of
each and every person's religious beliefs—and not simply as tolerance reluctantly given to other religions.

Baptists stand on the granite of the Bible. The Bible for them is
the Word of God, and on matters of theology and faith, it is the *sine
qua non* of Baptist piety. Translated from early texts, as written in
Hebrew, Greek, and Aramaic, the fidelity of transliterated texts to
the original meanings is truly astonishing. As a consequence, generations of faithful Baptists, most emphatically their biblical scholars,
rely on the New Testament for its testimony regarding the life and
atonement of Jesus Christ the Messiah.

The concept of Separation of Church and State is a unique Baptist doctrine—born of Thomas Helwys and Roger Williams, and
sustained by the golden orator from Texas, George W. Truitt. Those
Americans who do not understand the peril of Federal money given
to religious denominations for good and noble purposes should listen to John Leland and Isaac Backus: such national funds poison the
fellowship of religion, create vicious and selfish maneuvering by church
groups, and corrupt both the nation and the churches themselves.
Jefferson did not embrace the concept easily, but his great brain
welded to the ideal of Separation of Church and State for the pres-
ervation of a great new nation.

Few doctrines are more liberating and beloved by Baptists and those of kindred denominations than the concepts of the Priest-hood of the Believer and Soul Competency.

Unlike followers of the more sacerdotal religions, Baptists em-brace the certainty that between the sinner and God the Father there is absolutely no intermediary—no pastor, priest, bishop, cardinal, Virgin Mary, or church, only Christ Jesus the Savior and Lord. Only the blood of Christ is the noble element to wash away the sins of the sinner (in words taken from Holy Script: Revelation 1: 5).

Baptists baptize no infants, but only self-declaring children and adults, who answer of their own accord the call of the Holy Spirit to follow Jesus Christ; the response to the Heavenly Call must be by the free will of the convert. The petitioner is then accepted by the free vote of the church congregation. Total baptism, or immersion, as practiced by the early disciples, is precious to Baptists as a symbol of regeneration. Baptists, on the other hand, do not regard that baptism can have any role in salvation—but, manifestly, they give great im-portance to immersion for the witness it offers to the world of the new life of the believer. The Lord's Supper, a second ordinance, is observed in churches in remembrance of Christ's life, suffering, and death on the cross.

Many Baptists throughout the world are what they are because of enduring trials and ordeals while following Jesus Christ. In South America, in some Islamic nations, in China, Russia, India, and East-ern Europe, the road that believers have chosen is hard. Down through the centuries, the crucible of mistreatment has taught Baptists world-wide to be tolerant, to develop social and political goals that rein-force democracy, and foster the building of a moral society. However, in the twenty-first century, the greatest danger to numerous Baptists residing in the United States and the industrial countries may be presented by their increasing prosperity and the worldliness of their environment. So, Baptists of the future, if they would persevere as a sensitive, caring, godly people, are obliged to revisit their past, renew their visions, and remember the Christ-like Trailblazers, like John Bunyan, Luther Rice, and Billy Graham, who continue to cut the way through a harsh and pagan wilderness.

Notes

Chapter 1 John Smyth (1570-1612)

1. Henry C. Vedder, *Short History of the Baptists* (Chicago: The American Baptist Publication Company, 1963), p. 3.

2. H. Leon McBeth (1), *The Baptist Heritage. Four Centuries of Baptist Witness* (Nashville, Tenn.: Broadman Press, 1987), p. 32.

3. Robert G. Torbet, *A History of the Baptists* (Chicago: The Judson Press, 1955), pp. 62-63.

4. William R. Estep, *The Anabaptist Story* (Nashville, Tenn.: Broadman Press, 1963), p. 210.

5. McBeth (1), p. 33.

6. Torbet, p. 63.

7. McBeth (1), p. 33.

8. McBeth (1), p. 34.

9. Torbet, p. 63.

10. Torbet, pp. 63-64.

11. Torbet, p. 64.

12. Estep, p. 212, quoting Champlin Burrage, *The Early English Dissenters* (Cambridge: The University Press, 1912), I, p. 233.

13. Estep, p. 212

14. McBeth (1).

15. Estep, p. 213.

16. McBeth (1), p. 34.

17. McBeth (1), p. 36.

18. William Henry Brackney (2), *The Baptists* (New York: Greenwood Press, 1988), p. 4.

19. Estep, p. 212, quoting Champlin Burrage, I, p. 237.

20. Estep, pp. 217-18.

Chapter 2 Thomas Helwys (c.1570-c.1616)

1. Henry C. Vedder, *Short History of the Baptists* (Chicago: The American Baptist Publication Society, 1907), p. 266.

2. William R. Estep, *The Anabaptist Story* (Nashville, Tenn.: Broadman Press, 1963), p. 214.

3. Robert G. Torbet, *A History of the Baptists* (Philadelphia: The Judson Press, 1955), p. 65.

4. Estep, pp. 216-17.

5. Torbet, p. 65.

6. Torbet, pp. 65-66.

7. Torbet, p. 65.

8. Estep, pp. 214-17.

9. Estep, p. 216.

10. Torbet, p. 65.

11. Torbet, p. 65.

12. Estep, p. 215, quoting J. DeHoop Scheffer, *History of the Free Churchmen*, p. 170.

13. H. Leon McBeth (1), *The Baptist Heritage. Four Centuries of Baptist Witness* (Nashville, Tenn: Broadman Press, 1987.), p. 38.

14. Torbet, p. 65.

15. Estep, p. 216.

16. Vedder, pp. 216-17.

17. Torbet, p. 66.

18. Estep, p. 215, quoting Scheffer, p. 170.

19. Estep, p. 216. A copy of this document is preserved in the Bodleian Library, London.

20. McBeth (1), p. 103, quoting Thomas Helwys, *The Mistery of Iniquity* (London, 1612), p. 40.

21. A reproduction of *The Mistery of Iniquity* is found in the New York Public Library.

22. Torbet, p. 67.

23. Torbet, pp. 67-68.

24. McBeth (1), p. 38.

25. Estep, p. 218, quoting W. J. McGlothlin, *Baptist Confessions of Faith*, pp. 91-92.

26. Estep, p. 218.

27. Torbet, pp. 66-67.

28. Estep, p. 215, quoting Scheffer, p. 170.

29. Estep, pp. 215-18.

30. Estep, p. 217, quoting *The Mistery of Iniquity*.

31. McBeth (1), pp. 60-61, quoting Morgan W. Patterson, *Baptist Successionism*, p. 14.

32. McBeth (1), p. 73.

33. McBeth (1), p. 70, quoting William L. Lumpkin, *Baptist Confessions of Faith*, p. 122.

34. McBeth (1), p. 80, quoting Lumpkin, p. 120.

35. McBeth (1), p. 80, quoting Lumpkin, p. 137.

55. Richard L. Greaves *et al.*, *Civilizations of the World* (New York: Harper and Row, 1990), p. 447.

56. McBeth (1), p. 73, quoting Lumpkin, p. 127.

57. McBeth (1), p. 73

58. McBeth (1), p. 73

59. McBeth (1), p. 84.

60. McBeth (1), p. 86, quoting *The Mistery of Iniquity*, p. 69.

Chapter 3 John Bunyan (1628-1688)

1. Ola Elizabeth Winslow (1), *John Bunyan* (New York: The MacMillan Company, 1961), pp. 4-8.

2. Winslow (1) , pp. 13-15.

3. Henry C. Vedder, *Short History of the Baptists* (Chicago: The American Baptist Publication Society, 1907), p. 232.

4. Winslow (1), pp. 26-30.

5. Winslow (1), pp. 33-35.

6. Winslow (1), pp. 37-39.

7. Winslow (1), pp. 40-42.

8. Edwin S. Gaustad (1), *Baptist Piety: The Last Will and Testament of Obadiah Holmes* (Valley Forge, Pa: Judson Press, 1994), p. 140.

9. Winslow (1), p. 48.

10. Winslow (1), p. 63.

11. H. Leon McBeth (1), *The Baptist Heritage. Four Centuries of Baptist Witness* (Nashville, Tenn: Broadman Press, 1987), p. 82.

12. Winslow (1), pp. 57-59.

13. Winslow (1), p. 131.

14. Winslow (1), p. 22.

15. Winslow (1), p. 47.

16. *Compton's Picture Encyclopedia* (Chicago: William Benton Pub., 1967), pp. 376-77.

17. Winslow (1), pp. 88-91.

18. Winslow (1), p. 93.

19. Winslow (1), p. 106.

20. Winslow (1), p. 111.

21. Vedder, p. 233.

22. *Compton's Pictured Encyclopedia*, pp. 376-77.

23. Vedder, p. 233.

24. *Compton's Pictured Encyclopedia*, p. 378.

25. Winslow (1), p. 68.

26. Winslow (1), p. 71.

27. Winslow (1), p. 115, quoting *The Church-Book of Bunyan Meeting, 1650-1821.*

28. Winslow (1), pp. 114-16.

29. Winslow (1), pp. 74-84.

30. Winslow (1), pp. 129-32.

31. Winslow (1), p. 133.

32. Vedder, p. 232.

33. McBeth (1), pp. 64-65.

34. Burton L. Mack, *The Lost Gospel* (New York: Harper Collins, 1993), pp. 32-33.

35. McBeth (1), p. 81.

36. McBeth (1), p. 82.

37. Winslow (1), p. 203.

38. McBeth (1), p. 82, quoting Sydnor L. Stealey, ed., *A Baptist Treasury*, p. 69.

39. Winslow (1), p. 132, quoting *Differences in Judgment about Water Baptism, Works*, I, p. 459.

40. Vedder, p. 263.

41. McBeth (1), p. 82, quoting Stealey, p. 80.
42. McBeth (1), pp. 82-83.
43. McBeth (1), p. 94.
44. Winslow (1), pp. 136-39.
45. Winslow (1), p. 141.
46. Winslow (1), pp. 159-64.
47. Winslow (1), pp. 166-66.
48. Winslow (1), p. 199, quoting *Works*, IV, pp. 466-468.
49. Winslow (1), p. 203.

Chapter 4 William Kiffin (1616-1701)

1. H. Leon McBeth (1), *The Baptist Heritage. Four Centuries of Baptist Witness* (Nashville, Tenn.: Broadman Press, 1987), p. 44-45.

2. Henry C. Vedder, *Short History of the Baptists* (Chicago: The American Baptist Publication Company, 1963), p. 213.

3. McBeth (1), p. 44.

4. Robert G. Torbet, *A History of the Baptists* (Chicago: The Judson Press, 1955), p. 77.

5. Vedder, p. 214.

6. Vedder, p. 214.

7. Torbet, p. 86, quoting William T. Whitley, *The Baptists of London*, p. 51.

8. McBeth (1), p. 22.

9. McBeth (1), p. 39.

10. McBeth (1), p. 31.

11. Vedder, p. 206.

12. McBeth (1), p. 44.

13. Vedder, p. 207.

14. McBeth (1), p. 46.

15. McBeth (1), pp. 64-65.

16. McBeth (1), p. 80.

17. McBeth (1), p. 22.

18. Torbet, p. 72.

19. Vedder, p. 211.

20. McBeth (1), p. 81.

21. McBeth (1), pp. 82-85, quoting Syndnor L. Stealey, ed., *A Baptist Treasury*, pp. 79-84.

22. Vedder, pp. 262-63.

23. Richard L. Greaves *et al.*, *Civilizations of the World* (New York: Harper and Row, 1990), pp. 48-49.

24. Vedder, p. 221.

25. Vedder, p. 221.

26. Torbet, p. 77.

27. McBeth (1), pp. 86-90.

28. Vedder, p. 221.

29. McBeth (1), pp. 67-68, 72-73.

30. Vedder, p. 224.

31. Vedder, p. 225.

32. Vedder, p. 223.

33. Vedder, p. 225.

34. McBeth (1), p. 89, quoting B. S. Capp, *The Fifth Monarchy Men in England*, p. 101.

35. McBeth (1), p. 89, quoting Capp, p. 116.

36. McBeth (1), p. 89.

37. Vedder, p. 234.

38. Vedder, p. 213.

39. Vedder, p. 212.

40. Edwin S. Gaustad (1), *Baptist Piety: The Last Will and Testament of Obadiah Holmes* (Valley Forge, Pa: Judson Press, 1994), 140.

Chapter 5 Roger Williams (c.1603-1683)

1. H. Leon McBeth (1), *The Baptist Heritage. Four Centuries of Baptist Witness* (Nashville, Tenn.: Broadman Press, 1987), p. 124.

2. Ola Elizabeth Winslow (2), *Master Roger Williams* (New York: The MacMillan Company, 1957), pp. 28-30.

3. William Cathcart, ed., *The Baptist Encyclopedia* (Philadelphia: Louis H. Everts, 1881), Vol. I, p. 503.

4. McBeth (1), p. 125.

5. Winslow (2), p. 75.

6. Winslow (2), pp. 81-87.

7. Winslow (2), p. 90.

8. Jeanette Eaton, *Lone Journey, The Life of Roger Williams* (New York: Harcourt, Brace and Company, 1944), pp. 63-65.

9. Eaton, p. 67.

10. Eaton, p. 72.

11. Winslow (2), p. 93, quoting a 1652 letter to Anne Sadleir, n. c. p., VI, p. 239.

12. Eaton, pp. 79-81.

13. Winslow (2), p. 97.

14. Eaton, p. 88.

15. Winslow (2), p. 102.

16. Winslow (2), p. 144.

17. Eaton, pp. 89-90.

18. Winslow (2), pp. 104-05.

19. Winslow (2), pp. 107-08.

20. Winslow (2), pp. 116-17.

21. Winslow (2), pp. 117-19.

22. Winslow (2), pp. 119-20, quoting Winthrop's *Journal*, I, p. 204.

23. Winslow (2), pp. 121-23.

24. Winslow (2), p. 127.

25. Eaton, pp. 119-20.

26. Eaton, p. 120.

27. Eaton, pp. 122-23.

28. Eaton, pp. 86-87.

29. Winslow (2), quoting Williams, as contained in *George Fox Digg'd*, n.c.p., V, p. 447.

30. Winslow (2), pp. 169-70, quoting Key, n.c.p., I, pp. 155-58.

31. Winslow (2), p. 148.

32. Winslow (2), pp. 150-52.

33. Winslow (2), p. 152.

34. McBeth (1), pp. 138-39.

35. Wilbur Nelson, *Dr. John Clarke* (Newport, R. I. : Ward's Printer's, 1963 [booklet]), pp. 14-15.

36. McBeth (1), p. 139.

37. McBeth (2), p. 131. Mrs. Scott was the sister of famed Antinomian Preacher Anne Hutchinson.

38. George Washington Paschal, *History of North Carolina Baptists* (Raleigh: The General Board, North Carolina Baptist State Convention, 1930), I, p. 41.

39. Henry C. Vedder, *Short History of the Baptists* (Chicago: The American Baptist Publication Company, 1963), p. 291.

40. Vedder, p. 291.

41. Winslow (2), p. 113.

42. Winslow (2), p. 175.

43. Paschal, p. 42.

44. Robert G. Torbet, *A History of the Baptists* (Chicago: The Judson Press, 1955), p. 220.

45. Vedder, p. 292. Also Justo L. Gonzalez, *The Story of Christianity,* Vol. 2: *The Reformation to the Present Day* (New York: Harper & Row, 1985), p. 225. Roger Williams, according to Gonzalez, would become far more radical, reaching the conclusions that the Scripture was to be understood in purely spiritual terms and that all churches were false.

46. Winslow (2), pp. 274–75.

47. Eaton, p. 250.

48. Winslow (2), p. 259.

49. Winslow (2), p. 242.

50. Eaton, p. 251.

51. McBeth (1), pp. 133–34.

52. Eaton, pp. 177–78.

53. Eaton, pp. 197–98.

54. Winslow (2), pp. 182–83.

55. Winslow (2), pp. 187–88.

56. Winslow (2), p. 232.

57. McBeth (1), p. 140.

58. Winslow (2), p. 232.

59. Eaton, p. 223.

60. Eaton, p. 227.

61. Winslow (2), p. 244.

62. Winslow (2), pp. 236–37.

63. McBeth (1), pp. 136–37.

64. Vedder, p. 290.

65. Torbet, pp. 221–22.

66. Eaton, p. 256.
67. Paschal, Vol. I, p. 41.
68. Winslow (2), p. 291.

Chapter 6 Isaac Backus (1724-1806)

1. William G. McLoughlin, *New England Dissent 1630-1833, The Baptists and The Separation of Church and State*, Vols. I&II (Cambridge, Massachusetts: Harvard University, 1971), p. 264.

2. H. Leon McBeth (1), *The Baptist Heritage. Four Centuries of Baptist Witness* (Nashville, Tenn.: Broadman Press, 1987), p. 259.

3. Isaac Backus, *Church History of New England From 1620 to 1804* (Philadelphia: American Baptist Publication and S. S. Society, 1804), p. 4.

4. Morgan Edwards, "Materials Towards A History of The Baptists in The Province of North Carolina," *The North Carolina Historical Review* (Raleigh, 1924), Vol. IV, MDCCLXXI, p. 371.

5. McBeth(1), p. 205.
6. McBeth(1), p. 203.
7. Backus, p. 5.

8. William Cathcart (ed.), *The Baptist Encyclopedia* (Philadelphia: Louis H. Everts, 1881), Vol. I. , pp. 52-53.

9. McBeth (1), p. 204.
10. McLoughlin, pp. 465-66.
11. McBeth (1), p. 205.
12. Cathcart, p. 53.
13. Backus, p. 16.
14. Backus, p. 15.
15. McBeth (1), p. 260.
16. Backus, p. 7.

17. Robert G. Torbet, *A History of the Baptists* (Chicago: The Judson Press, 1955), p. 253.

18. McBeth (1), p. 258.
19. Cathcart, Vol. I. , p. 53.
20. Morgan Edwards, p. 371.
21. McLoughlin, pp. 549-50.
22. McBeth (1), pp. 242-43.

23. David Benedict, *A General History of the Baptist Denomination in America and Other Parts of the World* (New York: Lewis Colby, 1848), p. 422.

24. McLoughlin, p. 456.

25. McBeth (1), pp. 258-59.

26. O. K. and Marjorie Armstrong, *The Baptists in America* (Garden City, New York: Doubleday, 1979), p. 94.

27. Armstrong, p. 95, quoting Backus, *A History of New England with Particular Reference to the Denomination of Christians Called Baptists*, Vol. II.

28. Armstrong, p. 95.

29. McLoughlin, p. 458, quoting Backus.

30. Backus, pp. 173-74.

31. Armstrong, p. 94.

32. Backus, pp. 174-75.

33. McBeth (1), p. 263, quoting Backus, 2:155.

34. McBeth (1), p. 263.

35. McLoughlin, pp. 550-54.

36. McLoughlin, p. 549.

37. Backus, p. 11.

38. Gary B. Nash *et al.*, *The American People* (New York: Harper & Row, 1986), p. 150.

39. Backus, p. 193.

40. McBeth (1), pp. 242-43.

41. Armstrong, pp. 98-99.

42. Backus, pp. 192-93.

43. Armstrong, pp. 99-100, quoting Backus.

44. Armstrong, p. 100.

45. Backus, p. 196.

46. Backus, p. 197.

47. Armstrong, p. 106.

48. Armstrong, p. 106.

49. Armstrong, pp. 93-94.

50. Backus, pp. 11-12.

51. McBeth (1), p. 259

52. Backus, pp. 11-12.

53. McBeth (1), p. 131.

54. McBeth (1), pp. 138-39.
55. McBeth (1), p. 214.
56. McBeth (1), pp. 242-43.
57. Backus, p. 14.
58. Armstrong, p. 107.
59. McBeth (1), pp. 260-61.
60. Armstrong, p. 108.
61. Armstrong, p. 109.
62. McLoughlin, p. 920.
63. McLoughlin, p. 774.
64. McBeth (1), p. 204.
65. McLoughlin, p. 438.
66. Garnett Ryland, *The Baptists of Virginia 1699-1926* (Richmond, Virginia: The Virginia Baptist Board of Missions and Education, 1955), p. 143.
67. Benedict, p. 688.
68. McBeth (1), pp. 223-24.
69. McLoughlin, p. 774.
70. McBeth (1), p. 260.
71. McLoughlin, p. 936.
72. McLoughlin, pp. 936-37.
73. McLoughlin, p. 932.

Chapter 7 Martha Stearns Marshall (c.1722-1793)

1. H. Leon McBeth (1), *The Baptist Heritage. Four Centuries of Baptist Witness* (Nashville, Tenn.: Broadman Press, 1987), pp. 143-44.
2. William G. McLoughlin, "New England Dissent 1630-1833)" in *The Baptists and the Separation of Church and State* (Cambridge, Massachusetts: Harvard University, 1971), Vol. I, pp. 436-39.
3. Georgia Harkness, *Women in Church and Society* (Nashville: Abingdon Press, 1972), p. 211.
4. Merrill C. Tenney, *The ZonderVan Pictorial Bible Dictionary* (Grand Rapids: Regency Reference Library, 1967), p. 210.
5. Harkness, p. 73, quoting the Syrian Didascalia Apostolorum.
6. McBeth(1), p. 77.

7. H. Leon McBeth (2), *Women in Baptist Life* (Nashville, Tenn.: Broadman Press, 1979), pp. 164-65.

8. McBeth (2), pp. 165-66.

9. McBeth (2), pp. 166-67.

10. Waldo Harris and James Mosteller claim that the best records show that Daniel Marshall was a Congregationalist before becoming a Baptist. Waldo P. Harris, III, and James D. Mosteller, *Georgia's First Continuing Baptist Church* (College Park, Ga.: N & R Printing , Inc., 1997), pp. 57-59).

11. David Benedict, *A General History of the Baptist Denomination in America and Other Parts of the World* (New York: Lewis Colby, 1848), p. 683.

12. Benedict, p. 684.

13. Benedict, p. 724.

14. Morgan Edwards, "Materials Toward a History of the Baptists in the Province of North Carolina" in *The North Carolina Historical Review* (Raleigh: North Carolina Historical Commission, 1924), Vol. IV, MDCCLXXI, p. 386.

15. Barbara R. Allen, "Early Baptist Women and their Contribution to Georgia Baptist History" in *Viewpoints: Georgia Baptist History* (Atlanta: Georgia Baptist Historical Society), Vol. 9, 1984, p. 34.

16. Edwards, p. 386.

17. Allen, p. 34.

18. Garnett Ryland, *The Baptists of Virginia 1699-1926* (Richmond, Virginia: The Virginia Baptist Board of Missions and Education, 1955), p. 38., quoting Paschal, p. 227.

19. Edwards, p. 226.

20. Ryland, p. 37.

21. Ryland, p. 37.

22. Robert G. Torbet, *A History of the Baptists* (Chicago: The Judson Press, 1955), p. 245.

23. George Washington Paschal, *History of North Carolina Baptists* (Raleigh: The General Board, North Carolina Baptist State Convention, 1930), Vol. II, p. 197.

24. Paschal, Vol. II. , p. 48.

25. Paschal, Vol. II, pp. 48-49.

26. Paschal, Vol. II, p. 64.

27. Paschal, Vol. I, p. 228. Shubal, not Shubael, is the correct name used by Stearns on petitions regarding the Regulators.

28. Paschal, Vol. II, pp. 46-47.

29. McBeth (1), p. 222.

30. Ryland, p. 58.

31. Edwards, p. 384.

32. McBeth(1), pp. 231-32.

33. Paschal, Vol. I, p. 289, quoting Semple, *Virginia Baptists*, p. 375.

34. Allen, in *Viewpoints: Georgia Baptist History*, Vol. 9 (1984), p. 34.

35. Benedict, p. 684.

36. Paschal, Vol. II, p. 179.

37. Paschal, Vol. II, p. 201.

38. Paschal, Vol. II, p. 203.

39. Paschal, Vol. II, p. 35.

40. Henry C. Vedder, *Short History of the Baptists* (Chicago: The American Baptist Publication Company, 1963), pp. 321-24.

41. Vedder, pp. 321-24.

42. Paschal, Vol. II, pp. 170-71.

43. Paschal, Vol. II, p. 196.

44. Paschal, Vol. II, pp. 125-28.

45. Edwards, pp. 290-91.

46. Ryland, pp. 42-43.

47. Edwards, p. 399.

48. Benedict, pp. 687-88.

49. Benedict, p. 684.

50. Benedict, p. 687. Also Torbet, p. 247.

51. Allen, in *Viewpoints: Georgia Baptist History*, Vol. 9 (1984), p. 34.

52. Paschal, Vol. II, p. 187.

53. Paschal, Vol. II, p. 80.

54. Paschal, Vol. I, p. 403.

55. Paschal, Vol. II, p. 188.

56. Paschal, Vol. I, p. 390.

57. Paschal, Vol. I, p. 393.

58. Torbet, p. 247.

59. Paschal, Vol. II, pp. 260-61.

60. McBeth (1), p. 71.

61. *Baptist Advance* (Nashville, Tenn.: Broadman Press, 1964), pp. 12-13.

62. Paschal, Vol. I, p. 291.

63. B. D. Ragsdale, *Story of Georgia Baptists* (Atlanta: The Executive Committee of the Georgia Baptist Convention, 1951), Vol. 3., p. 209.

64. Paschal, Vol. II, pp. 14-15, 17, 32.

65. Paschal, Vol. II, p. 180.

66. Paschal, Vol. II, p. 168.

67. Paschal, Vol. II, p. 181.

68. Paschal, Vol. II, p. 181.

69. Paschal, Vol. II, pp. 178-79.

70. Paschal, Vol. I, pp. 385-86.

71. Paschal, Vol. I, pp. 386-87.

72. Paschal, Vol. I, p. 388.

73. Vedder, p. 332. Also McBeth (1), p. 220.

74. Torbet, p. 260.

75. Edwards, p. 369.

76. Torbet (p. 240) says the location is Guilford (now Randolph) County.

77. Edwards, pp. 396-97.

78. Paschal, Vol. II, pp. 53-56.

79. Paschal, Vol. II, p. 7.

80. Edwards, p. 385.

81. Paschal, Vol. II, p. 163-65.

82. Paschal, Vol. II, p. 57.

83. Paschal, Vol. II, pp. 66-67, quoting Morgan Edwards.

84. Paschal, Vol. II, p. 67, quoting Dr. Hufham.

85. Paschal, pp. 384-85.

86. Paschal, Vol. I, p. 223.

87. McBeth (1), p. 228, quoting Morgan Edwards.

88. Benedict, pp. 724, 727-29.

89. James Adams Lester, *A History of the Georgia Baptist Convention 1822-1972* (Atlanta: Executive Committee, Baptist Convention of the State of Georgia, 1972), p. 19, quoting Henry Holcombe.

90. Lester, p. 19. Prominent among the first Baptists in Georgia were

the Seventh-Day Baptists, who organized a church in 1759 at Tuckaseeking Creek, about forty miles north of Savannah, and a second group of Baptists converted by Nicholas Bedgegood about 1763, at Bethesda Orphanage near Savannah. Robert G. Gardner, "Primary Sources in the Study of Eighteenth Century Georgia Baptist History," *Viewpoints: Georgia Baptist History*, Vol. VII (1980), pp. 61-83.

91. Waldo P. Harris, III, *Viewpoints: Georgia Baptist History*, Vol. V (1976), pp. 54-55.

92. Paschal, Vol. I, p. 389.

93. Paschal, II, pp. 121-23.

94. Paschal, II, p. 123.

95. Paschal, II, p. 123-24.

96. Paschal, Vol. II, p. 86.

97. Paschal, Vol. I, p. 384.

98. Allan R. Millett & Peter Maslowski, *For The Common Defense: A Military History of the United States of America* (New York: Macmillan, Inc., 1984), pp. 71, 74.

99. Paschal, Vol. II, p. 90.

100. Torbet, p. 247.

101. Paschal, Vol. II, pp. 339-41.

102. Paschal, Vol. II, pp. 174-76.

103. Charles W. Koller, "George Washington's Baptism" in *The Christian Index*, 15 February 1996.

104. R. Ernest DuPuy and Trevor N. DuPuy, *The Encyclopedia of Military History from 3500 B.C. to the Present* (New York: Harper & Row), pp. 719-20.

105. O.K. and Marjorie Armstrong, *The Baptists in America* (Garden City, New York: Doubleday & Company, Inc., 1979), pp. 104-05.

106. Paschal, Vol. I, pp. 389-90.

107. Benedict, p. 725.

108. Benedict, p. 728.

109. Allen, *Viewpoints: Georgia Baptist History*, Vol. 9 (1984), p. 35.

110. The dates given for the birth and death of this remarkable woman are theoretical. John Newton's *Diary* confirms that she was alive in 1790. The commemorative marker stone at the Marshall Cemetery near Kiokee

bears 1793 as the date of Martha's death. Waldo Harris presents a reasonable basis to believe that the fifty-acre portion of Daniel Marshall's estate, containing Daniel's house, would not be conveyed to Abraham Marshall on October 26, 1793. unless the widow Martha had recently died. Waldo Harris, "Locations Associated with Daniel Marshall and the Kiokee Church, *Viewpoints: Georgia Baptist History*, Vol. 6 (1978), pp. 26-27.

Chapter 8 John Leland (1754-1841)

1. Garnett Ryland, *The Baptists of Virginia 1699-1926* (Richmond, Virginia: The Virginia Baptist Board of Missions and Education, 1955), p. 141.

2. Joseph Martin Dawson, *Baptists and the American Republic* (Nashville, Tennessee: Broadman Press, 1956), p. 96.

3. H. Leon McBeth (1), *The Baptist Heritage: Four Centuries of Baptist Witness* (Nashville, Tennessee: Broadman Press, 1987), p. 273.

4. McBeth (1), p. 274, quoting L. F. Greene, *The Writings of John Leland*, p. 35.

5. O. K. and Marjorie Armstrong, *The Baptists in America* (Garden City, New York: Doubleday & Company, Inc., 1979), p. 5.

6. William Cathcart, ed., *The Baptist Encyclopedia* (Philadelphia: Louis H. Everts, 1881), Vol. II, p. 682.

7. William G. McLoughlin, *New England Dissent 1630-1833: The Baptists and the Separation of Church and State* (Cambridge, Massachusetts: Harvard University, 1971), Vol. II, p. 928.

8. McBeth (1), p. 274, quoting L. F. Green, ed., *The Writings of John Leland* (New York: Arno Press, 1969), p. 27.

9. Armstrong, p. 5.

10. Cathcart, Vol. II, p. 683.

11. Ryland, p. 141.

12. Cathcart, Vol. II, p. 683.

13. Ryland, p. 141, quoting *Writings of Leland*, p. 114.

14. McBeth (1), pp. 255-56.

15. McBeth (1), p. 268.

16. McBeth (1), p. 269.

17. Dawson, p. 84.

18. McBeth (1), p. 269.

19. Dawson, p. 99, quoting Padover, *The Complete Jefferson*, p. 674.

20. McBeth (1), p. 270, quoting Lewis P. Little.

21. McLoughlin, Vol. II, p. 929.

22. McBeth (1), p. 230.

23. McBeth (1), p. 441.

24. McBeth (1), p. 233.

25. Robert G. Torbet, *A History of the Baptists* (Philadelphia: The Judson Press, 1955), pp. 82-84.

26. Torbet, pp. 258-59.

27. Torbet, p. 259.

28. Ryland, p. 92.

29. Ryland, p. 94, quoting letter of James Madison to William Bradford, Jr.

30. Ryland, p. 95.

31. Ryland, pp. 122-23.

32. McBeth (1), p. 276, quoting Semple, p. 493.

33. McBeth (1), p. 276, quoting Semple, p. 493.

34. McBeth (1), pp. 276-77.

35. McBeth (1), p. 277, quoting Semple, pp. 497-499.

36. Dawson, p. 95, quoting L. F. Greene, ed., *The Writings of John Leland, Including Some Events in His Life, Written by Himself,* p. 10.

37. Dawson, pp. 95-96.

38. McLoughlin, pp. 931-32.

39. Dawson, pp. 96-97.

40. Henry S. Burrage, *Baptist Hymn Writers and Their Hymns* (Portland, Maine: Brown Thurston & Company, 1888), p. 250.

41. McBeth (1), p. 274, quoting L. F. Greene, ed., pp. 179-92.

42. McBeth (1), p. 274.

43. McBeth (1), p. 274-75.

44. Richard L. Greaves *et al., Civilizations of the World* (New York: Harper & Row, 1990), p. 382.

45. McBeth (1), p. 275, quoting L. F. Greene, ed., *The Writings of John Leland* (New York: Arno Press, 1969), p. 184.

46. McBeth (1), p. 275, quoting Greene, p. 185.

47. McBeth (1), p. 275.

48. McBeth (1), p. 278.

49. McBeth (1), p. 278, quoting Semple, p. 96

50. McBeth (1), p. 279.

51. McBeth (1), p. 279, quoting Reuben E. Alley, *A History of Virginia*, pp. 372-73.

52. Armstrong, pp. 10-11.

53. *Compton's Pictured Encyclopedia* (Chicago: William Benton, Publisher, 1967), p. 488.

54. Armstrong, p. 1.

55. Armstrong, p. 9.

56. Armstrong, pp. 9-10.

57. Armstrong, p. 3.

58. McBeth (1), p. 280, quoting Dawson, p. 117.

59. McBeth (1), p. 281, quoting Dawson, p. 117.

60. McBeth (1), p. 281, quoting Dawson, p. 117.

61. Dawson, pp. 107-08.

62. Dawson, p. 109.

63. Dawson, p. 110, quoting from Madison Papers, Library of Congress.

64. Armstrong, pp. 4, 15.

65. Ryland, p. 102.

66. Dawson, pp. 110-11.

67. Ryland, p. 134.

68. Ryland, p. 134.

69. Dawson, p. 120.

70. Torbet, p. 299.

71. Dawson, p. 121.

72. Dawson, p. 121.

73. Dawson, pp. 162-63. Also Gary B. Nash *et al.*, *The American People* (New York: Harper & Row, 1986), 329, 473.

74. Dawson, pp. 167-68.

75. Dawson, p. 134.

76. McLoughlin, Vol. II, p. 928.

77. Dawson, pp. 123-25.

78. McLoughlin, Vol. II, p. 932.

79. McLoughlin, Vol. II, p. 930.

80. McBeth (1), p. 82, quoting Stealey, p. 80.

81. McBeth (1), p. 274.

82. McLoughlin, Vol. II, p. 928

83. Dawson, p. 31.

84. David Benedict, *A General History of the Baptist Denomination in America and Other Parts of the World* (New York: Lewis Colby, 1848), p. 259.

85. Wesley L. Forbis, ed., *Handbook To The Baptist Hymnal* (Nashville Convention Press, 1992), p. 39.

86. Forbis, ed., p. 39

87. McLoughlin, Vol. II, p. 928.

88. Armstrong, p. 107.

89. McLoughlin, Vol. II, pp. 698-99, quoting Isaac Backus.

90. McLoughlin, Vol. II, pp. 1068-69 and 1279.

91. McLoughlin, Vol. I, p. 625, quoting *Boston Gazette*, March 8, 1779.

92. McLoughlin, Vol. II., p. 1066.

93. Leah Townsend, *South Carolina Baptists 1670-1805* (Baltimore: Genealogical Publishing Company, Inc., 1978), pp. 176-78.

94. Loulie Latimer Owens, *Saints of Clay. The Shaping of South Carolina Baptists* (Columbia, South Carolina: R. L. Bryan Company, 1971), p. 52.

95. Ryland, p. 98, quoting an address by John S. Barbour.

96. McLoughlin, Vol. II, p. 1066.

97. McLoughlin, Vol. II, p. 1067.

98. Dawson, pp. 125-26.

99. Dawson, p. 129, quoting Hudson, *The Great Tradition of the American Churches*, p. 63-65.

100. Dawson, p. 132.

101. Dawson, p. 132, quoting S. E. Morrison, Massachusetts Historical Society, *Proceedings*, L (1917), 397.

102. Dawson, p. 133, quoting Leland, *Writings*, 233-55.

103. Dawson, pp. 133-34.

104. Dawson, p. 134.

105. Dawson, p. 135.

106. Dawson, p. 136, quoting *Writings*, pp. 651-56.

107. Dawson, p. 136.

108. Dawson, p. 95.

109. McLoughlin, Vol. II, p. 930.

Chapter 9 George Leile and the Black Church (c.1750-1815)

1. James M. Simms, *The First Colored Baptist Church in North America* (Philadelphia: J.B. Lippencott Co., 1888. Reprinted by Negro Universities Press, 1969), p. 14.

2. David Benedict, *A General History of the Baptist Denomination in America and Other Parts of the World* (New York: Lewis Colby, 1848), p. 740.

3. *The First African Baptist Church. Souvenir Journal* (Savannah, 1988), p. 29.

4. H. Leon McBeth (1), *The Baptist Heritage. Four Centuries of Baptist Witness* (Nashville, Tennessee: Broadman Press, 1987), p. 779.

5. Andrew Billingsley, *Mighty Like a River* (Oxford: Oxford University Press, 1999), p. 13.

6. Charles O. Walker, "Georgia's Religion in the Colonial Era, 1733-1790" in *Viewpoints: Georgia Baptist History* (Atlanta, Georgia: Baptist Historical Society), Vol. V (1976), p. 33.

7. Walker, *Viewpoints*, Vol. V (1976), p. 33.

8. Robert G. Gardner *et al.* (2), *A History of the Georgia Baptist Association 1784-1984*, Part I (Atlanta: Georgia Baptist Historical Society, 1988), pp. 15-16.

9. Gardner (2), p. 16.

10. Gardner (2), p. 16.

11. Leah Townsend, *South Carolina Baptists 1670-1805* (Baltimore: Genealogical Publishing Co., Inc., 1978), p. 256.

12. David C. Wooley, ed., *Baptist Advance* (Nashville: Broadman Press, 1964), quoting William E. Hatcher, p. 195.

13. William G. McLoughlin, *New England Dissent 1630-1833: The Baptists and The Separation of Church and State* (Cambridge, Massachusetts: Harvard University, 1971), Vol.II, pp. 1069, 1071.

14. Garnett Ryland, *The Baptists of Virginia 1699-1926* (Richmond, Virginia: The Virginia Baptist Board of Missions and Education, 1955), p. 155.

15. Townsend, p. 258.

16. Townsend, p. 257.

17. Townsend, p. 257.

18. Townsend, pp. 256-57.

19. McBeth (1), p. 778.

20. Townsend, pp. 259-60.

21. Gardner (2), pp. 12-13. Also Walker, *Viewpoints*, Vol. 5 (1976), p. 29.

22. Gardner (2), p. 13.

23. McBeth (1), p. 224.

24. Gardner (2), pp. 13-14.

25. Gardner (2), p. 15.

26. Townsend, p. 180.

27. Gardner (2), p. 17

28. *Souvenir Journal*, p. 28.

29. Gardner (2), p. 17.

30. Gardner (2), p. 17

31. Gardner (2), pp. 17-18.

32. Gardner (2), p. 18.

33. Gardner (2), pp. 18-19.

34. E. K. Love, *History of the First African Baptist Church From Its Organization* (Savannah, Georgia: The Morning News Print, 1888. Reprinted 1968.), pp. 35-36.

35. Love, p. 35.

36. Love, p. 36.

37. Gardner (2), p. 16

38. Billingsley, 15.

39. Simms, p. 14.

40. Simms, p. 15. Also Walker, *Viewpoints*, Vol. 5 (1976), p. 34.

41. Wanda Yancey (pamphlet), "Religion and Community. In Savannah, First African Baptist Church Means First" (August 1989; Main Library, Savannah, Georgia).

42. Billingsley, p. 15.

43. Simms, p. 15. Also E.K. Love, p. 34.

44. Billingsley, 15.

45. *Baptist Advance*, p. 194.

46. Simms, p. 15. Also see Walker, *Viewpoints*, Vol. 5 (1976), p. 39.

47. Simms, p. 15.

48. Yancey (pamphlet).

49. Simms, pp. 20 and 51.

50. Love, p. 31. Also Simms, p. 98.

51. Julia Floyd Smith, "Marching to Zion: The Religion of Black Baptists in Coastal Georgia prior to 1865" in *Viewpoints: Georgia Baptist History*, Vol. VI (1978), p. 48.

52. _____ (pamphlet, no author or date), "Past Will Live Again in Pilgrimage" (Main Library, Savannah).

53. Simms, p. 30.

54. Ryland, pp. 155-56.

55. Ryland, pp. 156-57.

56. Billingsley, p. 16.

57. Gardner (2), p. 27.

58. Simms, pp. 44-45.

59. Simms, pp. 35, 42-44.

60. Simms, pp. 38-39.

61. Gary B. Nash, *et al.*, *The American People* (New York: Harper & Row, 1986), p. 396.

62. Simms, p. 63-64.

63. Simms, p. 18.

64. Simms, p. 19.

65. Simms, p. 18.

66. Billingsley, p. 16. Also Simms, p. 21.

67. Simms, p. 21.

68. Simms, p. 22.

69. Yancey.

70. Simms, pp. 22-23.

71. *Souvenir Journal.*

72. Yancey.

73. Simms, p. 51.

74. Simms, pp. 46-47.

75. Simms, pp. 24-25.

76. Simms, pp. 24-25.

77. McBeth (1), pp. 780-81.

78. Simms, p. 39.

79. *Souvenir Journal.* Also Simms, p. 236.

80. Simms, p. 235.

81. Love, pp. 3-5.

82. Simms, p. 25.

83. Robert G. Torbet, *A History of the Baptists* (Philadelphia: The Judson Press, 1955), pp. 287-92. While Campbell may have correctly stressed that slaves and free persons were equal in the sight of God, his other doctrines posed a serious danger to the work of Missionary Baptists.

84. Simms, pp. 98-99, 108, 128.

85. Simms, pp. 106-07, 120.

86. Simms, pp. 68-69.

87. Simms, pp. 66, 70.

88. Simms, pp. 67-68.

89. Simms, p. 67.

90. *Savannah Morning News*, July 28, 1975. Also Simms, p. 71.

91. David Benedict, *A General History of the Baptist Denomination* (New York: Lewis Colby, 1848), p. 739.

92. Simms, p. 71.

93. Simms, pp. 74-75.

94. Whittington B. Johnson, "Andrew C. Marshall: A Black Religious Leader of Antebellum Savannah," in *The Georgia Historical Quarterly*, Vol. LXIX (Summer 1985), No. 2, pp. 172, 178.

95. Simms, pp. 82-83.

96. Love, pp. 8, 10.

97. Smith, p. 50.

98. Smith, p. 50.

99. Simms, p. 118.

100. Johnson, p. 182.

101. Love, p. 34.

102. *Baptist Advance* (1964), p. 194.

103. Love, p. 37.

104. Love, pp. 35-36.

105. *Baptist Advance* (1964), p. 194.

106. *Baptist Advance* (1964), p. 194.

107. *Baptist Advance* (1964), p. 194.

108. Love, p. 36.

109. Love, pp. 34-35.

110. Love, p. 35.

111. Simms, p. 100.

112. Yancey.

113. *Baptist Advance* (1964), p. 194.

Chapter 10 William Carey (1761-1834)

1. J. M. Roberts, *History of the World* (New York: Alfred A. Knopf, 1976), pp. 384-09.

2. H. Leon McBeth (1), *The Baptist Heritage: Four Centuries of Baptist Witness* (Nashville: Broadman Press, 1987), p. 781.

3. McBeth (1), p. 152.

4. McBeth (1), p. 153, quoting J.M.G. Owen, ed., *Records of an Old Association*, p. 37.

5. McBeth (1), pp. 172-73.

6. William Henry Brackney (2), *The Baptists* (New York: Greenwood Press, 1988), pp. 168-69. Also McBeth (1), pp. 152-82.

7. P. D. Kingdon *et al.*, *Baptist Heritage and Responsibility* (Mulhouse, France: Fellowship of Evangelical Churches in Europe, 1970), Vol. IV, p. 3.

8. Kingdon, Vol. IV, p. 4.

9. McBeth (1), p. 184.

10. Kingdon, Vol. IV, p. 3.

11. John Allen Moore, *Baptist Mission Portraits* (Macon, Georgia: Smyth & Helwys Publishing, Inc., 1994), p. 5.

12. McBeth (1), p. 184.

13. Moore, pp. 4, 6.

14. Kingdon, Vol. IV, p. 2.

15. Kingdon, Vol. IV, pp. 3, 4, 15.

16. Kingdon, Vol. IV, p. 2.

17. McBeth (1), p. 185.

18. Kingdon, Vol. IV, p. 5.

19. Moore, p. 4.

20. Kingdon, Vol. IV, p. 4. Also Moore, p. 7.

21. McBeth (1), p. 179.

22. McBeth (1), p. 179.

23. McBeth (1), p. 180.

24. Kingdon, Vol. IV, p. 5. Also McBeth (1), p. 185.

25. Moore, p. 7.

26. Kingdon, Vol. IV, p. 6.

27. Moore, p. 6.

28. McBeth (1), p. 185.

29. Kingdon, Vol. IV, p. 7.

30. Moore, p. 10.

31. McBeth (2), p. 185.

32. Kingdon, Vol. IV, pp. 8-9.

33. William L. Langer, *An Encyclopedia of World History* (Boston: Houghton Mifflin Company, 1948), p. 452.

34. Moore, p. 13.

35. Moore, p. 14.

36. Moore, p. 15.

37. Moore, p. 15.

38. Moore, p. 16.

39. Moore, p. 16.

40. Kingdon, Vol. IX, p. 10.

41. Moore, p. 17.

42. Moore, p. 17.

43. Kingdon, Vol. IV, p. 9.

44. Lawrence Holiday Harris, "India: A Study of National Integration" (Ph.D dissertation, University of Santo Tomas, Manila, 1970), pp. 48-52.

45. Kingdon, Vol. IV, p. 13; also McBeth (1), p. 186.

46. Langer, p. 535.

47. Kingdon, Vol. IV, p. 9.

48. Moore, p. 23.

49. Lawrence Holiday Harris, p. 54.

50. Moore, p. 21.

51. Moore, pp. 24-25.

52. Moore, p. 25.

53. Kingdon, Vol. IX, p. 10.

54. Moore, p. 25.

55. Moore, p. 22.

56. Kingdon, Vol. IV, p. 11.

57. Moore, p. 27.

58. Kingdon, Vol. IV, p. 12.

59. Moore, p. 25.

60. Moore, p. 26.

61. Kingdon, Vol. IX, p. 10.

62. Moore, p. 28.

63. Kingdon, Vol. IV, p. 11.

64. Kingdon, Vol. IV, p. 15.

65. Moore, p. 27.

66. Moore, p. 29.

67. Moore, p. 30.

68. Moore, pp. 30-31, 35.

69. Kingdon, Vol. IV, p. 12.

70. Moore, p. 31. Also Kingdon, Vol. IV, p. 12.

71. Kingdon, Vol. IV, p. 12.

72. Kingdon, Vol. IV, pp. 12-13.

73. Moore, p. 28.

74. Moore, pp. 32-33.

75. Kingdon, Vol. IV, p. 14.

76. Moore, p. 33.

77. Moore, p. 33.

78. Kingdon, Vol. IV, p. 14.

79. Moore, p. 33.

80. Kingdon, Vol. IV, p. 14.

81. Moore, p. 36.

82. Moore, pp. 37-38.

83. Kingdon, Vol. IV, p. 13.

84. Moore, pp. 34-35.

85. Kingdon, Vol. IV, p. 17.

86. Moore, pp. 40-41.

87. Moore, p. 41.

88. *Compton's Pictured Encyclopedia* (Chicago: William Benton, Publisher, 1967), Vol. VII, pp. 223-24.

89. Kingdon, Vol. IV, p. 15.

90. Moore, p. 40.

91. Kingdon, Vol. IV, p. 17.

Chapter 11 Luther Rice (1783-1836)

1. Robert G. Torbet, *A History of the Baptists* (Philadelphia: The Judson Press, 1955), pp. 332, 346.

2. Rufus W. Weaver, "The Place of Luther Rice in American Baptist Life," in *The Review and Expositor*, XXXIII, No. 2 (April 1936), pp. 121-122.

3. Weaver, pp. 131-32.

4. Evelyn Wingo Thompson, *Luther Rice: Believer in Tomorrow* (Nashville: Broadman Press, 1967), pp. 122-23.

5. Weaver, pp. 132-33.

6. Weaver, pp. 133-34.

7. William H. Brackney (1) (ed.), *Dispensations of Providence: The Journal and Selected Letters of Luther Rice* (Barre, Vermont: American Baptist Historical Society, 1984), pp. 1-2

8. Brackney (1), pp. 6, 13

9. Brackney (1), pp. 2, 27, 29.

10. Brackney (1), pp. 18, 26-27.

11. Brackney (1).

12. Brackney (1), pp. 1-3, 6.

13. Brackney (1), p. 3.

14. Brackney (1), pp. 2, 23-24, 33.

15. Brackney (1), pp. 2, 35.

16. Brackney (1), p. 29.

17. Brackney (1), p. 29.

18. H. Leon McBeth (1), *The Baptist Heritage* (Nashville: Broadman Press, 1987), p. 345, quoting Evelyn Wingo Thompson.

19. Thompson, pp. 40-41.

20. Thompson, p. 123.

21. McBeth (1), p. 345, quoting Claudius Buchanan.

22. McBeth (1), p. 345, quoting Evelyn Wingo Thompson.

23. McBeth (1), p. 345.

24. Brackney (1), p. 44.

25. Brackney (1), p. 44. Also Moore, p. 114.

26. Thompson, p. 59.

27. Thompson, p. 52.

28. Brackney (1), pp. 40, 41, 44.

29. Brackney (1), pp. 44-45.
30. Brackney (1), pp. 46-47.
31. Brackney (1), pp. 40-41.
32. Brackney (1), p. 74.
33. Thompson, p. 124.
34. Brackney (1), pp. 41-42.
35. Brackney (1), pp. 42-43.
36. Thompson, p. 122.
37. Thompson, p. 123.
38. Brackney (1), p. 75.
39. Thompson, p. 129.
40. Brackney (1), p. 43.
41. Brackney (1), pp. 43-44.
42. Brackney (1), p. 77. Also Thompson, p. 83.
43. Weaver, pp. 129-30.
44. Brackney (1), pp. 77-78.
45. Weaver, p. 135.
46. Weaver, pp. 129-30.
47. Weaver, pp. 129-30, 135-36.
48. Weaver, p. 136.
49. Brackney (1), p. 135.
50. McBeth (1), p. 352.
51. McBeth (1), p. 352, quoting Ann Judson, *Letter to Parents*, July 30, 1813.
52. Charles O. Walker *et al.*, "Historical Listing of Baptist Associations in Georgia, 1784 to 1994," in *Viewpoints: Georgia Baptist History*, Vol. 14 (1994), pp. 24-25.
53. Walter B. Shurden, *Not a Silent People: Controversies that Have Shaped Southern Baptists* (Nashville, Tenn.: Broadman Press, 1972), pp. 44-45.
54. Thompson, pp. 158-60.
55. Thompson, p. 161, quoting Babcock, p. 111.
56. Weaver, p. 137.
57. Brackney (1), pp. 77-78.
58. Shurden, p. 37.
59. McBeth (1), p. 318.
60. Shurden, p. 36.

61. McBeth (1), p. 350.
62. Brackney (1), p. 137.
63. Thompson, p. 103.
64. McBeth (1), p. 531.
65. Brackney (1), p. 80-81; also *Baptist Advance*, p. 13.
66. Thompson, p. 150.
67. Brackney (1), p. 81.
68. Thompson, p. 139.
69. Thompson, p. 138.
70. Shurden, p. 43, quoting Robert A. Baker, *A Baptist Source Book*, p. 80.
71. Brackney (1), pp. 83-115.
72. Brackney (1), pp. 78-80.
73. Brackney (1), p. 120.
74. Thompson, pp. 104-05.
75. Thompson, pp. 104-05, 108.
76. Brackney (1), pp. 149, 156.
77. Thompson, pp. 162-64.
78. Thompson, pp. 164-65.
79. Thompson, pp. 102-03.
80. Thompson, pp. 101-03. Also Brackney (1), p. 78.
81. Dawson, p. 201.
82. McBeth (1), pp. 353-54.
83. Thompson, p. 110.
84. Thompson, p. 110.
85. *The Christian Index*, Vol. 175, February 22, 1996.
86. Weaver, p. 139.
87. Thompson, p. 167.
88. Thompson, p. 172. Also McBeth (1), p. 362.
89. Thompson, pp. 110-11.
90. Weaver, pp. 138-39.
91. Thompson, pp. 111-12.
92. Thompson, p. 144.
93. Thompson, pp. 142-44.
94. Thompson, pp. 142-44.
95. Thompson, pp. 115-16.

96. Thompson, p. 118.

97. Brackney (1), pp. 79, 134.

98. McBeth (1), p. 355, quoting Thompson, p. 117.

99. Thompson, pp. 117-18, 121.

100. McBeth (1), p. 355.

101. Weaver, p. 141.

102. Thompson, p. 120, quoting the *Second Triennial Convention Report*.

103. Brackney (1), p. 151.

104. Thompson, p. 162.

105. Thompson, pp. 119, 120-22.

106. Thompson, p. 118.

107. Thompson, pp. 149-50, quoting Edward Kingsford, *The Baptist Banner and Pioneer*, February 16, 1841.

108. Thompson, pp. 161-62.

109. Torbet, p. 326.

110. Thompson, pp. 173-74.

111. Brackney (1), p. 79.

112. Brackney (1), p. 79.

113. Brackney (1), p. 79.

114. Thompson, pp. 168-69.

115. Thompson, p. 168.

116. Weaver, pp. 138-39.

117. Thompson, pp. 156-57.

118. Thompson, pp. 152-58.

119. Weaver, pp. 141-42.

120. Torbet, p. 270.

121. Weaver, p. 142.

122. Torbet, pp. 350-51.

123. McBeth (1), p. 359, quoting Winthrop S. Hudson.

124. Weaver, pp. 141-42.

125. Brackney (1), p. 80.

126. Thompson, pp. 165-66.

127. McBeth (1), p. 357.

128. McBeth (1), p. 358, quoting the Annual Report, Triennial Convention (1826), p. 20.

129. McBeth (1), p. 360.
130. Weaver, p. 143.
131. Brackney (1), p. 133.
132. McBeth (1), p. 356.
133. McBeth (1), p. 357.
134. McBeth (1), pp. 360-61.
135. McBeth (1), pp. 360-61.
136. McBeth (1), pp. 359-60.
137. Weaver, pp. 143-44.
138. Brackney (1), p. 80.
139. McBeth (1),m p. 360.
140. Thompson, p. 151.
141. Thompson, pp. 148-49.

Chapter 12 Johann Gerhard Oncken (1800-1884)

1. H. Leon McBeth (1), *The Baptist Heritage* (Nashville: Broadman Press, 1987), pp. 474-76.

2. J. H. Rushbrooke, *The Baptist Movement in the Continent of Europe* (London: Kingsgate Press, n.d.), pp. 18-19.

3. R. Ernest Depuy and Trevor N. Depuy, *The Encyclopedia of Military History* (New York: Harper & Row, 1986), p. 761.

4. Rushbrooke, *Baptist Movement*, pp. 18-19. Also Henry C. Vedder, *Short History of the Baptists* (Chicago: The American Baptist Publication Society, 1963), pp. 396-97.

5. David Benedict, *A General History of the Baptist Denomination in America and Other Parts of the World* (New York: Lewis Colby, 1848), p. 362.

6. Rushbrooke, *Baptist Movement*, pp. 19-20.

7. Rushbrooke, *Baptist Movement*, pp. 19-20.

8. Henry C. Vedder, *Short History of the Baptists* (Chicago: The American Baptist Publication Company, 1963), pp. 396-97.

9. Rushbrooke, *Baptist Movement*, p. 20.

10. Vedder, p. 396.

11. Rushbrooke, *Baptist Movement*, pp. 20-21.

12. Vedder, 397, quoting from Oncken's tract, "Triumphs of the Gospel," published at Hamburg, no date.

13. _____, *Centennial Story of Texas Baptists* (Dallas: Baptist General Convention of Texas, 1936), pp. 162-63. Also Vedder, pp. 397-398.

14. Benedict, pp. 360-361.

15. Vedder, p. 397, quoting from "Triumphs of the Gospel."

16. Vedder, p. 274. Also Rushbrooke, *Baptist Movement*, pp. 21-22.

17. Vedder, pp. 397-98. Also Rushbrooke, *Baptist Movement*, pp. 21-22.

18. Rushbrooke, *Baptist Movement*, pp. 22-23.

19. Benedict, pp. 360-61. Also Rushbrooke, *Baptist Movement*, p. 26.

20. Benedict, p. 361.

21. Rushbrooke, *Baptist Movement*, pp. 23-24.

22. Rushbrooke, *Baptist Movement*, pp. 24-25.

23. Vedder, pp. 398-99.

24. Benedict, p. 361.

25. Rushbrooke, *Baptist Movement*, p. 25.

26. Rushbrooke, *Baptist Movement*, p. 31.

27. Rushbrooke, *Baptist Movement*, pp. 32-33.

28. Rushbrooke, *Baptist Movement*, pp. 24-25.

29. Rushbrooke, *Baptist Movement*, pp. 28-29.

30. J.H. Rushbrooke, *Some Chapters of European Baptist History* (London: Kingsgate Press, 1929), pp. 18-19.

31. Rushbrooke, *Baptist Movement*, pp. 28-29.

32. Rushbrooke, *Baptist Movement*, pp. 29-30.

33. Benedict, p. 362.

34. Rushbrooke, *Some Chapters*, pp. 18-19. Also Vedder, p. 362.

35. Rushbrooke, *Baptist Movement*, pp. 30-31.

36. Rushbrooke, *Some Chapters*, pp. 17-18.

37. Rushbrooke, *Baptist Movement*, pp. 76-77. Also Vedder, pp. 404-05.

38. Rushbrooke, *Baptist Movement*, pp. 76-77

39. Vedder, pp. 404-05.

40. Rushbrooke, *Baptist Movement*, pp. 78-80.

41. Rushbrooke, *Baptist Movement*, pp. 36-37.

42. Rushbrooke, *Baptist Movement*, p. 36.

43. Vedder, pp. 400-01.

44. Vedder, pp. 400-01. Also Rushbrooke *Baptist Movement*, pp. 86-87, and Rushbrooke, *Some Chapters*, p. 20.

45. Rushbrooke, *Baptist Movement*, p. 87.

46. Vedder, p. 401.

47. Vedder, 402. Also Rushbrooke, *Baptist Movement*, 88.

48. Vedder, pp. 403-04.

49. Rushbrooke, *Baptist Movement*, pp. 32-33.

50. Vedder, pp. 398-99.

51. Rushbrooke, pp. 34-35.

52. Rushbrooke, *Baptist Movement*, pp. 33-34. Also Vedder, pp. 398-99.

53. Rushbrooke, *Baptist Movement*, pp. 37-38.

54. Rushbrooke, *Baptist Movement*, pp. 39-41.

55. Rushbrooke, *Baptist Movement*, 35.

56. Rushbrooke, *Baptist Movement*, pp. 35-36.

57. Klibanov, *Religious Sectarianism in Russia*, pp. 260-61.

58. Vedder, pp. 398-99.

59. Rushbrooke, *Baptist Movement*, p. 43.

60. Rushbrooke, *Baptist Movement*, pp. 43-44.

61. Vedder, 398.

62. Rushbrooke, *Baptist Movement*, pp. 32-33.

63. Rushbrooke, *Baptist Movement*, 42.

64. Rushbrooke, *pp. Some Chapters*, 72-74.

65. William F. Langer, *An Encyclopedia of World History* (Boston: Houghton Mifflin Company, 1948), p. 1042.

66. Rushbrooke, *Some Chapters*, pp. 58-59.

67. Rushbrooke, *Some Chapters*, pp. 60-61.

68. Rushbrooke, *Baptist Movement*, pp. 54-55.

69. Rushbrooke, *Baptist Movement*, pp. 55-56.

70. Rushbrooke, *Baptist Movement*, p. 57.

71. Rushbrooke, *Baptist Movement*, pp. 48-49.

72. Rushbrooke, *Baptist Movement*, pp. 49-50.

73. Rushbrooke, *Baptist Movement*, pp. 50-52. According to Rushbrooke, twenty thousand Anabaptists were put to death by the Austrians in the sixteenth century.

74. Rushbrooke, *Baptist Movement*, pp. 148-49, quoting Lehmann, Part I, pp. 210-14.

75. Rushbrooke, *Baptist Movement*, pp. 149-50.

76. Rushbrooke, *Baptist Movement*, pp. 154-55.

77. Rushbrooke, *Baptist Movement*, pp. 157-58.

78. McBeth (1), 470.

79. Vedder, pp. 399-400.

80. Ernest A. Payne, *Out of Great Tribulation: Baptists In the U.S.S.R.* (London: The Garden City Press Ltd., 1974), pp. 13-14.

81. A. I. Klibanov, *History of Religious Sectarianism in Russia (1860s-1917)* (Oxford: Pergamon Press, 1982), p. 250.

82. A. I. Klibanov, "The Dissident Denominations In The Past And Today," *Sovremenoe Sektansvo, Voprosy istorii Religii ateizma*, No. IX (1961), p. 57.

83. William A. Mueller, "Baptist Theological Thought," *Baptist Advance* (Nashville: Broadman Press, 1964), p. 450.

84. McBeth (1), p. 476.

Chapter 13 Vasili Gurevich Pavlov (1854-1924)

1. A. I. Klibanov, *History of Religious Sectarianism in Russia (1860s-1917)* (Oxford: Pergamon Press, 1982), p. 234.

2. Michael Bourdeaux (1), *Religious Ferment In Russia* (New York: St. Martin's Press, 1968), p. X; Bourdeaux reports date as September 1, 1867; Rushbrooke records it as August 20, 1867.

3. H. Leon McBeth (1), *The Baptist Heritage* (Nashville: Broadman Press, 1987), p. 490.

4. Klibanov, p. 234.

5. Klibanov, pp. 260-61. Also J. H. Rushbrooke, *The Baptist Movement in the Continent of Europe* (London: Kingsgate Press, 1923), p. 134.

6. McBeth (1), pp. 490-93.

7. Klibanov, p. 75.

8. Klibanov, p. 77.

9. Klibanov, pp. 88, 102.

10. William F. Langer, *An Encyclopedia of World History* (Boston: Houghton Mifflin Company, 1948), p. 704.

11. Klibanov, pp. 62-65.

12. Klibanov, pp. 64, 79, 106, 152.
13. Klibanov, p. 106.
14. Klibanov, pp. 105, 155.
15. Langer, p. 481. Also Klibanov, p. 148.
16. Klibanov, pp. 106-07.
17. Klibanov, pp. 107-08.
18. Klibanov, p. 110.
19. Klibanov, p. 109.
20. Klibanov, p. 119.
21. Klibanov, pp. 116-17, 124.
22. Klibanov, pp. 120-22.
23. Klibanov, pp. 124-25, 166-67.
24. L. A. Tultseva, "The Evolution of Old Russian Sectarianism," *Soviet Sociology*, Vol. 16 (1978?), Ormonk, N.Y., pp. 24-25.
25. Klibanov, pp. 64, 106.
26. Klibanov, "The Dissident Denominations In The Past and Today," *Sovremenoe Sektansvo, Voprosy Istorii Religii, Ateizma*, No. IX (1961), p. 48.
27. J. H. Rushbrooke, *Some Chapters of European Baptist History* (London: Kingsgate Press, 1929), p. 83.
28. Klibanov, pp. 48, 65.
29. Klibanov, p. 153.
30. Klibanov, pp. 106, 152-53.
31. Klibanov, p. 124.
32. Klibanov, pp. 160-63.
33. Klibanov, p. 249.
34. Klibanov, p. 158.
35. Klibanov, p. 182.
36. Klibanov, pp. 158-59.
37. Klibanov, pp. 198, 203-08.
38. Klibanov, p. 209.
39. Klibanov, p. 162.
40. Klibanov, p. 165.
41. Klibanov, p. 157.
42. Klibanov, pp. 159, 181-84.
43. Klibanov, pp. 156-57.
44. Klibanov, pp. 156-57.
45. Klibanov, pp. 268.

46. Klibanov, pp. 179-80.

47. Klibanov, pp. 159-60.

48. Klibanov, pp. 210.

49. Klibanov, p. 211.

50. Klibanov, pp. 214-15.

51. Klibanov, pp. 210, 222.

52. Tultseva, pp. 34, 39-40.

53. Tultseva, pp. 34-35.

54. Rushbrooke, *Some Chapters*, pp. 87-88. Also Michael Bourdeaux (2), *Faith on Trial in Russia* (New York: Harper & Row, 1971), p. 26.

55. Rushbrooke, *Some Chapters*, pp. 87-88.

56. Bourdeaux (2), p. 33.

57. Rushbrooke, *Some Chapters*, pp. 88-89.

58. Klibanov, p. 250.

59. A. I. Klibanov, "Dissident Denominations," p. 57.

60. Klibanov, p. 250-51.

61. Klibanov, pp. 251-52.

62. Charles T. Byford, *Peasants and Prophets, Baptist Pioneers in Russia and South Eastern Europe*, 2nd ed. (London: Kingsgate Press, 1912), p. 89.

63. Rushbrooke, *Some Chapters*, p. 89.

64. Rushbrooke, *Some Chapters*, pp. 98-99.

65. Byford, p. 77.

66. Byford, p. 77.

67. Rushbrooke, *Some Chapters*, pp. 84-85.

68. Blanche Sydnor White, *The Word of God* (Richmond, Virginia: Women's Missionary Union, Southern Baptist Convention, 1954 or 1955), p. 67.

69. Rushbrooke, *Baptist Movement*, pp. 132-33.

70. Bourdeaux (2), p. 27.

71. Henry C. Vedder, *Short History of the Baptists* (Chicago: The American Baptist Publication Society, 1907), pp. 405-06.

72. Vedder, p. 406.

73. Vedder, p. 406.

74. Klibanov, p. 234.

75. Klibanov, pp. 260-61.

76. Klibanov, p. 262.

77. Klibanov, p. 272.

78. Bourdeaux (2), p. 27.

79. Bourdeaux (2), p. 27.

80. Klibanov, 272. Also McBeth (1), pp. 492-39.

81. Rushbrooke, *Baptist Movement*, pp. 139-41. Also *Some Chapters*, pp. 96-98.

82. Vladimir Popov, "Vasilii Gurevich Pavlov and the Early Years of the Baptist World Alliance," *The Baptist Quarterly Journal of the Baptist Historical Society*, Vol. XXXVI (January 1995), pp. 4-5.

83. Rushbrooke, *Some Chapters*, p. 92.

84. David MacKenzie and Michael W. Curran, *A History of Russia and the Soviet Union* (Homewood, Illinois: The Dorsey Press, 1977), p. 384.

85. Rushbrooke, *Some Chapters*, 93.

86. Rushbrooke, *Some Chapters*.

87. Bourdeaux (2), p. 30.

88. Klibanov, pp. 257-58.

89. Popov.

90. Popov, 4. Also Rushbrooke, *Baptist Movement*, pp. 135-36.

91. Ernest A. Payne, *Out of Great Tribulation: Baptists in the U.S.S.R.* (London: The Garden City Press, 1974), pp. 19-20.

92. Klibanov, p. 273.

93. Popov, p. 6.

94. Popov, p. 5.

95. Popov, p. 5.

96. Payne, p. 55.

97. Klibanov, p. 276.

98. Popov, p. 8.

99. Byford, pp. 92-93.

100. Payne, p. 20.

101. Popov, p. 4.

102. Bourdeaux (2), p. 37. Also Popov, p. 4.

103. Popov, pp. 10-14.

104. Payne, p. 22.

105. Klibanov, pp. 284, 324.

106. Payne, p. 24.

107. Payne, pp. 16-17.

108. Payne, p. 26.

109. Payne, pp. 27-28.

110. Bourdeaux (2), p. 43.

111. Nikita Struve, *Christians in Contemporary Russia* (London: Harvill Press, 1963), p. 232.

112. Byford, pp. 78-81.

113. Payne, p. 29.

114. McBeth (1), p. 702. Also Payne, p. 9.

115. Bourdeaux (1), p. 2.

116. Klibanov, p. 229.

117. Payne, pp. 11-12.

118. Klibanov, p. 230.

119. Payne, pp. 29-30.

120. Byford, pp. 93-94.

Chapter 14 Philip P. Bliss (1838-1876)

1. Kenneth W. Osbeck (2), *101 More Hymn Stories* (Grand Rapids, Michigan: Kregel Publications, 1985),pp. 225-26 [hereafter designated Osbeck (2)].

2. E. E. Ryden, *The Story of Christian Hymnody* (Rock Island, Illinois: Augustana Press, 1959), p. 40.

3. Osbeck (2), p. 175.

4. Ryden, p. 558.

5. Harvey B. Marks, *The Rise and Growth of English Hymnody* (New York: Fleming H. Revell Company, 1938), pp. 29-30, 206.

6. Henry S. Burrage, *Baptist Hymn Writers and Their Hymns* (Portland, Maine: Brown Thurston & Company, 1888), p. 1.

7. Burrage, p. 4.

8. Winfred Douglas and Leonard Ellinwood, *Church Music in History & Practice* (New York: Charles Scribners Sons, 1962), p. 55.

9. Douglas, p. 60.

10. Douglas, p. 63.

11. Douglas, p. 63.

12. R. Ernest Depuy and Trevor N. Depuy, *The Encyclopedia of Military History* (New York: Harper & Row, 1986), pp. 538-39.

13. Ryden, p. 143.

14. Harvey B. Marks, *The Rise and Growth of English Hymnody* (New York: Fleming H. Revell Company, 1938), p. 86.

15. Douglas, pp. 69-71.

16. Douglas, pp. 64-65.

17. Douglas, p. 66.

18. Marks, pp. 78-80.

19. Marks, p . 81.

20. Kenneth W. Osbeck (1), *101 Hymn Stories* (Grand Rapids: Kregel Publications, 1982), p. 279.

21. Osbeck (1), *Hymn Stories*, pp. 281-83.

22. McBeth (1), pp. 94-95.

23. Marks, pp. 93, 98.

24. Marks, p. 100.

25. Douglas, p. 212.

26. Osbeck (1), p. 134.

27. Ryden, p. 557.

28. Osbeck (2), p. 175.

29. Osbeck (2), p. 226.

30. Osbeck (1), p. 93.

31. Marks, pp. 29, 206.

32. Osbeck (2), p. 175.

33. Ryden, p. 558.

34. Ryden, p. 558.

35. Osbeck (1), p. 134.

36. Osbeck (2), pp. 175-76.

37. Osbeck (2), p. 176.

38. Ryden, pp. 557, 564.

39. Ryden, p. 559.

40. Osbeck (1), p. 133.

41. Osbeck (1), p. 133.

42. Osbeck (1), p. 134.

43. Osbeck (2), p. 225.

44. Osbeck (2), pp. 225-26.

45. Osbeck (1), pp. 101-02.

46. Osbeck (1), p. 127.

47. Edmund D. Keith and Gaye L. McGlothlen, *Know Your Hymns* (Nashville: Convention Press, 1962), pp. 19-21.

48. Cecilia Margaret Rudin, *Stories of Hymns We Love* (Grand Rapids: Singspiration, Inc., 1972), pp. 69-70. Also Ryden, p. 559.

49. Osbeck (1), pp. 134, 165.

50. Ryden, pp. 438-39.

51. Ryden, p. 558.

52. Osbeck (1), p. 134.

53. Osbeck (2), p. 226.

Chapter 15 Lottie Moon (1841-1912)

1. William L. Langer, *An Encyclopedia of World History* (Boston: Houghton Mifflin Company, 1948, pp. 126, 346, 537.

2. Leon McBeth (2), *Women in Baptist Life* (Nashville: Broadman Press, 1979), pp. 75, 77.

3. Catherine B. Allen, *The New Lottie Moon Story* (Nashville: Broadman Press, 1980), p. 19.

4. William H. Brackney (1) (ed.), *Dispensations of Providence: The Journal and Selected Letters of Luther Rice* (Barre, Vermont: American Baptist Historical Society, 1984), p. 75.

5. Alma Hunt and Catherine B. Allen, *History of Woman's Missionary Union,* revised ed. (Nashville: Convention Press, 1976), pp. 4-5.

6. Allen, p. 12.

7. Allen, p. 11.

8. Irwin T. Hyatt, Jr., *Our Ordered Lives Confess: Three Nineteenth-Century American Missionaries in East Shantung* (Cambridge, Mass.: Harvard University Press, 1976), pp. 94-95.

9. Allen, pp. 1-19.

10. Allen, p. 20.

11. Allen, pp. 40, 46.

12. Allen, pp. 21-22.

13. Allen, pp. 21-23. Also Hyatt, 94.

14. Allen, p. 27.

15. Allen, p. 30.

16. Allen, pp. 30-31.

17. Allen, p. 32.

18. Allen, pp. 32-33.

19. Allen, pp. 37-38.
20. Allen, p. 30.
21. Allen, p. 35.
22. Allen, pp. 37-38.
23. Allen, pp. 37-38.
24. Allen, p. 39.
25. Hyatt, pp. 95.
26. Allen, pp. 47-48.
27. Allen, pp. 49-50.
28. Allen, p. 50.
29. Allen, pp. 48-49.
30. Allen, pp. 53-54.
31. Allen, p. 54.
32. Allen, p. 54.
33. Allen, p. 58.
34. Hyatt, p. 96. Also Allen, p. 62.
35. Allen, p. 62.
36. Hyatt, pp. 96-97.
37. Hunt and Allen, p. 13.
38. Hunt and Allen, p. 14.
39. Allen, p. 67.
40. Allen, pp. 62-65.
41. Hyatt, p. 96.
42. Allen, pp. 68-69.
43. Allen, pp. 69-70.
44. Hunt and Allen, pp. 14-15.
45. Allen, pp. 70-71.
46. Allen, p. 72, quoting the *Religious Herald* (September 18, 1873).
47. Allen, pp. 79-80.
48. Allen, p. 81.
49. Allen, pp. 82-83.
50. Allen, p. 83.
51. Allen, pp. 83-84.
52. Allen.
53. Allen, pp. 89-91.
54. Allen, p. 88.

55. Allen, p. 89.
56. Allen, p. 88.
57. Allen, pp. 87-88.
58. Hyatt, p. 97.
59. Allen, pp. 92-93.
60. Allen, p. 92.
61. Allen, pp. 95-96.
62. Allen, pp. 100-01.
63. Hyatt, p. 97. Also Allen, p. 88.
64. Allen, pp. 101-02.
65. Allen, p. 102.
66. Hyatt, p. 98.
67. Allen, pp. 110-11.
68. Allen, p. 113.
69. Allen, pp. 119-21.
70. Hyatt, pp. 98.
71. McBeth (1), 418.
72. Hyatt, pp. 98-99.
73. Allen, pp. 122-23. Also Hyatt 08-109.
74. Allen, pp. 104-105. Also Hyatt, pp. 5-14.
75. Hyatt, pp. 5-14.
76. Allen, p. 105.
77. Allen, pp. 104-06.
78. Hyatt, pp. 60, 76.
79. Allen, p. 150.
80. Hyatt, *op. cit.*
81. Allen, p. 151.
82. Hyatt, p. 101.
83. Allen, pp. 133-34.
84. Allen, pp. 131-32.
85. Allen, pp. 131-32.
86. McBeth (1), p. 746. Also Allen, p. 43.
87. Allen, p. 43.
88. Allen, pp. 143-44.
89. Allen, pp. 138-39.
90. Hyatt, p. 103.

91. Allen, pp. 144-49.

92. Allen, p. 141.

93. Allen, p. 140.

94. Allen, p. 140. Also Hyatt, p. 102.

95. Allen, pp. 141-42.

96. Hyatt, pp. 99-100.

97. Harry A. Franck, *Wandering In Northern China* (New York: Grosset & Dunlap, 1923), pp. 231, 251.

98. Hyatt, p. 100.

99. Hyatt, pp. 106-07.

100. Allen, p. 156.

101. Hyatt, pp. 105-06.

102. Allen, pp. 155-56.

103. Allen, p. 155.

104. Hyatt, p. 106.

105. Allen, p. 155.

106. Allen, pp. 156-57.

107. Hyatt, pp. 106-07.

108. Allen, pp. 157-58.

109. Hyatt, pp. 106-07.

110. Hyatt, pp. 117-18.

111. Hyatt, pp. 108-09. Also Allen, p. 159.

112. Allen, p. 162.

113. Hyatt, p. 109.

114. Hyatt, p. 107.

115. Hyatt, pp. 103-04.

116. Allen, p. 160.

117. Hyatt, pp. 112-13. Also Allen, p. 159.

118. Hyatt, pp. 112-13.

119. Hunt and Allen, pp. 23-24.

120. Allen, pp. 169-70.

121. Hunt and Allen, p. 24.

122. Hyatt, pp. 113-14.

123. Hyatt, p. 114. Also Hunt and Allen, pp. 39-44.

124. Hunt and Allen, p. 44.

125. Hunt and Allen, p. 45. Also Hyatt, p. 114.

126. Allen, pp. 161, 169.

127. Allen, pp. 169, 176.

128. Allen, pp. 161, 169.

129. Allen, p. 171.

130. Hyatt, p. 111.

131. Hyatt, pp. 111-12.

132. Allen, pp. 171-72. Also Hyatt, p. 111.

133. Hyatt, p. 115. Also Allen, p. 173.

134. Allen, p. 174.

135. Allen, pp. 181-83.

136. Hyatt, p. 116.

137. Allen, pp. 184-85.

138. Hyatt, pp. 115-16.

139. Allen, pp. 184-85.

140. Hyatt, p. 116. Also Allen pp. 183-84. Allen credits Li with ten thousand baptisms.

141. Hyatt, pp. 115-16.

142. Hyatt, p. 112.

143. Hyatt, p. 117. Also Allen, pp. 187-89.

144. Allen, p. 188.

145. Hyatt, pp. 114-15.

146. Allen, p. 188. Also Hyatt, p. 117.

147. Hyatt, pp. 124-25.

148. Hyatt, pp. 117-18.

149. R. Ernest Dupuy & Trevor N. Dupuy, *The Encyclopedia of Military History from 3500 B.C. to the Present* (New York, Harper & Row, 1985), pp. 864-66.

150. Allen, pp. 209-211.

151. Allen, p. 212.

152. Franck, p. 295.

153. Hyatt, p. 122.

154. Allen, pp. 214-215.

155. Allen, p. 268.

156. Allen, p. 122.

157. Allen, p. 258.

158. Allen, p. 266, quoting *Foreign Mission Journal*, December 1909.

159. Allen, pp. 267-68.
160. Hyatt, pp. 60, 67, 118.
161. Allen, p. 273.
162. Hyatt, pp. 122-23.
163. Allen, pp. 273-74.
164. Hyatt, p. 123.
165. McBeth (2), p. 92.
166. Hyatt, pp. 123-24. Also McBeth (2), p. 92.
167. Allen, p. 288.
168. Hyatt, pp. 124-25.
169. Hunt and Allen, pp. 18-19.
170. McBeth (2), pp. 90, 92.

Chapter 16 Benajah Harvey Carroll (1843-1914)

1. Robert A. Baker, *Tell The Generations Following. A History of Southwestern Baptist Theological Seminary 1908-1983* (Nashville: Broadman Press, 1983), pp. 54-55.
2. Baker, pp. 54-55.
3. Jeff D. Ray, *B. H. Carroll* (Nashville, Sunday School Board of the Southern Baptist Convention, 1927), p. 28.
4. Baker, p. 56.
5. Baker, p. 56.
6. Ray, p. 28.
7. Ray, p. 27.
8. Baker, p. 57.
9. Baker, p. 58.
10. Baker, pp. 58-60.
11. Baker, pp. 58-60.
12. Ray, pp. 16-17.
13. Ray, p. 29.
14. Baker, pp. 58-59.
15. Ray, pp. 16-17.
16. Ray, pp. 41-44. Also Baker, 64-65, quoting J. W. Crowder, *Dr. B. H. Carroll, the Colossus of Baptist History.*
17. Baker, p. 143.

18. Baker, pp. 59-60.

19. Baker, p. 60.

20. Baker, pp. 60-61.

21. Baker, p. 62.

22. Ray, p. 36.

23. Baker, p. 63.

24. Baker, p. 64.

25. Ray, pp. 43, 46-47.

26. Baker, pp. 64-65. Also Ray, pp. 41-44.

27. Baker, pp. 64-65, quoting J. W. Crowder, p. 78.

28. Baker, p. 65.

29. Baker, p. 63.

30. Baker, pp. 65-66.

31. Baker, pp. 63-64. Also Ray, pp. 72-74.

32. Baker, p. 66.

33. Baker, p. 66.

34. Ray, p. 79.

35. Baker, pp. 66-67.

36. Ray, pp. 63-64.

37. Baker, pp. 53-54.

38. Baker, pp. 14-75, quoting Ray, pp. 64-65.

39. Ray, pp. 69-70. Also Baker, p. 55.

40. Ray, pp. 72-74.

41. Baker, p. 70, quoting Frank E. Burkhalter, *A World-Visioned Church* (Nashville: Broadman Press, 1946), p. 88.

42. Ray, pp. 118-119.

43. Ray, pp. 151-152.

44. Ray, pp. 151-152.

45. Baker, p. 69.

46. Baker, pp. 71-72.

47. Baker, pp. 71-72.

48. Baker, pp. 70-71.

49. Baker, p. 71.

50. Baker, pp. 72-73.

51. Ray, pp. 121-123.

52. Baker, pp. 96-97.

53. Robert G. Torbet, *A History of the Baptists* (Chicago: The Judson Press, 1955), p. 340. Also Baker, pp. 98-100.

54. H. Leon McBeth (1), *The Baptist Heritage: Four Centuries of Baptist Witness* (Nashville, Tenn.: Broadman Press, 1987), p. 668.

55. L. R. Elliott (ed.), *Centennial Story of Texas Baptists* (Dallas: Baptist General Convention of Texas, 1936), pp. 160-61. Also McBeth (1), pp. 411-12.

56. McBeth (1), pp. 411-12.

57. Torbet, p. 340, quoting William W. Barnes in *The Review and Expositer*, Vol. XLIV, No. 2, p. 149.

58. *Centennial Story*, pp. 158-59.

59. Baker, 97-98.

60. Baker, pp. 97-98.

61. Torbet, p. 340. Also Baker, pp. 98-100.

62. Torbet, p. 340.

63. Baker, pp. 102-03.

64. Baker, pp. 102-03.

65. Baker, pp. 103-05.

66. Torbet, p. 340.

67. Baker, pp. 111-13.

68. Baker, pp. 103-05, 113-14.

69. Baker, pp. 111-13.

70. Baker, p. 117.

71. Baker, 117.

72. Baker, pp. 76-77.

73. Baker, pp. 83-84.

74. McBeth (1), pp. 450-53. Also Baker, pp. 79-80.

75. McBeth (1), pp. 450-53. Also Baker, pp. 79-80.

76. Baker, pp. 90-91.

77. Baker, pp. 82-83.

78. Baker, p. 82.

79. Baker, pp. 82-83.

80. Baker, pp. 82-83.

81. McBeth (1), pp. 458-59.

82. McBeth (1), pp. 458-59.

83. *Centennial Story*, p. 55.

84. Baker, pp. 80-81.

85. Baker, pp. 80-81.

86. McBeth (1) pp. 446, 670.

87. Baker, pp. 87-88.

88. Baker, pp. 88.

89. Baker, pp. 90-91.

90. Baker, pp. 91-93.

91. Baker, p. 90.

92. Baker, p. 93.

93. Baker, p. 93

94. Baker, p. 94-95.

95. Ray, pp. 101-02.

96. Baker, pp. 84-85.

97. Ray, pp. 97-98.

98. Baker, pp. 84-85.

99. Ray, pp. 98-99.

100. Ray, p. 100.

101. Baker, pp. 83-84.

102. McBeth (1), 432-33. Also Baker, p. 86.

103. McBeth (1), pp. 432-33. Also Baker, p. 86.

104. Baker, p. 87.

105. McBeth (1), pp. 677-78.

106. Ray, pp. 136-37.

107. McBeth (1), pp. 669-70, quoting Baker, pp. 24-25.

108. Ray, pp. 137-38.

109. Baker, pp. 119-20.

110. Ray, p. 107.

111. Baker, pp. 119-21.

112. Baker, p. 119, quoting Lee R. Scarborough, *A Modern School of the Prophets* (Nashville: Broadman Press, 1939), pp. 21-22.

113. Baker, p. 120.

114. Baker, p. 121.

115. Baker, p. 121.

116. Ray, p. 139.

117. Baker, p. 122.

118. Ray, p. 139.

119. Baker, p. 123.
120. Baker, p. 125.
121. Baker, pp. 126-28.
122. Baker, pp. 126-28.
123. Baker, p. 129.
124. Baker, pp. 132-33.
125. Ray, pp. 139-40.
126. Baker, pp. 133-36.
127. Baker, p. 138.
128. Baker, p. 139.
129. Baker, p. 236.
130. Baker, pp. 139-41.
131. Baker, pp. 143.
132. Baker, p. 143.
133. Baker, p. 144.
134. McBeth (1), pp. 679-80.
135. Baker, p. 178.
136. Baker, p. 178.
137. Baker, pp. 178-81.
138. Baker, pp. 178-81.
139. O. K. and Marjorie Armstrong, *The Baptists in America* (Garden City, New York: Doubleday & Company, Inc., 1979), p. 268.
140. Baker, pp. 178-81.
141. Armstrong, p. 268.
142. Armstrong, pp. 268-69.
143. Armstrong, p. 269.
144. Armstrong, p. 270-71.
145. Baker, pp. 145-46.
146. Baker, pp. 147-48.
147. Baker, pp. 148-50.
148. Baker, pp. 152-54.
149. Baker, pp. 154-57.
150. Baker, p. 144, quoting Proceedings, BGCT, pp. 58-59.
151. Ray, pp. 139-40.
152. Baker, pp. 157-58.
153. Baker, p. 161.
154. Baker, pp. 159-61.

155. Baker, p. 158.
156. Baker, p. 159.
157. Baker, pp. 162-63.
158. Baker, pp. 163-64.
159. Baker, p. 165.
160. Baker, p. 169.
161. Baker, p. 172.
162. Baker, p. 165.
163. Baker, p. 182.
164. Baker, p. 55.
165. Baker, p. 74.
166. Baker, p. 182.
167. Baker, p. 182.

Chapter 17 Walter Rauschenbusch (1861-1918)

1. Frank H. Woyke, *Heritage and Ministry of the North American Baptist Conference* (Oakbrook Terrace, Illinois: North American Baptist Conference, no date), p. 191.

2. Herman Von Berge [Foreword], *These Glorious Years* (Cleveland: Roger Williams Press, 1944), p. 104. Also Woyke, p. 45.

3. Woyke, pp. 47-48, 53.

4. Woyke, p. 53.

5. Woyke, pp. 52-56, 227.

6. Woyke, pp. 28-29, 33-34.

7. O. K. and Marjorie Armstrong, *The Baptists in America* (Garden City, New York: Doubleday & Company, Inc., 1979), pp. 194-95.

8. Gary B. Nash *et al.*, *The American People* (New York: Harper & Row, 1986), p. 417.

9. Armstrong, p. 220.

10. Von Berge, p. 114. Also Woyke, pp. 49-50.

11. Von Berge, pp. 51-52. Also Armstrong, pp. 220-221.

12. Von Berge, p. 117. Also Woyke, p. 290.

13. Armstrong, p. 221.

14. Armstrong, p. 221.

15. Woyke, p. 290.

16. Armstrong, p. 221.
17. Armstrong, p. 222.
18. Armstrong, p. 221.
19. Von Berge, p. 117.
20. Armstrong, p. 222.
21. Armstrong, p. 222-23.
22. Woyke, p. 227.
23. Armstrong, pp. 223-24.
24. Armstrong, pp. 219, 21.
25. Armstrong, p. 223.
26. Armstrong, p. 228.
27. William Henry Brackney (2), *The Baptists* (New York: Greenwood Press, 1988), p. 249.
28. Armstrong, pp. 228-29.
29. Armstrong, p. 223.
30. Armstrong, pp. 223-24.
31. Woyke, p. 290. Also Armstrong, p. 224.
32. Von Berge, p. 117. Also Armstrong, p. 226.
33. Woyke, pp. 51-52, 160.
34. Woyke, pp. 161-62.
35. Von Berge, p. 108.
36. Woyke, pp. 177-78, 180.
37. Woyke, pp. 227-29.
38. Woyke, p. 267.
39. Woyke, pp. 268-69.
40. Von Berge, p. 131.
41. Woyke, p. 226.
42. Woyke, p. 230-32.
43. Von Berge, pp. 228-29. Also Woyke, p. 227.
44. Woyke, pp. 236-37, 290. Also Von Berge, p. 230.
45. Armstrong, p. 233.
46. Woyke, pp. 27-33, 91.
47. Armstrong, p. 227, quoting D. R. Sharpe, *The Social Gospel of Rauschenbusch*, p. 273.
48. Armstrong, p. 225.
49. Armstrong, p. 228.

50. Armstrong, p. 227.

51. Armstrong, pp. 219-20.

52. Edwin S. Gaustad (2) (ed.), *A Documentary History of Religion in America Since 1865* (Grand Rapids: William B. Eerdmans Publishing Company, 1986), p. 490.

53. Armstrong, pp. 229-30.

54. Gaustad (2) (ed.), p. 125.

55. Gaustad (2), p. 125, quoting Rauschenbusch, *The Righteousness of the Kingdom*, pp. 70-72.

56. Gaustad (2), p. 126.

57. Gaustad (2), p. 126.

58. Armstrong, p. 226.

59. Armstrong, pp. 231-32.

60. Gaustad (2), pp. 99-100, 119-20.

61. Armstrong, pp. 231-32.

62. Armstrong, p. 232.

63. Armstrong, pp. 224-25.

64. Armstrong, p. 225.

65. Armstrong, p. 220, quoting Benson Y. Landis (ed.), *A Rauschenbusch Reader.*

66. Von Berge, pp. 64-66, 68, 70.

67. Von Berge, p. 93.

68. Nash, p. 650. Also Von Berge, pp. 118-19.

69. Von Berge, p. 82. Also Woyke, p. 243.

70. Armstrong, p. 226.

71. Armstrong, p. 226.

72. Woyke, p. 243.

73. Armstrong, p. 227.

74. Woyke, p. 191.

75. Woyke, pp. 195, 360-63.

76. Woyke, pp. 195-96.

77. VonBerge, pp. 41, 50.

78. Woyke, p. 182.

79. Woyke, pp. 201-02. Also Von Berge, pp. 64-66.

80. Von Berge, p. 84.

81. Woyke, pp. 360-61.

82. Woyke, pp. 180-81.

83. Von Berge, pp. 208-09.

84. Woyke, p. 258.

85. Woyke, pp. 198-99.

86. Von Berge, p. 134. Also Woyke, p. 212.

87. Woyke, pp. 181-82.

88. Woyke, p. 178

89. Von Berge, p. 51.

90. Woyke, pp. 360-62.

91. Woyke, pp. 194-95, 238.

92. Woyke, pp. 178-79.

93. Woyke, pp. 194-95.

94. Woyke, pp. 194-95.

95. Armstrong, pp. 233-34.

96. Von Berge, p. 119.

97. Armstrong, p. 232.

98. Armstrong, p. 93.

99. Von Berge, p. 93.

100. Armstrong, p. 229.

101. Armstrong, pp. 231-32.

102. Gaustad (2), pp. 119-20.

103. Gaustad (2), p. 120.

104. Armstrong, p. 231. Also Woyke, p. 290.

105. Armstrong, pp. 230-31.

106. Armstrong, p. 231.

107. Woyke, pp. 191-93.

108. Gaustad (2), p. 120.

109. Gaustad (2), pp. 120-21.

110. Armstrong, pp. 233-34.

111. Woyke, p. 290.

112. Von Berge, p. 120.

113. Taylor Branch (1), *Parting the Waters, America in the King Years 1954-63* (New York: Simon & Schuster, 1988), pp. 38-39.

114. Von Berge, p. 242.

115. McBeth (1), p. 568.

116. McBeth (1), pp. 568-69.

Chapter 18 Martin Luther King (1929-1968)

1. Taylor Branch (1), *Parting the Waters—America in the King Years 1954-63* (New York: Simon & Schuster, 1988), p. 40.
2. Branch (1), p. 40.
3. Branch (1), pp. 32-33.
4. Wilson Thomson, *The Autobiography of Elder Wilson Thompson: His Life and Travels, and Ministerial Labors* (Conley, Georgia: Old School Hymnal Co., republished, no date).
5. Branch (1), p. 30.
6. Branch (1), p. 33.
7. Branch (1), p. 30-32.
8. Branch (1), p. 32.
9. Branch (1), p. 34.
10. Branch (1), p. 34.
11. Branch, pp. 35-36.
12. Branch (1), p. 36.
13. Branch (1), p. 36.
14. Branch (1), p. 37.
15. Branch (1), p. 37-38.
16. Branch (1), p. 53-55.
17. Branch (1), pp. 55-56, 58.
18. Branch (1), pp. 41-43.
19. C. Eric Lincoln (ed.), *Martin Luther King, Jr., A Profile* (New York: Hill and Wang, 1970), p. 101, as narrated by James Baldwin.
20. Branch (1), pp. 43-44.
21. Branch (1), p. 48.
22. Branch (1), p. 58-59.
23. Branch (1), pp. 59-69.
24. Branch (1), pp. 60-61.
25. Branch (1), pp. 58, 61.
26. Branch (1), pp. 61-63.
27. Branch (1), p. 63.
28. *Compton's Pictured Encyclopedia* (Chicago: William Benton Publisher, 1967), pp. 272-81.
29. Branch (1), pp. 64-65.

30. Branch (1), p. 63.
31. Branch (1), p. 63.
32. Branch (1), pp. 64–65.
33. Branch (1), pp. 65–66.
34. Branch (1), p. 66.
35. Branch (1), pp. 67–68.
36. Branch (1), pp. 69–70.
37. Lincoln, p. 101, quoting James Baldwin. Also Branch (1), pp. 75–76.
38. Branch (1), pp. 79–80.
39. Branch (1), p. 81.
40. Branch (1), p. 82.
41. Branch (1), p. 83.
42. Branch (1), p. 85–87.
43. Dale Andrade, "Reflections on the Forgotten," *The Retired Officer Magazine* (June 2000), p. 59.
44. Branch (1), pp. 87–88.
45. Branch (1), pp. 90–91.
46. Branch (1), pp. 92–94.
47. Lincoln, p. 32.
48. Branch (1), p. 93.
49. Branch (1), pp. 92–94.
50. Branch (1), pp. 94–95.
51. Branch (1), pp. 95–98, 100–01.
52. Branch (1), pp. 98–101.
53. Branch (1), pp. 101–02.
54. Branch (1), pp. 98–101.
55. Branch (1), pp. 102, 326.
56. Branch (1), pp. 108–11.
57. Branch (1), pp. 1–12.
58. Branch (1), pp. 1–12, 15.
59. Branch (1), pp. 14–15.
60. Branch (1), pp. 19–22.
61. Branch (1), pp. 16–17.
62. Branch (1), pp. 22–25.
63. Branch (1), pp. 108–09.

64. Branch (1), pp. 22-25.

65. Branch (1), pp. 110-11.

66. Branch (1), p. 112.

67. Branch (1), p. 112-13.

68. Branch (1), pp. 114-16.

69. Branch, (1), p. 116.

70. Branch (1), p. 118.

71. Branch (1), p. 117.

72. Branch (1), pp. 118-19.

73. Branch (1), pp. 123-24.

74. Branch (1), p. 128.

75. Branch (1), p. 126.

76. Branch (1), pp. 106, 180.

77. Branch (1), p. 111.

78. Branch (1), p. 107.

79. Branch (1), pp. 124-25.

80. Branch (1), pp. 128-30.

81. Branch (1), pp. 130-31.

82. Branch (1), pp. 135-36.

83. Branch (1), pp. 138-40.

84. Branch (1), p. 140.

85. Branch (1), p. 142.

86. Branch (1), pp. 144-46.

87. Adam Fairclough, *Martin Luther King, Jr.* (Athens, Georgia: University of Georgia Press, 1995), p. 87, quoting "Lest We Forget," Folkways Records.

88. Lincoln, p. 52.

89. Branch (1), p. 261.

90. Branch (1), p. 16.

91. Branch (1), pp. 147-50.

92. Branch (1), pp. 152-54.

93. Branch (1), pp. 156-61.

94. Branch (1), pp. 161-62.

95. Branch (1), pp. 163-64.

96. Branch (1), pp. 164-66.

97. Branch (1), p. 167.

98. Branch (1), pp. 168-70, 260.
99. Branch (1), pp. 170-73.
100. Branch (1), pp. 174-78.
101. Branch (1), pp. 178-80.
102. Branch (1), pp. 184-85.
103. Branch (1), pp. 194-95.
104. Branch (1), pp. 186-87.
105. Branch (1), pp. 49-51.
106. Branch (1), p. 32.
107. Branch (1), p. 164.
108. Branch (1), pp. 186-87.
109. Branch (1), pp. 186-87.
110. Branch (1), p. 188.
111. Branch (1), p. 190.
112. Branch (1), pp. 190-91.
113. Branch (1), pp. 191-92.
114. Branch (1), pp. 194-95.
115. Branch (1), pp. 195.
116. Branch (1), pp. 196.
117. Branch (1), pp. 197-98.
118. Branch (1), pp. 197-99.
119. Lincoln, pp. 36-37.
120. Lincoln, p. 122. Also Branch, p. 222.
121. Branch (1), pp. 200, 206.
122. Lincoln, pp. 41-43.
123. Branch (1), pp. 202-203.
124. William Henry Brackney (2), *The Baptists* (New York: Greenwood Press, 1988), pp. 212-13.
125. Branch (1), pp. 214-15. Also Lincoln, pp. 44-46.
126. Lincoln, pp. 46-47 quoting from William Robert Miller, "The Broadening Horizons." Also Branch (1), pp. 217-18.
127. Branch (1), pp. 218-19.
128. Branch (1), p.106.
129. Branch (1), pp. 180, 220-22.
130. Branch (1), pp. 233-237.
131. Branch (1), p. 213.

132. Lincoln, p. 120. Also Fairclough, p. 50.

133. Branch (1), pp. 227-228.

134. Branch (1), pp. 227-228, 313-314.

135. Branch (1), pp, 101-102, 228.

136. Branch (1), pp. 55-56.

137. Branch (1), p. 228.

138. Branch (1), pp. 335-339.

139. Taylor Branch (2), *Pillar of Fire, America in the King Years 1963-65* (New York: Simon & Schuster, 1998).

140. Branch (1), p. 229.

141. Lincoln, pp. 58-61.

142. Lincoln, pp. 58-61.

143. Lincoln, pp. 63-67, 106.

144. Branch (1), pp. 252, 259.

145. Branch (1), p. 267. Also Lincoln, pp. 70-71.

146. Branch (1), p. 268.

147. Branch (1), p. 268.

148. Branch (1), pp. 207-08, 230.

149. Branch (1), pp. 271-73.

150. Branch (1), p. 276.

151. Lincoln, pp. 120-26, 149.

152. Lincoln, pp. 144-45, 149.

153. Branch (1), pp. 389-90.

154. Lincoln, pp. 145-46.

155. Branch (1), pp. 274-75, 276-78.

156. Branch (1), pp. 282-83.

157. Lincoln, pp. 160-61. Also Branch (1), pp. 294-97.

158. Branch (1), pp. 344, 348-49.

159. Branch (1), pp. 313-14.

160. Branch (1), pp. 303-04.

161. Branch (2), pp. 42-43. Also Branch (1), p. 312.

162. Branch (2), p. 49.

163. Branch (1), pp. 351-52, 357.

164. Branch (1), pp. 358-59.

165. Branch (1), pp. 360-62.

166. Branch (1), p. 363.

167. Branch (1), pp. 374-75.

168. Branch (1), pp. 360-62, 374-75. Also Lincoln, p. 126.

169. Branch (1), p. 366.

170. Branch (1), pp. 380-85.

171. Lincoln, pp. 69-70.

172. Lincoln, p. 159.

173. Lincoln, p. 124.

174. Fairclough, p. 68. Also Lincoln, pp. 161-63.

175. Branch (2), p. 62.

176. Branch (2), p. 90.

177. Branch (2), pp. 24-26.

178. Branch (2), p. 26.

179. Branch (2), pp. 144-45.

180. Branch (2), pp. 124-25.

181. Lincoln, p. 161-63.

182. Lincoln, p. 136.

183. Branch (2), pp. 46-48.

184. Lincoln, p. 140.

185. Branch (2), pp. 138-40.

186. Branch (2), pp. 76-78, 140.

187. Branch (2), pp. 88, 148.

188. Lincoln, p. 163.

189. Branch (2), p. 84.

190. Lincoln, p. 140.

191. David Levering Lewis, *King: A Biography* (Chicago: University of Illinois Press, 1978), p. 271. Also Branch (2), p. 16.

192. Branch (2), p. 48. Also Lincoln, p. 68.

193. Branch (2), p. 86. Also Branch (1), pp. 256-58.

194. Branch (2), pp. 98-100.

195. Branch (2), pp. 130-31.

196. Lewis, p. 271. Also Branch (2), pp. 184-85.

197. Branch (2), pp. 130-31, 184, 550, 596-97.

198. Branch (2), pp. 100-01.

199. Branch (2), pp. 130-31.

200. Branch (2), pp. 130-33.

201. Branch (2), p. 135.

202. Fairclough, p. 102.
203. Lincoln, p. 167.
204. Lewis, pp. 269-70, 274-81.
205. Francis C. Anderson, Jr., "Today we have everything in place but the dream," *Savannah Morning News*, January 17, 2000.
206. Fairclough, p. 102.
207. Lewis, pp. 274-81.
208. Lewis, pp. 282-90. Also Lincoln, pp. 150-51.
209. Chuck Stone, "Selma to Montgomery: The Road to Equality," *National Geographic*, Vol. 197, February 2000.
210. Fairclough, p. 103. Also Lewis, pp. 282-90.
211. Lewis, p. 306.
212. Fairclough, pp. 104-05.
213. Lewis, pp. 315-19, 321-22.
214. Lincoln, pp. 166-69.
215. Branch (2), p. 159.
216. Lincoln, p. 212.
217. Lewis, p. 296.
218. Lincoln, pp. 159-60.
219. Lewis, p. 387.
220. Lincoln, pp. 175-80.
221. Lewis, pp. 387-89.
222. Fairclough, pp. 124-25.
223. *Savannah Morning News*, January 17, 2000.
224. *USA Today*, January 17, 2000.
225. Fairclough, pp. 131-32.
226. Lincoln, p. 48.

Chapter 19 Jimmy Carter (b. 1924)

1. William A. Degregorio, *The Complete Book of U.S. Presidents from George Washington to Bill Clinton* (New York: Wingbooks, 1997), Appendix C.
2. *Savannah Morning News*, 21 February 2000.
3. Degregorio, pp. 617-18.

4. Degregorio, p. 618.

5. Degregorio, pp. 619-20.

6. Bruce Mazlish and Edwin Diamond, *Jimmy Carter, An Interpretive Biography* (New York: Simon and Schuster Inc., 1979), pp. 126-27.

7. Degregorio, pp. 619-20.

8. Mazlish, p. 127.

9. Mazlish, pp. 104-06.

10. Mazlish, pp. 107-08.

11. Mazlish, pp. 104-06. Also Degregorio, pp. 620-21.

12. Mazlish, pp. 107-08.

13. Degregorio, p. 628. Also Mazlish, p. 108.

14. Mazlish, p. 111.

15. Mazlish, p. 112.

16. Peter G. Bourne, *Jimmy Carter, A Comprehensive Biography From Plains to Postpresidency* (New York: Simon & Schuster Inc., 1997), p. 69.

17. Mazlish, p. 122.

18. Bourne, pp. 69-70.

19. Mazlish, pp. 115-19.

20. Mazlish, p. 106.

21. Mazlish, p. 121.

22. Mazlish, p. 121.

23. Mazlish, pp. 121-23.

24. Degregorio, pp. 620-21. Also Mazlish, pp. 124-25.

25. Mazlish, pp. 124-25. Also Degregorio, p. 621.

26. Mazlish, pp. 125-27.

27. Mazlish, p. 127.

28. Mazlish, pp. 127-29.

29. Mazlish, p. 129.

30. Mazlish, p. 130.

31. Mazlish, pp. 132-38.

32. Degregorio, p. 621.

33. Degregorio, p. 621.

34. Degregorio, p. 620.

35. Mazlish, pp. 130-31.

36. Mazlish, p. 131.

37. Degregorio, pp. 621-22.

38. Degregorio, p. 622.

39. Mazlish, pp. 109-11.

40. R Ernest DuPuy and Trevor N. DuPuy, *The Encyclopedia of Military History, from 3500 to the present*, 2nd Revised Edition (New York: Harper & Row, 1986), p. 63.

41. Mazlish, p. 138.

42. Margaret Truman, *First Ladies, An Intimate Group Portrait of White House Wives* (New York: Random House, 1995), p. 145.

43. Degregorio, pp. 622-23.

44. Degregorio, pp. 622-23.

45. David Rubel, *Encyclopedia of the Presidents and Their Times* (New York: Scholastic, Inc., 1994), pp. 189-90.

46. Degregorio, pp. 622-23.

47. Degregorio, pp. 623-24.

48. Mazlish, pp. 174-75.

49. Degregorio, pp. 623-24.

50. Bourne, p. 465.

51. Rubel, p. 190.

52. Degregorio, pp. 624-25.

53. Degregorio, pp. 620-21.

54. Rubel, p. 190.

55. Degregorio, p. 628.

56. Degregorio, p. 617.

57. Degregorio, p. 620.

58. Mazlish, pp.164-66.

59. Mazlish, p. 174.

60. Truman, p. 145-47.

61. Rubel, p. 190.

62. Rubel, p. 190.

63. Rubel, p. 191.

64. Mazlish, p. 228-31.

65. Degregorio, pp. 626-27.

66. Rubel, pp. 190-91. Also, Degregorio, p. 627.

67. Degregorio, p. 627.

68. Degregorio, p. 628. Also Rubel, p. 189.

69. Mazlish, p. 158.

70. Degregorio, p. 628.

71. Degregorio, p. 628. Also Rubel, pp. 191-92.

72. Degregorio, p. 628.

73. Rubel, p. 191.

74. Degregorio, 628-29. Also Rubel, 192.

75. Degregorio, p. 629.

76. Rubel, p. 192.

77. Degregorio, p. 629.

78. Rubel, p. 192.

79. Truman, p. 154.

80. Bourne, p. 466.

81. Rubel, pp. 190-91.

82. Bourne, pp. 467-68.

83. Bourne, p. 466.

84. Bourne, pp. 466-67.

85. Bourne, pp. 466-67.

86. Degregorio, p. 630 quoting Bill Adler, *The Wit and Wisdom of Jimmy Carter*, p. 72.

87. Truman, p. 149.

88. Bourne, p. 6.

89. Rubel, pp. 192-94.

90. Bourne, pp. 471-73.

91. Degregorio, p. 629.

92. Bourne, pp. 482-84.

93. Bourne, pp. 482-84.

94. Degregorio, p. 629.

95. Bourne, pp. 484-85.

96. Bourne, pp. 485-86.

97. Bourne, p. 486.

98. Bourne, p. 486.

99. Douglas Brinkley, *The Unfinished Presidency, Jimmy Carter's Journey Beyond the White House* (New York: Penguin Books, 1998), p. 347.

100. Brinkley, p. 347.

101. Anne Gearan, "Clinton Honors Korean War Veterans on 50th

Anniversary," *Savannah Morning News* (June 26, 2000). Also Brinkley, pp. 388-92.

102. Brinkley, pp. 392-94.
103. Brinkley, p. 394.
104. Brinkley, pp. 394-99.
105. Brinkley, pp. 399-409.
106. Brinkley, pp. 399-409.
107. Brinkley, pp. 409-11.
108. Brinkley, pp.391-92.
109. Brinkley, p. 407.
110. Brinkley, p. 413.
111. Brinkley, pp. 413-14.
112. Brinkley, pp. 415-20.
113. Brinkley, pp. 421-27.
114. Brinkley, pp. 427-29.
115. Brinkley, p. 442.
116. Brinkley, pp. 442-46.
117. Brinkley, p. 451.
118. Brinkley, pp. 451-52 quoting *Washington Post* (December 22, 1994).
119. Brinkley, p. 452.
120. Mazlish, pp. 153-54.
121. Mazlish, pp. 157-60.
122. Mazlish, pp. 153-55.
123. Lillian Craig Harris, *Keeping the Faith, Travels With Sudanese Women* (Limuru, Kenya: Paulines Publications, 1999), p. 23.
124. Degregorio, p. 617.
125. Walter F. Murphy and Michael N. Danielson, *American Democracy* (Hinsdale, Illinois: Dryden Press, 1977), pp. 323-24.
126. Degregorio, 630 quoting Bill Adler, *The Wit and Wisdom of Jimmy Carter*, p. 72.
127. Truman, p. 151.
128. Truman, pp. 147-49.
129. Brinkley, pp. 439-40.
130. Brinkley, pp. 372-73.
131. Degregorio, p. 630 quoting Thomas P. "Tip" O'Neill, Man of the House, p. 297.

Chapter 20 William Franklin Graham, Jr. (b. 1918)

1. John Pollock, *Billy Graham* (New York: McGraw-Hill Book Company, 1966), p. 42.

2. Pollock, p. 248.

3. Billy Graham, *Just As I Am: The Autobiography of Billy Graham* (New York: Harper Paperback, 1997), p. 3.

4. Graham, p. 4.

5. Pollock, p. 2.

6. Graham, p. 5.

7. Pollock, pp. 2-3.

8. Marshall Frady, *Billy Graham. A Parable of American Righteousness* (Boston: Little, Brown and Company, 1979), pp. 64-67.

9. Frady, pp. 67-68.

10. Frady, pp. 69-71.

11. Frady, pp. 71-73.

12. Frady, p. 76.

13. Janet Lowe, *Billy Graham Speaks. Insight From the World's Greatest Preacher* (New York: John Wiley & Sons, Inc. 1999), pp. 9-11. Also Frady, pp. 80-85.

14. Lowe, p. 10.

15. Frady, pp. 80-85.

16. Frady, pp. 87-90.

17. Frady, pp. 90-91. Also Lowe, pp. 11-12.

18. Frady, pp. 96-97.

19. Lowe, pp. 12-13.

20. Frady, pp. 96-98.

21. Frady, pp. 98-99.

22. Frady, pp. 99-100.

23. Frady, pp. 99-100. Also Lowe, pp. 12-13.

24. Frady, pp. 100-03.

25. Frady, pp. 105-07.

26. Frady, pp. 108-14.

27. Frady, pp. 126-28.

28. Frady, pp. 126-28.

29. Graham, p. 66.

30. Graham, p. 67. Also Pollock, p. 23.
31. Pollock, p. 23. Also Graham, pp. 67-68.
32. Frady, pp. 130-31.
33. Pollock, pp. 20-22.
34. Frady, pp. 131-32.
35. Frady, p. 133. Also Pollock, p. 26.
36. Frady, pp. 133-35.
37. Frady, pp. 135-36.
38. Frady, pp. 139-42.
39. Frady, pp. 136-39.
40. Pollock, p. 26.
41. Frady, pp. 139-42.
42. Pollock, p. 26.
43. Pollock, pp. 30-31.
44. Allan R. Millett and Peter Maslowski, *For the Common Defense.*
A Military History of the United States of America (New York: The Free Press, 1984), pp. 445-46.
45. Pollock, pp. 30-32.
46. Pollock, pp. 30-32. Also Frady, pp. 146-47.
47. Pollock, p. 32.
48. Frady, pp. 160-61.
49. Frady, p. 167.
50. Pollock, p. 39.
51. Pollock, pp. 39-41.
52. Frady, pp. 170-72.
53. Frady, pp. 173-74.
54. Frady, pp. 148-50.
55. Pollock, p. 43.
56. Frady, pp. 175-76. Also Pollock pp. 41-43.
57. Pollock, p. 44.
58. Pollock, pp. 44-45.
59. Frady, pp. 178-83.
60. Frady, p. 184.
61. Frady, p. 217.
62. Pollock, p. 246. Also Frady, pp. 217, 362.
63. Frady, p. 223.

64. Frady, pp. 217, 223, 346, 363. Also Pollock, 71.

65. Frady, pp. 194–96.

66. Frady, p. 198.

67. Pollock, p. 50.

68. Frady, p. 204.

69. Pollock, pp. 56–58. Also Frady, pp. 194–96.

70. Pollock, pp. 59–61.

71. Frady, p. 355.

72. Frady, pp. 357–58.

73. Frady, pp. 347–49, 364–65.

74. Graham, pp. 213, 217.

75. Frady, pp. 154–56. Also Pollock p. 78.

76. Frady, p. 225.

77. Frady, p. 221. Also Graham, p. 212.

78. Pollock, pp. 99–100.

79. Pollock, p. 91.

80. Pollock, p. 91.

81. Pollock, p. 90–92.

82. Pollock, p. 49.

83. Lowe, p. 165 quoting William Martin, *Christianity Today* (November 13, 1995).

84. Pollock, p. 48.

85. Pollock, pp. 48–49.

86. Pollock, p. 101. Also Frady, p. 225.

87. Pollock, pp. 101–02.

88. Pollock, p. 268.

89. Pollock, pp. 92–93.

90. Pollock, pp. 95–96.

91. Frady, p. 418.

92. Pollock, pp. 96–97.

93. Janet Lowe, p. 161 quoting the *New Yorker* (March 14, 1994).

94. Frady, pp. 396–97.

95. Frady, pp. 397–98.

96. Frady, p. 404.

97. Pollock, p. 20.

98. Frady, p. 509.

99. Pollock, Preface, VIII.

100. Lowe, pp. 72-73.

101. Lowe, p. 74.

102. Frady, pp. 320-23.

103. Pollock, p. 124.

104. Lowe, p. 75.

105. Lowe, pp. 75-76.

106. Lowe, pp. 75-76.

107. Frady, p. 319.

108. Lowe, p. 75.

109. Pollock, pp. 124, 139, 231.

110. Frady, p. 316. Also Lowe, p. 76.

111. Lowe, p. 76.

112. Pollock, p. 210.

113. Graham, p. 343.

114. Graham, pp. 347-49.

115. Pollock, pp. 142-44, 187.

116. Pollock, pp. 142-44.

117. Pollock, p. 147.

118. Pollock, p. 149.

119. Frady, pp. 337-41.

120. Frady, pp. 315-16.

121. Frady, pp. 293-98.

122. Frady, p. 303.

123. Frady, p. 309.

124. Frady, pp. 314-15. Also Graham, pp. 376-77 and Pollock, pp. 183-84.

125. Lowe, pp. 78-79.

126. Frady, p. 309.

127. Pollock, pp. 172-74.

128. Lowe, p. 80.

129. Frady, p.68.

130. Frady, p. 408.

131. Lowe, pp. 120-21.

132. Pollock, p. 98. Also Lowe, p. 121.

133. Frady, p. 408.

134. Pollock, p. 99. Also Lowe, p. 121.
135. Frady, pp. 409-10. Also Pollock, p. 225.
136. Frady, pp. 410-11.
137. Pollock, p. 262.
138. Frady, pp. 411-12. Also Pollock, pp. 229-30.
139. Frady, p. 414.
140. Pollock, pp. 228-29.
141. Frady, pp. 415-16.
142. Pollock, pp. 228-29.
143. Frady, p. 416.
144. Frady, p. 414.
145. Pollock, p. 97.
146. Pollock, pp. 224-25.
147. R. Ernest DePuy and Trevor N. DePuy, *The Encyclopedia of Military History from 3500 B.C. to the Present* (New York: Harper & Row, Publishers, Inc., 1986), pp. 1296-97.
148. DePuy, p. 1297. Also, Frady, pp. 420-21.
149. Frady, pp. 416, 425.
150. Frady, p. 423.
151. Frady, p. 428.
152. Frady, pp. 429-30.
153. Frady, p. 431.
154. Frady, pp. 429-30.
155. Frady, pp. 430-32. Also DePuy, p. 1220.
156. Frady, p. 343.
157. Frady, pp. 329-30.
158. Frady, pp. 332-34.
159. Pollock, pp. 230-32.
160. Pollock, pp. 232-33.
161. Graham, p. 668.
162. Graham, p. 673.
163. Graham, p. 676.
164. Graham, p. 680.
165. Graham, pp. 681-86.
166. Frady, pp. 497-99.
167. Frady, p. 328.

168. Lowe, pp. 81–82.
169. Lowe, pp. 104.
170. Pollock, p. 69. Also Lowe, p. 160.
171. Frady, pp. 320–21.
172. Frady, pp. 327, 428.
173. Frady, p. 200.
174. Pollock, pp. 69–71.
175. Pollock, p. 90. Also Frady, p. 452.
176. Frady, pp. 334–35.
177. Lowe, pp. 139–40 quoting Martin, *A Prophet with Honor*, p. 300.
178. Pollock, p. 92.
179. Lowe, p. 146 quoting Merle Miller, *Plain Speaking*, p. 363.
180. Graham, pp. 220–21.
181. Graham, pp. 234–35. Also Lowe, p. 122.
182. Graham, pp. 461–62.
183. Graham, p. 461.
184. Graham, p. 475.
185. Graham, pp. 488–90.
186. Graham, pp. 494–95.
187. Graham, pp. 553–55.
188. Graham, pp. 556–57.
189. Lowe, p. 154, quoting Martin, *A Prophet with Honor*, p. 463.
190. Lowe, p. 154.
191. Graham, pp. 582–83.
192. Graham, p. 590.
193. Graham, pp. 692–93.
194. Graham, pp.701–03.
195. Graham, pp. 744–47.
196. Frady, p. 438.
197. Frady, pp. 438–39.
198. Graham, pp. 422–23.
199. Frady, p. 443.
200. Frady, p. 445.
201. Frady, p. 450.
202. Frady, p. 454.
203. Frady, p. 474.

204. Frady, p. 479.

205. Frady, pp. 478-79.

206. Frady, p. 480.

207. Frady, p. 481.

208. Lowe, p. 90 quoting *Graham Makes Plea for an End to Intolerance*, p. 151.

209. Lowe, p. 136. Statement attributed to Bill Moyers, television personality.

210. Graham, pp. 682-83.

211. Pollock, p. 101.

212. Pollock, p. 183.

213. Pollock, p. 130.

214. Graham, pp. 773-74.

Bibliography

Books

Allen, Catherine B., *The New Lottie Moon Story* (Nashville, Tennessee: Broadman Press, 1980).

Armstrong, O. K. and Marjorie, *The Baptists in America* (Garden City, New York: Double Day & Company, Inc., 1979).

Backus, Isaac, *Church History of New England from 1620 to 1804* (Philadelphia: American Baptist Publication and S.S. Society, 1844).

Baker, Robert A. *et al*, *Baptist Advance* (Nashville: Broadman Press, 1964).

Baker, Robert A., *Tell the Generations Following. A History of Southwestern Baptist Theological Seminary 1908-1983* (Nashville, Tennessee: Broadman Press, 1983).

Baptist Advance (Nashville: Broadman Press, 1964).

Benedict, David, *A General History of the Baptist Denomination in America and Other Parts of the World* (New York: Lewis Colby, 1848).

Billingsley, Andrew, *Mighty Like a River, The Black Church and Social Reform* (Oxford: Oxford University Press, 1999).

Bourdeaux, Michael (1), *Religious Ferment in Russia* (London: MacMillan, 1968).

Bourdeaux, Michael (2), *Faith on Trial in Russia* (New York: Harper & Row, 1971).

Bourne, Peter G., *Jimmy Carter. A Comprehensive Biography from Plains to Postpresidency.* (New York: Simon & Schuster, Inc., 1997).

Brackney, William H. (1) (ed.), *Dispensations of Providence. The Journal and Selected Letters of Luther Rice.* (Barre, Vermont: American Baptist Historical Society, 1984).

Brackney, William H. (2), *The Baptists* (New York: Greenwood Press, 1988).

Branch, Taylor (1), *Parting the Waters. America in the King Years 1954-63* (New York: Simon & Schuster, 1988).

Branch, Taylor (2), *Pillar of Fire. America in the King Years 1963-65.* (New York: Simon & Schuster, 1988).

Brinkley, Douglas, *The Unfinished President. Jimmy Carter's Journey Beyond the White House* (New York: Penguin Books, 1998).

Burrage, Henry S., *Baptist Hymn Writers and Their Hymns* (Portland, Maine: Brown Thurston Company, 1888).

Butterfield, L. H., *Elder John Leland, Jeffersonian Itinerant* (Williamsburg, Va: Institute of Early American History).

Byford, Charles T., *Peasants and Prophets. Baptist Pioneers in Russia and South Eastern Europe,* 2nd Ed. (London: Kingsgate Press, 1912).

Carroll, J. M., *The Trail of Blood. Following the Christians Through the Centuries* (Booklet) (Lexington, Kentucky: Ashland Avenue Baptist Church, 1931). Reprinted April 1969.

Cathcart, William (ed.). *The Baptist Encyclopedia* (Philadelphia: Louis H. Everts, 1881).

Compton's Pictured Encyclopedia (Chicago: William Benton Publisher, 1967).

Cornwell, Patricia, *Ruth, A Portrait. The Story of Ruth Bell Graham* (New York: Doubleday, 1997).

Dawson, Joseph Martin, *Baptists and the American Republic* (Nashville, Tennessee: Broadman Press, 1956).

Degregorio, William A., *The Complete Book of U.S. Presidents from George Washington to Bill Clinton* (New York: Wings Books, 1997).

Douglas, Winfred and Ellinwood, Leonard, *Church Music in History and Practice* (New York: Charles Scribner's Sons, 1962).

DuPuy, R. Ernest and DuPuy, Trevor N., *The Encyclopedia of Military History from 3500 B.C. to the Present* (New York: Harper & Row, 1985).

Eaton, Jeanette, *Long Journey. The Life of Roger Williams* (New York: Harcourt, Brace and Company, 1944).

Elliott, L. R. (Ed.) *Centennial Story of Texas Baptists* (Dallas: Baptist General Convention of Texas, 1936).

Encyclopedia of Word Biography (New York: McGraw-Hill Book Company, 1973).

Estep, William R., *The Anabaptist Story* (Nashville, Tenn: Broadman Press, 1963).

Fairclough, Adam, *Martin Luther King, Jr.* (Athens, GA: University of Georgia Press, 1995).

Fletcher, William C. (ed.) and Strover, Anthony J., *Religion and the Search for New Ideals in the USSR* (New York: Frederick A. Praeger, 1967).

Forbis, Wesley L. (ed.), *Handbook to the Baptist Hymnal* (Nashville: Convention Press, 1992).

Franck, Harry A., *Wandering in Northern China* (New York: Grosset & Dunlap, 1923).

Gardner, Robert G. (2), Waldo P. Harris, III et al. *A History of the Georgia Baptist Association 1784-1984* Atlanta, Georgia Baptist Historical Society, 1988).

Gardner, Robert G. (ed.), *Viewpoints. Georgia Baptist History* (Atlanta: Georgia Baptist Historical Society, 1976, 1978, 1984).

Gaustad, Edwin S. (ed.) (1), *Baptist Piety—The Last Will and Testament of Obadiah Holmes* (Valley Forge, PA: Judson Press, 1994; #1, Monograph).

Gaustad, Edwin S. (ed.), *A Documentary History of Religion in America Since 1865* (Grand Rapids: William B. Eerdmans Publishing Company, Reprinted 1986; #2).

Gonzalez, Justo L., *The Story of Christianity, Vol. 2* (San Francisco: Harper & Row, 1985).

Graham, Billy, *Just As I Am. The Autobiography of Billy Graham* (New York: Harper Collins Publisher, 1997).

Greaves, Richard L., *et al. Civilizations of the World* (New York: Harper and Row, 1990).

Griffith, Gwilym O., *A Pocket History of the Baptist Movement* (London: Kingsgate Press, No Date).

Harkness, Georgia, *Women in Church and Society* (Nashville: Abingdon Press, 1972).

Harris, Lawrence H., *India: A Study of National Integration* (Ph.D dissertation, University of Santo Tomas, Manila, 1970).

Harris, Lillian Craig, *Keeping the Faith. Travels with Sudanese Women* (Limuru, Kenya: Paulines Publications Africa, 1999).

Harris, Waldo P. III and Mosteller, James D., *Georgia's First Continuing Baptist Church* (College Park, Georgia: N & R Printing, Inc., 1997).

Hays, Brooks and Steely, John E. *The Baptists' Way of Life* (Englewood Cliffs, N.J.: Prentice Hall, Inc., 1963).

Hobbs, Herschel, *The Herschel Hobbs Commentary* (Nashville: The Sunday School Board of the Southern Baptist Convention, July-September 1996, Vol. 28).

Hunt, Alma and Allen, Catherine B. *History of Woman's Missionary Union*, revised ed. (Nashville, Tennessee: Convention Press, 1976)

Frady Marshall, *Billy Graham. A Parable of American Righteouness* (Boston: Little, Brown and Company, 1979).

Hyatt, Irwin T., Jr., *Our Ordered Lives Confess. Three Nineteenth-Century American Missionaries in East Shantung* (Cambridge, Massachusetts: Harvard University Press, 1976).

James, Powhatan W., *George W. Truett* (New York: The MacMillan Company, 1939).

Johnson, Whittington B., "Andrew C. Marshall: A Black Religious Leader of Antebellum Savannah," *The Georgia Historical Quarterly*, Vol. LXIX, No. 2 (Summer 1985)

Keith, Edmond D. and McGlothlen, Gaye L., *Know Your Hymns* (Nashville: Convention Press, 1962).

King, Joe M., *A History of South Carolina Baptists* (Columbia, South Carolina: General Board of South Carolina Baptist Convention, 1964).

Kingdon, P. D. *et al*, *Baptist Heritage and Responsibility* (Mulhouse, France: Fellowship of Evangelical Churches in Europe, 1970).

Klibanov, A. I., *History of Religious Sectarianism in Russia (1860s-1917)* (Oxford: Pergamon Press, 1982).

Langer, William L., *An Encyclopedia of World History* (Boston: Houghton Mifflin Company, 1948).

Lester, James Adams, *A History of the Georgia Baptist Convention 1822-1972* (Atlanta: Executive Committee, Baptist Convention of the State of Georgia, 1972).

Lewis, David Levering, *King. A Biography* (Chicago: University of Illinois Press, 1978).

Life and Work Pursuits, Teacher Edition (Jan-March 1995) (Nashville: Sunday School Board of Southern Baptist Convention).

Lincoln, C. Eric (ed.) *Martin Luther King, Jr., A Profile* (New York: Hill and Wang, 1970).

Lord, F. Townley, *Baptist World Fellowship* (Nashville: Broadman Press, 1955).

Love, E. K., *History of the First African Baptist Church from Its Organization* (Savannah, Georgia: The Morning News Print, 1888).

Lowe, Janet, *Billy Graham Speaks. Insight from the World's Greatest Preacher* (New York: John Wiley & Sons, Inc., 1999).

Luckey, Hans, *Johann Gerhard Oncken Und Die Arnfaenge Des Deutschen Baptismus* (1934). This biography was not used in writing the chapter on Oncken but is regarded by scholars as a serious study of Oncken's place in Baptist history.

Mack, Burton L., *The Lost Gospel. The Book of Q and Christian Origins* (New York: Harper Collins, 1993).

Marks, Harvey B., *The Rise and Growth of English Hymnody* (New York: Fleming H. Revell Company, 1937).

Mazlish, Bruce and Diamond, Edwin, *Jimmy Carter. An Interpretive Biography* (New York: Simon and Schuster, Inc., 1979).

McBeth, H. Leon (1), *The Baptist Heritage. Four Centuries of Baptist Witness* (Nashville, Tenn: Broadman Press, 1987).

McBeth, H. Leon (2), *Women in Baptist Life* (Nashville, Tenn: Broadman Press, 1979).

MacKenzie, David and Curran, Michael W., *A History of Russia and the Soviet Union* (Homewood, Illinois: The Dorsey Press, 1977).

McLoughlin, William G., *New England Dissent 1630-1833. The Baptists and the Separation of Church and State* (Cambridge, Massachusetts: Harvard University, 1971).

Mercer, Jesse, *A History of the Georgia Baptist Association* (Reprint, Washington, Georgia: Georgia Baptist Association, 1980).

Millett, Allan R. and Maslowski, Peter, *For the Common Defense. A Military History of the United States of America* (New York: MacMillan, Inc., 1984).

Moore, John Allen, *Baptist Mission Portraits* (Macon, Georgia: Smyth & Helwy Publishing, Inc., 1994).

Murphy, Walter F. and Danielson, Michael N., *American Democracy* (Hinsdale, Illinois: Dryden Press, 1977).

Nash, Gary B. *et al*, *The American People* (New York: Harper & Row, 1986).

Nelson, Wilbur, *Dr. John Clarke* (Booklet; Newport, RI: Ward's Printer's, 1963).

Osbeck, Kenneth W. (1), *101 Hymn Stories* (Grand Rapids: Kregel Publications, 1982).

Osbeck, Kenneth W. (2), *101 More Hymn Stories* (Grand Rapids: Kregel Publications, 1985).

Owens, Loulie Latimer, Saints of Clay. *The Shaping of South Carolina Baptists* (Columbia, S.C: R. L. Bryan Co., 1971).

Paschal, George Washington, *History of North Carolina Baptist* (Raleigh: The General Board, North Carolina Baptists (Raleigh: The General Board, North Carolina Baptist State Convention, 1930) Vols I and II.

Payne, Ernest A., *Out of Great Tribulation. Baptists in the U.S.S.R.* (London: The Garden City Press, 1974).

Pollock, John, *Billy Graham* (New York: McGraw-Hill Book Company, 1966).

Ragsdale, B. D., *Story of Georgia Baptists.* Volume 3 (Atlanta: The Executive Committee of the Georgia Baptist Convention, 1951).

Ray, Jeff D., *B. H. Carroll* (Nashville: Sunday School Board of the Southern Baptist Convention, 1927).

Roberts, J. M., *History of the World* (New York: Alfred A. Knopf, 1976).

Rubel, David, *Encyclopedia of the Presidents and Their Times* (New York, Scholastic, Inc., 1994).

Rudin, Cecilia Margaret, *Stories of Hymns We Love* (Grand Rapids: Singspiration Inc., 1972).

Rushbrooke, J. H., *Some Chapters of European Baptist History* (London: Kingsgate Press, 1929).

Rushbrooke, J. H., *The Baptist Movement in the Continent of Europe* (London: Kingsgate Press, 1923).

Ryden, E. E., *The Story of Christian Hymnody* (Rock Island, Illinois: Augustana Press, 1959).

Ryland, Garnett, *The Baptists of Virginia 1699-1926* (Richmond, Virginia: The Virginia Baptist Board of Missions and Education, 1955).

Sadler, Lynn Veach, *Chronology of Bunyan* (Boston: Twayne Publishers, 1979).

Savannah Morning News, July 28, 1975.

Shurden Walter B., *Not a Silent People. Controversies That Have Shaped Southern Baptists* (Nashville, Tennessee: Broadman Press, 1972).

Simms, James M. *The First Colored Baptist Church in North America* (Philadelphia: J. B. Lippencott, 1888; reprinted in 1969 by Negro Universities Press).

Struve, Nikita, *Christians in Contemporary Russia* (London: Harvill Press, 1963).

Tenney, Merrill C., The Zondervan *Pictorial Bible Dictionary* (Grand Rapids: Regency Reference Library, 1967).

The Christian Index, Vol. 175, No. 7, 15 February 1996, Baptist Convention of State of Georgia, Atlanta.

Thompson, Evelyn Wingo, *Luther Rice: Believer in Tomorrow* (Nashville: Broadman Press, 1967).

Thompson, Wilson, *The Autobiography of Elder Wilson Thompson. His Life,*

Travels and Ministerial Labors (Conley, Georgia: Old School Hymnal Co., Inc.; republished 1978).

Torbet, Robert G. *A History of the Baptists* (Philadelphia: The Judson Press, 1955).

Townsend, Leah, *South Carolina Baptists 1607-1805* (Baltimore: Genealogical Publishing Co., Inc., 1978).

Truman, Margaret, *First Ladies. An Intimate Group Portrait of White House Wives* (New York: Random House, 1995).

Vedder, Henry C., *Short History of the Baptists* (Chicago: The American Baptist Publication Society, 1907).

Verdesi, Elizabeth Howell, *In But Still Out. Women in the Church* (Philadelphia: Westminister Press, 1976).

VonBerge, Herman (Foreword), *These Glorious Years: The Centenary History of German Baptists of North America* (Cleveland: Roger Williams Press, 1944).

Weaver, Rufus W., "The Place of Luther Rice In American Baptist Life" *(Review and Expositor*, XXXIII, No. 2, April 1936).

White, Blanche Sydnor, *The Word of God* (Richmond, Virginia: Women's Missionary Union, Southern Baptist Convention, 1954 or 1955).

Willison, George F., *Saints and Strangers. The Story of the Mayflower and the Plymouth Colony* (New York: Ballantine Books, Inc., 1965; paperback).

Winslow, Ola Elizabeth (1), *John Bunyan* (New York: The MacMillan Company, 1961).

Winslow, Ola Elizabeth (2), *Master Roger Williams* (New York: The MacMillan Company, 1957).

Woodward, Bob, *Shadow. Five Presidents and the Legacy of Watergate* (New York: Simon & Schuster, 1999).

Woyke, Frank H., *Heritage and Ministry of the North American Baptist Conference* (Oakbrook Terrace, Illinois: North American Baptist Conference, no date).

Yancey, Wanda, "Religion and Community in Savannah, First African

Baptist Church Means First," August, 1989 (Main Library, Savannah, Georgia; pamphlet).

Zundel, Veronica (compiler) *Fennans' Book of Christian Classics* (Grand Rapids, Michigan: William B. Eerdmanns Publishing Company, 1985).

Articles

Allen, Barbara R., "Early Baptist Women and Their Contribution to Georgia Baptist History," *Viewpoints. Georgia Baptist History,* Vol. 9 (Atlanta: Georgia Baptist Historical Society, 1984).

Allen, Barbara R., "Early Baptist Women and their Contribution to Georgia Baptist History," *Viewpoints. Georgia Baptist History*, Vol. 9 (1984).

Anderson, Francis C., Jr. "Today we have everything in place but the dream," *Savannah Morning News* (January 17, 2000).

Andrade, Dale, "Reflections on the Forgotten," *The Retired Officer Magazine* (June 2000).

Edwards, Morgan, "Materials Towards a History of the Baptists in the Province of North Carolina," *The North Carolina Historical Review*, Vol. IV, MDCCLXXI (Raleigh: North Carolina Historical Commission, 1924).

Gardner, Robert G., "Primary Sources in the Eighteenth-century Georgia Baptist History" *Viewpoints. Georgia Baptist History,* Vol. 7 (1980).

Gearan, Anne. "Clinton Honors Korean War Veterans on 501h Anniversary," *Savannah Morning News* (June 26, 2000).

Harris, Waldo P. III, "Daniel Marshall, Lone Georgia Baptist Pastor," *Viewpoints. Georgia Baptist History*, Vol. 5 (1976).

Harris, Waldo P. III, "Locations Associated with Daniel Marshall and the Kiokee Church," *Viewpoints. Georgia Baptist History*, Vol. 6 (1978).

Klibanov, A. I. and Matrokhin, L. N., "Schism of Contemporary Baptism," *Social Compass*, Vol. 21, 1974 (London: Sage).

Klibanov, A. I., "The Dissident Denominations in the Past and Today," Sovremenoe Sektansvo, Voprosy Istorii Religi i Ateizina, No. IX (1961).

Koller, Charles W., "George Washington's Baptism" (February 21, 1946), reprinted in *The Christian Index* (15 February 1996).

Lumpkin, William L., "The Role of Women in 18th Century Virginia Baptist Life," *Baptist History Heritage,* July 1973 (Nashville, Tennessee: Historical Commission of the Southern Baptist Conference).

Mueller, William A., "Baptist Theological Thought," (Nashville: Broadman Press, 1964), 450.

Popov, Vladimir, "Vasilii Gurevich Pavlov and the Early Years of the Baptist World Alliance," *The Baptist Quarterly, Journal of the Baptist Historical Sociejy,* Vol. XXXVI (January 1995).

Stone, Chuck, "Selma to Montgomery. The Road to Equality," *National Geographic,* Vol. 197 (February 2000).

The Review and Expositor, Vol. XXXIII, No. 2, April 1936 (Southern Baptist Theological Seminary, Louisville, Kentucky).

Tultseva, L. A., "The Evolution of Old Russian Sectarianism," *Soviet Sociology,* Vol. 16, 1978? (Ormonk, N.Y.).

USA Today, January 17, 2000.

Index